ABOUT THE AUTHOR

Bill Bryson's many books include, most recently, *In a Sunburned Country*, as well as *I'm a Stranger Here Myself, A Walk in the Woods, The Lost Continent, Notes from a Small Island, Neither Here Nor There, Made in America*, and *The Mother Tongue*. He edited *The Best American Travel Writing 2000*. Born in Des Moines, Iowa, in 1951, he lived in England for almost two decades. He now lives in Hanover, New Hampshire, with his wife and four children.

The Lost Continent

TRAVELS IN
SMALL-TOWN
AMERICA

Bill Bryson

HARPER **PERENNIAL**

To my father

HARPER **PERENNIAL**

A hardcover edition of this book was published in 1989 by Harper & Row, Publishers.

First HarperPerennial edition published 1990.

Reprinted in Perennial 2001.

The Library of Congress has catalogued the hardcover edition as follows:
Bryson, Bill
    The lost continent: travels in small-town America / Bill Bryson.
        p. cm.
    Includes index
    ISBN 0-06-016158-2
    1. United States—Description and travel—1981– 2. Cities and towns—United States. 3. United States—Social life and customs—1971– 4. Bryson, Bill—Journeys—United States.
    I. Title.
    E169.04.B78   1989
    917.3'0492–dc19   89-45027

ISBN-10: 0-06-092008-4 (pbk.)
ISBN-13: 978-0-06-092008-1 (pbk.)

08 09 10 RRD 70 69 68 67 66 65 64 63 62

Acknowledgments

I would like to thank the following people for their kind and various assistance in helping me during the preparation of this book: Hal and Lucia Horning, Robert and Rita Schmidt, Stan and Nancy Kluender, Mike and Sherry Bryson, Peter Dunn, Cynthia Mitchell, Nick Tosches, Paul Kingsbury, and, above all, my mother, Mary Bryson, who still has the best legs in Des Moines.

PART I

East

I

I COME FROM Des Moines. Somebody had to. When you come from Des Moines you either accept the fact without question and settle down with a local girl named Bobbi and get a job at the Firestone factory and live there forever and ever, or you spend your adolescence moaning at length about what a dump it is and how you can't wait to get out, and then you settle down with a local girl named Bobbi and get a job at the Firestone factory and live there forever and ever.

Hardly anyone ever leaves. This is because Des Moines is the most powerful hypnotic known to man. Outside town there is a big sign that says, WELCOME TO DES MOINES. THIS IS WHAT DEATH IS LIKE. There isn't really. I just made that up. But the place does get a grip on you. People who have nothing to do with Des Moines drive in off the interstate, looking for gas or hamburgers, and stay forever. There's a New Jersey couple up the street from my parents' house whom you see wandering around from time to time looking faintly puzzled but strangely serene. Everybody in Des Moines is strangely serene.

The only person I ever knew in Des Moines who wasn't serene was Mr. Piper. Mr. Piper was my parents' neighbor, a leering, cherry-faced idiot who was forever getting drunk and

3

crashing his car into telephone poles. Everywhere you went you encountered telephone poles and road signs leaning dangerously in testimony to Mr. Piper's driving habits. He distributed them all over the west side of town rather in the way dogs mark trees. Mr. Piper was the nearest possible human equivalent to Fred Flintstone, but less charming. He was a Shriner and a Republican—a Nixon Republican—and he appeared to feel he had a mission in life to spread offense. His favorite pastime, apart from getting drunk and crashing his car, was to get drunk and insult the neighbors, particularly us because we were Democrats, though he was prepared to insult Republicans when we weren't available.

Eventually, I grew up and moved to England. This irritated Mr. Piper almost beyond measure. It was worse than being a Democrat. Whenever I was in town, Mr. Piper would come over and chide me. "I don't know what you're doing over there with all those Limeys," he would say provocatively. "They're not clean people."

"Mr. Piper, you don't know what you're talking about," I would reply in my affected British accent. "You are a cretin." You could talk like that to Mr. Piper because (1) he *was* a cretin and (2) he never listened to anything that was said to him.

"Bobbi and I went over to London two years ago and our hotel room didn't even have a *bath*room in it," Mr. Piper would go on. "If you wanted to take a leak in the middle of the night you had to walk about a mile down the hallway. That isn't a clean way to live."

"Mr. Piper, the English are paragons of cleanliness. It is a well-known fact that they use more soap per capita than anyone else in Europe."

Mr. Piper would snort derisively at this. "That doesn't mean diddly-squat, boy, just because they're cleaner than a bunch of Krauts and Eye-ties. My God, a *dog's* cleaner than a bunch of Krauts and Eye-ties. And I'll tell you something else: If his daddy hadn't bought Illinois for him, John F. Kennedy would never have been elected president."

I had lived around Mr. Piper long enough not to be thrown by this abrupt change of tack. The theft of the 1960 presidential

4

election was a longstanding plaint of his, one that he brought into the conversation every ten or twelve minutes regardless of the prevailing drift of the discussion. In 1963, during Kennedy's funeral, someone in the Waveland Tap punched Mr. Piper in the nose for making that remark. Mr. Piper was so furious that he went straight out and crashed his car into a telephone pole. Mr. Piper is dead now, which is of course one thing that Des Moines prepares you for.

When I was growing up I used to think that the best thing about coming from Des Moines was that it meant you didn't come from anywhere else in Iowa. By Iowa standards, Des Moines is a mecca of cosmopolitanism, a dynamic hub of wealth and education, where people wear three-piece suits and dark socks, often simultaneously. During the annual state high-school basketball tournament, when the hayseeds from out in the state would flood into the city for a week, we used to accost them downtown and snidely offer to show them how to ride an escalator or negotiate a revolving door. This wasn't always so far from reality. My friend Stan, when he was about sixteen, had to go and stay with his cousin in some remote, dusty hamlet called Dog Water or Dunceville or some such improbable spot—the kind of place where if a dog gets run over by a truck everybody goes out to have a look at it. By the second week, delirious with boredom, Stan insisted that he and his cousin drive the fifty miles into the county town, Hooterville, and find something to do. They went bowling at an alley with warped lanes and chipped balls and afterwards had a chocolate soda and looked at a *Playboy* in a drugstore, and on the way home the cousin sighed with immense satisfaction and said, "Gee thanks, Stan. That was the best time I ever had in my whole life!" It's true.

I had to drive to Minneapolis once, and I went on a back road just to see the country. But there was nothing to see. It's just flat and hot, and full of corn and soybeans and hogs. Every once in a while you come across a farm or some dead little town where the liveliest thing is the flies. I remember one long, shimmering stretch where I could see a couple of miles down the highway and there was a brown dot beside the road. As I got closer I saw it was a man sitting on a box by his front yard, in some six-house town with a name like Spigot or Urinal watching my approach with inordinate interest. He watched me zip past and in the rearview mirror I could see him still watching me going on down the road until at last I disappeared into a heat haze. The whole thing must have taken about five minutes. I wouldn't be surprised if even now he thinks of me from time to time.

He was wearing a baseball cap. You can always spot an Iowa man because he is wearing a baseball cap advertising John Deere or a feed company, and because the back of his neck has been lasered into deep crevices by years of driving a John Deere tractor back and forth in a blazing sun. (This does not do his mind a whole lot of good either.) His other distinguishing feature is that he looks ridiculous when he takes off his shirt because his neck and arms are chocolate brown and his torso is as white as a sow's belly. In Iowa it is called a farmer's tan and it is, I believe, a badge of distinction.

Iowa women are almost always sensationally overweight— you see them at Merle Hay Mall in Des Moines on Saturdays, clammy and meaty in their shorts and halter tops, looking a little like elephants dressed in children's clothes, yelling at their kids, calling out names like Dwayne and Shauna. Jack Kerouac, of all people, thought that Iowa women were the prettiest in the country, but I don't think he ever went to Merle Hay Mall on a Saturday. I will say this, however—and it's a strange, strange thing—the teenaged daughters of these fat women are always utterly delectable, as soft and gloriously rounded and naturally fresh-smelling as a basket of fruit. I don't know what it is that happens to them, but it must be awful to marry one of those nubile cuties knowing that there is a time bomb ticking away in her that will at some unknown date make her bloat out into something huge and grotesque, presumably all of a sudden and without much notice, like a self-inflating raft from which the pin has been yanked.

Even without this inducement, I don't think I would have stayed in Iowa. I never felt altogether at home there, even when I was small. In about 1957, my grandparents gave me a View-Master for my birthday and a packet of disks with the title "Iowa—Our Glorious State." I can remember thinking even then that the selection of glories was a trifle on the thin side. With no natural features of note, no national parks, no battlefields or famous birthplaces, the View-Master people had to stretch their creative 3-D talents to the full. Putting the View-Master to your eyes and clicking the white handle gave you, as I recall, a shot of Herbert Hoover's birthplace, impressively three-dimensional, followed by Iowa's other great treasure, the Little Brown Church in the Vale (which inspired the song whose tune nobody ever quite knows), the highway bridge over the Mississippi River at Davenport (all the cars seemed to be hurrying towards Illinois), a field of waving corn, the bridge over the Missouri River at Council Bluffs and the Little Brown Church in the Vale again, taken from another angle. I can remember thinking even then that there must be more to life than that.

Then one gray Sunday afternoon when I was about ten I was watching TV and there was a documentary on about moviemaking in Europe. One clip showed Anthony Perkins walking along some sloping city street at dusk. I don't remember now if it was Rome or Paris, but the street was cobbled and shiny with rain and Perkins was hunched deep in a trench coat and I thought: "Hey, *c'est moi!*" I began to read—no, I began to *consume—National Geographic*s, with their pictures of glowing Lapps and mist-shrouded castles and ancient cities of infinite charm. From that moment, I wanted to be a European boy. I wanted to live in an apartment across from a park in the heart of a city, and from my bedroom window look out on a crowded vista of hills and rooftops. I wanted to ride trams and understand strange languages. I wanted friends named Werner and Marco who wore short pants and played soccer in the street and owned toys made of wood. I cannot for the life of me think why. I wanted my mother to send me out to buy long loaves of bread from a shop with a wooden pretzel hanging above the entrance. I wanted to step outside my front door and *be* somewhere.

As soon as I was old enough I left. I left Des Moines and Iowa and the United States and the war in Vietnam and Watergate, and settled across the world. And now when I came home it was to a foreign country, full of serial murderers and sports teams in the wrong towns (the Indianapolis Colts? the Phoenix Cardinals?)

and a personable old fart who was president. My mother knew that personable old fart when he was a sportscaster called Dutch Reagan at WHO Radio in Des Moines. "He was just a nice, friendly, kind of dopey guy," my mother says.

Which, come to that, is a pretty fair description of most Iowans. Don't get me wrong. I am not for a moment suggesting that Iowans are mentally deficient. They are a decidedly intelligent and sensible people who, despite their natural conservatism, have always been prepared to elect a conscientious, clearthinking liberal in preference to some cretinous conservative. (This used to drive Mr. Piper practically insane.) And Iowans, I am proud to tell you, have the highest literacy rate in the nation: 99.5 percent of grownups there can read. When I say they are kind of dopey I mean that they are trusting and amiable and open. They are a tad slow, certainly—when you tell an Iowan a joke, you can see a kind of race going on between his brain and his expression—but it's not because they're incapable of highspeed mental activity, it's only that there's not much call for it. Their wits are dulled by simple, wholesome faith in God and the soil and their fellow man.

Above all, Iowans are friendly. You go into a strange diner in the South and everything goes quiet, and you realize all the other customers are looking at you as if they are sizing up the risk involved in murdering you for your wallet and leaving your body in a shallow grave somewhere out in the swamps. In Iowa you are the center of attention, the most interesting thing to hit town since a tornado carried off old Frank Sprinkel and his tractor last May. Everybody you meet acts like he would gladly give you his last beer and let you sleep with his sister. Everyone is happy and friendly and strangely serene.

The last time I was home, I went to Kresge's downtown and bought a bunch of postcards to send back to England. I bought the most ridiculous ones I could find—a sunset over a feedlot, a picture of farmers bravely grasping a moving staircase beside the caption "We rode the escalator at Merle Hay Mall!" that sort of thing. They were so uniformly absurd that when I took them up to the checkout, I felt embarrassed by them, as if I were buying dirty magazines and hoped somehow to convey the impression

8

that they weren't really for me. But the checkout lady regarded each of them with interest and deliberation—just as they always do with dirty magazines, come to that.

When she looked up at me she was almost misty-eyed. She wore butterfly eyeglasses and a beehive hairdo. "Those are real nice," she said. "You know, honey, I've bin in a lot of states and seen a lot of places, but I can tell you that this is just about the purtiest one I ever saw." She really said "purtiest." She really meant it. The poor woman was in a state of terminal hypnosis. I glanced at the cards and to my surprise I suddenly saw what she meant. I couldn't help but agree with her. They *were* purty. Together, we made a little pool of silent admiration. For one giddy, careless moment, I was almost serene myself. It was a strange sensation, and it soon passed.

My father liked Iowa. He lived his whole life in the state, and is even now working his way through eternity there, in Glendale Cemetery in Des Moines. But every year he became seized with a quietly maniacal urge to get out of the state and go on vacation. Every summer, without a whole lot of notice, he would load the car to groaning, hurry us into it, take off for some distant point, return to get his wallet after having driven almost to the next state, and take off again for some distant point. Every year it was the same. Every year it was awful.

The big killer was the tedium. Iowa is in the middle of the biggest plain this side of Jupiter. Climb onto a rooftop almost anywhere in the state and you are confronted with a featureless sweep of corn for as far as the eye can see. It is a thousand miles from the sea in any direction, four hundred miles from the nearest mountain, three hundred miles from skyscrapers and muggers and things of interest, two hundred miles from people who do not habitually stick a finger in their ear and swivel it around as a preliminary to answering any question addressed to them by a stranger. To reach anywhere of even passing interest from Des Moines by car requires a journey that in other countries would be considered epic. It means days and days of unrelenting tedium, in a baking steel capsule on a ribbon of highway.

In my memory, our vacations were always taken in a big blue Rambler station wagon. It was a cruddy car—my dad always bought cruddy cars, until he got to the male menopause and started buying zippy red convertibles—but it had the great virtue of space. My brother, my sister and I in the back were miles away from my parents up front, in effect in another room. We quickly discovered during illicit forays into the picnic hamper that if you stuck a bunch of Ohio Blue Tip matches into an apple or hard-boiled egg, so that it resembled a porcupine, and casually dropped it out the tailgate window, it was like a bomb. It would explode with a small bang and a surprisingly big flash of blue flame, causing cars following behind to veer in an amusing fashion.

My dad, miles away up front, never knew what was going on or could understand why all day long cars would zoom up alongside him with the driver gesticulating furiously, before tearing off into the distance. "What was that all about?" he would say to my mother in a wounded tone.

"I don't know, dear," my mother would answer mildly. My mother only ever said two things. She said, "I don't know, dear." And she said, "Can I get you a sandwich, honey?" Occasionally on our trips she would volunteer other pieces of intelligence like "Should that dashboard light be glowing like that, dear?" or "I think you hit that dog/man/blind person back there, honey," but mostly she wisely kept quiet. This was because on vacations my father was a man obsessed. His principal obsession was with trying to economize. He always took us to the crummiest hotels and motor lodges and to the kind of roadside eating houses where they only washed the dishes weekly. You always knew, with a sense of doom, that at some point before finishing you were going to discover someone else's congealed egg yolk lurking somewhere on your plate or plugged between the tines of your fork. This, of course, meant cooties and a long, painful death.

But even that was a relative treat. Usually we were forced to picnic by the side of the road. My father had an instinct for picking bad picnic sites—on the apron of a busy truck stop or in a little park that turned out to be in the heart of some seriously deprived ghetto, so that groups of children would come and stand silently by our table and watch us eating Hostess cupcakes and crinkle-cut potato chips—and it always became incredibly windy the moment we stopped, so that my mother spent the whole of lunchtime chasing paper plates over an area of about an acre.

In 1957 my father invested $19.98 in a portable gas stove that took an hour to assemble before each use and was so wildly temperamental that we children were always ordered to stand well back when it was being lit. This always proved unnecessary, however, because the stove would flicker to life only for a few seconds before puttering out, and my father would spend many hours turning it this way and that to keep it out of the wind, simultaneously addressing it in a low, agitated tone normally associated with the chronically insane. All the while my brother, my sister and I would implore him to take us someplace with air-conditioning, linen tablecloths and ice cubes clinking in glasses of clear water. "Dad," we would beg, "you're a successful man. You make a good living. Take us to a Howard Johnson's." But he wouldn't have it. He was a child of the Depression and where capital outlays were involved he always wore the haunted look of a fugitive who has just heard bloodhounds in the distance.

Eventually, with the sun low in the sky, he would hand us hamburgers that were cold and raw and smelled of butane. We would take one bite and refuse to eat any more. So my father would lose his temper and throw everything into the car and drive us at high speed to some roadside diner where a sweaty man with a floppy hat would sling hash while grease fires danced on his grill. And afterwards, in a silent car filled with bitterness and unquenched basic needs, we would mistakenly turn off the main highway and get lost and end up in some no-hope hamlet with a name like Draino, Indiana, or Tapwater, Missouri, and get a room in the only hotel in town, the sort of run-down place where if you wanted to watch TV it meant you had to sit in the lobby and share a cracked leatherette sofa with an old man with big sweat circles under his arms. The old man would almost certainly have only one leg and probably one other truly arresting deficiency, like no nose or a caved-in forehead, which meant that although you were sincerely intent on watching "Laramie" or "Our Miss Brooks," you found your gaze being drawn, ineluctably and sneakily, to the amazing eaten-away body sitting beside you. You couldn't help yourself. Occasionally the man would turn out to have no tongue, in which case he would try to engage you in lively conversation. It was all most unsatisfying.

After a week or so of this kind of searing torment, we would fetch up at some blue and glinting sweep of lake or sea in a bowl of pine-clad mountains, a place full of swings and amusements and the gay shrieks of children splashing in water, and it would all almost be worth it. Dad would become funny and warm and even once or twice might take us out to the sort of restaurant where you didn't have to watch your food being cooked and where the glass of water they served you wasn't autographed with lipstick. This was living. This was heady opulence.

It was against this disturbed and erratic background that I became gripped with a curious urge to go back to the land of my youth and make what the blurb writers like to call a journey of discovery. On another continent, 4,000 miles away, I became quietly seized with that nostalgia that overcomes you when you have reached the middle of your life and your father has recently died and it dawns on you that when he went he took some of you with him. I wanted to go back to the magic places of my youth— to Mackinac Island, the Rocky Mountains, Gettysburg—and see if they were as good as I remembered them being. I wanted to hear the long, low sound of a Rock Island locomotive calling across a still night and the clack of it receding into the distance. I wanted to see lightning bugs, and hear cicadas shrill, and be inescapably immersed in that hot, crazy-making August weather that makes your underwear scoot up every crack and fissure and cling to you like latex, and drives mild-mannered men to pull out handguns in bars and light up the night with gunfire. I wanted to look for NeHi Pop and Burma Shave signs and go to a ball game and sit at a marble-topped soda fountain and drive through the kind of small towns that Deanna Durbin and Mickey Rooney used to inhabit in the movies. I wanted to travel around. I wanted to see America. I wanted to come home.

So I flew to Des Moines and acquired a sheaf of road maps, which I studied and puzzled over on the living room floor, drawing an immense circular itinerary that would take me all over this strange and giant semiforeign land. My mother, meantime, made me sandwiches and said, "Oh, I don't know, dear," when I asked her questions about the vacations of my childhood. And one September dawn in my thirty-sixth year I crept out of my childhood home, slid behind the wheel of an aging Chevrolet Chevette lent me by my sainted and trusting mother, and guided it out through the flat, sleeping streets of the city. I cruised down an empty freeway, the only person with a mission in a city of 250,000 sleeping souls. The sun was already high in the sky and promised a blisteringly hot day. Ahead of me lay about a million square miles of quietly rustling corn. At the edge of town I joined Iowa Highway 163 and with a light heart headed towards Missouri. And it isn't often you hear anyone say that.

2

IN BRITAIN it had been a year without summer. Wet spring had merged imperceptibly into bleak autumn. For months the sky had remained a depthless gray. Sometimes it rained, but mostly it was just dull, a land without shadows. It was like living inside Tupperware. And here suddenly the sun was dazzling in its intensity. Iowa was hysterical with color and light. Roadside barns were a glossy red, the sky a deep, hypnotic blue; fields of mustard and green stretched out before me. Flecks of mica glittered in the rolling road. And here and there in the distance mighty grain elevators, the cathedrals of the Middle West, the ships of the prairie seas, drew the sun's light and bounced it back as pure white. Squinting in the unaccustomed brilliance, I followed the highway to Otley.

My intention was to retrace the route my father always took to my grandparents' house in Winfield—through Prairie City, Pella, Oskaloosa, Hedrick, Brighton, Coppock, Wayland and Olds. The sequence was tattooed on my memory. Always having been a passenger before, I had never paid much attention to the road, so I was surprised to find that I kept coming up against odd turns and abrupt T-junctions, requiring me to go left here for a couple of miles, then right for a few miles, then left again and so on. It would have been much more straightforward to take High-way 92 to Ainsworth and then head south to Mount Pleasant. I couldn't imagine by what method of reasoning my father had ever settled on this route, and now of course I never would know. This seemed a pity, particularly as there was almost nothing he would have liked better than to cover the dining room table with maps and consider at length possible routings. In this he was like most Midwesterners. Directions are very important to them. They have an innate need to be oriented, even in their anecdotes. Any story related by a Midwesterner will wander off at some point into a thicket of interior monologue along the lines of "We were staying at a hotel that was eight blocks northeast of the state capitol building. Come to think of it, it was northwest. And I think it was probably more like nine blocks. And this woman without any clothes on, naked as the day she was born except for a coonskin cap, came running at us from the southwest . . . or was it the southeast?" If there are two Midwesterners present and they both witnessed the incident, you can just about write off the anecdote because they will spend the rest of the afternoon argu-ing points of the compass and will never get back to the original story. You can always tell a Midwestern couple in Europe because they will be standing on a traffic island in the middle of a busy intersection looking at a windblown map and arguing over which way is west. European cities, with their wandering streets and undisciplined alleys, drive Midwesterners practically insane.

This geographical obsession probably has something to do with the absence of landmarks throughout middle America. I had forgotten just how flat and empty it is. Stand on two phone books almost anywhere in Iowa and you get a view. From where I was now I could look out on a sweep of landscape about the size of Belgium, but there was nothing on it except for a few widely separated farms, some scattered stands of trees and two water towers, brilliant silver glints signifying distant, unseen towns. Far off in the middle distance a cloud of dust chased a car up a gravel road. The only things that stood out from the landscape were the grain elevators, but even they looked all the same, and there was nothing much to distinguish one view from another.

And it's so quiet. Apart from the ceaseless fidgeting of the corn, there is not a sound. Somebody could sneeze in a house three miles away and you would hear it ("Bless you!" "Thank you!"). It must nearly drive you crazy to live a life so devoid of stimulus, where no passing airplane ever draws your gaze and no car horns honk, where time shuffles forward so slowly that you half expect to find the people still watching Ozzie and Harriet on TV and voting for Eisenhower. ("I don't know how far you folks in Des Moines have got, but we're only up to 1958 here in Fudd County.")

Small towns are equally unhelpful in offering distinguishing features. About all that separates them are their names. They always have a gas station, a grocery store, a grain elevator, a place selling farm equipment and fertilizers, and something improbable like a microwave oven dealer or a dry cleaner's, so you can say to yourself as you glide through town, "Now what would they be doing with a dry cleaner's in Fungus City?" Every fourth or fifth community will be a county town, built around a square. A handsome brick courthouse with a Civil War cannon and a monument to the dead of at least two wars will stand on one side of the square and on the other sides will be businesses: a five-and-dime, a luncheonette, two banks, a hardware store, a Christian bookstore, a barber's, a couple of hairdressers, a place selling the sort of men's clothing that only someone from a very small town would wear. At least two of the businesses will be called Vern's. The central area of the square will be a park, with fat trees and a bandstand and a pole with an American flag and scattered benches full of old men in John Deere caps sitting around talking about the days when they had something else to do other than sit around and talk about the days when they had something else to do. Time in these places creaks along.

The best county town in Iowa is Pella, forty miles southeast of Des Moines. Pella was founded by Dutch immigrants and every May it still holds a big tulip festival for which they get somebody important like the mayor of The Hague to fly in and praise their bulbs. I used to like Pella when I was little because many of the residents put little windmills in their front yards, which made it kind of interesting. I wouldn't say it made it *outstandingly* interesting, but you learned from an early age to take what pleasures you could find on any trip across Iowa. Besides, Pella had a Dairy Queen on the edge of town where my father would sometimes stop and buy us ice cream cones dipped in chocolate, and for this alone I have always felt a special fondness for the place. So I was pleased to note, as I rolled into the town on this fine September morn, that there were still windmills whirling in many a front yard. I stopped at the square and got out to stretch my legs. It being a Sunday, the old men from the square had the day off—they would be on sleeping-in-front-of-the-TV duty all day—but in every other respect Pella was as perfect as I remembered it. The square was thick with trees and flowerbeds of blazing salvias and glowing marigolds. It had its own windmill, a handsome green one with white blades, nearly full-sized, standing on one corner. The stores around the square were of the cereal-box architecture favored by small-town stores throughout the Midwest, but with gingerbread cornices and other cheery embellishments. Every business had a solid, trustworthy Dutch name: Pardekooper's Drug Store, Jaarsma Bakery, Van Gorp Insurers, Gosselink's Christian Book Store, Vander Ploeg Bakery. All were shut, of course. Sundays are still closely observed in places like Pella. Indeed, the whole town was eerily quiet. It was steeped in that kind of dead silence that makes you begin to wonder, if you are of a suitably hysterical nature, if perhaps everybody has been poisoned in the night by a leak of odorless gas—which even now could be taking insidious control of your own central nervous system—turning Pella into a kind of Pompeii of the plains. I briefly imagined people from all over coming to look at the victims and being especially enthralled at the worried-looking young man in spectacles on the town square, forever clutching his throat and trying to get his car door open. But then I saw a man walking a dog at the far end of the square and realized that any danger was safely past.

I hadn't intended to linger, but it was such a splendid morning that I wandered off down a nearby street, past neat wooden-framed houses with cupolas and gables and front porches with two-seater swings that creaked in the breeze. There was no other sound, apart from the scuffling of my feet through dried leaves. At the bottom of the street, I came across the campus of Central

College, a small institution run by the Dutch Reformed Church, with a campus of red-brick buildings overlooking an ornamental pond with an arching wooden footbridge. The whole place was as tranquil as a double dose of Valium. It looked like the sort of tidy, friendly, clean-thinking college that Clark Kent would have attended. I crossed the bridge and at the far side of the campus found further evidence that I was not the only living person in Pella. From an open window high up in a dormitory building came the sound of a stereo turned up far too loud. It blared for a moment—something by Frankie Goes to Hollywood, I believe—and then from someplace indiscernible there came a booming voice that said, "IF YOU DON'T TURN THAT THING THE FUCK OFF RIGHT NOW I'M GONNA COME OVER THERE AND POUND YOUR HEAD IN!" It was the voice of a large person—someone, I fancied, with the nickname Moose. Immediately the music stopped and Pella slept again.

I continued on east, through Oskaloosa, Fremont, Hedrick, Martinsburg. The names were familiar, but the towns themselves awoke few memories. By this stage on most trips I was on the floor in a boredom-induced stupor, calling out at fifteen-second intervals, "How much longer? When are we going to be there? I'm bored. I feel sick. How much longer? When are we going to be there?" I vaguely recognized a bend in the road near Coppock, where we once spent four hours caught in a blizzard waiting for a snowplow to come through, and several spots where we had paused to let my sister throw up, including a gas station at Martinsburg where she tumbled out of the car and was lavishly sick in the direction of a pump attendant's ankles (boy, did that guy dance!), and another at Wayland where my father nearly left me at the side of the road after discovering that I had passed the time by working loose all the rivets on one of the back door panels, exposing an interesting view of the interior mechanisms, but unfortunately rendering both the window and door forever inoperable. However, it wasn't until I reached the turnoff for Winfield, just past Olds, a place where my father would announce with a sort of delirious joy that we were practically there, that I felt a pang of recognition. I had not been down this road for at least a dozen years, but its gentle slopes and isolated farms were as familiar to me as my own left leg. My heart soared. This was like going back in time. I was about to be a boy again.

Arriving in Winfield was always thrilling. Dad would turn off Highway 78 and bounce us down a rough gravel road at far too high a speed, throwing up clouds of white dust, and then to my mother's unfailing alarm would drive with evident insanity towards some railroad tracks on a blind bend in the road, remarking gravely, "I hope there's not a train coming." My mother didn't discover until years later that there were only two trains a day along those tracks, both in the dead of night. Beyond the tracks, standing alone in a neglected field, was a Victorian mansion like the one in the Charles Addams cartoons in *The New Yorker*. No one had lived in it for decades, but it was still full of furniture, under dank sheets. My sister and my brother and I used to climb in through a broken window and look through trunks of musty clothes and old *Collier's* magazines and photographs of strangely worried-looking people. Upstairs was a bedroom in which, according to my brother, lay the shriveled body of the last occupant, a woman who had died of heartbreak after being abandoned at the altar. We never went in there, though once, when I was about four, my brother peered through the keyhole, let out a howl, cried "She's coming!" and ran headlong down the stairs. Whimpering, I followed, squirting urine at every step. Beyond the mansion was a wide field, full of black-and-white cows, and beyond that was my grandparents' house, pretty and white beneath a canopy of trees, with a big red barn and acres of lawn. My grandparents were always waiting at the gate. I don't know whether they could see us coming and raced to their positions or whether they just waited there hour after hour. Quite possibly the latter because, let's face it, they didn't have a whole lot else to do. And then it would be four or five days of fun. My grandfather had a Model T Ford, which he let us kids drive around the yard, to the distress of his chickens and the older women. In the winter he would attach a sleigh to the back and take us for long cold rides down snowy roads. In the evenings we would all play cards around the kitchen table and stay up late. It was always

Christmas at my grandparents' house, or Thanksgiving, or the Fourth of July, or somebody's birthday. There was always happiness there.

When we arrived, my grandmother would scuttle off to pull something fresh-baked out of the oven. This was always something unusual. My grandmother was the only person I ever knew—possibly the only person who ever lived—who actually made things from the recipes on the backs of food packets. These dishes always had names like Rice Krispies 'n' Banana Chunks Upside Down Cake or Del Monte Lima Bean 'n' Pretzels Party Snacks. Generally they consisted of suspiciously large amounts of the manufacturer's own products, usually in combinations you wouldn't think of except perhaps in an especially severe famine. The one thing to be said for these dishes was that they were novel. When my grandmother offered you a steaming slab of cake or wedge of pie it might contain almost anything—Niblets sweet corn, chocolate chips, Spam, diced carrots, peanut butter. Generally it would have some Rice Krispies in it somewhere. My grandmother was particularly partial to Rice Krispies and would add a couple of shovelfuls to whatever she made, even if the recipe didn't call for it. She was about as bad a cook as you can be without actually being hazardous.

It all seems so long ago now. And it was. It was so long ago, in fact, that my grandparents had a crank telephone, the kind that hung on the wall and had a handle you turned and said, "Mabel, get me Gladys Scribbage. I want to ask her how she makes her Frosted Flakes 'n' Cheez Whiz Party Nuggets." And it would turn out that Gladys Scribbage was already listening in, or somebody else listening in would know how to make Frosted Flakes 'n' Cheez Whiz Party Nuggets. Everybody listened in. My grandmother often listened in when things were slow around the house, covering the mouthpiece with a hand and relaying to the rest of the room vivid accounts of colonic irrigations, prolapsed wombs, husbands who ran off to Burlington with the barmaid from Vern's Uptown Tavern and Supper Club, and other crises of small-town life. We always had to maintain the strictest silence during these sessions. I could never entirely understand why because if things got really juicy my grandmother would often butt in. "Well, I think Merle's a real skunk," she would say. "Yes, that's right, it's Maude Bryson here, and I just want to say that I think he's an absolute stinker to do that to poor Pearl. And I'll tell you something else, Mabel, you know you could get those support bras a dollar cheaper in Columbus Junction." In about 1962 the telephone company came and put a normal phone without a party line in my grandmother's house, possibly at the request of the rest of the town. It drove a hole right through her life from which she never entirely recovered.

I didn't really expect my grandparents to be waiting for me at the gate, on account of them both having been dead for many years. But I suppose I had vaguely hoped that another nice old couple might be living there now and would invite me in to look around and share my reminiscences. Perhaps they would let me be their grandson. At the very least, I had assumed that my grandparents' house would be just as I had last seen it.

It was not to be. The road leading to the house was still graveled with gleaming gypsum pebbles and still threw up satisfying clouds of dust, but the railroad tracks were gone. There was no sign that they had ever been there. The Victorian mansion was gone too, replaced by a ranch house–style home with cars and propane gas cylinders scattered around the yard like a toddler's playthings. Worse still, the field of cows was now an estate of box houses. My grandparents' home had stood well outside the town, a cool island of trees in an ocean of fields. Now cheap little houses crowded in on it from all sides. With shock, I realized that the barn was gone. Some jerk had torn down my barn! And the house itself—well, it was a shack. Paint had abandoned it in chunks. Bushes had been pointlessly uprooted, trees chopped down. The grass was high and littered with overspill from the house. I stopped the car on the road out front and just gaped. I cannot describe the sense of loss. Half my memories were inside that house. After a moment a hugely overweight woman in pink shorts, talking on a phone with an apparently endless cord, came and stood in the open doorway and stared at me, wondering what I was doing staring at her.

I drove on into the town. When I was growing up Main Street in Winfield had two grocery stores, a variety store, a tavern, a pool hall, a newspaper, a bank, a barbershop, a post office, two gas stations—all the things you would expect of any thriving little town. Everyone shopped locally; everyone knew everyone else. Now all that was left was a tavern and a place selling farm equipment. There were half a dozen vacant lots, full of patchy grass, where buildings had been torn down and never replaced. Most of the remaining buildings were dark and boarded up. It was like an abandoned film set which had long since been left to decay.

I couldn't understand what had happened. People now must have to drive thirty miles to buy a loaf of bread. Outside the tavern a group of young thuggy-looking motorcyclists were hanging out. I was going to stop to ask them what had happened to their town, but one of them, seeing me slow down, gave me the finger. For no reason. He was about fourteen. Abruptly, I drove on, back out towards Highway 78, past the scattered farms and gentle slopes that I knew like my own left leg. It was the first time in my life that I had turned my back on a place knowing that I would never see it again. It was all very sad, but I should have known better. As I always used to tell Thomas Wolfe, there are three things you just can't do in life. You can't beat the phone company, you can't make a waiter see you until he's ready to see you, and you can't go home again.

3

I DROVE ON, without the radio or much in the way of thoughts, to Mount Pleasant, where I stopped for coffee. I had the Sunday *New York Times* with me—one of the greatest improvements in life since I had been away was that you could now buy the *New York Times* out of machines on the day of publication in a place like Iowa, an extraordinary feat of distribution—and I spread out with it in a booth. Boy, do I love the Sunday *New York Times*. Apart from its many virtues as a newspaper, there is just something wonderfully reassuring about its very bulk. The issue in front of me must have weighed ten or twelve pounds. It could've stopped a bullet at twenty yards. I read once that it takes 75,000 trees to produce one issue of the Sunday *New York Times*—and it's well worth every trembling leaf. So what if our grandchildren have no oxygen to breathe? Fuck 'em.

My favorite parts of the *Times* are the peripheral bits—the parts that are so dull and obscure that they exert a kind of hypnotic fascination, like the home improvements column ("All You Need to Know About Fixings and Fastenings") and the stamps column ("Post Office Marks 25 Years of Aeronautic Issues"). Above all, I love the advertising supplements. If a Bulgarian asked me what life was like in America, I would without hesitation tell him to get ahold of a stack of *New York Times* advertising supplements. They show a life of richness and variety beyond the wildest dreams of most foreigners. As if to illustrate my point, the issue before me contained a gift catalog from the Zwingle Company of New York offering scores of products of the things-you-never-knew-you-needed variety—musical shoe trees, an umbrella with a transistor radio in the handle, an electric nail buffer. What a great country! My favorite was a small electric hot plate you could put on your desk to keep your coffee from going cold. This must be a real boon to people with brain damage, the sort of injuries that lead them to wander off and neglect their beverages. Really, who buys these things—silver toothpicks and monogrammed underpants and mirrors that say MAN OF THE YEAR on them? I have often thought that if I ran one of these companies I would produce a polished mahogany plaque with a brass plate on it saying, HEY, HOW ABOUT ME? I PAID $22.95 FOR THIS COMPLETELY USELESS PIECE OF CRAP. I'm certain they would sell like hotcakes.

Once in a deranged moment I bought something myself from one of these catalogs knowing deep in my mind that it would end in heartbreak. It was a little reading light that you clipped onto your book so as not to disturb your bedmate as she slumbered beside you. In this respect it was outstanding because it barely worked. The light it cast was absurdly feeble (in the catalog it looked like the sort of thing you could signal ships with if you got lost at sea) and left all but the first two lines of a page in darkness. I have seen more luminous insects. After about four minutes its little beam fluttered and failed altogether, and it has never been used again. And the thing is that I knew all along that this was how it was going to end, that it would all be a bitter disappointment. On second thought, if I ever ran one of those companies I would just send people an empty box with a note in it saying, "We have decided not to send you the item you've ordered because, as you well know, it would never properly work and you would only be disappointed. So let this be a lesson to you for the future."

From the Zwingle catalog I moved on to the food and household products advertisements. There is usually a wad of these bright and glossy inducements to try out exciting new products—

things with names like Hunk o' Meat Beef Stew 'n' Gravy ("with rich 'n' meaty chunks of beef-textured fiber") and Sniffa-Snax ("An Exciting New Snack Treat You Take Through the Nose!") and Country Sunshine Honey-Toasted Wheat Nut 'n' Sugar Bits Breakfast Cereal ("Now with Vitamin-Enriched Chocolate-Covered Raisin Substitute!"). I am endlessly fascinated by these new products. Clearly some time ago makers and consumers of American junk food passed jointly through some kind of sensibility barrier in the endless quest for new taste sensations. Now they are a little like those desperate junkies who have tried every known drug and are finally reduced to mainlining bathroom bowl cleanser in an effort to get still higher. All over America you can see countless flabby-butted couples quietly searching supermarket shelves for new combinations of flavors, hoping to find some untried product that will tingle in their mouths and excite, however briefly, their leaden taste buds.

The competition for this market is intense. The food inserts not only offered fifty-cent discounts and the like, but also if you sent off two or three labels the manufacturers would dispatch to you a Hunk o' Meat Beach Towel, or Country Sunshine Matching Apron and Oven Mitt, or a Sniffa-Snax hot plate for keeping your coffee warm while you slipped in and out of consciousness from a surfeit of blood sugar. Interestingly, the advertisements for dog food were much the same, except that they weren't usually chocolate flavored. In fact, every single product—from the lemon-scented toilet bowl cleansers to the scent-o'-pine trash bags—promised to give you a brief buzz. It's no wonder that so many Americans have a glazed look. They are completely junked out.

I drove on south on Highway 218 to Keokuk. This stretch of the road was marked on my map as a scenic route, though these things are decidedly relative. Talking about a scenic route in southeast Iowa is like talking about a good Barry Manilow album. You have to make certain allowances. Compared with an afternoon in a darkened room, it wasn't bad. But compared with, say, the coast road along the Sorrentine peninsula, it was perhaps a little tame. Certainly it didn't strike me as being any more or less scenic than any of the other roads I had been on today. Keokuk is a Mississippi River town where Iowa, Illinois and Missouri face each other across a broad bend in the river. I was heading towards Hannibal in Missouri and was hoping to see a bit of the town en route to the bridge south. But before I knew it, I found myself on a bridge going east to Illinois. I was so disconcerted by this that I only caught a glimpse of the river, a glistening smear of brown stretching off in two directions, and then, chagrined, I was in Illinois. I had really looked forward to seeing the Mississippi. Crossing it as a child had always been an adventure. Dad would call, "Here's the Mississippi, kids!" and we would scramble to the window to find ourselves on a bridge practically in the clouds, so high it made our breath catch, and the silvery river far, far below, wide, majestic, serene, going about its timeless business of just rolling on. You could see for miles—a novel experience in Iowa. You could see barges and islands and riverside towns. It looked wonderful. And then, abruptly, you were in Illinois and it was flat and full of corn and you realized with a sinking heart that that was it. That was your visual stimulation for the day. Now you had hundreds of miles more of arid cornland to cross before you would experience even the most fractional sense of pleasure.

And now here I was in Illinois, and it was flat and full of corn and boring. A childlike voice in my head cried, "When are we going to be there? I'm bored. Let's go home. When are we going to be there?" Having confidently expected at this stage to be in Missouri, I had my book of maps opened to the Missouri page, so I pulled over to the side of road, in a state of some petulance, to make a cartographical adjustment. A sign just ahead of me said, Buckle Up. Its the Law in Illinois. Clearly, however, it was not an offense to be unable to punctuate. Frowning, I studied my maps. If I turned off at Hamilton, just down the road, I could drive along the east bank of the river and cross into Missouri at Quincy. It was even marked on the map as a scenic route; perhaps my blundering would turn out to be no bad thing.

I followed the road through Warsaw, a run-down little river town. It plunged down a steep hill towards the river, but then turned inland and again I caught no more than a glimpse of the river. Almost immediately, the landscape spread out into a broad alluvial plain. The sun was sinking in the sky. To the left hills rose up, flecked with trees that were just beginning to show a blush of autumn color. To the right the land was as flat as a tabletop. Teams of combine harvesters labored in the fields, kicking up dust, working late to bring in the harvest. In the far distance, grain elevators caught the fading sun and glowed an opalescent white, as if lit from within. Somewhere out there, unseen, was the river.

I drove on. The road was completely unsignposted. They do this to you a lot in America, particularly on country roads that go from nowhere to nowhere. You are left to rely on your own sense of direction to find your way—which in my case, let us not forget, had only recently delivered me to the wrong state. I calculated that if I was going south the sun should be to my right (a conclusion I reached by imagining myself in a tiny car driving across a big map of America), but the road twisted and wandered, causing the sun to drift teasingly in front of me, first to this side of the road, then to that. For the first time all day, I had a sense of being in the heart of a vast continent, in the middle of nowhere.

Abruptly the highway turned to gravel. Gypsum nuggets, jagged as arrowheads, flew up against the underside of the car and made a fearful din. I had visions of hoses rupturing, hot oil spraying everywhere, me rolling to a steamy, hissing halt out here on this desolate road. The wandering sun was just settling onto the horizon, splashing the sky with faint pinks. Uneasily I drove on, and steeled myself for the prospect of a night spent beneath the stars, with doglike animals sniffing at my feet and snakes finding warmth up a trouser leg. Ahead of me on the road an advancing storm of dust became after a moment a pickup truck, which passed in a hellbent fashion, spraying the car with rocky projectiles, which thumped against the sides and bounced off the windows with a cracking sound, and then left me adrift in a cloud of dust. I trundled on, peering helplessly through the murk. It cleared just in time to show me that I was twenty feet from a T-junction with a stop sign. I was going fifty miles an hour, which on gravel leaves you with a stopping distance of about three miles. I jumped on the brakes with all my feet and made a noise like Tarzan missing a vine as the car went into a skid. It slide sideways past the stop sign and out onto a paved highway, where it came to a halt, rocking gently from side to side. At that instant an enormous semitrailer truck—all silver horns and flashing lights—blared mightily at me as it swept past, setting the car to rocking again. Had I slid out onto the highway three seconds earlier it would have crushed the car into something about the size of a bouillon cube. I pulled onto the shoulder and got out to examine the damage. It looked as if the car had been dive-bombed with bags of flour. Bits of raw metal showed through where paint had been pinged away. I thanked God that my mother was so much smaller than me. I sighed, suddenly feeling lost and far from home, and noticed ahead a road sign pointing the way to Quincy. I had come to a halt facing in the right direction, so at least something had come of it.

It was time to stop. Just down the road stood a little town, which I shall call Dullard lest the people recognize themselves and take me to court or come to my house and batter me with baseball bats. On the edge of town was an old motel which looked pretty seedy, though judging by the absence of charred furniture in the front yard it was clearly a step up from the sort of place my dad would have chosen. I pulled onto the gravel drive and went inside. A woman of about seventy-five was sitting behind the desk. She wore butterfly glasses and a beehive hairdo. She was doing one of those books that require you to find words in a mass of letters and circle them. I think it was called *Word Puzzles for Morons.*

"Help yew?" she drawled without looking up.

"I'd like a room for the night, please."

"That'll be thirty-eight dollars and fifty cents," she replied, as her pen fell greedily on the word *yup.*

I was nonplussed. In my day a motel room cost about twelve dollars. "I don't want to *buy* the room," I explained. "I just want to sleep in it for one night."

She looked at me gravely over the tops of her glasses. "The

28

room is thirty-eight dollars and fifty cents. Per night. Plus tax. You want it or not?" She had one of those disagreeable accents that add a syllable to every word. *Tax* came out as *tayax*.

We both knew that I was miles from anywhere. "Yes, please," I said contritely. I signed in and crunched across the gravel to my *suite du nuit.* There appeared to be no other customers. I went into my room with my bag and had a look around, as you do in a new place. There was a black-and-white TV, which appeared to get only one channel, and three bent coat hangers. The bathroom mirror was cracked, and the shower curtains didn't match. The toilet seat had a strip of paper across it saying SANITIZED FOR YOUR PROTECTION, but floating beneath it was a cigarette butt, adrift in a little circle of nicotine. Dad would have liked it here, I thought.

I had a shower—that is to say, water dribbled onto my head from a nozzle in the wall—and afterwards went out to check out the town. I had a meal of gristle and baked whiffle ball at a place called—aptly—Chuck's. I didn't think it was possible to get a truly bad meal anywhere in the Midwest, but Chuck managed to provide it. It was the worst food I had ever had—and remember, I've lived in England. It had all the attributes of chewing gum, except flavor. Even now when I burp I can taste it.

Afterwards I had a look around the town. There wasn't much. It was mostly just one street, with a grain silo and railroad tracks at one end and my motel at the other, with a couple of gas stations and grocery stores in between. Everyone regarded me with interest. Years ago, in the midst of a vivid and impressionable youth, I read a chilling story by Richard Matheson about a remote hamlet whose inhabitants waited every year for a lone stranger to come to town so that they could roast him for their annual barbecue. The people here watched me with barbecue eyes.

Feeling self-conscious, I went into a dark place called Vern's Tap and took a seat at the bar. I was the only customer, apart from an old man in the corner with only one leg. The barmaid was friendly. She wore butterfly glasses and a beehive hairdo. You could see in an instant that she had been the local good-time girl since about 1931. She had "Ready for Sex" written all over her face, but "Better Bring a Paper Bag" written all over her body. Somehow she had managed to pour her capacious backside into some tight red toreador pants and to stretch a clinging blouse over her bosom. She looked as if she had dressed in her granddaughter's clothes by mistake. She was about sixty. I could see why the guy with one leg had chosen to sit in the farthest corner.

I asked her what people in Dullard did for fun. "What exactly did you have in mind, honey?" she said and rolled her eyes suggestively. "Well, perhaps something in the way of legitimate theater or maybe an international chess congress," I croaked weakly. However, once we established that I was only prepared to love her for her mind, she became quite sensible and even rather charming. She told me in great and frank detail about her life, which seemed to have involved a dizzying succession of marriages to guys who were now in prison or dead as a result of shootouts, and dropped in breathtakingly candid disclosures like, "Now Jimmy kilt his mother, I never did know why, but Curtis never kilt nobody except once by accident when he was robbing a gas station and his gun went off. And Floyd—he was my fourth husband—he never kilt nobody neither, but he used to break people's arms if they got him riled."

"You must have some interesting family reunions," I ventured politely.

"I don't know what ever became of Floyd," she went on. "He had a little cleft in his chin rot year"—after a moment I realized that this was downstate Illinois for "right here, on this very spot indicated"—"that made him look kind of like Kirk Douglas. He was real cute, but he had a temper on him. I got a two-foot scar right across my back where he cut me with an ice pick. You wanna see it?" She started to hoist up her blouse, but I stopped her. She went on and on like that for ages. Every once in a while the guy in the corner, who was clearly eavesdropping, would grin, showing large yellow teeth. I expect Floyd had torn his leg off in a moment of high spirits. At the end of our conversation, the barmaid gave me a sideways look, as if I had been slyly trying to fool her, and said, "Say, where do you come from anyway, honey?"

I didn't feeling like giving her my whole life story, so I just said, "Great Britain."

"Well, I'll tell you one thing, honey," she said, "for a foreigner you speak English real good."

Afterwards I retired with a six-pack to my motel, where I discovered that the bed, judging by its fragrance and shape, had only recently been vacated by a horse. It had a sag in it so severe that I could see the TV at its foot only by splaying my legs to their widest extremity. It was like lying in a wheelbarrow. The night was hot and the air conditioner, an aged Philco window unit, expended so much energy making a noise like a steelworks that it could only manage to emit the feeblest and most occasional puffs of cool air. I lay with the six-pack on my chest, effectively immobilized, and drank the beers one by one. On the TV was a talk show presided over by some smooth asshole in a blazer whose name I didn't catch. He was the kind of guy for whom personal hair care was clearly a high priority. He exchanged some witless banter with the bandleader, who of course had a silvery goatee, and then turned to the camera and said in a solemn voice, "But seriously, folks. If you've ever had a personal problem or trouble at work or you just can't seem to get a grip on life, I know you're gonna be real interested in what our first guest has to tell you tonight. Ladies and gentlemen: Dr. Joyce Brothers."

As the band launched into a perky tune and Joyce Brothers strode onstage, I sat up as far as the bed would allow me and cried, "Joyce! Joyce Brothers!" as if to an old friend. I couldn't believe it. I hadn't seen Joyce Brothers for years and she hadn't changed a bit. Not one hair on her head had altered a fraction since the last time I saw her, droning on about menstrual flow, in 1962. It was as if they had kept her in a box for twenty-five years. This was as close as I would ever come to time travel. I watched agog as she and Mr. Smoothie chattered away about penis envy and fallopian tubes. I kept expecting him to say to her, "Now seriously, Joyce, here's a question all America has been wanting me to ask you: What sort of drugs do you take to keep yourself looking like that? Also, when are you going to do something about that hairstyle? And finally, why is it, do you think, that talk-show bozos like me all over America keep inviting you back again and again?" Because, let's be frank, Joyce Brothers is pretty dull. I mean, if you turn on the Johnny Carson show and she is one of the guests you know that absolutely everybody in town must be at some really big party or premiere. She is like downstate Illinois made flesh.

Still, like most immensely boring things, there is something wonderfully comforting about her. Her cheery visage on the glowing box at the foot of my bed made me feel strangely warm and whole and at peace with the world. Out here in this crud-bucket motel in the middle of a great empty plain I began for the first time to feel at home. I somehow knew that when I awoke I would see this alien land in a new but oddly familiar light. With a happy heart, I fell asleep and dreamed gentle dreams of southern Illinois and the rolling Mississippi River and Dr. Joyce Brothers. And it's not often you hear anyone say that either.

4

IN THE MORNING I crossed the Mississippi at Quincy; somehow it didn't look as big or majestic as I had remembered it. It was stately. It was imposing. It took whole minutes to cross. But it was also somehow flat and dull. This may have had something to do with the weather, which was likewise flat and dull. Missouri looked precisely the same as Illinois, which had looked precisely the same as Iowa. The only difference was that the car license plates were a different color.

Near Palmyra, I stopped at a roadside cafe for breakfast and took a seat at the counter. At this hour, just after eight in the morning, it was full of farmers. If there is one thing farmers sure do love it is to drive into town and spend half a day (a whole day in winter) sitting at a counter with a bunch of other farmers drinking coffee and teasing the waitress in a half-assed sort of way. I had thought that this was the busiest time of their year, but they didn't seem to be in any rush. Every once in a while one of them would put a quarter on the counter, get up with the air of a man who has just loaded six gallons of coffee into his belly, tell Tammy not to do anything he wouldn't do, and depart. A moment later we would hear the grip of his pickup truck's wheels on the gravel drive, someone would say something candid about him, provoking appreciative laughter, and the conversation would drift lazily back to hogs, state politics, Big Eight football and—when Tammy was out of earshot—sexual predilections, not least Tammy's.

The farmer next to me had only three fingers on his right hand. It is a little-noticed fact that most farmers have parts missing off them. This used to trouble me when I was small. For a long time I assumed that it was because of the hazards of farming life. After all, farmers deal with lots of dangerous machinery. But when you think about it, a lot of people deal with dangerous machinery, and only a tiny proportion of them ever suffer permanent injury. Yet there is scarcely a farmer in the Midwest over the age of twenty who has not at some time or other had a limb or digit yanked off and thrown into the next field by some noisy farmyard implement. To tell you the absolute truth, I think farmers do it on purpose. I think working day after day beside these massive threshers and balers with their grinding gears and flapping fan belts and complex mechanisms they get a little hypnotized by all the noise and motion. They stand there staring at the whirring machinery and they think, "I wonder what would happen if I just stuck my finger in there a little bit." I know that sounds crazy. But you have to realize that farmers don't have a whole lot of sense in these matters because they feel no pain. It's true. Every day in the *Des Moines Register* you can find a story about a farmer who has inadvertently torn off an arm and then calmly walked six miles into the nearest town to have it sewn back on. The stories always say, "Jones, clutching his severed limb, told his physician, 'I seem to have cut my durn arm off, Doc.'" It's never: "Jones, spurting blood, jumped around hysterically for twenty minutes, fell into a swoon and then tried to run in four directions at once," which is how it would be with you or me. Farmers simply don't feel pain—that little voice in your head that tells you not to do something because it's foolish and will hurt like hell and for the rest of your life somebody will have to cut up your food for you doesn't speak to them. My grandfather was just the same. He would often be repairing the car when the jack would slip and he would call out to you to come and crank it up again as he was having difficulty breathing, or he would run over his foot with the lawn mower, or touch a live wire, shorting out the whole of Winfield but leaving himself unscathed apart from a ringing in the ears and a certain lingering smell of burnt flesh. Like most people from the rural Midwest, he was practically indestructible. There are only three things that can kill a farmer: lightning, rolling over in a tractor and old age. It was old age that got my grandfather.

I drove on forty miles south to Hannibal, and went to see Mark Twain's boyhood home, a trim and tidy whitewashed house with green shutters set incongruously in the middle of the downtown. It cost two dollars to get in and was a disappointment. It purported to be a faithful reproduction of the original interiors, but there were wires and water sprinklers clumsily evident in every room. I also very much doubt that young Samuel Clemens's bedroom had Armstrong vinyl on the floor (the same pattern as in my mother's kitchen, I was interested to note) or that his sister's bedroom had a plywood partition in it. You don't actually go in the house; you look through the windows. At each window there is a recorded message telling you about that room as if you were a moron ("This is the kitchen. This is where Mrs. Clemens would prepare the family's meals. . . ."). The whole thing is pretty shabby, which wouldn't be so awful if it were owned by some underfunded local literary society and they were doing the best they could with it. In fact, it is owned by the city of Hannibal and it draws 135,000 visitors a year. It's a little gold mine for the town.

I proceeded from window to window behind a bald fat guy, whose abundant rolls of flesh made him look as if he were wearing an assortment of inner tubes beneath his shirt. "What do you think of it?" I asked him. He fixed me with that instant friendliness Americans freely adopt with strangers. It is their most becoming trait. "Oh, I think it's great. I come here whenever I'm in Hannibal—two, three times a year. Sometimes I go out of my way to come here."

"Really?" I tried not to sound dumbfounded.

"Yeah. I must have been here twenty, thirty times by now. This is a real shrine, you know."

"You think it's well done?"

"Oh, for sure."

"Would you say the house is just like Twain described it in his books?"

"I don't know," the man said thoughtfully. "I've never read one of his books."

Next door, attached to the house, was a small museum, which was better. There were cases of Twain memorabilia—first editions, one of his typewriters, photographs, some letters. There was precious little to link him to the house or the town. It is worth remembering that Twain got the hell out of both Hannibal and Missouri as soon as he could, and was always disinclined to come back. I went outside and looked around. Beside the house was a white fence with a sign saying, TOM SAWYER'S FENCE. HERE STOOD THE BOARD FENCE WHICH TOM SAWYER PERSUADED HIS GANG TO PAY HIM FOR THE PLEASURE OF WHITEWASHING. TOM SAT BY AND SAW THAT IT WAS WELL DONE. Really wakes up your interest in literature, doesn't it? Next door to the Twain house and museum—and I mean absolutely right next to it—was the Mark Twain Drive-In Restaurant and Dinette, with cars parked in little bays and people grazing off trays attached to their windows. It really lent the scene a touch of class. I began to understand why Clemens not just left town but also changed his name.

I strolled around the business district. The whole area was a dispiriting combination of auto parts stores, empty buildings and vacant lots. I had always thought that all river towns, even the poor ones, had something about them—a kind of faded elegance, a raffish air—that made them more interesting than other towns, that the river served as a conduit to the larger world and washed up a more interesting and sophisticated brand of detritus. But not Hannibal. It had obviously had better days, but even they couldn't have been all that great. The Hotel Mark Twain was boarded up. That's a sad sight—a tall building with every window plugged with plywood. Every business in town appeared to trade on Twain and his books—the Mark Twain Roofing Company, the Mark Twain Savings and Loan, the Tom 'n' Huck Motel, the Injun Joe Campground and Go-Kart Track, the Huck Finn Shopping Center. You could even go and be insane at the Mark Twain Mental Health Center—a possibility that would, I imagine, grow increasingly likely with every day spent in Hannibal. The whole place was sad and awful. I had been planning to stay for lunch, but the thought of having to face a Tom Sawyer Burger or Injun Joe Cola left me without any appetite for either food or Hannibal.

I walked back to the car. Every parked car along the street had a license plate that said, MISSOURI—THE SHOW ME STATE. I wondered idly if this could be short for "Show Me the Way to Any Other State." In any case, I crossed the Mississippi—still muddy, still strangely unimpressive—on a long, high bridge and turned my back on Missouri without regret. On the other side a sign said, BUCKLE UP. ITS THE LAW IN ILLINOIS. Just beyond it another said, AND WE STILL CAN'T PUNCTUATE.

I plunged east into Illinois. I was heading for Springfield, the state capital, and New Salem, a restored village where Abraham Lincoln lived as a young man. My dad had taken us there when I was about five and I thought it was wonderful. I wondered if it still was. I also wanted to see if Springfield was in any way an ideal town. One of the things I was looking for on this trip was the perfect town. I've always felt certain that somewhere out there in America it must exist. When I was small, WHO-TV in Des Moines used to show old movies every afternoon after school, and when other children were out playing kick-the-can or catching bullfrogs or encouraging little Bobby Birnbaum to eat worms (something he did with surprising amenability), I was alone in a curtained room in front of the TV, lost in a private world, with a plate of Oreo cookies on my lap and Hollywood magic flickering on my eyeglasses. I didn't realize it at the time, but the films WHO showed were mostly classics—*The Best Years of Our Lives, Mr. Smith Goes to Washington, Never Give a Sucker an Even Break, It Happened One Night.* The one constant in these pictures was the background. It was always the same place, a trim and sunny little city with a tree-lined Main Street full of friendly merchants ("Good morning, Mrs. Smith!") and a courthouse square, and wooded neighborhoods where fine houses slumbered beneath graceful arms. There was always a paperboy on a bike slinging papers onto front porches, and a genial old fart in a white apron sweeping the sidewalk in front of his drugstore and two men in suits striding briskly past. These two background men always wore suits, and they always strode smartly, never strolled or ambled, but strode in perfect synchrony. They were really good at it. No matter what was going on in the foreground—Humphrey Bogart blowing away a bad guy with a .45, Jimmy Stewart earnestly explaining his ambitions to Donna Reed, W. C. Fields lighting a cigar with the cellophane still on it—the background was always this timeless, tranquil place. Even in the midst of the most dreadful crises, when monster ants were at large in the streets or buildings were collapsing from some careless scientific experiment out at State U, you could still generally spot the paperboy slinging newspapers somewhere in the background and those two guys in suits striding along like Siamese twins. They were absolutely imperturbable.

And it wasn't just in the movies. Everybody on TV—Ozzie and Harriet, Wally and Beaver Cleaver, George Burns and Gracie Allen—lived in this middle-class Elysium. So did the people in the advertisements in magazines and on the commercials on television and in the Norman Rockwell paintings on the covers of the *Saturday Evening Post.* In books it was the same. I used to read Hardy Boys mysteries one after the other, not for the plots, which even at the age of eight I could see were ridiculously improbable ("Say, Frank, do you suppose those fellows with the funny accents that we saw at Moose Lake yesterday weren't really fisherman, but German spies, and that the girl in the bottom of their canoe with the bandage around her mouth wasn't really suffering from pyorrhea but was actually Dr. Rorshack's daughter? I've got a funny feeling those fellows might even be able to tell us a thing or two about the missing rocket fuel!"). No, I read them for Franklin W. Dixon's evocative, albeit incidental, descriptions of Bayport, the Hardy Boys' hometown, a place inexpressibly picturesque, where houses with porch swings and picket fences peeked out on a blue sweep of bay full of sailboats and skimming launches. It was a place of constant adventures and summers without end.

It began to bother me that I had never seen this town. Every year on vacation we would drive hundreds and hundreds of miles across the country, in an insane pursuit of holiday happiness, toiling over blue hills and brown prairies, through towns and cities without number, but without ever going through anywhere even remotely like that dreamy town in the movies. The places we passed through were hot and dusty and full of scrawny dogs, closed-down movie theaters, grubby diners and gas stations that looked as if they would be grateful to get two customers a week. But I felt sure that it must exist somewhere. It was inconceivable that a nation so firmly attached to small-town ideals, so dedicated in its fantasies to small-town notions, could not have somewhere built one perfect place—a place of harmony and industry, a place without shopping malls and oceanic parking lots, without factories and drive-in churches, without Kwik-Kraps and Jiffi-Shits and commercial squalor from one end to the other. In this timeless place Bing Crosby would be the priest, Jimmy Stewart the mayor, Fred MacMurray the high-school principal, Henry Fonda a Quaker farmer. Walter Brennan would run the gas station, a boyish Mickey Rooney would deliver groceries, and somewhere at an open window Deanna Durbin would sing. And in the background, always, would be the kid on a bike and those two smartly striding men. The place I was looking for would be an amalgam of all those towns I had encountered in fiction. Indeed, that might well be its name—Amalgam, Ohio, or Amalgam, North Dakota. It could exist almost anywhere, but it had to exist. And on this trip, I intended to find it.

I drove and drove, through flat farming country and little towns devoid of life: Hull, Pittsfield, Barry, Oxville. On my map, Springfield was about two inches to the right of Hannibal, but it seemed to take hours to get there. In fact, it does take hours to get there. I was only slowly adjusting to the continental scale of America, where states are the size of countries. Illinois is nearly twice as big as Austria, four times the size of Switzerland. There is so much emptiness, so much space between towns. You go through a little place and the dinette looks crowded, so you think, "Oh, I'll wait till I get to Fuddville before I stop for coffee," because it's only just down the road, and then you get out on the highway and a sign says, FUDDVILLE 102 MILES. And you realize that you are dealing with another scale of geography altogether. There is a corresponding lack of detail on the maps. On English maps every church and public house is dutifully recorded. Rivers of laughable minuteness—rivers you can step across—are landmarks of importance, known for miles around. In America whole towns go missing—places with schools, businesses, hundreds of quiet little lives, just vanish as effectively as if they had been vaporized.

And the system of roads is only cruelly hinted at. You look at the map and think you spy a shortcut between, say, Wienerville and Bewilderment, a straight gray line of county road that promises to shave thirty minutes from your driving time. But when you leave the main highway, you find yourself in a network of unrecorded back roads, radiating out across the countryside like cracks in a broken pane of glass.

The whole business of finding your way around becomes laden with frustration, especially away from the main roads. Near Jacksonville I missed a left turn for Springfield and had to go miles out of my way to get back to where I wanted to be. This happens a lot in America. The highway authorities are curiously reluctant to impart much in the way of useful information, like where you are or what road you are on. This is all the more strange when you consider that they are only too happy to provide all kinds of peripheral facts—NOW ENTERING BUBB COUNTY SOIL CONSERVATION DISTRICT, NATIONAL SPRAT HATCHERY 5 MILES, NO PARKING WED 3AM TO 6AM, DANGER: LOW FLYING GEESE, NOW LEAVING BUBB COUNTY SOIL CONSERVATION DISTRICT. Often on country roads you will come to a crossroads without signposts and then have to drive twenty miles or more without having any confidence in where you are. And then abruptly, without warning, you round a bend and find yourself at an eight-lane intersection with fourteen traffic lights and the most bewildering assortment of signs, all with arrows pointing in different directions. Lake Maggot State Park this way. Curtis Dribble Memorial Expressway over there. US Highway 41 South. US Highway 53 North. Interstate 11/78. Business District this way. Dextrose County Teachers' College that way. Junction 17 West. Junction 17 Not West. No U-Turn. Left Lane Must Turn Left. Buckle Your Seat Belt. Sit Up Straight. Did You Brush Your Teeth This Morning?

Just as you realize that you should be three lanes to the left, the lights change and you are swept off with the traffic, like a cork on a fast river. This sort of thing used to happen to my father all the time. I don't think Dad ever went through a really big and important intersection without getting siphoned off to somewhere he didn't want to be—a black hole of one-way streets, an expressway into the desert, a long and expensive toll bridge to some offshore island, necessitating an embarrassing and costly return trip. ("Hey, mister, didn't you come through here a minute ago from the other direction?") My father's particular specialty was the ability to get hopelessly lost without ever actually losing sight of his target. He never arrived at an amusement park or tourist attraction without first approaching it from several directions, like a pilot making passes over an unfamiliar airport. My sister and brother and I, bouncing on the back seat, could always see it on the other side of the freeway and cry, "There it is! There it is!" Then after a minute we would spy it from another angle on the far side of a cement works. And then across a broad river. And then on the other side of the freeway again. Sometimes all that would separate us from our goal would be a high chain-link fence. On the other side you could see happy, carefree families parking their cars and getting ready for a wonderful day. "How did they get in there?" my dad would cry, the veins on his forehead lively. "Why can't the city put up some signs, for Christ's sake? It's no wonder you can't find your way into the place," he would add, conveniently overlooking the fact that 18,000 other people, some of them of decidedly limited mental acuity, had managed to get onto the right side of the fence without too much difficulty.

Springfield was a disappointment. I wasn't really surprised. If it were a nice place, someone would have said to me, "Say, you should go to Springfield. It's a nice place." I had high hopes for it only because I had always thought it sounded promising. In a part of the world where so many places have harsh, foreign-sounding names full of hard consonants—De Kalb, Du Quoin, Keokuk, Kankakee—Springfield is a little piece of poetry, a name suggesting grassy meadows and cool waters. In fact, it was nothing of the sort. Like all small American cities, it had a downtown of parking lots and tallish buildings surrounded by a sprawl of shopping centers, gas stations and fast-food joints. It was neither offensive nor charming. I drove around a little bit, but finding nothing worth stopping for, I drove on to New Salem, twelve miles to the north.

New Salem had a short and not very successful life. The original settlers intended to cash in on the river trade that passed by, but in fact the river trade did just that—passed by—and the town never prospered. In 1837 it was abandoned and would no doubt have been lost to history altogether except that one of its residents from 1831 to 1837 was a young Abraham Lincoln. So now, on a 620-acre site, New Salem has been rebuilt just as it was when Lincoln lived there, and you can go and see why everybody was pretty pleased to clear off. Actually it was very nice. There were about thirty or forty log cabins distributed around a series of leafy clearings. It was a gorgeous autumn afternoon, with a warm breeze and soft sunlight adrift in the trees. It all looked impossibly quaint and appealing. You are not allowed to go in the houses. Instead you walk up to each one and peer through the windows or front door and you get an idea of what life was like for the people who lived there. Mostly it must have been pretty uncomfortable. Every house had a sign telling you about its residents. The historical research was impressively diligent. The only problem was that it all became a little repetitive after a while. Once you have looked through the windows of fourteen log cabins, you find yourself approaching number 15 with a certain diminution of enthusiasm, and by the time you reach number 20 it is really only politeness that impels you onward. Since they've taken the trouble to build all these cabins and scour the country digging out old rocking chairs and chamber pots, you feel that the least you can do is walk around and feign interest at each one. But in your heart you are really thinking that if you never saw a log cabin again you'd be pretty damn pleased. I'm sure that was what Lincoln was thinking when he packed his cases and decided not to be a backwoods merchant anymore, but to take up a more rewarding career emancipating Negroes and being president.

Down at the far end of the site, I met an older couple plodding towards me, looking tired. The man gave me a sympathetic look as he passed and said, "Only two more to go." Down the path from where they had come I could see one of the two remaining cabins, looking distant and small. I waited until the older couple were safely out of sight around a bend, and then sat down beneath a tree, a handsome oak into whose leaves the first trace of autumn gold was delicately bleeding. I felt a weight lifting from my shoulders and wondered why it was that I had been so enchanted by this place when I was five years old. Were childhoods so boring back then? I knew my own little boy, if driven to this place, would drop to the ground and start hyperventilating at the discovery that he had spent a day and a half sealed in a car only to come and see a bunch of boring log cabins. And looking at it now, I couldn't have blamed him. I mused for a few moments on the question of which was worse, to lead a life so boring that you are easily enchanted or a life so full of stimulus that you are easily bored.

But then it occurred to me that musing is a pointless waste of anyone's time, and instead I went off to see if I could find a Baby Ruth candy bar, a far more profitable exercise.

After New Salem, I took Interstate 55 south, and drove for an hour and a half towards St. Louis. It was boring, too. On a road as straight and as wide as an American interstate, fifty-five miles an hour is just too slow. It feels like walking speed. Cars and trucks coming towards you in the opposite direction seem to be traveling on one of those pedestrian conveyer belts you find in airports. You can see the people inside, get a long, lingering glimpse into their lives, as they slide past. And there's no sense of driving. You need to put a hand to the wheel occasionally just to confirm your course, but you can take time out to do the most intricate things—count your money, brush your hair, tidy up the car, use the rearview mirror to search and destroy blackheads, read maps and guidebooks, put on or discard articles of clothing. If your car possessed cruise control you could just about climb in the back and take a nap. It is certainly quite easy to forget that you are in charge of two tons of speeding metal, and it is only when you start to scatter emergency cones at roadwork sites or a truck honks at you as you drift into its path that you are jolted back to reality and you realize that henceforth you probably shouldn't leave your seat to search for snack food.

The one thing that can be said is that it leaves you time to think, and to consider questions like why is it that the trees along highways never grow? Some of them must have been there for forty years by now, and yet they are still no more than six feet tall and with only fourteen leaves on them. Is it a particular low-maintenance strain, do you suppose? And here's another one. Why can't they make cereal boxes with pouring spouts? Is some guy at General Foods splitting his sides at the thought that every time people pour out a bowl of cornflakes they spill some of them on the floor? And why is it that when you clean a sink, no matter how long you let the water run or how much you wipe it with a cloth, there's always a strand of hair and some bits of wet fluff left behind? And just what *do* the Spanish see in flamenco music?

In a forlorn effort to keep from losing my mind, I switched on the radio, but then I remembered that American radio is designed for people who have already lost their minds. The first thing I came across was a commercial for Folgers coffee. An announcer said in a confidential whisper, "We went to the world-famous Napa Valley Restaurant in California and—without telling the customers—served them Folgers instant coffee instead of the restaurant's usual brand. Then we listened in on hidden microphones." There followed an assortment of praise for the coffee along the lines of "Hey, this coffee is fantastic!" "I've never tasted such rich, full-bodied coffee before!" "This coffee is so good I can hardly stand it!" and that sort of thing. Then the announcer leaped out and told the diners that it was Folgers coffee, and they all shared a good laugh—and an important lesson about the benefits of drinking quality instant coffee. I twirled the dial. A voice said, "We'll return to our discussion of maleness in sixty seconds." I twirled the dial. The warbling voice of a female country singer intoned,

> His hands are tiny
> and his legs are short
> But I lean upon him
> For my child support.

I twirled the dial. A voice said, "This portion of the news is brought to you by the Airport Barber Shop, Biloxi." There was then a commercial for said barbershop, followed by thirty seconds of news, all of it related to deaths by cars, fires and gunfire in Biloxi in the last twenty-four hours. There was no hint that there might be a wider, yet more violent world beyond the city limits. Then there was another commercial for the Airport Barber Shop, in case you were so monumentally cretinous that you had forgotten about it during the preceding thirty seconds of news. I switched the radio off.

At Litchfield, I left the interstate, vowing not to get on one again if I could possibly help it, and joined a state highway, Illinois 127, heading south towards Murphysboro and Carbondale. Almost immediately life became more interesting. There were farms and houses and little towns to look at. I was still going fifty-five miles an hour, but now I seemed to be fairly skimming along. The landscape flashed past, more absorbing than before, more hilly and varied, and the foliage was a darker blur of green. Signs came and went: TEE PEE MINI MART, B-RITE FOOD STORE, BETTY'S BEAUTY BOX, SAV-A-LOT FOOD CENTER, PINCKNEYVILLE COON CLUB, BALD KNOB TRAILER COURT, DAIRY DELITE, ALL U CAN EAT. In between these shrines to dyslexia and free enterprise there were clearings on the hillsides where farmhouses stood. Almost every one had a satellite dish in the yard, pointed to the sky as if tapping into some life-giving celestial force. I suppose in a sense they were. Here in the hills, the light failed more quickly. I

45

noticed with surprise that it was past six o'clock and I decided that I had better find a room. As if on cue, Carbondale hove into view.

It used to be that when you came to the outskirts of a town you would find a gas station and a Dairy Queen, maybe a motel or two if it was a busy road or the town had a college. Now every town, even a quite modest one, has a mile or more of fast-food places, motor inns, discount cities, shopping malls—all with thirty-foot-high revolving signs and parking lots the size of Shropshire. Carbondale appeared to have nothing else. I drove in on a road that became a two-mile strip of shopping centers and gas stations, K Marts, J. C. Penneys, Hardees and McDonald's. And then, abruptly, I was in the country again. I turned around and drove back through town on a parallel street that offered precisely the same sort of things but in slightly different configurations and then I was in the country again. The town had no center. It had been eaten by shopping malls.

I got a room in the Heritage Motor Inn, then went out for a walk to try once more to find Carbondale. But there really was nothing there. I was perplexed and disillusioned. Before I had left on this trip I had lain awake at night in my bed in England and pictured myself stopping each evening at a motel in a little city, strolling into town along wide sidewalks, dining on the blue-plate special at Betty's Family Restaurant on the town square, then plugging a scented toothpick in my mouth and going for a stroll around the town, very probably stopping off at Vern's Midnite Tavern for a couple of draws and a game of eight-ball with the boys or taking in a movie at the Regal or looking in at the Val-Hi Bowling Alley to kibitz the Mid-Week Hairdressers' League matches before rounding off the night with a couple of games of pinball and a grilled cheese sandwich. But here there was no square to stroll to, no Betty's, no blue-plate specials, no Vern's Midnite Tavern, no movie theater, no bowling alley. There was no town, just six-lane highways and shopping malls. There weren't even any sidewalks. Going for a walk, as I discovered, was a ridiculous and impossible undertaking. I had to cross parking lots and gas station forecourts, and I kept coming up against little white-painted walls marking the boundaries between, say,

Long John Silver's Seafood Shoppe and Kentucky Fried Chicken. To get from one to the other, it was necessary to clamber over the wall, scramble up a grassy embankment and pick your way through a thicket of parked cars. That is if you were on foot. But clearly from the looks people gave me as I lumbered breathlessly over the embankment, no one had ever tried to go from one of these places to another under his own motive power. What you were supposed to do was get in your car, drive twelve feet down the street to another parking lot, park the car and get out. Glumly I clambered my way to a Pizza Hut and went inside, where a waitress seated me at a table with a view of the parking lot.

All around me people were eating pizzas the size of bus wheels. Directly opposite, inescapably in my line of vision, an overweight man of about thirty was lowering wedges into his mouth whole, like a sword swallower. The menu was dazzling in its variety. It went on for pages. There were so many types and sizes of pizza, so many possible permutations, that I felt quite at a loss. The waitress appeared. "Are you ready to order?"

"I'm sorry," I replied, "I need a little more time."

"Sure," she said. "You take your time." She went off to somewhere out of my line of vision, counted to four and came back. "Are you ready to order now?" she asked.

"I'm sorry," I said, "I really need just a little more time."

"OK," she said and left. This time she may have counted as high as twenty, but when she returned I was still nowhere near understanding the many hundreds of options open to me as a Pizza Hut patron.

"You're kinda slow, aren'tcha?" she observed brightly.

I was embarrassed. "I'm sorry. I'm out of touch. I've . . . just got out of prison."

Her eyes widened. "Really?"

"Yes. I murdered a waitress who rushed me."

With an uncertain smile she backed off and gave me lots and lots of time to make up my mind. In the end I had a medium-sized deep-dish pepperoni pizza with extra onions and mushrooms, and I can recommend it without hesitation.

Afterwards, to round off a perfect evening, I clambered over to a nearby K Mart and had a look around. K Marts are a chain of discount stores and they are really depressing places. You could take Mother Teresa to a K Mart and she would get depressed. It's not that there's anything wrong with the K Marts themselves, it's the customers. K Marts are always full of the sort of people who give their children names that rhyme: Lonnie, Donnie, Ronnie, Connie, Bonnie. The sort of people who would stay in to watch "The Munsters." Every woman there has at least four children and they all look as if they have been fathered by a different man. The woman always weighs 250 pounds. She is always walloping a child and bawling, "If you don't behave, Ronnie, I'm not gonna bring you back here no more!" As if Ronnie could care less about never going to a K Mart again. It's the place you would go if you wanted to buy a stereo system for under thirty-five dollars and didn't care if it sounded like the band was playing in a mailbox under water in a distant lake. If you go shopping at K Mart you know that you've touched bottom. My dad liked K Marts.

I went in and looked around. I picked up some disposable razors and a pocket notebook, and then, just to make an occasion of it, a bag of Reese's Peanut Butter Cups, which were attractively priced at $1.29. I paid for these and went outside. It was 7:30 in the evening. The stars were rising above the parking lot. I was alone with a small bag of pathetic treats in the most boring town in America and frankly I felt sorry for myself. I clambered over a wall and dodged across the highway to a Kwik-Krap mini-supermarket, purchased a cold six-pack of Pabst Blue Ribbon beer, and returned with it to my room where I watched cable TV, drank beer, messily ate Reese's Peanut Butter Cups (wiping my hands on the sheets) and drew meager comfort from the thought that in Carbondale, Illinois, that was about as good a time as you were ever likely to get.

5

IN THE MORNING I rejoined Highway 127 south. This was marked on my map as a scenic route and for once this proved to be so. It really was attractive countryside, better than anything I knew Illinois possessed, with rolling hills of wine-bottle green, prosperous-looking farms and deep woods of oak and beech. Surprisingly, considering I was heading south, the foliage here was more autumnal than elsewhere—the hillsides were a mixture of mustard, dull orange and pale green, quite fetching—and the clear, sunny air had an agreeable crispness to it. I could live here, in these hills, I thought.

It took me a while to figure out what was missing. It was billboards. When I was small, billboards thirty feet wide and fifteen feet high stood in fields along every roadside. In places like Iowa and Kansas they were about the only stimulation you got. In the 1960s Lady Bird Johnson, in one of those misguided campaigns in which presidents' wives are always engaging themselves, had most of the roadside billboards removed as part of a highway beautification program. In the middle of the Rocky Mountains this was doubtless a good thing, but out here in the lonesome heartland billboards were practically a public service.

Seeing one standing a mile off you would become interested to see what it said, and would watch with mild absorption as it advanced towards you and passed. As roadside excitements went, it was about on a par with the little windmills in Pella, but it was better than nothing.

The superior billboards would have a three-dimensional element to them—the head of a cow jutting out if it was for a dairy, or a cutout of a bowling ball scattering pins if it was for a bowling alley. Sometimes the billboard would be for some coming attraction. There might be a figure of a ghost and the words, VISIT SPOOK CAVERNS! OKLAHOMA'S GREAT FAMILY ATTRACTION! JUST 69 MILES! A couple of miles later there would be another sign saying, PLENTY OF FREE PARKING AT SPOOK CAVERNS. JUST 67 MILES! And so it would go with sign after sign promising the most thrilling and instructive afternoon any family could ever hope to have, at least in Oklahoma. These promises would be supported by illustrations showing eerily lit underground chambers, the size of cathedrals, in which the stalactites and stalagmites had magically fused into the shapes of witches' houses, bubbling caldrons, flying bats and Casper the Friendly Ghost. It all looked extremely promising. So we children in the back would begin suggesting that we stop and have a look, taking it in turns to say, in a sincere and moving way, "Oh, *please*, Dad, oh, pleeeeease."

Over the next sixty miles my father's position on the matter would proceed through a series of well-worn phases, beginning with a flat refusal on the grounds that it was bound to be expensive and anyway our behavior since breakfast had been so disgraceful that it didn't warrant any special treats, to studiously ignoring our pleas (this phase would last for up to eleven minutes), to asking my mother privately in a low voice what she thought about the idea and receiving an equivocal answer, to ignoring us again in the evident hope that we would forget about it and stop nagging (one minute, twelve seconds), to saying that we *might* go if we started to behave and kept on behaving more or less forever, to saying that we definitely would *not* go because, just look at us, we were already squabbling again and we hadn't even gotten there, to finally announcing—sometimes in an exasperated bellow, sometimes in a deathbed whisper—that all right we would go. You could always tell when Dad was on the brink of acceptance because his neck would turn red. It was always the same. He always said yes in the end. I never understood why he didn't just accede to our demands at the outset and save himself thirty minutes of anguish. Then he would always quickly add, "But we're only going for half an hour—and you're not going to buy anything. Is that clear?" This seemed to restore to him a sense that he was in charge of things.

By the last two or three miles, the signs for Spook Caverns would be every couple of hundred yards, bringing us to a fever pitch of excitement. Finally there would be a billboard the size of a battleship with a huge arrow telling us to turn right here and drive eighteen miles. "Eighteen miles!" Dad would cry shrilly, his forehead veins stirring to life in preparation for the inevitable discovery that after eighteen miles of bouncing down a dirt road with knee-deep ruts there would be no sign of Spook Caverns, that indeed after nineteen miles the road would end in a desolate junction without any clue of which way to turn, and that Dad would turn the wrong way. When eventually found, Spook Caverns would prove to be rather less than advertised—in fact, would give every appearance of being in the last stages of solvency. The caverns, damp and ill lit and smelling like a long-dead horse, would be about the size of a garage and the stalactites and stalagmites wouldn't look the least bit like witches' houses and Casper the Ghost. They would look like—well, like stalactites and stalagmites. It would all be a huge letdown. The only possible way of assuaging our disappointment, we would discover, would be if Dad bought us each a rubber Bowie knife and bag of toy dinosaurs in the adjoining gift shop. My sister and I would drop to the ground and emit mournful noises to remind him what a fearful thing unassuaged grief can be in a child.

So, as the sun sank over the brown flatness of Oklahoma and Dad, hours behind schedule, embarked on the difficult business of not being able to find a room for the night (ably assisted by my mother, who would misread the maps and mistakenly identify almost every passing building as a possible motel), we children would pass the time in back by having noisy and vicious knife fights, breaking off at intervals to weep, report wounds and complain of hunger, boredom and the need for toilet facilities. It was a kind of living hell. And now there appeared to be almost no billboards along the highways. What a sad loss.

I was headed for Cairo, which is pronounced "Kay-ro." I don't know why. They do this a lot in the South and Midwest. In Kentucky, Athens is pronounced "AY-thens" and Versailles is pronounced "Vur-SAYLES." Bolivar, Missouri, is "BAW-liv-er." Madrid, Iowa, is "MAD-rid." I don't know whether the people in these towns pronounce them that way because they are backward, undereducated shitkickers who don't know any better or whether they know better but don't care that everybody thinks they are backward undereducated shitkickers. It's not really the sort of question you can ask them, is it? At Cairo I stopped for gas and in fact I did ask the old guy who doddered out to fill my tank why they pronounced Cairo as they did.

"Because that's its *name*," he explained as if I were kind of stupid.

"But the one in Egypt is pronounced 'Ki-ro.'"

"So I've heard," agreed the man.

"And most people, when they see the name, think 'Ki-ro,' don't they?"

"Not in Kay-ro they don't," he said, a little hotly.

There didn't seem to be much to be gained by pursuing the point, so I let it rest there, and I still don't know why the people call it "Kay-ro." Nor do I know why any citizen of a free country would choose to live in such a dump, however you pronounce it. Cairo is at the point where the Ohio River, itself a great artery, joins the Mississippi, doubling its grandeur. You would think that at the confluence of two such mighty rivers there would be a great city, but in fact Cairo is a poor little town of 6,000 people. The road in was lined with battered houses and unpainted tenements. Aged black men sat on the porches and stoops on old sofas and rocking chairs, waiting for death or dinner, whichever came first. This surprised me. You don't expect to see tenements and porches full of black people in the Midwest—at least not outside big cities like Chicago and Detroit. But then I realized that I was no longer really in the Midwest. The speech patterns of southern Illinois are more Southern than Midwestern. I was nearly as far south as Nashville. Mississippi was only 160 miles away. And Kentucky was just across the river. I crossed it now, on a long, high bridge. From here on down to Louisiana the Mississippi is immensely broad. It looks safe and lazy, but in fact it is full of danger. Scores of people die in it every year. Farmers out fishing stare at the water and think, "I wonder what would happen if I just stuck my toe in there a little bit," and the next thing you know their bodies bob up in the Gulf of Mexico, bloated but looking strangely serene. The river is deceptively fierce. In 1927, when the Mississippi overflowed, it flooded an area the size of Scotland. That is a serious river.

On the Kentucky side of the river I was greeted by huge signs everywhere saying, FIREWORKS! In Illinois fireworks are illegal; in Kentucky they are not. So if you live in Illinois and want to blow your hand off, you drive across the river to Kentucky. You used to see a lot more of this sort of thing. If one state had a lower sales tax on cigarettes than a neighboring state, all the state-line gas stations and cafes would put big signs on their roofs saying, TAX-FREE CIGARETTES! 40 CENTS A PACK! NO TAX! and all the people from the next state would come and load their cars up with cut-price cigarettes. Wisconsin used to ban margarine to protect its dairy farmers, so everybody in Wisconsin, including all the dairy farmers, would drive to Iowa where there were big signs everywhere saying, MARGARINE FOR SALE! All the Iowans, in the meantime, were driving off to Illinois, where there was no sales tax on anything, or Missouri, where the sales tax on gasoline was 50 percent lower. The other thing you used to get a lot of was states going their own way in terms of daylight saving time, so in the summer Illinois might be two hours adrift from Iowa and one hour behind Indiana. It was all kind of crazy, but it made you realize to what an extent the United States is really fifty independent countries (forty-eight countries in those days). Most of that seems to have gone now, yet another sad loss.

I drove through Kentucky thinking of sad losses and was abruptly struck by the saddest loss of all—the Burma Shave sign. Burma Shave was a shaving cream that came in a tube. I don't know if it's still produced. In fact, I never knew anyone who ever used it. But the Burma Shave company used to put clever signs along the highway. They came in clusters of five, expertly spaced so that you read them as a little poem as you passed: IF HARMONY / IS WHAT YOU CRAVE / THEN GET / A TUBA / BURMA SHAVE. Or: BEN MET ANNA / MADE A HIT / NEGLECTED BEARD / BEN-ANNA SPLIT / BURMA SHAVE. Great, eh? Even in the 1950s the Burma Shave signs were pretty much a thing of the past. I can remember seeing only half a dozen in all the thousands of miles of highway we covered. But as roadside diversions went they were outstanding, ten times better than billboards and Pella's little twirling windmills. The only things that surpassed them for diversion value were multiple-car pileups with bodies strewn about the highway.

Kentucky was much like southern Illinois—hilly, sunny, attractive—but the scattered houses were less tidy and prosperous-looking than in the North. There were lots of wooded valleys and iron bridges over twisting creeks, and an abundance of dead animals pasted to the road. In every valley stood a little white Baptist church and all along the road were signs to remind me that I was now in the Bible Belt: JESUS SAVES. PRAISE THE LORD. CHRIST IS KING.

I was out of Kentucky almost before I knew it. The state tapers to a point at its western edge, and I was cutting across a chunk of it only 40 miles wide. In a veritable eyeblink in terms of American traveling time I was in Tennessee. It isn't often you can dispense with a state in less than an hour, and Tennessee would not detain me much longer. It is an odd-looking state, shaped like a Dutch brick, stretching more than 500 miles from east to west, but only 100 miles from top to bottom. Its landscape was much the same as that of Kentucky and Illinois—indeterminate farming country laced with rivers, hills and religious zealots—but I was surprised, when I stopped for lunch at a Burger

King in Jackson, at how warm it was. It was 83 degrees, according to a sign on the drive-in bank across the street, a good 20 degrees higher than it had been in Carbondale that morning. I was still obviously deep in the Bible Belt. A sign in the yard of a church next door said, CHRIST IS THE ANSWER. (The question, of course, is: What do you say when you strike your thumb with a hammer?) I went into the Burger King. A girl at the counter said, "Kin I hep yew?" I had entered another country.

6

JUST SOUTH OF Grand Junction, Tennessee, I passed over the state line into Mississippi. A sign beside the highway said, WELCOME TO MISSISSIPPI. WE SHOOT TO KILL. It didn't really. I just made that up. This was only the second time I had ever been to the Deep South and I entered it with a sense of foreboding. It is surely no coincidence that all those films you have ever seen about the South—*Easy Rider, In the Heat of the Night, Cool Hand Luke, Brubaker, Deliverance*—depict Southerners as murderous, incestuous, shitty-shoed rednecks. It really is another country. Years ago, in the days of Vietnam, two friends and I drove to Florida during college spring break. We all had long hair. En route we took a shortcut across the back roads of Georgia and stopped late one afternoon for a burger at a dinette in some dreary little crudville, and when we took our seats at the counter the place fell silent. Fourteen people just stopped eating, their food resting in their mouths, and stared at us. It was so quiet in there you could have heard a fly fart. A whole roomful of good ole boys with cherry-colored cheeks and bib overalls watched us in silence and wondered whether their shotguns were loaded. It was disconcerting. To them, out here in the middle of nowhere, we were a curiosity—some of them had clearly never seen no long-haired, nigger-loving, Northern, college-edjicated, commie hippies in the flesh before—and yet unspeakably loathsome. It was an odd sensation to feel so deeply hated by people who hadn't really had a proper chance to acquaint themselves with one's shortcomings. I remember thinking that our parents didn't have the first idea where we were, other than that we were somewhere in the continental vastness between Des Moines and the Florida Keys, and that if we disappeared we would never be found. I had visions of my family sitting around the living room in years to come and my mother saying, "Well, I wonder whatever happened to Billy and his friends. You'd think we'd have had a postcard by now. Can I get anybody a sandwich?"

That sort of thing did really happen down there, you know. This was only five years after three freedom riders were murdered in Mississippi. They were a twenty-one-year-old black from Mississippi named James Chaney and two white guys from New York, Andrew Goodman, twenty, and Michael Schwerner, twenty. I give their names because they deserve to be remembered. They were arrested for speeding, taken to the Neshoba County Jail in Philadelphia, Mississippi, and never seen again—at least not until weeks later when their bodies were hauled out of a swamp. These were kids, remember. The police had released them to a waiting mob, which had taken them away and done things to them that a child wouldn't do to an insect. The sheriff in the case, a smirking, tobacco-chewing fat boy named Lawrence Rainey, was acquitted of negligent behavior. No one was ever charged with murder. To me this was and always would be the South.

I followed Highway 7 south towards Oxford. It took me along the western edge of the Holly Springs National Forest, which seemed to be mostly swamp and scrubland. I was disappointed. I had half expected that as soon as I crossed into Mississippi there would be Spanish mosses hanging from the trees and women in billowy dresses twirling parasols and white-haired colonels with handlebar mustaches drinking mint juleps on the lawn while armies of slaves gathered the cotton and sang sweet hymns. But this landscape was just scrubby and hot and nondescript. Occasionally there would be a shack set up on bricks, with an old black man in a rocking chair on the porch, but precious little sign of life or movement elsewhere.

At the town of Holly Springs stood a sign for Senatobia, and I got briefly excited. Senatobia! What a great name for a Mississippi town! All that the old South stood for seemed to be encapsulated in those five golden syllables. Maybe things were picking up. Maybe now I would see chain gangs toiling in the sun and a prisoner in heavy irons legging it across fields and sloshing through creeks while pursued by bloodhounds, and lynch mobs roaming the streets and crosses burning on lawns. The prospect enlivened me, but I had to calm down because a state trooper pulled up alongside me at a traffic light and began looking me over with that sort of casual disdain you often get when you give a dangerously stupid person a gun and a squad car. He was sweaty and overweight and sat low in his seat. I assume he was descended from the apes like all the rest of us, but clearly in his case it had been a fairly gentle slope. I stared straight ahead with a look that I hoped conveyed seriousness of purpose mingled with a warm heart and innocent demeanor. I could *feel* him looking at me. At the very least I expected him to gob a wad of tobacco juice down the side of my head. Instead, he said, "How yew doin'?"

This so surprised me that I answered, in a cracking voice, "Pardon?"

"I said, how yew doin'?"

"I'm fine," I said. And then added, having lived some years in England, "Thank you."

"Y'on vacation?"

"Yup."

"Hah doo lack Miss Hippy?"

"Pardon?"

"I say, Hah doo lack Miss Hippy?"

I was quietly distressed. The man was armed and Southern and I couldn't understand a word he was saying to me. "I'm sorry," I said, "I'm kind of slow, and I don't understand what you're saying."

"I say"—and he repeated it more carefully—"how doo yew *lack* Mississippi?"

It dawned on me. "Oh! I like it fine! I like it heaps! I think it's wonderful. The people are so friendly and helpful." I wanted to add that I had been there for an hour and hadn't been shot at once, but the light changed and he was gone, and I sighed and thought, "Thank you, Jesus."

I drove on to Oxford, home of the University of Mississippi, or Ole Miss as it's known. The people named the town after Oxford in England in the hope that this would persuade the state to build the university there, and the state did. This tells you most of what you need to know about the workings of the Southern mind. Oxford appeared to be an agreeable town. It was built around a square, in the middle of which stood the Lafayette County Courthouse, with a tall clock tower and Doric columns, basking grandly in the Indian-summer sunshine. Around the perimeter of the square were attractive stores and a tourist information office. I went into the tourist information office to get directions to Rowan Oak, William Faulkner's home. Faulkner lived in Oxford for the whole of his life, and his home is now a museum, preserved as it was on the day he died in 1962. It must be unnerving to be so famous that you know they are going to come in the moment you croak and hang velvet cords across all the doorways and treat everything with reverence. Think of the embarrassment if you left a copy of Reader's Digest Condensed Books on the bedside table.

Behind the desk sat a large, exceptionally well dressed black woman. This surprised me a little, this being Mississippi. She wore a dark two-piece suit, which must have been awfully warm in the Mississippi heat. I asked her the way to Rowan Oak.

"You parked on the square?" she said. Actually she said, "You pocked on the skwaya?"

"Yes."

"Okay, honey, you git in yo' car and you makes the skwaya. You goes out the other end, twoads the university, goes three blocks, turns rat at the traffic lats, goes down the hill and you there, un'stan'?"

"No."

She sighed and started again. "You git in yo' car and you makes the skwaya—"

"What, I drive around the square?"

"That's rat, honey. You *makes* the skwaya." She was talking to me the way I would talk to a French person. She gave me the rest of the instructions and I pretended to understand, though they meant almost nothing to me. All I kept thinking was what funny sounds they were to be emerging from such an elegant-looking woman. As I went out the door she called out, "Hit doan really matter anyhow cuz hit be's closed now." She really said *hit;* she really said *be's.*

I said, "Pardon?"

"Hit be's closed now. You kin look around the grounz if you woan, but you cain't go insod."

I wint outsod thinking that Miss Hippy was goan be hard work. I walked around the square looking at the stores, most of them selling materials for a country club lifestyle. Handsome, well-dressed women bounded in and out. They were all tanned and rich-looking. On one of the corners was a bookstore with a magazine stand. I went in and looked around. At the magazine stand I picked up a *Playboy* and browsed through it. As one does. I was distressed to see that *Playboy* is now printed on that awful glossy paper that makes the pages stick together like wet paper towels. You can't flick through it anymore. You have to prise each page apart, like peeling paper off a stick of butter. Eventually I peeled my way to the main photo spread. It was of a naked paraplegic. I swear to God. She was sprawled—perhaps not the best choice of words in the context—in various poses on beds and divans, looking pert and indisputably attractive, but with satiny material draped artfully over her presumably withered legs. Now is it me, or does that seem just a little bit strange?

Clearly *Playboy* had lost its way, and this made me feel old and sad and foreign, because *Playboy* had been a cornerstone of American life for as long as I could remember. Every man and boy I knew read *Playboy.* Some men, like my dad, pretended not to. He used to get embarrassed if you caught him looking at it at the supermarket, and would pretend that he was really looking for *Better Homes and Gardens* or something. But he read it. He even had a little stash of men's magazines in an old hatbox at the back of his clothes closet. Every kid I knew had a father with a little stash of men's magazines which the father thought was secret and which the kid knew all about. Once in a while we would swap our dads' magazines among ourselves and then imagine their perplexity when they went to the closet and found that instead of last month's issue of *Gent* they now possessed a two-year-old copy of *Nugget* and, as a bonus, a paperback book called *Ranchhouse Lust.* You could do this knowing that your dad would never say a word to you about it. All that would happen would be that the next time you went back the stash would be in a different place. I don't know whether women in the fifties didn't sleep with their husbands or what, but this dedication to girlie magazines was pretty well universal. I think it may have had something to do with the war.

The magazines our fathers read had names like *Dude* and *Swell* and the women in them were unappealing, with breasts like deflated footballs and hips of abundant fleshiness. The women in *Playboy* were young and pretty. They didn't look like somebody you'd meet on shore leave. Beyond the incalculable public service *Playboy* performed by printing pictures of attractive naked women was the way it offered a whole attendant lifestyle. It was like a monthly manual telling you how to live, how to play the stock market and buy a hi-fi and mix sophisticated cocktails and intoxicate women with your wit and sense of style. Growing up in Iowa, you could use help with such matters. I used to read every issue from cover to cover, even the postal regulations at the bottom of the table of contents page. We all did. Hugh Hefner was a hero to all of us. Looking back now, I can hardly believe it because really—let's be frank—Hugh Hefner has always been kind of an asshole. I mean honestly, if you had all that money, would you want a huge circular bed and to spend your life in a silk dressing gown and carpet slippers? Would you want to fill a wing of your house with the sort of girls who would be happy to engage in pillow fights in the nude and wouldn't mind you taking pictures of them while so occupied for publication in a national magazine? Would you want to come downstairs of an evening and find Buddy Hackett, Sammy Davis, Jr., and Joey

Bishop standing around the piano in your living room? Do I hear a chorus of "Shit, no's" out there? Yet I bought it whole. We all did.

Playboy was like an older brother to my generation. And over the years, just like an older brother, it had changed. It had had a couple of financial reversals, a little problem with gambling, and had eventually moved out to the coast. Just like real brothers do. We had lost touch. I hadn't really thought about it for years. And then here suddenly, in Oxford, Mississippi, of all places, who should I run into but *Playboy* magazine. It was exactly like seeing an old high-school hero and discovering that he was bald and boring and still wearing those lurid V-neck sweaters and shiny black shoes with gold braid that you thought were so neat in about 1961. It was a shock to realize that both *Playboy* and I were a lot older than I had thought and that we had nothing in common anymore. Sadly I returned the *Playboy* to the rack and realized it would be a long time—well, thirty days anyway—before I picked up another one.

I looked at the other magazines. There were at least 200 of them, but they all had titles like *Machine Gun Collector, Obese Bride, Christian Woodworker, Home Surgery Digest.* There was nothing for a normal person, so I left.

I drove out South Lamar Street towards Rowan Oak, having first made the square, following the tourist lady's instructions as best I could, but I couldn't for the life of me find it. To tell you the truth, this didn't disturb me a whole lot because I knew it was closed and in any case I have never managed to read a William Faulkner novel beyond about page 3 (roughly halfway through the first sentence), so I wasn't terribly interested in what his house looked like. At any rate, in driving around I came across the campus of the University of Mississippi and that was much more interesting. It was a handsome campus, full of fine buildings that looked like banks and courthouses. Long shadows fell across the lawns. Young people, all looking as healthy and as wholesome as a bottle of milk, walked along with books tucked under their arms or sat at tables doing homework. At one table, a black student sat with white people. Things had clearly changed. It so happened that twenty-five years ago to the very week there had been a riot on this campus when a young black named James Meredith, escorted by 500 federal marshals, enrolled as a student at Ole Miss. The people of Oxford were so inflamed at the thought of having to share their campus with a *Niggra boy* that they wounded thirty of the marshals and killed two journalists. Many of the parents of these serene-looking students must have been among the rioters, hurling bricks and setting cars alight. Could that kind of hate have been extinguished in just one generation? It hardly seemed possible. But then it was impossible to imagine these tranquil students ever rioting over a matter of race. Come to that, it was impossible to imagine such a well-scrubbed, straight-arrow group of young people rioting over anything—except perhaps the number of chocolate chips in the dining hall cookies.

I decided on an impulse to drive on to Tupelo, Elvis Presley's hometown, thirty-five miles to the east. It was a pleasant drive, with the sun low and the air warm. Black woods pressed in on the road from both sides. Here and there in clearings there were shacks, usually with large numbers of black youngsters in the yard, passing footballs or riding bikes. Occasionally there were also nicer houses—white people's houses—with big station wagons standing in the driveways and a basketball hoop over the garage and large, well-mowed lawns. Often these houses were remarkably close—sometimes right next door—to a shack. You would never see that in the North. It struck me as notably ironic that Southerners could despise blacks so bitterly and yet live comfortably alongside them, while in the North people by and large did not mind blacks, even respected them as humans and wished them every success, just so long as they didn't have to mingle with them too freely.

By the time I reached Tupelo it was dark. Tupelo was a bigger place than I had expected, but by now I was coming to expect things to be not like I expected them to be, if you see what I mean. It had a long, bright strip of shopping malls, motels and gas stations. Hungry and weary, I saw for the first time the virtue of these strips. Here it all was, laid out for you—a glittering array of establishments offering every possible human convenience, clean, comfortable, reliable, reasonably priced places where you could rest, eat, relax and re-equip with the minimum of physical and mental exertion. On top of all this they give you glasses of iced water and free second cups of coffee, not to mention free matchbooks and scented toothpicks wrapped in paper to cheer you on your way. What a wonderful country, I thought, as I sank gratefully into Tupelo's welcoming bosom.

7

IN THE MORNING I went to the Elvis Presley birthplace. It was early, and I expected it to be closed, but it was open and there were already people there, taking photographs beside the house or waiting to file in at the front door. The house, tidy and white, stood in a patch of shade in a city park. It was amazingly compact, shaped like a shoebox, with just two rooms: a front room with a bed and dresser and a plain kitchen behind. But it looked comfortable and had a nice homey feel. It was certainly superior to most of the shacks I had seen along the highway. A pleasant lady with meaty arms sat in a chair and answered questions. She must get asked the same questions about a thousand times a day, but she didn't seem to mind. Of the dozen or so people there, I was the only one under the age of sixty. I'm not sure if this was because Elvis was so burned out by the end of his career that his fans were all old people or whether it is just that old people are the only ones with the time and inclination to visit the homes of dead celebrities.

A path behind the house led to a gift shop where you could buy Elvis memorabilia—albums, badges, plates, posters. Everywhere you looked his handsome, boyish face was beaming down at you. I bought two postcards and six books of matches, which

I later discovered, with a strange sense of relief, I had lost some-where. There was a visitors' book by the door. All the visitors came from towns with nowhere names like Coleslaw, Indiana; Dead Squaw, Oklahoma; Frigid, Minnesota; Dry Heaves, New Mexico; Colostomy, Montana. The book had a column for re-marks. Reading down the list I saw, "Nice," "Real nice," "Very nice," "Nice." Such eloquence. I turned back to an earlier page. One visitor had misunderstood the intention of the remarks col-umn and had written, "Visit." Every other visitor on that page and the facing page had written, "Visit," "Visit," "Re-visit," "Visit" until someone had turned the page and they got back on the right track.

The Elvis Presley house is in Elvis Presley Park on Elvis Presley Drive, just off the Elvis Presley Memorial Highway. You may gather from this that Tupelo is proud of its most famous native son. But it hadn't done anything tacky to exploit his fame, and you had to admire it for that. There weren't scores of gift shops and wax museums and souvenir emporia all trying to make a quick killing from Presley's fading fame, just a nice little house in a shady park. I was glad I had stopped.

From Tupelo I drove due south towards Columbus, into a hot and rising sun. I saw my first cotton fields, dark and scrubby but with fluffs of real cotton poking out from every plant. The fields were surprisingly small. In the Midwest you get used to seeing farms that sweep away to the horizon; here they were the size of a couple of vegetable patches. There were more shacks as well, a more or less continuous line of them along the highway. It was like driving through the world's roomiest slum. And these were real shacks. Some of them looked dangerously uninhabitable, with sagging roofs and walls that looked as if they had been cannonballed. Yet as you passed you would see someone lurking in the doorway, watching you. There were many roadside stores as well, more than you would have thought such a poor and scattered populace could support, and they all had big signs an-nouncing a motley of commodities: GAS, FIREWORKS, FRIED CHICKEN, LIVE BAIT. I wondered just how hungry I would have to be to eat fried chicken prepared by a man who also dealt in live bait. All the stores had Coke machines and gas pumps out front, and almost all of them had rusting cars and assorted scrap scattered around the yard. It was impossible to tell if they were still solvent or not by their state of dereliction.

Every once in a while I would come to a town, small and dusty, with loads of black people hanging around outside the stores and gas stations, doing nothing. That was the most arresting difference about the South—the number of black people everywhere. I shouldn't really have been surprised by it. Blacks make up 35 percent of the population in Mississippi and not much less in Alabama, Georgia and South Carolina. In some counties in the South, blacks outnumber whites by four to one. Yet until as recently as twenty-five years ago, in many of those counties not a single black person was registered to vote.

With so much poverty everywhere, Columbus came as a welcome surprise. It was a splendid little city, hometown of Tennessee Williams, with a population of 30,000. During the Civil War it was briefly the state capital, and it still had some large antebellum homes lining the well-shaded road in from the highway. But the real jewel was its downtown, which seemed hardly to have changed since about 1955. Crenshaw's Barber Shop had a rotating pole out front and across the street was a genuine five-and-dime called McCrory's and on the corner was the Bank of Mississippi in an imposing building with a big clock hanging over the sidewalk. The county courthouse, city hall and post office were all handsome and imposing edifices but built to a small-town scale. The people looked prosperous. The first person I saw was an obviously well-educated black man in a three-piece suit carrying a *Wall Street Journal.* It was all deeply pleasing and encouraging. This was a first-rate town. Combine it with Pella's handsome square and you would almost have my long-sought Amalgam. I was beginning to realize that I was never going to find it in one place. I would have to collect it piecemeal—a courthouse here, a fire station there—and here I had found several pieces.

I went for a cup of coffee in a hotel on Main Street and bought a copy of the local daily paper, the *Commercial Dispatch* ("Mississippi's Most Progressive Newspaper"). It was an old-fashioned paper with a banner headline across eight columns on page one that said TAIWANESE BUSINESS GROUP TO VISIT GOLDEN

TRIANGLE AREA, and beneath that a crop of related single-column subheadings all in different sizes, typefaces and degrees of coherence:

Visitors Are Looking
At Opportunities
For Investment

AS PART
OF TRADE
MISSION

**Group to Arrive in
Golden Triangle
Thursday**

STATE OFFICIALS
COORDINATE VISIT

All the stories inside suggested a city ruled by calmness and compassion: "Trinity Place Homemakers Give Elderly a Helping Hand," "Lamar Landfill Is Discussed," "Pickens School Budget Adopted." I read the police blotter. "During the past 24 hours," it said, "the Columbus Police Department had a total of 34 activities." What a wonderful place—the police here didn't deal with crimes, they had activities. According to the blotter the most exciting of these activities had been arresting a man for driving on a suspended license. Elsewhere in the paper I discovered that in the past twenty-four hours six people had died—or had death activities, as the police blotter might have put it—and three births had been recorded. I developed an instant affection for the *Commercial Dispatch* (which I rechristened in my mind the *Amalgam Commercial Dispatch*) and for the town it served.

I could live here, I thought. But then the waitress came over and said, "Yew honestly a breast menu, honey?" and I realized that it was out of the question. I couldn't understand a word these people said to me. She might as well have addressed me in Dutch. It took many moments and much gesturing with a knife and fork to establish that what she had said to me was "Do you want to see a breakfast menu, honey?" In fact I had been hoping to see a lunch menu, but rather than spend the afternoon trying to convey this notion, I asked for a Coca-Cola, and was enormously relieved to find that this did not elicit any subsidiary questions.

It isn't just the indistinctness with which Southerners speak that makes it so difficult to follow, it's also the slowness. This begins to get to you after a while. The average Southerner has the speech patterns of someone slipping in and out of consciousness. I can change my shoes and socks faster than most people in Mississippi can speak a sentence. Living there would drive me crazy. Slowly.

Columbus is just inside the state boundary line and I found myself, twenty minutes after leaving town, in Alabama, heading for Tuscaloosa by way of Ethelsville, Coal Fire and Reform. A sign by the highway said, Don't Litter. Keep Alabama the Beautiful. "OK, I the will," I replied cheerfully.

I put the radio on. I had been listening to it a lot in the last couple of days, hoping to be entertained by backward and twangy radio stations playing songs by artists with names like Hank Wanker and Brenda Buns. This is the way it always used to be. My brother, who was something of a scientific wizard, once built a shortwave radio from old baked-bean cans and that sort of thing, and late at night when we were supposed to be asleep he would lie in bed in the dark twiddling his knob (so to speak), searching for distant stations. Often he would pick up stations from the South. They would always be manned by professional hillbillies playing twangy music. The stations were always crackly and remote, as if the broadcasts were being beamed to us from another planet. But here now there were hardly any hillbilly-sounding people. In fact, there were hardly any Southern accents at all. All the disc jockeys sounded as if they came from Ohio.

Outside Tuscaloosa I stopped for gas and was surprised that the young man who served me also sounded as if he came from Ohio. In point of fact he did. He had a girlfriend at the University of Alabama, but he hated the South because it was so slow and backward. I asked him about the voices on the radio since he seemed to be an on-the-ball sort of guy. He explained that Southerners had become so sensitive about their reputation for being shit-squishing rednecks that all the presenters on TV and radio tried to sound as if they came from the North and had never in their whole lives nibbled a hush puppy or sniffed a grit. Nowadays it was the only way to get a job. Apart from anything else, the zippier Northern cadences meant the radio stations could pack in three or four commercials in the time it would take the average Southerner to clear his throat. That was certainly very true, and I tipped the young man thirty-five cents for his useful insight.

From Tuscaloosa, I followed Highway 69 south into Selma. All Selma meant to me was vague memories from the civil rights campaigns in the 1960s, when Martin Luther King led hundreds of blacks on forty-mile marches from there to Montgomery, the state capital, to register to vote. It was another surprisingly nice town—this corner of the South seemed to be awash with them. It was about the same size as Columbus, and just as shady and captivating. Trees had been planted along the streets downtown and the sidewalks had recently been repaved in brick. Benches had been set out, and the waterfront area, where the city ended in a sharp bluff overlooking the Alabama River, had been cleaned up. It all had an agreeable air of prosperity. At a tourist information office I picked up some pamphlets extolling the town, including one boasting of its black heritage. I was heartened by this. I had seen nothing even faintly praiseworthy of blacks in Mississippi. Moreover, blacks and whites here seemed to be on far better terms. I could see them chatting at bus stops, and I saw a black nurse and white nurse traveling together in a car, looking like old friends. Altogether, it seemed a much more relaxed atmosphere than in Mississippi.

I drove on, through rolling, open countryside. There were some cotton fields still, but mostly this was dairy country, with green fields and bright sunshine. In the late afternoon, almost the early evening, I reached Tuskegee, home of the Tuskegee Institute. Founded by Booker T. Washington and developed by George Washington Carver, it is America's premier college for blacks. It is also the seat of one of the poorest counties in America. Eighty-two percent of the county population is black. More than half the county residents live below the poverty level. Almost a third of them still don't have indoor plumbing. That is really poor. Where I come from you are poor if you can't afford a refrigerator that makes its own ice cubes and your car doesn't have automatic windows. Not having running water in the house is something beyond the realms of the imaginable to most Americans.

The most startling thing about Tuskegee was that it was completely black. It was in every respect a typical small American city, except that it was poor, with lots of boarded shopfronts and general dereliction, and that every person in every car, every pedestrian, every storekeeper, every fireman, every postman, every last soul was black. Except me. I had never felt so self-conscious, so visible. I suddenly appreciated what a black person must feel like in North Dakota. I stopped at a Burger King for a cup of coffee. There must have been fifty people in there. I was the only person who wasn't black, but no one seemed to notice or care. It was an odd sensation—and rather a relief, I must say, to get back out on the highway.

I drove on to Auburn, twenty miles to the northeast. Auburn is also a college town and roughly the same size as Tuskegee, but the contrast could hardly have been more striking. Auburn students were white and rich. One of the first sights I saw was a blonde sweeping past in a replica Duesenberg that must have cost her daddy $25,000. It was obviously a high-school graduation present. If I could have run fast enough to keep up, I would happily have urinated all down the side of it. Coming so soon after the poverty of Tuskegee, it made me feel strangely ashamed.

However, I must say that Auburn appeared to be a pleasant town. I've always liked college towns anyway. They are about the only places in America that manage to combine the benefits of a small-town pace of life with a dash of big-city sophistication. They usually have nice bars and restaurants, more interesting shops, an altogether more worldly air. And there is a pleasing sense of being around 20,000 young people who are having the best years of their lives.

In my day, the principal concerns of university students were sex, smoking dope, rioting and learning. Learning was something you did only when the first three weren't available, but at least you did it. Nowadays, American students' principal concerns seem to be sex and keeping their clothes looking nice. I don't think learning comes into it very much. At the time of my trip there was an outcry in America over the contagion of ignorance that appeared to be sweeping through the nation's young people. The principal focus of this nationwide wrist-wringing was a study by the National Endowment for the Humanities. It had recently tested 8,000 high-school seniors and found that they were as stupid as pig dribble. More than two-thirds of them did not know when the US Civil War took place, couldn't identify Stalin or Churchill, and didn't know who wrote *The Canterbury Tales*. Almost half thought World War I started before 1900. A third thought that Roosevelt was president during the Vietnam War and that Columbus sailed to America after 1750. Forty-two percent—this is my favorite—couldn't name a single country in Asia. I would scarcely have believed all this myself except that the summer before I had taken two American high-school girls for a drive around Dorset—bright girls, both of them now enrolled in colleges of high repute—and neither of them had ever heard of Thomas Hardy. How can you live to be eighteen years old and never have at least *heard* of Thomas Hardy?

I don't know the answer to that, but I suspect you could spend a week in Auburn kissing the ass of every person who had ever heard of Thomas Hardy and not get chapped lips. Perhaps that is a grossly unjustified comment. For all I know, Auburn may be a hotbed of Hardy scholarship. But what I do know, from having spent only a short while there, is that it hasn't got a single decent bookstore. How can a university town not have a decent bookstore? There was *a* bookstore, but all it sold was textbooks and a decidedly unliterary assortment of sweatshirts, stuffed animals and other paraphernalia bearing the Auburn University seal. Most American universities like Auburn have 20,000 students or more, and upwards of 800 or 1,000 professors and lecturers. How can any community with that many educated people not support a single decent bookstore? If I were the National Endowment for the Humanities, I would find that at least as compelling a question as why high-school seniors do so poorly on general knowledge tests.

Incidentally, I'll tell you why they do so poorly. They answer the questions as fast as they can, at random, and then sleep. We used to do it all the time. Once a year in high school, our principal, Mr. Toerag, would file the whole school into the auditorium and make us spend a tedious day answering multiple-choice questions on a variety of subjects for some national examination. It didn't take you long to deduce that if you filled in the circles without bothering to look at the questions, you could complete the work in a fraction of the time, and then shut your eyes and lose yourself in erotic eyelid movies until it was time for the next test. As long as your pencil was neatly stowed and you didn't snore, Mr. Toerag, whose job it was to wander up and down the rows looking for miscreants, would leave you alone. That was what Mr. Toerag did for a living, wander around all day looking for people misbehaving. I always imagined him at home in the evening walking around the dining room table and poking his wife with a ruler if she slouched. He must have been hell to live with. His name wasn't really Mr. Toerag, of course. It was Mr. Superdickhead.

8

I DROVE THROUGH bright early-morning sunshine. Here and there the road plunged into dense pine forests and led past collections of holiday cabins in the woods. Atlanta was only an hour's drive to the north and the people hereabouts were clearly trying to cash in on that proximity. I passed through a little town called Pine Mountain, which seemed to have everything you could want in an inland resort. It was attractive and had nice shops. The only thing it lacked was a mountain, which was a bit of a disappointment considering its name. I had intentionally chosen this route because Pine Mountain conjured up to my simple mind a vision of clean air, craggy precipices, scented forests and tumbling streams—the sort of place where you might bump into John-Boy Walton. Still, who could blame the locals if they stretched the truth a little in the pursuit of a dollar? You could hardly expect people to drive miles out of their way to visit something called Pine Flat-Place.

The countryside became gradually more hilly, though obstinately uncraggy, before the road made a gentle descent into Warm Springs. For years I had been harboring an urge to go there. I'm not sure why. I knew nothing about the place except that Franklin Roosevelt had died there. In the Register and Tribune

Building in Des Moines the main corridor was lined with historic front pages which I found strangely absorbing when I was small. One of them said PRESIDENT ROOSEVELT DIES AT WARM SPRINGS and I thought even then that it sounded like such a nice place to pass away.

In any event, Warm Springs was a nice place. There was just a main street, with an old hotel on one side and row of shops on the other, but they had been nicely restored as expensive boutiques and gift shops for visitors from Atlanta. It was all patently artificial—there was even outdoor Muzak, if you can stand it—but I quite liked it.

I drove out to the Little White House, about two miles outside town. The parking lot was almost empty, except for an old bus from which a load of senior citizens were disembarking. The bus was from the Calvary Baptist Church in some place like Firecracker, Georgia, or Bareassed, Alabama. The old people were noisy and excited, like schoolchildren, and pushed in front of me at the ticket booth, little realizing that I wouldn't hesitate to give an old person a shove, especially a Baptist. Why is it, I wondered, that old people are always so self-centered and excitable? But I just smiled benignly and stood back, comforted by the thought that soon they would be dead.

I bought my ticket and quickly overtook the old people on the slope up to the Roosevelt compound. The path led through a woods of tall pine trees that seemed to go up and up forever and sealed out the sunlight so effectively that the ground at their feet was bare, as if it had just been swept. The path was lined with large rocks from each state. Every governor had evidently been asked to contribute some hunk of native stone and here they were, lined up like a guard of honor. It's not often you see an idea that stupid brought to fruition. Many had been cut in the shape of the state, then buffed to a glossy finish and engraved. But others, clearly not catching the spirit of the enterprise, were just featureless hunks with a terse little plaque saying DELAWARE. GRANITE. Iowa's contribution was, as expected, carefully middling. The stone had been cut to the shape of the state, but by someone who had clearly never attempted such a thing before. I imagine he had impulsively put in the lowest bid and was surprised to get the contract. At least the state had found a rock to send. I had half feared it might be a clump of dirt.

Beyond this unusual diversion was a white bungalow, which had formerly been a neighboring home and was now a museum. As always with these things in America, it was well done and interesting. Photographs of Roosevelt at Warm Springs covered the walls and lots of his personal effects were on display in glass cases—his wheelchairs, crutches, leg braces and other such implements. Some of these were surprisingly elaborate and exerted a morbid interest because FDR was always most careful not to let the public see him as the cripple he was. And here we were viewing him with his trousers off, so to speak. I was particularly taken with a room full of all the handmade gifts that had been given to him when he was president and then presumably stuck at the back of a very large cupboard. There were carved walking sticks by the dozen and maps of America made of inlaid wood and portraits of FDR scratched on walrus tusks and etched with acid into slate. The amazing thing was how well done they all were. Every one of them represented hundreds of hours of delicate carving and tireless polishing, and all to be given away to a stranger for whom it would be just one more item in a veritable cavalcade of personalized keepsakes. I became so absorbed in these items that I scarcely noticed when the old people barged in, a trifle breathless but nonetheless lively. A lady with a bluish tint to her hair pushed in front of me at one of the display cases. She gave me a brief look that said, "I am an old person. I can go where I want," and then she dismissed me from her mind. "Say, Hazel," she called in a loud voice, "did you know you shared a birthday with Eleanor Roosevelt?"

"Is that so?" answered a grating voice from the next room.

"I share a birthday with Eisenhower myself," the lady with the bluish hair went on, still loudly, consolidating her position in front of me with a twitch of her ample butt. "And I've got a cousin who shares a birthday with Harry Truman."

I toyed for a moment with the idea of grabbing the woman by both ears and driving her forehead into my knee, but instead passed into the next room where I found the entrance to a small cinema in which they showed us a crackling black-and-white film all about Roosevelt's struggle with polio and his long stays at Warm Springs trying to rub life into his spindly legs, as if they had merely gone to sleep. It too was excellent. Written and narrated by a correspondent from UPI, it was moving without being mawkish, and the silent home movies, with their jerky movements that made all the participants look as if someone just out of camera range was barking at them to hurry up, exerted the same sort of voyeuristic fascination as FDR's leg braces. Afterwards we were at last released to see the Little White House itself. I fairly bounded ahead in order not to have to share the experience with the old people. It was down another path, through more pine trees and beyond a white sentry box. I was surprised at how small it was. It was just a little white cottage in the woods, all on one floor, with five small rooms, all paneled in dark wood. You would never believe that this could be the property of a president, particularly a rich president like Roosevelt. He did, after all, own most of the surrounding countryside, including the hotel on Main Street, several cottages and the springs themselves. Yet the very compactness of the cottage made it all the more snug and appealing. Even now, it looked comfy and lived in. You couldn't help but want it for yourself, even if it meant coming to Georgia to enjoy it. In every room there was a short taped commentary, which explained how Roosevelt worked and underwent therapy at the cottage. What it didn't tell you was that what he really came here for was a bit of rustic bonking with his secretary, Lucy Mercer. Her bedroom was on one side of the living room and his was on the other. The taped recording made nothing of this, but it did point out that Eleanor's bedroom, tucked away at the back and decidedly inferior to the secretary's, was mostly used as a guest room because Eleanor seldom made the trip south.

From Warm Springs I went some miles out of my way to take the scenic road into Macon, but there didn't seem to be a whole lot scenic about it. It wasn't unscenic particularly, it just wasn't scenic. I was beginning to suspect that the scenic route designations on my maps had been applied somewhat at random. I imagined some guy who had never been south of Jersey City sitting in an office in New York and saying, "Warm Springs to Macon? Oooh, that sounds nice," and then carefully drawing in the orange dotted line that signifies a scenic route, his tongue sticking ever so slightly out of the corner of his mouth.

Macon was nice—all the towns in the South seemed to be nice. I stopped at a bank for money and was served by a lady from Great Yarmouth, something that brought a little excitement to both of us, and then continued on my way over the Otis Redding Memorial Bridge. There is a fashion in many parts of America, particularly the South, to name things made out of concrete after some local worthy—the Sylvester C. Grubb Memorial Bridge, the Chester Ovary Levee, that sort of thing. It seems a very odd practice to me. Imagine working all your life, clawing your way to the top, putting in long hours, neglecting your family, stabbing people in the back and generally being thought a shit by everyone you came in contact with, just to have a highway bridge over the Tallapoosa River named after you. Doesn't seem right somehow. Still, at least this one was named after someone I had heard of.

I headed east for Savannah, down Interstate 16. It was a 173-mile drive of unspeakable tedium across the red-clay plain of Georgia. It took me five hot and unrewarding hours to reach Savannah. While you, lucky reader, have only to flit your eyes to the next paragraph.

I stood agog in Lafayette Square in Savannah, amid brick paths, trickling fountains and dark trees hung with Spanish moss. Before me rose up a cathedral of exquisite linen-fresh whiteness with twin Gothic spires, and around it stood 200-year-old houses of weathered brick, with hurricane shutters that clearly were still used. I did not know that such perfection existed in America. There are twenty such squares in Savannah, cool and quiet beneath a canopy of trees, and long straight side streets equally dark and serene. It is only when you stumble out of this urban rain forest, out into the open streets of the modern city, exposed to the glare of the boiling sun, that you realize just how sweltering the South can be. This was October, a time of flannel shirts and hot toddies in Iowa, but here summer was unrelenting. It was only eight in the morning and already businessmen were loosening their ties and mopping their foreheads. What must it be like in August? Every store and restaurant is air-conditioned. You step inside and the sweat is freeze-dried on your arms. Step back outside and the air meets you as something hot and unpleasant, like a dog's breath. It is only in Savannah's squares that the climate achieves a kind of pleasing equilibrium.

Savannah is a seductive city and I found myself wandering almost involuntarily for hours. The city has more than 1,000 historic buildings, many of them still lived in as houses. This was, New York apart, the first American city I had ever been in where people actually lived downtown. What a difference it makes, how much more vibrant and alive it all seems, to see children playing ball in the street or skipping rope on the front stoops. I wandered along the cobbled sidewalk of Oglethorpe Avenue to the Colonial Park Cemetery, full of moldering monuments and densely packed with the gravestones of people famous to the state's history—Archibald Bulloch, the first president of Georgia, James Habersham, "a leading merchant," and Button Gwinnett, who is famous in America for being one of the signatories of the Declaration of Independence and for having the silliest first name in Colonial history. The people of Savannah, in a careless moment, appear to have lost old Button. The historical marker said that he might be buried where I was standing now or then again he might be over in the corner or possibly somewhere else altogether. You could walk around all day and never know when you were on the Button, so to speak.

The business district in Savannah was frozen in a perpetual 1959—the Woolworth store didn't appear to have changed its stock since about then. There was a handsome old movie house, Weis's, but it was shut. Downtown movie houses are pretty much a thing of the past in America, alas, alas. You are always reading how buoyant the movie industry is in America, but all the theaters now are at shopping malls in the suburbs. You go to the movies there and you get a choice of a dozen pictures, but each theater is about the size of a large fridge-freezer and only marginally more comfortable. There are no balconies. Can you imagine that? Can you imagine movie theaters without balconies? To me going to the movies means sitting in the front row of the balcony with your feet up, dropping empty candy boxes onto the people below (or, during the more boring love scenes, dribbling Coke) and throwing Nibs at the screen. Nibs were a licorice-flavored candy, thought to be made from rubber left over from the Korean War, which had a strange popularity in the 1950s. They were practically inedible, but if you sucked on one of them for a minute and then threw it at the screen, it would stick with an interesting *pock* sound. It was a tradition on Saturdays for everybody to take the bus downtown to the Orpheum, buy a box of Nibs and spend the afternoon bombarding the screen.

You had to be careful when you did this because the theater manager employed vicious usherettes, dropouts from Tech High School whose one regret in life was that they hadn't been born into Hitler's Germany, who patrolled the aisles with high-powered flashlights looking for children who were misbehaving. Two or three times during the film their darting lights would fix on some hapless youngster, half out of his seat, poised in throwing position with a moistened Nib in his hand, and they would rush to subdue him. He would be carried off squealing. This never happened to my friends or me, thank God, but we always assumed that the victims were taken away and tortured with electrical instruments before being turned over to the police for a long period of mental readjustment in a reform school. Those were the days! You cannot tell me that some suburban multiplex with shoebox theaters and screens the size of bath towels can offer anything like the enchantment and community spirit of a cavernous downtown movie house. Nobody seems to have noticed it yet, but ours could well be the last generation for which moviegoing has anything like a sense of magic.

On this sobering thought I strolled down to Water Street, on the Savannah River, where there was a new riverside walk. The river itself was dark and smelly and on the South Carolina side opposite there was nothing to look at but down-at-heel warehouses and, further downriver, factories dispensing billows of smoke. But the old cotton warehouses overlooking the river on the Savannah side were splendid. They had been restored without being overgentrified. They contained boutiques and oyster bars on the ground floor, but the upper floors were left a tad shabby, giving them that requisite raffish air I had been looking for since Hannibal. Some of the shops were just a bit chichi, I must admit. One of them was called The Cutest Little Shop in Town, which made me want to have the quickest little dry heave in the county. A sign on the door said, ABSOTIVELY, POSILUTELY NO FOOD OR DRINK IN SHOP. I sank to my knees and thanked God that I had never had to meet the proprietor. The shop was closed so I wasn't able to go inside and see what was so cute about it.

Towards the end of the street stood a big new Hyatt Regency hotel, an instantly depressing sight. Massive and made of shaped concrete, it was from the Fuck You school of architecture so favored by the big American hotel chains. There was nothing about it in scale or appearance even remotely sympathetic to the old buildings around it. It just said, "Fuck you, Savannah." The city is particularly ill favored in this respect. Every few blocks you come up against some discordant slab—the De Soto Hilton, the Ramada Inn, the Best Western Riverfront, all about as appealing as spittle on a johnnycake, as they say in Georgia. Actually, they don't say anything of the sort in Georgia. I just made it up. But it has a nice Southern ring to it, don't you think? I was just about at the point where I was starting to get personally offended by the hotels, and in serious danger of becoming tiresome here, when my attention was distracted by a workman in front of the city courthouse, a large building with a gold dome. He had a leaf blower, a noisy contraption with miles of flex snaking back into the building behind him. I had never seen such a thing before. It looked something like a vacuum cleaner—actually, it looked like one of the Martians in *It Came from Outer Space*—and it was very noisy. The idea, I gathered, was that you would blow all the leaves into a pile and then gather them up by hand. But every time the man assembled a little pile of leaves, a breeze would come along and unassemble it. Sometimes he would chase one leaf half a block or more with his blower, whereupon all the leaves back at base would seize the opportunity to scuttle off in all directions. It was clearly an appliance that must have looked nifty in the catalog but would never work in the real world, and I vaguely wondered, as I strolled past, whether the people at the Zwingle Company were behind it in some way.

I left Savannah on the Herman Talmadge Memorial Bridge, a tall, iron-strutted structure that rises up and up and up and flings you, wide-eyed and quietly gasping, over the Savannah River and into South Carolina. I drove along what appeared on my map to be a meandering coast road, but was in fact a meandering inland road. This stretch of coast is littered with islands, inlets, bays and beaches of rolling sand dunes, but I saw precious little of it. The road was narrow and slow. It must be hell in the summer when millions of vacationers from all over the eastern seaboard head for the beaches and resorts—Tybee Island, Hilton Head, Laurel Bay, Fripp Island.

It wasn't until I reached Beaufort (pronounced "Bew-furt") that I got my first proper look at the sea. I rounded a bend to find myself, suddenly and breathtakingly, gazing out on a looking-glass bay full of boats and reed beds, calm and bright and blue, the same color as the sky. According to my Mobil Travel Guide, the three main sources of income in the area are tourism, the military and retired people. Sounds awful, doesn't it? But in fact Beaufort is lovely, with many mansions and an old-fashioned business district. I parked on Bay Street, the main road through town, and was impressed to find that the meter fee was only five cents. That must be just about the last thing a nickel will buy you in America—thirty minutes of peace of mind in Beaufort, South Carolina. I strolled down to a little park and marina, which had been recently built, from the look of it. This was only the fourth time I had seen the Atlantic from this side. When you come from the Midwest, the ocean is a thing rarely encountered. The park was full of signs instructing you not to enjoy yourself or do anything impertinent. They were every few yards, and said, No Swimming or Diving from Seawall. No Bike Riding in Park. Cutting or Damaging Flowers, Plants, Trees or Shrubs Prohibited. No Consumption or Possession of Beer, Wine, or Alcoholic Beverages in City Parks Without Special Permission of the City. Violators Will Be Prosecuted. I don't know what sort of mini-Stalin they have running the council in Beaufort, but I've never seen a place so officially unwelcoming. It put me off so much that I didn't want to be there anymore, and abruptly I left, which was a shame really because I still had twelve minutes of unexpired time on the meter.

As a result of this, I arrived in Charleston twelve minutes earlier than planned, which was good news. I had thought that Savannah was the most becoming American city I had ever seen, but it thumped into second place soon after my arrival in Charleston. At its harbor end, the city tapers to a rounded promontory which is packed solid with beautiful old homes, lined up one after the other along straight, shady streets like oversized books on a crowded shelf. Some are of the most detailed Victorian ornateness, like fine lace, and some are plain white clapboard with black shutters, but all of them are at least three stories high and imposing—all the more so as they loom up so near the road. Almost no one has any yard to speak of—though everywhere I looked there were Vietnamese gardeners minutely attending to patches of lawn the size of tablecloths—so children play on the street and women, all of them white, all of them young, all of them rich, gossip on the front steps. This isn't supposed to happen in America. Wealthy children in America don't play on the street; there isn't any need. They lounge beside the pool or sneak reefers in the $3,000 treehouse that Daddy had built for them for their ninth birthday. And their mothers, when they wish to gossip with a neighbor, do it on the telephone or climb into their air-conditioned station wagons and drive a hundred yards. It made me realize how much cars and suburbs—and indiscriminate wealth—have spoiled American life. Charleston had the climate and ambience of a Naples, but the wealth and style of a big American city. I was enchanted. I walked away the afternoon, up and down the peaceful streets, secretly admiring all these impossibly happy and good-looking people and their wonderful homes and rich, perfect lives.

The promontory ended in a level park, where children wheeled and bounced on BMXs and young couples strolled hand in hand and Frisbees sailed through the long strips of dark and light caused by the lowering sun filtering through the magnolia trees. Every person was youthful, good-looking and well scrubbed. It was like wandering into a Pepsi commercial. Beyond the park, a broad stone promenade overlooked the harbor, vast and shimmery and green. I went and peered over the edge. The water slapped the stone and smelled of fish. Two miles out you could see the island of Fort Sumter, where the Civil War began. The promenade was crowded with cyclists and sweating joggers, who weaved expertly among the pedestrians and shuffling tourists. I turned around and walked back to the car, the sun warm on my back, and had the sneaking feeling that after such perfection things were bound to be downhill from now on.

9

SOUTH CAROLINA was boring. For the sake of haste I got on Interstate 26, which runs in a 200-mile diagonal across the state, through a monotonous landscape of dormant tobacco fields and salmon-colored soil. According to my Mobil Travel Guide, I was no longer in the Deep South but in the Middle Atlantic states. But it had the heat and glare of the South and the people in gas stations and cafes along the way sounded Southern. Even the radio announcers sounded Southern, in attitude as much as accent. According to one news broadcast, the police in Spartanburg were looking for two black men "who raped a white girl." You wouldn't hear *that* outside the South.

As I neared Columbia, the fields along the road began to fill with tall signs advertising motels and quick-food places. These weren't the squat, rectangular billboards of my youth, with alluring illustrations and three-dimensional cows, but just large unfriendly signs standing atop sixty-foot-high metal poles. Their messages were terse. They didn't invite you to do anything interesting or seductive. The old signs were chatty and would say things like WHILE IN COLUMBIA, WHY NOT STAY IN THE MODERN SKYLINER MOTOR INN, WITH OUR ALL NEW SENSU-MATIC VIBRATING BEDS. YOU'LL LOVE 'EM! SPECIAL RATES FOR CHILDREN. FREE TV. AIR

COOLED ROOMS. FREE ICE. PLENTY OF PARKING. PETS WELCOME. ALL-U-CAN-EAT CATFISH BUFFET EVERY TUES 5–7 PM. DANCE NITELY TO THE VERNON STURGES GUITAR ORCHESTRA IN THE STARLITE ROOM. (PLEASE—NO NEGROES). The old signs were like oversized postcards, with helpful chunks of information. They provided something to read, a little food for thought, a snippet of insight into the local culture. Attention spans had obviously contracted since then. The signs now simply announced the name of the business and how to get there. You could read them from miles away: HOLIDAY INN, EXIT 26E, 4 MI. Sometimes these instructions were more complex and would say things like BURGER KING—31 MILES. TAKE EXIT 17B 5 MI TO US49 SOUTH, TURN RIGHT AT LIGHTS, THEN WEST PAST AIRPORT FOR 2½ MI. Who could want a Whopper that much? But the signs are effective, no doubt about it. Driving along in a state of idle mindlessness, suffering from hunger and a grease deficiency, you see a sign that says MCDONALD'S—EXIT HERE, and it's almost instinctive to swerve onto the exit ramp and follow it. Over and over through the weeks I found myself sitting at plastic tables with little boxes of food in front of me which I didn't want or have time to eat, all because a sign had instructed me to be there.

At the North Carolina border, the dull landscape ended abruptly, as if by decree. Suddenly the countryside rose and fell in majestic undulations, full of creeping thickets of laurel, rhododendron and palmetto. At each hilltop the landscape opened out to reveal hazy views of the Blue Ridge Mountains, part of the Appalachian chain. The Appalachians stretch for 2,100 miles from Alabama to Canada and were once higher than the Himalayas (I read that on a book of matches once and have been waiting years for an opportunity to use it), though now they are smallish and rounded, fetching rather than dramatic. All along their length they go by different names—the Adirondacks, Poconos, Catskills, Alleghenies. I was headed for the Smokies, but I intended to stop en route at the Biltmore Estate, just outside Asheville, North Carolina. Biltmore was built by George Vanderbilt in 1895 and was one of the biggest houses ever constructed in America—a 255-room pile of stone in the style of a Loire chateau, on grounds of 10,000 acres. When you arrive at Biltmore you are directed to park your car and go into a building by the gate to purchase your ticket before proceeding onto the estate. I thought this was curious until I went into the building and discovered that a gay afternoon at Biltmore would involve a serious financial commitment. The signs telling you the admission fee were practically invisible, but you could see from the ashen-faced look on people as they staggered away from the ticket windows that it must be a lot. Even so I was taken aback when my turn came and the unpleasant-looking woman at the ticket window told me that the admission fee was $17.50 for adults and $13 for children. *"Seventeen dollars and fifty cents!"* I croaked. "Does that include dinner and a floor show?"

The woman was obviously used to dealing with hysteria and snide remarks. In a monotone she said, "The admission fee includes admission to the George Vanderbilt house, of which 50 of the 250 rooms are open to the public. You should allow two to three hours for the self-guided tour. It also includes admission to the extensive gardens for which you should allow thirty minutes to one hour. It also includes admission and guided tour of the winery with audiovisual presentation and complimentary wine tasting. A guide to the house and grounds, available for a separate charge, is recommended. Afterwards you may wish to spend further large sums of money in the Deerpark Restaurant or, if you are a relatively cheap person, in the Stable Cafe, as well as avail yourself of the opportunity to buy expensive gifts and remembrances in the Carriage House Gift Shop."

But by this time I was already on the highway again, heading for the Great Smoky Mountains, which, thank God, are free.

I drove ten miles out of my way in order to spend the night in Bryson City, a modest self-indulgence. It was a small, nondescript place of motels and barbecue shacks strung out along a narrow river valley on the edge of the Great Smoky Mountains National Park. There is little reason to go there unless your name happens to be Bryson, and even then, I have to tell you, the pleasure is intermittent. I got a room in the Bennett's Court

Motel, a wonderful old place that appeared not to have changed a bit since 1956, apart from an occasional light dusting. It was precisely as motels always used to be, with the rooms spread out along a covered verandah overlooking a lawn with two trees and a tiny concrete swimming pool, which at this time of year was empty but for a puddle of wet leaves and one pissed-off-looking frog. Beside each door was a metal armchair with a scallop-shaped back. By the sidewalk an old neon sign thrummed with the sound of coursing neon gas and spelled out BENNETT'S COURT / VACANCY / AIR CONDITIONED / GUEST POOL / TV, all in green and pink beneath a tasteful blinking arrow in yellow. When I was small all motels had signs like that. Now you see them only occasionally in small forgotten towns on the edge of nowhere. Bennett's Court clearly would be the motel in Amalgam.

I took my bags inside, lowered myself experimentally onto the bed and switched on the TV. Instantly there came up a commercial for Preparation H, an unguent for hemorrhoids. The tone was urgent. I don't remember the exact words, but they were something like: "Hey, you! Have you got hemorrhoids? Then get some Preparation H! That's an order! Remember that name, you inattentive moron! Preparation H! And even if you haven't got hemorrhoids, get some Preparation H anyway! Just in case!" And then a voice-over quickly added, "Now available in cherry flavor." Having lived abroad so long, I was unused to the American hard sell and it made me uneasy. I was equally unsettled by the way television stations in America can jump back and forth between commercials and programs without hesitation or warning. You'll be lying there watching "Kojak," say, and in the middle of a gripping shootout somebody starts cleaning a toilet bowl and you sit up, thinking, "What the—" and then you realize it is a commercial. In fact, it is several minutes of commercials. You could go out for cigarettes and a pizza during commercial breaks in America, *and* still have time to wash the toilet bowl before the program resumed.

The Preparation H commercial vanished and a micro-instant later, before there was any possibility of the viewer reflecting on whether he might wish to turn to another channel, was replaced by a clapping audience, the perky sound of steel guitars and happy but mildly brain-damaged people in sequined outfits. This was "Grand Ole Opry." I watched for a couple of minutes. By degrees my chin dropped onto my shirt as I listened to their singing and jesting with a kind of numb amazement. It was like a visual lobotomy. Have you ever watched an infant at play and said to yourself, "I wonder what goes on in his little head"? Well, watch "Grand Ole Opry" for five minutes sometime and you will begin to have an idea.

After a couple of minutes another commercial break noisily intruded and I was snapped back to my senses. I switched off the television and went out to investigate Bryson City. There was more to it than I had first thought. Beyond the Swain County Courthouse was a small business district. I was gratified to note that almost everything had a Bryson City sign on it—Bryson City Laundry, Bryson City Coal and Lumber, Bryson City Church of Christ, Bryson City Electronics, Bryson City Police Department, Bryson City Fire Department, Bryson City Post Office. I began to appreciate how George Washington might feel if he were to be brought back to life and set down in the District of Columbia. I don't know who the Bryson was whom this town was so signally honoring, but I had certainly never seen my name spread around so lavishly, and I regretted that I hadn't brought a crowbar and monkey wrench because many of the signs would have made splendid keepsakes. I particularly fancied having the Bryson City Church of Christ sign beside my front gate in England and being able to put up different messages every week like REPENT NOW, LIMEYS.

It didn't take long to exhaust the possibilities for diversion in downtown Bryson City, and almost before I realized it I found myself on the highway out of town leading towards Cherokee, the next town along the valley. I followed it for a way but there was nothing to see except a couple of derelict gas stations and barbecue shacks, and hardly any shoulder to walk on so that cars shot past only inches away and whipped my clothes into a disconcerting little frenzy. All along the road were billboards and large hand-lettered signs in praise of Christ: GET A GRIP ON YOUR

LIFE—PRAISE JESUS; GOD LOVES YOU, AMERICA; and the rather more enigmatic WHAT WOULD HAPPEN IF YOU DIED TOMORROW? (Well, I thought, there would be no more payments on the freezer for a start.) I turned around and went back into town. It was 5:30 in the afternoon, Bryson City was a crypt with sidewalks and I was at a complete loss. Down a small hill, beside the rushing river, I spied an A&P supermarket, which appeared to be open, and I went down there for want of something better to do. I often used to hang out in supermarkets. Robert Swanson and I, when we were about twelve and so obnoxious that it would have been a positive mercy to inject us with something lethal, would often go to the Hinky-Dinky supermarket on Ingersoll Avenue in Des Moines during the summer because it was air-conditioned and pass the time by doing things I am now ashamed to relate— loosening the bottom of a bag of flour and then watching it pour onto the floor when some unsuspecting woman picked it up, or putting strange items like goldfish food and emetics in people's shopping carts when their backs were turned. I didn't intend to do anything like that in the A&P now—unless of course I got *really* bored—but I thought it would be comforting, in this strange place, to look at foodstuffs from my youth. And it was. It was almost like visiting old friends—Skippy Peanut Butter, Pop-Tarts, Welch's Grape Juice, Sara Lee cakes. I wandered the aisles, murmuring tiny cries of joy at each sighting of an old familiar nutrient. It cheered me up no end.

Then suddenly I remembered something. Months before, in England, I had noticed an ad for panty shields in the *New York Times Magazine*. These panty shields had dimples on them and the dimples had a name that was trademarked. This struck me as remarkable. Can you imagine being given the job of thinking up a catchy name for dimples on a panty shield? But I couldn't remember what it was. So now, for no reason other than that I had nothing better to do, I went over and had a look at the A&P's panty shield section. There was a surprising diversity of them. I would never have guessed that the market was so buoyant or indeed that there were so many panties in Bryson City that needed shielding. I had never paid much attention to this sort of thing before and it was really kind of interesting. I don't know how long I spent poking about among the various brands and reading the instructions for use, or whether I might even have started talking to myself a little, as I sometimes do when I am happily occupied. But I suppose it must have been quite some time. In any case, at the very moment that I picked up a packet of New Freedom Thins, with Funnel-Dot Protection ^{TM}, and cried triumphantly, "Aha! There you are, you little buggers!" I turned my head a fraction and noticed that at the far end of the aisle the manager and two female assistants were watching me. I blushed and clumsily wedged the packet back on the shelves. "Just browsing!" I called in an unconvincing voice, hoping I didn't look too dangerous or insane, and made for the exit. I remembered reading some weeks before that it is still against the law in twenty US states, most of them in the Deep South, for heterosexuals to engage in oral or anal intercourse. I had nothing like that in mind just now, you understand, but I think it indicates that some of these places can be doggedly unenlightened in matters pertaining to sex and could well have ordinances with respect to the unlawful handling of panty shields. It would be just my luck to pull a five-to-ten stretch for some unintended perversion in a place like North Carolina. At all events, I felt fortunate to make it back to my motel without being intercepted by the authorities, and spent the rest of my short stay in Bryson City behaving with the utmost circumspection.

The Great Smoky Mountains National Park covers 500,000 acres in North Carolina and Tennessee. I didn't realize it before I went there, but it is the most popular national park in America, attracting nine million visitors a year, three times as many as any other national park, and even early on a Sunday morning in October it was crowded. The road between Bryson City and Cherokee, at the park's edge, was a straggly collection of motels, junky-looking auto repair shops, trailer courts and barbecue shacks perched on the edge of a glittering stream in a cleft in the mountains. It must have been beautiful once, with the dark mountains squeezing in from both sides, but now it was just squalid. Cherokee itself was even worse. It is the biggest Indian reservation in the Eastern United States and it was packed from one end to the other with souvenir stores selling tawdry Indian trinkets, all of them with big signs on their roofs and sides saying, MOCCASINS! INDIAN JEWELRY! TOMAHAWKS! POLISHED GEMSTONES! CRAPPY ITEMS OF EVERY DESCRIPTION! Some of the places had a caged brown bear out front—the Cherokee mascot, I gathered—and around each of these was a knot of small boys trying to provoke the animal into a show of ferocity, encouraged from a safe distance by their fathers. At other stores you could have your photograph taken with a genuine, hung-over, flabby-titted Cherokee Indian in war dress for five dollars, but not many people seemed interested in this and the model Indians sat slumped in chairs looking as listless as the bears. I don't think I had ever been to a place quite so ugly, and it was jammed with tourists, almost all of them also ugly—fat people in noisy clothes with cameras dangling on their bellies. Why is it, I wondered idly as I nosed the car through the throngs, that tourists are always fat and dress like morons?

Then, abruptly, before I could give the question the consideration it deserved, I was out of Cherokee and in the national park and all the garishness ceased. People don't live in national parks in America as they do in England. They are areas of wilderness—often of enforced wilderness. The Smoky Mountains were once full of hillbillies who lived in cabins up in the remote hollows, up among the clouds, but they were moved out and now the park is sterile as far as human activities go. Instead of trying to preserve an ancient way of life, the park authorities eradicated it. So the dispossessed hillbillies moved down to valley towns at the park's edge and turned them into junkvilles selling crappy little souvenirs. It seems a very strange approach to me. Now a few of the cabins are preserved as museum pieces. There was one at a visitors' center just inside the park, which I dutifully stopped to have a look at. It was exactly like the cabins at the Lincoln village at New Salem in Illinois. I had not realized that it is actually possible to overdose on log cabins, but as I drew near the cabin I began to feel a sudden onset of brainstem death and I retreated to the car after only the briefest of looks.

The Smoky Mountains themselves were a joy. It was a perfect October morning. The road led steeply up through broad-leaved forests of dappled sunshine, full of paths and streams, and then, higher up, opened out to airy vistas. All along the road through the park there were lookout points where you could pull the car over and go "ooh!" and "wow!" at the views. They were all named for mountain passes that sounded like condominium developments for yuppies—Pigeon Gap, Cherry Cove, Wolf Mountain, Bear Trap Gap. The air was clear and thin and the views were vast. The mountains rolled away to a distant horizon, gently shading from rich green to charcoal blue to hazy smoke. It was a sea of trees—like looking out over a landscape from Colombia or Brazil, so virginal was it all. In all the rolling vastness there was not a single sign of humanity, no towns, no water towers, no plume of smoke from a solitary farmstead. It was just endless silence beneath a bright sky, empty and clear apart from one distant bluish puff of cumulus, which cast a drifting shadow over a far-off hill.

The Oconaluftee Highway across the park is only thirty miles long, but it is so steep and winding that it took me all morning to cross it. By 10 A.M. there was a steady stream of cars in both directions, and free spaces at the lookout points were hard to find. This was my first serious brush with real tourists—retired people with trailer homes heading for Florida, young families taking off-season vacations, honeymooners. There were cars and trailers, campers and motor homes from thousands of miles away—California, Wyoming, British Columbia—and at every lookout point people were clustered around their vehicles with the doors and trunks opened, feeding from ice coolers and portable fridges. Every few yards there was a Winnebago or Komfort Motor Home—massive, self-contained dwellings on wheels that took up three parking spaces and jutted out so far that cars coming in could only barely scrape past.

All morning I had been troubled by a vague sense of something being missing, and then it occurred to me what it was. There were no hikers such as you would see in England—no people in stout boots and short pants, with knee-high tasseled stockings. No little rucksacks full of sandwiches and flasks of tea.

And no platoons of cyclists in skintight uniforms and baker's caps laboring breathlessly up the mountainsides, slowing up traffic. What slowed the traffic here were the massive motor homes lumbering up and down the mountain passes. Some of them, amazingly, had cars tethered to their rear bumpers, like dinghies. I got stuck behind one on the long, sinuous descent down the mountain into Tennessee. It was so wide that it could barely stay within its lane and kept threatening to nudge oncoming cars off into the picturesque void to our left. That, alas, is the way of vacationing nowadays for many people. The whole idea is not to expose yourself to a moment of discomfort or inconvenience—indeed, not to breathe fresh air if possible. When the urge to travel seizes you, you pile into your thirteen-ton tin palace and drive 400 miles across the country, hermetically sealed against the elements, and stop at a campground where you dash to plug into their water supply and electricity so that you don't have to go a single moment without air-conditioning or dishwasher and microwave facilities. These things, these RVs, are like life-support systems on wheels. Astronauts go to the moon with less backup. RV people are another breed—and a largely demented one at that. They become obsessed with trying to equip their vehicles with gadgets to deal with every possible contingency. Their lives become ruled by the dread thought that one day they may find themselves in a situation in which they are not entirely self-sufficient. I once went camping for two days at Lake Darling in Iowa with a friend whose father—an RV enthusiast—kept trying to press labor-saving devices on us. "I got a great little solar-powered can opener here," he would say. "You wanna take that?"

"No thanks," we would reply. "We're only going for two days."

"How about this combination flashlight–carving knife? You can run it off the car cigarette lighter if you need to, and it doubles as a flashing siren if you get lost in the wilderness."

"No thanks."

"Well, at least take the battery-powered microwave."

"Really, we don't want it."

"Then how the hell are you going to pop popcorn out there in the middle of nowhere? Have you thought about that?"

A whole industry (in which no doubt the Zwingle Company of New York is actively involved) has grown up to supply this market. You can see these people at campgrounds all over the country, standing around their vehicles comparing gadgets—methane-powered ice-cube makers, portable tennis courts, anti-insect flame throwers, inflatable lawns. They are strange and dangerous people and on no account should be approached.

At the foot of the mountain, the park ended and suddenly all was squalor again. I was once more struck by this strange compartmentalization that goes on in America—a belief that no commercial activities must be allowed inside the park, but permitting unrestrained development outside, even though the landscape there may be just as outstanding. America has never quite grasped that you can live in a place without making it ugly, that beauty doesn't have to be confined behind fences, as if a national park were a sort of zoo for nature. The ugliness intensified to fever pitch as I rolled into Gatlinburg, a community that had evidently dedicated itself to the endless quest of trying to redefine the lower limits of bad taste. It is the world capital of tat. It made Cherokee look decorous. There is not much more to it than a single milelong main street, but it was packed from end to end with the most dazzling profusion of tourist clutter—the Elvis Presley Hall of Fame, Stars Over Gatlinburg Wax Museum, two haunted houses, the National Bible Museum, Hillbilly Village, Ripley's Believe It or Not Museum, the American Historical Wax Museum, Gatlinburg Space Needle, something called Paradise Island, something else called World of Illusions, the Bonnie Lou and Buster Country Music Show, Carbo's Police Museum ("See 'Walking Tall' Sheriff Buford Pusser's Death Car!"), Guinness Book of Records Exhibition Center and, not least, the Irlene Mandrell Hall of Stars Museum and Shopping Mall. In between this galaxy of entertainments were scores of parking lots and noisy, crowded restaurants, junk-food stalls, ice cream parlors and gift shops of the sort that sell "wanted" posters with YOUR NAME HERE and baseball caps with droll embellishments, like a coil of

95

realistic-looking plastic turd on the brim. Walking in an unhurried fashion up and down the street were more crowds of overweight tourists in boisterous clothes, with cameras bouncing on their bellies, consuming ice creams, cotton candy and corn dogs, sometimes simultaneously, and wearing baseball caps with plastic turds jauntily attached to the brim.

I loved it. When I was growing up, we never got to go to places like Gatlinburg. My father would rather have given himself brain surgery with a Black and Decker drill than spend an hour in such a place. He had just two criteria for gauging the worth of a holiday attraction: Was it educational and was it free? Gatlinburg was patently neither of these. His idea of holiday heaven was a museum without an admission charge. My dad was the most honest man I ever met, but vacations blinded him to his principles. When I had pimples scattered across my face and stubble on my chin he was still swearing at ticket booths that I was eight years old. He was so cheap on vacations that it always surprised me he didn't make us sift in litter bins for our lunch. So Gatlinburg to me was a heady experience. I felt like a priest let loose in Las Vegas with a sockful of quarters. All the noise and glitter, and above all the possibilities for running through irresponsible sums of money in a short period, made me giddy.

I wandered through the crowds, and hesitated at the entrance to the Ripley's Believe It or Not Museum. I could sense my father, a thousands miles away, beginning to rotate slowly in his grave as I looked at the posters. They told me that inside I would see a man who could hold three billiard balls in his mouth at once, a two-headed calf, a human unicorn with a horn protruding from his forehead and hundreds of other riveting oddities from all over the globe collected by the tireless Robert Ripley and crated back to Gatlinburg for the edification of discerning tourists such as myself. The admission fee was five dollars. The pace of my father's rotating quickened as I looked into my wallet and then sped to a whirring blur as I fished out a five-dollar bill and guiltily handed it to the unsmiling woman in the ticket booth. "What the hell," I thought as I went inside, "at least it will give the old man some exercise."

Well, it was superb. I know five dollars is a lot of money for a few minutes' diversion. I could just see my father and me standing outside on the sidewalk bickering. My father would say, "No, it's a big gyp. For that kind of money, you could buy something that would give you years of value."

"Like what—a box of carpet tiles?" I would reply with practiced sarcasm. "Oh, please, Dad, just this once don't be cheap. There's a two-headed calf in there."

"No, son, I'm sorry."

"I'll be good forever. I'll take out the garbage every day until I get married. Dad, there is a guy in there who can hold three billiard balls in his mouth at once. There is a *human unicorn* in there. Dad, we could be throwing away the chance of a lifetime here."

But he would not be moved. "I don't want to hear any more about it. Now let's all get in the car and drive 175 miles to the Molasses Point Historical Battlefield. You'll learn lots of worthwhile things about the little-known American war with Ecuador of 1802 and it won't cost me a penny."

So I went through the Ripley's Believe It or Not Museum and I savored every artifact and tasteless oddity. It was outstanding. I mean honestly, where else are you going to see a replica of Columbus's flagship, the *Santa Maria,* made entirely of chicken bones? And how can you possibly put a price on seeing an eight-foot-long model of the Circus Maximus constructed of sugar cubes, or the death mask of John Dillinger, or a room made entirely of matchsticks by one Reg Polland of Manchester, England (well done, Reg; Britain is proud of you)? We are talking lasting memories here. I was pleased to note that England was further represented by, of all things, a chimney pot, circa 1940. Believe it or not. It was all wonderful—clean, nicely presented, sometimes even believable—and I spent a happy hour there.

Afterwards, feeling highly content, I purchased an ice cream cone the size of a baby's head and wandered with it through the crowds of people in the afternoon sunshine. I went into a series of gift shops and tried on baseball caps with plastic turds on the brim, but the cheapest one I saw was $7.99 and I decided, out of deference to my father, that that would be just too much extravagance for one afternoon. If it came to it, I could always make my own, I thought as I returned to the car and headed for the dangerous hills of Appalachia.

IO

IN 1587, a group of 115 English settlers—men, women and children—sailed from Plymouth to set up the first colony in the New World, on Roanoke Island off what is now North Carolina. Shortly after they arrived, a child named Virginia Dare was born and thus became the first white person to arrive in America headfirst. Two years later, a second expedition set off from England to see how the settlers were getting on and to bring them their mail and tell them that the repairman from British Telecom had finally shown up and that sort of thing. But when the relief party arrived, they found the settlement deserted. There was no message of where the settlers had gone, nor any sign of a struggle, but just one word mysteriously scratched on a wall: "Croatoan." This was the name of a nearby island where the Indians were known to be friendly, but a trip to the island showed that the settlers had never arrived there. So where did they go? Did they leave voluntarily or were they spirited off by Indians? This has long been one of the great mysteries of the Colonial period.

I bring this up here because one theory is that the settlers pushed inland, up into the hills of Appalachia, and settled there. No one knows why they might have done this, but fifty years

later, when European explorers arrived in Tennessee, the Cherokee Indians told them that there was a group of pale people living
in the hills already, people who wore clothes and had long beards.
These people, according to a contemporary account, "had a bell
which they rang before they ate their meals and had a strange
habit of bowing their heads and saying something in a low voice
before they ate."

No one ever found this mysterious community. But in a
remote and neglected corner of the Appalachians, high up in the
Clinch Mountains above the town of Sneedville in northeastern
Tennessee, there still live some curious people called Melungeons
who have been there for as long as anyone can remember. The
Melungeons (no one knows where the name comes from) have
most of the characteristics of Europeans—blue eyes, fair hair,
lanky build—but a dark, almost Negroid skin coloring that is
distinctly non-European. They have English family names—Bro-
gan, Collins, Mullins—but no one, including the Melungeons
themselves, has any idea of where they come from or what their
early history might have been. They are as much of a mystery as
the lost settlers of Roanoke Island. Indeed, it has been suggested
that they may *be* the lost settlers of Roanoke.

Peter Dunn, a colleague at the *Independent* in London, put me
onto the Melungeon story when he heard that I was going to that
part of the world, and kindly dug out an article he had done for
the *Sunday Times Magazine* some years before. This was illustrated
with remarkable photographs of Melungeons. It is impossible to
describe them except to say that they looked like white Negroes.
They were simply white people with very dark skins. Their appearance was, to say the least, striking. For this reason they have
long been outcasts in their own county, consigned to shacks in
the hills in an area called Snake Hollow. In Hancock County,
"Melungeon" is equivalent to "Nigger." The valley people—who
are themselves generally poor and backward—regard the Melungeons as something strange and shameful, and the Melungeons
as a consequence keep to themselves, coming down from the
mountains only at widely scattered intervals to buy provisions.
They don't like outsiders. Neither do the valley people. Peter
Dunn told me that he and the photographer who accompanied

him were given a reception that ranged from mild hostility to outright intimidation. It was an uncomfortable assignment. A few months later a reporter from *Time* magazine was actually shot near Sneedville for asking too many questions.

So you can perhaps imagine the sense of foreboding that seeped over me as I drove up Tennessee Highway 31 through a forgotten landscape of poor and scattered tobacco farms, through the valley of the twisting Clinch River, en route to Sneedville. This was the seventh poorest county in the nation and it looked it. Litter was adrift in the ditches and most of the farmhouses were small and unadorned. In every driveway there stood a pickup truck with a gun rack in the back window, and where there were people in the yards they stopped what they were doing to watch me as I passed. It was late afternoon, nearly dusk, when I reached Sneedville. Outside the Hancock County Courthouse a group of teenagers were perched on the fronts of pickup trucks, talking to each other, and they too stared at me as I passed. Sneedville is so far from anywhere, such an improbable destination, that a stranger's car attracts notice. There wasn't much to the town: the courthouse, a Baptist church, some box houses, a gas station. The gas station was still open, so I pulled in. I didn't particularly need gas, but I wasn't sure when I would find another station. The guy who came out to pump the gas had an abundance of fleshy warts—a veritable crop—scattered across his face like button mushrooms. He looked like a genetic experiment that had gone horribly wrong. He didn't speak except to establish what kind of gas I wanted and he didn't remark on the fact that I was from out of state. This was the first time on the trip that a gas station attendant hadn't said in an engaging manner, "You're a long way from home, aren'tcha?" or "What brings you all the way here from I-o-way?" or something like that. (I always told them that I was on my way east to have vital heart surgery in the hope that they would give me extra Green Stamps.) I was very probably the first person from out of state this man had seen all year, yet he appeared resolutely uninterested in what I was doing there. It was odd. I said to him—blurted really—"Excuse me, but didn't I read somewhere that some people called Melungeons live around here somewhere?"

He didn't answer. He just watched the pump counter spin. I thought he hadn't heard me, so I said, "I say, excuse me, but didn't I hear that some people—"

"Don't know," he said abruptly without looking at me. Then he looked at me. "Don't know nothin' about that. You want your oil checked?"

I hesitated, surprised by the question. "No thank you."

"That's eleven dollars." He took my money without thanks and went back inside. I was fairly dumbfounded. I don't know quite why. Through the window I could see him pick up his telephone and make a call. He looked at me as he did it. Suddenly I felt alarmed. What if he was calling the police to tell them to come out and shoot me? I laid a small patch of rubber on his driveway as I departed—something you don't often see achieved with a Chevette—and made the pistons sing as I floored the accelerator and hurtled out of town at a breakneck twenty-seven miles an hour. But a mile or so later I slowed down. Partly this was because I was going up an almost vertical hill and the car wouldn't go any faster—for one breathless moment I thought it might actually start rolling backwards—and partly because I told myself not to be so jumpy. The guy was probably just calling his wife to remind her to buy more wart lotion. Even if he was calling the police to report an outsider asking impertinent questions, what could they do to me? It was a free country. I hadn't broken any laws. I had asked an innocent question, and asked it politely. How could anyone take offense at that? Clearly I was being silly to feel any sense of menace. Even so, I found myself glancing frequently into the rearview mirror and half expecting to see the hill behind me crawling with flashing squad cars and posses of volunteer vigilantes in pickup trucks coming after me. Judiciously, I stepped up my speed from eleven to thirteen miles an hour.

High up the hill I began to encounter shacks set back in clearings in the woods, and peered at them in the hope of glimpsing a Melungeon or two. But the few people I saw were white. They stared at me with a strange look of surprise as I lumbered past, the way you might stare at a man riding an ostrich, and generally made no response to my cheerful wave, though one or two did reply with an automatic and economical wave of their own, a raised hand and a twitch of fingers.

This was real hillbilly country. Many of the shacks looked like something out of "Li'l Abner," with sagging porches and tilting chimneys. Some were abandoned. Many appeared to have been handmade, with rambling extensions that had clearly been fashioned from scraps of plundered wood. People in these hills still made moonshine, or stump liquor as they call it. But the big business these days is marijuana, believe it or not. I read somewhere that whole mountain villages sometimes band together and can make $100,000 a month from a couple of acres planted in some remote and lofty hollow. That, more than the Melungeons, is an excellent reason not to be a stranger asking questions in the area.

Although I was clearly climbing high up into the mountains, the woods all around were so dense that I had no views. But at the summit the trees parted like curtains to provide a spectacular outlook over the valley on the other side. It was like coming over the top of the earth, like the view from an airplane. Steep green wooded hills with alpine meadows clinging to their sides stretched away for as far as the eye could see until at last they were consumed by a distant and colorful sunset. Before me a sinuous road led steeply down to a valley of rolling farms spread out along a lazy river. It was as perfect a setting as I had ever seen. I drove through the soft light of dusk, absorbed by the beauty. And the thing was, every house along the roadside was a shack. This was the heart of Appalachia, the most notoriously impoverished region of America, and it was just inexpressibly beautiful. It was strange that the urban professionals from the cities of the eastern seaboard, only a couple of hours' drive to the east, hadn't colonized an area of such arresting beauty, filling the dales with rusticky weekend cottages, country clubs and fancy restaurants.

It was strange, too, to see white people living in poverty. In America, to be white and impoverished really takes some doing. Of course, this was American poverty, this was white people's poverty, which isn't like poverty elsewhere. It isn't even like the poverty in Tuskegee. It has been suggested with more than a touch of cynicism that when Lyndon Johnson launched his great

War on Poverty in 1964, the focus was placed on Appalachia not because it was so destitute but because it was so white. A little-publicized survey at the time showed that 40 percent of the poorest people in the region owned a car and a third of those had been bought new. In 1964, my future father-in-law in England was, like most people there, years away from owning his first car and even now he has never owned a new one, yet no one ever called him destitute or sent him a free sack of flour and some knitting wool at Christmas. Still, I can't deny that by American standards the scattered shacks around me were decidedly modest. They had no satellite dishes in the yard, no Weber barbecues, no station wagons standing in the drive. And I daresay they had no microwaves in the kitchen, poor devils, and by American standards that is pretty damn deprived.

II

━━━━━━━━ I DROVE THROUGH a landscape of gumdrop hills, rolling roads, neat farms. The sky was full of those big fluffy clouds you always see in nautical paintings, and the towns had curious and interesting names: Snowflake, Fancy Gap, Horse Pasture, Meadows of Dan, Charity. Virginia went on and on. It never seemed to end. The state is nearly 400 miles across, but the twisting road must have added at least 100 miles to that. In any case, every time I looked at the map I seemed to have moved a remarkably tiny distance. From time to time I would pass a sign that said HISTORICAL MARKER AHEAD, but I didn't stop. There are thousands of historical markers all over America and they are always dull. I know this for a fact because my father stopped at every one of them. He would pull the car up to them and read them aloud to us, even when we asked him not to. They would say something like:

SINGING TREES SACRED BURIAL SITE

For centuries this land, known as the Valley of the Singing Trees, was a sacred burial site for the Blackbutt Indians. In recognition of this the US Government gave the land to the tribe in perpetuity in 1880. However, in 1882 oil was discovered beneath the singing trees and, after a series of skirmishes in which 27,413 Blackbutts perished, the tribe was relocated to a reservation at Cyanide Springs, New Mexico.

What am I saying? They were never as good as that. Usually they would commemorate something palpably obscure and uninteresting—the site of the first Bible college in western Tennessee, the birthplace of the inventor of the moist towelette, the home of the author of the Kansas state song. You knew before you got there that they were going to be boring because if they had been even remotely interesting somebody would have set up a hamburger stand and sold souvenirs. But Dad thrived on them and would never fail to be impressed. After reading them to us he would say in an admiring tone, "Well, I'll be darned," and then without fail would pull back onto the highway into the path of an oncoming truck, which would honk furiously and shed part of its load as it swerved past. "Yes, that was really very interesting," he would add reflectively, unaware that he had just about killed us all.

I was heading for the Booker T. Washington National Monument, a restored plantation near Roanoke where Booker T. Washington grew up. He was a remarkable man. A freed slave, he taught himself to read and write, secured an education and eventually founded the Tuskegee Institute in Alabama, the first college in America for blacks. Then, as if that were not achievement enough, he finished his career as a soul musician, churning out a series of hits in the 1960s on the Stax record label with the backup group the MGs. As I say, a remarkable man. My plan was to visit his monument and then zip over to Monticello for a leisurely look around Thomas Jefferson's home. But it was not to be. Just beyond Patrick Springs, I spied a side road leading to a place called Critz, which I calculated with a glance at the map could cut thirty miles off my driving distance. Impulsively I hauled the car around the corner, making the noise of squealing tires as I went. I had to make the noise myself because the Chevette couldn't manage it, though it did shoot out some blue smoke.

I should have known better. My first rule of travel is never go to a place that sounds like a medical condition and Critz clearly was an incurable disease involving flaking skin. The upshot is that I got hopelessly lost. The road, once I lost sight of the highway, broke up into a network of unsignposted lanes hemmed in by tall grass. I drove for ages, with that kind of glowering, insane resolve that you get when you are lost and become convinced that if you just keep moving you will eventually end up where you want to be. I kept coming to towns that weren't on my map—Sanville, Pleasantville, Preston. These weren't two-shack places. They were proper towns, with schools, gas stations, lots of houses. I felt as if I should call the newspaper in Roanoke and inform the editor that I had found a lost county.

Eventually, as I passed through Sanville for the third time, I decided I would have to ask directions. I stopped an old guy taking his dog out to splash urine around the neighborhood and asked him the way to Critz. Without batting an eyelid he launched into a set of instructions of the most breathtaking complexity. He must have talked for five minutes. It sounded like a description of Lewis and Clark's journey through the wilderness. I couldn't follow it at all, but when he paused and said "You with me so far?" I lied and said I was.

"Okay, well that takes you to Preston," he went on. "From there you follow the old drover's road due east out of town till you come to the McGregor place. You can tell it's the McGregor place because there's a sign out front saying: the McGregor Place. About a hundred yards further on there's a road going off to the left with a sign for Critz. But whatever you do don't go down there because the bridge is out and you'll plunge straight into Dead Man's Creek." And on he went like that for many minutes. When at last he finished I thanked him and drove off without conviction in the general direction of his last gesture. Within two hundred yards I had come to a T-junction and didn't have a clue which way to go. I went right. Ten minutes later, to the surprise of both of us, I was driving past the old guy and his ever-urinating dog again. Out of the corner of my eye I could see him gesturing excitedly, shouting at me that I had gone the wrong way, but as this was already abundantly evident to me, I ignored his hopping around and went left at the junction. This didn't get me any nearer Critz, but it did provide me with a new set of dead ends and roads to nowhere. At three o'clock in the afternoon, two hours after I had set off for Critz, I blundered back onto Highway 58. I was 150 feet further down the road than I had been when I left it. Sourly I pulled back onto the highway and drove for many long hours in silence. It was too late to go to the Booker T. Washington National Monument or to Monticello, even assuming I could summon the intelligence to find them. The day had been a complete washout. I had had no lunch, no life-giving infusions of coffee. It had been a day without pleasure or reward. I got a room in a motel in Fredericksburg, ate at a pancake house of ineffable crappiness and retired to my room in a dim frame of mind.

In the morning I drove to Colonial Williamsburg, a restored historic village near the coast. It is one of the most popular tourist attractions in the East and even though it was early on a Tuesday morning in October when I arrived, the parking lots were already filling up. I parked and joined a stream of people following the signs to the visitors' center. Inside it was cool and dark. Near the door was a scale model of the village in a glass case. Oddly, there was no you-are-here arrow to help you get oriented. Indeed, the visitors' center wasn't even shown. There was no way of telling where the village was in relation to where you were now. That seemed strange to me and I became suspicious. I stood back and watched the crowds. Gradually it became clear to me that the whole thing was a masterpiece of crowd management. Everything was contrived to leave you with the impression that the only way into Williamsburg was to buy a ticket, pass through a door ominously marked PROCESS-ING and then climb aboard a shuttle bus which would whisk you off to the historic site, presumably some distance away. Unless, like me, you pulled out of the river of people, you found yourself standing at the ticket counter making an instant decision on which of three kinds of tickets to buy—a Patriot's Pass for $24.50, a Royal Governor's Pass for $20 or a Basic

Admission Ticket for $15.50, each allowing entrance to a different number of restored buildings. Most visitors found themselves parted from a lot of money and standing in the line to the processing doorway before they knew what had hit them.

I hate the way these places let you get all the way there before disclosing just how steep and confiscatory the admission price is. They should be required to put up roadside signs saying, THREE MILES TO COLONIAL WILLIAMSBURG. GET YOUR CHECKBOOKS READY! or ONE MILE TO COLONIAL WILLIAMSBURG. IT'S PRETTY GOOD, BUT REAL EXPENSIVE. I felt that irritation, bordering on wild hate, that I generally experience when money is being tugged out of me through my nostrils. I mean honestly, $24.50 just to walk around a restored village for a couple of hours. I gave silent thanks that I had ditched the wife and kids at Manchester Airport. A day out here with the family could cost almost $75—and that's before paying for ice creams and soft drinks and sweatshirts saying, BOY, WERE WE SCREWED AT COLONIAL WILLIAMSBURG.

There was something wrong with the whole setup, something deeply fishy about the way it worked. I had lived in America long enough to know that if the only way into Williamsburg was to buy a ticket there would be an enormous sign on the wall saying, YOU MUST HAVE A TICKET. DON'T EVEN THINK ABOUT TRYING TO GET IN WITHOUT ONE. But there wasn't any such sign. I went outside, back out into the bright sunshine, and watched where the shuttle buses were going. They went down the driveway, joined a highway and disappeared around a bend. I crossed the highway, dodging the traffic, and followed a path through some woods. In a few seconds I was in the village. It was as simple as that. I didn't have to pay a penny. Nearby the shuttle buses were unloading ticketholders. They had had a ride of roughly 200 yards and were about to discover that what their tickets entitled them to do was join long, ill-humored lines of other ticketholders standing outside each restored historic building, sweating in silence and shuffling forward at a rate of one step every three minutes. I don't think I had ever seen quite so many people failing to enjoy themselves. The glacial lines put me in mind of Disney World, which was not altogether inappropriate since Williamsburg is really a sort of Disney World of American history. All the ticket takers and street sweepers and information givers were dressed in period costumes, the women in big aprons and muffin hats, the men in tricornered caps and breeches. The whole idea was to give history a happy gloss and make you think that spinning your own wool and dipping your own candles must have been bags of fun. I half expected to see Goofy and Donald Duck come waddling along dressed as soldiers in the Colonial army.

The first house I came to had a sign saying DR. McKENZIE'S APOTHECARY. The door was open, so I went inside, expecting to see eighteenth-century apothecary items. But it was just a gift shop selling overprecious reproductions at outrageous prices—brass candle snuffers at $28, reproduction apothecary jars at $35, that sort of thing. I fled back outside, wanting to stick my head in Ye Olde Village Puking Trough. But then, slowly and strangely, the place began to grow on me. As I strolled up Duke of Gloucester Street I underwent a surprising transformation. Slowly, I found that I was becoming captivated by it all. Williamsburg is big— 173 acres—and the size of it alone is impressive. There are literally dozens of restored houses and shops. More than that, it really is quite lovely, particularly on a sunny morning in October with a mild wind wandering through the ash and beech trees. I ambled along the leafy lanes and broad greens. Every house was exquisite, every cobbled lane inviting, every tavern and vine-clad shoppe remorselessly adrip with picturesque charm. It is impossible, even for a flinty-hearted jerk-off such as your narrator, not to be won over. However dubious Williamsburg may be as a historical document—and it is plenty dubious—it is at least a model town. It makes you realize what an immeasurably nice place much of America could be if only people possessed the same instinct for preservation as they do in Europe. You would think the millions of people who come to Williamsburg every year would say to each other, "Gosh, Bobbi, this place is beautiful. Let's go home to Smellville and plant lots of trees and preserve all the fine old buildings." But in fact that never occurs to them. They just go back and build more parking lots and Pizza Huts.

A lot of Williamsburg isn't as old as they like you to think it is. The town was the capital of Colonial Virginia for eighty years, from 1699 to 1780. But when the capital was moved to Richmond, Williamsburg fell into decline. In the 1920s John D. Rockefeller developed a passion for the place and began pouring money into its restoration—$90 million so far. The problem now is that you never quite know what's genuine and what's fanciful. Take the Governor's Palace. It looks to be very old—and, as I say, no one discourages you from believing that it is—but in fact it was only built in 1933. The original building burned down in 1781 and by 1930 had been gone for so long that nobody knew what it had looked like. It was only because somebody found a drawing of it in the Bodleian Library at Oxford that they were able to make a reasonable stab at reproducing it. But it isn't old and it may not even be all that accurate.

Everywhere you turn you are confronted, exasperatingly, with bogus touches. At the Bruton Parish Church, the gravestones looked like they were faked or at least the engravings had been reground. Rockefeller or someone else in authority had obviously been disappointed to discover that after a couple of centuries in the open air gravestones become illegible, so now the inscriptions are as fresh and deep-grooved as if they had been cut only last week, which they may well have been. You find yourself constantly wondering whether you are looking at genuine history or some Disneyesque embellishment. Was there really a Severinus Dufray and would he have had a sign outside his house saying, GENTEEL TAILORING? Possibly. Would Dr. McKenzie have a note in florid lettering outside his dispensary announcing, DR. McKENZIE BEGS LEAVE TO INFORM THE PUBLIC THAT HE HAS JUST RECEIVED A LARGE QUANTITY OF FINE GOODS, VIZ: TEA, COFFEE, FINE SOAP, TOBACCO, ETC., TO BE SOLD HERE AT HIS SHOP? Who can say?

Thomas Jefferson, a man of some obvious sensitivity, disliked Williamsburg and thought it ugly. (This is something else they don't tell you.) He called the college and hospital "rude, misshapen piles" and the Governor's Palace "not handsome." He can't have been describing the same place because the Williamsburg of today is relentlessly attractive. And for that reason I liked it.

I drove on to Mount Vernon, George Washington's home for most of his life. Washington deserves his fame. What he did in running the Colonial army was risky and audacious, not to say skillful. People tend to forget that the Revolutionary War dragged on for eight years and that Washington often didn't get a whole lot of support. Out of a populace of 5.5 million, Washington sometimes had as few as 5,000 soldiers in his army—one soldier for every 1,100 people. When you see what a tranquil and handsome place Mount Vernon is, and what an easy and agreeable life he led there, you wonder why he bothered. But that's the appealing thing about Washington, he is such an enigma. We don't even know for sure what he looked like. Almost all the portraits of him were done by, or copied from the works of, Charles Willson Peale. Peale painted sixty portraits of Washington, but unfortunately he wasn't very hot at faces. In fact, according to Samuel Eliot Morison, Peale's pictures of Washington, Lafayette and John Paul Jones all look to be more or less the same person.

Mount Vernon was everything Williamsburg should have been and was not—genuine, interesting, instructive. For well over a century it has been maintained by the Mount Vernon Ladies' Association and what a lucky thing it is we have them. Amazingly, when the house was put up for sale in 1853, neither the federal government nor the state of Virginia was prepared to buy it for the nation. So a group of dedicated women hastily formed the Mount Vernon Ladies' Association, raised the money to buy the house and two hundred acres of grounds, and then set about restoring it to precisely as it was in Washington's day, right down to the correct pigments of paint and patterns of wallpaper. Thank God John D. Rockefeller didn't get ahold of it. Today the association continues to run it with a dedication and skill that should be models to preservation groups everywhere, but alas are not. Fourteen rooms are open to the public and in each a volunteer provides an interesting and well-informed commentary—and is sufficiently clued up to answer almost any question—on how the room was used and decorated. The house was very much Washington's creation. He was involved in the daintiest questions of decor, even when he was away on military campaigns. It was strangely pleasing to imagine him at Valley Forge, with his troops dropping dead of cold and hunger, agonizing over the purchase of lace ruffs and tea cozies. What a great guy. What a hero.

12

I SPENT THE NIGHT on the outskirts of Alexandria and in the morning drove into Washington. I remembered Washington from my childhood as hot and dirty and full of the din of jackhammers. It had that special kind of grimy summer heat you used to get in big cities in America before air-conditioning came along. People spent every waking moment trying to alleviate it—wiping their necks with capacious handkerchiefs, swallowing cold glasses of lemonade, lingering by open refrigerators, sitting listlessly before electric fans. Even at night there was no relief. It was tolerable enough outside where you might catch a puff of breeze, but indoors the heat never dissipated. It just sat, thick and stifling. It was like being inside a vacuum cleaner bag. I can remember lying awake in a hotel in downtown Washington listening to the sounds of an August night wash in through the open window: sirens, car horns, the thrum of neon from the hotel sign, the swish of traffic, people laughing, people yelling, people being shot.

We once saw a guy who had been shot, one sultry August night when we were out for a late snack after watching the Washington Senators beat the New York Yankees 4–3 at Griffith Stadium. He was a black man and he was lying among a crowd of legs in what appeared to me at the time to be a pool of oil, but which was of course the blood that was draining out of the hole in his head. My parents hustled us past and told us not to look, but we did of course. Things like that didn't happen in Des Moines, so we gaped extensively. I had only ever seen murders on TV on programs like "Gunsmoke" and "Dragnet." I thought it was something they did just to keep the story moving. It had never occurred to me that shooting someone was an option available in the real world. It seemed such a strange thing to do, to stop someone's life just because you found him in some way disagreeable. I imagined my fourth-grade teacher, Miss Bietlebaum, who had hair on her upper lip and evil in her heart, lying on the floor beside her desk, stilled forever, while I stood over her with a smoking gun in my hand. It was an interesting concept. It made you think.

At the diner where we went for our snack, there was yet another curious thing that made me think. White people like us would come in and take seats at the counter, but black people would place an order and then stand against the wall. When their food was ready, it would be handed to them in a paper bag and they would take it home or out to their car. My father explained to us that Negroes weren't allowed to sit at luncheon counters in Washington. It wasn't against the law exactly, but they didn't do it because Washington was enough of a Southern city that they just didn't dare. That seemed strange too and it made me even more reflective.

Afterwards, lying awake in the hot hotel room, listening to the restless city, I tried to understand the adult world and could not. I had always thought that once you grew up you could do anything you wanted—stay up all night or eat ice cream straight out of the container. But now, on this one important evening of my life, I had discovered that if you didn't measure up in some critical way, people might shoot you in the head or make you take your food out to the car. I sat up on one elbow and asked my dad if there were places where Negroes ran lunch counters and made white people stand against the wall.

My dad regarded me over the top of a book and said he didn't think so. I asked him what would happen if a Negro tried to sit at a luncheon counter, even though he wasn't supposed to. What would they do to him? My dad said he didn't know and told me I should go to sleep and not worry about such things. I lay down and thought about it for a while and supposed that they would shoot him in the head. Then I rolled over and tried to sleep, but I couldn't, partly because it was so hot and I was confused and partly because earlier in the evening my brother had told me that he was going to come over to my bed when I was asleep and wipe boogers on my face because I hadn't given him a bite of my frosted malt at the ball game, and I was frankly unsettled by this prospect, even though he seemed to be sleeping soundly now.

The world has changed a lot since those days, of course. Now if you lie awake in a hotel room at night, you don't hear the city anymore. All you hear is the white sound of your air conditioner. You could be in a jet over the Pacific or in a bathysphere beneath the sea for all you hear. Everywhere you go is air-conditioned, so the air is always as cool and clean as a freshly laundered shirt. People don't wipe their necks much anymore or drink sweating glasses of lemonade or lay their bare arms gratefully on cool marble soda fountains because nowadays summer heat is something out there, something experienced only briefly when you sprint from your parking lot to your office or from your office to the luncheon counter down the block. Nowadays, black people sit at luncheon counters, so it's not as easy to get a seat, but it's more fair. And no one goes to Washington Senators games anymore because the Washington Senators no longer exist. In 1972 the owner moved the team to Texas because he could make more money there. Alas. But perhaps the most important change, at least as far as I am concerned, is that my brother no longer threatens to wipe boogers on me when I annoy him.

Washington feels like a small city. Its metropolitan population is three million, which makes it the seventh largest in America. And if you add Baltimore, right next door, it rises to over five million. But the city itself is quite small, with a population of just 637,000, less than Indianapolis or San Antonio. You feel as if you are in some agreeable provincial city, but then you turn a corner and come up against the headquarters of the FBI or the World Bank or the IMF and you realize what an immensely important place it is. The most startling of all these surprises is the White House. There you are, shuffling along downtown, looking in department store windows, browsing at cravats and negligees, and you turn a corner and there it is—the White House—right in the middle of the downtown. So handy for shopping, I thought. It's smaller than you expect. Everybody says that.

Across the street there is a permanent settlement of disaffected people and crazies, living in cardboard boxes, protesting at the Central Intelligence Agency controlling their thoughts from outer space. (Well, wouldn't you?) There was also a guy panhandling for quarters. Can you believe that? Right there in our nation's capital, right where Nancy Reagan could have seen him from her bedroom window. I refused to give him a penny. "Why don't you go and mug somebody?" I told him. "It has more dignity."

Washington's most fetching feature is the Mall, a broad, grassy strip of parkland which stretches for a mile or so from the Capitol building at the eastern end to the Lincoln Memorial at the western side, overlooking the Potomac. The dominant landmark is the Washington Monument. Slender and white, shaped like a pencil, it rises 555 feet above the park. It is one of the simplest and yet handsomest structures I know, and all the more impressive when you consider that its massive stones had to be brought from the Nile delta on wooden rollers by Sumerian slaves. I'm sorry, I'm thinking of the Great Pyramids at Giza. Anyway, it is a real feat of engineering and very pleasing to look at. I had hoped to go up it, but there was a long line of people, mostly restive schoolchildren, snaked around the base and some distance into the park, all waiting to squeeze into an elevator about the size of a telephone booth, so I headed east in the direction of Capitol Hill, which isn't really much of a hill at all.

Scattered around the Mall's eastern end are the various museums of the Smithsonian Institution—the Museum of American History, the Museum of Natural History, the Air and Space Museum and so on. The Smithsonian—which, incidentally, was donated to America by an Englishman who had never been there—used to be all in one building, but they keep splitting off sections of it and putting them in new buildings all over town. Now there are fourteen Smithsonian museums. The biggest ones are arrayed around the Mall, the others are mostly scattered around the city. Partly they had to do this because they get so much stuff every year—about a million items. In 1986, just to give you some idea, the Smithsonian's acquisitions included ten thousand moths and butterflies from Scandinavia, the entire archives of the Panama Canal Zone postal service, part of the old Brooklyn Bridge and a MiG-25 jet fighter. All of this used to be kept in a wonderful old Gothic brick building on the Mall called the Castle, but now the Castle is just used for administration and to show an introductory film.

I strolled down towards the Castle now. The park was full of joggers. I found this a little worrying. I kept thinking, shouldn't they be running the country, or at least destabilizing some Central American government? I mean to say, don't you usually have something more important to do at 10:30 on a Wednesday morning than pull on a pair of Reeboks and go sprinting around for forty-five minutes?

At the Castle I found the entrance area blocked with wooden trestles and lengths of rope. American and Japanese security men in dark suits were standing around. They all looked as if they spent a lot of time jogging. Some of them had headphones on and were talking into radios. Others had dogs on long leashes or mirrors on poles and were checking out cars parked along Jefferson Drive in front of the building. I went up to one of the American security men and asked him who was coming, but he said he wasn't allowed to tell me. I thought this was bizarre. Here I was in a country where, thanks to the Freedom of Information Act, I could find out how many suppositories Ronald Reagan's doctor had prescribed for him in 1986,* but I couldn't be told which foreign dignitary would shortly be making a public appearance on the steps of a national institution. The lady next to me said, "It's Nakasone. President of Japan."

"Oh, really," I replied, always ready to see a celebrity. I asked the security man when he would be arriving. "I'm not allowed to tell you that either, sir," he said and passed on.

---

*1,472.

I stood with the crowd for a while and waited for Mr. Nakasone to come along. And then I thought, "Why am I standing here?" I tried to think of anyone I knew who would be impressed to hear that I had seen with my own eyes the prime minister of Japan. I imagined myself saying to my children, "Hey, kids, guess who I saw in Washington—Yasuhiro Nakasone!" and being met with silence. So I walked on to the National Air and Space Museum, which was more interesting.

But not nearly as interesting as it ought to be, if you ask me. Back in the 1950s and '60s, the Smithsonian *was* the Castle. Everything was crammed into this one wonderfully dark and musty old building. It was like the nation's attic and, like an attic, it was gloriously random. Over here was the shirt Lincoln was wearing when he was shot, with a dried brown bloodstain above the heart. Over there was a diorama showing a Navajo family fixing dinner. Up above you, hanging from the gloomy rafters, were the *Spirit of St. Louis* and the Wright brothers' first plane. You didn't know where to look next or what you would find around each corner. Now it is as if everything has been sorted out by a fussy spinster, folded neatly and put in its proper place. You go to the Air and Space Museum and you see the *Spirit of St. Louis* and the Wright brothers' plane and lots of other famous planes and rocket ships and it's all highly impressive, but it is also clinical and uninspired. There is no sense of discovery. If your brother came running up to you and said, "Hey, you'll never guess what I found in this room over here!" you would in fact guess, more or less, because it would have to be either an airplane or a rocket ship. At the old Smithsonian it could have been absolutely anything—a petrified dog, Custer's scalp, human heads adrift in bottles. There's no element of surprise anymore. So I spent the day trudging around the various museums dutifully and respectfully, with interest but not excitement. Still, there was so much to see that a whole day passed and I had seen only a part of it.

In the evening I came back to the Mall, and walked across it to the Jefferson Memorial. I had hoped to see it at dusk, but I arrived late and the darkness fell like a blanket. Before I was very far into the park it was pitch dark. I expected to be mugged—indeed, I took it as my due wandering into a city park like this on a dark night—but evidently the muggers couldn't see me. The only physical risk I ran was being bowled over by one of the many joggers who sprinted invisibly along the dark paths. The Jefferson Memorial was beautiful. There's not much to it, just a large marble rotunda in the shape of Monticello, with a gigantic statue of Jefferson inside and his favorite sayings engraved on the walls ("Have a nice day," "Keep your shirt on," "You could have knocked me over with a feather," etc.), but when it is lit up at night it is entrancing, with the lights of the memorial smeared across the pool of water called the Tidal Basin. I must have sat for an hour or more just listening to the rhythmic swish of the distant traffic, the sirens and car horns, the distant sounds of people shouting, people singing, people being shot.

I lingered so long that it was too late to go to the Lincoln Memorial and I had to come back in the morning. The Lincoln Memorial is exactly as you expect it to be. He sits there in his big high chair looking grand and yet kindly. There was a pigeon on his head. There is always a pigeon on his head. I wondered idly if the pigeon thought that all the people who came every day were there to look at him. Afterwards, as I strolled across the Mall, I spied yet more trestles and draped ropes, with security men hanging about. They had closed off a road across the park and had brought in two helicopters with the presidential seal on their sides and seven cannons and the Marine Corps Band. It was quite early in the morning and there were no crowds, so I went and stood beside the roped enclosure, the only spectator, and none of the security men bothered me or even seemed to notice me.

After a couple of minutes, a wailing of sirens filled the air and a cavalcade of limousines and police motorcycles drew up. Out stepped Nakasone and some other Japanese men, all in dark suits, escorted by some junior-looking Aryans from the State Department. They all stood politely while the Marine Corps Band blared a lively tune, which I didn't recognize. Then there was a twenty-one-gun salute, but the cannons didn't go "BOOM!" as you would expect. They went "PUFF." They were filled with some kind of noiseless powder, presumably so as not to waken the president in the White House across the way, so when the battery commander shouted, "Ready, steady, go!" or whatever it was he shouted, there followed seven quick *puff* sounds and then a dense cloud of smoke drifted over us and went on a long slow waft across the park. This was done three times because there were only seven cannons. Then Nakasone gave a friendly wave to the crowd—which is to say, to me—and sprinted with his party to the presidential helicopters, whose blades were already whirring to life. After a moment they rose up, tilted past the Washington Monument and were gone, and everyone back on the ground relaxed and had a smoke.

Weeks afterwards, back in London, I told people about my private encounter with Nakasone and the Marine Corps Band and the noiseless cannons and how the prime minister of Japan had waved to me alone. Most of them would listen politely, then allow a small pause and say, "Did I tell you that Mavis has to go back into hospital next week to have her feet done?" or something like that. The English can be so crushing sometimes.

From Washington I took US 301 out past Annapolis and the US Naval Academy and over a long, low bridge across the Chesapeake Bay into eastern Maryland. Before 1952, when the bridge was built, the eastern side of the bay had enjoyed centuries of isolation. Ever since then, people have been saying that outsiders will flood in and ruin the peninsula, but it still looked pretty unspoiled to me, and my guess is that it's the outsiders who have kept it that way. It's always the outsiders who are the most fiercely opposed to shopping malls and bowling alleys, which the locals in their simple, trusting way tend to think might be kind of handy.

Chestertown, the first town of any size I came to, confirmed this. The first thing I saw was a woman in a bright pink track suit zipping past on a bicycle with a wicker basket on the front. Only an urban émigré would have a bicycle with a wicker basket. A local person would have a Subaru pickup truck. There seemed to be a lot of these bike ladies about and between them they had clearly made Chestertown into a model community. The whole place was as neat as a pin. The sidewalks were paved with brick and lined with trees, and there was a well-tended park in the middle of the business district. The library was busy. The movie theater was still in business and not showing a *Death Wish* movie. Everything about the place was tranquil and appealing. This was as nice a town as I had seen. This was almost Amalgam.

I drove on through the low, marshy flatlands, much taken with the simple beauty of the Chesapeake peninsula, with its high skies and scattered farms and forgotten little towns. Late in the morning I crossed into Delaware, en route to Philadelphia. Delaware may well be the most obscure of all the American states. I once met a girl from Delaware and couldn't think of a single thing to say to her. I said, "So you come from Delaware? Gosh. Wow." And she moved quickly on to someone more verbally dextrous, and also better-looking. For a while it troubled me that I could live in America for twenty years, have the benefit of an expensive education and not know anything at all about one of the fifty states. I went around asking people if they had ever heard Delaware mentioned on television or seen a story pertaining to it in the newspaper or read a novel set there and they'd say, "You know, I don't think I ever have," and then they'd look kind of troubled too.

I determined that I would read up on Delaware so that the next time I met a girl from there I could say something droll and apposite and she might go to bed with me. But I could find almost nothing written about Delaware anywhere. Even the entry in the *Encyclopaedia Britannica* was only about two paragraphs long and finished in the middle of a sentence, as I recall. And the funny thing was that as I drove across Delaware now I could feel it vanishing from my memory as I went, like those children's drawing slates on which you erase the picture by lifting the transparent sheet. It was as if a giant sheet were being lifted up behind me as I drove, expunging the experience as it unfolded. Looking back now, I can just vaguely recall some semi-industrial land-scape and some signs for Wilmington.

And then I was in the outskirts of Philadelphia, the city that gave the world Sylvester Stallone and Legionnaires' disease, among other things, and was too preoccupied with the disturbing thoughts that this called up to give Delaware any further consideration.

13

WHEN I WAS a child, Philadelphia was the third biggest city in America. What I remembered of it was driving through endless miles of ghettos, one battered block after another, on a hot July Sunday, with black children playing in the spray of fire hydrants and older people lounging around on the street corners or sitting on the front stoops. It was the poorest place I had ever seen. Trash lay in the gutters and doorways, and whole buildings were derelict. It was like a foreign country, like Haiti or Panama. My dad whistled tunelessly through his teeth the whole time, as he always did when he was scared, and told us to keep the windows rolled up even though it was boiling in the car. At stoplights people would stare stonily at us and Dad would whistle in double time and drum the steering wheel with his fingers and smile apologetically at anyone who looked at him, as if to say, "Sorry, we're from out of state."

Things have changed now, naturally. Philadelphia is no longer the third biggest city in America. Los Angeles pushed it into fourth place in the 1960s, and now there are freeways to whisk you into the heart of town without soiling your tires in the ghettos. Even so, I managed a brief, inadvertent visit to one of the poorer neighborhoods when I wandered off the freeway in search of a gas station. Before I could do anything about it, I found myself sucked into a vortex of one-way streets that carried me into the most squalid and dangerous-looking neighborhood I had ever seen. It may have been, for all I know, the very ghetto we passed through all those years before—the brownstone buildings looked much the same—but it was many times worse than the one I remembered. The ghetto of my childhood, for all its poorness, had the air of a street carnival. People wore colorful clothes and seemed to be having a good time. This place was just bleak and dangerous, like a war zone. Abandoned cars, old refrigerators, burned-out sofas littered every vacant lot. Garbage cans looked as if they had been thrown to the street from the rooftops. There were no gas stations—I wouldn't have stopped anyway, not in a place like this, not for a million dollars—and most of the storefronts were boarded with plywood. Every standing object had been spray-painted with graffiti. There were still a few young people on the stoops and corners, but they looked listless and cold—it was a chilly day—and they seemed not to notice me. Thank God. This was a neighborhood where clearly you could be murdered for a pack of cigarettes—a fact that was not lost on me as I searched nervously for a way back onto the freeway. By the time I found it, I wasn't whistling through my teeth so much as singing through my sphincter.

It really was the most uncomfortable experience I had had in many years. God, what it must be like to live there and to walk those streets daily. Do you know that if you are a black man in urban America you now stand a one-in-nineteen chance of being murdered? In World War II, the odds of being killed were one in fifty. In New York City there is one murder every four hours. Murder there has become the most common cause of death for people under thirty-five—and yet New York isn't even the most murderous city in America. At least eight other cities have a higher murder rate. In Los Angeles there are more murders on schoolgrounds alone each year than there are in the whole of London. So perhaps it is little wonder that people in American cities take violence as routine. I don't know how they do it.

On my way to Des Moines to start this trip, I passed through O'Hare Airport in Chicago, where I ran into a friend who worked for a St. Louis newspaper. He told me he had been working extra hard lately because of something that had happened to his boss. The boss had been driving home from work late one Saturday night when he had stopped at some traffic lights. As he waited for the lights to change, the passenger door opened and a man with a gun got in. The gunman made the boss drive down to the riverfront, where he shot him in the head and took his money. The boss had been in a coma for three weeks and they weren't sure whether he was going to live.

My friend was telling me this not because it was such an incredible story, but simply by way of elucidating why he was having to work so damned hard lately. As for his boss, my friend's attitude seemed to be that if you forget to lock your car doors when you're driving through St. Louis late at night, well, you've got to expect to take a bullet in the head from time to time. It was very odd, his deadpan attitude, but it seems to be more and more the way in America now. It made me feel like a stranger.

I drove downtown and parked near City Hall. On top of the building is a statue of William Penn. It's the main landmark downtown, visible from all around the city, but it was covered in scaffolding. In 1985, after decades of neglect, the city fathers decided to refurbish the statue before it fell down. So they covered it in scaffolding. However, this cost so much that there was no money left to do the repairs. Now, two years later, the scaffolding was still there and not a lick of work had been done. A city engineer had recently announced with a straight face that before long the scaffolding itself would need to be refurbished. This is more or less how Philadelphia works, which is to say not very well. No other city in America pursues the twin ideals of corruption and incompetence with quite the same enthusiasm. When it comes to asinine administration, Philadelphia is in a league of its own.

Consider: in 1985, a bizarre sect called MOVE barricaded itself into a tenement house on the west side of town. The police chief and mayor considered the options open to them and decided that the most intelligent use of their resources would be to blow up the house—but of course!—even though they knew there were children inside and it was in the middle of a densely populated district. So they dropped a bomb on the house from a helicopter. This started a fire that quickly grew out of control and burned down most of the neighborhood—sixty-one houses in all—and killed eleven people, including all the children in the barricaded home.

When they aren't being incompetent, city officials like to relax with a little corruption. Just as I was driving into town I heard on the radio that a former city councilman had been sentenced to ten years in jail and his aide to eight years for attempted extortion. The judge called it a gross breach of public trust. He should know. Across town a state review board was calling for the dismissal of nine of the judge's colleagues for taking cash gifts from members of the roofers' union. Two of those judges were already awaiting trial on extortion charges. This sort of thing is routine in Philadelphia. A few months earlier when a state official named Bud Dwyer was similarly accused of corruption, he called a press conference, pulled out a gun and, as cameras rolled, blew his brains out. This led to an excellent local joke. *Q.* What is the difference between Bud Dwyer and Bud Lite? *A.* Bud Lite has a head on it.

Yet for all its incompetence and criminality, Philadelphia is a likable place. For one thing, unlike Washington, it feels like a big city. It had skyscrapers and there was steam rising through vents in the sidewalk and on every corner stood a stainless steel hot-dog stand, with a chilly-looking guy in a stocking cap bobbing around behind it. I wandered over to Independence Square—actually it's now called Independence National Historical Park—and looked respectfully at all the historic buildings. The main building is Independence Hall, where the Declaration of Independence was drawn up and the Constitution ratified. When I had first been there in 1960, there was a long line stretching out of the building. There still was—in fact, it seemed not to have moved in twenty-seven years. Deep though my respect is for both the Constitution and the Declaration of Independence, I was disinclined to spend my afternoon in such a long and immobile line. I went instead to the visitors' center. Nationalpark visitors' centers are always the same. They always have some displays in glass cases that manage to be both boring and uninformative, a locked auditorium with a board out front saying that the next showing of the free twelve-minute introductory film will be at 4 P.M. (just before 4 P.M. somebody comes and changes it to 10 A.M.), some racks of books and brochures with titles like *Pewter in History* and *Vegetables of Old Philadelphia*, which are too boring even to browse through, much less buy, and a drinking fountain and rest rooms, which everyone makes use of because there's not much else to do. Every visitor to every national park goes into the visitors' center, stands around kind of stupidly for a while, then has a pee and a drink of water and wanders back outside. That is what I did now.

From the visitors' center I ambled along Independence Mall to Franklin Square, which was full of winos, many of whom had the comical idea that I might be prepared to give them twenty-five cents of my own money. According to my guidebook, Franklin Square had "lots of interesting things" to see—a museum, a working book bindery, an archaeological exhibit and "the only post office in the United States which does not fly the American flag" (don't ask me why)—but my heart wasn't in it, especially with piteous and unwashed winos tugging at my sleeves all the while, and I fled back to the real world of downtown Philadelphia.

Late in the afternoon, I found my way to the offices of the *Philadelphia Inquirer*, where an old friend from Des Moines, Lucia Herndon, was lifestyle editor. The *Inquirer* offices were like newspaper offices everywhere—grubby, full of junk, littered with coffee cups in which cigarette butts floated like dead fish in a polluted lake—and Lucia's desk, I was impressed to note, was one of the messiest in the room. This may have accounted in part for her impressive rise at the *Inquirer*. I only ever knew one journalist with a truly tidy desk, and he was eventually arrested for molesting small boys. Make of that what you will—but just bear it in mind the next time somebody with a tidy desk invites you camping.

We drove in my car out to the district of Mount Airy, where, conveniently for me—and for her too, come to that—Lucia lived with another old friend of mine from Des Moines, her husband, Hal. All day long I had been wondering, vaguely and intermittently, why Hal and Lucia liked Philadelphia so much—they had moved there about a year before—but now I understood. The road to Mount Airy led through the most beautiful city park I had ever been in. Called Fairmount Park and covering almost 9,000 acres, it is the largest municipal park in America and it is full of trees and flowering shrubs and bosky glades of infinite charm. It stretches for miles along the banks of the Schuylkill River. We drove through a dreamy twilight. Boats sculled along the water. It was perfection.

Mount Airy was out in the Germantown section of the city. It had a nice settled feeling to it, as if people had lived there for generations—which is in fact the case in Philadelphia, Lucia told me. The city was still full of the sort of neighborhoods where everybody knew everybody else. Many people scarcely ever ventured more than a few hundred yards from their homes. It was not uncommon to get lost and find that hardly anybody could reliably direct you to a neighborhood three miles away. Philadelphia also had its own vocabulary—downtown was called "center city," sidewalks were called "pavements," as in England—and peculiarities of pronunciation.

In the evening I sat in Hal and Lucia's house, eating their food, drinking their wine, admiring their children and their house and furniture and possessions, their easy wealth and comfort, and felt a sap for ever having left America. Life was so abundant here, so easy, so convenient. Suddenly I wanted a refrigerator that made its own ice cubes and a waterproof radio for the shower. I wanted an electric orange juicer and a room ionizer and a wristwatch that would keep me in touch with my biorhythms. I wanted it all. Once in the evening I went upstairs to go to the bathroom and walked past one of the children's bedrooms. The door was open and a bedside light was on. There were toys everywhere—on the floor, on shelves, tumbling out of a wooden trunk. It looked like Santa's workshop. But there was nothing extraordinary about this: it was just a typical middle-class American bedroom.

And as for American closets, they seem to be always full of

yesterday's enthusiasms: golf clubs, scuba diving equipment, tennis rackets, exercise machines, tape recorders, darkroom equipment, objects that once excited their owner and then were replaced by other objects even more shiny and exciting. That is the great, seductive thing about America—the people always get what they want, right now, whether it is good for them or not. There is something deeply worrying, and awesomely irresponsible, about this endless self-gratification, this constant appeal to the baser instincts.

I should point out that I am not talking about Hal and Lucia in all this. They are good people and lead modest and responsible lives. Their closets aren't full of scuba diving equipment and seldom-used tennis rackets. They are full of mundane items like buckets and galoshes, ear muffs and scouring powders. I know this for a fact because late in the night when everyone was asleep I crept out of bed and had a good look.

In the morning, I dropped Hal at his office downtown—correction, center city—and the drive through Fairmount Park was as enchanting in the morning sunshine as it had been at dusk. All cities should have parks like this, I thought. He told me some more interesting things about Philadelphia: that it spent more money on public art than any other city in America—1 percent of the total city budget—and yet it had an illiteracy rate of 40 percent. He pointed out to me, in the middle of Fairmount Park, the palatial Philadelphia Museum of Art, which had become the city's top tourist attraction, not because of its collection of 500,000 paintings, but because its front steps were the ones Sylvester Stallone sprinted up in *Rocky*. People were actually coming to the museum in buses, looking at the steps and leaving without ever going inside to see the pictures. As we were driving we listened to a radio talk show hosted by a man named Howard Stern. Howard Stern had a keen interest in sex and was engagingly direct with his callers. "Good morning, Marilyn," he would say to a caller, "are you wearing panties?" This, we agreed, beat most early-morning talk shows hands down. Howard queried his callers with arresting candor and a measure of prurience I had not before encountered on American radio.

Unfortunately, I lost the station soon after dropping Hal off and spent the rest of the morning searching for it without success, and eventually ended up listening to a competing program in which an ear specialist gave advice to callers with hearing difficulties. Later there was a woman who was an expert on dealing with intestinal worms in dogs. As this principally consisted of giving the dogs a tablet to make the worms die, it was not long before I felt as if I were something an expert on the matter too. And so the morning passed.

I drove to Gettysburg, where the decisive battle of the American Civil War was fought over three days in July 1863. There were over 50,000 casualties. I parked at the visitors' center and went inside. It contained a small, ill-lit museum with glass cases containing bullets, brass buttons, belt buckles and that sort of thing, each with a yellowed typed caption beside it saying, "Buckle from uniform of 13th Tennessee Mountaineers. Found by Festus T. Scrubbins, local farmer, and donated by his daughter, Mrs. Marienetta Stumpy." There was precious little to give you any sense of the battle itself. It was more like the gleanings of a treasure hunt.

The only truly interesting thing was a case devoted to the Gettysburg Address, where I learned that Lincoln was invited to speak only as an afterthought and that everyone was taken aback when he accepted. It was only ten sentences long and took just two minutes to deliver. I was further informed that he gave the address many months after the battle. I had always imagined him making it more or less immediately afterwards, while there were still bodies lying around and wraiths of smoke rising from the ruins of distant houses and people like Festus T. Scrubbins poking around among the twitching casualties to see what useful souvenirs they could find. The truth, as so often in this life, was disappointing.

I went outside and had a look at the battlefield, which sprawls over 3,500 acres of mostly flat countryside, fringed by the town of Gettysburg with its gas stations and motels. The battlefield had the great deficiency common to all historic battlefields. It was just countryside. There was nothing much to distinguish this stretch of empty fields from that one. You had to take their word for it that a great battle was fought there. There were a lot of cannons scattered about, I'll give them that. And along the road leading to the site of Pickett's charge, the attack by Confederate troops that turned the tide of battle in the Union's favor, many of the regiments had erected obelisks and monuments to their own glory, some of them very grand. I strolled down there now. Through my dad's old binoculars I could clearly see how Pickett's troops had advanced from the direction of the town, a mile or so to the north, sweeping across the Burger King parking lot, skirting the Tastee Delite Drive-In and regrouping just outside the Crap-o-Rama Wax Museum and Gift Shop. It's all very sad. Ten thousand soldiers fell there in an hour; two out of every three Confederate soldiers didn't make it back to base. It is a pity, verging on the criminal, that so much of the town of Gettysburg has been spoiled with tourist tat and that it is so visible from the battlefield.

When I was little, my dad bought me a Union cap and a toy rifle and let me loose on the battlefield. I was in heaven. I dashed about the whole day crouching behind trees, charging over to Devil's Den and Little Round Top, blowing up parties of overweight tourists with cameras around their necks. My dad was in heaven too because the park was free and there were literally hundreds of historical plaques for him to read. Now, however, I just found it boring.

I was about to depart, feeling guilty that I had come so far without getting anything much out of the experience, when I saw a sign at the visitors' center for tours to the Eisenhower home. I had forgotten that Ike and Mamie Eisenhower had lived on a farm just outside Gettysburg. Their old home was now a national historical monument and could be toured for $2.50. Impulsively I bought a ticket and went outside where a bus was just about to depart to take half a dozen of us to the farm four or five miles away down a country lane.

Well, it was great. I can't remember the last time I had such a good time in a Republican household. You are greeted at the door by a fragrant woman with a chrysanthemum on her bosom, who tells you a little about the house, about how much Ike and Mamie loved to sit around and watch TV and play canasta, and then gives you a leaflet describing each room and lets you wander off on your own so that you can linger or stride on as it pleases you. Each doorway was blocked off with a sheet of clear plastic, but you could lean against it and gaze into the interior. The house has been preserved precisely as it was when the Eisenhowers lived there. It was as if they had simply wandered off and never come back (something that either of them was quite capable of doing towards the end). The decor was quintessentially early 1960s Republican. When I was growing up we had some neighbors, the McGibbonses, who were rich Republicans and this was practically a duplicate of their house. There was a big TV console in a mahogany cabinet, table lamps made out of pieces of driftwood, a padded leather cocktail bar, French-style telephones in every room, bookshelves containing about twelve books (usually in matching sets of three) and otherwise filled with large pieces of flowery gilt-edged porcelain of the sort favored by homosexual French aristocrats.

When the Eisenhowers bought the place in 1950, a 200-year-old farmhouse stood on the site, but it was drafty and creaked on stormy nights, so they had it torn down and replaced with the present building, which *looks* like a 200-year-old farmhouse. Isn't that great? Isn't that just so Republican? I was enchanted. Every room contained things I hadn't seen for years—1960s kitchen appliances, old copies of *Life* magazine, boxy black-and-white portable TVs, metal alarm clocks. Upstairs the bedrooms were just as Ike and Mamie had left them. Mamie's personal effects were on her bedside table—her diary, reading glasses, sleeping pills—and I daresay that if you knelt down and looked under the bed you would find all her old gin bottles.

In Ike's room his bathrobe and slippers were laid out and the book he had been reading on the day he died was left open on the chair beside the bed. The book was—and I ask you to remember for a moment that this was one of the most important men of this century, a man who held the world's destiny in his hands throughout much of World War II and the Cold War, a man chosen by Columbia University to be its president, a man venerated by Republicans for two generations, a man who throughout the whole of my childhood had his finger on The Button—the book was *West of the Pecos* by Zane Grey.

From Gettysburg, I headed north up US 15 towards Bloomsburg, where my brother and his family had recently moved. For years they had lived in Hawaii, in a house with a swimming pool, near balmy beaches, beneath tropical skies and whispering palms, and now, just when I had landed a trip to America and could go anywhere I wanted, they had moved to the Rust Belt. Bloomsburg, as it turned out, was actually very nice—a bit short on balmy beaches and hula girls with swaying hips, but still nice for all that.

It's a college town, with a decidedly sleepy air. You feel at first as if you should be wearing slippers and a bathrobe. Main Street was prosperous and tidy and the surrounding streets were mostly filled with large old houses sitting on ample lawns. Here and there church spires poked out from among the many trees. It was pretty well an ideal town—one of those rare American places where you wouldn't need a car. From almost any house in town it would be a short and pleasant stroll to the library and post office and stores. My brother and his wife told me that a developer was about to build a big shopping mall outside town and most of the bigger merchants were going to move out there. People, it appeared, didn't want to stroll to do their shopping. They actually wanted to get in their cars and drive to the edge of town, where they could then park and walk a similar distance across a flat, treeless parking lot. That is how America goes shopping and they wanted to be part of it. So now downtown Bloomsburg is likely to become semiderelict and another nice little town will be lost. So the world progresses.

Anyway, it was a pleasure to see my brother and his family, as you can imagine. I did all the things you do when you visit relatives—ate their food, used their bathtub, washing machine and telephone, stood around uselessly while they searched for spare blankets and grappled with a truculent sofa bed, and of course late at night when everyone was asleep I crept out of my room and had a good look in their closets. (Nothing very interesting, I'm afraid.)

As it was the weekend and as they had some spare time, my brother and his wife decided to take me down to Lancaster County to show me the Amish country. It was a two-hour drive. En route, my brother pointed out the Three Mile Island nuclear reactor at Harrisburg, where a few years before some careless employees had very nearly irradiated the whole of the eastern seaboard, and then forty-five miles further on we passed the Peach Bottom nuclear facility, where seventeen employees had recently been dismissed after it had been revealed that they spent their working hours sleeping, taking drugs, having rubber-band fights and playing video games. At some times every person in the plant was dozing, according to investigators. Allowing state utilities in Pennsylvania to run nuclear power stations is a bit like letting Prince Philip fly through London air space. In any case, I made a mental note to bring an antiradiation suit with me next time I came to Pennsylvania.

Lancaster County is the home of the Pennsylvania Dutch, the Amish and Mennonites. The Mennonites are named after a well-known brand of speed-stick deodorant. They aren't really. I just made that up. They are named after Menno Simons, one of their early leaders. In Europe they were called Anabaptists. They came to Lancaster County 250 years ago. Today there are 12,500 Amish people in the county, almost all of them descended from 30 original couples. The Amish split from the Mennonites in 1693, and there have been countless subdivisions since then, but the thing that they all have in common is that they wear simple clothes and shun modern contrivances. The problem is that since about 1860 they've been squabbling endlessly over just how rigorous they should be in their shunning. Every time anybody invents something useful or notable, like television or rubber gloves, they argue about whether it is ungodly or not, and the ones who don't like it go off and form a new sect. First, they argued over whether they should have steel rims or rubber rims on their buggies, then whether they should have tractors, then electricity, then telephones and television. Now presumably they argue over whether they should have a frost-free refrigerator and whether their instant coffee should be powdered or freeze-dried.

The most splendid thing about the Amish is the names they

give their towns. Everywhere else in America towns are named after either the first white person to get there or the last Indian to leave. But the Amish obviously gave the matter of town names some thought and graced their communities with intriguing, not to say provocative, appellations: Blue Ball, Bird in Hand, and Intercourse, to name but three. Intercourse makes a good living by attracting passersby such as me who think it the height of hilarity to send their friends and colleagues postcards with an Intercourse postmark and some droll sentiment scribbled on the back.

Americans are so fascinated by the Amish way of life, by the idea of people living 200 years in the past, that they come quite literally by the millions to gawk. There were hundreds and hundreds of tourists thronging Intercourse when we arrived, and cars and buses choking the roads into town. Everyone hoped to see and photograph some genuine Amish. Up to five million people a year visit the county and non-Amish businessmen have erected vast souvenir palaces, replica farms, wax museums, cafeterias and gift shops to soak up the $350 million that the visitors are happy to spend each year. Now there is almost nothing left in these towns for the Amish themselves to buy, so they don't come in and the tourists have nothing to do but take pictures of each other.

Travel articles and movies like *Witness* generally gloss over this side of things, but the fact is that Lancaster County is now one of the most awful places in America, especially on weekends when traffic jams sometimes stretch for miles. Many of the Amish themselves have given up and moved to places like Iowa and upper Michigan where they are left alone. Out in the countryside, particularly on the back roads, you can still sometimes see the people in their funny dark clothes working in the fields or driving their distinctive black buggies down the highway, with a long line of tourist cars creeping along behind, pissed off because they can't get by and they really want to be in Bird in Hand so they can get some more funnel cakes and Sno-Cones and perhaps buy a wrought-iron wine rack or combination mailbox–weather vane to take back home to Fartville with them. I wouldn't be surprised if a decade from now there isn't a real Amish person left in the county. It is an unspeakable shame. They should be left in peace.

In the evening, along with everyone else in the whole of Pennsylvania, we went to one of the many barnlike family-style Pennsylvania Dutch restaurants that are scattered across the county. The parking lot was packed with buses and cars and there were people waiting everywhere, inside the building and out. We went in and were given a ticket with the number 621 on it and went with it to a tiny patch of floor space just vacated by another party. Every few minutes a man would step to the door and call out a series of numbers ridiculously lower than ours—220, 221, 222—and a dozen or so people would follow him into the dining room. We debated leaving, but a party of fat people beside us told us not to give up because it was worth the wait, even if we had to stay there until eleven o'clock. The food was that good, they said, and where food was concerned these people clearly had some experience. Well, they were right. Eventually our number was called and we were ushered into the dining room with nine strangers and all seated together at one big trestle table.

There must have been fifty other such tables in the room, all with a dozen or so people at them. The din and bustle were enormous. Waitresses rushed back and forth with outsized trays and everywhere you looked people were shoveling food into their mouths, elbows flapping, as if they hadn't eaten for a week. Our waitress made us introduce ourselves to each other, which everybody thought was kind of dopey, and then she started bringing food, great platters and bowls of it—thick slabs of ham, mountains of fried chicken, buckets of mashed potatoes and all kinds of vegetables, rolls, soups and salads. It was incredible. You helped yourself and with two hands heaved the platter on to the next person. You could have as much of anything as you wanted—indeed, when a bowl was empty the waitress brought back another and practically ordered you to clear it.

I've never seen so much food. I couldn't see over the top of my plate. It was all delicious and pretty soon everybody knew everybody else and was having a great time. I ate so much my armpits bulged. But still the food kept coming. Just when I thought I would have to summon a wheelchair to get me to the car, the waitress took away all the platters and bowls, and started bringing desserts—apple pies, chocolate cakes, bowls of homemade ice cream, pastries, flans and God knows what else.

I kept eating. It was too delicious to pass up. Buttons popped off my shirt; my trousers burst open. I barely had the strength to lift my spoon, but I kept shoveling the stuff in. It was grotesque. Food began to leak from my ears. And still I ate. I ate more food that night than some African villagers eat in a lifetime. Eventually, mercifully, the waitress prised the spoons out of our hands and took the dessert stuff away, and we were able to stumble zombielike out into the night.

We got in the car, too full to speak, and headed towards the greenish glow of Three Mile Island. I felt as if I had eaten the contents of a cement mixer. I lay on the back seat of the car, my feet in the air, and moaned softly. I vowed that I would never eat again, and meant it. But two hours later, when we arrived back at my brother's house, the agony had abated and my brother and I were able to begin a new cycle of gross overconsumption, beginning with a twelve-pack of beer and bucket of pretzels from his kitchen and concluding, in the early hours of the morning, with a plate of onion rings and two-foot-long submarine sandwiches, full of goo and spices, at an all-night eatery out on Highway 11.

14

IT WAS TEN MINUTES to seven in the morning and it was cold. Standing outside the Bloomsburg bus station, I could see my breath. The few cars out this early trailed clouds of vapor. I was hung over and in a few minutes I was going to climb onto a bus for a five-hour ride into New York. I would sooner have eaten cat food.

My brother had suggested that I take the bus because it would save having to find a place to park in Manhattan. I could leave the car with him and come back for it in a day or two. At two in the morning, after many beers, this had seemed a good plan. But now, standing in the early-morning chill, I realized I was making a serious mistake. You only go on a long-distance bus in the United States because either you cannot afford to fly or—and this is really licking the bottom of the barrel in America—you cannot afford a car. Being unable to afford a car in America is the last step before living out of a plastic sack. As a result, most of the people on long-distance buses are one of the following: mentally defective, actively schizoid, armed and dangerous, in a drugged stupor, just released from prison or nuns. Occasionally you will also see a pair of Norwegian students. You can tell they are Norwegian students because they are so pink-faced and healthy-looking and they wear little pale blue ankle socks with their sandals.

By and large a ride on a long-distance bus in America combines most of the shortcomings of prison life with those of an ocean crossing in a troopship. So when the bus pulled up before me, heaving a pneumatic sigh, and its doors flapped open, I boarded it with some misgivings. The driver himself didn't look any too stable. He had the sort of hair you associate with people who have had accidents involving live wires. There were about half a dozen other passengers, though only two of them looked seriously dangerous and just one was talking to himself. I took a seat near the back and settled down to get some sleep. I had drunk far too many beers with my brother the night before, and the hot spices from the submarine sandwich were now expanding ominously inside my abdomen and drifting around like that stuff they put in lava lamps. Soon from one end or the other it would begin to seep out.

I felt a hand on my shoulder from behind. Through the gap in the seat I could see it was an Indian man—by that I mean a man from India, not an American Indian. "Can I smoke on this bus?" he asked me.

"I don't know," I said. "I don't smoke anymore, so I don't pay much attention to these things."

"But do you *think* I can smoke on this bus?"

"I really don't know."

He was quiet for a few minutes, then his hand was on my shoulder again, not tapping it but resting there. "I can't find an ashtray," he said.

"No fooling," I responded wittily, without opening my eyes.

"Do you think that means we're not allowed to smoke?"

"I don't know. I don't care."

"But do you *think* it means we're not allowed to smoke?"

"If you don't take your hand off my shoulder I am going to dribble vomit on it," I said.

He removed his hand quickly and was silent for perhaps a minute. Then he said, "Would you help me look for an ashtray?"

It was seven in the morning and I was deeply unwell. I

jumped up. "WILL YOU PLEASE JUST LEAVE ME ALONE!" I said to him. Two seats back a pair of Norwegian students looked shocked. I gave them a look as if to say, "And don't you try anything either, you wholesome little shits!" and sank back into my seat. It was going to be a long day.

I slept fitfully, that dissatisfying, semiconscious sleep in which you incorporate into your dreams the things going on around you—the grinding of gears, the crying of babies, the mad swervings of the bus back and forth across the highway as the driver gropes for a dropped cigarette or lapses into a psychotic episode. Mostly I dreamed of the bus plunging over a cliff face, sailing into a void; in my dream, we fell for miles, tumbling through the clouds, peacefully, with just the sound of air whisking past outside, and then the Indian saying to me, "Do you think it would be all right if I smoked *now?*"

When I awoke there was drool on my shoulder and a new passenger opposite me, a haggard woman with lank gray hair who was chain-smoking cigarettes and burping prodigiously. They were the sort of burps children make to amuse themselves—rich, resonant, basso profundo burps. The woman was completely unself-conscious about it. She would look at me and open her mouth and out would roll a burp. It was amazing. Then she would take a drag of her cigarette and burp a large puff of smoke. That was amazing too. I glanced behind me. The Indian man was still there, looking miserable. Seeing me, he started to lean forward to ask a supplementary question, but I stopped him with a raised finger and he sank back. I stared out the window, feeling ill, and passed the time by trying to imagine circumstances less congenial than this. But apart from being dead or at a Bee Gees concert I couldn't think of a single thing.

We reached New York in the afternoon. I got a room in a hc el near Times Square. The room cost $110 a night and was so small I had to go out into the corridor to turn around. I had never been in a room where I could touch all four walls at once. I did all the things you do in hotel rooms—played with the lights and TV, looked in the drawers, smelled the little cake of soap in the bathroom, put all the towels and ashtrays in my suitcase—and then wandered out to have a look at the city.

The last time I had been in New York was when I was sixteen and my friend Stan and I came out to visit my brother and his wife, who were living there then. They had an apartment in a strange, Kafkaesque apartment complex in Queens called Lefrak City. It consisted of about a dozen identical tall, featureless buildings clustered around a series of lonesome quadrangles, the sort of quadrangles where rain puddles stand for weeks and the flowerbeds are littered with supermarket carts. Each building was like a vertical city, with its own grocery store, drugstore, laundromat and so on. I don't remember the details except that each building was taller than the tallest building in Des Moines and that the total population was something like 50,000—bigger than most Iowa towns. I had never conceived of so many people gathered in one place. I couldn't understand why in such a big, open country as America people would choose to live like that. It wasn't as if this were something temporary, a place to spend a few months while waiting for their ranch house in the suburbs to be built. This was home. This was it. Thousands and thousands of people would live out their lives never having their own backyard, never having a barbecue, never stepping out the back door at midnight to have a pee in the bushes and check out the stars. Their children would grow up thinking that supermarket carts grew wild, like weeds.

In the evenings, when my brother and his wife went out, Stan and I would sit with binoculars and scan the windows of the neighboring buildings. There were hundreds of windows to choose from, each containing a ghostly glow of television, a separate glimpsed life, another chapter in the endless story of the naked city. What we were looking for, of course, were naked women—and to our amazement we did actually see some, though usually this resulted in such excited grappling for control of the binoculars that the women had dressed and gone out for the evening by the time we got their windows back in view. Mostly what we saw, however, were other men with binoculars scanning the windows of our building. It was all very strange. This was

August 1968. In the background, I remember, the television was filled with news of the Russian invasion of Czechoslovakia and Mayor Daley's men kicking the crap out of demonstrators at the Democratic convention in Chicago. It was a strange time to be young, full of lust and bodily juices.

What I particularly remember was the sense of menace whenever we left the building. Groups of hoody-looking teenagers with no place to go would sit on the walls around the complex watching anyone who passed. I always expected them to fall in behind us as we went by and to take our money and stick us with knives they had made in the prison workshop, but they never bothered us, they just stared.

New York still frightened me. I felt the same sense of menace now as I walked down to Times Square. New York scared me. I had read so much for so long about murders and street crime that I felt a personal gratitude to everyone who left me alone. I wanted to hand out cards that said, "Thank you for not killing me."

But the only people who assaulted me were panhandlers. There are 36,000 vagrants in New York and in two days of walking around every one of them asked me for money. Some of them asked twice. People in New York go to Calcutta to get some relief from begging. I began to regret that I didn't live in an age when a gentleman could hit such people with his stick. One guy, my favorite, came up and asked if he could borrow a dollar. That knocked me out. I wanted to say, "Borrow a dollar? Certainly. Shall we say interest at 1 percent above prime and we'll meet back here on Thursday to settle?" I wouldn't give him a dollar, of course—I wouldn't give my closest friend a *dollar*—but I pressed a dime into his grubby mitt and gave him a wink for his guile.

Times Square is incredible. You've never seen such lights, such hustle. Whole sides of buildings are given over to advertisements that blink and ripple and wave. It's like a storm on an electronic sea. There are perhaps forty of these massive inducements to spend and consume, and all but two of them are for Japanese companies: Mita Copiers, Canon, Panasonic, Sony. My mighty homeland was represented by just Kodak and Pepsi-Cola. The war is over, Yankee dog, I thought bleakly.

143

The most riveting thing about New York is that anything can happen there. Only the week before a woman had been eaten by an escalator. Can you beat that? She had been on her way to work, minding her own business, when suddenly the stair beneath her gave way and she plummeted into the interior mechanisms, into all the whirring cogs and gears, with the sort of consequences you can well imagine. How would you like to be the cleaner in *that* building? ("Bernie, can you come in early tonight? And listen, you'd better bring along a wire brush and a *lot* of Ajax.") New York is always full of amazing and unpredictable things. A front-page story in the *New York Post* was about a pervert with AIDS who had been jailed that day for raping little boys. Can you believe that? "What a city!" I thought. "Such a madhouse!" For two days I walked and stared and mumbled in amazement. A large black man on Eighth Avenue reeled out of a doorway, looking seriously insane, and said to me, "I been smoking ice! Big bowls of ice!" I gave him a quarter real fast, even though he hadn't asked for anything, and moved off quickly. On Fifth Avenue I went into the Trump Tower, a new skyscraper. A guy named Donald Trump, a developer, is slowly taking over New York, building skyscrapers all over town with his name on them, so I went in and had a look around. The building had the most tasteless lobby I had ever seen—all brass and chrome and blotchy red and white marble that looked like the sort of thing that if you saw it on the sidewalk you would walk around it. Here it was everywhere—on the floors, up the walls, on the ceiling. It was like being inside somebody's stomach after he'd eaten pizza. "Incredible," I muttered and walked on. Next door a store sold pornographic videos, right there on Fifth Avenue. My favorite was *Yiddish Erotica,* Volume 2. What could this possibly consist of—rabbis with their trousers down, tarty women lying spread-eagled and saying, "You wanna fuck already?" "Superb, incredible," I mumbled and plodded on.

In the evening, as I strolled back along Times Square, my eye was caught by a striptease club with a photograph of the strippers in the window. They were nice-looking girls. One of the photos was of Samantha Fox. Since Ms. Fox was at this time being paid something like £250,000 a year to show off her comely udders to readers of British newspapers such as the *Sun,* it seemed to me improbable, to say the least, that she would be peeling off for strangers in a smoky basement room on Times Square. In fact, I would go so far as to suggest that there was a little fraud at work here. It's a mean trick to play on a horny person.

They always used to do this to you at the Iowa State Fair. The strippers' tents at the back of the midway would be covered with wildly erotic paintings of the most beautiful, silky-haired, full-breasted, lithe-bodied women you ever saw—women whose moist and pouty lips seemed to be saying, "I want you—yes, you there, with the zits and glasses. Come and fulfill me, little man." Aged fourteen and delirious with lust, you would believe these pictures with all your heart and many of the neighboring organs. You would hand over a crumpled dollar and go inside into a dusty tent that smelled of horse manure and rubbing alcohol and find onstage a weary stripper looking not unlike your own mother. It was the sort of disappointment from which you never really recover, and my heart went out now to the lonely sailors and Japanese photocopier salesmen who were down there drinking sweet, warm cocktails and having a night of overpriced disappointment. "We learn from our mistakes," I remarked sagely to myself with a rueful smile and told a panhandler to piss off.

I went back to my room, pleased not to have been mugged, more pleased not to have been murdered. On top of my television was a card saying that for $6.50 I could have an in-room movie. There was, as I recall, a choice of four—*Friday the Thirteenth, Part 19,* in which a man with a personality disorder uses knives, hatchets, Cuisinarts and a snowblower to kill a succession of young women just as they are about to step into the shower; *Death Wish 11,* in which Charles Bronson tracks down and kills Michael Winner; *Bimbo,* in which Sylvester Stallone as Rambo has a sex-change operation and then blows up a lot of Oriental people; and, on the adult channel, *My Panties Are Dripping,* a sensitive study of interpersonal relationships and social conflict in postmodern Denmark, with a lot of vigorous bonking thrown in for good measure. I toyed for a moment with the idea of watching a bit of the last one—just to help me relax, as they say in evangelical circles—but I was too cheap to spend $6.50, and, anyway, I've always suspected that if I did punch the requisite button (which was worn to a nubbin, I can tell you), the next day a bellboy would confront me with a computer printout and tell me that if I didn't give him fifty dollars he would send a copy of the room receipt to my mother with "Miscellaneous charges: Deviant Porno Movie, $6.50" circled in red. So instead I lay on the bed and watched a rerun on normal television of "Mr. Ed," a 1960s comedy series about a talking horse. Judging by the quality of the jokes, I would guess that Mr. Ed wrote his own material. But at least there was nothing in it that would get me blackmailed.

And thus ended my day in New York, the most exciting and stimulating city in the world. I couldn't help but reflect that I had no reason to feel superior to my fellow lonely hearts in the strip-tease club twenty floors below. I was just as lonesome as they were. Indeed, all over this big, heartless city there were no doubt tens of thousands of people just as solitary and friendless as me. What a melancholy thought.

"But I wonder how many of them can do this?" I remarked to myself and with my hands and feet reached out and touched all four walls at once.

15

IT WAS THE Columbus Day weekend and the roads were busy. Columbus has always seemed to me an odd choice of hero for a country that celebrates success as America does because he was such a dismal failure. Consider the facts: he made four long voyages to the Americas, but never once realized that he wasn't in Asia and never found anything worthwhile. Every other explorer was coming back with exciting new products like potatoes and tobacco and nylon stockings, and all Columbus found to bring home were some puzzled-looking Indians—and he thought they were Japanese. ("Come on, you guys, let's see a little sumo.")

But perhaps Columbus's most remarkable shortcoming was that he never actually saw the land that was to become the United States. This surprises a lot of people. They imagine him trampling over Florida, saying, "You know, this would make a nice resort." But in fact his voyages were all spent in the Caribbean and bouncing around the swampy, bug-infested coasts of Central America. If you ask me, the Vikings would make far more worthy heroes for America. For one thing, they did actually discover it. On top of that, the Vikings were manly and drank out of skulls and didn't take any crap from anybody. Now *that's* the American way.

When I lived in America Columbus Day was one of those semibogus holidays that existed only for the benefit of public workers with strong unions. There was no mail on Columbus Day and if you innocently drove all the way over to the east side of town to the Iowa State Vehicle Licensing Center to renew your driver's license you would find the door locked and a notice hanging in the window saying, CLOSED FOR COLUMBUS DAY HOLIDAY. SO TOUGH SHIT TO YOU. But otherwise life was no different than on any other day. Now, however, it appeared that the Columbus Day holiday had spread. There were lots of cars and recreational vehicles on the highway and the radio announcers kept talking about things like the number of fatalities that were expected "this Columbus Day weekend." (How do they know these things anyway? Is there some kind of secret quota?) I had been looking forward to reaching New England because I wanted to see the autumn color. In addition, the states would be small and varied and there wouldn't be that awful rolling tedium that comes with all the other American states, even the attractive ones. But I was wrong. Of course, New England states are indubitably tiny—Connecticut is only eighty miles across; Rhode Island is smaller than London—but they are crowded with cars, people and cities. Connecticut appeared to be just one suburb. I drove up US 202 towards Litchfield, which was marked on my map as a scenic route, and it was, to be sure, more scenic than a suburb, but it wasn't exactly spectacular.

Perhaps I was expecting too much. In the movies in the 1940s people were always going to Connecticut for the weekend, and it always looked wonderfully green and rustic. It was always full of empty roads and stone cottages in leafy glades. But this was just semisuburban: ranch houses with three-car garages and lawns with twirling sprinklers and shopping centers every six blocks. Litchfield itself was very handsome, the quintessential New England town, with an old courthouse and a long sloping green with a cannon and a memorial to the war dead. On one side of the green stood pleasant shops and on the other was a tall, white, steepled church, dazzling in the October sunshine. And there was color—the trees around the green were a rich gold and lemon. This was more like it.

I parked in front of MacDonald Drug and crossed the green through a scuffle of fallen leaves. I strolled along residential streets where big houses squatted on wide lawns. Each was a variation on the same theme: rambling clapboard with black shutters. Many had wooden plaques on them pertaining to their history—OLIVER BOARDMAN 1785; 1830 COL. WEBB. I spent over an hour just poking around. It was a pleasant town for poking.

Afterwards I drove east, sticking to back highways. Soon I was in the suburbs of Hartford, and then in Hartford itself, and then in the suburbs on the other side of Hartford. And then I was in Rhode Island. I stopped beside a sign saying WELCOME TO RHODE ISLAND and stared at the map. Was that really all there was to Connecticut? I considered turning back and having another sweep across the state—there had to be more to it than that—but it was getting late, so I pressed on, venturing into a deep and rather more promising pine forest. Considering Rhode Island's microscopic size it seemed to take me ages to find my way out of the forest. By the time I hit Narragansett Bay, a heavily islanded inlet which consumes almost a quarter of the state's modest square mileage, it was almost dark, and there were lights winking from the villages scattered along the shoreline.

At Plum Point a long bridge crossed the sound to Conanicut Island, which rode low and dark on the water, like a corpse. I crossed the bridge and drove around the island a little, but by now it was too dark to see much. At one place where the shore came in near the road, I parked and walked to the beach. It was a moonless night and I could hear the sea before I could see it, coming in with a slow, rhythmic *whoosh-whoosh*. I went and stood at the water's edge. The waves fell onto the beach like exhausted swimmers. The wind played at my jacket. I stared for a long time out across the moody sea, the black vastness of the Atlantic, the fearsome, primordial, storm-tossed depths from which all of life has crawled and will no doubt one day return, and I thought, "I could murder a hamburger."

In the morning I drove into Newport, America's premier yachting community, home of the America's Cup races. The old part of town had been fixed up in recent years, by the look of it. Shops with hanging wooden signs out front lined the streets. They all had jauntily nautical names like the Flying Ship and Shore Thing. The harbor was almost too picturesque, with its crowds of white yachts and bare masts undulating beneath a sky in which gulls danced and reeled. But all around the fringe of the downtown there were unsightly parking lots, and a busy four-lane road, more freeway than city street, divided the waterfront from the town. Spindly trees stood along it like scrawny afterthoughts. The city had also built a little park, Perrott Park, but it was unkempt and full of graffiti. I had not encountered this kind of neglect before. Most American towns are spotless, and this really surprised me, especially considering the importance of tourism to Newport. I walked up Thames Street, where some fine old sea captains' homes were fighting a losing battle with litter and dog shit and the encroachment of gas stations and car transmission places. It was all very sad. This was a place where the people didn't seem to care, or perhaps just didn't notice, how shabby they had let things grow. It reminded me of London.

I drove out to Fort Adams State Park across the bay. From there Newport looked another town altogether—a charming cut-out of needle-shaped church spires and Victorian rooftops pro-truding from a parkland of trees. The bay glittered in the sunshine and its scores of sailboats bobbed on the gentle waves. It was captivating. I drove on along the shore road, past Brenton Point, and then down Bellevue Avenue, where the most fabulous summer homes ever built line the road on both sides and spill over onto many of the streets beyond.

Between about 1890 and 1905, America's richest families—the Vanderbilts, the Astors, the Belmonts, dozens of others—tried to outdo each other by building magnificent homes, which they insisted on calling cottages, all along this half-mile strip of imposing cliffs. Most were loosely modeled on French chateaux and filled with furniture, marble and tapestries shipped at huge expense from Europe. Hostesses routinely spent $300,000 or more on entertainment for a season that listed only six or eight weeks. For forty years or so this was the world headquarters of conspicuous consumption.

Most of the houses are now run as museums. They charge an arm and a leg to get in and in any case the lines outside most of them were enormous (this was the Columbus Day weekend, remember). You can't see much from the street—the owners didn't want common people staring at them as they sat on the lawn counting their money, so they put up dense hedges and high walls—but I discovered quite by chance that the city had built an asphalt footpath all along the cliff edge, from which I could see the backs of the grander mansions, as well as enjoy giddying views of the ocean breaking onto the rocks far below. I had the path almost to myself and walked along it in a state of quiet amazement, with my mouth open. I had never seen such a succession of vast houses, such an excess of architecture. Every house looked like a cross between a wedding cake and a state capitol building. I knew that the grandest of all the houses was The Breakers, built by the Vanderbilts, and I kept thinking, "Well, *this* must be it" and "Now surely *this* must be it," but then the next house along would be even more awesome. When at last I reached The Breakers, it was absolutely enormous, a mountain with windows. You can't look at it without thinking that nobody, with the possible exception of oneself, deserves to be that rich.

On the other side of the fence, the lawns and terraces were full of pudgy tourists in Bermuda shorts and silly hats, wandering in and out of the house, taking pictures of each other and trampling the begonias, and I wondered what Cornelius Vanderbilt would make of that, the dog-faced old prick.

I drove on to Cape Cod, another place I had never been and for which I had high expectations. It was very picturesque, with its old salt-box homes, its antique shops and wooden inns, its pretty villages with quaint names: Sagamore, Sandwich, Barnstable, Rock Harbor. But it was jam-packed with tourists in overloaded cars and rumbling motor homes. Boy, do I hate motor homes! Especially on crowded peninsulas like Cape Cod where they clog the streets and block the views—and all so that some guy and his dumpy wife can eat lunch and empty their bladders without stopping.

The traffic was so dense and slow moving that I almost ran out of gas and just managed to limp into a two-pump station outside West Barnstable. It was run by a man who was at least ninety-seven years old. He was tall and rangy and very spry. I've never seen anybody pump gas with such abandon. First he slopped a quantity of it down the side of the car and then he got so engaged in talking about where I came from—"Ioway, eh? We don't get many from Ioway. I think you're the first this year. What's the weather like in Ioway this time of year?"—that he let the pump run over and I had to point out to him that gasoline was cascading down the side of the car and gathering in a pool at our feet. He withdrew the nozzle, sloshing another half-gallon over the car and down his trousers and shoes, and kind of threw it back at the pump, where it dribbled carelessly.

He had a cigarette butt plugged into the side of his mouth and I was terrified he would try to light it. And he did. He pulled out a crumpled book of matches and started to fidget one of them to life. I was too stunned to move. All I could think of was a television newscaster saying, "And in West Barnstable today a tourist from Iowa suffered third-degree burns over 98 percent of his body in an explosion at a gas station. Fire officials said he looked like a marshmallow that had fallen on the campfire. The owner of the gas station has still not been found." But we didn't explode. The little stub of cigarette sprouted smoke, which the man puffed up into a good-sized billow, and then he pinched out the match with his fingers. I suppose after all these decades of pumping gas he had become more or less incombustible, like those snake handlers who grow immune to snake venom. But I wasn't inclined to test this theory too closely. I paid him hastily and pulled straight back onto the highway, much to the annoy-ance of a man in a forty-foot motor home who dripped mustard on his lap in braking to avoid me. "That'll teach you to take a building on vacation," I muttered uncharitably and hoped that something heavy had fallen on his wife in back.

Cape Cod is a long, thin peninsula that sprouts out of the base of Massachusetts, runs out to sea for twenty miles or so and then curls back in on itself. It looks like an arm flexed to make a muscle—in fact, it looks remarkably like my arm because there's almost no muscle in it. There are three roads along the lower part of the peninsula—one along the north shore, one along the south shore and one up the middle—but at the peninsula's elbow at Rock Harbor, where it narrows and abruptly turns north, the three roads come together and there is just one long slow highway up the forearm to Provincetown at the fingertips. Provincetown was swarming with tourists. The town has just one route in and one route out. Only a few hundred people live there, but they get as many as 50,000 visitors a day during the summer and on holiday weekends such as this one. Parking was not allowed in the town itself—there were mean-spirited towaway warnings everywhere—so I paid a couple of bucks to leave my car with several hundred others out in the middle of nowhere and trudged a long way into town.

Provincetown is built on sand. All around it stand rolling dunes broken only by occasional clumps of straw-colored grass. The names of the businesses—Windy Ridge Motel, Gale Force Gift Shop—suggested that wind might be something of a local feature, and indeed there was sand drifted across the roads and piled in the doorways, and with every whipping breeze it flew in your eyes and face and dusted whatever food you happened to be eating. It must be an awful place to live. I might have disliked it less if Provincetown had tried just a little harder to be charming. I had seldom seen a place so singularly devoted to sucking money out of tourists. It was filled with ice cream parlors and gift shops and places selling T-shirts, kites and beach paraphernalia.

I walked around for a while and had a hot dog with mustard and sand and a cup of coffee with cream and sand and had a look in a window of a real estate agency, where I noticed that a basic two-bedroom house by the beach was on offer at $190,000, though it did include a fireplace and all the sand you could eat. The beaches looked nice enough, but apart from that I couldn't see a single real attraction in the place.

Provincetown is where the Pilgrim fathers first touched American soil in 1620. There's a big campanile-type tower in the middle of the town to commemorate the event. The Pilgrims, curiously enough, didn't mean to land on Cape Cod at all. They were aiming for Jamestown in Virginia, but missed their target by a mere 600 miles. I think that is a considerable achievement. Here's another curious thing: they didn't bring with them a single plow or horse or cow or even a fishing line. Does that strike you as just a little bit foolish? I mean to say, if you were going to start a new life in a land far, far away, don't you think you would give some thought to how you were going to fend for yourself once you got there? Still, for all their shortcomings as planners, the Pilgrim fathers were sufficiently on the ball not to linger in the Provincetown area and at the first opportunity they pushed on to mainland Massachusetts. So did I.

I had hoped to go to Hyannis Port, where the Kennedys had their summer home, but the traffic was so slow, especially around Woods Hole, where the ferry to Martha's Vineyard departs, that I dared not. Every motel I passed—and there were hundreds—said No Vacancy. I got on Interstate 93, thinking I would follow it for a few miles just to get away from Cape Cod, and start looking for a room, but before I knew it I was in Boston, caught in the evening rush hour. Boston's freeway system was insane. It was clearly designed by a person who had spent his childhood crashing toy trains. Every few hundred yards I would find my lane vanishing beneath me and other lanes merging with it from the right or left, or sometimes both. This wasn't a road system, it was mobile hysteria. Everybody looked worried. I had never seen people working so hard to keep from crashing into each other. And this was a Saturday—God knows what it must be like on a weekday.

Boston is a big city and its outer suburbs dribble on and on all the way up to New Hampshire. So, late in the evening, without having any clear idea of how I got there, I found myself in one of those placeless places that sprout up along the junctions of interstate highways—purplishly lit islands of motels, gas stations, shopping centers and fast-food places—so brightly lit they must be visible from outer space. This one was somewhere in the region of Haverhill. I got a room in a Motel 6 and dined on greasy fried chicken and limp french fries at a Denny's Restaurant across the way. It had been a bad day, but I refused to get depressed. Just a couple of miles down the road was New Hampshire and the start of the real New England. Things could only get better.

16

══════════ I HAD ALWAYS thought that New England was nothing but maple trees and white churches and old guys in checkered shirts sitting around iron stoves in country general stores swapping tall tales and spitting in the cracker barrel. But if lower New Hampshire was anything to go by, clearly I had been misinformed. There was just modern commercial squalor— shopping centers, gas stations, motels. Every once in a while there would be a white church or clapboard inn standing incongruously in the midst of Burger Kings and Texacos. But far from mollifying the ugliness, it only intensified it, reminding you what had been thrown away for the sake of drive-through burgers and cheap gasoline.

At Salisbury, I joined old Route 1, intending to follow it up the coast through Maine. Route 1, as the name suggests, is the patriarch of American roads, the first federal highway. It stretches for 2,500 miles from the Canadian border to the Florida Keys. For forty years it was the main highway along the eastern seaboard, connecting all the big cities of the North—Boston, New York, Philadelphia, Baltimore, Washington—with the beaches and citrus groves of the South. It must have been wonderful in the 1930s and 1940s to drive from Maine to Florida on vacation, going through all those big marvelous cities and then passing on to the hills of Virginia and the green mountains of the Carolinas, getting warmer with the passing miles. But by the 1960s Route 1 had become too congested to be practical—a third of all Americans live within twenty miles of it—and Interstate 95 was built to zip traffic up and down the coast with only the most fleeting sense of a changing landscape. Today Route 1 is still there, but you would need weeks to drive its entire length. Now it is just a local road, an endless city street, an epic stretch of shopping malls.

I had hoped that here in rural New England it would retain something of its former charm, but it seemed not to. I drove through a chill morning drizzle and wondered if ever I would find the real New England. At Portsmouth, an instantly forgettable little town, I crossed over into Maine on an iron bridge over the gray Piscataqua River. Seen through the rhythmic swish of windshield wipers, Maine too looked ominously unpromising, a further sprawl of shopping centers and muddy new housing developments.

Beyond Kennebunkport the suburbs at last gave way to forest. Here and there massive brown boulders emerged eerily from the earth, like subterranean creatures coming up for air, and occasionally I caught glimpses of the sea—a gray plane, cold and bleak. I drove and drove, thinking that any moment now I would encounter the fabled Maine of lobster pots and surf-battered shores and lonely lighthouses standing on rocks of granite, but the towns I passed through were just messy and drear, and the countryside was wooded and unmemorable. Once, outside Falmouth, the road ran for a mile or so along a silvery bay with a long, low bridge leading over it to a landscape of snug farms nestled in a fold of hills, and I got briefly excited. But it was a false alarm and the landscape quickly grew dull again. The rest of the time the real Maine eluded me. It was always just over there, like the amusement parks my dad used to miss.

At Wiscasset, a third of the way up the coast to New Brunswick, I lost heart altogether. Wiscasset bills itself on the signboard at the edge of town as the prettiest village in Maine, which doesn't say a whole lot for the rest of the state. I don't mean to suggest that Wiscasset was awful, because it wasn't. It had a steep main street lined with craft shops and other yuppie emporia sloping down to a placid inlet of the Atlantic Ocean. Two old wooden ships sat rotting on the bank. It was OK. It just wasn't worth driving four hours to get there.

Abruptly I decided to abandon Route 1 and plunge northward, into the dense pine forests of central Maine, heading in an irregular line for the White Mountains, on a road that went up and down, up and down, like a rucked carpet. After a few miles I began to sense a change of atmosphere. The clouds were low and shapeless, the daylight meager. Winter clearly was closing in. I was only seventy miles or so from Canada and it was evident that winters here were long and severe. It was written in the crumbling roads and in the huge stacks of firewood that stood outside each lonely cabin. Many chimneys were already sprouting wintry wisps of smoke. It was barely October, but already the land had the cold and lifeless feel of winter. It was the kind of atmosphere that makes you want to turn up your collar and head for home.

Just beyond Gilead I passed into New Hampshire and the landscape became more interesting. The White Mountains rose up before me, big and round, the color of wood ash. Presumably they take their name from the birch trees that cover them. I drove on an empty highway through a forest of trembling leaves. The skies were still flat and low, the weather cold, but at least I was out of the monotony of the Maine woods. The road rose and fell and swept along the edge of a boulder-strewn creek. The scenery was infinitely better—but still there was no color, none of the brilliant golds and reds of autumn that I had been led to expect. Everything from the ground to the sky was a dull, cadaverous gray.

I drove past Mount Washington, the highest peak in the northeastern United States (6,288 feet, for those of you who are keeping notes). But its real claim to fame is as the windiest place in America. It's something to do with . . . well, with the way the wind blows, of course. Anyway, the highest wind speed ever recorded anywhere on earth was logged on the top of Mount Washington in April 1934 when a gust of—pencils ready?—231 miles an hour whistled through. That must have been an experience and a half for the meteorologists who worked up there. Can you imagine trying to describe a wind like that to somebody? "Well, it was, you know, real . . . *windy*. I mean, *really* windy. Do you know what I'm saying?" It must be very frustrating to have a truly unique experience.

Just beyond it, I came to Bretton Woods, which I had always pictured as a quaint little town. But in fact there was no town at all, just a hotel and a ski lift. The hotel was huge and looked like a medieval fortress, but with a bright red roof. It looked like a cross between Monte Cassino and a Pizza Hut. It was here in 1944 that economists and politicians from twenty-eight nations got together and agreed to set up the International Monetary Fund and the World Bank. It certainly looked a nice place to make economic history. As John Maynard Keynes remarked at the time in a letter to his brother, Milton, "It has been a most satisfactory week. The negotiations have been cordial, the food here is superb and the waiters are ever so pretty."

I stopped for the night at Littleton, which, as the name suggests, is a little town near the Vermont border. I pulled into the Littleton Motel on the main street. On the office door was a sign that said, "If you want ice or advice, come before 6:30. I'm taking the wife to dinner. ('And about time too!'—wife)." Inside was an old guy on crutches who told me I was very lucky because he had just one room left. It would be forty-two dollars plus tax. When he saw me start to froth and back off, he hastily added, "It's a real nice room. Got a brand-new TV. Nice carpets. Beautiful little shower. We've got the cleanest rooms in town. We're famous for that." He swept an arm over a selection of testimonials from satisfied customers which he displayed under glass on the countertop. "Our room must have been the cleanest room in town!"— A.K., Aardvark Falls, Ky. "Boy, was our room ever clean! And such nice carpets!"—Mr. and Mrs. J.F., Spotweld, Ohio. That sort of thing.

Somehow I doubted the veracity of these claims, but I was too weary to return to the road, so with a sigh I said all right and signed in. I took my key and a bucket of ice (at forty-two dollars plus tax I intended to have everything that was going) and went with them to my room. And by golly, it *was* the cleanest room in town. The TV was brand-new and the carpet was plush. The bed was comfortable and the shower really was a beauty. I felt instantly ashamed of myself and retracted all my bad thoughts about the proprietor. ("I was a pompous little shit to have doubted you."—Mr. B.B., Des Moines.)

I ate fourteen ice cubes and watched the early evening news. This was followed by an old episode of "Gilligan's Island," which the TV station had thoughtfully put on as an inducement to its non-brain-damaged viewers to get up immediately and go do something more useful. This I did. I went out and had a look around the town. The reason I had chosen to stop for the night at Littleton was that an American Heritage book I had with me referred to it as picturesque. In point of fact, if Littleton was characterized by anything it was a singular lack of picturesqueness. The town consisted principally of one long street of mostly undistinguished buildings, with a supermarket parking lot in the middle and the shell of a disused gas station a couple of doors away. This, I think we can agree, does not constitute picturesqueness. Happily, the town had other virtues. For one thing, it was the friendliest little place I had ever seen. I went into the Topic of the Town restaurant. The other customers smiled at me, the lady at the cash register showed me where to put my jacket, and the waitress, a plump and dimpled little lady, couldn't do enough for me. It was as if they had all been given some kind of marvelous tranquilizer.

The waitress brought me a menu and I made the mistake of saying thank you. "You're welcome," she said. Once you start this there's no stopping. She came and wiped the table with a damp cloth. "Thank you," I said. "You're welcome," she said. She brought me some cutlery wrapped in a paper napkin. I hesitated, but I couldn't stop myself. "Thank you," I said. "You're welcome," she said. Then came a place mat with "Topic of the Town" written on it, and then a glass of water, and then a clean ashtray, and then a little basket of saltine crackers wrapped in cellophane, and at each we had our polite exchange. I ordered the fried chicken special. As I waited I became uncomfortably aware that the people at the next table were watching me and smiling at me in a deranged fashion. The waitress was watching me too, from a position by the kitchen doorway. It was all rather unnerving. Every few moments she would come over and top up my iced water and tell me that my food would only be a minute.

"Thank you," I'd say.

"You're welcome," she'd say.

Eventually the waitress came out of the kitchen with a tray the size of a tabletop and started setting down plates of food in front of me—soup, salad, a platter of chicken, a basket of steaming rolls. It all looked delicious. Suddenly I realized that I was starving.

"Can I get you anything else?" she said.

"No, this is just fine, thank you," I answered, knife and fork plugged in my fists, ready to lunge at the food.

"Would you like some ketchup?"

"No thank you."

"Would you like a little more dressing for your salad?"

"No thank you."

"Have you got enough gravy?"

There was enough gravy to drown a horse. "Yes, plenty of gravy, thank you."

"How about a cup of coffee?"

"Really, I'm fine."

"You sure there's nothing I can do for you?"

"Well, you might just piss off and let me eat my dinner," I wanted to say, but I didn't, of course. I just smiled sweetly and said no thank you and after a while she withdrew. But she stood with a pitcher of iced water and watched me closely the whole meal. Every time I took a sip of water, she would come forward and top up my glass. Once when I reached for the pepper, she misread my intentions and started forward with the water pitcher, but then had to retreat. After that, whenever my hands left the cutlery for any reason, I would semi-mime an explanation to her of what I was about to do—"I'm just going to butter my roll now"—so that she wouldn't rush over to give me more water. And all the while the people at the next table watched me eat and smiled encouragingly. I couldn't wait to get out of there.

When at last I finished the waitress came over and offered me dessert. "How about a piece of pie? We've got blueberry, blackberry, raspberry, boysenberry, huckleberry, whortleberry, cherry berry, hairy berry, chuckberry and berry-berry."

"Gosh, no thanks, I'm too full," I said placing my hands on my stomach. I looked as if I had stuffed a pillow under my shirt.

"Well, how about some ice cream? We've got chocolate chip, chocolate fudge, chocolate ripple, chocolate-vanilla fudge, chocolate nut fudge, chocolate marshmallow swirl, chocolate mint with fudge chips, and fudge nut with or without chocolate chips."

"Have you got just plain chocolate?"

"No, I'm afraid there's not much call for that."

"I don't think I'll have anything then."

"Well, how about a piece of cake? We've got—"

"Really, no thank you."

"A cup of coffee?"

"No thank you."

"You sure now?"

"Yes, thank you."

"Well, I'll just get you a little more water then," and she was off for the water jug before I could get her to give me my bill. The people at the next table watched this with interest and smiled a smile that said, "We are completely off our heads. How are you?"

Afterwards, I had a walk around the town—that is to say, I walked up one side of the street and down the other. For the size of the place it was a nice town. It had two bookstores, a picture gallery, a gift shop, a movie house. People on the sidewalk smiled at me as I passed. This was beginning to worry me. Nobody, even in America, is *that* friendly. What did they want from me? Up at the far end of the street there was a BP service station, the first one I had seen in America. Feeling vaguely homesick for Blighty, I walked up to have a look at it and was disappointed to see that there wasn't anything particularly British about it. The guy behind the counter wasn't even wearing a turban. When he saw me looking in the window he smiled at me with that same strange, unsettling smile. Suddenly I realized what it was—it was the look of someone from outer space, that odd, curiously malevolent B-movie smile of a race of interplanetary creatures who have taken over a small town in the middle of nowhere as their first step towards becoming . . . *Earth Masters.* I know this sounds improbable, but crazier things have happened—look who was in the White House, for Christ's sake. As I strolled back to the motel, I gave everyone I passed that same eerie smile, thinking I ought to keep on their good side, just in case. "And you never know," I remarked to myself in a low voice, "if they do take over the planet, there might be some openings for a guy of your talents."

In the morning I arose very early to a day that promised splendor. I peered out of my motel window. A pink dawn was spilled across the sky. I dressed quickly and hit the road before Littleton had even begun to stir. A few miles out of town I crossed the state line. Vermont presented an altogether greener, tidier prospect than New Hampshire. The hills were fat and soft, like a sleeping animal. The scattered farms looked more prosperous and the meadows climbed high up the rolling hillsides, giving the valleys an alpine air. The sun was soon high and warm. On a ridge overlooking an expanse of hazy foothills, I passed a sign that said PEACHAM, SETTLED 1776 and beyond that stood a village. I parked beside a red general store and got out to have a look around. There was no one about. Presumably the people of Littleton had come in the night and taken them off to the planet Zog.

I walked past the Peacham Inn—white clapboard, green shutters, no sign of life—and wandered up a hill, past a white Congregational church and pleasant, dozing houses. At the crest of the hill stood a broad green, with an obelisk and flagpole, and beside it an old cemetery. A zephyr wind teased the flag. Down the hill, across a broad valley, a series of pale green and brown hills rolled away to the horizon, like the swells of a sea. Below me the church bell tolled the hour, but otherwise there was not a sound. This was as perfect a spot as I had ever seen. I had a look at the obelisk. COMMEMORATING PEACHAM SOLDIERS 1869, it said, and had names carved in it, good New England names like Elijah W. Sargent, Lowell Sterns, Horace Rowe. There were forty-five names in all, too many surely for a mere hamlet in the hills. But then the cemetery beside the green also looked far too large for the size of town. It covered the hillside and the grandeur of many of the monuments suggested that this had once been a place of wealth.

I went through the gate and had a look around. My eye was caught by one particularly handsome stone, an octagonal marble column surmounted by a granite sphere. The column logged the copious deaths of Hurds and their near relatives from Capt. Nathan Hurd in 1818 to Frances H. Bement in 1889. A small panel on the back said:

> Nathan H. died July 24 1852 AE. 4 Y'S 1 M'O.
> Joshua F. died July 31 1852 AE. 1 YR 11 M'S.
> Children of J. & C. Pitkin.

What could it have been, I wondered, that carried off these two little brothers just a week apart? A fever? It seemed unlikely in July. An accident in which one died and the other lingered? Two unrelated events? I pictured the parents crouched at Joshua F.'s bedside, watching his life ebb, praying to God not to take him as well, and having their hopes crushed. Isn't life shitty? Everywhere I looked there was disappointment and heartbreak recorded in the stones: JOSEPH, SON OF EPHRAIM AND SARAH CARTER, DIED MARCH 18 1846, AGED 18 YRS, ALMA FOSTER, DAUT. OF ZADOCK AND HANNAH RICHARDSON, D. MAY 22, 1847, AE. 17 YRS. So many were so young. I became infected with an inexpressible melancholy as I wandered alone among these hundreds of stilled souls, the emptied lives, the row upon row of ended dreams. Such a sad place! I stood there in the mild October sunshine, feeling so sorry for all these luckless people and their lost lives, reflecting bleakly on mortality and on my own dear, cherished family so far away in England, and I thought, "Well, fuck this," and walked back down the hill to the car.

I drove west across Vermont, into the Green Mountains. The mountains were dark and round and the valleys looked rich. Here the light seemed softer, sleepier, more autumnal. There was color everywhere—trees the color of mustard and rust, meadows of gold and green, colossal white barns, blue lakes. Here and there along the highways roadside produce stands brimmed with pumpkins and squash and other autumn fruits. It was like a day trip to heaven. I wandered around on back roads. There was a surprising lot of small houses, some little better than shacks. I supposed there couldn't be much work in a place like Vermont. The state has hardly any towns or industry. The biggest city, Burlington, has a population of just 37,000. Outside Groton I stopped at a roadside cafe for coffee and listened along with the other three customers to a fat young woman with a pair of ill-kempt children moaning in a loud voice about her financial problems to the woman behind the counter. "I still only get four dollars an hour," she was saying. "Harvey, he's been at Fibberts for three years and he's only just got his first raise. You know what he gets now? Four dollars and sixty-five cents an hour. Isn't that pathetic? I told him, I said, 'Harvey, they're just walkin' all over you.' But he won't do nothin' about it." She broke off here to rearrange the features on one of her children's faces with the back of her hand. "HOW MANY TIMES HAVE I TOLD YOU NOT TO INNARUP ME WHEN I'M *TALKING?*" she inquired rhetorically of the little fellow, and then in a calmer voice turned back to the cafe lady and launched into a candid list of Harvey's other shortcomings, which were manifold.

Only the day before in Maine I had seen a sign in a McDonald's offering a starting wage of five dollars an hour. Harvey must have been immensely moronic and unskilled—doubtless both—not to be able to keep pace with a sixteen-year-old burger jockey at McDonald's. Poor guy! And on top of that here he was married to a woman who was slovenly and indiscreet, and had a butt like a barn door. I hoped old Harvey had sense enough to appreciate all the incredible natural beauty with which God had blessed his native state because it didn't sound as if He had blessed Harvey very much. Even his kids were ugly as sin. I was half tempted to give one of them a clout myself as I went out the door. There was just something about his nasty little face that made you itch to smack him.

I drove on, thinking what an ironic thing it was that the really beautiful places in America—the Smoky Mountains, Appalachia, and now Vermont—were always inhabited by the poorest, most undereducated people. And then I hit Stowe and realized that when it comes to making shrewd generalizations, I am a cretin. Stowe was anything but poor. It was a rich little town, full of chichi boutiques and expensive ski lodges. In fact, for most of the rest of the day, as I wandered around and through the Green Mountain ski resorts, I saw almost nothing but wealth and beauty—rich people, rich houses, rich cars, rich resorts, beautiful scenery. I drove around quite struck by it all, wandered over to Lake Champlain—also immensely beautiful—and idled down the western side of the state, just over the border from New York State.

Below Lake Champlain the landscape became more open, more rolling, as if the hills had been flattened out from the edges, like someone pulling a crease out of a bedspread. Some of the towns and villages were staggeringly pretty. Dorset, for instance, was an exquisite little place, standing around an oval green, full of beautiful white clapboard houses, with a summer playhouse and an old church and an enormous inn. And yet. And yet there was something about these places. They were too perfect, too rich, too yuppified. At Dorset there was a picture shop called the Dorset Framery. At Bennington, just down the road, I passed a place called the Publyk House Restaurant. Every inn and lodge had a quaint and picturesque name—the Black Locust Inn, the Hob Knob, the Blueberry Inn, the Old Cutter Inn—and a hanging wooden sign out front. There was always this air of quaint artifice pushing in on everything. After a while I began to find it oddly oppressive. I longed to see a bit of neon and a restaurant with a good old family name—Ernie's Chop House, Zweiker's New York Grille—with a couple of blinking beer signs in the front window. A bowling alley or drive-in movie theater would have been most welcome. It would have made it all seem real. But this looked as if it had been designed in Manhattan and brought in by truck.

One village I went through had about four stores and one of them was a Ralph Lauren Polo Shop. I couldn't think of anything worse than living in a place where you could buy a $200 sweater but not a can of baked beans. Actually, I could think of a lot of worse things—cancer of the brain, watching every episode of a TV miniseries starring Joan Collins, having to eat at a Burger Chef more than twice in one year, reaching for a glass of water in the middle of the night and finding that you've just taken a drink from your grandmother's denture cup, and so on. But I think you get my point.

17

══════════════ I SPENT THE night in Cobleskill, New York, on the northern fringes of the Catskills, and in the morning drove to Cooperstown, a small resort on Lake Otsego. Cooperstown was the home of James Fenimore Cooper, from whose family the town takes its name. It was a handsome town, as handsome as any I had seen in New England, and more replete with autumn color, with a main street of square-topped brick buildings, old banks, a movie theater, family stores. The Cooperstown Diner, where I went for breakfast, was busy, friendly and cheap—all that a diner should be. Afterwards I went for a stroll around the residential streets, shuffling hands-in-pockets through the dry leaves, and down to the lakeside. Every house in town was old and pretty; many of the larger ones had been converted into inns and expensive B&Bs. The morning sunlight filtered through the trees and threw dappled shadows across the lawns and sidewalks. This was as nice a little town as I had seen on the trip; it was almost Amalgam.

The only shortcoming with Cooperstown is that it is full of tourists, drawn to the town by its most famous institution, the Baseball Hall of Fame, which stands by a shady park at the far end of Main Street. I went there now, paid $8.50 admission and walked into its cathedral-like calm. For those of us who are baseball fans and agnostics, the Hall of Fame is as close to a religious experience as we may ever get. I walked serenely through its quiet and softly lit halls, looking at the sacred vestments and venerated relics from America's national pastime. Here, beautifully preserved in a glass case, was "the shirt worn by Warren Spahn when registering win No. 305, which tied him with Eddie Plank for most by a left-hander." Across the aisle was "the glove used by Sal Maglie in September 25, 1958, no-hitter vs. Phillies." At each case people gazed reverently or spoke in whispers.

One room contained a gallery of paintings commemorating great moments in baseball history, including one depicting the first professional night game under artificial lighting, played in Des Moines, Iowa, on May 2, 1930. This was exciting news to me. I had no idea that Des Moines had played a pivotal role in the history of both baseball and luminescence. I looked closely to see if the artist had depicted my father in the press box, but then I realized that my father was only fifteen years old in 1930 and still in Winfield. This seemed kind of a pity.

In an upstairs room I suppressed a whoop of joy at the discovery of whole cases full of the baseball cards that my brother and I had so scrupulously collected and cataloged, and which my parents, in an early flirtation with senility, had taken to the dump during an attic spring cleaning in 1981. We had the complete set for 1959 in mint condition; it is now worth something like $1,500. We had Mickey Mantle and Yogi Berra as rookies, Ted Williams from the last year he hit .400, the complete New York Yankees teams for every year between 1956 and 1962. The whole collection must have been worth something like $8,000—enough, at any rate, to have sent Mom and Dad for a short course of treatment at a dementia clinic. But never mind! We all make mistakes. It's only because everyone throws these things out that they grow so valuable for the lucky few whose parents don't spend their retirements getting rid of all the stuff they spent their working lives accumulating. Anyway it was a pleasure to see all the old cards again. It was like visiting an old friend in the hospital.

The Hall of Fame is surprisingly large, much larger than it looks from the road, and extremely well presented. I wandered through it in a state of complete contentment, reading every label, lingering at every display, reliving my youth, cocooned in a happy nostalgia, and when I stepped back out onto Main Street and glanced at my watch I was astonished to discover that three hours had elapsed.

Next door to the Hall of Fame was a shop selling the most wonderful baseball souvenirs. In my day all we could get were pennants and baseball cards and crummy little pens in the shape of baseball bats that stopped working about the second time you tried to sign your name with them. But now little boys could get everything with their team's logo on it—lamps, towels, clocks, throw rugs, mugs, bedspreads and even Christmas tree ornaments, plus of course pennants, baseball cards and pens that stop working about the second time you use them. I don't think I have ever felt such a pang of longing to be a child again. Apart from anything else, it would mean I'd get my baseball cards back and I could put them somewhere safe where my parents couldn't get at them; then when I got to my age I could buy a Porsche.

I was so taken with all the souvenirs that I began to fill my arms with stuff, but then I noticed that the store was full of Do Not Touch signs and on the counter by the cash register had been taped a notice that said, Do Not Lean on Glass—If You Break, Cost to You is $50. What a jerky thing to say on a sign. How could you expect kids to come into a place full of wonderful things like this and not touch them? This so elevated my hackles that I deposited my intended purchases on the counter and told the girl I didn't want them after all. This was perhaps just as well because I'm not altogether sure that my wife would have wanted St. Louis Cardinals pillowcases.

My ticket to the Hall of Fame included admission to a place on the edge of town called the Farmers Museum, where a couple of dozen old buildings—a schoolhouse, a tavern, a church and the like—have been preserved on a big site. It was about as exciting as it sounds, but having bought the ticket I felt obliged to go and have a look at it. If nothing else, the walk through the afternoon sunshine was pleasant. But I was relieved to get back in the car and hit the road again. It was after four by the time I left town. I drove on across New York State for several hours, through the Susquehanna Valley, which was very beautiful, especially at this time of day and year in the soft light of an autumn afternoon: watermelon-shaped hills, golden trees, slumbering towns. To make up for my long day in Cooperstown, I drove later than usual, and it was after nine by the time I stopped at a motel on the outskirts of Elmira.

I went straight out for dinner, but almost every place I approached was closed, and I ended up eating in a restaurant attached to a bowling alley—in clear violation of Bryson's second rule of dining in a strange town. Generally, I don't believe in doing things on principle—it's kind of a principle of mine—but I do have six rules of public dining to which I try to adhere. They are:

1. Never eat in a restaurant that displays photographs of the food it serves. (But if you do, never believe the photographs.)
2. Never eat in a restaurant attached to a bowling alley.
3. Never eat in a restaurant with flocked wallpaper.
4. Never eat in a restaurant where you can hear what they are saying in the kitchen.
5. Never eat in a restaurant that has live entertainers with any of the following words in their titles: Hank, Rhythm, Swinger, Trio, Combo, Hawaiian, Polka.
6. Never eat in a restaurant that has bloodstains on the walls.

In any event, the bowling alley restaurant proved quite acceptable. Through the wall I could hear the muffled rumblings of falling bowling pins and the sounds of Elmira's hairdressers and grease monkeys having a happy night out. I was the only customer in the restaurant. In fact, I was quite clearly the only thing standing between the waitresses and their going home. As I waited for my food, they cleared away the other tables, removing the ashtrays, sugar bowls and tablecloths, so that after a while I found myself dining alone in a large room, with a white table-cloth and flickering candle in a little red bowl, amid a sea of barren Formica tabletops.

The waitresses stood against the wall and watched me chew my food. After a while they started whispering and tittering, still watching me as they did so, which frankly I found a trifle unsettling. I may only have imagined it, but I also had the distinct impression that someone was little by little turning a dimmer switch so that the light in the room was gradually disappearing. By the end of my meal I was finding my food more or less by touch and occasionally by lowering my head to the plate and sniffing. Before I was quite finished, when I just paused for a moment to grope for my glass of iced water somewhere in the gloom beyond the flickering candle, my waitress whipped the plate away and put down my bill.

"You want anything else?" she said in a tone that suggested I had better not. "No thank you," I answered politely. I wiped my mouth with the tablecloth, having lost my napkin in the gloom, and added a seventh rule to my list: never go into a restaurant ten minutes before closing time. Still, I never really mind bad service in a restaurant. It makes me feel better about not leaving a tip.

In the morning I awoke early and experienced that sinking sensation that overcomes you when you first open your eyes and realize that instead of a normal day ahead of you, with its scatterings of simple gratifications, you are going to have a day without even the tiniest of pleasures; you are going to drive across Ohio.

I sighed and arose. I shuffled around the room in my old-man posture, gathered up my things, washed, dressed and without enthusiasm hit the highway. I drove west through the Alleghenies and then into a small, odd corner of Pennsylvania. For 200 miles the border between New York and Pennsylvania is a straight line, but at Pennsylvania's northwestern corner, where I was now, it abruptly juts north, as if the draftsman's arm had been jogged. The reason for this small cartographical irregularity was to let Pennsylvania have its own outlet onto Lake Erie so that its residents wouldn't have to cross New York State, and it remains today a 200-year-old reminder of how the early states weren't at all confident that the Union was going to work. That it did was far more of an achievement than is often appreciated nowadays.

Just inside the Pennsylvania state line, the highway merged with Interstate 90. This is the main northern route across America, stretching 3,016 miles from Boston to Seattle, and there were lots of long-distance travelers on it. You can always tell long-distance travelers because they look as if they haven't been out of the car for weeks. You only glimpse them when they pass, but you can see that they have already started to set up home inside—there are pieces of washing hanging in the back, remnants of takeout meals on the windowsill and books, magazines and pillows scattered around. There's always a fat woman asleep in the front passenger seat, her mouth hugely agape, and a quantity of children going crazy in the back. You and the father exchange dull but not unsympathetic looks as the two cars slide past. You glance at each other's license plates and feel envy or sympathy in proportion to your comparative distances from home. One car I saw had Alaska plates on it. This was unbelievable. I had never seen Alaska license plates before. The man must have driven over 4,500 miles, the equivalent of going from London to Zambia. He was the most forlorn-looking character I had ever seen. There was no sign of a wife and children. I expect by now he had killed them and put their bodies in the trunk.

A drizzly rain hung in the air. I drove along in that state of semimindlessness that settles over you on interstate highways. After a while Lake Erie appeared on the right. Like all the Great Lakes, it is enormous, more an inland sea than a lake, stretching 200 miles from west to east and about 40 miles across. Twenty-five years ago Lake Erie was declared dead. Driving along its southern shore, gazing out at its flat gray immensity, I thought this appeared to be a remarkable achievement. It hardly seemed possible that something as small as man could kill something as large as a Great Lake. But just in the space of a century or so we managed it. Thanks to lax factory laws and the triumph of greed over nature in places like Cleveland, Buffalo, Toledo, Sandusky and other bustling centers of soot and grit, Lake Erie was transformed in just three generations from a bowl of blue water into a large toilet. Cleveland was the worst offender. Cleveland was so vile that its river, a slow-moving sludge of chemicals and half-digested solids called the Cuyahoga, once actually caught fire and burned out of control for four days. This also was a remarkable achievement, I feel. Things are said to be better now. According to a story in the *Cleveland Free Press*, which I read during a stop for coffee near Ashtabula, an official panel with the ponderous title of the International Joint Commission's Great Lakes Water Quality Board had just released a survey of chemical substances in the lake, and it had found only 362 types of chemicals in the lake compared with more than a thousand the last time they had counted. That still seemed an awful lot to me and I was surprised to see a pair of fishermen standing on the shore, hunched down in the drizzle, hurling lines out onto the greenish murk with long poles. Maybe they were fishing for chemicals.

Through dull rain I drove through the outer suburbs of Cleveland, past signs for places that were all called Something Heights: Richmond Heights, Maple Heights, Garfield Heights, Shaker Heights, University Heights, Warrensville Heights, Parma Heights. Curiously, the one outstanding characteristic of the surrounding landscape was its singular lack of eminences. Clearly what Cleveland was prepared to consider the heights was what others would regard as distinctly middling. Somehow this did not altogether surprise me. After a time Interstate 90 became the Cleveland Memorial Shoreway, and followed the sweep of the bay. The windshield wipers of the Chevette flicked hypnotically and other cars threw up spray as they swished past. Outside my window the lake sprawled dark and vast until it was consumed by a distant mist. Ahead of me the tall buildings of downtown Cleveland appeared and slid towards me, like shopping on a supermarket conveyor belt.

Cleveland has always had a reputation for being a dirty, ugly, boring city, though now they say it is much better. By "they" I mean reporters from serious publications like the *Wall Street Journal, Fortune* and the *New York Times* Sunday magazine, who visit the city at five-year intervals and produce long stories with titles like "Cleveland Bounces Back" and "Renaissance in Cleveland." No one ever reads these articles, least of all me, so I couldn't say whether the improbable and highly relative assertion that Cleveland is better now than it used to be is wrong or right. What I can say is that the view up the Cuyahoga as I crossed it on the freeway was of a stew of smoking factories that didn't look any too clean or handsome. And I can't say that the rest of the town looked such a knockout either. It may be improved, but all this talk of a renaissance is clearly exaggerated. I somehow doubt that if the Duc d'Urbino were brought back to life and deposited in downtown Cleveland he would say, "Goodness, I am put in mind of fifteenth-century Florence and the many treasures therein."

And then, quite suddenly, I was out of Cleveland and on the James W. Shocknessy Ohio Turnpike in the rolling rural emptiness between Cleveland and Toledo, and highway mindlessness once more seeped in. To relieve the tedium I switched on the radio. In fact, I had been switching it on and off all day, listening for a while but then giving up in despair. Unless you have lived through it, you cannot conceive of the sense of hopelessness that comes with hearing "Hotel California" by the Eagles for the fourteenth time in three hours. You can feel your brain cells disappearing with little popping sounds. But it's the disc jockeys that make it intolerable. Can there anywhere be a breed of people more irritating and imbecilic than disc jockeys? In South America there is a tribe of Indians called the Janamanos, who are so backward they cannot even count to three. Their counting system goes, "One, two . . . oh, gosh, a whole bunch." Obviously disc jockeys have a better dress sense and possess a little more in the way of social skills, but I think we are looking at a similar level of mental acuity.

Over and over I searched the airwaves for something to listen to, but I could find nothing. It wasn't as if I was asking for all that much. All I wanted was a station that didn't play endless songs by bouncy prepubescent girls, didn't employ disc jockeys who said "H-e-y-y-y-y" more than once every six seconds and didn't keep telling me how much Jesus loved me. But no such station existed. Even when I did find something halfway decent, the sound would begin to fade after ten or twelve miles, and the old Beatles song that I was listening to with quiet pleasure would gradually be replaced by a semidemented man talking about the word of God and telling me that I had a friend in the Lord.

Many American radio stations, particularly out in the hinterland, are ridiculously small and cheap. I know this for a fact because when I was a teenager I used to help out at KCBC in Des Moines. KCBC had the contract to broadcast the Iowa Oaks professional baseball games, but it was too cheap to send its sportscaster, a nice young guy named Steve Shannon, on the road with the team. So whenever the Oaks were in Denver or Oklahoma City or wherever, Shannon and I would go out to the KCBC studio—really just a tin hut standing beside a tall transmitter tower in a farmer's field somewhere southeast of Des Moines—and he would broadcast from there as if he were in Omaha. It was bizarre. Every couple of innings someone at the ballpark would call me on the phone and give me a bare summary of the game, which I would scribble into a scorebook and pass to Shannon, and on the basis of this he would give a two-hour broadcast.

It was a remarkable experience to sit there in a windowless hut on a steaming August night listening to the crickets outside and watching a man talking into a microphone and saying things like, "Well, it's a cool evening here in Omaha, with a light breeze blowing in off the Missouri River. There's a special guest in the crowd tonight, Governor Warren T. Legless, who I can see sitting with his pretty young wife, Bobbi Rae, in a box seat just below us here in the press box." Shannon was a genius at this sort of thing. I remember one time the phone call from the ballpark didn't come through—the guy at the other end had gotten locked in a toilet or something—and Shannon didn't have anything to tell the listeners. So he delayed the game with a sudden downpour, having only a moment before said that it was a beautiful cloudless evening, and played music while he called the ballpark and begged somebody there to let him know what was going on.

Funnily enough, I later read that the exact same thing had happened to Ronald Reagan when he was a young sportscaster in Des Moines. In Reagan's case he had the batter hit foul balls one after the other for over half an hour while pretending there was nothing implausible in this, which when you think about it is more or less how he ran the country as president.

Late in the afternoon, I happened onto a news broadcast by some station in Crudbucket, Ohio, or some such place. American radio news broadcasts usually last about thirty seconds. It went like this: "A young Crudbucket couple, Dwayne and Wanda Dreary, and their seven children, Ronnie, Lonnie, Connie, Donnie, Bonnie, Johnny and Tammy-Wynette, were killed in a fire after a light airplane crashed into their house and burst into flames. Fire Chief Walter Water said he could not at this stage rule out arson. On Wall Street, shares had their biggest one-day fall in history, losing 508 points. And the weather outlook for greater Crudbucket: clear skies with a 2 percent chance of precipitation. You're listening to radio station K-R-U-D where you get more rock and less talk." There then followed "Hotel California" by the Eagles.

I stared at the radio, wondering whether I had heard that second item right. The biggest one-day fall in shares in history? The collapse of the American economy? I twirled the dial and found another news broadcast: ". . . but Senator Poontang denied that the use of the four Cadillacs and the trips to Hawaii were in any way connected with the $120 million contract to build the new airport. On Wall Street, shares suffered their biggest one-day fall in history, losing 508 points in just under three hours. And the weather outlook here in Crudbucket is for cloudy skies and a 98 percent chance of precipitation. We'll have more music from the Eagles after this word."

The American economy was coming apart in shreds and all I could get were songs by the Eagles. I twirled and twirled the dial, thinking that surely somebody somewhere must be giving the dawn of a new Great Depression more than a passing mention—

and someone was, thank goodness. It was CBC, the Canadian network, with an excellent and thoughtful program called "As It Happens," which was entirely devoted that evening to the crash of Wall Street. I will leave you, reader, to consider the irony in an American citizen, traveling across his own country, having to tune in to a foreign radio network to find out the details of one of the biggest domestic news stories of the year. To be scrupulously fair, I was later told that the public-radio network in America—possibly the most grossly underfunded broadcast organization in the developed world—also devoted a long report to the crash. I expect it was given by a man sitting in a tin hut in a field somewhere, reading scribbled notes off a sheet of paper.

At Toledo, I joined Interstate 75, and drove north into Michigan, heading for Dearborn, a suburb of Detroit, where I intended spending the night. Almost immediately I found myself in a wilderness of warehouses and railroad tracks and enormous parking lots leading to distant car factories. The parking lots were so vast and full of cars that I half wondered if the factories were there just to produce sufficient cars to keep the parking lots full, thus eliminating any need for consumers. Interlacing all this were towering electricity pylons. If you have ever wondered what becomes of all those pylons you see marching off to the horizon in every country in the world, like an army of invading aliens, the answer is that they all join up in a field just north of Toledo, where they discharge their loads into a vast estate of electrical transformers, diodes and other contraptions that looks for all the world like the inside of a television set, only on a rather grander scale, of course. The ground fairly thrummed as I drove past and I fancied I felt a crackle of blue static sweep through the car, briefly enlivening the hair on the back of my neck and leaving a strangely satisfying sensation in my armpits. I was half inclined to turn around at the next intersection and go back for another dose. But it was late and I pressed on. For some minutes I thought I smelled smoldering flesh and kept touching my head tentatively. But this may only have been a consequence of having spent too many lonely hours in a car.

At Monroe, a town halfway between Toledo and Detroit, a big sign beside the highway said, WELCOME TO MONROE—HOME OF GENERAL CUSTER. A mile or so later there was another sign, even larger, saying, MONROE, MICHIGAN—HOME OF LA-Z-BOY FURNITURE. Goodness, I thought, will the excitement never stop? But it did, and the rest of the journey was completed without drama.

18

══════════ **I SPENT THE NIGHT** in Dearborn for two reasons. First, it would mean not having to spend the night in Detroit, the city with the highest murder rate in the country. In 1987, there were 635 homicides in Detroit, a rate of 58.2 per 100,000 people, or eight times the national average. Just among children, there were 365 shootings in which both the victim and gunman were under sixteen (of whom 40 died). We are talking about a tough city—and yet it is still a rich one. What it will become like as the American car industry collapses in upon itself doesn't bear thinking about. People will have to start carrying bazookas for protection.

My second and more compelling reason for going to Dearborn was to see the Henry Ford Museum, a place my father had taken us when I was small and which I remembered fondly. After breakfast in the morning, I went straight there. Henry Ford spent his later years buying up important Americana by the truckload and crating it to his museum, beside the big Ford Motor Company Rouge Assembly Plant. The parking lot outside the museum was enormous—on a scale to rival the factory parking lots I had passed the day before—but at this time of year there were few cars in it. Most of them were Japanese.

I went inside and discovered without surprise that the entrance charge was steep: $15 for adults and $7.50 for children. Americans are clearly prepared to fork out large sums for their pleasures. Grudgingly I paid the admission charge and went in. But almost from the moment I passed through the portals I was enthralled. For one thing, the scale of it is almost breathtaking. You find yourself in a great hangar of a building covering twelve acres of ground and filled with the most indescribable assortment of stuff—machinery, railway trains, refrigerators, Abraham Lincoln's rocking chair, the limousine in which John F. Kennedy was killed (nope, no bits of brains on the floor), George Washington's campaign chest, General Tom Thumb's ornate miniature billiard table, a bottle containing Thomas Edison's last breath. I found this last item particularly captivating. Apart from being ridiculously morbid and sentimental, how did they know which breath was going to be Edison's last one? I pictured Henry Ford standing at the deathbed shoving a bottle in his face over and over and saying, "Is that it?"

This was the way the Smithsonian once was and still should be—a cross between an attic and a junk shop. It was as if some scavenging genius had sifted through all the nation's collective memories and brought to this one place everything from American life that was splendid and fine and deserving fondness. It was possible here to find every single item from my youth—old comic books, lunchpails, bubblegum cards, Dick and Jane reading books, a Hotpoint stove just like the one my mom used to have, a soda pop dispenser like the one that used to stand in front of the pool hall in Winfield.

There was even a collection of milk bottles exactly like those that Mr. Morrisey, the deaf milkman, used to bring to our house every morning. Mr. Morrisey was the noisiest milkman in America. He was about sixty years old and wore a large hearing aid. He always traveled with his faithful dog, Skipper. They would arrive like clockwork just before dawn. Milk had to be delivered early, you see, because in the Midwest it spoiled quickly once the sun came up. You always knew when it was 5:30 because Mr. Morrisey would arrive, whistling for all he was worth, waking all the dogs for blocks around, which would get Skipper very excited and set him to barking. Being deaf, Mr. Morrisey tended not to notice his own voice and you could hear him clinking around on your back porch with his rack of milk bottles and saying to Skipper, "WELL, I WONDER WHAT THE BRYSONS WANT TODAY! LET'S SEE . . . FOUR QUARTS OF SKIMMED AND SOME COTTAGE CHEESE. WELL, SKIPPER, WOULD YOU FUCKING BELIEVE IT, I LEFT THE COTTAGE CHEESE ON THE GODDAMN TRUCK!" And then you would look out the window to see Skipper urinating on your bicycle and lights coming on in houses all over the neighborhood. Nobody wanted to get Mr. Morrisey fired, on account of his unfortunate disability, but when Flynn Dairies discontinued home deliveries in about 1960 on economic grounds ours was one of the few neighborhoods in the city from which there was no outcry.

I walked through the museum in a state of sudden, deep admiration for Henry Ford and his acquisitive instincts. He may have been a bully and an anti-Semite, but he sure could build a nifty museum. I could happily have spent hours picking around among the memorabilia. But the hangar is only a fractional part of it. Outside there is a whole village—a little town—containing eighty homes of famous Americans. These are the actual homes, not replicas. Ford crisscrossed the country acquiring the residences and workshops of the people he most admired—Thomas Edison, Harvey Firestone, Luther Burbank, the Wright brothers and of course himself. All these he crated up and shipped back to Dearborn where he used them to build this 250-acre fantasyland—the quintessential American small town, a picturesque and timeless community where every structure houses a man of genius (almost invariably a white, Christian man of genius from the Middle West). Here in this perfect place, with its broad greens and pleasing shops and churches, the lucky resident could call on Orville and Wilbur Wright for a bicycle inner tube, go to the Firestone farm for milk and eggs (but not for rubber yet—Harvey's still working on it!), borrow a book from Noah Webster and call on Abraham Lincoln for legal advice, always assuming he's not too busy with patent applications for Charles Steinmetz or emancipating George Washington Carver, who lives in a tiny cabin just across the street.

It is really quite entrancing. For a start, places like Edison's workshop and the boardinghouse where his employees lodged have been scrupulously preserved. You can really see how these people worked and lived. And there is a certain undeniable convenience in having the houses all brought together. Who in a million years would go to Columbiana, Ohio, to see the Harvey Firestone birthplace, or to Dayton to see where the Wright brothers lived? Not me, brother. Above all, bringing these places together makes you realize just how incredibly inventive America has been in its time, what a genius it has had for practical commercial innovation, often leading to unspeakable wealth, and how many of the comforts and pleasures of modern life have their roots in the small towns of the American Middle West. It made me feel proud.

I drove north and west across Michigan, lost in a warm afterglow of pleasure from the museum. I was past Lansing and Grand Rapids and entering the Manistee National Forest, 100 miles away, almost before I knew it. Michigan is shaped like an oven mitt and is often about as exciting. The Manistee forest was dense and dull—endless groves of uniform pine trees—and the highway through it was straight and flat. Occasionally I would see a cabin or little lake in the woods, both just glimpsable through the trees, but mostly there was nothing of note. Towns were rare and mostly squalid—scattered dwellings and ugly prefab buildings where they made and sold ugly prefab cabins, so that people could buy their own little bit of ugliness and take it out into the woods.

After Baldwin, the road became wider and emptier and the commercialism grew sparser. At Manistee, the highway ran down to Lake Michigan, and then followed the shoreline off and on for miles, going through rather more pleasant little communities of mostly boarded-up summer homes—Pierport, Arcadia, Elberta ("A Peach of A Place"), Frankfort. At Empire I stopped to look at the lake. The weather was surprisingly cold. A blustery wind blew in from Wisconsin, seventy miles away across the steely gray water, raising whitecaps and wavelets. I tried to go for a stroll, but I was out for only about five minutes before the wind blew me back to the car.

I went on to Traverse City, where the weather was milder, perhaps because it was more sheltered. Traverse City looked to be a wonderful old town that seemed not to have changed since about 1948. It still had a Woolworth's, a J. C. Penney, an old-fashioned movie theater called the State and a timeless café, the Sydney, with black booths and a long soda fountain. You just don't see places like that anymore. I had coffee and felt very pleased to be there. Afterwards I drove north on a road running up one side of Grand Traverse Bay and down the other, so that you could always see where you were going or where you had been, sometimes veering inland past farms and cherry orchards for a couple of miles and then sweeping back down to the water's edge. As the afternoon progressed, the wind settled and the sun came out, tentatively at first, like a shy guest, and then stayed on, giving the lake bright patches of silver and blue. Far out over the water, perhaps twenty miles away, dark clouds dumped rain on the lake. It fell in a pale gray curtain. And high above a faint rainbow reached across the sky. It was inexpressibly beautiful. I drove transfixed.

In the early evening I reached Mackinaw City, on the tip of the oven mitt, the point where the shorelines of southern and northern Michigan pinch together to form the Straits of Mackinac, which separate Lake Michigan from Lake Huron. A suspension bridge, five miles long, spans the gap. Mackinaw City—they are fairly casual about how they spell the word up this way—was a scattered and unsightly little town, full of gift shops, motels, ice cream parlors, pizzerias, parking lots and firms operating ferries to Mackinac Island. Almost every place of business, including the motels, was boarded up for the winter. The Holiday Motel, on the shore of Lake Huron, seemed to be open so I went inside and rang the desk bell. The young guy who came out looked surprised to have a customer. "We were just about to close up for the season," he said. "In fact, everybody's gone out to dinner to celebrate. But we've got rooms if you want one."

"How much?" I asked.

He seemed to snatch a figure from the air. "Twenty dollars?" he said.

"Sounds good to me," I said and signed in. The room was small but nice and it had heating, which was a good thing. I went out and had a walk around, to look for something to eat. It was only a little after seven, but it was dark already and the chill air felt more like December than October. I could see my breath. It was odd to be in a place so full of buildings and yet so dead. Even the McDonald's was closed, with a sign in the window telling me to have a good winter.

I walked down to the Shepler's Ferry terminal—really just a big parking lot with a shed—to see what time the ferry to Mackinac Island would depart in the morning. That was my reason for being here. There was one at eleven. I stood beside the pier, facing into the wind, and gazed for a long time out across Lake Huron. Mackinac Island was berthed a couple of miles out in the lake like a glittering cruise ship. Nearby, even larger but with no lights, was Bois Blanc Island, dark and round. Off to the left, Mackinac Bridge, lit up like a Christmas decoration, spanned the strait. Everywhere the lights shimmered on the water. It was odd that such a nothing little town could have such a wonderful view.

I ate dinner in a practically empty restaurant and then had some beers in a practically empty bar. Both places had turned on the heating. It felt good, cozy. Outside the wind beat against the plate-glass windows, making a *woppa-woppa* sound. I liked the quiet bar. Most bars in America are dark and full of moody characters—people drinking alone and staring straight ahead. There's none of that agreeable coffeehouse atmosphere that you find in bars in Europe. American bars are, by and large, just dark places to get drunk in. I don't like them much, but this one was OK. It was snug and quiet and well lit, so I could sit and read. Before too long I was fairly well lit myself. This was also OK.

In the morning I awoke early and gave the steamy window a wipe with my hand to see what kind of day it was. The answer was: not a good one. The world was full of sleety snow, dancing about in the wind like a plague of white insects. I switched on the TV and crept back into the warm bed. The local PBS station came on. PBS is the Public Broadcasting System, what we used to call educational TV. It is supposed to show quality stuff, though because it is always strapped for funds this consists mostly of BBC melodramas starring Susan Hampshire and domestically produced programs that cost about twelve dollars to make—cookery programs, religious discussions, local high-school wrestling matches. It's pretty well unwatchable most of the time, and it's getting worse. In fact, the station I was watching was holding a telethon to raise funds for itself. Two middle-aged men in casual clothes were sitting in swivel chairs, with a pair of phones on a table between them, asking for money. They were trying to look perky and cheerful, but there was a kind of desperation in their eyes.

"Wouldn't it be tragic for your children if they didn't have 'Sesame Street' anymore?" one of them was saying to the camera. "So come on, moms and dads, give us a call and make a pledge now." But nobody was calling. So the two talked to each other about all the wonderful programs on PBS. They had clearly been having this conversation for some time. After a while one of them had a phone call. "I've had my first caller," he said as he put the phone down. "It was from Melanie Bitowski of Traverse City and it's her fourth birthday today. So happy birthday, honey. But next time you or any of you other kids call in, why don't you get your mom or dad to pledge some money, sweetheart?" These guys were clearly begging for their jobs, and the whole of northern Michigan was turning a blind eye to their pleadings.

I showered and dressed and packed up my bag, all the while keeping an eye on the TV to see if anyone made a pledge, and no one ever did. When I switched off, one of them was saying, with just a hint of peevishness, "Now come on, I can't believe that *nobody* out there is watching us. Somebody must be awake out there. Somebody must want to preserve quality public television for themselves and their children." But he was wrong.

I had a large breakfast in the same place I had eaten the night before and then, because there was absolutely nothing else to do, I went and stood on the quayside, waiting for the ferry. The wind had died. The last sleet melted as it hit the ground and then stopped falling altogether. Everywhere there was the *tip-tip-tip* sound of dripping, off the roofs, off branches, off me. It was only ten o'clock and nothing was happening at the quayside—the Chevette, dressed with sleety snow, stood alone and forlorn in the big parking lot—so I went and walked around, down to the site of the original Fort Mackinac and then along residential streets full of treeless lawns and one-story ranch houses. When I returned to the ferry site, about forty minutes later, the Chevette had gained some company and there was a fair crowd of people—twenty or thirty at least—already boarding the boat.

We all sat on rows of seats in one small room. The hydrofoil started up with a noise like a vacuum cleaner, then turned and slid out onto the green bleakness of Lake Huron. The lake was choppy, like a pan of water simmering on a low heat, but the ride was smooth. The people around me were strangely excited. They kept standing up to take pictures and point things out to each other. It occurred to me that many of them had never been on a ferry before, perhaps had never even seen an island, not one big enough to be inhabited anyway. No wonder they were excited. I was excited too, though for a different reason.

I had been to Mackinac Island before. My dad took us there when I was about four and I remembered it fondly. In fact, it was probably my oldest clear memory. I remembered that it had a big white hotel with a long porch and banks of flowers, positively dazzling in the July sunshine, and I could remember a big fort on a hill, and that the island had no cars, but just horse-drawn carriages, and that there was horse manure everywhere, and that I stepped in some, warm and squishy, and that my mother cleaned my shoe with a twig and a Kleenex, gagging delicately, and that as soon as she put the shoe back on my foot, I stepped backwards into some more with my other shoe, and that she didn't get cross. My mother never got cross. She didn't exactly do cartwheels, you understand, but she didn't shout or snap or look as if she were suppressing apoplexy, as I do with my children when they step in something warm and squishy, as they always do. She just looked kind of tired for a moment, and then she grinned at me and said it was a good thing she loved me, which was very true. She's a saint, my mother, especially where horse shit is concerned.

Mackinac Island is small—only about five miles long, a couple of miles wide—but like most islands it seems bigger when you are on it. Since 1901, no cars or motorized vehicles of any type have been allowed on the island, so when you step off the boat onto Main Street you find a lineup of horse-drawn carriages waiting at the curb—a fancy one to take customers to the Grand Hotel, open phaetons to take people on expensive tours of the island, and a kind of sledge to deal with luggage and freight. Mackinac village was just as perfect as I remembered it, a string of white Victorian buildings along a sloping Main Street, snug cottages climbing up the steep hill to old Fort Mackinac, built in 1780 to defend the strait, still standing guard over the town.

I wandered off through the town, picking my way around little piles of horse manure. Without cars, the silence was almost complete. The whole island appeared to be on the brink of a six-month coma. Almost all the stores and restaurants along Main Street were shut for the season. I expect it's awful there in the summer with all the thousands of day-trippers. A brochure that I picked up by the harbor listed sixty gift shops alone and more than thirty restaurants, ice cream parlors, pizzerias and cookie stalls. But now at this time of year it all looked quaint and restful and incredibly pretty.

For a while, Mackinac Island was the biggest trading post in the New World—John Jacob Astor's fur trading company was based here—but its real glory dates from the late nineteenth century when wealthy people from Chicago and Detroit came to escape the city heat and enjoy the pollen-free air. The Grand Hotel, the biggest and oldest resort hotel in America, was built and the country's wealthiest industrialists constructed ornate summer houses on the bluffs overlooking Mackinac village and Lake Huron. I walked up there now. The views across the lake were fantastic, but the houses were simply breathtaking. They are some of the grandest, most elaborate houses ever built of wood, twenty-bedroomed places with every embellishment known to the Victorian mind—cupolas, towers, domes, dormers, gables, turrets, and front porches you could ride a bike around.

Some of the cupolas had cupolas. They are just incredibly splendid and there are scores of them, standing side by side on the bluffs flanking Fort Mackinac. What it must be to be a child and play hide-and-seek in those houses, to have a bedroom in a tower and be able to lie in bed and gaze out on such a lake, and to go bicycling on carless roads to little beaches and hidden coves, and above all to explore the woodlands of beech and birch that cover the back three-quarters of the island.

I wandered into them now, along one of the many paved paths that run through the dark woods, and felt like a seven-year-old on a grand adventure. Every turn in the path brought up some exotic surprise—Skull Cave, where, according to a sign beside it, an English fur trader hid from the Indians in 1763; Fort Holmes, an old British redoubt on the highest point on the island, 325 feet above Lake Huron; and two mossy old cemeteries out in the middle of nowhere, one Catholic and one Protestant. Both seemed impossibly big for such a small island, and they consisted mostly of the same few names going back generations—the Truscotts, Gables, Sawyers. I happily wandered for three hours without seeing a soul or hearing a sound made by man, and only barely sampled the island. I could easily have stayed for days. I returned to the village by way of the Grand Hotel, quite the most splendid and obnoxiously hoity-toity such institution I have ever come across. A rambling white wooden building with the biggest porch in the world (660 feet), it is indubitably swish and expensive. A single room at the time I was there cost $135 a night. A sign in the street leading down to the hotel said, GRAND HOTEL— PROPER DRESS REQUIRED AT THE HOTEL AND HOTEL-OWNED STREET. GENTLEMEN AFTER 6 P.M. MUST BE ATTIRED IN A COAT AND TIE. LADIES MAY NOT BE ATTIRED IN SLACKS. This is possibly the only place in the world where you are told how to dress just to walk down the street. Another sign said a charge would be levied on anyone coming into the hotel just to gawp. Honestly. I suppose they have a lot of trouble with day-trippers. I walked stealthily down the road towards the hotel half expecting to see a sign saying, "ANYONE PASSING BEYOND THIS POINT WEARING PLAID PANTS OR WHITE SHOES WILL BE ARRESTED." But there wasn't anything. I had it in my mind to put my head in the front door, just to see what life is like for really rich people, but there was a liveried doorman standing guard, so I had to beat a retreat.

I caught the afternoon ferry back to the mainland, and drove over the Mackinac Bridge to the chunk of land Michigan people call the Upper Peninsula. Before the bridge was built in 1957, this bit of Michigan was pretty well cut off from its own state, and even now it has an overwhelming sense of remoteness. It is mostly just a bleak and sandy peninsula, 150 miles long, squeezed between three of the Great Lakes, Superior, Huron and Michigan. Once again, I was almost in Canada. Sault Ste. Marie was just to the north. Its great locks connect Lake Huron and Lake Superior and are the busiest in the world, carrying a greater volume of tonnage than the Suez and Panama canals combined, believe it or not.

I was on Route 2, which follows the northern shoreline of Lake Michigan for most of its length. It is impossible to exaggerate the immensity of the Great Lakes. There are five of them, Erie, Huron, Michigan, Superior and Ontario, and they stretch 700 miles from top to bottom, 900 miles from east to west. They cover 94,500 square miles, making them almost precisely the size of the United Kingdom. Together they form the largest expanse of fresh water on earth.

More squally storms were at work far out on the lake, though where I was it was dry. About twenty miles offshore were a group of islands—Beaver Island, High Island, Whiskey Island, Hog Island and several others. High Island was once owned by a religious sect called the House of David, whose members all had beards and specialized, if you can believe it, in playing baseball. In the 1920s and '30s they toured the country taking on local teams wherever they went and I guess they were just about unbeatable. High Island was reputedly a kind of penal colony for members of the sect who committed serious infractions—grounded into too many double plays or something. It was said that people were sent there and never heard from again. Now, like all the other islands in the group except Beaver, it is uninhabited. I felt a strange pang of regret that I couldn't go over and explore them. In fact, the whole of the Great Lakes was exerting a strange hold on me, which I couldn't begin to understand. There was something alluring about the idea of a great inland sea, about the thought that if you had a boat you could spend years just bouncing around from one Great Lake to another, chugging from Chicago to Buffalo, Milwaukee to Montreal, pausing en route to investigate islands, bays and towns with curious names like Deadman's Point, Egg Harbor, Summer Island. A lot of people do just that, I guess—buy a boat and disappear. I can see why.

All over the peninsula I kept encountering roadside food stands with big signs on them saying PASTIES. Most of them were closed and boarded up, but at Menominee, the last town before I crossed into Wisconsin, I passed one that was open and impulsively I turned the car around and went back to it. I had to see if they were real Cornish pasties or something else altogether but with the same name. The guy who ran the place was excited to have a real Englishman in his store. He had been making pasties for thirty years but he had never seen a real Cornish pasty or a real Englishman, come to that. I didn't have the heart to tell him that actually I came from Iowa, the next state over. Nobody ever gets excited at meeting an Iowan. The pasties were the real thing, brought to this isolated corner of Michigan by nineteenth-century Cornishmen who came to work in the local mines. "Everybody eats them up here in the Upper Peninsula," the man told me. "But nobody's ever heard of them anywhere else. You cross the state line into Wisconsin, just over the river, and people don't know what they are. It's kind of strange."

The man handed me the pasty in the paper bag and I went with it out to the car. It did seem to be a genuine Cornish pasty except that it was about the size of a rugby ball. It came on a Styrofoam platter with a plastic fork and some sachets of ketchup. Eagerly I tucked into it. Apart from anything else I was starving.

It was awful. There wasn't anything wrong with it exactly— it was a genuine pasty, accurate in every detail—it was just that after more than a month of eating American junk food it tasted indescribably bland and insipid, like warmed cardboard. "Where's the grease?" I thought. "Where's the melted cheese patty and pan-fried chicken gravy? Where, above all, is the chocolate fudge frosting?" This was just meat and potatoes, just natural unenhanced flavor. "No wonder it's never caught on over here," I grumbled and pushed it back into the bag.

I started the car and drove on into Wisconsin, looking for a motel and a restaurant where I could get some real food—something that would squirt when I bit into it and run down my chin. That, of course, is the way food should be.

19

================= "AT NORTHERN WISCONSIN General Hospital, we'll help you to achieve your birthing goals," said a voice on the radio. Oh, God, I thought. This was yet another new development since I had left America—the advent of hospital advertising. Everywhere you go you now encounter hospital ads. Who are they for? A guy gets hit by a bus, does he say, "Quick, take me to Michigan General. They've got a magnetic resonance imager there"? I don't understand it. But then I don't understand anything to do with American health care.

Just before I left on this trip, I learned that my uncle was in Mercy Hospital in Des Moines. So I looked up the number in the phone book and under Mercy Hospital there were ninety-four telephone numbers listed. The phone numbers started with Admitting and proceeded alphabetically through Biofeedback, Cancer Hotline, Impotency Program, Infant Apnea Hotline, Osteoporosis Program, Public Relations, something called Share Care Ltd., Sleep Referral Services, Smoke Stoppers and on and on. Health care in America is now a monolithic industry and it is completely out of control.

The person I was visiting, my elderly uncle, had just suffered a severe heart attack. As a complication arising from this, he also had pneumonia. As you might imagine, he looked a trifle under the weather. While I was with him, a social worker came in and gently explained to him some of the costs involved in his treatment. My uncle could, for instance, have Medicine A, which would cost five dollars a dose, but which he would have to take four times a day, or he could have Medicine B, which would cost eighteen dollars a dose, but which he would have to take only once a day. That was the social worker's job, to act as a liaison between the doctor, the patient and the insurance company, and to try to see to it that the patient wasn't hit with a lot of bills that the insurance company wouldn't pay. My uncle would, of course, be billed for this service. It seemed so crazy, so unreal, to be watching him sucking air from an oxygen mask, all but dead, and giving weak yes-or-no nods to questions concerning the continuance of his own life based on his ability to pay.

Contrary to popular belief abroad, it is possible, indeed quite easy, to get free treatment in America by going to a county hospital. They aren't very cheery places, in fact they are generally pretty grim, but they are no worse than any National Health Service hospital. There has to be free treatment because there are 40 million people in America without hospital insurance. God help you, however, if you try to sneak into a county hospital for a little free health care if you've got money in the bank. I worked for a year at the county hospital in Des Moines and I can tell you that they have batteries of lawyers and debt collectors whose sole job is to dig into the backgrounds of the people who use their facilities and make sure they really are as destitute as they claim to be.

Despite the manifest insanities of private health care in America, there is no denying that the quality of treatment is the best in the world. My uncle received superb and unstinting care (and, not incidentally, they restored his health). He had a private room with a private bath, a remote control television and video recorder, his own telephone. The whole hospital was carpeted and full of exotic palms and cheerful paintings. In government hospitals in Britain, the only piece of carpet or color TV you find is in the nursing officers' lounge. I worked in an NHS hospital years ago and once late at night I sneaked into the nursing officers' lounge just to see what it was like. Well, it was like the queen's sitting room. It was all velvety furniture and half-eaten boxes of Milk Tray chocolates.

The patients, in the meantime, slept beneath bare light bulbs in cold and echoing barrack halls, and spent their days working on jigsaw puzzles that had at least a fifth of the pieces missing, awaiting a fortnightly twenty-second visit by a swift-moving retinue of doctors and students. Those were, of course, the good old days of the NHS. Things aren't nearly so splendid now.

Forgive me. I seem to have gone off on a little tangent there. I was supposed to be guiding you across Wisconsin, telling you interesting facts about America's premier dairy state, and instead I go off and make unconstructive remarks about British and American health care. This was unwarranted.

Anyway, Wisconsin is America's premier dairy state, producing 17 percent of the nation's cheese and milk products, by golly, though as I drove across its rolling pleasantness I wasn't particularly struck by an abundance of dairy cows. I drove for long hours, south past Green Bay, Appleton and Oshkosh and then west towards Iowa. This was quintessential Midwestern farming country, a study in browns, a landscape of low wooded hills, bare trees, faded pastures, tumble-down corn. It all had a kind of muted beauty. The farms were large, scattered and prosperous looking. Every half-mile or so I would pass a snug-looking farmhouse, with a porch swing and a yard full of trees. Standing nearby would be a red barn with a rounded roof and a tall grain silo. Everywhere corncribs were packed to bursting. Migrating birds filled the pale sky. The corn in the fields looked dead and brittle, but often I passed large harvesters chewing up rows and spitting out bright yellow ears.

I drove through the thin light of afternoon along back highways. It seemed to take forever to cross the state, but I didn't mind because it was so fetching and restful. There was something uncommonly alluring about the day, about the season, the sense that winter was drawing in. By four o'clock the daylight was going. By five the sun had dropped out of the clouds and was slotting into the distant hills, like a coin going into a piggy bank. At a place called Ferryville, I came suddenly up against the Mississippi River. It fairly took my breath away, it was so broad and beautiful and graceful lying there all flat and calm. In the setting sun it looked like liquid stainless steel.

On the far bank, about a mile away, was Iowa. Home. I felt a strange squeeze of excitement that made me hunch up closer to the wheel. I drove for twenty miles down the eastern side of the river, gazing across to the high dark bluffs on the Iowa side. At Prairie du Chien I crossed the river on an iron bridge full of struts and crossbars. And then I was in Iowa. I actually felt my heart quicken. I was home. This was my state. My license plate matched everyone else's. No one would look at me as if to say, "What are you doing here?" I belonged.

In the fading light, I drove almost randomly around northeast Iowa. Every couple of miles I would pass a farmer on a tractor juddering along the highway, heading home to dinner on one of the sprawling farms up in these sheltered hills above the Mississippi. It was Friday, one of the big days of the farmer's week. He would wash his arms and neck and sit down with his family to a table covered with great bowls of food. They would say grace together. After dinner the family would drive into Hooterville and sit out in the cold October air and through their steamy breath watch the Hooterville High Blue Devils beat Kraut City 28–7 at football. The farmer's son, Merle, Jr., would score three of the touchdowns. Afterwards Merle senior would go to Ed's Tavern to celebrate (two beers, never more) and receive the admiration of the community for his son's prowess. Then it would be home to bed and up early in the frosty dawn to go out hunting for deer with his best friends, Ed and Art and Wally, trudging across the fallow fields, savoring the clean air and companionship. I was seized with a huge envy for these people and their unassuming lives. It must be wonderful to live in a safe and timeless place, where you know everyone and everyone knows you, and you can all count on each other. I envied them their sense of community, their football games, their bring-and-bake sales, their church socials. And I felt guilty for mocking them. They were good people.

I drove through the seamless blackness, past Millville, New Vienna, Cascade, Scotch Grove. Every once in a while I would pass a distant farmhouse whose windows were pools of yellow light, warm and inviting. Occasionally there would be a larger town, with a much larger pool of light scooped out of the darkness—the high-school football field, where the week's game was in progress. These football fields lit up the night; they were visible from miles off. As I drove through each town, it was clear that everybody was out at the game. There was nobody on the streets. Apart from one forlorn teenaged girl standing behind the counter in the local Dairy Queen, waiting for the postgame rush, everyone in town was at the football game. You could drive in with a fleet of trucks and strip the town during a high-school football game in Iowa. You could blow open the bank with explosives and take the money out in wheelbarrows and no one would be there to see it. But of course nobody would think of such a thing because crime doesn't exist in rural Iowa. Their idea of a crime in these places would be to miss the Friday football game. Anything worse than that only exists on television and in the newspapers, in a semimythic distant land called the Big City.

I had intended to drive on to Des Moines, but on an impulse I stopped at Iowa City. It's a college town, the home of the University of Iowa, and I still had a couple of friends living there—people who had gone to college there and then never quite found any reason to move on. It was nearly ten o'clock when I arrived, but the streets were packed with students out carousing. I called my old friend John Horner from a street-corner phone and he told me to meet him in Fitzpatrick's Bar. I stopped a passing student and asked him the way to Fitzpatrick's Bar, but he was so drunk that he had lost the power of speech. He just gazed numbly at me. He looked to be about fourteen years old. I stopped a group of girls, similarly intoxicated, and asked them if they knew the way to the bar. They all said they did and pointed in different directions, and then became so convulsed with giggles that it was all they could do to stand up. They moved around in front of me like passengers on a ship in heavy seas. They looked about fourteen years old too.

"Are you girls always this happy?" I asked.

"Only at homecoming," one of them said.

Ah, that explained it. Homecoming. The big social event of the college year. There are three ritual stages attached to homecoming celebrations at American universities: (1) Get grossly intoxicated; (2) throw up in a public place; (3) wake up not knowing where you are or how you got there and with your underpants on backwards. I appeared to have arrived in town somewhere between stages one and two, though in fact a few of the more committed revelers were already engaged in gutter serenades. I picked my way through the weaving throngs in downtown Iowa City asking people at random if they knew the way to Fitzpatrick's Bar. No one seemed to have heard of it—but then many of the people I encountered probably could not have identified themselves in a roomful of mirrors. Eventually I stumbled onto the bar myself. Like all bars in Iowa City on a Friday night, it was packed to the rafters. Everybody looked to be fourteen years old, except one person—my friend John Horner, who was standing at the bar looking all of his thirty-five years. There is nothing like a college town to make you feel old before your time. I joined Horner at the bar. He hadn't changed a lot. He was now a teacher and a respectable member of the community, though there was still a semiwild glint in his eye. In his day, he had been one of the most committed drug takers in the community, and indeed he still had a faintly burnt-out look about him. We had been friends almost forever, since first grade at least. We exchanged broad smiles and warm handshakes and tried to talk, but there was so much noise and throbbing music that we were just two men watching each other's mouths move. So we gave up trying to talk and instead had a beer and stood smiling inanely at each other, the way you do with someone you haven't seen for years, and watching the people around us. I couldn't get over how young and fresh-looking they all seemed. Everything about them looked brand-new and unused—their clothes, their faces, their bodies. When we had drained our beer bottles, Horner and I stepped out onto the street and walked to his car. The fresh air felt wonderful. People were leaning against buildings everywhere and puking.

"Have you ever seen so many twerpy little assholes in all your life?" Horner asked me rhetorically.

"And they're all just fourteen years old," I added.

"Physically they are fourteen years old," he corrected me, "but emotionally and intellectually they are still somewhere shy of their eighth birthday."

"Were we like that at their age?"

"I used to wonder that, but I don't think so. I may have been that stupid once, but I was never that shallow. These kids wear button-down-collar shirts and penny loafers. They look like they're on their way to an Osmonds concert. And they don't know *anything*. You talk to them in a bar and they don't even know who's running for president. They've never heard of Nicaragua. It's scary."

We walked along thinking about the scariness of it all. "But there's something even worse," Horner added. We were at his car. I looked at him across the top of it. "What's that?" I asked.

"They don't smoke dope. Can you believe that?"

Well, I couldn't. The idea of students at the University of Iowa not smoking dope is . . . well, simply inconceivable. On any list of reasons for going to the University of Iowa, smoking dope took up at least two of the first five places. "Then what are they here for?"

"They're getting an *education*," Horner said in a tone of wonder. "Can you believe that? They *want* to be insurance salesmen and computer programmers. That's their dream in life. They want to make a lot of money so they can go out and buy more penny loafers and Madonna albums. It terrifies me sometimes."

We got in his car and drove through dark streets to his house. Horner explained to me how the world had changed. When I left America for England, Iowa City was full of hippies. Difficult as it may be to believe, out here amid all these cornfields, the University of Iowa was for many years one of the most radical colleges in the country, at its peak exceeded in radicalness only by Berkeley and Columbia. Everybody there was a hippie, the professors as much as the students. It wasn't just that they smoked dope and frequently rioted; they were also open-minded and intellectual. People cared about things like politics and the environment and where the world was going. Now, from what Horner was telling me, it was as if all the people in Iowa City had had their brains laundered at the Ronald McDonald Institute of Mental Readjustment.

"So what happened?" I asked Horner when we were settled at his house with a beer. "What made everyone change?"

"I don't know exactly," he said. "The main thing, I guess, is that the Reagan Administration has this obsession with drugs. And they don't distinguish between hard drugs and soft drugs. If you're a dealer and you're caught with pot, you get sent away for just as long as if it were heroin. So now nobody sells pot. All the people who used to sell it have moved on to crack and heroin because the risk is no worse and the profits are a lot better."

"Sounds crazy," I said.

"Of course it's crazy!" Horner answered, a little hotly. Then he calmed down. "Actually a lot of people just stopped dealing in pot altogether. Do you remember Frank Dortmeier?"

Frank Dortmeier was a guy who used to ingest drugs by the sackful. He would snort coke through a garden hose given half a chance. "Yeah, sure," I said.

"I used to get my pot from him. Then they brought in this law that if you are caught selling dope within a thousand yards of a public school they put you in jail forever. It doesn't matter that you may only be selling one little reefer to your own mother, they still put you away for eternity just as if you were standing on the school steps shoving it down the throats of every sniveling little kid who passed by. Well, when they brought this law in, Dortmeier started to get worried because there was a school up the street from him. So one night under cover of darkness, he goes out with a hundred-foot tape measure and measures the distance from his house to the school and damn me but it's 997 yards. So he just stops selling dope, just like that." Horner drank his beer sadly. "It's really frustrating. I mean, have you ever tried to watch American TV without dope?"

"It must be tough," I agreed.

"Dortmeier gave me the name of his supplier so I could go and get some myself. Well, this guy was in Kansas City. I had no idea. So I drove all the way down there, just to buy a couple of ounces of pot, and it was crazy. The house was full of guns. The guy kept looking out the window like he was expecting the police to tell him to come out with his hands up. He was half convinced that I was an undercover narcotics officer. I mean here I am, a thirty-five-year-old family man, with a college education and a respectable job, I'm 180 miles from home and I'm wondering if I'm going to get blown away, and all so that I can just have a little something to help me get through 'Love Boat' reruns on TV. It was too crazy for me. You need somebody like Dortmeier for a situation like that—somebody with a lust for drugs and no brain." Horner shook the beer can by his ear to confirm that it was empty and then looked at me. "You wouldn't by any wild chance have any dope with you?" he asked.

"I'm sorry, John," I said.

"Shame," said Horner and went out to the kitchen to get us more beers.

I spent the night in Horner's spare room and in the morning stood with him and his pleasant wife in the kitchen drinking coffee and chatting while small children swirled about our legs. Life is odd, I thought. It seemed so strange for Horner to have a wife and children and a paunch and a mortgage and to be, like me, approaching the cliff face of middle age. We had been boys for so long together that I suppose I had thought the condition was permanent. I realized with a sense of dread that the next time we met we would probably talk about gallstone operations and the relative merits of different brands of storm windows. It put me in a melancholy mood and kept me there as I reclaimed my car from its parking space downtown and returned to the highway.

I drove along old Route 6, which used to be the main highway to Chicago, but now with Interstate 80 just three miles to the south, it is all but forgotten, and I hardly saw a soul along its length. I drove for an hour and a half without much of a thought in my head, just a weary eagerness to get home, to see my mom, to have a shower, and not to touch a steering wheel for a long, long time.

Des Moines looked wonderful in the morning sunshine. The dome on the state capitol building gleamed. The trees were still full of color. They've changed the city completely—downtown now is all modern buildings and bubbling fountains and whenever I'm there now I have to keep looking up at the street signs to get my bearings—but it felt like home. I suppose it always will. I hope so. I drove through the city, happy to be there, proud to be part of it.

On Grand Avenue, near the governor's mansion, I realized I was driving along behind my mother, who had evidently borrowed my sister's car. I recognized her because the right turn signal was blinking pointlessly as she proceeded up the street. My mother generally puts the turn signal on soon after pulling out of the garage and then leaves it on for pretty much the rest of the day. I used to point this out to her, but then I realized it is actually a good thing because it alerts other motorists that they are approaching a driver who may not be entirely on top of matters. I followed along behind her. At Thirty-First Street the blinking turn signal jumped from the right side of the car to the left—I had forgotten that she likes to move it around from time to time—as we turned the corner for home, but then it stayed cheerily blinking on the left for the last mile, down Thirty-First Street and up Elmwood Drive.

I had to park a fair distance from the house and then, despite a boyish eagerness to see my mother, I took a minute to log the final details of the trip in a notebook I had been carrying with me. It always made me feel oddly important and professional, like a jumbo-jet pilot at the end of a transatlantic flight. It was 10:38 A.M., and I had driven 6,842 miles since leaving home 34 days earlier. I circled this figure, then got out, grabbed my bags from the trunk and walked briskly to the house. My mother was already inside. I could see her through the back window, moving around in the kitchen, putting away groceries and humming. She is always humming. I opened the back door, dropped my bags and called out those four most all-American words: "Hi, Mom, I'm home!"

She looked real pleased to see me. "Hello, dear!" she said brightly and gave me a hug. "I was just wondering when I'd be seeing you again. Can I get you a sandwich?"

"That would be great," I said even though I wasn't really hungry.

It was good to be home.

PART II

West

20

I WAS HEADED for Nebraska. Now there's a sentence you don't want to have to say too often if you can possibly help it. Nebraska must be the most unexciting of all the states. Compared with it, Iowa is paradise. Iowa at least is fertile and green and has a hill. Nebraska is like a 75,000-square-mile bare patch. In the middle of the state is a river called the Platte, which at some times of the year is two or three miles wide. It looks impressive until you realize that it is only about four inches deep. You could cross it in a wheelchair. On a landscape without any contours or depressions to shape it, the Platte just lies there, like a drink spilled across a tabletop. It is the most exciting thing in the state.

When I was growing up, I used to wonder how Nebraska came to be lived in. I mean to say, the original settlers, creaking across America in their covered wagons, had to have passed through Iowa, which is green and fertile and has, as I say, a hill, but stopped short of Colorado, which is green and fertile and has a mountain range, and settled instead for a place that is flat and brown and full of stubble and prairie dogs. Doesn't make a lot of sense, does it? Do you know what the original settlers made their houses of? Dried mud. And do you know what happened to all those mud houses when the rainy season came every year? That's correct, they slid straight into the Platte River.

For a long time I couldn't decide whether the original settlers in Nebraska were insane or just stupid, and then I saw a stadium full of University of Nebraska football fans in action on a Saturday and realized that they must have been both. I may be a decade or so out of touch here but when I left America, the University of Nebraska didn't so much play football as engage in weekly ritual slaughters. They were always racking up scores of 58–3 against hapless opponents. Most schools, when they get a decent lead, will send in a squad of skinny freshmen in unsoiled uniforms to let them run around a bit and get dirty and, above all, to give the losers a sporting chance to make the score respectable. It's called fair play.

Not Nebraska. The University of Nebraska would send in flamethrowers if it were allowed. Watching Nebraska play football every week was like watching hyenas tearing open a gazelle. It was unseemly. It was unsporting. And of course the fans could never get enough of it. To sit among them with the score 66–0 and watch them bray for more blood is a distinctly unnerving experience, particularly when you consider that a lot of these people must work at the Strategic Air Command in Omaha. If Iowa State ever upset Nebraska, I wouldn't be at all surprised if they nuked Ames. All of these thoughts percolated through my mind on this particular morning and frankly left me troubled.

I was on the road again. It was a little after 7:30 A.M. on a bright but still wintry Monday morning in April. I drove west out of Des Moines on Interstate 80, intending to zip across the western half of Iowa and plunge deep into Nebraska. But I couldn't face Nebraska just yet, not this early in the morning, and abruptly at De Soto, just fifteen miles west of Des Moines, I pulled off the interstate and started wandering around on back roads. Within a couple of minutes I was lost. This didn't altogether surprise me. Getting lost is a family trait.

My father, when behind the wheel, was more or less permanently lost. Most of the time he was just kind of lost, but whenever we got near something we were intent on seeing he would become seriously lost. Generally it would take him about an hour to realize that he had gone from the first stage to the second. All during that time, as he blundered through some unfamiliar city, making sudden and unpredictable turns, getting honked at for going the wrong way down one-way streets or for hesitating in the middle of busy intersections, my mother would mildly suggest that perhaps we should pull over and ask directions. But my father would pretend not to hear her and would press on in that semiobsessional state that tends to overcome fathers when things aren't going well.

Eventually, after driving the wrong way down the same one-way street so many times that merchants were beginning to come and watch from their doorways, Dad would stop the car and gravely announce, "Well, *I* think we should ask directions" in a tone that made it clear that this had been his desire all along.

This was always a welcome development, but seldom more than a partial breakthrough. Either my mom would get out and stop a patently unqualified person—a nun on an exchange visit from Costa Rica usually—and come back with directions that were hopelessly muddled or my father would go off to find somebody and then not come back. The problem with my dad was that he was a great talker. This is always a dangerous thing in a person who gets lost a lot. He would go into a cafe to ask the way to Giant Fungus State Park and the next thing you knew he would be sitting down having a cup of coffee and a chat with the proprietor or the proprietor would be taking him out back to show him his new septic tank or something. In the meantime the rest of us would have to sit in a quietly baking car, with nothing to do but sweat and wait and listlessly watch a pair of flies copulate on the dashboard.

After a very long time my father would reappear, wiping crumbs from around his mouth and looking real perky. "Darnedest thing," he would say, leaning over to talk to my mom through the window. "Guy in there collects false teeth. He's got over seven hundred sets down in his basement. He was so pleased to have someone to show them to that I just couldn't say no. And then his wife insisted that I have a piece of blueberry pie and see the photographs from their daughter's wedding. They'd never heard of Giant Fungus State Park, I'm afraid, but the guy said his brother at the Conoco station by the traffic lights would know. *He* collects fan belts, of all things, and apparently has the largest collection of prewar fan belts in the upper Midwest. I'm just going down there now." And then, before anybody could stop him, he'd be gone again. By the time he finally returned my father would know most of the people in town and the flies on the dashboard would have a litter of infants.

Eventually I found what I was looking for: Winterset, birthplace of John Wayne. I drove around the town until I found his house—Winterset is so small that this only took a minute—and slowed down to look at it from the car. The house was tiny and the paint was peeling off it. Wayne, or Marion Morrison as he then was, only lived there for a year or so before his family moved to California. The house is run as a museum now, but it was shut. This didn't surprise me as pretty much everything in the town was shut, quite a lot of it permanently from the look of things. The Iowa Movie Theater on the square was clearly out of business, its marquee blank, and many of the other stores were gone or just hanging on. It was a depressing sight because Winterset was really quite a nice-looking little town with its county courthouse and square and long streets of big Victorian houses. I bet, like Winfield, it was a different place altogether fifteen or twenty years ago. I drove back out to the highway past the Gold Buffet ("Dancing Nitely") feeling an odd sense of emptiness.

Every town I came to was much the same—peeling paint, closed businesses, a deathly air. Southwest Iowa has always been the poorest part of the state and it showed. I didn't stop because there was nothing worth stopping for. I couldn't even find a place to get a cup of coffee. Eventually, much to my surprise, I blundered onto a bridge over the Missouri River and then I was in Nebraska City, in Nebraska. And it wasn't at all bad. In fact, it was really quite pleasant—better than Iowa by a long shot, I was embarrassed to admit. The towns were more prosperous-looking and better maintained, and the roadsides everywhere were full of bushes from which sprang a profusion of creamy flowers. It was all quite pretty, though in a rather monotonous way. That is the problem with Nebraska. It just goes on and on, and even the good bits soon grow tedious. I drove for hours along an undemanding highway, past Auburn, Tecumseh, Beatrice (a town of barely 10,000 people but which produced two Hollywood stars, Harold Lloyd and Robert Taylor), Fairbury, Hebron, Deshler, Ruskin.

At Deshler I stopped for coffee and was surprised at how cold it was. Where the weather is concerned, the Midwest has the worst of both worlds. In the winter the wind is razor sharp. It skims down from the Arctic and slices through you. It howls and swirls and buffets the house. It brings piles of snow and bone-cracking cold. From November to March you walk leaning forward at a twenty-degree angle, even indoors, and spend your life waiting for your car to warm up, or digging it out of drifts or scraping futilely at ice that seems to have been applied to the windows with superglue. And then one day spring comes. The snow melts, you stride about in shirtsleeves, you incline your face to the sun. And then, just like that, spring is over and it's summer. It is as if God has pulled a lever in the great celestial powerhouse. Now the weather rolls in from the opposite direction, from the tropics far to the south, and it hits you like a wall of heat. For six months, the heat pours over you. You sweat oil. Your pores gape. The grass goes brown. Dogs look as if they could die. When you walk downtown you can feel the heat of the pavement rising through the soles of your shoes. Just when you think you might very well go crazy, fall comes and for two or three weeks the air is mild and nature is friendly. And then it's winter and the cycle starts again. And you think, "As soon as I'm big enough, I'm going to move far, far away from here."

At Red Cloud, home of Willa Cather, I joined US 281 and headed south towards Kansas. Just over the border is Smith Center, home of Dr. Brewster M. Higley, who wrote the words to "Home on the Range." Wouldn't you just know that "Home on the Range" would be written by somebody with a name like Brewster M. Higley? You can see the log cabin where he wrote the words. But I was headed for something far more exciting—the geographical center of the United States. You reach it by turning off the highway just outside the little town of Lebanon and following a side road for about a mile through the wheat fields. Then you come to a forlorn little park with picnic tables and a stone monument with a wind-whipped flag atop it and a plaque saying that this is the centermost point in the continental United States, by golly. Beside the park, adding to the sense of forlornness, was a closed-down motel, which had been built in the evident hope that people would want to spend the night in this lonely place and send postcards to their friends saying, "You'll never guess where we are." Clearly the owner had misread the market.

I climbed onto a picnic table and could instantly see for miles across the waving fields. The wind came at me like a freight train. I felt as if I were the first person to come there for years. It was a strange feeling to think that of all the 230 million people in the United States I was the most geographically distinctive. If America were invaded, I would be the last person captured. This was it, the last stand, and as I climbed down off the table and returned to the car I felt an uneasy sense of guilt for leaving the place undefended.

I drove into the gathering evening gloom. The clouds were low and swift. The landscape was a sea of white grass, fine as a child's hair. It was strangely beautiful. By the time I reached Russell, it was dark and rain was falling. The headlights swept over a sign that said, WELCOME TO BOB DOLE COUNTRY. Russell is the hometown of Bob Dole, who was at this time running for the Republican nomination for president. I stopped and got a room for the night, figuring that if Dole were elected president, I could tell my children that I had once spent the night in his hometown and perhaps thereby deepen their respect for me. Also, every time Russell was shown on TV over the next four years I could say, "Hey, I was there!" and make everybody in the room stop talking while I pointed out things I had seen. In the event, Dole dropped out of the race two days later, primarily because nobody could stand him, apart from his family and some other people around Russell, and the town, alas, lost its chance at fame.

I awoke to a more promising day. The sun was bright and the air was clear. Bugs exploded colorfully against the windshield, a sure sign of spring in the Midwest. In the sunshine Kansas seemed an altogether more agreeable place, which surprised me a little. I had always thought one of the worst things anyone could say to you was, "We're transferring you to Kansas, son." Kansas calls itself "the Wheat State." That kind of says it all, don't you think? It really makes you want to cancel that Barbados trip, doesn't it? But in fact Kansas was okay. The towns I went through all looked trim and prosperous and quintessentially American. But then Kansas is the most quintessential of American states. It is, after all, where Superman and Dorothy from *The Wizard of Oz* grew up, and all the towns I went through had a cozy, leafy, timeless air to them. They looked like the sort of places where you could still have your groceries delivered by a boy on a bike and people would still say things like "by golly" and "gee whillikers." At Great Bend, I stopped on the square beside the Barton County Courthouse and had a look around. It was like passing through a time warp. The place appeared not to have changed a fraction since 1965. The Crest Movie Theater was still in business. Nearby stood the *Great Bend Daily Tribune* and the Brass Buckle Clothing Store, with a big sign on it that said, FOR GUYS AND GALS. Gee whillikers. A man and his wife passed me on the sidewalk and said good morning like old friends. The man even tipped his hat. From a passing car came the sound of the Everly Brothers. This was almost too eerie. I half expected Rod Serling to step out from behind a tree and say, "Bill Bryson doesn't know it, but he's just driven into a community that doesn't exist in time or space. He's just embarked on a one-way trip into . . . The Twilight Zone."

I had a look in the window of the Family Pharmacy and Gift Shop, which had an interesting and unusual display that included a wheelchair, a packet of disposable absorbent underpants (it isn't often you find a store catering to the incontinent impulse shopper), teddy bears, coffee mugs bearing wholesome sentiments like "World's Best Grandma," Mother's Day cards and a variety of porcelain animals. In one corner of the window was a poster for a concert by—you are never going to believe this—Paul Revere and the Raiders. Can you beat that? There they were, still dressed up like Continental soldiers, prancing about and grinning, just like when I was in junior high school. Goodness me, what assholes. They would be performing at the Civic Auditorium in Dodge City in two weeks. Tickets started at $10.75. This was all becoming too much for me. I was glad to get in the car and drive on to Dodge City, which at least is intentionally unreal.

Somewhere during the seventy miles between Great Bend and Dodge City you leave the Midwest and enter the West. The people in the towns along the way stop wearing baseball caps and shuffling along with that amiable dopeyness characteristic of the Midwest and instead start wearing cowboy hats and cowboy boots, walking with a lope and looking vaguely suspicious and squinty, as if they think they might have to shoot you in a minute. People in the West like to shoot things. When they first got to the West they shot buffalo.* Once there were 70 million buffalo on the plains and then the people of the West started blasting away at them. Buffalo are just cows with big heads. If you've ever looked a cow in the face and seen the unutterable depths of trust and stupidity that lie within, you will be able to guess how difficult it must have been for people in the West to track down buffalo and shoot them to pieces. By 1895, there were only 800 buffalo left, mostly in zoos and touring Wild West shows. With no buffalo left to kill, Westerners started shooting Indians. Between 1850 and 1890 they reduced the number of Indians in America from two million to 90,000.

Nowadays, thank goodness, both have made a recovery. Today there are 30,000 buffalo and 300,000 Indians, and of course you are not allowed to shoot either, so all the Westerners have left to shoot at are road signs and each other, both of which they do rather a lot. There you have a capsule history of the West.

When they weren't shooting things, the people of the West went into towns like Dodge City for a little social and sexual

---

*Many people will tell you that you mustn't call them buffalo, that they are really bison. Buffalo, these people will tell you, actually live in China or some other distant country and are a different breed of animal altogether. These are the same people who tell you that you must call geraniums pelargoniums. Ignore them.

intercourse. At its peak, Dodge City was the biggest cow town and semen sink in the West, full of drifters, drovers, buffalo hunters and the sort of women that only a cowboy could find attractive. But it was never as tough and dangerous as you were led to believe on "Gunsmoke" and all those movies about Bat Masterson and Wyatt Earp. For ten years it was the biggest cattle market in the world; that's all.

In all those years, there were only thirty-four people buried in Boot Hill Cemetery and most of those were just drifters found dead in snowdrifts or of natural causes. I know this for a fact because I paid $2.75 to go and see Boot Hill and the neighboring "Historic Front Street," which has been rebuilt to look like it did when Dodge City was a frontier town and Bat Masterson and Wyatt Earp were the sheriffs. Matt Dillon never existed, I was distressed to learn, though Bat Masterson and Wyatt Earp were both real enough. Bat Masterson ended his life as sports editor of the *New York Morning Telegraph.* Isn't that interesting? And here's another interesting fact, which I didn't tell you about earlier because I've been saving it: Wyatt Earp was from Pella, the little Iowa town with the windmills. Isn't that great?

Fifty miles beyond Dodge City is Holcomb, Kansas, which gained a small notoriety as the scene of the murders described with lavish detail in the Truman Capote book *In Cold Blood.* In 1959, two small-time crooks broke into the house of a wealthy Holcomb rancher named Herb Clutter because they had heard he had a safe full of money. In fact he didn't. So, chagrined, they tied Clutter's wife and two teenaged children to their beds and took Clutter down to the basement and killed them all. They slit Clutter's throat (Capote describes his gurglings with a disturbing relish) and shot the others in the head at point-blank range. Because Clutter had been prominent in state politics, the *New York Times* ran a small story about the murders. Capote saw the story, became intrigued and spent five years interviewing all the main participants—friends, neighbors, relatives, police investigators and the murderers themselves. The book, when it came out in 1965, was considered an instant classic, largely because Capote told everyone it was. In any case, it was sufficiently seminal, as we used to say in college, to have made a lasting impact and it occurred to me that I could profitably reread it and then go to Holcomb and make a lot of trenchant observations about crime and violence in America.

I was wrong. I quickly realized there was nothing typical about the Clutter murders: they would be as shocking today as they were then. And there was nothing particularly seminal about Capote's book. It was essentially just a grisly and sensational murder story that pandered, in a deviously respectable way, to the reader's baser instincts. All that a trip to Holcomb would achieve would be to provide me with the morbid thrill of gawping at a house in which a family had long before been senselessly slaughtered. Still, that's about all I ask out of life, and it was bound, at the very least, to be more interesting than Historic Front Street in Dodge City.

In Capote's book, Holcomb was a tranquil, dusty hamlet, full of intensely decent people, a place whose citizens didn't smoke, drink, lie, swear or miss church, a place in which sex outside marriage was unforgivable and sex before marriage unthinkable, in which teenagers were home at eleven on a Saturday night, in which Catholics and Methodists didn't mingle if they could possibly help it, in which doors were never locked, and children of eleven or twelve were allowed to drive cars. For some reason I found the idea of children driving cars particularly astonishing. In Capote's book, the nearest town was Garden City, five miles down the highway. Things had clearly changed. Now Holcomb and Garden City had more or less grown together, connected by an umbilicus of gas stations and fast-food places. Holcomb was still dusty, but no longer a hamlet. On the edge of town was a huge high school, obviously new, and all around were cheap little houses, also new, with barefooted Mexican children running around in the front yards. I found the Clutter house without too much trouble. In the book it stood apart from the town, down a shady lane. Now the lane was lined with houses. There was no sign of occupancy at the Clutter house. The curtains were drawn. I hesitated for a long time and then went and knocked at the front door, and frankly was relieved that no one answered. What could I have said? Hello, I'm a stranger passing through town with a morbid interest in sensational murders and I just wondered if you could tell me what it's like living in a house in which several people have had their brains spattered onto the walls? Do you ever think about it at mealtimes, for instance?

I got back in the car and drove around, looking for anything that was familiar from the book, but the shops and cafes all seemed to have gone or been renamed. I stopped at the high school. The main doors were locked—it was four in the afternoon—but some students from the track team were drifting about on the playing fields. I accosted two of them standing along the perimeter and asked them if I could talk to them for a minute about the Clutter murders. It was clear that they didn't know what I was talking about.

"You know," I prompted. *In Cold Blood*. The book by Truman Capote."

They looked at me blankly.

"You've never heard of *In Cold Blood?* Truman Capote?" They hadn't. I could scarcely believe it. "Have you ever heard of the Clutter murders—a whole family killed in a house over there beyond that water tower?"

One of them brightened. "Oh, yeah," he said. "Whole family just wiped out. It was, you know, weird."

"Does anybody live in the house now?"

"Dunno," said the student. "Somebody used to live there, I think. But now I think maybe they don't. Dunno really." Talking was clearly not his strongest social skill, though compared with the second student he was a veritable Cicero. I thought I had never met two such remarkably ignorant young men, but then I stopped three others and none of them had heard of *In Cold Blood* either. Over by the pole-vaulting pit I found the coach, an amiable young social sciences teacher named Stan Kennedy. He was supervising three young athletes as they took turns sprinting down a runway with a long pole and then crashing with their heads and shoulders into a horizontal bar about five feet off the ground. If knocking the hell out of a horizontal bar was a sport in Kansas, these guys could be state champions. I asked Kennedy if he thought it odd that so many of the students had never heard of *In Cold Blood*.

"I was surprised at that myself when I first came here eight years ago," he said. "After all, it was the biggest thing that ever happened in the town. But you have to realize that the people here hated the book. They banned it from the public library and a lot of them even now won't talk about it."

This surprised me. A few weeks before I had read an article in an old *Life* magazine about how the townspeople had taken Truman Capote to their hearts even though he was a mincing little fag who talked with a lisp and wore funny caps. In fact, it turns out, they disdained him not only as a mincing little fag, but as a meddler from the big city who had exploited their private grief for his own gain. Most people wanted to forget the whole business and discouraged their children from developing an interest in it. Kennedy had once asked his brightest class how many of the students had read the book, and three-quarters of them had never even looked at it.

I said I thought that was surprising. If I had grown up in a place where something famous had happened I would want to read about it. "So would I," Kennedy said. "So would most people from our generation. But kids these days are different."

We agreed that this was, you know, weird.

There is nothing much to be said for the far west of Kansas except that the towns are small and scattered and the highways mostly empty. Every ten miles or so there is a side road, and at every side road there is an old pickup truck stopped at a stop sign. You can see them from a long way off—in Kansas you can see everything from a long way off—glinting in the sunshine. At first you think the truck must be broken down or abandoned, but just as you get within thirty or forty feet of it, it pulls out onto the highway in front of you, causing you to make an immediate downward adjustment in your speed from sixty miles an hour to about twelve miles an hour and to test the resilience of the steering wheel with your forehead. This happens to you over and over. Curious to see what sort of person could inconvenience you in this way out in the middle of nowhere, you speed up to overtake it and see that sitting at the wheel is a little old man of eighty-seven, wearing a cowboy hat three sizes too large for him, staring fixedly at the empty road as if piloting a light aircraft through a thunderstorm. He is of course quite oblivious of you. Kansas has more drivers like this than any other state in the nation, more than can be accounted for by simple demographics. Other states must send them their old people, perhaps by promising them a free cowboy hat when they get there.

21

=============== I SHOULD HAVE known better, but I had it in my mind that Colorado was nothing but mountains. Somehow I thought that the moment I left Kansas I would find myself amid the snow-topped Rockies, in lofty meadows of waving buttercups, where the skies were blue and the air was as crisp as fresh celery. But it was nothing like that at all. It was just flat and brown and full of remote little towns with charmless names: Swink, Ordway, Manzanola. They in turn were all full of poor-looking people and mean-looking dogs nosing around on the margins of liquor stores and gas stations. Broken bottles glittered among the stubble in the roadside ditches and the signs along the way were pocked from shotgun blasts. This sure wasn't the Colorado John Denver was forever yodeling on about.

I was imperceptibly climbing. Every town along the highway announced its elevation, and each was several hundred feet higher than the previous one, but it wasn't until I had nearly reached Pueblo, 150 miles into the interior, that I at last saw mountains. Suddenly there they were, blue and craggy and heavy with snow.

My plan was to take State Highway 67 north up to Victor

and Cripple Creek, two old gold-mining towns. The road was marked on my map as scenic. What I didn't realize was that it was unpaved and that it led through a mountain pass ominously called Phantom Canyon. It was the most desolate and bone-shaking road I have ever been on, full of ruts and rocks—the kind of road that makes everything in the car dance about and doors fly open. The problem was that there was no way to turn around. One side of the road hugged a wall of rock, rising up and up, like the side of a skyscraper; the other fell sharply away to a creek of excited water. Meekly I pressed on, driving at a creeping pace and hoping that things would improve in a while. But of course they didn't. The road grew ever steeper and more perilous. Here and there the two sides of the canyon would narrow and I would be hemmed in for a while by walls of fractured stone that looked as if they had been struck with a hammer, and then suddenly it would open out again to reveal hair-raising views down to the twisting canyon floor far, far below.

Everywhere above me house-sized boulders teetered on pin-heads of rock, just waiting to tumble down the mountainside and make a doormat of me. Rock slides were evidently common. The valley floor was a graveyard of boulders. I prayed that I would not meet another vehicle coming down the hill and have to re-verse all the way to the valley floor. But I needn't have worried because of course not a single other person in the whole of North America was sufficiently moronic to drive through Phantom Can-yon at this time of year, when a sudden storm could turn the road to mud and bog the car down for months—or send it slipping and sliding over the void. I wasn't used to dealing with landscapes that can kill you. Cautiously I pressed on.

High up in the mountains I crossed a wooden bridge of laughable ricketyness over a deep chasm. It was the sort of bridge on which, in the movies, a slat always breaks, causing the heroine to plunge through up to her armpits with her pert legs wiggling helplessly above the chasm, until the hero dashes back to save her, spears falling all around them. When I was twelve years old, I could never understand why the hero, oper-ating from this position of superiority, didn't say to the lady,

"OK, I'll save your life, but later you have to let me see you naked. Agreed?"

Beyond the bridge wet snow began to fly about. It mixed with the hundreds of insects that had been flinging themselves into the windshield since Nebraska (what a senseless waste of life!) and turned it into a brown sludge. I attacked it with window washer solution, but this just converted it from a brown sludge to a creamy sludge and I still couldn't see. I stopped and jumped out to wipe at the window with my sleeve, certain that at any moment a bobcat, seeing the chance of a lifetime, would drop onto my shoulders and rip off my scalp with a sound like two strips of Velcro being parted. I imagined myself, scalpless, stumbling whimpering down the mountainside with the bobcat nipping at my heels. This formed such a vivid image in my mind that I jumped back into the car, even though I had only created a small rectangle of visibility about the size of an envelope. It was like looking out of a tank turret.

The car wouldn't start. Of course. Drily I said, "Oh, thank you, God." Up here in the thin air, the Chevette just gasped and wheezed and quickly became flooded. While I waited for the flooding to subside, I looked at the map and was dismayed to discover that I still had twenty miles to go. I had done only eight miles so far and I had been at it for well over an hour. The possibility that the Chevette might not make it to Victor and Cripple Creek took root in my skull. For the first time it occurred to me that perhaps no one ever came along this road. If I died out here, I reflected bleakly, it could be years before anyone found me or the Chevette, which would obviously be a tragedy. Apart from anything else the battery was still under warranty.

But of course I didn't die out there. In fact, to tell you the truth, I don't intend ever to die. The car started up and I crept up over the last of the high passes and thence into Victor without further incident. Victor was a wonderful sight, a town of Western-style buildings perched incongruously in a high green valley of the most incredible beauty. Once it and Cripple Creek, six miles down the road, were boom towns to beat all boom towns. At their peak, in 1908, they had 500 gold mines between them and a population of 100,000. Miners were paid in gold. In 25 years or so the mines produced $800 million worth of gold and made a lot of people rich. Jack Dempsey lived in Victor and started his career there.

Today only a couple of working mines are left and the population is barely a thousand. Victor had the air of a ghost town, though at least the streets were paved. Chipmunks darted among the buildings and grass was growing through cracks in the sidewalk. The town was full of antique stores and craft shops, but almost all of them were closed, evidently waiting for the summer season. Quite a few were empty and one, the Amber Inn, had been seized for nonpayment of taxes. A big sign in the window said so. But the post office was open and one cafe, which was full of old men in bib overalls and younger men with beards and ponytails. All the men wore baseball caps, though here they advertised brands of beer—Coors, Bud Lite, Olympia—rather than brands of fertilizers.

I decided to drive on to Cripple Creek for lunch, and then wished I hadn't. Cripple Creek stands in the shadows of Mount Pisgah and Pikes Peak and was far more touristy than Victor. Most of the stores were open, though they weren't doing much business. I parked on the main street in front of the Sarsaparilla Saloon and had a look around. Architecturally, Cripple Creek was much the same as Victor, but here the businesses were almost all geared to tourists: gift shops, snack bars, ice cream parlors, a place where children could pan for gold in an artificial creek, a miniature golf course. It was pretty awful, and made worse by the bleakening weather. Flurries of snow were still swirling about. It was cold and the air was thin. Cripple Creek is nearly two miles up. At that altitude, if you're not used to it, you feel uncomfortably breathless a lot of the time and vaguely unwell all of the time. Certainly the last thing I wanted was an ice cream or a game of miniature golf, so I returned to the car and pressed on.

At the junction of US 24, I turned left and headed west. Here the weather was superb. The sun shone, the sky was blue. Out of the west, a flotilla of clouds sailed in, fluffy and benign, skimming the peaks. The highway was of pink asphalt; it was like driving along a strip of bubblegum. The road led up and over the Wilkerson Pass and then down into a long valley of rolling meadows with glittering streams and log cabins set against a backdrop of muscular mountains. It looked like a scene out of a deodorant commercial. It was glorious, and I had it almost all to myself. Near Buena Vista the land dramatically dropped away to reveal a plain and beyond it the majestic Collegiate Peaks, the highest range in the United States, with 16 peaks over 14,000 feet along a stretch of 30 miles. I fell with the highway down the mountainside and crossed the plain towards the Collegiate range, tall and blue and snow-peaked. It was like driving into the opening credits of a Paramount movie.

I had intended to make for Aspen, but at the turning at Twin Lakes I found a white barrier barring the way and a sign saying that the highway to Aspen over Independence Pass was closed because of snow. Aspen was just 20 miles away down the closed road, but to reach it by the alternative northern route would have required a detour of 150 miles. Disappointed, I looked for someplace else to go for the night and drove on to Leadville, a place about which I knew nothing and indeed had never even heard of.

Leadville was outstanding. The outskirts of the town were ragged and shabby—there's a surprising amount of poverty in Colorado—but the main street was broad and lined with sturdy Victorian buildings, many of them with turrets and towers. Leadville was another gold-and-silver-mining town; it was here that the Unsinkable Molly Brown got her start, as did Meyer Guggenheim. Like Cripple Creek and Victor, it now catered to tourists—every place in the Rockies caters to tourists—but it had a much more genuine feel to it. Its population was 4,000, enough to give it an independent life apart from what the tourists brought it.

I got a room in the Timberline Motel, had a stroll around the town and a creditable meal at the Golden Burro Cafe—not the greatest food in the world, or even possibly in Leadville, but at six dollars for soup, salad, chicken-fried steak, mashed potatoes, green beans, coffee and pie, who's bitching?—followed by a moonlight stroll back to the motel, a hot shower and a little TV. If only life could always be so simple and serene. I was asleep by ten, dreaming happy dreams in which I manfully dealt with pouncing bobcats, swaying wooden bridges and windshields full of sticky insects. The heroine even let me see her with her clothes off. It was a night to remember.

22

IN THE MORNING, the weatherman on the TV said that a "frunnal system" was about to dump many inches of snow on the Rockies. This seemed to please him a lot. You could see it in his twinkling eyes. His map showed a band of unpleasantness sitting like a curse over almost the whole of the West. Roads would be shut, he said, a hint of grin tugging at the corners of his mouth, and travel advisories would be issued. Why are television weathermen always so malicious? Even when they are trying to be sincere, you can see that it's a front—that just under the surface there lurks a person who spent his childhood pulling the wings off insects and snickering whenever another child fell under the wheels of a passing vehicle.

Abruptly, I decided to head south for the arid mountains of New Mexico, over which the weather map showed nothing much in particular happening. I had a niece at a small, exclusive college in Santa Fe whom I hadn't seen for a long time and I was sure she would be delighted for all her friends on campus to witness a slobby, overweight man pull up in a cheap, dusty car, leap out and embrace her, so I decided to drive straight there.

I headed south on US 285, which runs along the line of the Continental Divide. All around me was the most incredible natural beauty, but the landscape was constantly blemished by human intrusions—ugly trailer parks, untidy homesteads, even junkyards. Every town was mostly a collection of fast-food places and gas stations, and all along the road for many miles stood signs the size of barns saying, CAMPGROUND, MOTEL, RAFTING.

The farther south I went the more barren the landscape grew, and after a while the signs disappeared. Beyond Saguache the wide plain between the mountains became a sweep of purple sage, interspersed with dead brown earth. Here and there a field of green had been snatched from the scrub with the aid of massive wheeled water sprinklers. In the middle of these oases would stand a neat farmhouse. But otherwise the landscape between the distant mountain ranges was as featureless as a dried seabed. Between Saguache and Monte Vista lies one of the ten or twelve longest stretches of straight road in America: almost forty miles without a single bend or kink. That may not sound such a lot on paper, but it feels endless on the road. There is nothing like a highway stretching off to an ever-receding vanishing point to make you feel as if you are going nowhere. At Monte Vista, the road takes a left turn—this makes you perk up and grip the wheel—and then there is another twenty-mile stretch as straight as a ruler's edge. And so it goes. Two or three times in an hour you zip through a dusty little town—a gas station, three houses, one tree, a dog—or encounter a fractional bend in the road which requires you to move the steering wheel an inch to the right or left for two seconds, and that's your excitement for the hour. The rest of the time you don't move a muscle. Your buttocks grow numb and begin to feel as if they belong to another person.

In the early afternoon I crossed over into New Mexico—one of the high points of the day—and sighed at the discovery that it was just as unstimulating as Colorado had been. I switched on the radio. I was so far from anywhere that I could pick up only scattered stations, and those were all Spanish-speaking ones playing that kind of *aye-yi-yi* Mexican music that's always sung by strolling musicians with droopy mustaches and big sombreros in the sort of restaurants where high-school teachers take their wives for their thirtieth wedding anniversaries—the sort of places where they like to set your food alight to impress you. It had

never once occurred to me in thirty-six years of living that anyone listened to Mexican music for pleasure. Yet here there were
a dozen stations blaring it out. After each song, a disc jockey
would come on and jabber for a minute or two in Spanish in the
tone of a man who has just had his nuts slammed in a drawer.
There would then be a break for an advertisement, read by a man
who sounded even more urgent and excited—he clearly was having his nuts repeatedly slammed in a drawer—and then there
would be another song. Or rather, it would be the same song
again, as far as I could tell. That is the unfortunate thing about
Mexican musicians. They seem to know only one tune. This may
explain why they have difficulty finding work anywhere other
than at second-rate restaurants.

At a hamlet called Tres Piedras—almost every place in New
Mexico has a Spanish name—I took Highway 64 to Taos, and
things began to improve. The hills grew darker and the sage
became denser and lusher. Everyone always talks about the sky
around Taos, and it is astonishing. I had never seen a sky so vivid
and blue, so liquid. The air in this part of the desert is so clear
you can sometimes see 180 miles, or so my guidebook said. In any
case, you can certainly see why Taos has always attracted artists
and writers—or at least you can until you get to Taos itself. I had
expected it to be a sweet little artists' colony, full of people with
smocks and easels, and it was just a tourist trap, with slow-
moving traffic and stores selling ugly Indian pottery and big silver
belt buckles and postcards. There were a couple of interesting
galleries, but mostly it was hot and dusty and full of silver-haired
hippies. It was mildly amusing to see that hippies still existed—
indeed were now grandparents—but it was scarcely worth the
bother of getting there. So I drove on to Santa Fe, fearful that it
would be much the same. But it was not. In fact, it was quite
beautiful, and I was instantly charmed.

The first nice thing about Santa Fe is that it has trees. It has
trees and grass and shade and cool plazas full of flowers and
plants and the soothing burble of running water. After days of
driving across the barren wastes of the West this is a treat beyond
dimension. The air is warm and clean and the reddish Sangre de
Cristo mountains at the city's back are just sensational, especially

at sunset when they simply glow, as if lit from within, like jack-o'-lanterns. The town itself is just too rich and pretty for words. It is the oldest continuously inhabited city in America—it was founded in 1610, a decade before the Pilgrims set off from Plymouth—and takes great pride in its age. Everything in Santa Fe, and I mean everything, is made out of adobe. There's an adobe Woolworth's, an adobe multistory parking lot, an adobe six-story hotel. When you pass your first adobe gas station and adobe supermarket, you think, "Hey, let's get out of here," but then you realize that it isn't something laid on for the tourists. Adobe is simply the indigenous building material, and using it everywhere gives the town a uniformity of appearance few other places achieve. Besides, Santa Fe is filthy rich, so everything is done tastefully and well.

I drove up into the hills looking for St. John's College, where my niece was a student. It was four in the afternoon and the streets were full of long shadows. The sun was settling onto the mountains and the adobe houses on every hillside were lit with a rich orange-brown glow. St. John's is a small college perched high up in the hills, with the finest view in town, looking down over Santa Fe and the rolling mountains beyond. It has only 300 students on its sleepy campus, but my niece, on this fine spring afternoon, was not among them. No one knew where she was, but everyone promised to let her know that a slobby, overweight person with dusty shoes and tropical armpits had come looking for her and would call back in the morning.

I went back into town, got a room, had a deep, hot bath, changed into clean clothes and spent the evening shambling happily around the tranquil streets of downtown Santa Fe, gazing admiringly at the window displays in the expensive galleries and boutiques, savoring the warm evening air, and disconcerting people in the more exclusive restaurants by pressing my face up against the windows and looking critically at their food. The heart of Santa Fe is the Plaza, a Spanish-style square with white benches and a tall obelisk commemorating the battle of Valverde, whatever that was. On the base was an engraved inscription in which

February had been misspelled as *Febuary;* this pleased me very much. Another pleasing thing about the Plaza was a place on the corner called the Ore House. Downstairs it is a restaurant, but upstairs there is a bar with an open porch where you can sit—where indeed I did sit—for many tranquil hours drinking beers brought to your table by a pleasant waitress with a nice bottom, enjoying the mild evening and watching the stars fill the pale blue desert sky. Through the open door into the bar I could also watch the pianist, a well-groomed young man who played a seemingly endless series of chords and tinkling arpeggios that never really developed into anything you could call a song. But he cruised suavely up and down the keyboard and he had a winning smile and excellent teeth, which I suppose is the main thing in a cocktail bar pianist. Anyway, the ladies clearly liked him.

I don't know how many beers I had, but—I will be frank here—it was too many. I had not allowed for the fact that in the thin mountain air of Santa Fe you get drunk much faster. In any case, I was surprised to discover as I arose a couple of hours after entering that the relationship between my mind and legs, which was normally quite a good one, had broken down. More than that, my legs now didn't seem to be getting on at all well with each other. One of them started for the stairs, as instructed, but the other, in a burst of petulance, decided to make for the rest room. The result was that I lurched through the bar like a man on stilts, grinning inanely as if to say, "Yes, I know I look like an asshole. Isn't this amusing?"

En route, I bumped into the table of a party of middle-aged rich people, slopping their drinks, and could only broaden my brainless smile and burble that I was ever so sorry. I patted one of the ladies affectionately on the shoulder with that easy familiarity that overcomes me when I am drunk and used her as a kind of springboard to propel myself towards the stairs, where I smiled a farewell to the room—everyone was by now watching me with interest—and descended the stairs in one fluid motion. I didn't exactly fall, but then again I didn't exactly walk down. It was more like surfing on the soles of my shoes, and was, I believe, not unimpressive. But then I often perform my best stunts while intoxicated. Once, many years ago during a party at John

230

Horner's house, I fell backwards out of an upstairs window and bounced to my feet with an élan that is still widely talked about south of Grand Avenue.

In the morning, chastened with a hangover, I drove back to the campus of St. John's, found my niece and embarrassed her—possibly even grossed her out—with a hug. We went to breakfast in a fancy restaurant downtown and she told me all about St. John's and Santa Fe and afterwards showed me the sights of the town: St. Francis's Cathedral (very beautiful), the Palace of the Governors (very boring, full of documents about territorial governors) and the famous staircase at the Loretto Chapel. This is a wooden staircase that rise 21½ feet in a double spiral up to a choir loft. The remarkable thing about it is that it is not supported by anything except its own weight. It looks as if it ought to fall down. The story is that the nuns of the chapel prayed for someone to build them a staircase and an anonymous carpenter turned up, worked on the staircase for six months and then disappeared without payment as mysteriously as he had arrived. For a hundred years the nuns milked this story for all it was worth, and then one day a few years ago they abruptly sold the chapel to a private company, which now runs it for a profit and charges you fifty cents to get in. This kind of soured me on the place, and it didn't do a whole lot for my respect for nuns.

Generally speaking—which is of course always a dangerous thing to do, generally speaking—Americans revere the past only as long as there is some money in it somewhere and it doesn't mean going without air-conditioning, free parking and other essential conveniences. Preserving the past for its own sake doesn't come into it much. There is little room for sentiment. When somebody comes along and offers a group of nuns good money for their staircase, they don't say, "Certainly not, it is a hallowed shrine, built for us by a mysterious and rather hunky-looking courier of Jesus." They say, "How much?" And if the offer is good enough they sell it and use the money to build a new convent on a bigger site, with air-conditioning, lots of parking space and a games room. I don't mean to suggest for a moment that nuns are worse than other Americans in this regard. They are simply behaving in the customary American way. I find that very sad. It is no wonder that so few things last for more than a generation in America.

I left Santa Fe and drove west along Interstate 40. This used to be Route 66. Everybody loved Route 66. People used to write songs about it. But it was only two lanes wide, not at all suitable for the space age, hopelessly inadequate for people in motor homes, and every fifty miles or so it would pass through a little town where you might encounter a stop sign or a traffic light—what a drag!—so they buried it under the desert and built a new superhighway that shoots across the landscape like a four-lane laser and doesn't stop for anything, even mountains. So something else that was nice and pleasant is gone forever because it wasn't practical—like passenger trains and milk in bottles and corner shops and Burma Shave signs. And now it's happening in England, too. They are taking away all the nice things there because they are impractical, as if that were reason enough—the red phone boxes, the pound note, those open London buses that you can leap on and off. There's almost no experience in life that makes you look and feel more suave than jumping on or off a moving London bus. But they aren't practical. They require two men (one to drive and one to stop thugs from kicking the crap out of the Pakistani gentleman at the back) and that is un-economical, so they have to go. And before long there will be no more milk in bottles delivered to the doorstep or sleepy rural pubs, and the countryside will be mostly shopping centers and theme parks. Forgive me. I don't mean to get upset. But you are taking my world away from me, piece by little piece, and some-times it just pisses me off. Sorry.

I drove west along Interstate 40, through an impoverished land-scape. Habitations were few. Such towns as existed were mostly just scatterings of trailer homes dumped along the roadside, as if dropped from a great height. They had no yards, no fences, noth-ing to separate them from the desert. Much of the land was given over to Indian reservations. Every twenty or thirty miles I would pass a lone hitchhiker, sometimes an Indian but usually a white person, laden with bags. I had seen hardly any hitchhikers before now, but here there were many, the men looking dangerous, the women looking crazy. I was entering a land of drifters: dreamers, losers, vagrants, crazy people—they all always go west in America. They all have this hopeless idea that they will get to the coast and make a fortune as a movie star or rock musician or game-show contestant or something. And if things don't work out they can always become a serial murderer. It's strange that no one ever goes east, that you never encounter anyone hitchhiking to New York in pursuit of some wild and crazy dream to be a certified public accountant or make a killing in leveraged buyouts.

The weather worsened. Dust began to blow across the road. I was driving into the storm that the weatherman had spoken of on television the morning before. Beyond Albuquerque the skies darkened and a sleety rain began to dart about. Tumbleweeds bounced across the desert and over the highway, and the car was knocked sharply sideways with each gust of wind.

I had always thought that deserts were hot and dry the year around. I can tell you now that they are not. I suppose because we always took our vacations between June and August it implanted in me the idea that everywhere in America outside the Midwest was hot the year around. Wherever you went in the summer in America it was murder. It was always ninety degrees. If you closed the windows you baked, but if you left them open everything blew everywhere—comic books, maps, loose articles of clothing. If you wore shorts, as we always did, the bare skin on your legs became part of the seat, like cheese melted onto toast, and when it was time to get up, there was a ripping sound and a screaming sensation of agony as the two parted. If in your sun-baked delirium you carelessly leaned your arm against the metal part of the door onto which the sun had been shining, the skin where it made contact would shrivel and disappear, like a plastic bag in a flame. This would always leave you speechless. It was a truly amazing, and curiously painless, spectacle to watch part of your body just vanish. You didn't know whether to shriek at your mother as if you had been gravely wounded or do it again, in a spirit of scientific inquiry. In the end, usually, you would do nothing, but just sit listlessly, too hot to do anything else.

So I was surprised to find myself in wintry weather, in a landscape as cold as it was bleak. The darting sleet thickened as the highway climbed up and into the Zuni Mountains. Beyond Gallup it turned to snow. Wet and heavy, it fell from the sky like scattered feathers, and the afternoon became like night.

Twenty miles beyond Gallup, I entered Arizona and the farther I drove into that state the more evident it became that I was entering a storm of long standing. The snow along the roadside became ankle-deep and then knee-deep. It was odd to think that only a couple of hours before I had been strolling around Santa Fe in bright sunshine and shirtsleeves. Now the radio was full of news of closed roads and atrocious weather—snow in the mountains, torrential rain elsewhere. It was the worst spring storm in decades, the weatherman said with ill-disguised glee. The Los Angeles Dodgers had been rained out at home for the third day in a row—the first time this had happened since they moved to the coast from Brooklyn thirty years before. There was nowhere I could turn to escape this storm. Bleakly, I pushed on towards Flagstaff, a hundred miles to the west.

"And there's fourteen inches of snow on the ground at Flagstaff—with more expected," the weatherman said, sounding very pleased.

23

NOTHING PREPARES YOU for the Grand Canyon. No matter how many times you read about it or see it pictured, it still takes your breath away. Your mind, unable to deal with anything on this scale, just shuts down and for many long moments you are a human vacuum, without speech or breath, but just a deep, inexpressible awe that anything on this earth could be so vast, so beautiful, so silent.

Even children are stilled by it. I was a particularly talkative and obnoxious child, but it stopped me cold. I can remember rounding a corner and standing there agog while a mouthful of half-formed jabber just rolled backwards down my throat, forever unuttered. I was seven years old and I'm told it was only the second occasion in all that time that I had stopped talking, apart from short breaks for sleeping and television. The one other thing to silence me was the sight of my grandfather dead in an open coffin. It was such an unexpected sight—no one had told me that he would be on display—and it just took my breath away. There he was all still and silent, dusted with powder and dressed in a suit. I particularly remember that he had his glasses on (what did they think he was going to do with those where he was going?) and that they were crooked. I think my grandmother had knocked them askew during her last blubbery embrace and then everyone else had been too squeamish to push them back into place. It was a shock to me to realize that never again in the whole of eternity would he laugh over "I Love Lucy" or repair his car or talk with his mouth full (something for which he was widely noted in the family). It was awesome.

But not nearly as awesome as the Grand Canyon. Since, obviously, I could never hope to relive my grandfather's funeral, the Grand Canyon was the one vivid experience from my childhood that I could hope to recapture, and I had been looking forward to it for many days. I had spent the night at Winslow, Arizona, fifty miles short of Flagstaff, because the roads were becoming almost impassable. In the evening the snow had eased to a scattering of flakes and by morning it had stopped altogether, though the skies still looked dark and pregnant. I drove through a snow-whitened landscape towards the Grand Canyon. It was hard to believe that this was the last week of April. Mists and fog swirled about the road. I could see nothing at the sides and ahead of me except the occasional white smear of oncoming headlights. By the time I reached the entrance to Grand Canyon National Park, and paid the five-dollar admission, snow was dropping heavily again, thick white flakes so big that their undersides carried shadows.

The road through the park followed the southern lip of the canyon for thirty miles. Two or three times I stopped in turnouts and went to the edge to peer hopefully into the silent murk, knowing that the canyon was out there, just beyond my nose, but I couldn't see anything. The fog was everywhere—threaded among the trees, adrift on the roadsides, rising steamily off the pavement. It was so thick I could kick holes in it. Glumly I drove on to the Grand Canyon village, where there was a visitors' center and a rustic hotel and a scattering of administrative buildings. There were lots of tour buses and recreational vehicles in the parking lots and people hanging around in entranceways or picking their way through the slushy snow, going from one building to another. I went and had an overpriced cup of coffee in the hotel cafeteria and felt damp and dispirited. I had really been looking forward to the Grand Canyon. I sat by the window and bleakly watched the snow pile up.

Afterwards, I trudged towards the visitors' center, perhaps 200 yards away, but before I got there I came across a snow-spattered sign announcing a lookout point half a mile away along a trail through the woods, and impulsively I went down it, mostly just to get some air. The path was slippery and took a long time to traverse, but on the way the snow stopped falling and the air felt clean and refreshing. Eventually I came to a platform of rocks, marking the edge of the canyon. There was no fence to keep you back from the edge, so I shuffled cautiously over and looked down, but could see nothing but gray soup. A middle-aged couple came along and as we stood chatting about what a dispiriting experience this was, a miraculous thing happened. The fog parted. It just silently drew back, like a set of theater curtains being opened, and suddenly we saw that we were on the edge of a sheer, giddying drop of at least a thousand feet. "Jesus!" we said and jumped back, and all along the canyon edge you could hear people saying, "Jesus!" like a message being passed down a long line. And then for many moments all was silence, except for the tiny fretful shiftings of the snow, because out there in front of us was the most awesome, most silencing sight that exists on earth.

The scale of the Grand Canyon is almost beyond comprehension. It is ten miles across, a mile deep, 180 miles long. You could set the Empire State Building down in it and still be thousands of feet above it. Indeed you could set the whole of Manhattan down inside it and you would still be so high above it that buses would be like ants and people would be invisible, and not a sound would reach you. The thing that gets you—that gets everyone—is the silence. The Grand Canyon just swallows sound. The sense of space and emptiness is overwhelming. Nothing happens out there. Down below you on the canyon floor, far, far away, is the thing that carved it: the Colorado River. It is 300 feet wide, but from the canyon's lip it looks thin and insignificant. It looks like an old shoelace. Everything is dwarfed by this mighty hole.

And then, just as swiftly, just as silently as the fog had parted, it closed again and the Grand Canyon was a secret once more. I had seen it for no more than twenty or thirty seconds, but at least I had seen it. Feeling semisatisfied, I turned around and walked back towards the car, content now to move on. On the way, I encountered a young couple coming towards the edge. They asked me if I'd had any luck and I told them all about how the fog had parted for a few seconds. They looked crushed. They said they had come all the way from Ontario. It was their honeymoon. All their lives they had wanted to see the Grand Canyon. Three times every day for the past week they had put on their moon boots and honeymoon winterwear and walked hand in hand to the canyon's edge, but all they had seen so far was an unshifting wall of fog.

"Still," I said, trying to help them look on the bright side, "I bet you've gotten in a lot of good shagging." I didn't really say that. Even I wouldn't say that. I just made sympathetic noises and said what a shame it was about the weather and wished them luck. I walked on in a reflective mood to the car, thinking about the poor honeymooners. As my father always used to tell me, "You see, son, there's always someone in the world worse off than you."

And I always used to think, "So?"

I headed north on Highway 89 towards Utah. The radio was full of more news of bad weather in the Rockies and Sierra Nevadas, and of roads closed by rock slides and heavy snow, though here in northern Arizona there was no snow at all. Absolutely none. Ten miles beyond the Grand Canyon it just disappeared and a few miles after that it was like spring. The sun came out. The world was warm. I rolled the window down a little.

I drove and drove. That is what you do in the West. You drive and you drive and you drive, advancing from one scattered town to the next, creeping across a landscape like Neptune. For long, empty hours your one goal in life is to get to Dry Gulch or Cactus City or wherever. You sit there watching the highway endlessly unfurl and the odometer advancing with the speed of centuries and all you think about is getting to Dry Gulch and hoping by some miracle it will have a McDonald's or at least a coffee shop. And when at last you get there, all there is is a two-pump gas station and a stall with an old Indian woman selling Navajo trinkets and you realize that you have to start the process all over again with another impossibly isolated hamlet with a depressingly unpromising name: Coma, Doldrum, Dry Well, Sunstroke.

The distances are almost inconceivable. There is often thirty miles between houses and a hundred miles or more between towns. What would it take to make you live in a place where you had to drive seventy-five miles just to buy a pair of shoes—and even then they would look as if they came from a funeral home?

The answer to my question, of course, is that not many people do want to live in such a place, except for Indians, who were never given much choice. I was now driving across the largest Indian reservation in America—a Navajo reservation stretching for 150 miles from north to south and 200 miles from east to west—and most of the few cars along the highway were driven by Indians. Almost without exception these were big old Detroit cars in dreadful condition, with all the trim gone or flopping loosely, and with at least one mismatched door and important-looking pieces hanging from the undercarriage, clattering on the highway, shooting out sparks or dense smoke. They never seemed to be able to get over about forty miles an hour, but they were always difficult to pass because of the way they drifted around on the highway.

Occasionally they would drift far off to the right, sometimes even kicking up desert dust, and I would shoot past. Always it was the same sight: a car packed with Indian men and boys and a driver drunk beyond repair, sitting there with a wet-dream look on his face—the look of a man who is only barely conscious but having a splendid time nonetheless.

At Page, Arizona, home of the Glen Canyon Dam, I passed into Utah and almost immediately the landscape improved. The hills grew purplish and red and the desert took on a blush of color. After a few miles, the sagebrush thickened and the hills became darker and more angular. It all looked oddly familiar.

Then I consulted my Mobil guidebook and discovered that this was where all the Hollywood Westerns were made. More than a hundred film and television companies had used Kanab, the next town down the road, as their headquarters for location shooting.

This excited me, and when I got to Kanab, I stopped and went into a cafe to see if I could find out more. A voice from the back called out that she would be just a minute, so I had a look at the menu on the wall. It was the strangest menu I had ever seen. It was full of foods I had never heard of: potato logs ("small, medium and family size"), cheese sticks for 89 cents, pizza pockets for $1.39, Oreo shakes for $1.25. The special offer was "8oz log, roll and slaw, $7.49." I decided I would have coffee. After a moment the woman who ran the cafe came out wiping her hands on a towel. She told me some of the films and TV shows that had been shot around Kanab: *Duel at Diablo, Butch Cassidy and the Sundance Kid,* "My Friend Flicka," "The Rifleman," some Clint Eastwood movies. I asked her whether any Hollywood stars ever came in for some potato logs or cheese sticks. She shook her head wistfully and said no. Somehow this didn't altogether surprise me.

I spent the night at Cedar City and in the morning drove to Bryce Canyon National Park, which was invisible on account of fog and snow, and then, in a surly mood, to Zion National Park, where it was like summer. This was very odd because the two parks are only about forty miles apart, and yet they seemed to inhabit different continents as far as the weather went. If I live forever I will not begin to understand the weather of the West.

Zion was incredibly beautiful. Whereas at the Grand Canyon you are on the top looking down, at Zion you are at the bottom looking up. It is just a long, lush canyon, dense with cottonwood trees along the valley floor, hemmed in by towering copper-colored walls of rock—the sort of dark, forbidding valley you would expect to pass through in a hunt for the lost city of gold. Here and there long, thin waterfalls emerged from the rock face and fell a thousand feet or more down to the valley, where the water collected in pools or tumbled onward into the swirling Virgin River. At the far end of the valley the high walls squeezed together until they were only yards apart. In the damp shade, plants grew out of cracks in the rock, giving the whole the appearance of hanging gardens. It was very picturesque and exotic.

The sheer walls on either side looked as if they might rain boulders at any moment—and indeed they sometimes do. Halfway along the path the little river was suddenly littered with rocks, some of them the size of houses. A sign said that on July 16, 1981, more than 15,000 tons of rock fell 1,000 feet into the river here, but it didn't say whether there were any people squashed beneath them. I daresay there were. Even now in April there were scores of people all along the path; in July there must have been hundreds. At least a couple of them must have got caught. When the rocks came tumbling down, there would be no place to run.

I was standing there reflecting on this melancholy thought when I became aware of a vaguely irritating whirring noise beside me. It was a man with a camcorder, taking footage of the rocks. It was one of the early, primitive models, so he had all kinds of power packs and auxiliary paraphernalia strapped to his body, and the camera itself was enormous. It must be like going on vacation with your vacuum cleaner. Anyway, it served him right. My first rule of consumerism is never buy anything you can't make your children carry. The man looked exhausted, but of course having spent a ridiculously inflated sum to buy the camera he was now determined to film everything that passed before his eyes, even at the risk of acquiring a hernia (and when that happened he would of course get his wife to film the operation).

I can never understand these people who rush to buy new gadgets; surely they must see that they are going to look like idiots in about a year when the manufacturers come up with tiny lightweight versions of the same thing at half the price. Like the people who paid $200 for the first pocket calculators and then a few months later they were being given away at gas stations. Or the people who bought the first color televisions.

One of our neighbors, Mr. Sheitelbaum, bought a color TV in 1958 when there were only about two color programs a month. We used to peek through his window when we knew one was coming on, and it was always the same—people with orange faces and clothes that kept changing hue. Mr. Sheitelbaum kept bobbing up to fiddle with the many little knobs with which the thing was equipped while his wife shouted encouragement from across the room.

For a few moments the color would be pretty fair—not accurate exactly, but not too disturbing—and then just as Mr. Sheitelbaum placed his butt back on the sofa it would all go haywire and we would have green horses and red clouds, and he'd be back at the control panel again. It was hopeless. But having spent such a huge amount of money on this thing, Mr. Sheitelbaum would never give up on it, and for the next fifteen years whenever you walked past his living room window you would see him fiddling with the controls and muttering.

In the late afternoon, I drove on to St. George, a small city not far from the state line. I got a room in the Oasis Motel and dined at Dick's Cafe. Afterwards, I went for a stroll. St. George had a nice old-town feel about it, though in fact most of the buildings were new except for the Gaiety Movie Theater (ALL SEATS $2) and Dixie Drugstore next door. The drugstore was closed, but I was brought up short by the sight of a soda fountain inside, a real marble-topped soda fountain with twirly stools and straws in paper wrappers—the sort in which you tear off one end and then blow, sending the wrapper on a graceful trajectory into the cosmetics department.

I was crushed. This must be just about the last genuine drugstore soda fountain in America and the place was closed. I would have given whole dollars to go in and order a Green River or a chocolate soda and send a few straw wrappers wafting about and then challenge the person on the next stool to a twirling contest. My personal best is four full revolutions. I know that doesn't sound much, but it's a lot harder than it looks. Bobby Wintermeyer did five once and then threw up. It's a pretty hairy sport, believe me.

On the corner was a big brick Mormon church, or temple or tabernacle or whatever they call them. It was dated 1871 and looked big enough to hold the whole town—and indeed it probably often does since absolutely everybody in Utah is a Mormon. This sounds kind of alarming until you realize that it means Utah is the one place on the planet where you never have to worry about young men coming up to you and trying to convert you to Mormonism. They assume you are one of them already. As long as you keep your hair cut fairly short and don't say, "Oh, shit!" in public when something goes wrong, you may escape detection for years. It makes you feel a little like Kevin McCarthy in *Invasion of the Body Snatchers*, but it is also strangely liberating.

Beyond the Mormon church things became mostly residential. Everything was green and fresh after the recent rains. The town smelled of spring, of lilacs and fresh-mown grass. The evening was creeping in. It was that relaxed time of day when people have finished their dinners and are just pootling about in the yard or garage, not doing much of anything in preparation for shortly doing even less.

The streets were the widest I'd ever seen in any town, even out here in the residential neighborhoods. Mormons sure do love wide streets. I don't know why. Wide streets and lots of wives for bonking, those are the foundation stones of Mormonism. When Brigham Young founded Salt Lake City one of the first things he did was decree that the streets be 100 feet wide, and he must have said something similar to the people of St. George. Young knew the town well—he had his winter home there—so if the townspeople ever tried anything slack with the streets he'd have been onto them right away.

24

=============== HERE'S A RIDDLE for you. What is the difference between Nevada and a toilet? Answer: You can flush a toilet.

Nevada has the highest crime rate of any state, the highest rape rate, the second highest violent crime rate (it's just nosed out by New York), the highest highway fatality rate, the second highest rate of gonorrhea (Alaska is the trophy holder) and the highest proportion of transients—almost 80 percent of the state's residents were born elsewhere. It has more prostitutes than any other state in America. It has a long history of corruption and strong links with organized crime. And its most popular entertainer is Wayne Newton. So you may understand why I crossed the border from Utah with a certain sense of disquiet.

But then I got to Las Vegas and my unease vanished. I was dazzled. It's impossible not to be. It was late afternoon, the sun was low, the temperature was in the high eighties, and the Strip was already thronged with happy vacationers in nice clean clothes, their pockets visibly bulging with money, strolling along in front of casinos the size of airport terminals. It all looked fun and oddly wholesome. I had expected it to be nothing but hookers and high rollers in stretched Cadillacs, the sort of people who wear white leather shoes and drape their jackets over their shoulders, but these were just ordinary folks like you and me, people who wear a lot of nylon and Velcro.

I got a room in a motel at the cheaper end of the Strip, showered lavishly, danced through a dust storm of talcum powder, pulled on my cleanest T-shirt, and went straight back out, tingling with clean skin and childlike excitation. After days of driving across the desert you are ready for a little stimulus, and Las Vegas certainly provides it. Now, in the oven-dry air of early evening, the casino lights were coming on—millions and millions of them, erupting into walls of bilious color and movement, flashing, darting, rippling, bursting, all of them competing for my attention, for the coins in my pocket. I had never seen such a sight. It is an ocular orgasm, a three-dimensional hallucination, an electrician's wet dream. It was just as I had expected it to be but multiplied by ten.

The names on the hotels and casinos were eerily familiar: Caesar's Palace, the Dunes, the Sands, the Desert Inn. What most surprised me—what most surprises most people—is how many vacant lots there were. Here and there among the throbbing monoliths there were quarter-mile squares of silent desert, little pockets of dark calm, just waiting to be developed. When you have been to one or two casinos and seen how the money just pours into them, like gravel off a dump truck, it is hard to believe that there could be enough spare cash in the world to feed still more of them, yet more are being built all the time. The greed of mankind is practically insatiable, mine included.

I went into Caesar's Palace. It is set well back from the street, but I was conveyed in on a moving sidewalk, which rather impressed me. Inside the air was thick with unreality. The decor was supposed to be like a Roman temple or something. Statues of Roman gladiators and statesmen were scattered around the place and all the cigarette girls and ladies who gave change were dressed in skimpy togas, even if they were old and overweight, which most of them were, so their thighs wobbled as they walked. It was like watching moving Jell-O. I wandered through halls full of people intent on losing money—endlessly, single-mindedly feeding coins into slot machines or watching the clattering dance of a steel ball on a roulette wheel or playing games of blackjack that had no start or finish but were just continuous, like time. It all had a monotonous, yet anxious rhythm. There was no sense of pleasure or fun. I never saw anyone talking to anyone else, except to order a drink or cash some money. The noise was intense—the crank of one-armed bandits, the spinning of thousands of wheels, the din of clattering coins when a machine paid out.

A change lady Jell-O'd past and I got $10 worth of quarters from her. I put one in a one-armed bandit—I had never done this before; I'm from Iowa—pulled the handle and watched the wheels spin and thunk into place one by one. There was a tiny pause and then the machine spat six quarters into the payout bucket. I was hooked. I fed in more quarters. Sometimes I would lose and I would put in more quarters. Sometimes the machine would spit me back some quarters and I would put those in as well. After about five minutes I had no quarters left. I flagged down another ample-hipped vestal virgin and got $10 more. This time I won $12 worth of quarters straight off. It made a lot of noise. I looked around proudly, but no one paid any attention to me. Then I won $5 more. Hey, this is all right, I thought. I put all my quarters in a little plastic bucket that said CAESAR'S PALACE on it. There seemed to be an awful lot of them, gleaming up at me, but in about twenty minutes the bucket was empty. I went and got another $10 worth of quarters, and started feeding them in. I won some and lost some. I was beginning to realize that there was a certain pattern to it: for every four quarters I put in, I would on average get three back, sometimes in a bunch, sometimes in dribbles. My right arm began to ache a little. It was boring really, pulling the handle over and over, watching the wheels spin and thunk, thunk, thunk, spin and thunk, thunk, thunk. With my last quarter I won $3 worth of quarters, and was mildly disappointed because I had been hoping to go for dinner and now here I had a mittful of quarters again. So I dutifully fed the quarters into the machine and won some more money. This really was getting tiresome. Finally, after about thirty minutes I got rid of the last quarter and was able to go and look for a restaurant.

On the way out my attention was caught by a machine making a lot of noise. A woman had just won $600. For ninety seconds the machine just poured out money, a waterfall of silver. When it stopped, the woman regarded the pile without pleasure and began feeding it back into the machine. I felt sorry for her. It was going to take her all night to get rid of that kind of money.

I wandered through room after room trying to find my way out, but the place was clearly designed to leave you disoriented. There were no windows, no exit signs, just endless rooms, all with subdued lighting and with carpet that looked as if some executive had barked into a telephone, "Gimme twenty thousand yards of the ugliest carpet you got." It was like woven vomit. I wandered for ages without knowing whether I was getting closer to or farther from an exit. I passed a little shopping center, restaurants, a buffet, cabarets, dark and silent bars where people brooded, bars with live music and astonishingly untalented entertainers ("And gimme some astonishingly untalented entertainers while you're at it") and one large room in which the walls were covered with giant TV screens showing live sporting events—major league baseball, NBA basketball, boxing matches, a horse race. A whole wallful of athletes were silently playing their hearts out for the benefit of the room's lone spectator, and he was asleep.

I don't know how many gaming rooms there were, but there were many. It was often hard to tell whether I was seeing a new room or an old room from another angle. In each one it was the same—long ranks of people dully, mechanically losing money. It was as if they had been hypnotized. None of them seemed to see that everything was stacked against them. It is all such an incredible con. Some of the casinos make profits of $100 million a year—that's the kind of money many large corporations make—and without having to do anything but open their doors. It takes almost no skills, no intelligence, no class to run a casino. I read in *Newsweek* that the guy who owns the Horseshoe casino downtown has never learned how to read and write. Can you believe that? That gives you some idea of the sort of levels of intellectual attainment you need to be a success in Vegas. Suddenly, I hated the place. I was annoyed with myself for having been taken in by it all, the noise and sparkle, for having so quickly and mindlessly lost thirty dollars. For that kind of money I could have bought a baseball cap with a plastic turd on the brim *and* an ashtray in the shape of a toilet saying, PLACE YOUR BUTT HERE. SOUVENIR OF LAS VEGAS, NEVADA. This made me deeply gloomy.

I went and ate in the Caesar's Palace buffet, hoping that some food would improve my outlook. The buffet cost eight dollars, but you could eat all you wanted, so I took a huge amount of everything, determined to recoup some of my loss. The resultant plate was such a mixture of foods, gravies, barbecue sauces and salad creams that it was really just a heap of tasteless goo. But I shoveled it all down and then had an outsized platter of chocolate goo for dessert. And then I felt very ill. I felt as if I had eaten a beanbag. Clutching my distended abdomen, I found my way to an exit. There was no moving sidewalk to return me to the street—there's no place in Las Vegas for losers and quitters—so I had to make a long weaving walk down the floodlit driveway to the Strip. The fresh air helped a little, but only a little. I limped through the crowds along the Strip, looking like a man doing a poor imitation of Quasimodo, and went into a couple of other casinos, hoping they would re-excite my greed and make me forget my swollen belly. But they were practically identical to Caesar's Palace—the same noise, the same stupid people losing all their money, the same hideous carpets. It all just gave me a headache. After a while, I gave up altogether. I plodded back to my motel and fell heavily onto the bed and watched TV with that kind of glazed immobility that overcomes you when your stomach is grossly overloaded and there's no remote control device and you can't quite reach the channel switch with your big toe.

So I watched the local news. Principally this consisted of a rundown of the day's murders in Las Vegas accompanied by film from the various murder scenes. These always showed a house with the front door open, some police detectives shuffling around and a group of neighborhood children standing on the fringes, waving happily at the camera and saying hi to their moms. In between each report the anchorman and anchorwoman would trade witless quips and then say in a breezy tone something like, "A mother and her three young children were hacked to death by a crazed axman at Boulder City today. We'll have a filmed report after these words." Then there would be many long minutes of commercials, mostly for products to keep one's bowels sleek, followed by filmed reports on regional murders, house fires, light airplane crashes, multiple car pileups on the Boulder Highway and other bits of local carnage, always with film of mangled vehicles, charred houses, bodies under blankets and a group of children standing on the fringes, waving happily at the cameras and saying hi to their moms. It may only have been my imagination, but I would almost swear that it was the same children in every report. Perhaps American violence had bred a new kind of person—the serial witness.

Finally there was a special report about a man awaiting release from prison who ten years before had raped a young woman and then, for reasons of obscure gratification, had sawed off her arms at the elbows. No kidding. This was so shocking even to the hardened sensibilities of Nevadans that a mob was expected to be waiting for the man when he was released at 6 A.M. the next day, according to the TV reporter, who then gave all the details necessary to enable viewers to go down and join in. The police, the reporter added with a discernible trace of pleasure, were refusing to guarantee the man's safety. The report concluded with a shot of the reporter talking to camera in front of the prison gate. Behind her a group of children were jumping up and down and waving hellos to their moms. This was all becoming too bizarre for me. I got up heavily and switched the TV to "Mr. Ed." At least you know where you are with Mr. Ed.

In the morning I took Interstate 15 south out of Las Vegas, a long, straight drive through the desert. It's the main route between Las Vegas and Los Angeles, 272 miles away, and it's like driving across the top of an oven. After about an hour I passed over into California, into a shimmering landscape of bleached earth and patchy creosote bushes called the Devils Playground. The sunlight glared. The far-off Soda Mountains quivered and distant cars coming towards me looked like balls of fire, so brilliant was their reflection, and always ahead on the road there was a slick smear of mirage that disappeared as I drew near and reappeared further on. Along the shoulder of the road, sometimes out on the desert itself, were cars that had failed to complete the journey. Some of them looked to have been there for a long time.

What an awful place to break down. In the summer, this was one of the hottest spots on earth. Off to the right, over the parched Avawatz Mountains, was Death Valley, where the highest temperature ever recorded in America, 134 degrees Fahrenheit, was logged in 1913 (the world record, in 1922 in Libya, is just 2 degrees higher). But that was the shade temperature. A thermometer lying on the ground in the sun has gone over 200 degrees. Even now in April the temperature was nudging 90 and it was very unpleasant. It was impossible to imagine it almost half as hot again. And yet people live out there, in awful little towns like Baker and Barstow, where the temperature often stays over 90 degrees for 100 days in a row and where they can go ten years without a drop of rain. I pressed on, longing for clear water and green hills.

One good thing about California is that it doesn't take long to find a complete contrast. The state has the strangest geography. At Death Valley you have the lowest point in America—282 feet below sea level—and yet practically overlooking it is the highest point in the country (not counting Alaska)—Mount Whitney, at 14,495 feet. You could, if you wished, fry an egg on the roof of your car in Death Valley, then drive thirty miles into the mountains and quick-freeze it in a snowbank. My original intention was to cross the Sierra Nevadas by way of Death Valley (breaking off from time to time to perform experiments with eggs), but a weather lady on the radio informed me that the mountain passes were all still closed on account of the recent nasty weather. So I had to make a long and unrewarding detour across the Mojave Desert, on old Highway 58. This took me past Edwards Air Force Base, which runs for almost forty miles along the highway behind a seemingly endless stretch of chain-link fence. The Space Shuttle lands at Edwards, and Chuck Yeager broke the sound barrier there, so it's really quite a hotshot place, but from the highway I couldn't see anything at all—no planes, no hangars, just mile after mile of tall chain-link fence.

Beyond the little town of Mojave, the desert ended and the landscape erupted in smooth hills and citrus groves. I crossed the Los Angeles Aqueduct, which carries water from northern California to Los Angeles, fifty miles to the south. Even out here the city's smog was threaded through the hills. Visibility was no more than a mile. Beyond that there was just a wall of brownish-gray haze. On the other side of it the sun was a bleary disk of light. Everything seemed to be bled of color. Even the hills looked jaundiced. They were round and covered with boulders and low-growing trees. There was something strangely familiar about them—and then I realized what it was. These were the hills that the Lone Ranger and Zorro and Roy Rogers and the Cisco Kid used to ride around on in the TV shows of the 1950s. I had never noticed until now that the West of the movies and the West of television were two quite different places. Movie crews had obviously gone out into the real West—the West of buttes and bluffs and red river valleys—while television companies, being cheap, had only just driven a few miles into the hills north of Hollywood and filmed on the edges of orange groves.

Here clearly were the very boulders that Tonto, the Lone Ranger's faithful sidekick, used to creep around on. Every week the Lone Ranger would send Tonto off to creep around on some boulders in order to spy on an encampment of bad guys and every week Tonto would get captured. He was hopeless. Every week the Lone Ranger would have to ride in and save Tonto, but he didn't mind doing that because he and Tonto were very close. You could see it in the way they looked at each other.

Those were the days all right. Now children sit and watch people having their vitals sprayed around the room with a chain saw and think nothing of it. I know that makes me sound very old and crotchety to all you youngsters out there, but I think it's a pity that we can't have some good wholesome entertainment like we had when I was a boy, when the heroes wore masks and capes, and carried whips, and liked other men a whole bunch. Seriously, have you ever stopped to think what strange role models we were given when we were children? Like Superman. Here's a guy who changes his clothes in public. Or Davy Crockett, a man who conquered the frontier, fought valiantly at the Alamo and yet never noticed that he had a dead squirrel on his head. It's no wonder people my age grew up confused and got heavily involved with drugs. My favorite hero of all was Zorro, who whenever he was peeved with someone would whip out his sword and with three deft strokes carve a *Z* in the offending party's shirt. Wouldn't you just love to be able to do that?

"Waiter, I specifically asked for this steak rare."

Slash, slash, slash!

"Excuse me, but I believe I was here before you."

Slash, slash, slash!

"What do you mean you don't have it in my size?"

Slash, slash, slash!

For weeks, my friend Robert Swanson and I tried to master this useful trick by practicing with his mother's kitchen knives, but all we had to show for it were some torn shirts and ragged wounds across our chests, and after a time we gave it up as both painful and impossible, a decision that even now I rue from time to time.

As I was so close to Los Angeles, I toyed with the idea of driving on in, but I was put off by the smog and the traffic and above all by the thought that in Los Angeles someone might come up to me and carve a *Z* in my chest for real. I think it's only right that crazy people should have their own city, but I cannot for the life of me see why a sane person would want to go there. Besides, Los Angeles is passé. It has no surprises. My plan was to drive up through the hidden heart of California, through the fertile San Joaquin Valley. Nobody ever goes there. There is a simple reason for this, as I was about to discover. It is really boring.

25

══════════════ I WOKE UP quietly excited. It was a bright clear morning and in an hour or two I was going to go to Sequoia National Park and drive through a tree. This excited me, in a calm, unshowy sort of way. When I was five, my Uncle Frank and Aunt Fern from Winfield went to California on vacation—this was, of course, before it turned out that Frank was a homosexual, the old devil, and ran off to Key West, Florida, with his barber, which rather shocked and upset a lot of people in Winfield, especially when they realized that from now on they would have to drive all the way to Mount Pleasant to get their hair cut—and they sent us a postcard showing a redwood tree of such enormous girth that a road had been cut right through the base of it. The postcard pictured a handsome young couple in a green Studebaker convertible driving through the tree and looking as if they were having something approximating a wholesome orgasm. It made an immediate impression on me. I went to my dad and asked him if we could go to California on our next vacation and drive through a tree and he looked at the card and said, "Well . . . maybe one day," and I knew then that I had about as much chance of seeing the road through the tree as I had of sprouting pubic hair.

Every year my father would call a family powwow (can you believe this?) to discuss where we were going on vacation and every year I would push for going to California and the tree with a road through it, and my brother and sister would sneer cruelly and say that that was a really mega-dumb idea. My brother always wanted to go to the Rocky Mountains, my sister to Florida and my mother said she didn't care where we went as long as we were all together. And then my dad would pull out some brochures with titles like "Arkansas—Land of Several Lakes" and "Arkansas—the Sho' Nuff State" and "Important Vacation Facts About Arkansas" (with a foreword by Governor Luther T. Smiley), and suddenly it would seem altogether possible that we might be going to Arkansas that year, whatever our collective views on the matter might be.

When I was eleven, we went to California, the very state that housed my dream tree, but we only went to places like Disneyland and Hollywood Boulevard and Beverly Hills. (Dad was too cheap to buy a map showing the homes of the movie stars, so we just drove around and speculated.) A couple of times at breakfast I asked if we could drive up and see the tree with a road through it, but everybody was so dismissive—it was too far away, it would be too stupendously boring for words, it would probably cost a lot of money—that I lost heart and stopped asking. And in fact I never asked again. But it stayed at the back of my mind, one of my five great unfulfilled dreams from childhood. (The others, it goes without saying, were to have the ability to stop time, to possess the gift of X-ray vision, to be able to hypnotize my brother and make him be my slave, and to see Sally Ann Summerfield without a stitch of clothing on.)

Not surprisingly, none of these dreams came true. (Which is perhaps just as well. Sally Ann Summerfield is a blimp now. She turned up at my high-school reunion two years ago and looked like a shipping hazard.) But now here at last I was about to fulfill one of them. Hence the tingle of excitement as I slung my suitcase in the trunk and headed up Highway 63 for Sequoia National Park.

I had spent the night in the little city of Tulare, in the heart of the San Joaquin Valley. This is the richest and most fertile farming country in the world. They grow over 200 kinds of crops in the San Joaquin Valley. That very morning, on the local news on TV, they reported that the farming income for Tulare County for the previous year was $1.6 billion and yet it was only the second highest figure for the state. Fresno County, just up the road, was richer still. Even so, the landscape didn't look all that brilliant. The valley was as flat as a tennis court. It stretched for miles in every direction, dull and brown and dusty, and a permanent haze hung on the horizon, like a dirty window. Perhaps it was the time of year, or perhaps it was the drought that was just beginning to choke central California, but it didn't look rich or fruitful. And the towns that speckled the plain were equally dull. They looked like towns from anywhere. They didn't look rich or modern or interesting. Except that there were oranges the size of grapefruits growing on trees in the front yards, I could have been in Indiana or Illinois or anywhere. That surprised me. On our family trip to California it had been like driving into the next decade. It had all looked sleek and modern. Things that were still novelties in Iowa—shopping centers, drive-in banks, McDonald's restaurants, miniature golf courses, kids on skateboards— were old and long established in California. Now they just looked older. The rest of the country had caught up. The California of 1988 had nothing that Iowa didn't have. Except smog. And beaches. And oranges growing in front yards. And trees you could drive through.

I joined Highway 198 at Visalia and followed it as it shot through fragrant lemon groves, ran along the handsome shoreline of Lake Kaweah and climbed up into the foothills of the Sierra Nevada Mountains. Just beyond Three Rivers I entered the park, where a ranger in a wooden booth charged me a five-dollar entrance fee and gave me a brochure detailing the sights beyond. I looked quickly through it for a photograph of a road through a tree, but there weren't any pictures, just words and a map bearing colorful and alluring names: Avalanche Pass, Mist Falls, Farewell Gap, Onion Valley, Giant Forest. I made for Giant Forest.

Sequoia National Park and Kings Canyon National Park are contiguous. Effectively they are one national park and, like all national parks in the West, it is a good-sized one—seventy miles from top to bottom, thirty miles across. Because of the twisting roads as I climbed up into the mountains, progress was slow, though splendidly scenic.

I drove for two hours on lofty roads through boulder-strewn mountains. Snow was still lying about in broad patches. At last I entered the dark and mysterious groves of the giant sequoia (*Sequoiadendron giganteum,* according to my brochure). The trees were tall, no doubt about it, and fat around the base, though not fat enough to take a highway. Presumably they would get fatter as I moved deeper into the forest. Sequoias are ugly trees. They soar up and up and up, but their branches are sparse and stubby, so they look silly, like the sort of trees three-year-olds draw. In the middle of the Giant Forest stands the General Sherman Tree—the biggest living thing on earth. Surely the General Sherman was the one I was looking for.

"Oh boy, Chevette, have I got a treat for you!" I called out and patted the steering wheel fondly. When at last I neared the General Sherman, I found a small parking lot and a path leading to the tree through the woods. Evidently it was no longer possible to drive through the tree. This was a disappointment—name me something in life that isn't—but never mind, I thought. I'll walk through it; the pleasure will last longer. Indeed, I'll walk through it severally. I will stroll and saunter and glide, and if there aren't too many people about, I might well dance around it in the light-footed manner of Gene Kelly splashing through puddles in *Singin' in the Rain.*

So I banged the car door shut and walked up the trail to the tree and there it was, with a little fence around it to keep people from getting too close. It was big all right—tall and fat—but not *that* tall, not *that* fat. And there was no hole through its base. You might just about have managed to cut a modest road through it, but—and here's the important thing—no one ever had. Beside the tree was a large wooden board with an educational message on it. It said, "The giant General Sherman is not only the biggest tree in the world, but also the biggest living thing. It is at least 2,500 years old, and thus also one of the oldest living things. Even so, it is surprisingly boring, isn't it? That is because it isn't all that tall or all that fat. What sets it apart from other redwoods is that it doesn't taper very much. It stays pretty fat all the way up. Hence it has a greater bulk than any other tree. If you want to see really impressive redwoods—ones with roads driven through their bases—you have to go to Redwood National Park, way up near the Oregon border. Incidentally, we've erected a fence around the base of the tree to keep you well back from it and intensify your disappointment. As if that were not enough, there is a party of noisy young Germans coming up the path behind you. Isn't life shitty?"

As you will appreciate, this is somewhat paraphrased, but that was the gist of it. The Germans came and were obnoxious and unthoughtful, as adolescents tend to be, and stole the tree from me. They perched on the fence and started taking pictures. I derived some small pleasure from wandering in front of the cameraman whenever he was about to click the shutter, but this is an activity from which it is difficult to extract sustained amusement, even with Germans, and after a minute or two I left them there jabbering away about *die Pop Musik* and *das Drugs Scene* and their other adolescent preoccupations.

In the car I looked at the map and was disheartened to discover that Redwood National Park was almost 500 miles away. I could hardly believe it. Here I was 300 miles north of Los Angeles and yet I could drive another 500 miles and *still* be in California. It is 850 miles from top to bottom—about the distance between London and Milan. It would take me a day and a half to get to Redwood National Park, plus a day and a half to get back to where I was now. I didn't have that kind of time. Gloomily, I started the car and drove on to Yosemite National Park, seventy miles up the highway.

And what a disappointment that proved to be. I'm sorry to moan, I truly am, but Yosemite was a letdown of monumental proportions. It is incredibly, mouth-gawpingly beautiful. Your first view of the El Capitan valley, with its towering mountains and white waterfalls spilling hundreds of feet down to the meadows of the valley floor, makes you think that surely you have expired and gone to heaven. But then you drive on down into

Yosemite village and realize that if this is heaven you are going to spend the rest of eternity with an awful lot of fat people in Bermuda shorts.

Yosemite is a mess. The National Park Service in America—let's be candid here—does a pretty half-assed job of running many of the national parks. This is surprising because in America most leisure-time activities are about a million times better than anywhere else. But not national parks. The visitors' centers are usually dull, the catering is always crappy and expensive, and you generally come away having learned almost nothing about the wildlife, geology and history of the places you've driven hundreds of miles to see. The national parks are supposed to be there to preserve a chunk of America's wilderness, but in many of them the number of animals has actually fallen. Yellowstone has lost all its wolves, mountain lions and white-tailed deer, and the numbers of beaver and bighorn sheep are greatly depleted. These animals are thriving outside Yellowstone, but as far as the park service itself is concerned they are extinct.

I don't know why it should be, but the National Park Service has a long history of incompetence. In the 1960s, if you can believe it, the park service invited the Walt Disney Corporation to build a development in Sequoia National Park. Mercifully, that plan was quashed. But others have succeeded, most notably in 1923 when, after a long fight between conservationists and businessmen, the Hetch Hetchy Valley in the northern part of Yosemite—which was said to be even more spectacularly beautiful than Yosemite Valley itself—was flooded to create a reservoir to provide drinking water for San Francisco, 150 miles to the west. So for the last sixty years one of the half-dozen or so most breathtaking stretches of landscape on the planet has lain under water for commercial reasons. God help us if they ever find oil there.

The great problem at Yosemite today is simply finding your way around. I've never seen a place so badly signposted. It's as if they are trying to hide the park from you. At most parks the first thing you want to do is go to the visitors' center and have a look at the big map to get your bearings and decide what you want to see. But at Yosemite the visitors' center is almost impossible to find. I drove around Yosemite village for twenty-five minutes before I discovered a parking lot and then it took me a further twenty minutes, and a long walk in the wrong direction, to find the visitors' center. By the time I found it I knew my way around and didn't need it anymore.

And everything is just hopelessly, depressingly crowded—the cafeterias, the post office, the stores. This was in April; what it must be like in August doesn't bear guessing at. I have never been anywhere that was simultaneously so beautiful and so awful. In the end, I had a nice long walk and a look at the waterfalls and the scenery and it was outstanding. But I cannot believe that it can't be better run.

In the evening I drove on to Sonora, through a tranquil sunset, along sinuous mountain roads. I reached the town after dark and had difficulty finding a room. It was only the middle of the week, but most places were full. The motel I finally found was grossly overpriced and the TV reception was terrible. It was like watching people moving around in front of funhouse mirrors. Their bodies would proceed across the screen and their heads would follow a moment later, as if connected by elastic. I was paying forty-two dollars for this. The bed was like a pool table with sheets. And the toilet seat didn't have a SANITIZED FOR YOUR PROTECTION wrapper on it, denying me my daily ritual of cutting it with my scissors and saying, "I now declare this toilet open." These things become important to you when you have been alone on the road for a while. In a sour mood I drove into town and went to a cheap restaurant for dinner. The waitress made me wait a long time before she came and took my order. She looked tarty and had an irritating habit of repeating everything I said to her.

"I'd like the chicken-fried steak," I said.

"You'd like the chicken-fried steak?"

"Yes. And I would like french fries with it."

"You want french fries with it?"

"Yes. And I would like a salad with Thousand Island dressing."

"You want a salad with Thousand Island dressing?"

"Yes, and a Coke to drink."

"You want a Coke to drink?"

"Excuse me, miss, but I've had a bad day and if you don't stop repeating everything I say, I'm going to take this ketchup bottle and squirt it all down the front of your blouse."

"You're going to take that ketchup bottle and squirt it all down the front of my blouse?"

I didn't really threaten her with ketchup—she might have had a large boyfriend who would come and pummel me; also, I once knew a waitress who told me that whenever a customer was rude to her she went out to the kitchen and spat in his food, and since then I have never spoken sharply to a waitress or sent undercooked food back to the kitchen (because then the cook spits in it, you see)—but I was in such a disagreeable mood that I put my chewing gum straight into the ashtray without wrapping it in a piece of tissue first, as my mother always taught me to do, and pressed it down with my thumb so that it wouldn't fall out when the ashtray was turned over, but would have to be prised out with a fork. And what's more—God help me—it gave me a tingle of satisfaction.

In the morning I drove north from Sonora along Highway 49, wondering what the day would bring. I wanted to head east over the Sierra Nevadas, but many of the passes were still closed. Highway 49, as it turned out, took me on an agreeably winding journey through hilly country. Groves of trees and horse pastures overlooked the road, and occasionally I passed an old farmhouse, but there was little sign that the land was used for anything productive. The towns I passed through—Tuttletown, Melones, Angels Camp—were the places where the California Gold Rush took place. In 1848, a man named James Marshall found a lump of gold at Sutter Creek, just up the road, and people went crazy. Almost overnight, 40,000 prospectors poured into the state and in a little over a decade, between 1847 and 1860, California's population went from 15,000 to nearly 400,000. Some of the towns have been preserved as they were at the time—Sonora is not too bad in this regard—but mostly there's not much to show that this was once the scene of the greatest gold rush in history. I suppose this is largely because most of the people lived in tents and when the gold ran out so did they. Now most of the little towns offered the customary stretch of gas stations, motels and hamburger emporia. It was Anywhere, USA.

At Jackson, I found that Highway 88 was open through the mountains—the first open passage through the Sierras in almost 300 miles—and I took it. I had expected that I would have to take the next but one pass along, the infamous Donner Pass, where in 1846 a party of settlers became trapped by a blizzard for several weeks and survived by eating each other, an incident that caused a great sensation at the time. The leader of the group was named Donner. I don't know what became of him, but I bet he took some ribbing whenever he went into a restaurant after that. At any rate, it got his name on the map. The Donner Pass was also the route taken by the first transcontinental railroad, the Southern Pacific, and first transcontinental highway, old Route 40, the Lincoln Highway, on their 3,000-mile journey from New York to San Francisco. As with Route 66 further south, Route 40 had been callously dug up and converted into a dull, straight interstate highway, so I was pleased to find a back road open through the mountains.

And it was very pleasant. I drove through pine-forested scenery, with occasional long views across unpeopled valleys, heading in the general direction of Lake Tahoe and Carson City. The road was steep and slow and it took me much of the afternoon to drive the hundred or so miles to the Nevada border. Near Woodfords I entered the Toiyabe National Forest, or at least what once had been the Toiyabe National Forest. For miles and miles there was nothing but charred land, mountainsides of dead earth and stumps of trees. Occasionally I passed an undamaged house around which a firebreak had been dug. It was an odd sight, a house with swings and a wading pool in the middle of an ocean of blackened stumps. A year or so before, the owners must have thought they were the luckiest people on the planet, to live in the woods and mountains, amid the cool and fragrant pines. And now they lived on the surface of the moon. Soon the forest would be replanted and for the rest of their lives they could watch it grow again, inch by annual inch.

I had never seen such devastation—miles and miles of it—

and yet I had no recollection of having read about it. That's the thing about America. It's so big that it just absorbs disasters, muffles them with its vastness. Time and again on this trip I had seen news stories that would elsewhere have been treated as colossal tragedies—a dozen people killed by floods in the South, ten crushed when a store roof collapsed in Texas, twenty-two dead in a snowstorm in the East—and each of them treated as a brief and not terribly consequential diversion between ads for hemorrhoid unguents and cottage cheese. Partly it is a consequence of that inane breeziness common to local TV newscasters in America, but mostly it is just the scale of the country. A disaster in Florida is regarded in California in the same way that a disaster in Italy is regarded in Britain—as something briefly and morbidly diverting, but too far away to be tragic in any personal sense.

I entered Nevada about ten miles south of Lake Tahoe. Las Vegas had so put me off that I had no desire to go to another sink of iniquity, though I was later told that Tahoe is a really nice place and not at all like Las Vegas. Now I shall never know. I can tell you, however, that Carson City was just about the most nothing little city you could ever hope to zip through. It's the state capital, but mostly it was just Pizza Huts and gas stations and cheap-looking casinos.

I headed out of town on US 50, past Virginia City and towards Silver Springs. This was more or less the spot on "Bonanza" where the map used to burst into flames. Remember that? It has been many years since I've seen the program, but I recall Pa and Hoss and Little Joe and the surly-looking one whose name I forget all living in a landscape that was fruitful and lush, in a Western, high-chaparral sort of way. But out here there was nothing but cement-colored plains and barren hills and almost no habitations at all. Everything was gray, from the sky to the ground. This was to remain the pattern for the next two days.

It would be difficult to conceive of a more remote and cheerless state than Nevada. It has a population of just 800,000 in an area about the size of Britain and Ireland combined. Almost half of that population is accounted for by Las Vegas and Reno, so most of the rest of the state is effectively just empty. There are only 70 towns in the entire state—the British Isles have 40,000, just to give you some comparison—and some of them are indescribably remote. For instance, Eureka, a town of 1,200 in the middle of the state, is sixty miles in any direction from the nearest town. Indeed, the whole of Eureka County has just three towns and a total population of under 2,500—and this in an area of a couple of thousand square miles.

I drove for a while across this fearsome emptiness, taking a back highway between Fallon and a spot on the map called Humboldt Sink, where I gratefully joined Interstate 80. This was a cowardly thing to do, but the car had been making odd noises off and on for the past couple of days—a sort of faint *clonk clonk oh god help me clonk I'm dying oh god oh god clonk* noise—which wasn't covered in the troubleshooting section of the owner's manual. I couldn't face the prospect of breaking down and being stranded for days in some godforsaken dust hole while waiting for an anticlonk device to be shipped in from Reno on the weekly Greyhound. In any case, Highway 50, the nearest alternative road, would have taken me 150 miles out of my way and into Utah. I wanted to go a more northerly route across Montana and Wyoming—the Big Sky country. So it was with some relief that I joined the interstate, though even this was remarkably empty—usually I could see one car in the distance far ahead and one in the distance far behind—considering it was the main artery across the country. Indeed, with a sufficiently capacious fuel tank and bladder, you could drive the whole way between New York and San Francisco without stopping.

At Winnemucca I pulled off for gas and coffee and called my mother to let her know that I hadn't been killed yet and was doing all right for underwear—a matter of perennial concern to my mother. I was able to reassure her on this score and she reassured me that she hadn't willed her money to the International Guppy Institute or anything similarly rash (I just like to check!), so we were able to continue our respective days with light hearts.

In the phone booth was a poster with a photograph of a

young woman on it under the caption, HAVE YOU SEEN THIS GIRL? She was attractive and looked youthful and happy. The poster said she was nineteen years old and had been driving from Boston to San Francisco on her way home for Christmas when she disappeared. She had called her parents from Winnemucca to tell them to expect her the next afternoon and that was the last anyone had heard of her. Now, she was almost certainly dead, somewhere out there in that big empty desert. Murder is terrifyingly easy in America. You can kill a stranger, dump the body in a place where it will never be found and be 2,000 miles away before the murdered person is even missed. At any given time there are an estimated twelve to fifteen serial murderers at large in the country, just drifting around, snatching random victims and then moving on, leaving behind few clues and no motives. A couple of years earlier in Des Moines, some teenaged boys were cleaning out an office downtown for one of their fathers on a Sunday afternoon when a stranger came in, took them into a back room and shot each of them once in the back of the head. For no reason. That guy was caught, as it happens, but he could as easily have gone off to another state and done the same thing again. Every year in America 5,000 murders go unsolved. That is an incredible number.

I spent the night in Wells, Nevada, the sorriest, seediest, most raggedy-assed town I've ever seen. Most of the streets were unpaved and lined with battered-looking trailer homes. Everyone in town seemed to collect old cars. They sat rusting and windowless in every yard. Almost everything in town appeared to exist on the edge of dereliction. Such economic life as Wells could muster came from the passing traffic of I-80. A number of truck stops and motels were scattered around, though many of these were closed down and those that remained were evidently struggling. Most of the motel signs had letters missing or burnt out, so that they said, LONE ST R MOT L—V CAN Y. I had a walk around the business district before dinner. This consisted mostly of closed-down stores, though a few places appeared still to be in business: a drugstore, a gas station, a Trailways bus depot, the Overland Hotel—sorry, H tel—and a movie house called the Nevada, though this proved upon closer inspection also to be deceased. There were dogs everywhere, sniffing in doorways and peeing on pretty much everything. It was cold, too. The sun was setting behind the rough, distant peaks of the Jackson Mountains and there was a decided chill in the air. I turned up my collar and trudged the half-mile from the town proper to the interstate junction with US 93, where the most prosperous-looking truck stops were gathered, forming an oasis of brightness in the pinkish dusk.

I went into what looked to be the best of them, the 4-Way Cafe, which I gather took its name from the fact that it consisted of a gift shop, restaurant, casino and bar. The casino was small, just a room with a couple of dozen slot machines, mostly nickel ones, and the gift shop was about the size of a closet. The cafe was crowded and dense with smoke and chatter. Steel-guitar music drifted out of the jukebox. I was the only person in the room who didn't have a cowboy hat on, apart from a couple of the women.

It was absolutely, in my opinion, the worst food I have ever had in America, at any time, under any circumstances, and that includes hospital food, gas station food and airport coffee shop food. It even includes Greyhound bus station food and Woolworth's luncheon counter food. It was even worse than the pastries they used to put in the food dispensing machines at the Register and Tribune Building in Des Moines and those tasted like somebody had been sick on them. This food was just plain terrible, and yet everybody in the room was shoveling it away as if there were no tomorrow. I picked at it for a while—bristly fried chicken, lettuce with blackened veins, french fries that had the appearance and appeal of albino slugs—and gave up, despondent. I pushed the plate away and wished that I still smoked. The waitress, seeing how much I had left, asked me if I wanted a doggy bag.

"No thank you," I said through a thin smile, "I don't believe I could find a dog that would eat it."

On reflection, I can think of one eating experience even more dispiriting than dining at the 4-Way Cafe and that was the lunchroom at Callanan Junior High School in Des Moines. The lunchroom at Callanan was like something out of a prison movie. You would shuffle forward in a long, silent line and have lumpen, shapeless food dolloped onto your tray by lumpen, shapeless women—women who looked as if they were on day release from a mental institution, possibly for having poisoned food in public places. The food wasn't merely unappealing, it was unidentifiable. Adding to the displeasure was the presence of the deputy principal, Mr. Snoyd, who was always stalking around behind you, ready to grab you by the neck and march you off to his office if you made gagging noises or were overheard inquiring of the person across from you, "Say, what is this shit?" Eating at Callanan was like having your stomach pumped in reverse.

I went back to the motel feeling deeply hungry and unsatisfied. I watched some TV and read a book, and then slept that fitful sleep you get when all of your body is still and resting except your stomach, which is saying, "WHERE THE FUCK IS MY DINNER? HEY, BILL, ARE YOU LISTENING TO ME? WHERE THE F-U-C-K IS MY EVENING SUSTENANCE?"

26

=============== HERE, APROPOS OF nothing at all, is a true story. In 1958, my grandmother got cancer of the colon and came to our house to die. At this time my mother employed a cleaning lady named Mrs. Goodman, who didn't have a whole lot upstairs but was possessed of a good Catholic heart. After my grandmother's arrival, Mrs. Goodman grew uncharacteristically sullen. Then one afternoon at finishing time she told my mother that she would have to quit because she didn't want to catch cancer from my grandmother. My mother soothingly reassured Mrs. Goodman that you cannot "catch cancer" and gave her a small pay increase to compensate for the extra work occasioned by my grandmother's clammy and simpering presence. So with ill-disguised reluctance Mrs. Goodman stayed on. And about three months later she caught cancer and with alarming swiftness died.

Well, as you can imagine, since it was my family that killed the poor woman, I've always wanted to commemorate her in some small way and I thought that here would be as good a place as any, especially as I had nothing of interest to tell you about the drive from Wells, Nevada, to Twin Falls, Idaho.

So, goodbye, Mrs. Goodman, it was nice knowing you. And we're all very, very sorry.

Twin Falls was a nice enough place—Mrs. Goodman, I've no doubt, would have liked it; but then when you think about it a dead person would probably appreciate any change of scenery— and the landscape in southern Idaho was greener and more fertile than anything Nevada had to offer. Idaho is known for its potatoes, though in fact Maine, just a third its size, produces more. Its real wealth comes from mining and timber, particularly in the higher reaches of the Rockies, up towards Canada, over 500 miles north of where I was now. I was headed for Sun Valley, the famous resort up in the Sawtooth Mountains, and the neighboring town of Ketchum, where Ernest Hemingway spent the last year of his life and blew his brains out. This has always seemed to me (not that it's any of my business, mind you) a particularly thoughtless and selfish way to kill oneself. I mean to say, your family is going to be upset enough that you are dead without your having to spoil the furniture and gross everyone out on top of that.

In any case, Ketchum was touristy, though Sun Valley itself proved to be most agreeable. It was built as a ski resort in the 1930s by the Union Pacific Railroad as a way of enticing people to travel to the region during the winter. It certainly has a beautiful setting, in a bowl of jagged mountains, and is supposed to have some of the best skiing in the country. People like Clint Eastwood and Barbra Streisand have houses there. I looked in a window in a real estate office and didn't see anything for sale for less than $250,000.

The town part of Sun Valley—it's really just a little shopping center—is built to look like a Bavarian village. I found it oddly charming. As so often with these things in America, it was superior to a real Bavarian village. There were two reasons for this: (1) It was better built and more picturesque; and (2) the inhabitants of Sun Valley have never adopted Adolf Hitler as their leader or sent their neighbors off for gassing. Were I a skier and rich, I would on these grounds alone unhesitatingly choose it over Garmisch-Partenkirchen, say. In the meantime, being poor and skiless, there was nothing much for me to do but poke around in the shops. For the most part these sold swish skiing outfits and expensive gifts—things like large pewter elk for $200 and lead crystal paperweights at $150—and the people who ran them were those snooty types who watch you as if they think you might do a poo in the corner given half a chance. Understandably, this soured me on the place and I declined to make any purchases. "Your loss, not mine," I murmured sniffily as I left.

Idaho is another big state—550 miles from top to bottom, 300 miles across at the base—and it took me the rest of the day just to drive to Idaho Falls, near the border with Wyoming. En route I passed the little town of Arco, which on December 20, 1951, became the first town in the world to be lighted with nuclear-powered electricity, supplied by the world's first peacetime nuclear reactor at a site ten miles southwest of town at the Idaho National Engineering Laboratory. The name is misleading because the so-called laboratory covers several hundred square miles of scrubby chaparral and is actually the biggest nuclear dump in the country. The highway between Arco and Idaho Falls runs for forty miles alongside the complex, but it is lined by high fences interspersed with military-style checkpoints. In the far distance stand large buildings where, presumably, workers in white spacesuits wander around in rooms that look like something out of a James Bond film.

I didn't realize it at the time, but the US government had recently admitted that plutonium had been found to be leaking from one of the storage facilities on the site and was working its way downward through the ground to a giant subterranean reservoir, which supplies the water for tens of thousands of people in southern Idaho. Plutonium is the most lethal substance known to man—a spoonful of it could wipe out a city. Once you make some plutonium, you have to keep it safe for 250,000 years. The United States government had managed to keep its plutonium safe for rather less than 36 years. This, it seems to me, is a convincing argument for not allowing your government to mess with plutonium.

And this was only one leak out of many. At a similar facility in the state of Washington, 500,000 gallons of highly radioactive substances drained away before anyone thought to put a dipstick in the tank and see how things were doing. How do you lose 500,000 gallons of anything? I don't know the answer to that question, but I do know that I would not like to be a real estate agent trying to sell houses in Pocatello or Idaho Falls five years from now when the ground starts to glow and women are giving birth to human flies.

For the time being, however, Idaho Falls remains an agreeable little city. The downtown was attractive and still evidently prospering. Trees and benches had been set out. A big banner was draped across one of the streets saying, IDAHO FALLS SAYS NO TO DRUGS. That's really going to keep the kids off the hard stuff, I thought. Small-town America is obsessed with drugs, yet I suspect that if you strip-searched every teenager in Idaho Falls you would come up with nothing more illicit than some dirty magazines, a packet of condoms and a half-empty bottle of Jack Daniel's. It will help them to cope when they find out there's plutonium in their drinking water.

I had an excellent dinner at Happy's Chinese Restaurant. The room was empty except for one other party consisting of a middle-aged couple, their teenage daughter and a Swedish exchange student who was simply radiant—blond, tanned, soft-spoken, hypnotically beautiful. I stared at her helplessly. I had never seen anyone so beautiful in a Chinese restaurant in Idaho before. After a while a man came in who was evidently a passing acquaintance of the family and stopped at their table to chat. He was introduced to the Swedish girl and asked her about her stay in Idaho Falls and if she had been to the local sights—the lava caves and hot springs. (She had. Zey were vairy nice.) Then he asked The Big Question. He said, "Well, Greta, which do you like better, the United States or Sweden?"

The girl blushed. She obviously had not been in the country long enough to expect this question. Suddenly she looked more child than woman. With an embarrassed flutter of hands she said, "Oh, I sink Sweden," and a pall fell over the table. Everyone looked uncomfortable. "Oh," said the man in a flat, disappointed tone, and the conversation turned to potato prices.

People in middle America always ask that question. When

you grow up in America you are inculcated from the earliest age with the belief—no, the *understanding*—that America is the richest and most powerful nation on earth because God likes us best. It has the most perfect form of government, the most exciting sporting events, the tastiest food and amplest portions, the largest cars, the cheapest gasoline, the most abundant natural resources, the most productive farms, the most devastating nuclear arsenal and the friendliest, most decent and most patriotic folks on earth. Countries just don't come any better. So why anyone would want to live anywhere else is practically incomprehensible. In a foreigner it is puzzling; in a native it is seditious. I used to feel this way myself. In high school I shared a locker with a Dutch exchange student and I remember him asking me one day in a peevish tone why everybody, absolutely everybody, wanted him to like America better than the Netherlands. "Holland is my home," he said. "Why can't people understand that it's where I want to live?"

I considered his point. "Yes," I said, "but deep down, Anton, wouldn't you really rather live here?" And funnily enough, in the end, he decided he did. The last I heard he was a successful realtor in Florida, driving a Porsche, wearing wraparound sunglasses and saying, "Hey, what's happening?" which of course is a considerable improvement on wearing wooden shoes, carrying pails of milk on a yoke over your shoulder and being invaded by Germany every couple of generations.

In the morning I drove on to Wyoming, through scenery that looked like an illustration from some marvelous children's book of Western tales—snowy peaks, pine forests, snug farms, a twisting river, a mountain vale with a comely name: Swan Valley. That is the one thing that must be said for the men and women who carved out the West. They certainly knew how to name a place. Just on this corner of the map I could see Soda Springs, Massacre Rocks, Steamboat Mountain, Wind River, Flaming Gorge, Calamity Falls—places whose very names promised adventure and excitement, even if in reality all they contained were a DX gas station and a Tastee-Freez drive-in.

Most of the early settlers in America were oddly inept at devising place names. They either chose unimaginative, semirecycled names—New York, New Hampshire, New Jersey, New England—or toadying, kiss-ass names like Virginia, Georgia, Maryland and Jamestown in a generally pitiable attempt to secure favor with some monarch or powdered aristocrat back home. Or else they just accepted the names the Indians told them, not knowing whether Squashaninsect meant "land of the twinkling lakes" or "place where Big Chief Thunderclap paused to pass water."

The Spanish were even worse because they gave everything religious names, so that every place in the Southwest is called San this or Santa that. Driving across the Southwest is like an 800-mile religious procession. The worst name on the whole continent is the Sangre de Cristo Mountains in New Mexico, which means "the Blood of Christ Mountains." Have you ever heard of a more inane name for any geographical feature? It was only here in the real West, the land of beaver trappers and mountain men, that a dollop of romance and color was brought to the business of giving names. And here I was about to enter one of the most beautiful and understatedly romantic of them all: Jackson Hole.

Jackson Hole isn't really a hole at all; it's just the name for a scenic valley that runs from north to south through the Grand Tetons, very probably the most majestic range in the Rockies. With their high white peaks and bluish-gray bases they look like some kind of exotic confection, like blueberry frappés. At the southern edge of Jackson Hole is the small town of Jackson, where I stopped now for lunch. It was a strange place, with an odd combination of bow-legged Yosemite Sams and upmarket stores like Benetton and Ralph Lauren, which are there for the benefit of the many well-heeled tenderfeet who come for the skiing in the winter and to dude ranches in the summer. Every place in town had a Wild West motif—the Antler Motel, the Silver Dollar Saloon, the Hitching Post Lodge. Even the Bank of Jackson, where I went to cash a traveler's check, had a stuffed buffalo head on the wall. Yet it all seemed quite natural. Wyoming is the most fiercely Western of all the Western states. It's still a land of cowboys and horses and wide open spaces, a place where a man's gotta do what a man's gotta do, which on the face of it primarily consists of driving around in a pickup truck and being kind of slow. I had never seen so many people in cowboy apparel, and almost everybody owns a gun. Only a couple of weeks before, the state legislature in Cheyenne had introduced a rule that all legislators would henceforth have to check their handguns at the front desk before being allowed into the state-house. That's the sort of state Wyoming is.

I drove on to Grand Teton National Park. And there's another arresting name for you. Tetons means tits in French. That's an interesting fact—a topographical tit-bit, so to speak—that Miss Mucous, my junior-high-school geography teacher, failed to share with us in the eighth grade. Why do they always keep the most interesting stuff from you in school? If I'd known in high school that Thomas Jefferson kept a black slave to help him deal with sexual tension or that Ulysses S. Grant was a hopeless drunk who couldn't button his own fly without falling over, I would have shown a livelier interest in my lessons, I can assure you.

At any rate, the first French explorers who passed through northwestern Wyoming took one look at the mountains and said, *"Zut alors!* Hey, Jacques, clock those mountains. They look just like my wife's tetons."* Isn't it typical of the French to reduce everything to a level of sexual vulgarity? Thank goodness they didn't discover the Grand Canyon, that's all I can say. And the remarkable thing is that the Tetons look about as much like tits as . . . well, as a frying pan or a pair of hiking boots. In a word, they don't look like tits at all, except perhaps to desperately lonely men who have been away from home for a very long time. They looked a little bit like tits to me.

Grand Teton National Park and Yellowstone National Park run together to form one enormous area of wilderness stretching over a hundred miles from north to south. The road connecting them, Route 191, had only just been reopened for the year, and the Teton visitors' centers were still closed. There were hardly any other people or cars around and for forty miles I drove in splendid isolation along the wild meadows of the Snake River, where herds of elk grazed against the backdrop of the tall and jagged Tetons. As I climbed into Yellowstone the clouds grew moody and looked heavy with snow. The road I was on is closed for six months of the year, which gives you some idea of the sort of winters they have there. Even now the snow along the roadside was five or six feet deep in places.

Yellowstone is the oldest national park in the world (it was created in 1872) and it is enormous, about the size of Connecticut. I drove for over an hour without seeing anyone, except for a park warden in a wooden hut who charged me ten dollars to get in. That must be an exciting job for a college graduate, to sit in a hut in the middle of nowhere and take ten dollars off a tourist every two or three hours. Eventually I came to a turnoff for Grant Village, and I followed it for a mile through the snowy woods. The village was good-sized, with a visitors' center, motel, stores, post office and campgrounds, but everything was shut and every window was boarded. Snowdrifts rose almost to the rooftops of some of the buildings. I had now driven seventy miles without seeing an open place of business, and gave silent thanks that I had filled up with gasoline at Jackson.

Grant Village and the neighboring village of West Thumb are on the banks of Yellowstone Lake, which the highway runs alongside. Steam was rising from fumaroles in the lake and bubbling up through the mud by the roadside. I was in the area of the park called the caldera. Once there was a great mountain here. But 600,000 years ago it blew up in a colossal volcanic eruption that sent 240 cubic miles of debris into the atmosphere. The geysers, fumaroles and steaming mud pots for which Yellowstone is famous are the spluttering relics of that cataclysm.

Just beyond West Thumb the highway split in two. One branch went to Old Faithful, the most famous of all the geysers, but a chain had been strung across the road with a red sign hanging from it saying, ROAD CLOSED. Old Faithful was seventeen miles away down the closed road, but eighty miles away down the alternative road. I drove on to Hayden Valley, where you can stop the car at frequent turnouts and look out upon the plain of the Yellowstone River. This is where the grizzly bears roam and buffalo graze.

When you enter the park you are given a set of stern instructions telling you not to approach the animals as they are likely to kill or maim you, though I read later that more people have been killed in the park by other people than by animals. Even so, grizzlies are still a real threat to campers, one or two of whom get carried off every year. If you camp in the park you are instructed to change your clothes after eating or cooking and put them and all your food in a bag suspended from a branch 10 feet above the ground 100 yards from your tent. Stories abound of peckish campers who eat a bar of chocolate at bedtime and five minutes later a grizzly bear puts his head in the tent and says, "Hey, have you guys got some chocolate in here?" According to the park literature, there is even evidence that sexual intercourse and menstruation attract grizzlies. This seemed a bit rough to me.

I peered through my dad's binoculars but I didn't see any bears, possibly because they were still hibernating, and possibly because there aren't very many left in the park. Most of them have been driven out by the crush of visitors in the summer, even though large tracts of Yellowstone have been closed to people to encourage the bears to stay. There were, however, herds of buffalo everywhere. They are quite an extraordinary animal, with such big heads and shoulders on tiny legs. It must have been something to see when herds numbering in the millions filled the plains.

I drove on to Geyser Basin. This is the most volatile and unstable landscape in the world. A few miles to the east the land is rising by almost an inch a year, suggesting that another big blowout is on the way. Geyser Basin presented the most fantastic and eerie prospect, a lunar landscape of steam vents, hissing geysers and shallow pools of the deepest blue aquamarine. You can wander all over along wooden sidewalks built above the ground. If you were to step off them, according to the signs, you would sink into the crusty soil and be scalded to death by the water just below the surface. The whole place stank of sulfur.

I walked down to Steamboat Geyser, the biggest in the

world. According to the sign, it shoots water up to 400 feet into the air, though only at widely spaced intervals. The last big eruption was three and a half years earlier, on September 26, 1984. As I was watching it erupted—suddenly I understood the expression "to jump out of one's skin." The steamy mudpack before me made a flapping sound like a colossal palpitating sphincter (my own sphincter, I can tell you, began to beat a modest counterpoint) and then with a whoosh like a whale coming up for air shot out a great, steaming plume of white water. It went up only about twenty or thirty feet, but it poured forth for many seconds. Then it died and came again, and it repeated this four times, filling the cool air with blankets of steam, before it went dormant. When it finished, I shut my mouth with my hand and walked back to the car, knowing that I had seen one of the more arresting sights of my life.

There was no need now to drive on to Old Faithful, still forty miles down the road. I headed instead up the steep road over Roaring Mountain, past Nymph Lake, Grizzly Lake and Sheepeater Cliff—oh, how I love those names—and on down into Mammoth Hot Springs, home of the park headquarters. Here there was a visitors' center open, so I had a look around, and a pee and a drink of water, before driving on. When I emerged from the park at its northern end, by the little town of Gardiner, I was in a new state, Montana. I drove the sixty miles or so to Livingston through a landscape that was less wild but more beautiful than anything Yellowstone had offered. Partly this was because the sun came out and filled the late afternoon with a sudden springlike warmth. Long, flat shadows lay across the valley. There was no snow here, though the first infusion of green was just beginning to seep into the grassy and still yellow pastures along the highway. It was almost the first of May and winter was only just now withdrawing.

I got a room in the Del Mar Motel in Livingston, had some dinner and went for a walk out along the highway at the edge of town. With the sun sinking behind the nearby mountains, the evening quickly grew cold. A bleak wind came whipping down from the emptiness of Canada, 300 miles to the north, the kind of wind that slips up the back of your jacket and humiliates your hair. It resonated down the telephone lines, like a man whistling through his teeth, and made the tall grass seethe. Somewhere a gate creaked and banged, creaked and banged. The highway stretched out flat and straight ahead of me until it narrowed to a vanishing point some miles away. Every so often a car would come at me down the highway from behind, sounding eerily like a jet taking off. As it came nearer and nearer I would half wonder for one moment if it was going to hit me—it sounded that close—and then it would flash past and I would watch its taillights disappear into the gathering gloom.

A freight train came along on some tracks that ran parallel to the highway. At first it was a distant light and short bursts of horn, and then it was rolling past me, slow and stately, on its nightly procession through Livingston. It was enormous—American trains are twice the size of European ones—and at least a mile long. I counted sixty freight cars on it before I lost track, all of them with names on them like Burlington Northern, Rock Island, Santa Fe. It struck me as curious that train lines were so often named after towns that never amounted to much. I wondered how many people a century ago lost their shirts buying property in places like Atchison and Topeka on the assumption that one day they would be as big as Chicago and San Francisco. Towards the end of the train one car went by with its door open and I could see three shadowy figures inside: hobos. I was amazed to find that such people still existed, that it was still possible to ride the rails. In the dusk it looked a very romantic way to spend your life. It was all I could do to keep from sprinting along and climbing aboard and just disappearing with them into the night. There is nothing like an evening train rolling past to make you take leave of your senses. But instead I just turned around and trudged back along the tracks into town, feeling oddly content.

27

THE NEXT DAY I was torn between driving back into Wyoming further east along Interstate 90 and going to the little town of Cody or staying in Montana and visiting the Custer National Battlefield. Cody takes its name from Buffalo Bill Cody, who agreed to be buried there if they named the town after him. There were presumably two further stipulations: (1) that they waited until he was dead before they buried him, and (2) that they filled the town with as much tourist tat as they could possibly manage. Seeing the chance to collect a little lucre, the townspeople happily acceded and they have been cashing in on Cody's fame ever since. Today the town offers half a dozen cowboy museums and other diversions and of course many opportunities to purchase small crappy trinkets to take back home with you.

The people of Cody like you to think that Buffalo Bill was a native son. In fact, I'm awfully proud to tell you, he was an Iowa native, born in the little town of Le Claire in 1846. The people of Cody, in one of the more desperate commercial acts of this century, bought Buffalo Bill's birthplace and re-erected it in their town, but they are lying through their teeth when they hint that he was a local. And the thing is, they have a talented native son of their own. Jackson Pollock, the artist, was born in Cody. But they don't make anything of that because, I suppose, Pollock was a complete wanker when it came to shooting buffalo.

So that was option one. Alternatively, as I say, I had the choice of driving on across Montana to Little Bighorn, where Custer came a cropper. To be perfectly frank, neither one of them seemed terribly exciting—I would have preferred something more in the way of a tall drink on a terrace overlooking the sea—but in Wyoming and Montana you don't get a lot to choose from. In the end, I opted for Custer's last stand. This rather surprised me because as a rule I don't like battlefields. I fail to see the appeal in them once they have carted off the bodies and swept up. My father used to love battlefields. He would go striding off with a guidebook and map, enthusiastically retracing the ebb and flow of the Battle of Lickspittle Ridge, or whatever.

Once I had the choice of going with my mother to a museum and looking at dresses of the presidents' wives or staying with my dad and I rashly chose the latter. I spent a long afternoon trailing behind him certain that he had lost his mind. "Now this must be the spot where General Goober accidentally shot himself in the armpit and had to be relieved of command by Lieutenant Colonel Bowlingalley," he would say as we hauled ourselves to the top of a steep summit. "So that means Pillock's forces must have been regrouping over there at those trees"—and he would point to a grove of trees three hills away and stride off with his documents fluttering in the wind and I would think, "Where's he going *now?*" Afterwards, to my great disgust, I discovered that the museum of First Ladies' dresses had taken only twenty minutes to see and my mother, brother and sister had spent the rest of the afternoon in a Howard Johnson's restaurant eating hot fudge sundaes.

So the Custer Battlefield National Monument came as a pleasant surprise, even though it cost three dollars to get in. There's not much to it, but then there wasn't much to the battle. The visitors' center contained a small but absorbing museum with relics from both the Indians and soldiers, and a topographical model of the battlefield, which employed tiny light bulbs to show you how the battle progressed. Mostly this consisted of a string of blue lights moving down the hill in a confident fashion and then scurrying back up the hill pursued by a much larger number of red lights. The blue lights formed into a cluster at the top of the hill where they blinked furiously for a while, but then one by one they winked out as the red lights swarmed over them. On the model the whole thing was over in a couple of minutes; in real life it didn't take much longer. Custer was an idiot and a brute and he deserved his fate. His plan was to slaughter the men, women and children of the Cheyenne and Sioux nations as they camped out beside the Little Bighorn River and it was just his bad luck that they were much more numerous and better armed than he had reckoned. Custer and his men fled back up the hill on which the visitors' center now stands, but there was no place to hide and they were quickly overrun. I went outside and up a short slope to the spot where Custer made his last stand and had a look around.

It occupies a bleak and treeless hill, a place where the wind never stops blowing. From the hilltop I could see for perhaps fifty or sixty miles and there was not a tree in sight, just an unbroken sweep of yellowish grassland rolling away to a white horizon. It was a place so remote and lonely that I could see the wind coming before I felt it. The grass further down the hill would begin to ripple and a moment later a gust would swirl around me and be gone.

The site of Custer's last stand is enclosed by a black cast-iron fence. Inside this little compound, about fifty yards across, are scattered white stones to mark the spots where each soldier fell. Behind me, fifty yards or so down the far side of the hill, two white stones stood together where a pair of soldiers had obviously made a run for it and been cut down. No one knows where or how many Indians fell because they took their dead and injured away with them. In fact, nobody really knows what happened there that day in June 1876 because the Indians gave such conflicting accounts and none of the white participants lived to tell the tale. All that is known for sure is that Custer screwed up in a mighty big way and got himself and 260 men killed.

Scattered as they are around such a desolate and windy bluff, the marker stones are surprisingly, almost disturbingly, poignant. It's impossible to look at them and not imagine what a strange and scary death it must have been for the soldiers who dropped there, and it left me yet again in a reflective frame of mind as I walked back down the hill to the car and returned to the endless American highway.

I drove to Buffalo, Wyoming, through a landscape of mossy brown hills. Montana is enormously vast and empty. It is even bigger and emptier than Nevada, largely because there are no population centers to speak of. Helena, the state capital, has a population of just 24,000. In the whole state there are fewer than 800,000 people—this in an area of slightly more than 147,000 square miles. Yet it has a kind of haunting beauty with its endless empty plains and towering skies. Montana is called the Big Sky country, and it really is true. I had always thought of the sky as something fixed and invariable, but here it seemed to have grown by a factor of at least ten. The Chevette was a tiny particle beneath a colossal white dome. Everything was dwarfed by that stupendous sky.

The highway led through a big Crow Indian reservation, but I saw no sign of Indians either on the road or off it. Beyond Lodge Grass and Wyola I passed back into Wyoming. The landscape stayed the same, though here there were more signs of ranching, and the map once again filled up with diverting names: Spotted Horse, Recluse, Crazy Woman Creek, Thunder Basin.

I drove into Buffalo. In 1892 it was the scene of the famous Johnson County War, the incident that inspired the movie *Heaven's Gate,* though in fact the term *war* is a gross overexaggeration of events. All that happened was that the local ranchers, in the guise of the Wyoming Stock Growers' Association, hired a bunch of thugs to come to Johnson County and rough up some of the homesteaders who had recently, and quite legally, begun moving in. When the thugs killed a man, the homesteaders rose up and chased them to a ranch outside town, where they laid siege until the cavalry rode in and gave the humbled bullies safe passage out of town. And that was it: just one man killed and hardly any shots fired. That was the way the West really was, by and large. It was just farmers. That's all.

I reached Buffalo a little after four in the afternoon. The town has a museum dedicated to the Johnson County War, which I was hoping to see, but I discovered when I got there that it is only open from June to September. I drove around the business district, toying with the idea of stopping for the night, but it was such a dumpy little town that I decided to press on to Gillette, seventy miles down the road. Gillette was even worse. I drove around it for a few minutes, but I couldn't face the prospect of spending a Saturday night there, so I decided to press on once again.

Thus it was that I ended up in Sundance, thirty miles further down the road. Sundance is the town from which the Sundance Kid took his name, and from all appearances that was the only thing in town worth taking. He wasn't born in Sundance; he just spent some time in jail there. It was a small, charmless place, with just one road in and one road out. I got a room in the Bear Lodge Motel on Main Street, and it was pleasant in a basic sort of way. The bed was soft; the television was hooked up to HBO, the cable movie network; and the toilet had a "Sanitized for Your Protection" banner across the seat. On the far side of the street was a restaurant that looked acceptable. Clearly I was not about to have the Saturday night of a lifetime here, but things could have been worse. And indeed very soon they were.

I had a shower and afterwards as I dressed I switched on the television and watched the Reverend Jimmy Swaggart, a TV evangelist who had recently been caught dallying with a prostitute, the old rascal. Naturally this had put a certain strain on his credibility and he had taken to the airwaves, more or less continuously as far as I could tell, to beg for mercy. Here he was once again appealing for money and forgiveness, in that order. Tears rolled from his eyes and glistened on his cheeks. He told me he was a miserable sinner. "No argument there, Jimbo," I said and switched off.

I stepped out onto Main Street. It was "ten of seven," as they say in this part of the world. The evening was warm and in the still air the aroma of charbroiled steaks floated over from the restaurant across the street and berthed in my nostrils. I hadn't eaten all day and the whiff of sirloin made me realize just how hungry I was. I smoothed down my wet hair, needlessly looked both ways before stepping off the sidewalk—there was nothing moving on the road for at least a hundred miles in either direction—and went over. I opened the door and was taken aback to discover that the place was packed with Shriners.

The Shriners, if you are not familiar with them, are a social organization composed of middle-aged men of a certain disposition and mentality—the sort of men who like to give each other hotfoots and pinch the bottoms of passing waitresses. They seem to get drunk a lot and drop water balloons out of hotel windows. Their idea of advanced wit is to stick a cupped hand under their armpits and make farting noises. You can always tell a Shriner because he's wearing a red fez and his socks don't match. Ostensibly, Shriners get together to raise money for charities. This probably is what they tell their wives. However, here's an interesting fact that may help you to put this claim into perspective. In 1984, according to *Harper's Magazine,* the amount of money raised by the Shriners was $17.5 million; of this sum, the amount they donated to charities was $182,000. In short, what Shriners do is get together and be assholes. So you can perhaps conceive of my disquiet at the prospect of eating dinner amid a group of fifty bald-headed men who are throwing pats of butter around the room and setting fire to one another's menus.

The hostess came over. She was chewing gum and didn't look overfriendly. "Help you?" she said.

"I'd like a table for one, please."

She clicked her chewing gum in an unattractive fashion. "We're closed."

I was taken aback once more. "You look pretty open to me."

"It's a private party. They've reserved the restaurant for the evening."

I sighed. "I'm a stranger in town. Can you tell me where else I can get something to eat?"

She grinned, clearly pleased to be able to give me some bad news. "We're the only restaurant in Sundance," she said. Some beaming Shriners at a nearby table watched my unfolding discomfort with simple-minded merriment. "You might try the gas station down the street," the lady added.

"The gas station serves food?" I responded in a tone of quiet amazement.

"No, but they've got potato chips and candy bars."

"I don't believe this is happening," I muttered.

"Or else you can go about a mile out of town on Highway 24 and you'll come to a Tastee-Freez drive-in."

This was great. This was just too outstanding for words. The woman was telling me that on a Saturday night in Sundance, Wyoming, all I could have for dinner was potato chips and ice cream.

"What about another town?" I asked.

"You can try Spearfish. That's thirty-one miles down Route 14 over the state line in South Dakota. But you won't find much there either." She grinned again, and clicked her gum, as if proud to be living in such a turdy place.

"Well, thank you *so* much for your help," I said with elaborate insincerity and departed.

And there you have the difference between the Midwest and the West, ladies and gentlemen. People in the Midwest are nice. In the Midwest the hostess would have felt bad about my going hungry. She would have found me a table at the back of the room or at least fixed me up with a couple of roast beef sandwiches and a slab of apple pie to take back to the motel. And the Shriners, subimbecilic assholes that they may be, would have been happy to make room for me at one of their tables, and probably would even have given me some pats of butter to throw. People in the Midwest are good and they are kind to strangers. But here in Sundance the milk of human kindness was exceeded in tininess only by the size of the Shriners' brains.

I trudged up the road in the direction of the Tastee-Freez. I walked for some way, out past the last of the houses and onto an empty highway that appeared to stretch off into the distance for miles, but there was no sign of a Tastee-Freez, so I turned around and trudged back into town. I intended to get the car, but then I couldn't be bothered. There was something about the way they can't even spell freeze right that's always put me off these places. How much faith can you place in a company that can't even spell a monosyllable? So instead I went to the gas station and bought about six dollars' worth of potato chips and candy bars, which I took back to my room and dumped on the bed. I lay there and pushed candy bars into my face, like logs into a sawmill, watched some plotless piece of violent Hollywood excrescence on HBO, and then slept another fitful night, lying in the dark, full and yet unsatisfied, staring at the ceiling and listening to the Shriners across the street and to the ceaseless bleating of my stomach: "Hey, what is all this crap in here? It's nothing but chocolate. This is disgusting. I want some real food. I want steak and mashed potatoes. Really, this is just too gross for words. I've a good mind to send this all back. I'm serious, you'd better go and stand by the toilet because this is coming straight back up in a minute. Are you listening to me, butt-face?"

And so it went all night long. God, I hate my stomach.

I awoke early and peeked, shivering, through a gap in the curtains. It was a drizzly Sunday dawn. Not a soul was about. This would be an excellent time to firebomb the restaurant. I made a mental note to pack gelignite the next time I came to Wyoming. And sandwiches. Switching on the TV, I slipped back into bed and pulled the covers up to just below my eyeballs. Jimmy Swaggart was still appealing for forgiveness. Goodness me, but that man can cry. He is a human waterfall. I watched for a while, but then got up and changed the channel. On all the other channels it was just more evangelists, usually with their dumpy wives sitting at their sides. You could see why they all went out for sex. Generally, the program would also feature the evangelist's son-in-law, a graduate of the Pat Boone school of grooming, who would sing a song with a title like "You've Got A Friend in Jesus And Please Send Us Lots of Money." There can be few experiences more dispiriting than to lie alone in a darkened motel room in a place like Wyoming and watch TV early on a Sunday morning.

I can remember when we didn't even have TV on Sunday

mornings; that's how old I am. You would turn on WOI and all you would get was a test pattern and you would sit there and watch that because there was nothing else. Then after a while they would take off the test pattern and show "Sky King," which was an interesting and exciting program, at least compared to a test pattern. Nowadays they don't show test patterns at all on American TV, which is a shame because given a choice between test patterns and TV evangelists, I would unhesitatingly choose the test patterns. They were soothing in an odd way and, of course, they didn't ask you for money or make you listen to their son-in-law sing.

It was just after eight when I left the motel. I drove through the drizzle to Devils Tower, about twenty-five miles away. Devils Tower was the mountain used by Steven Spielberg in *Close Encounters of the Third Kind,* the one on which the aliens landed. It is so singular and extraordinary that you cannot imagine what Spielberg would have used as an alternative if it hadn't been available. You can see it long before you get to it, but as you draw nearer the scale of it becomes really quite awesome. It is a flat-topped cone of rock 865 feet high, soaring out of an otherwise flat and featureless plain. The scientific explanation is that it was a volcanic fluke—an outsized lump of warm rock that shot out of the earth and then cooled into its present arresting shape. In the moonlight it is said to glow, though even now on a wet Sunday morning with smoky clouds brushing across its summit it looked decidedly supernatural, as if it were placed there eons ago for the eventual use of aliens. I only hope that when they do come they don't expect to eat out.

I stopped at a lay-by near the tower and got out to look at it, squinting through the drizzle. A wooden sign beside the road said that the tower was considered sacred by the Indians and that in 1906 it became the first designated national monument in America. I stared at the tower for a long time, hypnotized both by its majesty and by a dull need for coffee, and then realized that I was getting very wet, so I returned to the car and drove on.

Having gone without dinner the night before, I intended to indulge myself in that greatest of all American gustatory pleasures—going out for Sunday breakfast.

Everybody in America goes out for Sunday breakfast. It is such a popular pastime that you generally have to line up for a table, but it's always worth the wait. Indeed, the inability to achieve instant oral gratification is such an unusual experience in America that lining up actually intensifies the pleasure. You wouldn't want to do it all the time, of course, you wouldn't want to get British about it or anything, but once a week for twenty minutes is "kinda neat," as they say. One reason you have to line up is that it takes the waitress about thirty minutes just to take each order. First you have to tell her whether you want your eggs sunny-side up, over easy, scrambled, poached, parboiled, or in an omelette, and in an omelette, whether you want it to be a plain, cheese, vegetable, hot-spicy, or chocolate-nut-'n'-fudge omelette; and then you have to decide whether you want your toast on white, rye, whole wheat, sourdough, or pumpernickel bread and whether you want whipped butter, pat butter, or low-cholesterol butter substitute; and then there's a complicated period of negotiation in which you ask if you can have cornflakes instead of the cinnamon roll and link sausages instead of patties. So the waitress, who is only sixteen years old and not real smart, has to go off to the manager and ask him whether that's possible, and she comes back and tells you that you can't have cornflakes instead of the cinnamon roll, but you can have Idaho fries instead of the short stack of pancakes, or you can have an English muffin and bacon instead of whole wheat toast, but only if you order a side of hashed browns and a large orange juice. This is unacceptable to you, and you decide that you will have waffles instead, so the waitress has to rub everything out with her nubby eraser and start all over again. And across the room the line on the other side of the "Please Wait to Be Seated" board grows longer and longer, but the people don't mind because the food smells so good and, anyway, all this waiting is, as I say, kinda neat.

I drove along Highway 24 through a landscape of low hills, in a state of tingly anticipation. There were three little towns over the next twenty miles and I felt certain that one of them would have a roadside restaurant. I was nearly to the South Dakota state line. I was leaving the ranching country and entering more conventional farmland. Farmers cannot exist without a roadside restaurant every couple of miles, so I had no doubt that I would find one just around the next bend. One by one I passed through the little towns—Hulett, Alva, Aladdin—but there was nothing to them, just sleeping houses. No one was awake. What kind of place was this? Even on Sundays farmers are up at dawn. Beyond Beulah I passed the larger community of Belle Fourche and then St. Onge and Sturgis, but still there was nothing. I couldn't even get a cup of coffee.

At last I came to Deadwood, a town that, if nothing else, lived up to its first syllable. For a few years in the 1870s, after gold was discovered in the Black Hills, Deadwood was one of the liveliest and most famous towns in the West. It was the home of Calamity Jane. Wild Bill Hickock was shot dead while playing cards in a local saloon. Today the town makes a living by taking large sums of money off tourists and giving them in return some crappy little trinket to take home and put on their mantlepiece. Almost all the stores along the main street were souvenir emporia, and several of them were open even though it was a Sunday morning. There were even a couple of coffee shops, but they were closed.

I went in the Gold Nugget Trading Post and had a look around. It was a large room where nothing but souvenirs were sold—moccasins, beaded Indian bags, arrowheads, nuggets of fool's gold, Indian dolls. I was the only customer. I didn't see anything to buy, so I left and went in another store a couple of doors away—The World Famous Prospectors Gift Shop—and found exactly the same stuff at identical prices and again I was the only customer. At neither place did the people running things say hello or ask me how I was doing. They would have in the Midwest. I went back out into the miserable drizzle and walked around the town looking for a place to eat, but there was nothing. So I got back in the car and drove on to Mount Rushmore, forty miles down the road.

Mount Rushmore is just outside the little town of Keystone, which is even more touristy than Deadwood, but at least there were some restaurants open. I went into one and was seated immediately, which rather threw me. The waitress gave me a menu and went off. The menu had about forty breakfasts on it. I had only read to number seventeen ("Pigs in a Blanket") when the waitress returned with a pencil ready, but I was so hungry that I just decided, more or less arbitrarily, that I would have breakfast number three. "But can I have link sausages instead of hashed browns?" I added. She tapped her pencil against a notice on the menu. It said NO SUBSTITUTIONS. What a drag. That was the most fun part. No wonder the place was half empty. I started to make a protest, but I fancied I could see her forming a bolus of saliva at the back of her mouth and I broke off. I just smiled and said "Okay, never mind, thank you!" in a bright tone. "And please don't spit in my food!" I wanted to add as she went off, but somehow I felt this would only encourage her.

Afterwards I drove to Mount Rushmore, a couple of miles outside town up a steep road. I had always wanted to see Mount Rushmore, especially after watching Cary Grant clamber over Thomas Jefferson's nose in *North by Northwest* (a film that also left me with a strange urge to strafe someone in a cornfield from a low-flying airplane). I was delighted to discover that Mount Rushmore was free. There was a huge terraced parking lot, though hardly any cars were in it. I parked and walked up to the visitors' center. One whole wall was glass, so that you could gaze out at the monument, high up on the neighboring mountainside. It was shrouded in fog. I couldn't believe my bad luck. It was like peering into a steam bath. I thought I could just make out Washington, but I wasn't sure. I waited for a long time, but nothing happened. And then, just as I was about to give up and depart, the fog mercifully drifted away and there they were—Washington, Jefferson, Lincoln, and Teddy Roosevelt, staring glassily out over the Black Hills.

The monument looked smaller than I had expected. Everybody says that. It's just that positioned as you are well below the monument and looking at it from a distance of perhaps a quarter of a mile, it looks more modest than it is. In fact, Mount Rushmore is enormous. Washington's face is 60 feet high, his eyes 11 feet wide. If they had bodies, according to a sign on the wall, the Rushmore figures would be 465 feet tall.

In an adjoining room there was an excellent and more or less continuous movie presentation giving the history of Mount Rushmore, with lots of impressive statistics about the amount of rock that was shifted, and terrific silent film footage showing the work in progress. Mostly this consisted of smiling workmen packing dynamite into the rock face followed by a big explosion; then the dust would clear and what had been rock was now revealed to be Abraham Lincoln. It was remarkable. The whole thing is an extraordinary achievement, one of America's glories, and surely one of the great monuments of this century.

The project took from 1927 to 1941 to complete. Just before it was finished, Gutzon Borglum, the man behind it all, died. Isn't that tragic? He did all that work for all those years and then just when they were about to crack open the champagne and put out the little sausages on toothpicks, he keeled over and expired. On a bad luck scale of 0 to 10, I would call that an 11.

I drove east across South Dakota, past Rapid City. I had intended to stop off and see Badlands National Park, but the fog and drizzle were so dense that it seemed pointless. More than that, according to the radio I was half a step ahead of another perilous "frunnal" system. Snow was expected on the higher reaches of the Black Hills. Many roads in Colorado, Wyoming, and Montana were already shut by fresh snowfalls, including the highway between Jackson and Yellowstone. If I had gone to Yellowstone a day later, I would now be stranded, and if I didn't keep moving, I could well be stranded for a couple of days in South Dakota. On a bad luck scale of 0 to 10, I would call that a 12.

Fifty miles beyond Rapid City is the little town of Wall, home of the most famous drug store in the West, Wall Drug. You know it's coming because every hundred yards or so along the whole of that fifty miles you pass a big billboard telling you so: STEAKS AND CAKES—WALL DRUG, 47 MILES, HOT BEEF SANDWICHES—WALL DRUG, 36 MILES, FIVE CENT COFFEE—WALL DRUG, 25 MILES, and so on. It is the advertising equivalent of the Chinese water torture. After a while the endless drip, drip, drip of billboards so clouds your judgment that you have no choice but to leave the interstate and have a look at it.

It's an awful place, one of the world's biggest tourist traps, but I loved it and I won't have a word said against it. In 1931, a guy named Ted Hustead bought Wall Drug. Buying a drugstore in a town in South Dakota with a population of three hundred people at the height of the Great Depression must be about as stupid a business decision as you can make. But Hustead realized that people driving across places like South Dakota were so delirious with boredom that they would stop and look at almost anything. So he put up a lot of gimmicks like a life-size dinosaur, a 1908 Hupmobile, a stuffed buffalo, and a big pole with arrows giving the distances and directions from Wall Drug to places all over the world, like Paris and Hong Kong and Timbuktu. Above all, he erected hundreds of billboards all along the highway between Sioux Falls and the Black Hills, and filled the store with the most exotic and comprehensive assortment of tourist crap human eyes have ever seen, and pretty soon people were pouring in. Now Wall Drug takes up most of the town and is surrounded by parking lots so enormous that you could land a jumbo jet on them. In the summer they get up to 20,000 visitors a day, though when I arrived things were decidedly more quiet and I was able to park right out front on Main Street.

I was hugely disappointed to discover that Wall Drug wasn't just an overgrown drugstore as I had always imagined. It was more a mini shopping mall, with about forty little stores selling all kinds of different things—postcards, film, western wear, jewelry, cowboy boots, food, paintings, and endless souvenirs. I bought a very nice kerosene lamp in the shape of Mount Rushmore. The wick and glass jar that encloses it sprout directly out of George Washington's head. It was made in Japan and the four presidents have a distinctly oriental slant to their eyes. There were many other gifts and keepsakes of this type, though none quite as beautiful or charming. Sadly, there were no baseball caps with plastic turds on the brim. Wall Drug is a family store, so that sort of thing is right out. It was a pity because this was the last souvenir place I was likely to encounter on the trip. Another dream would have to go unfulfilled.

28

================ **I DROVE ON** and on across South Dakota. God, what a flat and empty state. You can't believe how remote and lonely it feels out in the endless fields of yellow grass. It is like the world's first drive-through sensory deprivation chamber. The car was still making ominous clonking noises, and the thought of breaking down out here filled me with disquiet. I was in a part of the world where you could drive hundreds of miles in any direction before you found civilization, or at least met another person who didn't like accordion music. In a forlorn attempt to pass the time, I thumbed through my Mobil guides, leaning them against the steering wheel while drifting just a trifle wildly in and out of my lane, and added up the populations and sizes of the four states of the high plains: North and South Dakota, Montana and Wyoming. Altogether they take up 385,000 square miles— an area about the size of France, Germany, Switzerland and the Low Countries combined—but they have a total population of just 2.6 million. There are almost four times as many people in Paris alone. Isn't that interesting? Here's another interesting fact for you. The population density of Wyoming is 1.9 people per square kilometer; in South Dakota it is a little over 2 people per square kilometer. In Britain, there are 236.2 people per square kilometer. The number of people airborne in the United States at any given time (136,000) is greater than the combined populations of the largest cities in each of these four states. And finally here's a really interesting fact. According to a survey by *Current Health* magazine, the percentage of salad bar customers in the United States seen "touching or spilling food or otherwise being unsanitary" is 60 percent. I am of course aware that this has nothing to do with the population of the northern plains states, but I thought a brief excursion into irrelevancy was a small price to pay for information that could change your life. It certainly has changed mine.

I stopped for the night in a nothing little town called Murdo, got a room in a Motel 6 overlooking Interstate 90 and went for dinner in a big truck stop across the highway. A highway patrol car was parked by the restaurant door. There is always a highway patrol car parked by the restaurant door. As you walk past it you can hear muffled squawking on the radio. "Attention, attention! Zero tango charlie! A Boeing 747 has just crashed into the nuclear power plant on Highway 69. People are wandering around with their hair on fire. Do you read me?" Inside, oblivious of all this, are the two highway patrolmen, sitting at the counter eating apple pie with ice cream and shooting the breeze with the waitress. Every once in a great while—perhaps twice in a day—the two patrolmen will get up from the counter and drive out to the highway to ticket some random motorists for trying to cross the state at seven miles an hour above the permitted limit. Then they will go and have some more pie. That is what it is to be a highway patrolman.

In the morning I continued on across South Dakota. It was like driving over an infinite sheet of sandpaper. The skies were low and dark. The radio said there was a tornado watch in effect for the region. This always freaks out visitors from abroad—chambermaids in hotels in the Midwest are forever going into rooms and finding members of Japanese trade delegations cowering under the bed because they've heard a tornado siren—but locals pay no attention to these warnings because after years of living in the tornado belt you just take it as part of life. Beside, the chances of being hit by a tornado are about one in a million.

The only person I ever knew who came close was my grandfather. He and my grandmother (this is an absolutely true story, by the way) were sleeping one night when they were awakened by a roaring noise like the sound of a thousand chain saws. The whole house shook. Pictures fell off the walls. A clock toppled off the mantelpiece in the living room. My grandfather plodded over to the window and peered out, but he couldn't see a thing, just pitch blackness, so he climbed back into bed, remarking to my grandmother that it seemed a bit stormy out there, and went back to sleep. What he didn't realize was that a tornado, the most violent force in nature, had passed just beyond his nose. He could literally have reached out and touched it—though of course had he done so he would very probably have been sucked up and hurled into the next county.

In the morning, he and Grandma woke up to a fine clear day. They were surprised to see trees lying everywhere. They went outside and discovered, with little murmurings of astonishment, a swath of destruction stretching across the landscape in two directions and skirting the very edge of their house. Their garage was gone, but their old Chevy was standing on its concrete base without a scratch on it. They never saw a single splinter of the garage again, though later in the day a farmer brought them their mailbox, which he had found in a field two miles away. It just had a tiny dent in it. That's the sort of things tornadoes do. All those stories you've ever read about tornadoes driving pieces of straw through telegraph poles or picking up cows and depositing them unharmed in a field four miles away are entirely true. In southwest Iowa there is a cow that has actually had this happen to it twice. People come from miles around to see it. This alone tells you a lot about the mysteries of tornadoes. It also tells you a little something about what there is to do for fun in southwest Iowa.

In midafternoon, just beyond Sioux Falls, I at last left South Dakota and passed into Minnesota. This was the thirty-eighth state of my trip and the last new one I would visit, though really it hardly counted because I was just skimming along its southern edge for a while. Off to the right, only a couple of miles away over the fields, was Iowa. It was wonderful to be back in the Midwest, with its rolling fields and rich black earth. After weeks in the empty West, the sudden lushness of the countryside was almost giddying. Just beyond Worthington, Minnesota, I passed back into Iowa. As if on cue, the sun emerged from the clouds. A swift band of golden light swept over the fields and made everything instantly warm and springlike. Every farm looked tidy and fruitful. Every little town looked clean and friendly. I drove on spellbound, unable to get over how striking the land-scape was. There was nothing much to it, just rolling fields, but every color was deep and vivid: the blue sky, the white clouds, the red barns, the chocolate soil. I felt as if I had never seen it before. I had no idea Iowa could be so beautiful.

I drove to Storm Lake. Somebody once told me that Storm Lake was a nice little town, so I decided to drive in and have a look. And by golly, it was wonderful. Built around the blue lake from which it takes its name, it is a college town of 8,000 people. Maybe it was the time of year, the mild spring air, the fresh breeze, I don't know, but it seemed just perfect. The little down-town was solid and unpretentious, full of old brick buildings and family-owned stores. Beyond it a whole series of broad, leafy streets, all of them lined with fine Victorian homes, ran down to the lakefront where a park stood along the water's edge. I stopped and parked and walked around. There were lots of churches. The whole town was spotless. Across the street, a boy on a bike slung newspapers onto front porches and I would almost swear that in the distance I saw two guys in 1940s suits cross the street without breaking stride. And somewhere at an open window, Deanna Durbin sang.

Suddenly I didn't want the trip to be over. I couldn't stand the thought that I would go to the car now and in an hour or two I would crest my last hill, drive around my last bend, and be finished with looking at America, possibly forever. I pulled my wallet out and peered into it. I still had almost seventy-five dollars. It occurred to me to drive up to Minneapolis and take in a Minnesota Twins baseball game. Suddenly this seemed an excellent idea. If I drove just a little bit maniacally, I could be there in three hours—easily in time for a night game. I bought a copy of USA Today from a street-corner machine and went with it into a coffee shop. I slid into a booth and eagerly opened it to the sports pages to see if the Twins were at home. They were not. They were in Baltimore, a thousand miles away. I was desolate. I couldn't believe I had been in America all this time and it hadn't occurred to me before now, the last day of the trip, to go to a ball game. What an incredibly stupid oversight.

My father always took us to ball games. Every summer he and my brother and I would get in the car and drive to Chicago or Milwaukee or St. Louis for three or four days and go to movies in the afternoon and to ball games in the evening. It was heaven. We would always go to the ballpark hours before the game started. Because Dad was a sportswriter of some standing—no, to hell with the modesty, my dad was one of the finest sportswriters in the country and widely recognized as such—he could go into the press box and onto the field before the game and to his eternal credit he always took us with him. We got to stand beside him at the batting cage while he interviewed people like Willie Mays and Stan Musial. We got to sit in the dugouts (they always smelled of tobacco juice and urine; I don't know what those guys got up to down there) and we got to go in the dressing rooms and watch the players dress for the games. I've seen Ernie Banks naked. Not a lot of people can say that, even in Chicago.

The best feeling was to walk around the field knowing that kids in the stands were watching us enviously. Wearing my Little League baseball cap with its meticulously creased brim and a pair of very sharp plastic sunglasses, I thought I was Mr. Cool. And I was. I remember once at Comiskey Park in Chicago some kids calling to me from behind the first base dugout, a few yards away. They were big-city kids. They looked like they came from the Dead End Gang. I don't know where my brother was this trip, but he wasn't there. The kids said to me, "Hey, buddy, how come you get to be down there?" and "Hey, buddy, do me a favor, get me Nellie Fox's autograph, will ya?" But I paid no attention to them because I was . . . Too Cool.

So I was, as I say, desolate to discover that the Twins were a thousand miles away on the East Coast and that I couldn't go to a game. My gaze drifted idly over the box scores from the previous day's games and I realized with a kind of dull shock that I didn't recognize a single name. It occurred to me that all these players had been in junior high school when I left America. How could I go to a baseball game not knowing any of the players? The essence of baseball is knowing what's going on, knowing who's likely to do what in any given situation. Who did I think I was fooling? I was a foreigner now.

The waitress came over and put a paper mat and cutlery in front of me. "Hi!" she said in a voice that was more shout than salutation. "And how are you doin' today?" She sounded as if she really cared. I expect she did. Boy, are Midwestern people wonderful. She wore butterfly glasses and had a beehive hairdo.

"I'm very well, thank you," I said. "How are you?"

The waitress gave me a sideways look that was suspicious and yet friendly. "Say, you don't come from around here, do ya?" she said.

I didn't know how to answer that. "No, I'm afraid I don't," I replied, just a trifle wistfully. "But, you know, it's so nice I sometimes kind of wish I did."

Well, that was my trip, more or less. I visited all but ten of the lower forty-eight states and drove 13,978 miles. I saw pretty much everything I wanted to see and a good deal that I didn't. I had much to be grateful for. I didn't get shot or mugged. The car didn't break down. I wasn't once approached by a Jehovah's Witness. I still had sixty-eight dollars and a clean pair of underpants. Trips don't come much better than that.

I drove on into Des Moines and it looked very large and handsome in the afternoon sunshine. The golden dome of the state capitol building gleamed. Every yard was dark with trees.

People were out cutting the grass or riding bikes. I could see why strangers came in off the interstate looking for hamburgers and gasoline and stayed forever. There was just something about it that looked friendly and decent and nice. I could live here, I thought, and turned the car for home. It was the strangest thing, but for the first time in a long time I almost felt serene.

INDEX

Des Moines *(cont.)*
  county hospitals and free care, 194
  high school tests, 73
  KCBC radio baseball-game broadcasts,
    176–77
  lighting of night baseball, 169
  Mercy Hospital, 193–94
  Merle Hay Mall, 6, 8
  movie-going in, 79–80
  murder of teenage boys, 264
  return to, after Eastern trip, 202–3
  return to, after Western trip, 298–99
  WHO radio and TV, 8, 37
De Soto, Iowa, 208
De Soto Hilton Hotel, Savannah, 81
Detroit, Michigan, 53, 178, 180
Devils Tower, Wyoming, 286
Dick's Cafe, St. George, Utah, 242
Dillinger, John, 97
Dillon, Matt, 215
Dining-out rules, 171–72
Disc jockeys, 175–76
Disneyland, 254
Disney World, 109–10, 111
Dixon, Franklin W., 38
Dodge City, Kansas, 214–15
Dole, Bob, 212
Donald Duck, 110
Donner Pass, 261
Dope, smoking of, 72, 199–200
Dorset, Vermont, 166
Dortmeier, Frank, 200–201
Douglas, Kirk, 30
"Dragnet," 115
Drugs, 198–201
  small-town obsession with, 270
Drugstore soda fountains, 242
Dude magazine, 61
Duel at Diablo (film), 240
"Dullard," Illinois, 28–32
Dunes (casino), 245
Dunn, Peter, 100
Du Quoin, Illinois, 42
Durbin, Deanna, 12, 39, 296
Dwyer, Bud, 127

Eagles, 175, 176
Earp, Wyatt, 215
Eastwood, Clint, 240, 268
Easy Rider (film), 56
Edison, Thomas, 181–83
Edwards Air Force Base, 250
Egg Harbor, Michigan, 191
Eisenhower, Dwight, 16, 76
  farm outside Gettysburg, 132–34
Eisenhower, Mamie, 132–33
Elberta, Michigan, 183
El Capitan Valley, 257
Elmira, New York, 171

Empire, Michigan, 183
Empire State Building, 237
Encyclopaedia Britannica, 122
England, 4, 14, 97, 129
  first colonies in New World, 99
  national parks in, 92–94
  and newfound practicality, 232
  See also Britain
English people, 121
Erie, Lake, 172, 173–74, 190
Eureka, Nevada, 263
Europe, 7, 15, 135, 150
  bars in, 185
  historic preservation in, 110
  and size of trains, 277
Everly Brothers, 213

Fairburg, Nebraska, 211
Fairmount Park, Philadelphia, 129–30
Fallon, Nevada, 263
Falmouth, Maine, 157
Fancy Gap, Virginia, 105
Farewell Gap, Sequoia National Park,
    255
Farmers, 33–35
  and ability to endure pain, 33–34
  Fridays, and football games, 196–97
  John Deere caps and tans, 6
  and roadside restaurants, 288
Farmers Museum, Cooperstown, 170
Father (author's), 238
  and author's baseball card collection,
    169
  on driving vacations, 9–12
    and choice of destination, 254
    frugality, 10–12, 96–98
    getting lost, 41, 208–10
    and historical markers, 105–6
    love of battlefields, 279
    reaction to billboard signs, 50–51
  and men's magazines, 60–61
  as sportswriter, 297–98
  trips to Winfield, 18–19
  in Washington, D.C., 114–16
Faulkner, William, 59, 62
Fern (author's aunt), 253
Ferryville, Wisconsin, 196
Fields, W. C., 38
Firestone, Harvey, 182–83
Firestone factory, 3
Fitzpatrick's Bar, Iowa City, 197–98
Flagstaff, Arizona, 234, 236
Flaming Gorge, Wyoming, 271
Flintstone, Fred, 4
Florida, 156, 254, 262, 271
  spring-break trip to, 56–57
Flynn Dairies, Des Moines, 182
Folger's Coffee radio commercial, 44
Fonda, Henry, 39

Hebron, Nebraska, 211
Hedrick, Iowa, 14, 18
Hefner, Hugh, 61
Helena, Montana, 281
Hemingway, Ernest, 268
Hemorrhoids commercial, 88
Henry Ford Museum, 180–83
Heritage Motor Inn, Carbondale, 46
Herman Talmadge Memorial Bridge, 82
Herndon, Hal, 129
Herndon, Lucia, 128–30
Heroin, 200
Hetch Hetchy Valley, 258
Hickock, Wild Bill, 288
High Island, Michigan, 190
High school
  and football games, 196–97
  and multiple-choice tests, 73
  students, and Clutter murders, 217–18
  testing of senior students, 72–73
Highway patrolmen, 294
Highways
  fatalities, 148, 244
  55-mile-per-hour speed limit, 43–44
  tedium while driving on, 9, 44, 173,
    175
Higley, Dr. Brewster M., 211
Hikers, 93
Hillbillies, 92, 103–4
Hilton Head, South Carolina, 82
Himalayas, 86
Hippies, 199, 228
Historical markers, 105–6
"Historic Front Street," Dodge City,
  215–16
Hitchhikers, 233
Hitler, Adolf, 268
Hobos, 277
Hog Island, Michigan, 190
Holiday Inn signs, 86
Holiday Motel, Mackinac, 184–85
Holly Springs National Forest, 58
Hollywood Boulevard, 254
Hollywood Western films, 240
Homecoming celebrations, 198
"Home on the Range" (song), 211
Hong Kong, 291
Hooterville, Iowa, 5
Hoover, Herbert, 7
Horner, John, 197–201, 231
Horse Pasture, Virginia, 105
Horseshoe (casino), 247
Hospital advertisements, 193
"Hotel California" (song), 175, 176
Hotels
  architecture of, 81
  movies in, 145–46
House of David sect, 190

Howard Johnson's, 11, 279
Hulett, Wyoming, 288
Hull, Missouri, 39
Humboldt Sink, Nevada, 263
Huron, Lake, 184–85, 187–90
Hustead, Ted, 291
Hyannis Port, Massachusetts, 154
Hyatt Regency, Savannah, 81

Idaho, 266–70
  potatoes, 268
Idaho Falls, 269–70
Idaho National Engineering Laboratory,
  269
Illinois, 26, 33, 37, 39–48, 54–55
  sales taxes and daylight saving time,
    53
  size of, 39
In Cold Blood (Capote), 215–18
Independence National Historical Park,
  Philadelphia, 127–28
Independence Pass, Colorado, 224
Indiana, 53, 255
Indianapolis, Indiana, 116
Indians, 100, 214, 272
  Cherokee reservation, 92
  Crow reservation, 281
  and Custer's last stand, 279–81
  and Devils Tower, 286
  Navajo reservation, 239
  Western reservations, 232
Intercourse, Pennsylvania, 136
International Joint Commission's Great
  Lakes Water Quality Board, 174
International Monetary Fund (IMF), 159
Interplanetary creatures, 162–63
In the Heat of the Night (film), 56
Invasion of the Body Snatchers (film), 243
Iowa, 5–9, 14, 196, 255
  Amish in, 136
  and billboards, 49
  camping out, and gadgets for, 94–95
  on Columbus Day, 148
  crime in rural areas, 197
  and daylight saving time, 53
  getting lost in, 208
  and New York Times delivery, 23
  return to, after Eastern states trip,
    195–203
  return to, after Western states trip,
    296, 298–99
  Roosevelt commemoration stone at
    Warm Springs, 75–76
  Southeast, 25–26
  Southwest, 210
    cows and tornadoes, 295
  State Fair, and strippers, 145
  University, 197–99
    and Nebraska football games, 208

306

Virgin River, 240
Visalia, California, 255

Wall Drug, South Dakota, 290–92
Wall Street crash, 177–78
Wall Street Journal, 67, 175
Walt Disney Corporation, 258
Walton, John-Boy, 74
Wanker, Hank, 69
Warm Springs, Georgia, 74–75
War on Poverty (1964), 104
Warsaw, Illinois, 26
Washington, Booker T., 71, 106
Washington, D.C., 127, 156
   the Mall, 117, 119–20 -
   size of, 116–17
   and summer heat, 114–16
Washington, George, 89, 112–13, 181,
   289–90
Washington, Mount, 158–59
Washington Monument, 117, 121
Washington Senators, 114, 116
Washington (state), 269–70
Watergate scandal, 7
Water pollution, 173–74
Wayland, Iowa, 14, 18
Wayne, John, 210
Wealth
   and Jackson Hole dude ranches, 272
   in New England ski-resort towns, 166
   in the South, 83
Weather
   April in the Rockies, 226
   in Cripple Creek, Colorado, 223
   Death Valley temperatures, 250
   at Grand Canyon, 236–38
   in Nebraska, 211
   storms, in New Mexico and Arizona,
      233–34, 238
   summer heat, 233–34
   and Washington, D.C., summers,
      114–16
Weathermen, 226, 234
Webster, Noah, 182
Welch's Grape Juice, 90
Wells, Nevada, 264–66
West Barnstable, Massachusetts, 152
Westerners
   compared with Midwesterners, 284
   and naming of towns, 271
   and shooting of buffalo and Indians,
      214
Western states, 296
   and driving distances, 238–39
   hitchhikers to, 233
   national parks, 255–56
   See also names of states; Westerners

West of the Pecos (Grey), 134
West Thumb, Wyoming, 274
Whiskey Island, Michigan, 190
White House, 117, 121, 163
White Mountains, New Hampshire, 158
Whitney, Mount, 250
Wilkerson Pass, Colorado, 224
Williams, Ted, 169
Williams, Tennessee, 67
Williamsburg. *See* Colonial Williamsburg
Wilmington, Delaware, 123
Wind River, Wyoming, 271
Winfield, Iowa, 14, 18–22, 181, 210, 253
Winnemucca, Nevada, 263–64
Winner, Michael, 145
Winslow, Arizona, 236
Wintermeyer, Bobby, 242
Winterset, Iowa, 210
Wiscasset, Maine, 157–58
Wisconsin, 53, 183, 191–93
   and dairy farms, 195
Witness (film), 136
Wizard of Oz (film), 213
Wolfe, Thomas, 22
Woodfords, California, 261
Woods Hole, Massachusetts, 154
Woolworth's stores, 184, 265
World Bank, 159
The World Famous Prospectors Gift
      Shop, Deadwood, Wyoming, 288
World War I, 72
World War II, 125, 133
Worthington, Minnesota, 296
Wright, Orville and Wilbur, 119, 182–83
Wyola, Montana, 281
Wyoming, 263, 269, 271–76, 278–79,
      290
   most "Western" of states, 272
   population and size, 293
Wyoming Stock Growers' Association,
   281

Yeager, Chuck, 250
Yellowstone Lake, 274
Yellowstone National Park, 258, 273–76,
      290
Yellowstone River, 275
Yiddish Erotica (pornographic video), 144
Yosemite National Park, 257–58
Yosemite village, 258–59
Young, Brigham, 243

Zion National Park, 240–41
"Zorro," 251–52
Zuni Mountains, 234
Zwingle Company gift catalogue, 24, 81,
      95

ALSO BY JOEL OSTEEN

Your Best Life Now

Become a
Better
You

---

7 Keys to Improving Your Life Every Day

JOEL OSTEEN

FREE PRESS

New York   London   Toronto   Sydney

The names and identifying details of some individuals mentioned
in this book have been changed.

FREE PRESS
A Division of Simon & Schuster, Inc.
1230 Avenue of the Americas
New York, NY 10020

First Free Press export edition August 2008

FREE PRESS and colophon are trademarks of Simon & Schuster, Inc.

For information about special discounts for bulk purchases,
please contact Simon & Schuster Special Sales at 1-800-456-6798
or business@simonandschuster.com

Manufactured in the United States of America

1   3   5   7   9   10   8   6   4   2

Library of Congress Cataloging-in-Publication Data
Osteen, Joel.
Become a better you : 7 keys to improving your life every day / Joel Osteen.—1st Free
Press hardcover ed.
p.   cm.
Includes bibliographical references.
1. Self-actualization (Psychology)—Religious aspects—Christianity.
2. Christian life.   I. Title.
BV4598.2.O86   2007
248.4—dc22   2007020823
ISBN-13: 978-1-4391-0224-4
ISBN-10:   1-4391-0224-4

To Victoria, the love of my life.

Thanks for believing in me and inspiring me to greater things. Your love, friendship, and your kind, gentle spirit make living with you each day a gift. I would not be who I am without the seeds you have sown in my life.

I respect you, admire you, and look forward to spending the rest of our lives together.

To Jonathan.

Thanks for being such an incredible son! You are kind, respectful, and have a great sense of humor. You amaze me with your wisdom, your insight, and your talent. I treasure the time we share together. You are going to make a significant impact on our world. I am proud to call you my son.

To Alexandra, my little jewel.

You are not only beautiful on the outside, but you are beautiful on the inside. You have such a tender heart, filled with kindness and compassion. You are smart and funny, and have a voice like an angel. When you sing, we feel God's love. I am proud of you and I will always be your number one fan!

CONTENTS

ACKNOWLEDGMENTS

Writing a book is a bit like gathering some raw materials and through an extensive refining process, shaping them into a finely tuned, high performance automobile—it takes a great team of skilled and dedicated people to see a concept, and then turn it into reality. I've been blessed to have just such a team working with me on *Become a Better You,* and I appreciate each person who has contributed.

First, I want to thank the many people who have poured spiritual wisdom into my life. Growing up in a pastor's home as I did, I was privileged to meet and talk with a wide variety of "world-changers," individuals from around the world, ministers and their families, men and women who wanted their lives to count, to make a difference, and who believed that our best days were still ahead of us. Many of the people who visited with us or ministered to our community were humorous and interesting, and all possessed a wide repertoire of incredibly fascinating stories, laced with life principles and truth. To them, along with my mother and father, I am grateful for laying the strong foundations on which much that I do today is built.

Next, I want to thank the many great authors and speakers whose books and audio messages have helped shape my life, as well. These mentors "built the infrastructure," and contributed greatly to my continuing education, and I thank each one for the investment you have made in me. With every life that is touched through my books, speaking, audio or video ministries, you share the credit; any success

I have known, and any eternal impact I may have is part of your legacy.

Special thanks to Carolyn Reidy, Dominick Anfuso, and Martha Levin of Simon & Schuster, for believing in this project and for going the extra mile to make sure it happened. Thanks, too, to Jason Madding, for a great cover design.

I am immensely grateful to Jan Miller and Shannon Marven, of Dupree/Miller, who caught the vision for what could be, and then patiently oversaw all our negotiations.

Special thanks to collaborator Ken Abraham, who provided key editorial assistance as well as valuable insights and perspectives to my material.

Thanks also to the Lakewood Church family—the thousands of faithful who attend each week as well as the those who watch our services on television, the internet, pod casts, or who listen on radio. I'm so grateful to the devoted staff of Lakewood Church, for facilitating much of the research and logistical details involved with this project. Michelle Trevino, my executive assistant, coordinated so many important aspects of the book-writing process. Paul Osteen, Kevin Comes, Don Iloff, and Duncan Dodds—my inner circle of mighty men—deserve great credit. These men smoothly manage the myriad aspects of the ministry while allowing me to do what I do best.

Heartfelt thanks to my mom, Dodie Osteen, who loves me, prays for me, and always encourages me. And to Georgine Iloff, the best mother-in-law a man could ever want! Thanks to my sister, Lisa Comes, whose excellence and integrity inspire me; to Gary and April Simons of High Point Church and Jim and Tamara Graff of Faith Family Church, my sisters and brothers-in-law. God has richly blessed me through each of you. Last, but certainly not least, thanks to my sisters-in-law, Jackelyn Iloff and Jennifer Osteen, for your constant support and encouragement.

INTRODUCTION

Whether life is going well for you or collapsing right before your eyes, we all want to be better. We want to be more effective in our lives. We want to know God better; we want to be better spouses and parents, better lovers, better encouragers, better community leaders, better employees, and better bosses and managers. God put something deep down inside us that evokes a desire to be more like Him. In our inner being, we hear a voice saying, "You were born for better than this; you are meant to live at a higher level than you are currently. Don't be satisfied with less. You can be better."

The question is: "How? What must I do to become a better me?"

In my first book, *Your Best Life Now*, I presented seven steps to living at your full potential. Today many people are developing a greater vision for their future and are experiencing more of God's blessings and favor. But even if you are living your best life now, it is important that you do not become stagnant. God always wants to increase us, to do more in and through us. He always wants to take us deeper into self-discovery and then wants to raise us to a higher level of living. He didn't create us to be average. He doesn't want us to settle for "good enough." He wants us to keep stretching, to keep pressing forward into the next level.

Now, in *Become a Better You*, I want to help you do just that. I want to take you deeper; I'm hoping to help you look inside yourself and discover the priceless seeds of greatness that God has placed within you. In this book, I will reveal to you seven keys that you can use to unlock those seeds of greatness, allowing them to burst forth in an abundantly blessed life. These keys are not complicated or difficult; in fact, their sheer simplicity often causes them to elude many people's notice. Nevertheless, they are seven key principles that have helped shape me and continue to keep me expecting good things in my personal life, in my relationships, in my family, and in my career. I know these principles work, because I have experienced them firsthand in my own life.

Too many people settle for mediocrity in their thoughts, attitudes, or actions. It's time to put off those negative mind-sets and rise higher. Remember, God has put in you everything you need to live a victorious life. Now, it's up to you to draw it out. We can't let wrong mind-sets, a negative past, or other people's opinions discourage us or cause us to give up and quit pressing forward. People who want to live at their full potential have discovered that the good can often be the enemy of the best.

Have you ever noticed a person and thought, *What a great attitude! She's a great mother,* or *He's a tremendous employee.* Most likely, that person you admired was a walking, talking example of someone who is becoming a better person.

What does it mean to become a better you? First, you understand that God wants you to become all that He created you to be. Second, it is imperative that you realize that God will do His part, but you must do your part as well. To become a better you, you must:

1. Keep pressing forward.
2. Be positive toward yourself.
3. Develop better relationships.
4. Form better habits.
5. Embrace the place where you are.
6. Develop your inner life.
7. Stay passionate about life.

Most of us make some effort to improve in these areas, but to truly see the kind of marked improvement we want, we must start focusing on them in a more deliberate manner. In the pages ahead, I'll explain each of these principles in depth: how they work and how you can use them to improve your life and affect generations to come. I'll help you see where you are, where you have been, and where you are going. As we grow together, God will continue to pour good things into our lives, and He will indeed take us to places that we never dreamed possible.

If you are going through a tough time, take heart. There are better days ahead! God wants to bring you through, to bring you out even better, and to restore everything you have lost, plus give you more!

If you are thriving and enjoying life, you can use these principles to help guard your heart and mind, and to maintain an attitude and lifestyle that is pleasing to God. Be quick to acknowledge God's goodness in your life, keeping in mind that it is His blessing that you are enjoying and that you are blessed to be a blessing to someone else, and He will continue to fill your life with immeasurable love, joy, and peace.

Get ready! You are about to embark on an inner journey through which you will explore parts of yourself that perhaps you've rarely or never previously tested. Every step is about your head, your heart, and your soul, but you will be surprised to see how your inner journey influences your "outer" life, producing better quality relationships, a more productive use of your gifts and talents, and ultimately a totally better life.

I must warn you: Practicing the seven keys within this book could be a potentially life-changing process! And while I can't guarantee that you will become rich or famous, I can assure you that if you follow this plan, you will live a more fulfilled life.

Becoming a better you is all about growing, learning, and improving. The more you learn to trust God, the better you will be. He will continually expand your horizons, and you can become a better you!

PART ONE

KEEP PRESSING FORWARD

CHAPTER 1

Stretching to the Next Level

The famous architect Frank Lloyd Wright designed many beautiful buildings, homes, and other magnificent structures. Toward the end of his career, a reporter asked him, "Of your many beautiful designs, which one is your favorite?"

Without missing a beat, Frank Lloyd Wright answered, "My next one."

Frank Lloyd Wright understood the principle of stretching, constantly pressing forward, never being satisfied simply with past successes. The entire world is waiting for your next adventure.

Too many people are living far below their potential. They have many gifts and talents, and so much more going for them. But they've gotten comfortable, settled where they are, and lately become too easily satisfied.

I often hear people making excuses for stagnating in their personal growth:

"I've achieved as much as most."

"Compared to other people, I'm doing pretty well in my career."

"I've gone as far as my parents did."

That's great, but God wants you to go further. He's a progressive God, and He wants every generation to be increasing in happiness, success, and significance. No matter where we are in life, God has more in store. He never wants us to quit growing. We should always be reaching for new heights in our abilities, in our spiritual walk, in our finances, careers, and personal relationships. We all have areas where we can come up higher. We may have achieved a certain level of success, but there are always new challenges, other mountains to climb. There are new dreams and goals that we can pursue.

No doubt, God has already done a lot in your past. He's opened doors for you that nobody else could open. Maybe He's given you a wonderful family and home. Perhaps He's caused you to be promoted, given you favor with your employer or supervisors. That is marvelous, and you should thank God for all that He has done for you. But be careful: Sometimes when you are enjoying life, it is easy to become complacent, to get satisfied, and think, *Yes, God's been good to me. I can't complain. I've achieved my goals; I've reached my limits.* But God never performs His greatest feats in your yesterdays.

He may have done wonders in the past, but you haven't seen anything yet! The best is yet to come. Don't allow your life to become dull. Keep dreaming, hoping, and planning for new projects, experiences, and adventures with God.

God never performs His greatest feats in your yesterdays.

I've discovered that God likes to outdo Himself. He wants to show His favor in your life in greater ways today than He did yesterday. He wants you to be more blessed tomorrow than you are today. He intends for you to have a greater impact on the world than you have had. That means if you're a teacher, you haven't taught your best lesson yet. If you're a builder, you haven't built your best home yet. If you're a businessperson, you haven't negotiated your best deal yet. It's time to get your hopes up; enlarge your vision, and get ready for the new things that God has on the horizon. Your best days are not behind you. They're in front of you.

But if this is going to happen, we have to keep pressing forward, stretching ourselves. Get rid of low expectations. Don't make little plans for your life. Don't have little dreams. Don't go around thinking, *Everybody gets good breaks except me. I've reached my limits. I'll probably never get this promotion. I don't know why I'm not as talented as that other person.*

No, get rid of that defeated mind-set. You are a child of the Most High God. God has breathed His life into you. He planted seeds of greatness in you. You have everything you need to fulfill your God-given destiny. God has already put in the talent, the creativity, the discipline, the wisdom, and the determination. It's all in you. You are full of potential. But you have to do your part and start tapping into it. You have to make better use of the gifts and talents that God has given you.

The Scripture teaches that we have a valuable treasure on the inside. You have a gift. You have something to offer that nobody else has. You didn't just show up on planet Earth by accident. You were handpicked by Almighty God. He saw you before you were formed in your mother's womb and placed you here for a reason. You have an assignment. There's something that God wants you to accomplish. Somebody needs your touch. Somebody needs what you have.

Don't live with that treasure undiscovered, and don't die with the treasure still in you. Press forward. Give birth to the dreams and desires that God has placed in your heart.

Neurologists have discovered that the average person uses less than 10 percent of his or her mind. That means more than 90 percent of the mind's capability lies dormant. It never gets tapped into. But if we could just understand what we have: God has deposited a part of Himself in you. When it came time for you to be born, God said, "Let Me give you some of this gift; some of this talent; some of this creativity." You have the seed of Almighty God on the inside of you. You were never created to be average. You were never created to reach a certain level and then plateau. You were created to excel. There's no limit to how high you can go in life. There's no limit to what you can accomplish, if you will just learn to shake off complacency and keep stretching into the next level.

But it all starts in our hearts and minds. We have to believe that we have what it takes. We have to believe that we have a gift, a treasure on the inside. People may have tried to push you down. Circumstances may have soured your outlook on life.

Maybe you've tried to succeed in life but have hit a brick wall again and again. Try again. Somebody may have told you "no" a thousand times; ask again. Keep asking until you get the "yes" that you've been waiting to hear. You've got to keep pressing. Too many people grow satisfied with far less than God's best for their lives. Sometimes they get discouraged, but all too often, they simply get comfortable. They stop stretching anymore; they are not exercising their faith, and like a once muscular, toned body that no longer exercises, they grow flabby. One of the main reasons for this sort of complacency is that people don't really understand what they have on the inside. They don't understand their God-given potential.

Years ago, a friend of mine and a passenger were in Europe driving on the Autobahn, the superhighway across Germany. Unlike American freeways, the Autobahn has no speed limits. You can travel as fast as you want to drive.

My friend was so excited as he pressed down on the accelerator and took the car up to 80 miles an hour, then 90, 100, 110. He felt like the king of the road, zooming past people left and right.

A few minutes later, another car streaked down the freeway. This car was the exact same model as my friend's car, but it blew by him like he was standing still. That second automobile must have been going 170 per hour.

The passenger traveling with my friend laughed and said, "See; you're not going as fast as you can. You're just going as fast as you will."

Think about that: My friend's car possessed tremendous potential. It too was capable of going 180 miles per hour. The manufacturer put in the potential. How fast my friend drove didn't have anything to do with the car's capability. In other words, the potential was not lessened just because he chose not to use it. And simply having the potential on board did not affect his future.

It's the same way with us. Our potential has been put in us by our Manufacturer, our Creator, Almighty God. Whether we use it or not does not diminish it, but it does impact our future. The events of your past do not reduce your potential. How somebody has treated you or what he or she said about you doesn't change your potential. Maybe you've been through some disappointments, or have had some unfair things happen in life. None of that affects your potential. It has been put in you permanently by the Creator of the Universe. When we believe, we take a step of faith and stretch ourselves; that's when we start to tap into it. That's when we'll rise higher.

The capability is in you. The real question is: Are you willing to break free from your self-imposed limitations and start stretching to the next level?

Too often, we allow experiences from the past to keep us from pressing forward. Perhaps a business partner, a coach, a relative, or a friend said, "Hey, do you really think you can do that? Maybe that opportunity is not right for you. What if you try and fail? What if it doesn't work out?"

These negative words may haunt you and stymie your progress in pressing forward. Understand that none of those statements can change your potential on the inside. It's still in you. Don't allow other people to talk you out of using what God has given you and doing what you know God wants you to do.

Many people have had negative comments spoken over them, such as "You don't have what it takes. You're not very talented. I don't think you'll ever be successful."

If we're not careful, we'll allow those negative words to play over and over in our minds. They can create a stronghold.

A young woman named Sherry came to me for advice. She had tolerated an abusive relationship for years in which she was repeatedly told, "You can't do anything right. You're so slow. You're not attractive." After hearing that for so long, it had totally beaten her down physically, emotionally, and spiritually. She had no joy, little confidence, and extremely low self-esteem.

I told her what I'm telling you: "Your value, your gifts, and talents have been put in you by Almighty God. And it doesn't matter what anyone else has spoken over you. The good news is God has the final authority. He says you have a treasure on the inside. He says you have a gift. He says you are valuable. You've got to quit playing that old tune and put on a new one. You need to be dwelling on thoughts like: I am creative. I am talented. I am valuable. I have a bright future. My best days are still out in front of me. You have to get your mind going in this new direction. Because dwelling on negative thoughts about yourself will keep you from becoming all God has created you to be."

Regardless of who has spoken negative words into your life—a parent, a spouse, a coach, or a teacher—you must cast those words down. Words are powerful. They can create barriers in your heart and mind. Sometimes one little phrase can hold us back for years.

A friend of mine used to travel as an assistant with a well-known minister. One day, a man came to the hotel and wanted the minister to pray for him. The associate told the man, "I'm sorry, but the minister can't be disturbed. He's resting and getting prepared for the meeting tonight."

But this man refused to take no for an answer. He was extremely aggressive and determined. My friend remained kind and courteous, trying to placate the unexpected visitor. But the caller continued to press.

Finally, my friend said, "How about this? I will pray for you. I work with the minister every day. I'll be glad to pray for you."

At that, the obnoxious man turned his nose up. He said, "I don't think so. *You* won't do."

The words stung: "You won't do." The implicit message was "You are not good enough. Your prayers can't get the job done."

My friend later told how those words seared through his heart and mind day after day. "You won't do." Lying in bed at night, he'd think, *You don't have what it takes. You're not anointed like the famous preacher. You can't help a soul.*

The young man already struggled with his confidence, but now he was allowing these negative words to play repeatedly in his subconscious mind. He couldn't shake them off, and instead allowed those negative words to hold him down for years.

Too many people don't have the confidence and the self-esteem they should because they're constantly dwelling on negative thoughts about themselves. I don't say this arrogantly, but in my mind, all day long I try to remind myself: *I am anointed. I am creative. I am talented. I am successful. I have the favor of God. People like me. I'm a victor and not a victim.*

Try it! If you go around thinking those kinds of thoughts, low self-esteem, lack of confidence, or inferiority won't have a chance with you. Throw your shoulders back, put a smile on your face, and be looking for opportunities to stretch into the next level.

Back in the Garden of Eden, after Adam and Eve ate the forbidden fruit, they hid. In the cool of the day, God came to them and said, "Adam, Eve, where are you?"

They said, "God, we're hiding because we are naked."

I love the way God answered them. He said, "Adam, who told you that you were naked?" In other words, "Who told you that something was wrong with you?" God immediately knew the enemy had been talking to them.

God is saying to you today, "Who told you that you don't have what it takes to succeed? Who told you that the best grades you could make in school would be C's rather than A's? Who told you that you are not attractive enough to succeed in your personal relationships or talented enough to flourish in your career? Who told you that your marriage is never going to last?"

Who told you that something was wrong with you?

Those are lies from the enemy. You need to reject those ideas and discover what God says about you.

"Well, I don't think I could ever get this promotion, Joel."

Who told you that? God said, "No good thing will He withhold when you walk uprightly."

"Well, I don't think I'll ever get married, Joel. I haven't had a date in so long I don't think I'll ever find someone who would love me for who I am, and with whom I would be compatible."

Who told you that? God said, "When you delight yourself in Him, He will give you the desires of your heart."

"Well, I don't think I could ever be in management. I don't think I could be a leader."

Who told you that? God says, "You can do all things through Christ." The potential is inside you. It doesn't change just because you don't believe it or just because you've been through some negative experiences in the past. It has been deposited in you permanently by the Creator of the Universe. The Scripture says, "God's gifts and His callings are irrevocable." [1] That means God is never going to take back the potential He has poured into you. He's never going to say, "I'm tired of dealing with you. You've tried and failed too many times. You've made so many mistakes. Let me just have the gifts back."

No, those gifts, and the calling on your life, will be with you till the day you leave this earth. But it is up to you to decide whether you tap into them and use them or not.

If You Only Knew

In John 4, Jesus met a woman at a well in Samaria, and He asked her for a drink of water. She was surprised, because back then, the Jews didn't have anything to do with the Samaritans. She said, "How can you ask me for a drink?"

Jesus said, "If you knew who I was, you would ask me for a drink, and I would give you living water."

The woman thought that Jesus was talking about literal water. She said, "Sir, you don't even have anything with which to draw water. You don't have a bucket, and the well is deep. How can you possibly give me water?"

I wonder how many times God tells us that He wants to do something great in our lives, that we are going to be healthy and well; we are going to get out of debt. We feel it strongly, but like the woman at the well, we start thinking about what we don't have, and all the obstacles in our path, and before long, we've talked ourselves out of God's best.

"That could never happen for me. I don't have the education; I don't have the talent; I don't have the discipline. I'll never break this addiction; I'll never accomplish my dreams." No, you must quit looking at what you don't have, and start believing that all things are possible.

I never dreamed that I'd be doing what I am doing today, encouraging people around the world. For seventeen years, my father tried to get me to speak at our home church, but I had no desire. I'm naturally quiet and reserved and would much prefer working behind the scenes.

But when my father went to be with the Lord, I knew that I was supposed to step up. Although I had never preached before, never had been to seminary, and had no formal training, I said, "God, I'm not going to look at what I don't have. I'm looking unto you. I know in my weakness, you show up the strongest." I took that step of faith, and God has taken me places I never dreamed.

He can do the same for you. Don't get stuck in a rut in your attitude, your career, or your marriage. You have incredible potential within you—much more than you may realize! God is not limited to the laws of nature. He can do what human beings cannot. The key is to get your eyes off your problems and onto your God.

When God puts a dream in your heart, it may look impossible in the natural. Every voice may tell you it will never happen. "You'll never break that addiction. You'll never accomplish your dreams. You'll never be happy." But if you will believe and stay in faith, and expect good things, you too can defy the odds.

I talked to a famous tightrope walker, who comes from a family of seven generations of circus entertainers. I asked him, "What is the key to walking on the tightrope? You make it look so easy."

He said, "Joel, the secret is to keep your eyes fixed on where you are going. You never look down. Where your head goes, that's where your body is going, too. If you look down, there's a good chance you will fall. So you always have to look to where you want to be."

It's the same principle in life. Some people are always looking back, focused on their hurts and pains. Other people are looking down, living in self-pity, and complaining that life is not fair. The key to rising higher is to keep looking to where you want to go. Dream big dreams! Don't focus on where you are today; keep a positive vision and see yourself accomplishing your goals and fulfilling your destiny.

As a young man, growing up, Pete loved playing baseball. That was his passion. But when he tried out for the team, the coach didn't even give him a chance. He said, "I'm sorry, son; you're just too small. You will never be able to play on this team."

Pete was devastated. His heart was set on playing baseball. His mom picked him up from school, and he and his best friend climbed into the backseat of the car. Poor Pete was doing all he could to keep his composure, trying not cry, and then his friend—who was much bigger than Pete—said, "Hey, did you tell your mom you didn't make the team because you're too little?"

The friend's words pierced Pete's heart. He hated being small. He went home feeling low and dejected. Later that week, though, the school made a special announcement: "Since so many boys tried out for the team, we are going to create a second team; a B team." Pete tried out and made the B team.

That season, those two teams ended up in a play-off for the championship, and the second team, the B team, beat the A team. Guess who the winning pitcher was. That's right; the B team won the championship thanks to Pete's great pitching ability.

Now, consider this question: How much potential did Pete have when he was rejected for the A team? Was his potential any different when he began pitching for the B team?

Other people do not determine your potential.

The point is: Other people's opinions do not determine your potential. What they said or what they think about you does not change what God has placed on the inside. Don't allow negative words or attitudes to take root and keep you from pressing forward. God may be asking you today, "Who told you that you were too small? Who told you that you aren't intelligent? Who told you that you don't have the necessary talent?"

God would not have put the dream in your heart if He had not already given you everything you need to fulfill it. That means if I have a dream or a desire, and I know it's from God, I don't have to worry whether I have what it takes to see that dream fulfilled. I know God doesn't make mistakes. He doesn't call us to do something without giving us the ability or the wherewithal to do it.

You have to realize that God has matched you with your world. In other words, even though at times you may not feel that you are able to accomplish your dreams, you have to get beyond those feelings and know deep inside, *I have the seed of Almighty God in me.* Understand, God will never put a dream in your heart without first equipping you with everything you need to accomplish it. If you feel that you don't have the necessary wisdom, talent, ability, or resources, simply remind yourself, *God has matched me with my world. He has already put in me what I need.*

A minister once handed a man a twenty-dollar bill and asked him to hide it secretly in his wife's Bible. "Be sure she doesn't see you do it," he emphasized.

Later, during the sermon, the minister asked the woman to stand up. "Do you trust me, ma'am?" he asked.

"Yes, of course," she replied.

"Will you do what I ask you to do?"

"Yes, I will," she answered.

"Good, then please open your Bible, and give me the twenty-dollar bill inside."

The woman cringed, as she said, "Oh, I'm sorry. I don't have a twenty-dollar bill."

"I thought you said that you trusted me?" the minister asked with feigned incredulity.

"Yes, I do," the woman replied.

"Then please open your Bible and give me the twenty-dollar bill."

The woman opened her Bible with no small measure of reticence, and to her complete surprise, she discovered a twenty-dollar bill within the pages. Her eyes brightened as she looked at the minister and asked, "But how did it get there?"

"I gave it to you," the minister said with a smile, "and now I'm simply asking you to draw out the gift I have already given, and use that twenty dollars for something good."

In a similar way, God will never ask you for something without first depositing it within you. If you will dare to take a step of faith, you will discover gifts inside that you never before realized were there.

Some people almost miss the great things God wants to do in and through them because they talk themselves out of believing for better things. In the Old Testament, when God told Moses to confront Pharaoh, the ruler of Egypt, and command him to free God's people who had been living in slavery, Moses balked. "God, I can't do such a thing," Moses said. "I stutter and stammer. I'm not a good speaker."

I love how God answered Moses' protests and excuses. God asked, "Moses, who made your tongue? Who made your voice?"

With these poignant questions, God was reminding His man, "Moses, I have already put in you exactly what you need. Now draw out what I've given you, and use it for my honor, for the good of your family and friends, and your own good."

God said something similar to Gideon, another Old Testament hero. God told Gideon that he would deliver the Hebrew people from oppression. God even called Gideon a mighty man of valor.

Nevertheless, Gideon cowered in fear and insecurity. "No, not me, God," he fretted. "I'm the least in my family. Everybody around me is more talented than I am."

Yet God gave Gideon exactly what he needed to do what God had asked him to do.

Don't let the size of your dreams or the vastness of God's calling on your life intimidate you. Moreover, don't allow naysayers in your path to keep you from pressing forward. When people attempted to discourage the Apostle Paul, trying to talk him out of his dreams, telling him what he couldn't do, Paul responded, "What if they don't believe? Will their unbelief make the promise of God of no effect in my life?"

Paul was saying, "If other people don't want to believe God for better things in their lives, fine; but that won't keep me from believing. I know the promises of God are in me."

That's the attitude we need to have as well. So what if other people say I can't succeed? So what if someone tries to pull me down; so what if a person doesn't believe? I am not going to allow their actions, attitudes, or comments to cause me to give up on my God-given dreams. I'll not allow their unbelief to influence my faith.

Don't Let Rejection Keep You Down

Too often, when we suffer some kind of rejection or disappointment, we get so discouraged that we settle right where we are. "I guess it wasn't meant to be," we rationalize. Or "I thought I could go out with that attractive person, but maybe I am not good-looking enough." Or "I thought I could get the promotion, but I tried and failed. Maybe I don't have the talent. It didn't work out."

When disappointment or rejection knocks you down, get back up and go again. We give up too easily on our dreams. We need to understand that just as God supernaturally opens doors, sometimes God supernaturally closes doors. And when God closes a door, it's always because He has something better in store. So just because you've come to a dead end, that's not the time to give up. Find a different route and keep pressing forward.

Often, out of our greatest rejection comes our greatest direction. When you come to a closed door, or something doesn't work out in your life, instead of seeing that as the end, regard that as God nudging you into a better direction. Yes, sometimes it's uncomfortable; sometimes we may not like it. But we cannot make the mistake of just sitting back and settling where we are.

Out of our greatest rejection comes our greatest direction.

Back in 1959, my father was the pastor of a successful church with a thriving congregation. They had just built a beautiful new sanctuary and my father had a bright future. About that time, my sister Lisa was born with something like cerebral palsy. Hungry for a fresh touch from God, my dad went away for a while and got alone with God. He searched the Scriptures in a new way, and he began to see how God was a good God, a healing God, and that God could still perform miracles today. My dad went back to his church and he preached with a new fire, a new enthusiasm. He thought everybody would be thrilled, but the congregation's reaction was just the opposite. They didn't like his new message. It didn't fit in with their tradition. After suffering much persecution, heartache, and pain, my father knew the best thing for him to do was to leave that church.

Naturally, my dad was disappointed. He didn't understand why such a thing should happen. But remember, out of rejection comes direction. When one door closes, God is about to open up a bigger and a better door.

My father went down the street to an abandoned feed store.

There, he and ninety other people formed Lakewood Church on Mother's Day, 1959. The critics said it would never last, but today, nearly fifty years later, Lakewood Church has grown to become one of the largest churches in America and is still going strong.

I don't believe that my father would have enjoyed the ministry he had, and I don't believe he would have become all God created him to be, if he would have stayed in that limited environment. Here's a key: The dream in your heart may be bigger than the environment in which you find yourself. Sometimes you have to get out of that environment in order to see that dream fulfilled.

The dream in your heart may be bigger than the environment in which you find yourself.

Consider an oak tree. If you plant it in a pot, its growth will be limited. Once its roots fill that pot, it can grow no further. The problem is not with the tree; it is with the environment. It is stifling growth. Perhaps you have bigger things in your heart than your present environment can facilitate. That's why, at times, God will stir you out of a comfortable situation. When you go through persecution and rejection, it's not always because somebody has it in for you. Sometimes, that's God's way of directing you into His perfect will. He's trying to get you to stretch to the next level. He knows you're not going to go without a push, so He'll make it uncomfortable for you to stay where you are currently. The mistake we make at times is getting negative and sour; we focus on what didn't work out. When we do that, we inhibit the opening of new doors.

A few years ago, Lakewood Church was trying to buy some property on which we could build a new sanctuary. We had looked for months, and finally had found a wonderful one-hundred-acre tract of land. We were so excited. However, the day we were to close the deal, the people sold the land right out from under us.

I was terribly disappointed, and I had to tell myself, "Joel, God has closed this door for a reason. He has something better in store." Sure, I was down, and I admit that I was discouraged, but I had to shake that off and say, "No, I'm not settling here. I'm going to keep pressing forward."

A few months later, we found another nice piece of property. It would have worked as well, but a similar series of events transpired and the owner refused to sell it to us. Another disappointment. I didn't understand it, but I said, "God, I'm trusting you. I know your ways are not my ways. This doesn't seem right. It doesn't seem fair. But I'm going to stay in an attitude of faith and keep expecting good things."

Not long after that, the door to the Compaq Center, a sixteen-thousand-seat sports arena, opened up in downtown Houston, right in the middle of one of the busiest sections of the city. Then it became clear why God had closed the other doors. Had we purchased either of those properties, those choices might have kept us from God's best.

Throughout life, we're not always going to understand everything that happens along the way. But we've got to learn to trust God. We've got to believe that He has us in the palm of His hand, that He is leading and guiding us, that He always has our best interests at heart.

I know people who have experienced rejection in their personal relationships. Maybe their marriage didn't work out. They put all those years into it and now they're hurt, dejected, going around defeated and not expecting anything good.

I don't believe that divorce is God's best. Unfortunately, sometimes it is unavoidable. If you have been through a divorce, understand that God still has another plan for your life. Just because somebody rejected you or walked out of your life and left you hurt, that doesn't mean you should retreat and settle where you are. That rejection did not change what God put on the inside of you. It doesn't mean that you cannot yet be happy. When one door closes, if you will keep the right attitude, God will open another door. But you have to do your part and keep pressing forward. Too many people get bitter, they get angry, and they start to blame God. Instead, let that hurt go. You may not understand it, but trust God and move on with your life. Don't look at it as the end. Look at it as a new beginning. Somebody may have rejected you, but you can hold your head up high knowing this: God accepts you. God approves you. And He has something better in store.

Friend, don't die with the treasure still inside you. Keep pressing forward. Keep reaching for new heights. Give birth to what God has placed in your heart. Don't let other people talk you out of your dreams. Listen to what God says about you, not all the negative voices. When you face rejection and disappointment, don't stay there. Know that God has another plan. That closed door simply means God has something better in store. You may not have experienced God's favor in the past, but this is a new day. You have not seen, heard, or imagined the wonderful things God has in store for you. Don't be weighed down by the distractions and disappointments in life; instead, keep stretching to the next level, reaching for your highest potential. If you do that, I can tell you with confidence your best days are in front of you. God is going to show you more of His blessings and favor, and you will become a better *you*, better than you ever dreamed possible.

CHAPTER 2

Give Your Dreams a New Beginning

Years ago, I went into a government building that had two sets of double doors spaced about fifteen feet apart. The doors opened automatically as I approached, but for security reasons, when I went through the first set of doors, I had to let them close tightly before the next set of doors would open in front of me. As long as I stayed at the first set of doors, the second set would not open.

In many ways, life operates in a manner similar to those automatic doors. You have to let go of your disappointments, let go of your failures, and let those doors totally close behind you. Step forward, into the future that God has for you, knowing there's nothing you can do about past disappointments. You cannot change the past, but you can do something about the future. What's in front of you is far more important than what is behind you. Where you are going is more significant than where you came from or where you have been.

If you will have the right attitude, you will give birth to more in the future than you've lost in the past. Quit looking back. This is a new day. It may seem like your dreams have died, but God can resurrect your dead dreams or give you brand-new ones. He is a supernatural God and when we believe, all things are possible.

You will give birth to more in the future than you've lost in the past.

God has not given up on you; He knows that He put seeds of greatness in you. You have something to offer that nobody else has. He's given you noble dreams and desires. Too often, however, we allow adversities, disappointments, and setbacks to deter us, and before long, we find that we're not pressing forward anymore. We're not stretching; we're not believing we will rise any higher in life.

Ironically, some of the most gifted, talented people go through some of the most unfair, unfortunate experiences: divorce, abuse, neglect. And it's easy for such a person to think, *Why is this happening to me? What did I do to deserve any of this?*

Unfortunately, the enemy knows something about what's on the inside of you, as well. He knows the potential you're carrying, so he does everything he can to keep that seed from taking root. He doesn't want your gifts and talents to flourish. He doesn't want you to accomplish your dreams. He wants you to live an average, mediocre life.

But understand this: God did not create any person without putting something extremely valuable on the inside. Life may have tried to push you down through disappointments or setbacks. In the natural, you don't know how you could rise any higher. You don't see how you're ever going to be happy. You need to dig your heels in and say, "I know what I have on the inside. I'm a child of the Most High God. I'm full of His 'can-do' power, and I'm going to rise up to become everything God has created me to be."

The Apostle Paul urged his young understudy, Timothy, "Stir up the gift within you." Similarly, you need to stir up your gifts, talents, dreams, and desires—in short, the potential within you. Maybe these qualities and traits are buried beneath depression and discouragement, negative voices of people telling you that you can't; beneath weaknesses; beneath failures or fears.

But the good things of God are still there. Now you've got to do your part and start digging them out.

God wants to do a new thing.

You may have had more than your share of unfair, negative experiences. But know this: God wants to do a new thing. He wants to give you a new beginning. Don't give up. Don't go around thinking that you've peaked; that you've reached your limits in life. "Well,

Joel, you don't know my situation. I've gone as far as my education can take me. You don't know my struggles."

No, I may not know any of that. But I do know our God, and He is all-powerful. He has more in store for you. My question for you is: Can you perceive it? Can you make room for it? The first place it starts is in your thinking. If your thinking is limited, then your life is going to be limited.

"But, Joel, I've gone through bankruptcy. I've tried and failed."

Well, let it go. This is a new day.

"My marriage didn't work out. I'm so disappointed. I never thought that I'd be in this situation at this point in my life."

That's unfortunate, but it's not the end. When one door closes, God will always open another. If all the doors close, He'll open a window! God always wants to give you a fresh beginning. He still has a great plan for your life. Do you know when that's going to happen? It will commence the moment you quit looking back. Whenever you quit grieving over what you've lost. Nothing will keep you from the good things of God as much as living in the past.

You may feel that life has knocked you down through disappointments or other unfair situations. But whatever you do, don't stay down. Get back up again, dust yourself off. If you can't find anybody to encourage you, learn to encourage yourself. Get up in the morning, put your shoulders back, look in the mirror, and say, "I've come too far to stop now. I may be knocked down, but I'm not knocked out. I'm going to get back up again. I know I'm a victor, not a victim."

You must keep yourself stirred up if you're going to see these new doors open. I know too many people who are living in the land of "good enough."

"Joel, I don't like my job, but it's good enough." "My husband and I, we don't get along well, but it's good enough; we're surviving." "I'm not using my gifts. I'm not doing what I like, but it's good enough; at least I'm working."

No, don't ever let "good enough" be good enough. Keep pressing. Keep believing. You were not made to be average; you were made to excel. You were made to leave your mark on this generation. At the start of each new day, remind yourself: "I am talented. I am creative.

I am greatly favored by God. I am equipped. I am well able. I will see my dreams come to pass." Declare those statements by faith and before long, you will begin to see them in reality.

Understand that throughout life we will always have forces opposing us, trying to keep us from becoming all God's created us to be. And many times, the adversities, the unfair situations are the results of the enemy's efforts, attempting to discourage us and to deceive us into giving up on our dreams. You may feel as if you're at an empty place in life today. Not much is going your way. You've been through severe difficulties. But God wants to restore you, to encourage you, to fill you with His hope. He wants to resurrect your dreams. He wants to do a new thing.

Continually remind yourself that you have a gift on the inside. You are talented. You are creative. That's exactly why the enemy is trying to push you down, to keep your gifts, your creativity, your joy, your smile, your personality, and your dreams from ever seeing the light of day. He would love for them to lie dormant your whole lifetime. Thank God, it's not up to your enemy: it's up to you.

Granted, you may have gotten off to a rough start in life. You may have had more than your share of unfair things happen. But it's not how you start that counts. It's how you finish. Shake off the past; shake off discouragement. Remind yourself that God is still in complete control of your life. If you'll keep your trust in Him, He promises that no weapon formed against you will prosper. Your situation may seem unfair, it may be difficult; it may seem that the forces working against you are winning momentarily, but God said He'd turn your circumstances around and use them to your advantage.

Don't get complacent. Don't let "good enough" be good enough. Keep yourself stirred up. The forces that are for you are greater than the forces that are against you. The Scripture says, "Weeping may endure for a night, but joy is coming in the morning." [2]

Don't let "good enough" be good enough.

You've got to get your dreams back. Get your fire back. Don't just survive your marriage; get a new vision for it today. Don't just drag into work doing the same thing: start taking some steps of faith. You've got more in you. Push yourself a bit. What you are hoping for may not have happened in the past, but this is a new day. If you'll keep pressing, hoping, believing, not only will you rise higher, but also you'll see things begin to change in your favor.

"Joel, I tried and I failed. My dream was dashed."

Well, dream another dream.

"But I've suffered a big loss, a major setback."

Get back up and go again. That's what we all have to do.

Imagine the disappointment and devastation Adam and Eve must have felt when they discovered that their son Cain had killed their son Abel. Despite their pain, they said in Genesis 4:25, "God has appointed another seed unto us." They were saying in effect, "We are horrified that something like this could happen in our family, and we feel wiped out. But we're not going to mourn forever, because we know God has another seed."

In your difficult times, when you feel like conditions couldn't get any worse, God still says, "Take heart. I'm going to appoint another seed. I'm going to do a new thing."

You may have received a bad report from the doctor; or perhaps a relationship didn't work out. For everything that you've lost, everything that's been stolen, everything that's been taken away, know this: God has another plan. He has another seed.

God uses the word *seed* because that hints at what is coming. Remember, if you will do your part to let go of the old, and start pressing forward, you will give birth to more in the future than you've lost in the past.

Many people have a tough time letting go of what lies behind. They're always focused on who hurt them or how unfairly they have been treated. "Why did this happen to me?" Meanwhile, their gifts, talents, and dreams are pressed down. All the potential is lying dormant.

That almost happened to my father. My dad was married at an early age, but, unfortunately, the relationship didn't work out. My father was devastated. He felt certain that his days of ministry were over and that he'd never have a family again. He thought sure that he had ruined his life and destroyed any future impact for good that he might hope to have. He spent long hours just sitting around depressed, defeated, and dejected.

Then one day, he did what I'm asking you to do. Instead of settling for good enough, instead of focusing on all his mistakes and dwelling on his failures, he decided to let it go. Years later, he told me the hardest thing for him to do was to receive God's mercy. But the Bible says that when we confess our sins, God not only forgives us, He chooses not to remember them anymore. If somebody keeps bringing up your past, you need to know it is not God. If God has let go of it, why don't you let go of it, too?

That's what my father did. One day, he got up, dusted himself off, and said, "Yes, I've made some mistakes. I've made some poor choices. But I know God has another seed. I know He has another plan." Shortly after that, he met my mother. Eventually, they got married and over the years, God blessed them with five children!

Many people who, like my father, have experienced hurt and pain are sitting around wallowing in their mistakes, feeling guilty, condemned, and frustrated. Feeling like they're washed up in life, they allow their gifts and talents to waste away; they place their dreams on hold.

Please, don't let that be you. If you've made mistakes, know this: God is the God of a second chance, a third chance, a fourth, and more. I'm not saying to take the easy path and bail out of a marriage. No, if at all possible, stick with that marriage and make it work. However, if you're already past that point, don't sit around thinking that life is over and that you're never going to be happy. No, God has another seed. He wants to give you a new beginning.

Let the door close completely and step forward into the future God has for you. Quit looking back. Instead, receive God's mercy and start pressing forward in life.

The car you drive has a large windshield, but only a relatively small rearview mirror. The implication is obvious: What happened in your past is not nearly as important as what is in your future. Where you are going is much more important than where you've been. If you stay focused on the past, you're liable to miss numerous excellent opportunities ahead.

What happened in your past is not nearly as important as what is in your future.

How do we let go of the past? First, discipline your thoughts to stop thinking about it. Quit talking about it. Quit reliving every negative experience.

If you have been through a loss or one of your dreams has died, of course there's a proper time for grieving. But at some point, you need to get up, dust yourself off, put on a fresh attitude, and start pressing forward in life. Don't let disappointment become the central theme of your life. Quit mourning over something you can't change. God wants to give you a new beginning, but you have to let go of the old before you'll ever see the new. Let that door close behind you and step through the door in front of you.

Maybe you've allowed other people to convince you that you're never going to rise higher, that you will never see your dreams come to pass. It's been too long. You've messed up too severely.

Don't believe those lies. Instead, take courage from the Old Testament character Caleb. When Caleb was a young man, he and Joshua were part of an exploratory spy mission to determine the strength of the enemy before God's people moved into the land that God had promised them. Of the twelve spies, only Caleb and Joshua presented a positive report to Moses. They said, "We are well able to take the land." The other ten spies said, "No, Moses, there are giants in the land; the opposition is too formidable; the obstacles to overcome are too large." And the majority tried to talk Moses and the rest of the children of Israel out of pressing forward into the blessings that God promised them. They were all too willing to settle for second best, to dwell for the rest of their lives right where they were. Unfortunately, that group of negative thinkers never did make it into the Promised Land. They spent the next forty years spinning their wheels and wandering around aimlessly in a desert. Eventually, most of them died with their dream still in them, as God raised up an entire new generation of people.

By then, Caleb was eighty-five years old, but he hadn't given up on the dream God had placed in his heart. A lot of people that age would be sitting back in a rocking chair, thinking about the good old days, but not Caleb. He kept himself stirred up, and he kept himself in shape as well. He told Joshua that he was still as strong as he was when the promise first came to him.

Caleb went back to the exact same place; the same mountain that the others had feared to climb. He said, "God, give me this mountain." Caleb was saying in effect "I don't want another place to live. I still have this dream in my heart."

Interestingly, Caleb did not ask for an easy inheritance. In fact, the mountain he claimed had five giants living on it. Surely, he could have found a place less fortified, more accessible, or more easily occupied. But Caleb said, "No, I don't care how many obstacles are there. God promised me this place. Although it is forty years later, I'm going to keep pressing; I'm going to keep believing until I see that promise fulfilled."

That's the kind of attitude we need to have. We give up too easily. "Well, I didn't get the promotion I wanted; I guess it's not going to happen."

"My husband and I can't get along. I guess it's over."

No, keep pressing forward and keep believing. Keep yourself stirred up. You've got the gifts, the talents, and the dreams. Don't allow complacency to keep you from seeing God's promises fulfilled in your life.

Stay in a Healthy Environment

Another important key to reaching your full potential is putting yourself in an environment where the seed can grow. I know people who are extremely talented. They have incredible potential. But they insist on hanging around the wrong sort of people. If you are close friends with people who are lazy and undisciplined, people who don't have great dreams, people who are negative and critical, they will rub off on you. Moreover, that environment in which you place yourself will prevent you from rising any higher. You cannot hang out with negative people and expect to live a positive life. If all your friends are depressed and defeated and have given up on their dreams, make some changes. Let's be honest: You're probably not going to pull them up; more likely, if you continue to spend too much time in their presence, they will pull you down.

You cannot hang out with negative people and expect to live a positive life.

Certainly, you love your friends; you can pray for them and try to encourage them to make positive changes in their lives, but sometimes the best thing you can do is break away from negative people and put yourself in a healthy, positive, faith-filled environment. This is extremely critical, because it doesn't matter how great the potential in the seed, if you don't put it in good soil, it will not take root and grow.

Natalie was living in an extremely negative environment, complete with physical, emotional, and verbal abuse. Although her husband Thomas was domineering and controlling, and refused to seek help, Natalie remained in that marriage year after year. She was afraid to leave; afraid she'd be lonely, afraid she couldn't support herself and her two daughters, afraid she'd never meet another man who would be willing to love and accept her, let alone her children.

When Natalie asked me if I thought she should stay in that abusive relationship, I replied, "I don't believe that's God's best. I'm all for sticking together and trying to make things work out, Natalie. But understand that God did not create you to be mistreated and abused. Your mother was in an abusive relationship, and now you are, and unless you make some changes, your daughters will be as well."

It was heartrending for her, but Natalie finally mustered her courage and let the door close on that relationship. She made a fresh start, went back to school, and graduated with honors. She found a good job and met a man who fell in love not only with her but with her children as well. Today, Natalie is happily married and is thriving. Yet none of that would have happened had she not let one door close and walked through another.

I've had people tell me, "Joel, I don't know why I'm drawn to abusive people like that. I get out of one bad relationship and I get into another one that's twice as bad. I know I should get out. I know it's not good for me. But I just can't leave. I'd feel guilty."

I usually answer, "No, you have a responsibility to keep yourself healthy and whole. You have a gift. God has entrusted you with His talents, with His dreams. And it may be painful, but the best thing you can do is get away from somebody that is a constant drag on your spirit. Don't allow somebody to treat you that way. You are extremely valuable. You are made in the image of Almighty God."

"Joel, if I take a stand and set some boundaries, that person may leave; he or she may walk away." In truth, that would be the best thing that could ever happen. I heard somebody say there's something called "the gift of good-bye." That means when somebody who is pulling you down chooses to leave, you may not realize it, but he just did you a great favor. Don't look back; instead keep looking forward. Get ready for the new thing God wants to do in your life.

Your destiny is not tied to the people who walk away from you.

At times, all of us will have people who leave our lives. They may not be bad people. It's just that the season for that relationship is over. We may not understand it, but God knows what He's doing. Maybe that person is holding you back. Maybe she's keeping you from spreading your wings. Maybe he is not a good influence. You may discover that, sometimes, if you don't keep things stirred up, God will stir things for you. When somebody leaves your life or a relationship is over—whether it is a business partner, a friend, a neighbor, or a coworker who parts company—don't get upset. Don't try to talk them into staying. Let God do the new thing. Understand that your destiny is not tied to the people who walk away from you.

You may think, "But I need that person in my life. He's a great friend. I depend on her to be there for me. She's a great business partner."

No, that person is not the key to you becoming a better you. When God is finished with something, there's no amount of glue that can hold it together. You might as well let it go and get ready for something new that God wants to do in and through your life.

Keep yourself in a healthy physical environment. If you tend to struggle with discouragement and depression, don't sit around in a dark house all day long thinking about your problems. Open the windows; let the sun shine in. Put on some good uplifting music. Create a positive environment. When you're tempted to get discouraged, don't you dare go find five other friends who are discouraged and sit around discussing your problems. Find somebody happy to cheer you up. Get around people who will inspire you to rise higher. Be careful with whom you associate, especially when you feel emotionally vulnerable, because negative people can steal the dream right out of your heart.

When I first considered the move of Lakewood Church to our present location in the former Compaq Center in downtown Houston, numerous people told me that we'd never move into that facility. Business leaders and other "experts" said, "Joel, don't waste your time and money. It's not going to happen."

I could have easily given up and thought, *They're probably much smarter than I am in this area. They have much better business acumen than I have. Maybe I should just let it go.*

But I said, "No. I believe God put this dream in my heart, and I'm not going to look up fifty years from now and say, 'I wonder what would have happened if I'd have just believed? I wonder what would have happened if I hadn't let them talk me out of that dream?' "

I can't think of anything worse than coming to the end of your life and having a bunch of regrets: What could have happened? What might have happened? What should have happened?

Beware of the negative influences around you as you pursue your dreams. I remember one consultant we hired during our quest to secure the Compaq Center. Every time we met, he told us all the reasons why it wasn't going to work out. He always had a negative report. When I finally realized the profound impact that consultant was having, I said, "We don't need that man on our team. He is contaminating our environment. He's pulling everybody down."

Surround yourself with people who encourage you, people who will build you up. Certainly, you need people who will be honest enough to tell you when you are making a poor choice or a bad decision. Don't surround yourself with a bunch of "yes-men." On the other hand, don't tolerate a bunch of negative, critical, "can't do it" people. Sometimes the people who will discourage you the most are the people who are closest to you.

Remember King David? When he was just a boy, he told his older brother Eliab that he wanted to fight the huge Philistine giant, Goliath. Eliab tried to discourage David by putting him down. He said, "David, what are you doing out here on the battlefield? You're supposed to be at home taking care of our father's few sheep." He was really saying, "David, you're never going to do anything great. You don't have what it takes."

Right there, David had to make a crucial choice: Would he believe that negative assessment from his brother, or would he believe what God had put in his heart? He could have said, "Well, maybe my brother is right. He's older than I am, more experienced, more knowledgeable about the obstacles we're facing. I'm just a kid. I don't feel too talented. Maybe I will get killed out there."

But no, David said, "Eliab, I don't care what you say about me. I know who I am. I know what God has placed inside me. I'm going to step out and fulfill my God-given destiny." He did just that, facing and felling the giant with a few pebbles from the brook.

Isn't it interesting that even Jesus had to leave His hometown of Nazareth because the people there were so filled with unbelief? Jesus knew that if he stayed in that negative environment, it would hold Him back.

You, too, may have family members or relatives who lack vision and can't imagine you achieving greatness. Don't get angry with them. Most likely, they're good people. You love them and treat them with respect, but understand that you cannot be around them on a daily basis. You have to love them from a distance. Life is too short for you to be pulled down by negative, jealous, cynical people. It doesn't matter how great your gift is or how much potential is locked inside your seeds of greatness, if you don't put that seed in an environment conducive to growth, it will not take root. It will be nearly impossible for your dream to flourish.

Some people you have to love from a distance.

You need to hang around other dreamers—not daydreamers, but people with big goals, people who plan to do something significant with their lives. Hang around people who are going to help you become all God created you to be.

God is saying this is a time of new beginnings. Get your fire back. Get your passion back. You may have been sick a long time, but this is your day to get well. You may have struggled with depression and discouragement, but this is the time to break free. You may come from a family of defeat, failure, and negativism, but this is your time to rise above that morass.

Start stretching your faith once again. Get up each morning expecting good things to happen. And remember, God is on your side. He loves you. He's for you. The Scripture says, "If you put your trust in him, you will not be disappointed."[3]

My father often quoted a simple yet profound statement by Edwin Markham (1852–1940) that sums up the attitude we need: "Ah, great it is to believe the dream as we stand in youth by the starry stream; but a greater thing is to fight life through and say at the end, the dream is true!"

Don't settle for mediocrity; never let good enough be good enough. You too will discover that the dream is true!

CHAPTER 3

The Power of Your Bloodline

I read recently about some famous racehorses, the kind you might see at the Kentucky Derby or other prestigious horse races. I never realized how much time, effort, and resources went into the making of one of those championship horses. I had always thought that somebody was out riding and one day, he or she discovered that a certain horse was fast and gifted. So they decided to enter the horse in some races. Of course, the development of a champion racehorse takes much more than that.

These are not ordinary horses; these are thoroughbreds. They have generation after generation of winners on the inside. These horses have been carefully studied and bred for generations. The breeders, trainers, and veterinarians may search data and statistics for the past fifty or sixty years to check the animal's bloodline. It's no coincidence that a horse raced in the Kentucky Derby.

In horse racing, the "blood stock agent" focuses his attention on the animal's bloodline. He or she will spend months studying a particular line of horses, researching the lineage. The blood stock agent will examine how the horse's father fared as a racer, how long his stride was, how fast he could run, what size he was, and on and on. The breeders understand that winners don't randomly happen. Winning is in the blood.

Simply to breed one of these world champion thoroughbreds can cost up to half a million dollars. And there's no guarantee that the colt will win. In fact, when that newborn colt is born, his legs are all wobbly, he can barely stand up, and his eyes are glazed. The uninformed observer might say, "Those poor owners wasted their money. That horse couldn't win anything. He looks like an average, ordinary horse."

But the owners know that on the inside, in his blood, that colt has a legacy of championship genes. In fact, he may have a dozen world champions on the inside. It's all in the blood. That's why the owners are not necessarily concerned about the colt's initial weakness. They don't really care what color he is, how pretty he is, or even how large he is. They know that deep down on the inside, that colt has the blood of a winner.

Friend, that is how God looks at you and me. Our external appearance is irrelevant. It doesn't matter what color your skin is or what your ethnic background is. It doesn't matter how many weaknesses or flaws you have. You have the DNA of Almighty God. You come from a long line of champions.

Consider this: Your Heavenly Father spoke the galaxies into existence. Your elder brother defeated the enemy. Think about some of your natural ancestors:

Moses parted the Red Sea. There's great faith in your bloodline.

David, a shepherd boy, defeated Goliath with only a few pebbles he picked up from a brook. That is courage in your bloodline.

Samson toppled a building. There's supernatural strength in your bloodline.

Daniel spent an entire night in a lion's den and wasn't harmed. Divine protection flows through your bloodline.

Nehemiah rebuilt the walls of Jerusalem when all the odds were against him. Determination and persistence pulsate through your bloodline.

Queen Esther put her life on the line to save God's people. Sacrifice and heroism are in your bloodline.

Do you understand? You come from a bloodline of champions. You are not ordinary; you are a thoroughbred. It doesn't matter what your present condition looks like; you need to know that inside you flows the blood of a winner. On the inside of you are seeds of greatness. Take a better look at your bloodline. On the inside of you is champion after champion. You are the seed of Almighty God.

You come from a bloodline of champions.

That's why you must quit focusing on your weaknesses and get a bigger vision for your life. Understand that God sees you already at the Winner's Circle. He's already seen them putting the roses around your neck. That's what David was talking about when he said, "God, all of my days you ordained before one of them came to be."[4] In other words, you may be a mere thirty, forty, or fifty years of age, but God has been working on you for a long time. He had you planned long before you were born. You are extremely valuable; you are not ordinary; you come from great stock. You've been destined to live in victory, destined to overcome, destined to leave your mark on this generation.

Sometimes you hear people say, "Well, he's just got good genes. He just comes from good stock." Let me tell you, you come from superior stock. God brought you out of His best.

Interestingly, to most people, the famous racehorses don't look much different from ordinary horses. Certainly, they are beautiful animals, but the average person couldn't ascertain the champion from the merely well-bred horse. The difference is in the blood. That's what makes them extremely valuable.

It's the same way with us. The Scripture says we overcome by the blood of the Lamb, the Word of our testimony, and a willingness to lay down our lives.[5] Because of what God has done, every one of us is a thoroughbred.

"But you don't know the life I've led," I hear you saying. "I've failed here and I've made mistakes over there, and I still have this addiction."

That doesn't change your bloodline; it doesn't change what's in you. You may never have realized how valuable you are. Perhaps you never realized the price God paid for you. You need to recognize what you have on the inside. It says in First Corinthians that you were bought with a high price. God gave His very best for you, His only Son. So please don't go around thinking that you are worthless, that you don't have a future. You are a champion on the inside. It's in your blood.

One time, years ago, my father went to a meeting at a friend's church. My father arrived a little late, so he simply sat down on the back row. A few minutes later, a young man came in and sat down not too far from my father. Daddy noticed that the young man looked extremely distraught. My father's heart went out to the young man; he was deeply concerned about him. Daddy thought to himself that after the service he would speak to the young man and try to encourage him in some way. In the middle of the meeting, however, the young man got up and left.

My father felt compelled to follow him; Daddy got up from where he was sitting and went looking for him. He looked all over the front lobby of the church but couldn't find him. My dad searched the parking lot and still couldn't find him. He came back in and was about to give up, but he decided to check the restroom. A few other people were in there, so my father just waited. Sure enough, a few minutes later, the young man came out.

He looked surprised to see my father, so Daddy said, "I know you don't know me, and I don't mean to get in your business, but I'm very concerned about you. And I want you to know that God loves you and you are extremely valuable to Him."

The young man stared back at my father, and suddenly tears began to flow down his face. He said, "My life is so messed up. I'm addicted to so many drugs that I can't take it anymore. I decided to come to church one last time, and then I was going home to take every pill that I could find and end it all."

Later, he told how he had seen my father sitting down the row from him. He didn't know who Daddy was, but he was impressed by the dress shoes my father wore. Those shoes left an impression in his mind, and when he went out there, he knew Daddy was coming after him. He said, "I tried everything to get away, but everywhere I looked, those same shoes kept following me."

My father told him, "It doesn't matter where you are right now. You may have made mistakes. You may have failed a thousand times, but understand that it does not change your value in God's eyes. You are not here on earth by accident. God has a plan and a purpose for your life. He has an assignment for you. And it's not just to drift around in mediocrity."

My father and the young man prayed together, and that night was a turning point in his life. Today, more than thirty years later, that man is a pastor of a church, and he has helped thousands of other people to make a difference in our world.

Maybe you are like that young man. Perhaps you have never fully considered what you have on the inside. You may have made mistakes, but don't let your mistakes keep you down. Get back up and go again. Your errors or wrong choices do not change your bloodline. They don't change what's in you. Oftentimes, society will write a person off when he or she fails or makes poor choices, but God is not that way. God sees your potential. He knows what you're capable of being. He's the one who designed you, and He knows that you can still do great things. It's in your blood.

He has programmed you with everything you need for victory. That's why every day you can say things like, "I have what it takes. I am more than a conqueror. I am intelligent; I am talented. I am successful; I am attractive; I am an overcomer." God put all those things in your bloodline.

Your spiritual bloodline is more powerful than your natural bloodline.

Granted, you may have to overcome some negative elements in your family's natural bloodline, but always remember your spiritual bloodline is more powerful than your natural bloodline. You have been handpicked by Almighty God. You have His royal blood flowing through your veins. Put your shoulders back and hold your head up high knowing that you have been chosen. You've been set apart before the foundation of the world. Understand your value and shake off inferiority or insecurity. The "champion" is already within you, just waiting to be discovered. It's in your blood.

What About Bad Blood?

Where I grew up, folks often described a troublemaker by saying, "Well, he's just got bad blood." Really, there's some truth to that. What's in our bloodline is extremely important. We all have a natural bloodline flowing from our parents, grandparents, great-grandparents, and other family members in our family tree.

But we also have a spiritual bloodline. The good news is that our spiritual bloodline can override our natural bloodline. The Scripture talks about all things becoming new. The old is passed away.[6] In other words, we have entered into a new bloodline. When you really understand all God has done for you, and you begin to act on it, then you can rise up out of any adversity; you can overcome anything negative from your past. There's power in your spiritual bloodline.

David said in Psalm 139:13, "God, you created my inmost being; you knit me together in my mother's womb." Verse 16 of that psalm says, "All the days ordained for me were written in your book before one of them came to be." Notice, David is saying that God saw us before we were born. Before Adam and Eve, before Abraham, before Moses or your grandparents, God knew you. In other words, your parents didn't simply get together and decide to have a child. You were preordained to be here before the foundation of the world.

God is the great architect of the universe. He planned everything, and prearranged for you to be here at this particular time in history. That's one reason why we should feel a sense of destiny and value.

Understand that your value is not based on how somebody else has treated you or on how perfect of a life you have lived, or even how successful you are. Your value is based solely on the fact that you are a child of the Most High God. No, we're not perfect, we make mistakes; we all have weaknesses. But that doesn't change our value in God's eyes. We are still the apple of His eye. We are still His most prized possession.

Sometimes "religion" tries to beat people down and make them feel bad about themselves. "You've done this and you failed here, and you didn't treat this person right, and you didn't raise your kids as well as you should have." Many people wallow in that condemnation and they go around with low self-esteem and a sense of unworthiness. Their attitude is *God could never bless me. I've made too many mistakes. I blew it.*

No, God knew you weren't going to be perfect. Why don't you lighten up and give yourself a break? Quit beating yourself up over everything you've done wrong. After all, you can't change the past. If you've made mistakes, just say, "God, I'm sorry; I repent. Help me to do better next time." Then let it go and move on. If you hold on to it, you open the door to guilt and condemnation. Before long, you'll be going around with a "poor old me" mentality.

"I don't deserve anything. I'm just a weak worm of the dust," I hear people say. No, you're not a weak worm of the dust; you are a child of the Most High God. Hold your head up high, put your shoulders back, and start acting like a child of Almighty God.

God was thinking about you before you were ever even born.

Friend, you've got to believe in yourself and believe that you have something to offer this world that nobody else has. You've been made in the image of Almighty God. That means you're not like another animal—a dog, a cat, a horse. No, the Scripture says that God breathed His life into you.[7] You are a person of destiny. You didn't just happen to show up. God was thinking about you before you were even born. The Bible says that He has meticulously made everything about you.

Some people are always finding fault with themselves. "I wish I didn't look like this. I wish had her personality, and I wish I had his talent."

No, God designed you as you are on purpose. You are an original. Quit being negative and critical toward yourself and start enjoying yourself as the unique creation of God.

I hope you take this in the right sense, but I like being me. I know I'm not perfect, and I have areas in which I need to improve. Overall, though, I enjoy being myself. I realize I am valuable to God.

You, too, may have some things you wish you could change, but rather than focus on those areas, take what God has given you and make the most of it. You are valuable to God. I heard somebody put it like this: If God had a refrigerator, your picture would be on it. If God carried a wallet, your photo would be in it.

You may say, "Joel, I haven't gotten good breaks in life, and my parents struggled with these same problems. I think this is my lot in life."

No, your lot in life is to be a victor and not a victim. Your lot in life is to be happy, healthy, and whole. Sure, you may have some things to overcome in that natural bloodline, but your spiritual bloodline looks very good. Your Father spoke the worlds into existence. He could have chosen anybody, but He chose you. He equipped you and approved you.

I love the Scripture that says, "If we belong to Christ, we are Abraham's seed, and heirs according to the promise." [8] That means we can all experience the blessings of Abraham. If you study Abraham's record, you'll discover that he was prosperous, healthy, and lived a long, productive life. Even though he didn't always make the best choices, he enjoyed God's blessings and favor.

No matter how many mistakes you've made, you need to know that on the inside, you have the seed of Almighty God. Your attitude should be, "I may have a lot to overcome, people may have tried to push me down, maybe I didn't get the best breaks, but that does not change who I am. I know I can fulfill my destiny." You should go out each day expecting good things, anticipating God's blessings and favor. God has planned all of your days for good, not evil.

"I don't really see that happening in my life," you say. "I've endured so much adversity."

Maybe so, but if you will keep pressing forward, if you'll keep believing, God says He'll take those negative experiences, turn them around, and He will use them to your advantage.

Remember, we are called overcomers. That means we're going to have obstacles to overcome. You can't have great victories without having difficult battles. You'll never have a great *testimony* without going through a few *tests*. The enemy always fights the hardest when he knows God has something great in store for you.

If you've had unfair things happen to you, or people have robbed or cheated you, the Scripture says that God will bring you out with twice what you had before.[9] If you are struggling through tough times, start declaring, "I'm coming out of this experience with twice the joy, twice the peace, twice the honor, twice the promotion." Every day when you get up, declare, "This is going to be a day of victory in my life. I'm expecting God's unprecedented favor. Promotion, favor, increase, they're all on the way."

Tap into God's Power

I've had people tell me, "Joel, I know that someday I'll be happy. I know one day I'll enjoy my life in the sweet by and by."

I appreciate what they are saying, but God wants us to enjoy our lives right here in the nasty now and now. He wants us to have a little heaven on earth, right where we are. One of the reasons Christ came was that we might live an abundant life. You can be happy and free in this life, not simply in heaven one of these days; you can accomplish your dreams before you go to heaven!

How can you do that? By tapping into God's power inside of you.

The Bible says, "Christ has redeemed us from the curse of the law."[10] The curse is behind any kind of defeat—sin, mistakes, wrong choices, fear, worry, constant sickness, unhealthy relationships, or bad attitudes. Please understand that those are all things from which you have already been set free. But here's the catch: If you don't appreciate and take advantage of your freedom, if you don't get your thoughts, your words, your attitudes going in the right direction, it won't do you any good.

You may be sitting back waiting on God to do something supernatural in your life, but the truth is, God is waiting on you. You must rise up in your authority, have a little backbone and determination, and say, "I am not going to live my life in mediocrity, bound by addictions, negative and defeated. No, I'm going to do like the Apostle Paul and start pressing forward. I'm going to take hold of everything God has in store for me."

I heard a story about a little dog that had been kept on a twenty-foot leash for years, tied to a tree. He had his home there and the owner came out to feed him and play with him occasionally. But the dog remained on the leash. He would see the other dogs, and he would run right out to the end of his leash. He knew exactly how far he could go. He wanted to chase them. He wanted to go play, but he knew he was limited. If he went too far, the leash jerked him back into place.

One day, the owner felt sorry for the dog, so he decided to let him off that leash. Instead of removing the whole leash, however, the owner simply unfastened the leash from the dog's collar. The collar remained around the dog's neck, but it wasn't buckled anymore. The owner thought sure the dog would take off running, happy and free. Another dog came along, and sure enough, his dog got up and took off running. Much to the owner's surprise, when his dog got to where the leash would have ended, he stopped right where he always did.

A few minutes later, a cat came strutting by. This cat had tormented the dog for years. But that cat knew where to walk—just a couple of feet outside of the leash's range. Again the dog took off running but stopped right where he normally did.

The dog was free; he just didn't realize it. The leash was loosed. All he had to do was go one step farther than he was used to going and he could have walked right out of it.

Many times, that's similar to what we are doing. God has loosed our chains of addictions, of personal defeats, of bad attitudes. The problem is we're not walking out of them.

"I've always been this way. I've always had a problem with my temper. I've always had this addiction," some people lament.

No, you need to realize you have already been set free. Two thousand years ago, God loosened your collar. Now, it's up to you to start walking out of it.

How do you do it? Change your attitude. Quit saying, "I can't do it; I'll never be well; I'll always be in debt. I've got too much to overcome."

Every enemy in your life has already been defeated—enemies of worry, depression, addiction, financial lack—and you have power over all of them. The same power that raised Christ from the dead is inside you. There is nothing in your life that you cannot overcome; no hurt is too deep that you cannot forgive. You have the power to let go of the negative things of your past. You may have been knocked down a thousand times, but you have the power to get back up again. The medical report may not look good, but you have the power to stand strong.

Refuse to sit back and accept things that are less than God's best. Your attitude should be, "I know my chains have been removed; I know the price has been paid, and even if I have to believe my whole lifetime, even if I have to stand in faith till the day I die, I'm not going to sit back and accept a life of mediocrity. I'm going to keep pressing forward."

Too many people learn to function in their dysfunction. They embrace all kinds of things that are not God's best. They're argumentative, bitter, and resentful; they allow strife in their home, and they're critical and judgmental. Instead of dealing with it and being willing to change, they merely put a bandage on it and continue living in bondage, functioning in their dysfunction.

Too many people learn to function in their dysfunction.

You can never change what you tolerate. As long as you accept it and accommodate it, you're going to stay right where you are. But you don't have to live that way. You are learning to function in your dysfunction. I encourage you to go one step further. Try giving up one cigarette a day. Forgive one person who has offended you. Strive to be just a little more disciplined today than you were yesterday.

"Well," you say, "Joel, I've been this way so long. I don't see how I could ever change." No, your freedom has already been purchased, but you have to rid yourself of that defeated mentality and start thinking power thoughts. Start saying, "I'm free. This addiction does not control me. Greater is He who is in me than he that's in the world." Don't ever say, "I'll never see my dreams come to pass; I'll probably never get married." Or "My bills are so high, and my income is so low, I don't think I'll ever get out of debt." No, turn that around. You need to be saying, "I am more than a conqueror. I will fulfill my destiny. God is supplying all of my needs."

You must press in if you're going to take hold of everything God has in store for you. It's easy to get passive, to say, "That's a lot of work; that's hard. I don't want to change that much. I know I'm prone to be negative, but I don't feel like having a good attitude. I know I shouldn't eat this junk food, but I enjoy it. I know I need to quit smoking, but I'm tired of trying."

You can never change what you tolerate.

Those kinds of attitudes will keep you from becoming a better you. You *can* rise higher. You *can* be a better person, a better parent, spouse, coworker, or a better leader. God has more in store for you.

You may have had many negative things in your family line for generations. They just keep being passed down from one generation to the next: sicknesses, bad attitudes, addictions, financial stress, low self-esteem, and other chronic conditions. Please understand those are some of the things from which you have been redeemed. Those things are under the curse, and that curse has been broken.

No doubt, the people who went before you—your parents, family members, your ancestors—were good people. But when a person doesn't understand what God has done for him or her, it's easy just to accept a life of mediocrity.

A young man named Eric told me, "Joel, my grandfather was an alcoholic and my dad was an alcoholic. Now, I've got the same problem. I just can't beat it."

"No, you can beat it," I encouraged him. "The power in you is greater than that addiction. But you've got to change your attitude. You've got to start saying, 'I'm free.' Declare that every day. Don't talk about the way you are, talk about the way you want to be."

Often you hear people say, "Once you're addicted, you're always addicted." "Once an alcoholic, always an alcoholic." People may spout such nonsense, but God's Word says, "Whom the Son sets free is free indeed." [11] God's help can overcome any evil in your life. You can break any bad habit. You can overcome any obstacle.

"Well, Joel, my grandmother had diabetes. My mother has diabetes. It looks like I'm going to have it, too."

When you think like that, you're planning to be diabetic. You're inviting that malady into your life. You need to put your foot down and say, "Grandmother may have had it. Mother may have had it. But as for me and my house, we're redeemed from diabetes. I'm going to live under the blessing and not the curse." Don't make plans for negative things.

In my family, on my father's side, as far back as we can trace, there has been a history of heart disease—people in my family dying early deaths because of heart problems. But I'm not planning to have heart disease. I'm planning to live a long, healthy life. I do my part to stay healthy; I try to eat right and exercise regularly. And I declare every day, "I will fulfill my destiny in good health."

Maybe Alzheimer's disease runs in your family genes, but don't succumb to it. Instead, say every day, "My mind is alert. I have clarity of thought. I have a good memory. Every cell in my body is increasing and getting healthier." If you'll rise up in your authority, you can be the one to put a stop to the negative things in your family line.

Don't talk about the way you are, talk about the way you want to be.

Vanessa is a medical doctor who attends Lakewood Church. In 1995, she was practicing medicine in Washington, DC, when she began to feel terrible pain in her joints. The pain intensified to the point where she could hardly stand it. She came to Houston to have an operation on her knees, hoping the surgical procedure would fix the problem, but, unfortunately, it grew worse. Her body continued to decline. Although she was not yet thirty years of age, Vanessa walked with a cane. She told us that she felt and looked like a ninety-year-old woman.

Interestingly, Vanessa's father had the same disease in his early twenties, and he ended up dying from it at the age of forty-three. Her grandmother had the exact same ailment and lived as a paraplegic. It looked as though Vanessa was headed down that same path.

When she attended church at the old Lakewood campus, it took her forty-five minutes to get from her car to her seat inside the sanctuary. It took most other people about two or three minutes. After the service, she usually waited until the crowd cleared out, so nobody could see how bad her condition was. During the week, she would get up at three in the morning to start getting dressed, and start getting her joints loosened up so she could be at the hospital by seven.

The easy thing for her to do was to just sit back and think, *Too bad for me. Daddy had it. Grandmother had it. I guess this is my lot in life.*

But Vanessa didn't do that. She was a warrior.

She said, "I'm going to rise up and take hold of everything that God has in store for me." She started praying, believing, and declaring every day: "I'm getting better and better. God is restoring health unto me. I will live and not die." For three years, she didn't see any sign of change. It didn't look as though anything was happening. That didn't deter Vanessa; she just kept on believing.

Sometimes you have to show the enemy that you're more determined than he is. That's what Vanessa was doing.

One day, out of the clear blue, she noticed the pain wasn't quite as bad. She could move her joints a little easier. The next day, she felt slightly better. The following day, she moved a bit easier. It didn't happen overnight, but over that next three months, Vanessa got better and better, and today she's totally free. Dr. Vanessa is happy, healthy, and whole.

She took a stand and she broke the curse of that sickness. Now, her children, her grandchildren, generations to come will benefit because she made a decision to live under the blessing and not the curse.

"Well, Joel, I don't know if that would happen for me. You don't know my circumstances."

You're right. It's not going to happen if you are negative and doubtful. This type of blessing is for believers, not doubters. You need to rise up like Dr. Vanessa, look that obstacle in the eye, and say, "I will defeat you. I am a child of the Most High God, and I am going to become all that He has created me to be."

Get rid of that weakness mentality. Start thinking powerful

thoughts, such as *I can do all things through Christ. I am a victor and not a victim*. Remember, the same power that raised Christ from the dead is inside you. Your collar has already been loosed. The price has already been paid. It's up to you to rise up and walk in your authority.

Don't settle for anything less than God's best.

What's holding you back in life? Addictions, bad attitudes, low self-esteem? Recognize what it is. Don't just learn to function in your dysfunction. Be willing to make some changes. The Old Testament prophet Joel said, "Wake up the mighty men." You are a mighty man or woman; don't settle for anything less than God's best. Stir up the gift on the inside. Keep your dreams alive. Make a decision today that from now on, you are going to live under the blessing and not the curse. As you do, you'll discover that Almighty God has already loosened the leash in your life and has given you the power to break free from things that have held you back in the past.

CHAPTER 4

Breaking Free from the Strongholds of Your Past

It is startling but true: The decisions we make today don't simply affect ourselves; they affect our children and our children's children for multiplied generations. The Bible talks about how the iniquity of the fathers can be passed down for three or four generations. That means bad habits, addictions, negativity, wrong mind-sets and other types of iniquities can be passed down.

Perhaps you are struggling in certain areas right now because people who came before you made poor choices. Many times, you can look back and see the results of those choices somewhere in your family line. It is important that we recognize what has happened and that we not passively accept these negative patterns. "Well, this is just the way I am. This poverty and sickness has been in my family for years."

No, you need to rise up and do something about it. It may have been there for years, but the good news is it doesn't have to stay there. You can be the one to put a stop to it. You can be the one to choose the blessing and not the curse.

Recent research seeks to identify specific genes and determine how genes for traits such as addiction, eating disorders, even depression, are passed down. The researchers can see definite patterns, but they cannot conclusively determine whether the cause is genetic, environmental, or hereditary, or some combination of those factors.

Certainly, all those things can be factors, but I believe the root cause is spiritual. The Bible calls it an *iniquity*.

We have to understand that just as the strong physical characteristics can be inherited, the negative things in our family's bloodline will continue from generation to generation until somebody rises up and puts a stop to it. For example, when Adam and Eve disobeyed God, that decision didn't just affect them; it affected their children. Do you know who the first murderer was in the Bible? It was Adam's son Cain. The second murderer was one of Cain's descendants, a man by the name of Lamech. That iniquity kept getting passed down through generations of Cain's offspring. It was in their family line.

Similarly, many of the things we struggle with today may be traced to somebody in our family line who gave in to it, and now we have to deal with it. We shouldn't use that as an excuse or a rationalization for continuing that pattern, but we must recognize what has happened, and we need to be more determined than ever that we are going to be the ones to put a stop to it.

A beautiful young woman named Betsy struggles with anorexia. She explained to me how her mother had succumbed to it, several of her aunts had it, her sisters had it, and several cousins did too. This one sickness was practically tearing this family apart. That was not just a coincidence; that's a negative, destructive spirit that keeps getting passed down in that family. It probably would have continued to decimate the family had Betsy not made a choice to live under the blessings of God rather than a curse. Betsy realized that her struggle against anorexia was not merely a physical battle; it was a spiritual battle as well. As she took authority over those issues in the name of Jesus, Betsy broke free from the bondage she had inherited.

Examine the areas in your life where you constantly struggle, in the areas where it seems as though something is trying to drag your family down. Maybe it's a pattern of divorce, poverty, addictions, abuse, depression, even sicknesses.

Nearly every male in Tim's family has had a heart attack and died by the time he was fifty years old. Tim is currently forty-eight, so you can imagine how concerned and worried he is. "Tim, you can be the one to break that curse," I told him. "Don't start planning your funeral. Don't assume that you will have a heart attack. Take a stand against it."

I said, "Eat right, exercise regularly, and every day, declare, 'With long life, God is satisfying me and showing me His salvation.' "

Friend, you have to make the choice whether you will receive the blessing and not the curse. If these negative patterns exist in your family line, recognize what's happening and do something about it. Don't just keep passing it down. The pattern may not have been initiated from any horrible wrong that was done. Sometimes these things are a result of somebody opening the door to the enemy. Perhaps one of your ancestors opened the door to fear, anxiety, or worry, and everyone else has picked up on it for years. Regardless of how the negative pattern began, you can be the one to stop it.

Stephen and Susan's son Bradley started first grade, and he was so excited about it. He was outgoing and energetic and met many new friends. After a couple of months, however, Bradley began having intense panic attacks at school. He would get so upset and afraid that his parents weren't going to come back and pick him up. Bradley's teacher tried to calm him down by getting Stephen or Susan on the phone, so one of them could tell him how much they loved him and, of course, that they'd be back to pick him up as soon as school was over. But nothing his parents said calmed Bradley. Time after time, the parents would have to rush to the school and assure their child that everything was okay.

There was no reason for Bradley's unexplainable fear. Stephen and Susan were loving parents, and they had never before left him anyplace. Nevertheless, the panic attacks continued month after month. The situation got so bad that when Bradley was at home, he would not leave Susan's side. He'd follow her from room to room. If she went outside, he was right there. If for some reason he couldn't find her, he would burst into another panic attack.

The couple was frustrated and heartbroken, wondering what they had done to cause this awful condition, and what they could do to help Bradley. Then one day, Stephen was talking with his father, the child's grandfather, and as he explained the situation, it was as though a light turned on in the grandfather's mind. "Stephen, I know exactly what's wrong with Bradley," the grandfather said. "When I was a little boy in the first grade, my father died suddenly. I was so afraid that when my mother would try to walk me to school, I would cry so hard, thinking that she may not come back. Many times, she would just turn around and take me back home. I believe that somehow Bradley's fear is connected to mine."

Stephen and Susan realized that Bradley's fear didn't originate with him; it was passed down because of that traumatic event in the grandfather's life. They began to understand that things could get passed down from one generation to the next, things that they didn't have anything to do with. You can't simply deal with such conditions medically, psychologically, or in any other physical sense. You can't merely apply sheer willpower to overcome this condition; it is a spiritual battle. Stephen and Susan began to pray; daily they bound the stronghold of fear in their family's line, and they stood against that curse. Today, Bradley is a young man and is completely free, living a normal, healthy life.

Some people are living under a spirit of depression that gets passed from generation to generation. Their lives are characterized by a lack of joy and little enthusiasm. I've seen it even in little children. Other kids can be out laughing, playing, having a good time, but the child from the depressed family languishes in the doldrums, so serious and solemn, not even enjoying his childhood. That's a spirit of depression.

I've known men that have everything in the world going for them. They have great families, they make plenty of money, they're successful in their careers, yet they're never really happy or fulfilled. It's as though something is always gnawing at them, stealing their joy, peace, and victory. Friend, that is not normal. That is a spirit of defeat, a spirit of discouragement. And you have to deal with it in a manner similar to what Stephen and Susan did—rise up and stand against it through prayer and positive, biblically based affirmations.

You can be the one to break the curse in your family. Don't just sit back and say, "Well, we've always been negative." "I've always had this addiction." "Everybody in my family gets married and divorced three or four different times."

No, be the one to say, "Enough is enough. I'm sick and tired of being sick and tired. As for my family and me, we're choosing the blessing and not the curse."

You can be the one to stand against the forces of darkness and to break those strongholds that are keeping you and your family in bondage. The Scripture says, "The curse does not come without a cause." [12] That means when we are dealing with issues such as addictions, bad habits, and dysfunctions, either we've made bad choices or somebody in our family line has made some bad choices. There's a reason a child grows up to become an alcoholic. There's a reason a child becomes an abusive parent. There's a reason a young man commits crimes until he is sent off to prison, and when he is released, he goes right back to a life of crime. Certainly, societal issues may have an impact, but these things don't randomly happen in the spirit realm. Somebody, somewhere, opened the door to the enemy.

Overcoming Negative History

Understand, if you are struggling with one or more of these things, that does not make you a bad person. You need not mope around guilty and condemned because you have some obstacles to overcome. Many times, it may not even be your fault. Somebody else made the poor choices, and now you have to deal with the repercussions. Nevertheless, be careful that you don't use that as an excuse to perpetuate negative lifestyle patterns. You have to dig your heels in and do something about it.

One of the first steps to overcoming these generational curses is to recognize what you're dealing with. Identify it. Don't ignore it. Don't try to sweep it under the rug and hope that it will go away. It won't.

If you're lazy and undisciplined, don't make excuses; just admit it and say, "I'm going to deal with this." If you have an anger problem, or if you don't treat other people with honor and respect, don't try to convince yourself that everything is okay. Admit it and deal with it.

The Bible says, "Confess your faults one to another and pray for one another that you may be healed." [13] Notice, you must be honest enough with yourself to confess your faults. Notice, too, that you're going to have to find a good mature friend and say, "I need your help. I'm struggling in this area, and I need you to pray with me."

Too often, we do just the opposite. We think, *I'm not going to tell anybody about this problem. What would they think of me? I'd be embarrassed.*

Instead, swallow your pride, confess your weakness, and get the help you need so you can be free. It is not easy to admit that we need help, but it is necessary, and it is liberating.

Robert grew up in a violent, angry home. As a young man, he got hooked on drugs and began selling them to support his habit. He lived dangerously, in a perpetual self-destruct mode, following his family's pattern of violence and anger.

Then, in his mid-twenties, Robert gave his life to the Lord. As he studied the Bible, he began sharing the good news with others and eventually became a pastor. He was doing great personally, and the church grew in strength and numbers. Robert became one of the most respected citizens in the community as well as traveling and sharing his story of how God had changed his life.

People did not know that he still had a serious anger problem. God had delivered him from all sorts of other bad habits, addictions, drugs, and alcoholism, but Robert still struggled with this anger. He would never show it in public, but if something went wrong at home, he'd fly into a violent fit of uncontrollable rage. Many times, something insignificant would set him off and he would erupt. He was extremely abusive to his wife physically and verbally. He would throw things and treat her horribly, often placing her in physical danger. Then when he finally calmed down, he begged for her forgiveness, which she readily granted. She would say to him, "Honey, we have got to go get some help. We've got to go talk to somebody about this problem."

"I'm too embarrassed," he told her. "I'm the pastor of the church. I'm supposed to be the example. How could I ever tell anybody I have this terrible problem?"

His wife drew up every bit of courage she could muster and said, "But the Scripture says, 'Confess your faults so you can be healed.' Robert, you will never overcome what you're struggling with all by yourself. You've got to find a friend, a mentor, a pastor, a counselor. Find somebody that will stand with you. Find somebody that will pray with you. Find somebody that will hold you accountable."

Robert's wife was absolutely right. Just because you are dealing with some tough things doesn't mean that you're a bad person. We have to get past the misconception that because we love God and people look up to us, we're supposed to be perfect. It doesn't always work that way.

If you have an anger problem or a problem with alcohol, or some other kind of hidden addiction, don't try to beat that problem on your own. Don't hide it because you're too embarrassed. Find a godly person that will stand in faith with you. I'm not saying that you have to announce it to the world. But you need to find one person that you can really trust. As you do your part, God will help you to overcome the negative patterns in your life.

Pastor Robert later admitted that he wouldn't tell anybody about his anger problem because he thought that something was wrong with him. He couldn't understand how God had delivered him from all the other bad addictions, but he still had this serious anger problem. Robert later confided that even when he was enraged and out of control, deep down on the inside, he would be saying to himself, "Why am I doing this? Why can't I stop? What is wrong with me?"

The problem was that anger had been in his family line a long time. It wasn't as easy to overcome as some of those other habits were. Beyond that, he had to get past his fears of what everybody was going to think of him. Finally, Pastor Robert went for help. As he confessed his faults and stood against the forces of darkness, God set him free completely. Today he's one of the kindest, gentlest men you would ever want to meet.

In the same way, you can beat anything that's come against you. No addiction is too difficult for our God. No stronghold is impenetrable to Him. It doesn't matter how long you've had it, or how many times you've tried and failed, today is a new day. If you will be honest with yourself, recognize what you're dealing with, and find somebody to hold you accountable, then you too can start living under the blessing and not the curse. You can free yourself from those negative generational patterns, and start a new pattern of goodness and love for your descendants.

Take responsibility for your actions. God has given you free will. You can choose to change. You can choose to set a new standard. Every right choice you make will overturn the wrong patterns that other people in your family's lineage have made. Every time you resist a temptation, you are one step closer to your victory. You may have a negative history, but you don't have to perpetuate it. We can't change the past, but we can change the future by making right choices today.

Sadly, hurting people end up hurting other people. You might think that when we come out of a negative environment, we would be quick to change. You hear people say it all the time: "Well, I'm never going to raise my kids like that." Or "I'll never treat my wife the way my father treated my mother." The truth is, more often than not, they end up doing exactly what they said they would never do. That spirit is passed down.

If you grew up in a negative environment, unless you break that spiritual pattern, there's a high probability that you will treat your children the same way you were treated. I know people that were abused physically and verbally growing up. You would think that since they suffered so much and went through all that pain, they would stay far away from it. However, studies confirm the opposite. People who have been abused are the most likely to become abusers. Why is that? It's not because they want to. They know how destructive it is. It's because that negative spirit keeps being passed down.

Thank God, you and I can do something about it. The Scripture says in Ephesians that our fight is not against flesh and blood, but we fight in the spiritual realm.[14] You have to rise up and say, "I'm taking authority over this thing and I am not going to live this way any longer." God will give you the power to do what you need to do. Don't just sit back and accept the status quo. Do something about it.

Many people play the blame game today. "It's his fault or her fault." "Well, I'm depressed because my mother was depressed." Or "I can't break these addictions because everybody in my family has these addictions." Or "I'm angry because you made me angry."

Avoid that mess. Take responsibility for your own actions. You may have experienced some unfair things in the past that have made life more difficult for you, but your attitude should be, "I'm not going to sit around and moan and complain about how I was raised or about how somebody mistreated me. No, this is the life God gave me, and I'm going to make the most of it. I'm going to make good choices starting today."

We've heard a lot about the generational curse, but equally as important is our generational choice. We don't have to stay the way we are.

**This is the life God has given me,
and I'm going to make the very most of it.**

Put a stop to any of the negative patterns in your family's bloodline. It may have been there for years, but you can be the one to make a difference. Remember, this is a spiritual battle. You must take authority over all the strongholds that are keeping you in bondage. One of the first things you must do is recognize what it is, identify it, get it out in the open, and deal with it. As you do, you will see God's blessings and favor in your life, and you will pass down those good things to the generations to follow. In the next chapter, I'll show you how you can leave a lasting positive legacy.

CHAPTER 5

The Generational Blessing

Most of us don't give much thought to the plethora of decisions we make as we go through each day. Yet the decisions we make today will affect our children, our grandchildren, and the generations to come.

Too often, we think only about the here and now. "Well, Joel, it's my life. I know I have some bad habits. I know I'm kind of hot-tempered. I know I don't treat everybody right. But that's okay; I can handle it."

The problem with that kind of thinking is it's not just hurting you; it's making life more difficult on those who come after you. The things that we don't overcome, the issues we leave on the table, so to speak, will be passed down for the next generation to deal with. None of us lives or dies to ourselves. A person's good habits as well as their poor choices—the addictions, bad attitudes, and wrong mind-sets—all are passed down.

But the good news is: Every right decision we make, every time we resist temptation, every time we honor God, when we do the right thing, not only are we going to come up higher ourselves, but we're making it a little easier on the generations that will come after us.

Think of it like this: Each of us has a spiritual bank account. By the way we live, we're either storing up equity or storing up iniquity. Equity would be anything good: our integrity, our determination, our godliness. That's storing up blessings. On the other hand, iniquity includes our bad habits, addictions, selfishness, lack of discipline. All of these things, either good or bad, will be passed down to future generations.

I like to look at my life as a few laps in the marathon that our family line is running. When my life is done, I'm going to hand the baton to my children. Contained in that baton will be my physical DNA, my traits, hair color, size, and weight. It will also hold my spiritual and emotional DNA. It will include my tendencies, attitudes, habits, and mind-sets. My children will take the baton, run a few laps, and hand it to their children, and on and on. Every lap that we run with purpose, passion, and integrity is one more lap that can be used for good by those that come after us. In a sense, the laps we run well put future generations further down the road toward significance and success.

We need to think about the big picture. I want to leave my family line better off than they were before. I don't want selfishness, addictions, or bad habits to diminish my life. I want everything about my life now to make it easier on those who will come after me.

Even if you don't have children, you're going to live on through the people you influence. Your habits, attitudes, and what you stand for will all be passed down to somebody.

I read of an interesting study done in 1993 by the United States military. They were curious about what traits get passed down from one generation to the next. We know that our physical traits do. What about emotional, mental, and spiritual characteristics? What about bad attitudes and addictions? Or what about good qualities such as integrity, compassion, and godliness? Can they be passed down as well?

The researchers extracted some white blood cells from a volunteer and they carefully placed them in a test tube. They then put a probe from a lie detector machine down in that test tube, to measure the person's emotional response.

Next, they instructed this same volunteer to go a couple of doors down and watch some violent scenes from an old war movie on television. When this man watched the scenes, even though the blood that was being tested was in another room, when he got all uptight and tense, that lie detector test shot off the page. It was detecting his emotional response even though the blood was no longer in his body.

The experimenters did this with person after person with the same results. They concluded that the blood cells seem to "remember" where they came from.

Now, if sicknesses and addictions and wrong mind-sets can be passed down, how much more can God's blessings, favor, and good habits be passed down through our blood?

As important as it may be to understand the generational curse, it is vital that we understand the generational blessings we can obtain. I know that much of the favor and blessing on my life did not come to me by my own effort; I didn't accumulate all that I am currently enjoying on my own. It was because my father and mother passed it down to me. They left me not just a physical inheritance; they imparted a spiritual inheritance to me as well.

We can build on the past. My father put me forty years down the road when he passed the baton, handing over the ministry of Lakewood Church. My dream is to place my children far, far down the road. And I'm not talking financially; I'm talking about their attitudes, helping them along in their work habits, in their character, and in their walk with God.

We need to understand that the generations are connected. You are sowing seeds for future generations. Whether you realize it or not, everything you do counts. Every time you persevere, every time you are faithful, every time you serve others, you are making a difference; you're storing up equity in your "generational account."

It's easy in life to think, "Well, I'm just a businessman." Or "I'm just a housewife." Or "I'm just a single mom raising my kids, going to work. I'm not going to do anything great. Be realistic."

No, you've got to learn to think more generationally. The fact that you're a hard worker, faithful to your spouse and family, giving it your all—you are sowing seeds for those to come after you. You may not see it *all* happen in your lifetime. You may very well be sowing a seed for a child or for a grandchild to do something great. But don't get discouraged. It's your family legacy. It's not just your life you are changing; you are literally changing your family tree!

My grandmother on my father's side worked extremely hard most of her life. My grandparents were cotton farmers and they lost everything they had in the Great Depression. They didn't have much money, had little food, and no future to speak of. My grandmother worked twelve hours a day earning ten cents an hour washing people's clothes: a dollar-twenty a day.

But Grandmother never complained about her plight. She didn't go around with a "poor-me" mentality; she just kept doing her best, giving it her all. She was determined and persistent. She may not have realized it, but she was sowing seeds for her children. She passed down hard work, determination, and persistence, which my father built upon. Because Grandmother laid the foundation, Daddy was able to break out of poverty and depression and raise our family to a completely new level.

My grandmother never really enjoyed the blessings and the favor that her descendants did. Had she not been willing to pay the price, my father may never have escaped poverty, and I might not be enjoying the season of usefulness that I am experiencing today.

These days, Victoria and I tend to get a lot of credit for the successful lives we are leading, but we have learned to look back and give credit to whom credit is due: our forefathers and -mothers. Many people in our family lines gave us some help along the way.

My grandmother never received a lot of fanfare during her lifetime. She didn't get a lot of glory, but she ran some important laps in our family's race. When she passed that baton down, it contained determination, persistence, a never-give-up attitude, and a can-do mentality. Now those traits are instilled in our family's legacy. I believe that four or five generations from now, people in my family line will be better off because of Grandmother Osteen.

In the same way, when you get up early, work hard, and have a spirit of excellence, you are making a difference in your family's future. Don't be shortsighted and so ingrown that if it doesn't happen right now, you're not going to be happy. No, you are sowing seeds that will reap a great harvest for generations to come.

"But, Joel, I'm working hard," one single mom told me. "I'm trying to send my kid to college and I'm so tired."

I could sympathize with that dear single mom and many more like her. Nobody said it would be easy, but keep being faithful. You don't know how God may use that child to impact the world. Somebody in your family line may become a great businessman, leader, teacher, minister, statesman, or author. It may be in this generation or it may be four or five generations down the line. But it will happen partly because you were willing to pay the price.

Any time you see somebody who's successful or has accomplished something great, you can be sure they didn't do it all by themselves. Somebody else helped pay the price along the way. Somebody passed down those qualities that they needed.

When you live your life with excellence, going the extra mile, nobody else may notice. It may seem as though you are not reaping any of the benefits, but know this: In the bloodline being formed in your DNA are that fortitude, strength, and excellent spirit. They will be passed down to future generations. You are making a difference.

I have a friend who pastors a large church in another state. He and his wife established it fourteen or fifteen years ago, and today several thousand people attend services there regularly. It's a strong, healthy church.

But my friend has big dreams in his heart. He wants to see that church grow to thousands and thousands of people. Moreover, he has a dream of writing books that will affect the world.

After a few years of working at the church, he became extremely discouraged. The energy and enthusiasm had leveled off, not too much exciting was happening; the church's numerical growth had slowed. On top of that, when my friend drives to work each morning, he passes by another large church. This congregation numbers between fifteen thousand to twenty thousand people, and has a big, beautiful campus with many new buildings, exactly what my friend has been dreaming about and working toward.

On one particular day, my friend was sitting in traffic, staring at the big church's beautiful campus, and he felt as though salt were being rubbed in a wound. He was so discouraged, he said, "God, it's just not fair. I poured my heart and soul into the dream that You gave me, but I don't think I'll ever measure up to this man's success. Why won't my church grow?"

He honestly expressed his feelings as he continued. "God, I feel like I'm being laughed at. I don't even know if I should stay in the race."

Just then, God spoke to him, not aloud, but down inside his heart and mind. He said, "Son, what would you think if your son saw your dream come to pass? What if your daughter wrote a book that influenced the world? How would you feel if your children were to enjoy the success for which you are longing?"

My friend's eyes lit up. He said, "God, that would be great. That would be a dream come true." My friend later told me that this experience changed his perspective. He began to think more about investing in the future generations. "Maybe I'm sowing the seeds for my children," he said. "Maybe I'm laying the groundwork for my grandchildren to do something great."

Remember, every lap we run is one less lap for those who come after us. Every day you stay faithful, every test you pass or obstacle you overcome, you are storing up equity and blessings for future generations. You're making it easier on your children, and on your grandchildren. Your dreams may not come to pass exactly as you would hope, but the seeds you sow may be harvested by your sons and your daughters.

Interestingly, the pastor of the big church that my friend passed every day was a fourth-generation pastor. His father, his grandfather, and his great-grandfather had faithfully led smaller congregations of a few hundred people. Why did this man have such a large church, making such a tremendous impact?

Somebody paid the price. Yes, that pastor is talented and gifted. But his forefathers, those that went before him, are the ones who stored up the equity. Now the favor is being released on this generation.

Let me ask you: Are you willing to pay the price so your children and their children as well as future generations can rise higher and accomplish more? If you're like me, nothing would make you happier than to see your children go further and achieve more than you thought possible for yourself. Or to see your grandchildren go further than you ever dreamed.

Your Children Will Do Even More!

Oftentimes, you may see further than you're going to go personally. God may put something bigger in you than you can accomplish on your own. Don't be surprised if your children or your grandchildren come along and finish what you started. I heard somebody say, "Nothing truly great can ever be accomplished in just one lifetime." At the time, I didn't understand that saying, because obviously, every generation can do something great. But I've learned since that sometimes God's plans span more than one generation.

Many times, I heard my father say, "One day we're going to build an auditorium to hold twenty thousand people. One day, we're going to have a big place where we can all come together and worship." My father had the vision, but God used his children to complete it. Nevertheless, had he not stayed faithful—had he not stayed determined and kept that excellent spirit—I don't believe the fulfillment would have come to pass. Daddy sowed the seeds; he paved the way, and my family members—as well as millions of other people—have enjoyed the blessings as a result.

You may have a big dream in your heart. Keep in mind that God may have put that seed in you to get it started. Your children and your grandchildren may take it further than you ever thought possible.

In the Old Testament, King David had a dream to build a permanent temple where God's people could worship. David gathered the supplies, brought in huge cedar trees from Lebanon, amassed a fortune in gold and other precious metals. But God never allowed David to build the temple. Instead, God instructed David's son Solomon to construct His house of worship.

If not everything is happening in your timing the way you want, keep doing your best. God is still in control. In addition, as you continue sowing seeds and living with excellence, know this: You are making a difference. In God's perfect timing, the fruit of your labor will be seen.

The Scripture says that God's people left the place better off than it was when they found it.[15] That should be our goal as well: I'm going to leave my family with more integrity, more joy, more faith, more favor, and with more victory. I'm going to leave my loved ones free from bondage and closer to God.

Maybe you weren't raised by parents who set you up for success by planting positive characteristics in your family line. Possibly you've inherited attitudes of defeat, mediocrity, addictions, and negativity. But thank God, you can start a new family line. You can be the one to set a new standard.

Somebody has to be willing to pay the price. Somebody has to step up and clear the leftovers off the table. Negative things may have been in your bloodline, but they don't have to stay in your bloodline. All it takes is for one person to rise up and start making better choices. Every right choice you make begins to overturn the wrong choices of those who have gone before you.

Nobody else may have done so, but if you'll make positive changes, one day, people in your family line will look back and say, "It was because of this man. It was because of that woman. They were the turning point. We were defeated up till then. We were addicted up to that point. However, look what happened when they came along. Everything changed. We came up higher."

What happened? The curse was broken and the blessings began. That's what you can do for your family.

I know I am where I am today because somebody in my family line prayed. Somebody took a stand for righteousness. Somebody stuck with his or her commitments. Somebody lived a life of integrity. My forefathers, most of whom I have never met, have sown seeds into my life.

"Oh, Joel, you just got some lucky breaks," somebody might say.

Luck had nothing to do with it. My life is blessed today because somebody in my family line was praying, persevering even when times were tough, and honoring God through it all.

If you have godly parents, godly grandparents, you should be extremely grateful because you have innumerable advantages today. You have more of God's favor, more of His blessings because of what they've done. They've paid the price to invest in your future.

Moreover, when you have this godly heritage, you will sometimes stumble into blessings. Great things will happen, and you won't even be able to figure out why. Seemingly impenetrable doors will open supernaturally. You'll get the promotion, and you know you didn't deserve it. That's not a lucky break. It's because that grandmother was praying. It's because your parents lived lives marked by excellence. Or your great-grandparents sowed seeds of integrity and success.

Certainly, each of us is responsible for our own actions, and you and I must work diligently to make use of the opportunities afforded us. But the Bible also indicates that when we have this heritage of faith, we will live in houses that we did not build. We will enjoy vineyards that we didn't plant. God's blessings will chase us down and overtake us. I thank God every day for my parents and my grandparents. Because of the way they lived and what they've done, I know I'm not living under a generational curse; I'm living under a generational blessing.

You can do something similar for your family. Money, houses, cars, or other material possessions may be part of your legacy to your children—if you leave those things to your heirs, that's great. Living a life of integrity and excellence that honors God is worth more than all of that. To pass on the favor and blessings of God to your future generations is worth more than anything else in this world.

Don't take the easy way out. Keep doing your best even when it's difficult. Keep loving, giving, and serving. Your faithfulness is noticed in heaven. You are storing up equity for both yourself and generations to come.

First Samuel, chapter 25, relates how David and his men protected the family and the workers of a man by the name of Nabel from their enemies. One day, David sent his men to ask Nabel for some food and supplies. David thought that Nabel would be grateful and that he would freely give David's troops the supplies for which they asked. But when David's men arrived, Nabel treated them rudely and disrespectfully. He said, "I don't even know who you are. I never asked you to do any of this, so just be on your way. Don't bother me."

When those men got back and told David how insolently they had been treated, David was furious. He said, "All right, men. Get your swords. We're going to go take care of Nabel. We're going to wipe him out."

But on the way there, Nabel's wife, Abigail, stopped David. She had heard about her husband's insulting behavior, so she brought a bountiful supply of gifts and food, hoping to reduce David's anger. She said, "David, my husband is a rude and ungrateful man. He shouldn't have treated you like that." In verse 28, she said, "But David, if you will forgive this wrong, I know that God will give you an enduring house."

I like that phrase "an enduring house." Abigail was saying, "David, I know you have a right to be angry. I know my husband paid you back evil for your good, but if you can overlook it, take the high road, and let it go, I know God will bless you for generations to come. I know He will give you an enduring house."

David swallowed his pride, walked away, and overlooked the offense. He let it go, and God did indeed bless him and his future children as a result.

Throughout life, we're all going to have situations where we can find some excuse to be angry, some rationale to be bitter. You may say, "Joel, I've got a good reason to walk out of my marriage. I've been horribly mistreated." Or "I have every right to live with a chip on my shoulder. I've been forced to endure so much pain and unfairness."

Indeed, you may have good reason for feeling the way you do and for responding to life negatively. Still, I'm asking you to take the high road; don't give in to it. That stuff can get into your blood; it can be passed down. Your children and grandchildren already have enough to overcome without you adding to it.

It may be difficult, but you have the power to overcome the wrong choices made by your family members in previous generations. Beyond that, you can make life better for the generations that follow you. Every offense that you forgive, every bad habit you break, every victory you win is one less lap for those who come after you. Even if you don't do it for yourself, do it for your children, do it for your grandchildren. Do it so you can have an enduring house.

I heard somebody say, "Your blood always speaks." What they meant is your blood is charged with your experiences. It remembers, as was illustrated by that military study I mentioned earlier, where it has come from. A hundred years from now, your blood will still speak to future generations. In some way, either positively or negatively, your bloodline will affect others in your family line.

What will your blood say? Defeat. Mediocrity. Unforgiveness. Bitterness.

No, I believe your blood will speak Determination. Persistence. Integrity. Godliness. Generosity. Favor. Faith and victory!

Determine that you will pass down a godly heritage. Leave your family a legacy of good things. You may have inherited negative input from the past, but thank God, today is a new day. Draw a line in the sand and declare, "I am done with the generational curse. As for me and my family, we're going to live under the generational blessing."

Do it so you can have an enduring house.

Get up every day and give it your best effort. If you will do that, not only will you rise higher and accomplish more, but God has promised that your seed, your family line for up to a thousand generations, is going to have the blessings and the favor of God—all because of the life that you've lived.

CHAPTER 6

Discovering Your Destiny

Before you were born, God saw you, and He endowed you with gifts and talents uniquely designed for you. He's given you ideas and creativity, as well as specific areas in which you can excel.

Why, then, do so many people today feel unfulfilled in their lives, merely going to work at some mundane job, trying to earn a living, stuck in a career they don't even like? The answer is simple: They are not pursuing the dreams and desires God has placed within their hearts.

If we are not moving toward our God-given destiny, tension and dissatisfaction will always exist in our inner being. It won't go away with time; it will be there as long as you live. I can't think of anything more tragic than to come to the end of life on earth and realize that you have not really "lived," that you have not become what God created you to be. You simply endured an average, mediocre life. You got by, but you lived without passion or enthusiasm, allowing your inner potential to lie dormant and untapped.

I heard somebody say the wealthiest place on earth is not Fort Knox or the oil fields of the Middle East. Nor is it the gold and diamond mines in South Africa. Ironically, the wealthiest places on earth are the cemeteries, because lying in those graves are all kinds of dreams and desires that will never be fulfilled. Buried beneath the ground are books that will never be written, businesses that will never be started, and relationships that will never be formed. Sadly, the incredible power of potential is lying in those graves.

A major reason why so many people are unhappy and lacking enthusiasm is that they are not fulfilling their destiny. Understand,

God deposited a gift, a treasure inside you, but you have to do your part to bring it forth.

How can you do that? Simple: Determine that you are going to start focusing on your divine destiny and taking steps toward the dreams and desires that God has placed in your heart. Our goal should be that we're going to live life to the fullest, pursuing our passions and dreams, and when it comes our time to go, we will have used as much of our potential as possible. We're not going to bury our treasures; instead, we're going to spend our lives well.

How do you discover your sense of divine destiny? It's not complicated. Your destiny has to do with what excites you. What are you passionate about? What do you really love doing? Your destiny will be a part of the dreams and desires that are in your heart—part of your very nature. Because God made you and He is the One who put those desires within you in the first place, it shouldn't surprise you that your destiny will involve something that you enjoy. For instance, if you really love children, your destiny will probably be connected to something that has to do with kids—teaching, coaching, caring for them, mentoring them.

Or maybe you love seeing things built or renovated. Most likely, your destiny will probably fall into the fields of construction, design, or architecture. I know people who are extremely helpful, so compassionate, and caring. No doubt, their destiny will probably push them toward some field of social work, or possibly even a medical field, as a doctor, a nurse, a caregiver, minister, or counselor. Your destiny will usually follow the dream about which you are most passionate.

From the time I was ten or eleven years old, I was fascinated with television production. I loved the cameras, editing, and the production of television shows and movies. Every part of the process excited me. As a young man, I spent most of my weekends at Lakewood Church, where my father was the senior pastor. At the time, the church owned some small industrial cameras, and I'd spend all day Saturday playing with the television equipment. I didn't really know how to run it, but I was fascinated by it. I'd turn the camera on and off, unplug it, plug it back in, coil the cables, and get the equipment ready for Sunday. I was passionate about it because it was what came naturally to me.

When I got old enough—maybe thirteen or fourteen years of age—I began helping to run the camera during the services; I became pretty good at it, too. In fact, I soon became one of the best cameramen that we had. It wasn't hard for me; quite the contrary, I loved it; to me working behind the camera seemed almost like a hobby.

Looking back, I see now that my love for television production was part of my God-given destiny. God had hardwired that into me before the foundation of the world.

I went to college and studied broadcasting for a year, returned home, and started a full-fledged television ministry at Lakewood Church. Today, I am on the other side of the cameras, and I can see how God was guiding my steps and preparing me for the fulfillment of my destiny.

Maybe you don't like the field in which you are working; you awaken each morning dreading going to your job. The work is meaningless and mundane.

If that sounds like you, it may be time to reexamine what you are doing. You are not meant to live a miserable and unfulfilled life. Make sure that you are in a field that is a part of your destiny. Don't spend twenty-five years in a meaningless existence, doing something you dislike, staying there simply because it is convenient and you don't want to rock the boat. No, step into your divine destiny.

We should love what we're doing. We should go to work every day with enthusiasm, passionate about what we do. I'm not saying we don't have to work hard, or there are not going to be some frustrating days, and some people with whom we'd rather not deal. That's all a part of life. Ultimately, we should enjoy what we're doing. When you get home at night, you should feel that you've accomplished something, that you've helped to make the world a better place. I believe that when you discover your destiny, and start working in some realm associated with it, you will thrive.

We should love what we're doing.

Think about a good hunting dog—it's natural for that breed of dog to hunt. Put a hunting dog in a cooped-up area, and he'll lie around the yard all day long, lazy, unmotivated, with no enthusiasm, just dragging through the day. But when the owner comes home and opens up the bed of his pickup truck, and the dog realizes he is about to go hunting, he comes alive. He'll start barking, jumping, and running around the yard in excitement. It's a night-and-day difference.

Why? Because God designed hunting dogs that way. He put that passion inside them, so there's a natural excitement and enthusiasm. They don't have to get themselves all worked up to be happy. They don't have to say, "Well, let me go listen to a sermon or a motivational message. I need to work up some zest and zeal to go hunting today."

No, when those dogs know they're going hunting, they're excited about it. The Creator of the universe hardwired that desire into them.

I really believe when we get into our destiny and we are doing what we know we're called to do, enthusiasm and excitement will exude from us naturally. We may not jump up and down every day, but deep within, we're going to know: This is what I was called to do. This is why I was born. This is my destiny.

You have a sense of destiny hardwired into you, a divine purpose installed by the Creator of the universe. It is a part of your nature, who you really are.

I like to think of it like this: God made all sorts of animals and He's given each one unique characteristics and personality traits. For instance, the owl is nocturnal—it likes to be out at night. God has given the owl eyes that can see as well in the dark as human beings can see in the daylight. But if that owl decided that he wanted to start sleeping at night and staying out during the day, he would be working against his God-given destiny, and problems would certainly follow him. For one thing, he'd have a hard time finding food. He'd struggle all day, not enjoying his life, because he'd not be doing what God created him to do. He would have stepped outside his destiny.

On the other hand, when you're really in line with your destiny, many things come naturally to you. Continuing my analogy, nobody has to tell the owl to stay up at night. God made it nocturnal, so it is natural for an owl to operate in the darkness, and it has the equipment to do so.

In a similar fashion, God has installed certain traits in every one of us. If we can discover our destiny and do what we're good at naturally, life becomes much more enjoyable. It won't be a struggle or a headache.

If you have ever heard great singers, their performance sounds effortless. Why is that? Because they are doing what they are good at naturally.

On the other hand, if you're doing something that is not natural, it's always a struggle. If you try, train, practice, and push, and you still can't seem to get a skill down, recognize that's not in your nature.

Of course, at times we must persevere even though success doesn't come quickly or easily. Sometimes you must push through and learn things that are hard, and those lessons are often extremely beneficial. In general, though, life should not be a constant struggle. When you're living within your purpose, one of the most noticeable results will be how natural it feels. Learn to appreciate and use the skills, gifts, or abilities at which you are naturally talented.

Two friends of mine went to Bible school together, both young men planning to become pastors. When they graduated, Craig started a church, and he asked his friend Ron to come along and help. Ron was set on starting his own church, but since no opportunity had opened for him, he decided to help Craig for a while. Ron was a phenomenal musician, a tremendous piano player, songwriter, and singer.

Craig put Ron in charge of the music ministry at the church, and for several years, he excelled in that area. The church was known around the countryside for its outstanding music. The crowds grew larger, and the congregation thrived.

Nevertheless, Ron kept telling himself, "I've got to get out there and start my church."

Both Craig and Ron's wife recognized how his music was positively affecting people, but Ron wouldn't hear it. To him, music was too easy. He had always done that. It came naturally to him, and he excelled in that area. Ron felt sure he had to get out and try something more challenging, more difficult—something new.

One day, he realized that everything he hoped to impart to people, he was giving them through his music. He began to feel a sense of destiny about what he was already doing. In fact, when Ron really thought about being a pastor, he acknowledged that many aspects of that position weren't appealing to him at all.

Ron decided he would stay right where he was and continue using his God-given gifts and talents. He and his family have been blessed as a result, and many people have been encouraged and inspired through his music. But he almost missed his divine destiny because he was too close to it. It seemed too "normal" for him.

Similarly, God has given you certain talents, gifts, or skills that you can do well, specific areas in which you excel. Don't take them for granted. It may be in sales or communications, or in encouraging people or in athletics or in marketing; whatever it is, don't denigrate it simply because it comes naturally to you. That may well be precisely what God has hardwired into you. It may be an important part of your destiny. Make sure that you explore it to the fullest, keeping in mind that what seems boring to one person may be exhilarating to another for whom that area is part of his or her destiny.

My brother-in-law Kevin is the administrator at Lakewood Church, and he is a tremendous help to our entire staff. Kevin is a "detail person," extremely organized and efficient. He plans wisely and uses his time well. It is not merely something he learned at a time-management seminar; it is a God-given gift. (In my opinion, it is not normal to be that organized! But I'm glad that Kevin is.)

When we were overseeing the $100 million renovation of the Compaq Center into Lakewood Church, Kevin knew every detail of the construction project. He knew where every penny was spent, and he could explain why it was spent. Beyond that, he could tell you three other ways that we tried to accomplish the same thing while saving money. Kevin is a detail person.

When Victoria, I, and our children go on vacation with Kevin and Lisa's family, Kevin sends me an advance itinerary. He'll send me my tickets as well as a weather report. He'll send me rental car information and traffic instructions. He reminds me to bring my driver's license. The morning of our flight, he calls to tell me where traffic is backed up on the freeway.

One time I got to the airport and realized that I had forgotten my driver's license, so now Kevin sends me instructions—in writing—regarding matters that I never even think about. He is gifted in being detail oriented.

Kevin stays in his area of strength. He excels as our administrator. Kevin could think in the back of his mind, *Well, if I could get up there and preach, I'd really be making a difference.* But no. If Kevin got up and preached, we might not need the Compaq Center! He can't preach, and I can't administrate. He's doing what he's good at naturally. He's often told me, "Joel, this job is a dream come true." Kevin loves coming to work every day. He's passionate about it. It's what he's good at. It's a part of his destiny.

You need to be aware of your natural strengths as well and to use them to your best advantage and to the benefit of others. It says in Romans 12, verse 6, in *The Living Bible*, "God has given each of us the ability to do certain things well." You can't do everything well, but you can do *something* well. Focus on your strengths and make sure that you are not missing out on your destiny because you are always getting involved in something that doesn't come naturally. When you are truly in your destiny, it is not a constant struggle. It just feels right.

Your Destiny Will Fit You

My father loved traveling to India. That was one of his main passions. Two or three times a year, Victoria and I would travel with him. Oftentimes, after we landed in one of India's major cities, we would travel for four or five more hours, deep into the country, to one of the little villages. Of course, there weren't any nice hotels—or often, any hotels at all—back in there. Nor was there any food that we might want to eat. Added to that, the weather was usually hot and sticky, and within minutes after our arrival, we felt dirty and uncomfortable. But my father had a great love for the people of India, so we went year after year.

We sometimes stayed at this old, run-down Indian army barracks. It was nothing more than four concrete walls, with no inside bathroom, no air-conditioning, no sheets on the bed—in fact, it had no beds, just dingy, narrow, uncomfortable cots. At night, all sorts of bugs and other bothersome insects seemed to take over. Victoria and I never complained about the conditions, but we could not wait until we got out of there.

On one of Victoria's first trips to India, shortly after she and I had married, we were staying at those army barracks. Early one morning, my father and I were out on the front lawn eating breakfast. Suddenly, we heard Victoria screaming at the top of her lungs. I'd never heard a woman scream like that before.

Daddy and I dropped our breakfast plates and ran toward the building. As we approached, we saw Victoria running outside and down the stairs violently shaking her long blond hair just as hard and rapidly as she could. About that time, we saw the problem: A large iguanalike lizard was hanging in Victoria's hair. Noble newlywed husband that I was, all I could think of was, *Girl, just keep on shaking! If you're looking at me to get that thing off you, you're looking at the wrong person!*

Finally, much to my relief, my lovely Victoria shook that lizard out of her hair. I thought I was going to have to resuscitate her.

But my father barely seemed to notice the uncomfortable surroundings. Daddy acted as though he were staying in a fancy hotel. He didn't smell the smells. He didn't feel the heat. He didn't see the bugs. He was as happy as he could be. In fact, I had never seen my father any happier than when he was in the villages of India.

He told me one time, "Joel, if I didn't know I was supposed to pastor Lakewood Church, I'd live right here."

Why was that? Why wasn't he uncomfortable? It's because it was a part of his destiny. He was passionate about it. Just as God had hardwired television production into me, God had hardwired missionary work into him.

Proverbs 18:16 says that your gift will make room for you. I'm convinced if you'll get into your destiny, no matter where you are, you won't have any problem getting hired or getting happy. You won't have any problem finding work, friends, or opportunity. In fact, if you'll focus on your strengths and do what you're gifted to do, you'll probably have to turn down opportunities.

If you are not fulfilled, it may well be because you are not pursuing your destiny. Make sure that you are fulfilling the dreams that God has placed in your heart. Are you tapping into the potential that's on the inside? Have you discovered what you do best, what comes naturally? Are you excelling in that area?

If you are called to be a stay-at-home mom and raise your children, do it to the best of your ability. Don't allow society to pressure you into some career simply because your friends are doing it. Recognize your purpose and do it well.

If you are gifted in the area of sales, don't sit behind a desk all day long in a room by yourself. Get into the area of your gifting and do it to the best of your ability. If you're going to fulfill your destiny, you must do what God hardwired you to do. Make sure you operate in a realm where you are passionate.

One of my favorite old movies is *Chariots of Fire*. In this film, Eric Liddell is a gifted runner whose dream is to compete in the Olympics, but he feels called to be a missionary in China. Yet he knows that God has given him his gift of running. When he runs, he feels that he is dedicating himself to God. In one of the classic lines from the movie, Liddell says, "When I run, I feel God's pleasure." He was saying, when I do what I know I'm called to do, when I'm using my gifts and talents, when I'm pursuing my destiny, I can feel God smiling down on me.

Another of my favorite lines in the film is when Liddell says, "To win is to honor God." I believe we should live by that same philosophy, striving to excel, pursuing our destiny, becoming the best that we can possibly be, and as we do, we will honor God. If you're called to be a businessman, excel at it and you honor God. If you're called to teach children, excel in it and you honor God. Whatever you are called to do, if you'll do it to the best of your ability and excel at it, you are honoring God.

You may not have yet stepped into your divine destiny. You're still doing many things for which you have little passion and no enthusiasm. It is time to become a better you.

Certainly, you can't just snap your fingers and change careers, but at least examine your life and be aware of how you're spending your time. Are you pursuing your passion? Are you doing what you are good at naturally? If not, why don't you make some changes? Time is short. Find one thing that you're passionate about and start giving yourself to it. And God will lead you one step at a time.

I mentioned earlier how God put the desire in me for television production as a young man. I followed that passion, then when my father went to be with the Lord, I had the desire to step up and pastor the church and I followed that passion. I can honestly say today that I believe I've stepped into my God-given destiny. I know this is why God put me here; this is why I was born.

My desire for you is that you will follow God's divine destiny for your life, discover your calling, and stay in your purpose. Make a decision to keep pressing forward, keep believing, and keep stretching until you see your dreams fulfilled. Then one day, you will look back and say with confidence, "This is why God put me here."

ACTION POINTS

PART 1: KEEP PRESSING FORWARD

1. Today I will meditate on thoughts such as these:

   "I have everything I need to fulfill my destiny."

   "God accepts me; He approves me; I know God has good things in store for me."

   "I am valuable; I have royal blood in my bloodline; I have a bright future!"

   "My best days are ahead of me."

2. I will take time this week to examine my life carefully, identifying any negative patterns that have been part of my family's past. I have decided that I will be the one to set a new standard; I will shake off negative mind-sets and begin living under the blessings of God rather than under the curse.

3. With God's help, I will overcome any challenges I face that might inhibit my growth as I stretch toward the next level in specific areas of my life.

4. I will be more aware that the decisions I make today will affect future generations as well as my own life. I will be more careful and deliberate about making wise decisions. I will pray, search the Scripture for guidance, seek godly advice, and take time to think before making major decisions. I will make choices based on my desire to leave my family better off than they were previously.

PART TWO

BE POSITIVE
TOWARD YOURSELF

CHAPTER 7

Stop Listening to Accusing Voices

If you truly want to become a better you, it is imperative that you learn to feel good about yourself. Too many people live under condemnation, constantly listening to the wrong voices. The Bible refers to the enemy as "the accuser of the brethren" who would love for us to live our lives guilty and condemned. He constantly brings accusations against us, telling us what we didn't do or what we should have done. He'll remind us of all our past mistakes and failures.

"You lost your temper last week."

"You should have spent more time with your family."

"You went to church, but you arrived late."

"You gave, but you didn't give enough."

Many people swallow these lines with little or no defense. Consequently, they walk around feeling guilty, condemned, and extremely discontented with themselves. They go through the day without joy, without confidence, expecting the worst and often receiving it.

Granted, no human being is perfect. We've all sinned, failed, and made mistakes. But many people don't know they can receive God's mercy and forgiveness. Instead, they allow themselves to be beaten up on the inside. They tune in to that voice telling them, "You blew it. You messed up." They are so hard on themselves. Instead of believing that they're growing and improving, they believe that voice telling them, "You can't do anything right. You'll never break this habit. You're just a failure." When they wake up in the morning, a voice is telling them what they did wrong yesterday and how they'll probably do something wrong today. As a result, they become extremely critical toward themselves, and that usually spills over to other people as well.

If we're going to live in peace with ourselves, we must learn to put our foot down and say, "I may not be perfect, but I know I'm growing. I may have made mistakes, but I know I am forgiven. I have received God's mercy."

Sure, we all want to be better human beings, but we needn't beat ourselves up over our shortcomings. I may not have a perfect performance, but I know my heart is right. Other people may not always be pleased with me, but I'm confident that God is.

Similarly, as long as you're doing your best and desire to do what's right according to God's Word, you can be assured God is pleased with you. Certainly, He wants you to improve, but He knows that we all have weaknesses. We all do things that we know in our hearts we shouldn't do. When our human foibles and imperfections poke through our idealism, it's normal to get down on ourselves. *After all, we tend to think, we don't deserve to be happy; we have to prove that we're really sorry.*

But no, we should learn to receive God's forgiveness and mercy. Don't allow those condemning voices to play repeatedly in your mind. That will only accentuate a negative attitude toward yourself. If you have a bad attitude toward you, it will hinder every area of your life.

Negative accusations take various forms: "You're not as spiritual as you should be." "You didn't work hard enough last week." Or "God can't bless you because of your past."

Those are all lies. Don't make the mistake of dwelling on that rubbish, not for a moment. Sometimes when I walk off the platform, having spoken at Lakewood and around the world by means of television, the first thought that comes to my mind is, *Joel, that message just wasn't good today. Nobody got anything out of that. You practically put them to sleep.*

I've learned to shake that off. I turn it around and say, "No, I believe it was good! I did my best. I know that at least one person really got something out of it. I did. I thought it was good."

As long as we're doing our best, we don't have to live condemned, even when we make mistakes or fail. There's a time to repent, but there's also a time to shake it off and press forward. Don't live with regrets. Don't go around saying, "Well, I should have done this or that. I should have gone back to college." Or "I should have spent more time with my family." "I should have taken better care of myself."

No, quit condemning yourself. Your analysis and observations may be true, but it doesn't do you any good to put yourself down. Let the past be the past. You cannot change it, and if you make the mistake of living in guilt today because of something that happened yesterday, you won't have the strength you need to live this day in victory.

The Apostle Paul once said, "The things I know I should do, I don't. The things I know I shouldn't do, I end up doing." [16] Even this great man of God who wrote half the New Testament struggled in this regard. That tells me God does not disqualify me merely because I don't perform perfectly, 100 percent of the time. I wish I did, and I'm constantly striving to do better. I don't do wrong on purpose, but like anyone else, I too have weaknesses. Sometimes I make mistakes or wrong choices, but I have learned not to beat myself up over those things. I don't wallow in condemnation; I refuse to listen to the accusing voice. I know God is still working on me, that I'm growing, learning, and becoming a better me. I have made up my mind that I'm not going to live condemned during the process.

That accusing voice will come to you and tell you, "You lost your temper last week in traffic."

Your attitude should be, "That's okay. I'm growing."

"Well, you said some things yesterday you shouldn't have."

"Yes, that's true. I wish I wouldn't have spoken like that, but I have repented. Now, I know I'm forgiven. I'm going to do better next time."

"Well, what about that failure you went through two years ago in your relationship and in your business?"

"That's in the past. I've received God's mercy. This is a new day. I'm not looking back, I'm looking forward."

When we have that kind of attitude, we take away the lethal

power of the accuser. He can't control us when we don't believe his lies.

Perhaps you need to shake off that old guilty feeling. You need to quit listening to the voice that's telling you, "God is not pleased with you. You have too many weaknesses. You've made too many mistakes."

No, as long as you have asked God to forgive you, and you are pressing forward in the direction He wants you to go, you can know with confidence God is pleased with you. When that accusing voice taunts, "You've blown it; you don't have a future; you're so undisciplined . . ." don't sit back and agree, *Yeah, that's right.*

No, you need to start talking back to the accuser. You need to rise up in your authority and say, "Wait a minute. I am the righteousness of God. God has made me worthy. I may have made mistakes, but I know I am forgiven. I know I am the apple of God's eye. I know God has great things in store for me."

Scripture tells us to "put on the breastplate of God's approval."[17] That's one of the most important pieces of our armor. Think about what the breastplate covers. It covers your heart, the center of your being, the way you think and feel about yourself deep inside. If you're going around with that gnawing feeling, thinking, *I don't have much of a future. I've blown it too many times. God couldn't be pleased with me,* I can tell you this: You're listening to the wrong voice. That's the accuser.

You need to start getting up every morning and saying with confidence: "God is pleased with me. God approves me. God accepts me just the way I am."

Understand that you are not a surprise to God. God is not up in the heavens scratching His head saying, "What did I get myself into? I never dreamed he'd have that problem. I never dreamed she'd have that many weaknesses."

God made us. He knows everything about you, and He still approves you. He is pleased with you. You may have faults, but you are still the apple of God's eye. You may not be where you should be, but at least you're not where you used to be. Quit condemning yourself.

The Bible tells us, "He that began a good work in you will continue to perform it until the day of Jesus Christ." [18] God is still working on us.

Take the pressure off yourself; give yourself the right to have some weaknesses and not to perform perfectly 100 percent of the time. When you make a mistake, don't sit around guilty for two or three weeks. Immediately go to God and say, "Father, I'm sorry. I repent. Help me to do better next time."

Here's the key: Then you have to receive God's forgiveness and mercy.

Sam asks God to forgive him every day for something he did three years ago. He has asked for forgiveness more than five hundred times for the same thing. Sam fails to grasp the fact that God forgave him the first time he asked. The problem is, Sam didn't receive the forgiveness and mercy. He continues listening to the accusing voices. "You blew it. God can't bless you. You know what you did a few years ago."

Instead, Sam needs to get up every morning and say something like, "Father, thank You that Your mercy endures forever. I may have made mistakes in the past, but I know nothing I've done is too much for Your mercy. I may have even made mistakes yesterday. But I know Your mercy is fresh and new every single morning. So I receive it by faith today."

If you get ahold of this truth, it will break the bondage that has held you back for years. Quit listening to the accusing voices. Quit going around feeling wrong about yourself. If you're living your life condemned, that's telling me you're not receiving God's mercy. At times, you may think, *I don't feel like I deserve it. I don't feel like I'm worthy.*

But that's what grace is all about. None of us deserves it. It's a free gift. We're not worthy in ourselves. The good news is, God has made us worthy. You are not a weak worm of the dust. You are a child of the Most High God. Refuse to listen to accusing voices anymore.

"Well, Joel, I've got a lot of things to overcome."

Who doesn't? We all have areas in which we need to improve. However, God does not focus on what's wrong with you. He focuses on what's right with you. He's not looking at all your faults and weaknesses. He's looking at how far you've come, and how much you're growing. You need to put your foot down today and say, "I'm not living condemned anymore. I'm not going through life feeling guilty and unworthy. No mistake I've made is too horrible. I've repented. I've asked for forgiveness. Now, I'm going to take it one step further and start receiving God's mercy."

As a parent, I don't focus on what our children do wrong. Our child can strike out a thousand times at the Little League field, but we'll go around bragging about the one hit he got all year long. As I write these words, our son Jonathan is twelve years old. If somebody asks me about him, I immediately think of all the things I love about Jonathan. I'll tell you he's smart, talented, and funny. He has a quick sense of wit.

I once mentioned in a sermon that most people use only 10 percent of their minds. Jonathan leaned over to Victoria and said, "Mom, I'm above average. I use eleven percent!"

Jonathan is not perfect. He makes mistakes, and it is my joy to teach him, to train him, to help him come up higher. That's the way God is with us. He loves us unconditionally.

What if Jonathan came in one day and said, "Daddy, I just don't feel like I deserve your blessings anymore. I don't feel like I'm worthy of your love. You know, back when I was three years old, I told that lie. Back when I was four, I hit my baby sister."

If he said something like that, I would check his temperature. Jonathan knows how to receive. He knows he's loved. He knows Victoria and I want to bless him.

A couple of years ago, we bought him a guitar, and he couldn't wait till we got home and set up the amplifier. A few minutes later, Jonathan came over and gave me a big hug. He said, "Daddy, thank you so much for this new guitar. And by the way, when do you think we can get my new keyboard?" My son certainly is not shy!

It would do us all good to have some of that boldness. The Scripture urges, "Let us come boldly to the throne of grace."[19] Why?

"To receive mercy for our failures."

Don't pray, "Oh, God, I blew it again. I'm a miserable failure as a parent. I lost my temper. I yelled at my kids. I know I don't deserve anything good in life."

No, if you want to receive something good from God, come to Him humbly and with reverence, but come to Him with boldness. "God, I've made mistakes, but I know You love me, and I'm asking for forgiveness; I'm receiving Your mercy." Then go out expecting God's blessings and favor.

I am bold enough to believe that I am a friend of Almighty God, and that He is smiling down on me right now. I've accepted the fact that I don't perform perfectly all the time, but I know my heart is right. To the best of my ability, I'm doing what pleases Him. That means I don't have to listen to the accusers. I don't have to live my life condemned. When I make mistakes, all I have to do is go to God, ask for forgiveness, then receive His mercy and keep pressing forward.

Maybe you are beaten down because of negative experiences. Perhaps it wasn't even your fault; somebody mistreated you, or somebody rejected you.

The enemy loves to twist that around, insinuating there's something wrong with you. I've seen it with people who were mistreated during their childhood. They weren't even old enough to know what was going on, but the enemy taunts them, "You brought this on yourself. It's your fault." Especially in relationships that don't work out, you may hear that voice telling you, "You are to blame. You're not good enough. You're not attractive enough. You didn't try hard enough."

Have you ever thought that perhaps that other person may have had some problems? Quit receiving all the accusations. Quit allowing the condemning voices to take root, crowding out the good things of God in your life. Some people are practically addicted to guilt. They don't know what it's like to feel good about themselves, to believe they are loved, forgiven, or to believe that they have a bright future.

"Joel, you don't know what I've done in my past," Regan told me. "You don't know what I've been through."

"Maybe not, Regan," I said, "but there's no need for you to internalize all the guilt, shame, and blame. You need to understand that when you came to Christ, when you received His forgiveness, God cleaned out all of your closets. He chooses not to remember your mistakes, your sins, your failures. My question is, Why don't you quit remembering them? Why don't you quit listening to the voice of the accuser?"

I love the story Jesus told about the prodigal son. This young man made a lot of mistakes. He told his dad that he wanted his share of the inheritance. When the father gave the son his money, the boy left home, went out, and lived a wild life. Eventually, those poor choices caught up to him. When his money ran out, so did his friends. He didn't have anything to eat, any place to stay, and he ended up working in a hog pen feeding the pigs. He got so desperate and low, he had to eat the hog food just to stay alive.

One day, sitting in that filth and shame, he said to himself, "I will arise and go back to my father's." That was the best decision that he ever made. When you make mistakes, when you go through failures and disappointments, don't sit around in self-pity. Don't go month after month condemning yourself, rejecting yourself. The first step to victory is to get back up again and go back to your Heavenly Father's loving arms.

The young man headed home, and I'm sure in the back of his mind, he thought, *I'm just wasting my time. My father is never going to receive me back. He's going to be so put out with me. I've made so many terrible choices.* I can imagine that he tried to talk himself out of it three or four times along the way. No doubt, he told himself, "I'm such a failure. My father will never forgive me."

The Scripture says, "When the father saw him a long way off." [20] That tells me the father must have been looking for him. The father must have gotten up every morning and said to himself, "Maybe today will be the day my son comes back home." Morning, noon, and night, the father was on the lookout. When he saw his son, he took off running toward him. He couldn't wait to see him. The parallels in the story are obvious, with the father representing God.

That intrigues me, since this is the only picture of God running in the Bible. To whom or what was God running? One of the disciples? One of the apostles? A famous religious leader? No, the Father is running to a young man that needs mercy. He's running to a person who has made grievous mistakes, a person who has failed miserably.

When the father got there, he embraced his son; he hugged him. He was so happy to see him, but the son just hung his head in shame. He started to say, "Dad, I've really blown it. I've made some terrible decisions. And I know I don't deserve any of this, but maybe you could take me back as one of your hired servants. I'll work out in the fields for you."

The father would have nothing to do with that. He said, "What are you talking about? You are my son. I want to celebrate the fact that you are home."

Perhaps you think that God could never forgive you. You've made too many mistakes, blown it too many times. But let me assure you, nothing that you've done is too much for the mercy of God. Your heavenly Father is not looking for ways to condemn you or to chew you out. He stands before you with His arms held open wide. If you are far from where you know you ought to be, you need to know that God is waiting for you, and the moment you take one step toward Him, your Father will come running to you.

Nothing that you've done is too much for the mercy of God.

Maybe you have been away for a long time, living in guilt and condemnation, feeling that God could never make anything out of your life.

Today can be a new beginning. God has mercy for any mistake that you've ever made.

The father said to one of his servants, "Go get the best robe and put it on my son." One translation says, "Put the robe of honor on him."

Similarly, you may have made foolish mistakes and suffered some severe setbacks. However, God doesn't simply want to restore you. He doesn't merely want to give you a new beginning. He wants to put the robe of honor on you. That's just the way our God is. In other words, even when we make mistakes, even when we bring the trouble on ourselves, God is so good, when we return to Him, He will not hold that against us. He will receive us back and make something great out of our lives.

The only way this can happen, though, is if we have the right attitude. We cannot continue wallowing in the dirt and expect to have God's best. You may not be where you should be in life, but don't sit around in self-pity. Do as that prodigal son did and say, "I'm going to arise and go back to my father." In other words, "I'm done with living in guilt, shame, and condemnation. I'm going to get up out of this mess, and start receiving God's mercy."

Sure, it will take faith, because everything in you will say, "You know what you've done. You know the mistakes you've made. Do you really think God is going to bless you?"

Precisely at that point, put your shoulders back and say, "I don't think so, I know so. I know God is a good God. I know His mercy is bigger than any mistake I've made. So, I'm going to start receiving His mercy and expecting good things in my life."

A lot of people think God is mad at them, that He's keeping a record of everything they have ever done wrong, and they may have blown it one too many times. When they make poor choices, they wouldn't dare go to God and ask Him for forgiveness and help. They assume they must pay for their own mistakes. Unfortunately, the way most people attempt to do so is by giving up on their dreams; they perpetually feel disqualified, depressed, and defeated, thinking they are paying God back by living at a much lower level than He intended them to enjoy.

But the good news is that the debt has already been paid. Why not accept God's mercy? Why don't you believe that God still has great things in store for you? Yes, you may have made mistakes, but nothing you have done is too much for the mercy of God.

Imagine that I hear my son Jonathan calling out to me, "Daddy! Come help me!"

I look out the window and I see my son hanging on to a tree limb high off the ground, and he looks as though he is about to fall. I instantly recognize that Jonathan could get hurt badly if he should hit the ground from that height.

How do you think I would respond?

I wouldn't say, "Mmm, let me think about this. How good has he been lately?"

I wouldn't ask, "Victoria? Has Jonathan been keeping up with his chores? Let me go check on his bedroom to see if everything is as neat and clean as we expect."

Meanwhile, Jonathan is hanging tenuously from the tree limb, crying out to me, "Daddy, please! Please help me, I'm in trouble."

"Just hang on a while longer, Jonathan; I want to go check your report card."

No, of course I wouldn't say or do such a thing. Jonathan is my son, and I love him (as I do our daughter Alexandra). If one of Victoria's and my children needs me, I'm going to do all I can to help.

That's the way God looks at you. He does not focus on your mistakes or your failures. He does not desire to make your life miserable or to see how much frustration you can take. God wants you to succeed; He created you to live abundantly.

You needn't go through life with that nagging feeling, *God is not pleased with me. I'd be a hypocrite to ask for His help after all the mistakes I've made.*

Quite the contrary, you are the apple of God's eye. You are His prized possession. Nothing you have ever done, or will ever do, can keep God from loving you and wanting to be good to you.

Dare to believe that. Shake off those feelings of guilt and unworthiness. It doesn't please God for us to drag through life feeling like miserable failures, trying to show God how sorry we are for our wrong choices. Instead, recognize that you are His child, that He loves you and would do almost anything to help you. Dust yourself off, straighten up, and throw your shoulders back, knowing that you are forgiven. Declare, "I may have made some mistakes; I may have blown it badly, but I know God is full of mercy and He still has a great plan for my life."

Develop this new attitude free from guilt and condemnation, and—most of all—free from the accusing voice. No matter how long it has been lying to you, telling you that you're washed up, that you've made too many mistakes, God still has a great plan for your life. You may have missed Plan A, but the good news is that God has a Plan B, a Plan C, and a Plan D. You can turn your face toward Him, knowing that He has already turned His face toward you.

My parents often told our family members a poignant story of when my oldest brother Paul was just a small boy, before any of us siblings were born. Mother and Dad would put Paul in bed at night and then they'd go get in their own bed. Their room was just a few feet down the hall, and every night, my parents would say, "Good night, Paul."

Paul would answer, "Good night, Mother. Good night, Daddy." One night for some reason, Paul was afraid. After they had said their good nights, a few minutes later, Paul said, "Daddy, are you still in there?"

My father said, "Yes, Paul. I'm still in here."

Then Paul said, "Daddy, is your face turned toward me?"

Somehow, the assurance that Daddy was looking in his direction made Paul feel more secure. He could sleep peacefully knowing that my father's face was turned toward him.

"Yes, Paul, my face is turned toward you."

Paul soon drifted off to sleep, knowing that he was under Daddy's watchful care and protection.

Friend, please know your heavenly Father's face is turned toward you. The good news is that God's face will always be turned toward you, regardless of what you have done, where you have been, or how many mistakes you've made. He loves you and is turned in your direction, looking for you.

God's face will always be turned toward you.

Maybe you used to be excited about your life, but along the way, you experienced failures, disappointments, and setbacks. Perhaps those accusatory voices have been nagging at you, keeping you down, discouraged, guilty, condemned. You need to know today that God is running toward you. His face is turned in your direction. He is not an angry, condemning God. He is a loving, merciful, forgiving God. He's your heavenly Father and He still has a great plan for your life.

Moreover, God can restore anything that's been stolen from you. You may have failed a thousand times or lost everything you once held dear. But God has not run out of mercy. You can receive it today. It all starts by changing your attitude. Quit being negative toward yourself. Stop accepting the accusations and start receiving God's mercy. Stop dwelling on your past and quit listening to condemning voices. Instead, start putting on God's approval, knowing that He is pleased with you, knowing that you are forgiven and that He has a bright future in store for you. When you do that, you will diffuse the power of the accuser and you will experience a new sense of freedom. You can even learn to like yourself and begin feeling good about yourself. In the chapters ahead, I'll show you how.

CHAPTER 8

Learning to Like Yourself

We all have areas that we need to improve, but as long as we're pressing forward, getting up each day and doing our very best, we can be assured that God is pleased with us. He may not be pleased with every decision we make, but He is pleased with us. I know it is difficult for some people to believe, but God wants us to feel good about ourselves. He wants us to be secure and to have healthy self-images, but so many people focus on their faults and weaknesses. When they make mistakes, they're extremely critical of themselves. They live with that nagging feeling that chides, "You're not what you're supposed to be. You don't measure up. You've blown it too many times."

Guess what. God knew that you were not going to be perfect. He knew that you were going to have weaknesses, faults, and wrong desires—He knew all that before you were even born—and He still loves you!

One of the worst things you could do is to go through life being against yourself. This is a major problem today. Many people have a war going on inside themselves. They don't really like who they are. "Well, I'm slow, I'm undisciplined, I'm unattractive, and I'm not as smart as other people." They focus on their weaknesses, not realizing that this negative introspection is a root cause of many of their difficulties. They can't get along in relationships, they're insecure, they don't enjoy their life, and it's largely because they're not at peace with who they are.

Jesus said, "Love your neighbor as you love yourself." [21] Notice, the prerequisite to loving others is to love yourself. If you don't have a healthy respect for who you are, and if you don't learn to accept yourself faults and all, you will never be able to properly love other people. Unfortunately, self-loathing destroys many relationships nowadays.

I've met many people who think their spouse is the reason they can't get along in their marriage. Or they're sure that it's their coworker's fault, but the fact is they have a civil war raging on the inside. They don't like their looks, they don't like where they are in life, they're upset because they haven't broken a bad habit, and that poison spills out into their other relationships.

Understand, you can't give away what you don't have. If you don't love yourself, you're not going to be able to love others. If you're at strife on the inside, feeling angry or insecure about yourself, feeling unattractive, feeling condemned, then that's all you can give away. On the other hand, if you'll recognize that God is working on you, and in spite of your flaws and weaknesses, you can learn to accept yourself. Then you can give that love away and have healthy relationships.

This basic principle could save your marriage; it could change your relationships with the people around you. You think everybody else is the problem, but before you can make significant progress in life, you must come to peace with who you are. Please recognize that if you're negative toward yourself, it's not only affecting you; it is influencing every relationship you have, and it will affect your relationship with God.

That's why it's so important that you feel good about who you are. You may have some faults. You may have some things you wish you could change about yourself. Well, join the crowd. We all do. But lighten up and quit being so hard on yourself. Interestingly, we might never criticize another person or tell him or her, "You are really dumb; you're unattractive, you're undisciplined. I don't like you." Yet we don't have any problem saying it to ourselves. But understand that when you criticize yourself, you are criticizing God's ultimate creation.

"I'm trying to live right," Pete said, "but, Joel, I'm so impatient. I can't control my temper and I get upset so easily."

"Obviously, losing your temper never helps matters, Pete," I told him. "But remember, God is still working on you. You're not a finished product. It's okay to like yourself while God is in the process of changing you. I don't know one person who's arrived just yet, who doesn't need to change in some area of his or her life. But as long as you are negative and critical toward yourself, the process slows down; you make matters worse."

I'm not talking about living a sloppy life, or having a flippant, unconcerned attitude toward sin and mistakes. The fact that you are reading this book indicates that you want to be better, that you are striving for excellence, and that you have a heart to please God. If that's you, don't live under mounds of condemnation merely because you are still struggling in some areas. When you make mistakes, simply go to God and say, "Father, I'm sorry. I repent. Help me to do better next time." Then let it go. Don't beat yourself up for two weeks, or two months, or two years. Shake it off and move on.

Many people are their own worst enemies. "Well, I'm so overweight. I've blown my diet. I don't spend enough time with my children. I'm so undisciplined I didn't even clean my house last week. Surely, God is not pleased with me."

Don't step into that trap. The Scripture indicates that God has already approved and accepted you. It doesn't say God approves you as long as you live a perfect life. No, it says God approves you unconditionally, just as you are. Frankly, it's not because of what you have or haven't done; God loves you because of who you are and because of who he is. God *is* love. You are a child of the Most High God. If God approves you, why don't you start approving yourself? Shake off guilt, condemnation, inadequacies, and a sense that you can't measure up, and start feeling good about who you are.

If God approves you, why don't you start approving yourself?

"Well, Joel, I don't know if I believe that," a dear, well-meaning man told me. "We're just poor old sinners."

No, we used to be poor old sinners, but when we came to Christ, He washed away our sins. He made us new creatures. Now, we are no longer poor old sinners, we are sons and daughters of the Most High God. Instead of crawling around the floor with that "poor old me" mentality, you can step up to the dinner table. God has an incredible banquet prepared for you. He has an abundant life for you. No matter how many mistakes you've made in the past, or what sort of difficulties you struggle with right now, you have been destined to live in victory. You may not be all you want to be, but at least you can look back and say, "Thank You, God; I'm not what I used to be."

The enemy doesn't want you to understand that you have been made righteous. He much prefers you to have a sin consciousness, but God wants you to have a righteousness consciousness. Start dwelling on the fact that you've been chosen, set apart, approved, and accepted in heaven—and that you have been made righteous on earth.

Every morning, no matter how we feel, we need to get out of bed and boldly declare, "Father, I thank You that You have approved me. Thank You that You are pleased with me. Thank You that I am forgiven. I know that I am a friend of God."

Just as you put on your clothes, consciously put on the breastplate of God's approval. All through the day, everywhere you go, imagine big bold letters right across your chest saying "Approved by Almighty God." When those condemning voices attempt to pummel your self-image with comments such as "You're not this, you're not that, you blew it over here," simply look in the mirror and see that affirmation: Approved by Almighty God.

I know my children aren't perfect. They have faults and weaknesses, and they sometimes make mistakes. But I also know that they're growing. They're learning. Imagine you asking me, "Joel, are you pleased with your children?"

How do you think I would answer?

I would not list all their faults. I wouldn't think about what they have done wrong over their young lives or even the time they may have disobeyed last week. No, without hesitation, I would tell you, "Yes, I am pleased with them. They are great children." Then I'd tell you everything I like about them. I'd tell you they are loving, caring, attractive, talented. I mean, they're just like their father!

Seriously, that's exactly the way God sees you. He's not focused on your faults. He's not keeping a list of your shortcomings. God is not looking at everything you've done wrong over your entire life or your disobedience last week. He's looking at what you're doing right. He's looking at the fact that you have made a conscious decision to be better, to live right, and to trust Him. He is pleased that you are kind and courteous to people. He's looking at the fact that you have a desire to know Him better.

It's time for you to get in agreement with God and start feeling good about who you are. Certainly, you may have some areas in which you need to improve, and you will because you're growing. You're making progress. You can live free from the heaviness that has weighed you down in the past.

Get in agreement with God and start feeling good about who you are.

Keep in mind, the enemy accuses that you're never doing enough. "You're not working hard enough, not being a good enough marriage partner or parent; you did fairly well on your diet yesterday, but you shouldn't have eaten that dessert late last night."

Don't take that stuff. You have a multitude of good qualities to every one negative quality.

"But, Joel, I'm so impatient."

Well, that may be true, but have you ever thought about the fact that you're always on time? You're persistent. You're determined.

"I don't think I'm as good a mom as I should be."

Maybe not, but have you noticed that your children are doing great in school? Your children never miss a meal. They are healthy, well rounded socially, and busy in sports, school, and church activities.

"Well, I'm not a very good husband, Joel."

Okay, maybe you work too much, but you've never missed a house payment. You provide a great living for your family.

"But I've made a lot of mistakes in life."

Yes, but you picked up this book and began reading, learning, seeking to change for the better. That's a pretty great choice. Give yourself the benefit of the doubt. Take off those rags of condemnation and start putting on your robe of righteousness. Put on the breastplate of God's approval.

You can, you should feel good about yourself. When you regard yourself positively, you are in agreement with God.

"What about that mistake I made last week? What about that time I failed last year?"

The moment you repented, God not only forgave you, He forgot about it. He chooses not to remember it anymore. Quit bringing up what God has already forgotten; let it go and start feeling good about who you are. We tend to think God is keeping a list of all of our mistakes. In your mind, you can see Him up there in heaven. "Oops! They failed there, let me get that down." And "Uh-oh, I heard that comment. Gabriel, make a special note of that one."

That's not God's heart at all. God is for you; He is on your side. He is the best friend you could ever have. God is not looking at what you've done wrong; He's looking at what you've done right. He's not focused on what you are; He's focused on what you can become.

You can be assured that God is pleased with you. He's in the process of changing you. That's why I can get up every morning and even though I make mistakes, I can boldly say, "God, I know you approve me, so I feel good about who I am."

**God is not looking at what you've done wrong;
He's looking at what you've done right.**

"Joel, you're making it too easy," an older man complained. "You're giving people a license to sin."

No, you don't need a license. If you want to sin, you can sin. I sin all I want to. The good news is that I don't want to. I want to live a life that's pleasing to God. I want to live a life of excellence and integrity.

Stop dwelling on everything that's wrong with you and taking an inventory of what you're not. The Scripture says in Hebrews, "To look away from everything that distracts." [22] If you constantly pick yourself apart, you're bound to be depressed and defeated. Look away from that; recognize that you are changing, that you're making progress. Accept the truth that spiritual growth is a process, not an overnight flash. The Bible says God changes us little by little.

"But, Joel, I've got all these weaknesses," I hear you saying. "If you only knew me . . ."

Here's some good news: God's power shows up the greatest in our weaknesses. When we are weak, He is strong. You can learn to lean on God, and instead of being negative and critical toward yourself, say, "Father, I'm leaning on You. I'm asking You to help me to beat this bad habit. God, I know I'm weak in this area, but I believe You are strong in and through me. I'm asking You to help me have a better opinion about myself."

In your weaknesses, whatever they may be, instead of getting down on yourself, simply ask God to help you, and you'll see His power show up like never before.

I believe God allows us to have some weaknesses so we'll always have to trust Him. If you're waiting until you get rid of everything you struggle with and until you feel like you're perfect, before you begin to like yourself, you're going to be waiting your whole lifetime.

"Well, Joel, I'd feel good about myself if I could drop twenty pounds. I'd feel good about myself if I would be a little more patient, if I'd be a little more understanding."

No, you can start feeling good about yourself right now. You're not perfect, but you are trying to live better, and God looks at your heart. He sees the inside, and He is changing you little by little.

We're all at different stages in our spiritual maturity. That's why each of our attitudes can be, "God, I know I have these areas I need to improve, but I'm doing my best. I also know that You have already accepted and approved me, so I'm going to start accepting myself. I'm making up my mind that I am going to go through this day feeling good about me."

I heard a story about a man and his small son who were hiking up a mountain. Suddenly, the little boy slipped and slid about thirty yards down the mountainside, getting caught in some brush. Unhurt but frightened, he called out, "Somebody, help me!"

A voice called back, "Somebody, help me!"

The youngster looked surprised and confused. He said, "Who are you?"

The voice shouted back, "Who are you?"

The boy began to get aggravated. "You're a coward!" he yelled.

The voice shouted back, "You're a coward!"

The boy shot back, "You're a fool."

The voice repeated, "You're a fool."

By then, the boy's father had reached him and helped extricate his son from the brush. The boy looked up and said, "Dad, who is that?"

The father chuckled and said, "Son, that's called an echo, but it's also called life." He said, "Son, let me show you something." The dad shouted out, "You're a winner!"

The voice shouted back, "You're a winner!"

The dad's voice boomed, "You've got what it takes."

The voice boomed back, "You've got what it takes."

The dad shouted, "You can make it."

The voice shouted back, "You can make it."

"Son, that's exactly how it is in life," the father explained. "Whatever you send out always comes back to you."

Let me ask: What messages are you sending out about yourself?

"I'm a failure, I'm unattractive. I'm undisciplined. I'm broke. I've got a terrible temper. Nobody likes to be around me."

Start sending out "I'm approved, I'm accepted, I am the righteousness of God. I am creative. I am talented. I am more than a conqueror." Make sure you are transmitting good messages about yourself.

Whatever you send out always comes back to you.

When Jesus was baptized, He came up out of the water and a voice boomed out of the heavens, saying, "This is my beloved son in whom I am well pleased." [23] Of course, Jesus was uniquely God's Son, but I believe God is saying that to you, too. He is well pleased with you.

"Oh, God couldn't say that to me. You can't imagine the life I've lived. You don't know the things I struggle with right now."

No, let this sink deep down into your heart, mind, and soul: God is pleased with you. He has already accepted and approved you. He may not be pleased with every decision you make, but if you have entrusted your life to Him, God is pleased with you.

What a tragedy to go through life being against yourself, especially when there is no rational reason to do so. Understand that it is not that God will be pleased with you one of these days, when you finally get your stuff together. No, God is pleased with you right now. The war within is over; God has won! That's why it's okay to feel good about who you are today, right now, this very moment.

CHAPTER 9

Making Your Words
Work for You

God didn't create any of us to be average. He didn't make us to barely get by. We were created to excel. The Scripture teaches that before the foundation of the world, God not only chose us, but He equipped us with everything we need to live His abundant life.[24] You have seeds of greatness inside of you, but it is up to you to believe and act on them.

I see too many people today going around with low self-esteem, feeling inferior, as if they don't have what it takes. As long as we have that poor self-image, we're not going to experience God's best. You will never rise above the image that you have of yourself. That's why it is so important that we see ourselves as God sees us.

You need to have an image of a champion on the inside. You may not be there yet; you may have some areas to overcome, but you need to know deep down inside that you are a victor and not a victim.

One of the best ways that we can improve our self-image is with our words. Words are like seeds. They have creative power. It says in Isaiah that "We will eat the fruit of our words." That's amazing when you stop to consider that truth: Our words tend to produce what we're saying.

Every day, we should make positive declarations over our lives. We should say things such as, "I am blessed. I am prosperous. I am healthy. I am talented. I am creative. I am wise." When we do that, we are building up our self-image. As those words permeate your heart and mind, and especially your subconscious mind, eventually they will begin to change the way you see yourself.

The Scripture says, "With our tongue, we can either bless our life or we can curse our life." [25]

Some individuals curse their own future by saying things such as, "I don't have what it takes. I'm so clumsy I can't get anything right. I'm so undisciplined. I'll probably never lose this weight."

We must be extremely careful what we allow out of our mouth. Our words set the direction for our lives.

Which direction are you going? Are you declaring good things? Are you blessing your life, speaking words of faith over your future and your children's future? Or are you prone to saying negative things? "Nothing good ever happens to me. I'll probably never get out of debt. I'll never break this addiction."

When you talk like that, you are setting the limits for your life.

Our words set the direction for our lives.

Many people suffer a poor self-image because of their own words. They've gone around for years putting themselves down, and now they've developed these wrong mind-sets that prevent them from rising higher in their careers or in their personal lives.

"Joel, I've made so many mistakes I don't see how God could bless me," Catherine said through her tears. "I just don't feel like I deserve it."

"No, we don't deserve God's blessings," I told her. "They are part of the free gift of God's salvation. The best thing you could do is to accept His offer, and all through the day start saying to yourself, 'I am a new creation. I am forgiven. I am valuable to God. He has made me worthy.' If you keep saying that long enough, you're going to start believing it. And you will begin expecting good things."

You may be lonely, but you shouldn't go around talking about it all the time. "Well, I'm so lonely. I'm discouraged. Nobody likes to be around me. I'll probably never get married."

No, get up every day and say, "I am fun to be around; I am attractive and friendly; I have a good personality, I'm an engaging person; people are drawn to me." As you speak such positive statements day after day, you will soon discover your self-image is changing for the better. You'll feel better about yourself, and you'll not only have more confidence, you'll be friendlier; you will attract other positive people to yourself.

Maybe you have had other people speak negative, destructive words over you. Perhaps a parent, coach, or teacher said things like, "You don't have what it takes, you're never going to be successful, you can't go to that college; you're not smart enough." Now those words have taken root and they are setting the limits for your life. Unfortunately, you've heard those comments for so long they have seeped down into your self-image. The only way you can change the effects of those words is for you to get on the offensive and start speaking these faith-filled words over your own life. Moreover, the best eraser you can ever find is God's Word. Start speaking out of your own mouth what God says about you: "I am anointed; I am approved; I am equipped; I've been chosen, set apart, destined to live in victory."

When you speak such faith-filled words, you will bless your life. Furthermore, your self-image will begin to improve.

Positively or negatively, creative power resides in your words, because you believe your words more than you believe anybody else's. Think about it. Your words go out of your mouth and they come right back into your own ears. If you hear those comments long enough, they will drop down into your spirit, and those words will produce exactly what you're saying.

That's why it is so important that we get in a habit of declaring good things over our lives every day. When you get up in the morning, instead of looking at that mirror and saying, "Oh, I can't believe I look like this. I'm getting so old, so wrinkled," you need to smile and say, "Good morning, you good-looking thing!" No matter how you feel, look at yourself in that mirror, and say, "I am strong. I am healthy. God is renewing my strength like the eagles. And I am excited about this day."

In the natural, physical realm, those statements may not seem to be true. You may not feel up to par that day. Or you may have many obstacles to overcome. The Scripture tells us that we are to "call the things that are not as if they already were." [26]

In other words, don't talk about the way you are; talk about the way you want to be. That's what faith is all about. In the physical realm, you have to see it to believe it, but God says you have to believe it, and then you'll see it.

For instance, you may be undisciplined in a certain area, but instead of complaining about it and talking badly about yourself, start calling in what you need.

Change the way you speak about yourself and you can change your life. Start each day with saying things such as, "I am disciplined. I have self-control. I make good decisions. I'm an overcomer. This problem didn't come to stay; it came to pass." All through the day—as you're driving to work, taking a shower, or cooking dinner—under your breath, declare positive, biblically accurate statements about yourself: "I am more than a conqueror. I can do what I need to do. I'm a child of the Most High God."

**Change the way you speak about yourself
and you can change your life.**

As you speak affirmatively about yourself, you'll be amazed to discover that you are getting stronger emotionally and spiritually, and that image on the inside is changing for the better.

Jacqueline is a bright young high school student, but she did not believe that she could ever make good grades. "I'm just a C student," she lamented. "That's the best I've ever done. I don't understand math. My teacher is the hardest one around."

Fortunately, Jacqueline learned to stop limiting herself by her words. Now each day on the way to school, she says, "I excel in school. I am a quick learner. I have good study habits. I am a good student; I am full of God's wisdom."

Maybe you tend to be critical and judgmental toward people. Don't sit back and say, "That's the way I am."

Instead, look in that mirror and say, "I am compassionate; I am kind. I am sympathetic and understanding; I believe the best in people." As you consistently make these positive declarations, the new attitudes will get down inside you and your relationships will begin to change.

When God told Abraham and Sarah they were going to have a child, they were both well beyond the childbearing years. No wonder Sarah laughed. She must have said, "Abraham, what are you talking about? Me? Have a child. I'm an old woman. I don't think so."

God had to change the image Abraham and Sarah had of themselves before they could ever have that child. How did God do that? He changed their names; He changed the words they were hearing. He changed Sarai to Sarah, which means "princess." He changed Abram to Abraham, which means "father of many nations." Think about it. Before Abraham had a single child, God called him by faith the father of many nations. Every time somebody said, "Hey, Abraham. How you doing?" they were saying, "Hello, father of many nations." He heard that so often, it began to sink down inside him.

Sarah was an older woman who had never had any children. She probably didn't feel much like a princess, but every time somebody said, "Hello, Sarah," they were saying, "Hello, princess." Over time, that changed her self-image. Now, she no longer saw herself as an older, barren woman; she began to see herself as a princess. Eventually, she gave birth to a child, whom the parents named Isaac, as God had instructed.

Perhaps God has whispered something to your heart that seems totally impossible. It may seem impossible for you to ever be well again, or impossible for you to get out of debt, to get married, to lose weight, to start that new business. In the natural, physical realm, all the odds are against you; you don't see how it could happen. But if you're going to see those dreams come to pass, you have to get your mouth moving in the right direction and use your words to help you develop a new image on the inside. No matter how impossible something looks, no matter how you feel, start boldly declaring, "I am strong in the Lord. I can do all things through Christ. I am well able to fulfill my destiny." Call in what God has promised you. The Scripture says, "Let the weak say I am strong." You may not feel well today, but don't go around saying, "I don't think I'm ever going to get over this sickness."

Instead, start boldly declaring, "God is restoring health unto me. I am getting better every day in every way."

Or maybe your financial situation doesn't look good. Start declaring, "I am blessed. I am prosperous. I'm the head and not the tail. I will lend and not borrow."

Don't merely use your words to describe your situation; use your words to change your situation.

Victoria and I have some friends who were trying to have another child. They had a daughter, and they really wanted to have a son. Unfortunately, every time the wife became pregnant, she had a miscarriage. This happened five times over a nine-year period. As the couple grew older, they also grew discouraged and frustrated.

The husband's name was Joe, and he had gone by that name his whole lifetime. But one day it came to his attention that his full given name, Joseph, meant "God will add." When Joe heard that, something clicked inside of him. He knew that was God speaking to him. Joe decided to start using his full name

He told his friends, family members, and coworkers, "Please don't call me Joe anymore; start calling me Joseph." They didn't know what he was doing, and several wrote off Joe's desire to be called Joseph as some sort of midlife crisis. But Joseph didn't care. He knew that every time somebody said, "Hello, Joseph," they were saying, "God will add." They were speaking faith into his life. Joseph took that to mean that "God is going to add to us a son."

Several months after Joseph began believing his name, his wife became pregnant again. And for the first time in ten years, she carried the child full term, and gave birth to a healthy baby boy.

As a testimony to what God had done for them, they named their baby "Joseph" as well—"God will add."

With our words, we can prophesy our own future. Unfortunately, many people predict defeat, failure, lack, and mediocrity. Avoid those kinds of comments and use your words to declare good things. Declare health, joy, financial blessing, happy and whole relationships. All through the day, you can declare, "I have the favor of God. I can do what I need to do." As you do so, you will be blessing your own life and strengthening your self-image.

If you struggle with depression, use your words to change your situation. You may have been through a lot of disappointments. You may have gone through some setbacks in the past. More than anybody, you need to get up every day and boldly declare, "This is going to be a great day. I may have been defeated in the past, but this is a new day. God is on my side. Things are changing in my favor."

When discouraging thoughts attack, instead of complaining and expecting the worst, say it again and again: "Something good is going to happen to me. I'm a victor and not a victim." It's not enough to merely think positively: You need to speak positively about yourself. You need to hear it over and over again. "Good things are coming my way. God is fighting my battles for me. New doors of opportunity are opening."

As you speak affirmatively, you will develop a new image on the inside, and things will begin to change in your favor.

If you will set aside five minutes a day and simply declare good things over your life, you may be astounded at the results. Before you start your busy day, before you leave the house, drive to work, or take the kids to school, take a few minutes to speak blessings over your life. You may prefer to write the statements, so you can have a record of them. It says in Habakkuk to write down your vision. Make a list of your dreams, goals, and aspirations as well as the areas you want to improve, the things you want to see changed. Always make sure you can back it up with God's Word. Then get alone with God and take a few minutes every day to declare good things over your life. Remember, it's not enough to read it or merely think about it. Something supernatural happens when we speak it out. That's how we give life to our faith.

Maybe you struggle with worry. You're always upset about something and your mind tends to fret over insignificant, minor concerns. Start declaring, "I have the peace of God. My mind is at rest. I have a relaxed and easygoing attitude." Declare it by faith and use your words to change that situation.

Betty had tried to quit smoking for years and years. She had good intentions, and she did her best, but she just couldn't seem to break the habit. She was always saying, "I just don't have what it takes. This is too hard for me; I'll never break this addiction." She even told her friends, "If I ever do quit smoking, I know I will gain so much weight." She was constantly speaking negative words over her life, and this went on for years.

One day somebody encouraged Betty to change what she was saying, to call the things that are not as if they already were. She didn't know any better, so she just started saying, "I don't like to smoke. I can't stand the taste of nicotine. And when I do quit smoking, I'm not going to gain one bit of weight." She said that day after day, month after month.

She later told me, "Joel, I'd be sitting there smoking a cigarette and enjoying it, yet I'd say out of my mouth, 'I can't stand to smoke. I can't stand this nicotine.' " She wasn't talking about the way she was; she was talking about the way she wanted to be. She did that month after month, and then one day, she woke up and lit up a cigarette and it tasted differently—slightly bitter. Before long, the taste grew worse and worse. Eventually, the cigarettes tasted so bad to Betty, she couldn't stand the taste anymore, and she was able to lay them down and not pick them up again.

Amazingly, Betty did not gain one bit of weight because of kicking the smoking habit. Today, she's totally free from nicotine. Betty broke that addiction in part by the power of her words. She prophesied her own future.

Like Betty, maybe you have spent years saying negative things about yourself. "I can't break this addiction. I can't lose weight. I'll never get out of debt. I'll never get married."

Understand, those words have created a stronghold in your heart and mind. You have developed the wrong picture of yourself on the inside. You must begin to change that image and start seeing yourself with the victory or else you will remain in bondage, right where you are.

Decide today that you will speak only positive affirmations about yourself. You may have a thousand bad habits, but don't let another critical word come out of your mouth toward yourself. Use your words to bless your life. Look in that mirror and call in what you need. The image of your life must change on the inside before it can change on the outside.

Use your words to bless your life.

Start saying every day, "I am excelling in my career. I have the favor of God. I make good decisions. I'm a hard worker and I'm going to rise to new heights." If you hear that long enough, it will create a new image within, an image of victory, an image of success.

Every day, whether I feel like it or not, I declare, "I am anointed. My gifts and talents are coming out to the full. Every message gets better and better. People are drawn to me. People want to listen to me."

Occasionally, I receive letters from people who say, "Joel, I never watch TV ministers. I don't even like them. But for some reason, when I turn you on, I just can't turn you off."

A man wrote, telling me that his wife had been trying to get him to watch me on television for years, but he wouldn't do it. He was quite cynical and sarcastic toward the things of God. One day, however, he was flipping through the channels and came across our program. As usual, he immediately pressed the remote control to change the channel, but for some reason his remote control quit working and he was stuck watching the program. Frustrated and aggravated, he manipulated that remote control, but nothing helped. He changed the batteries and it still didn't work.

In his letter, he admitted, "Joel, even though I acted like I wasn't listening, what you were saying was applying directly to me." He continued, "Funny thing, the minute the program was over, my remote control started working again." As I read his letter, I thought, *God works in mysterious ways.* Now, that man never misses church on Sunday.

Learn to declare good things over your life. If you are negative and critical toward yourself, your own words can stop God's best plan from coming to pass in your life. That is what almost happened to the Old Testament prophet Jeremiah. God said, "Jeremiah, I saw you before you were ever formed in your mother's womb and I have chosen you to be a prophet to the nations."

Jeremiah was young, and he didn't have a great deal of self-confidence. When he heard God's promise, rather than feeling blessed, Jeremiah was afraid. He said, "God I can't do that. I can't speak to the nations. I'm too young. I wouldn't even know what to say."

God answered, "Jeremiah, say not that you are too young."[27] Notice, God immediately stopped Jeremiah's negative words. Why? God knew that if Jeremiah went around saying, "I can't do this. I don't have what it takes. I'm too young," those negative words would thwart the plan and prevent the promise from coming to pass. God simply said, "Jeremiah, do not say that anymore. Don't use those words to curse your future." Jeremiah changed his words about himself and became a courageous spokesman to a generation that had settled for less than God's best.

God has called you to do great things, as well. He's put dreams and desires in your heart. Sure, there are areas where you want to improve, things that you want to accomplish. Be careful that you don't make excuses: "God, I can't do it. I've made too many mistakes. I'm too young. I'm too old. God, I come from the wrong side of the tracks."

No, God is saying to us the same thing He said to Jeremiah: Stop it. Those negative words can keep you from experiencing My best plan.

Decide right now that today will be a turning point in your life. Prior to now, you rarely have said anything good about yourself. But starting today, get on the offensive and start making positive declarations over your own life. Every day, say things like "I am blessed. I am healthy and prosperous. I am competent; I am called. I'm anointed. I'm creative. I'm talented. I am well able to fulfill my destiny."

Start making positive declarations over your own life.

If you want to know where you are going to be five years from now, listen to your words. You are prophesying your future. If you want to be stronger, healthier, happier, if you want to break addictions, then start declaring it right now. Remember, you will eat the fruit of your own words, so bless your future. Get in agreement with God, and learn to speak words of faith and victory over your own life. Not only will you develop a better self-image, you will become a better you!

CHAPTER 10

Have Confidence in Yourself

Each of us has an internal dialogue, an inner conversation going on with ourselves throughout the day. In fact, we talk more to ourselves than we do to anybody else. The question is, What are you saying to yourself? What do you meditate on? Positive thoughts? Empowering thoughts? Affirming thoughts? Or do you go around thinking negative, defeated thoughts, telling yourself things like "I'm unattractive. I'm not talented. I've made many mistakes. I'm sure God is displeased with me." That kind of negative self-talk keeps millions of people from rising higher.

We usually talk to ourselves subconsciously, without even thinking about it. But in the back of your mind, you have these reoccurring thoughts. And for most people those thoughts are negative: I'm clumsy. I'll never overcome my past. I don't have what it takes.

All through the day they allow defeated messages to permeate their mind and self-talk. They see somebody that's successful, somebody that's achieving, and that inner voice tells them, "That will never happen for me. I'm not as smart as that person; I'm not that talented." Or they see somebody that is in good physical shape, somebody that looks healthy, fit, and attractive. That voice tells them, "I'm just not that disciplined. I'll never get back in shape." There's a negative voice on the inside that's constantly telling the person that something is wrong with them.

"You're not a good mother." "You didn't work hard enough last week." "You are a weak person." If we make the mistake of allowing this negative self-talk to take root, it not only saddens our spirit, but it also limits how high we can go in life. Many people are living in mediocrity because they are playing that negative recording day after day, over and over again.

I've discovered that often these wrong-thinking patterns stem from childhood. The people who should have been nurturing us and telling us what we could become, building our confidence, did just the opposite. I know people who are stuck in a rut because as they were growing up, somebody mistreated them, or somebody rejected them. A parent, a coach, or even a peer spoke negative words over the person. They didn't know any better. They just let it take root. Now those wrong-thinking patterns are keeping that person from becoming all God intends him or her to be.

We have to reprogram our minds. Please don't lay in bed every morning thinking about everything that's wrong with you. Don't lie there and rehearse all your mistakes—thinking about what you can't do or how you don't have what it takes. It doesn't matter how many times you've tried and failed. You have to shake off those negative messages and experiences, and put on a new recording. Remind yourself often: "I am a child of the Most High God. I have a bright future. God is pleased with me. I am talented; I am creative; I have what it takes. I will fulfill my destiny." We should be talking to ourselves that way, not in arrogance but in a quiet confidence. Deep down on the inside, all through the day, we should hear things like "I am anointed. I am called. I am chosen. I am equipped. This is my season."

Our internal dialogue should always be positive and hopeful. We should always talk to ourselves with empowering, affirming thoughts. We have to get out of the habit of thinking negative thoughts about ourselves. Don't ever say, "I'm so slow. I'm unattractive. I'll never overcome my past."

No, get those phrases out of your vocabulary. If you make the mistake of dwelling on that junk, it will set the limits for your life. You may have suffered horrible pain in the past. You may have had some unfair things happen to you, but don't allow that to pull you down by constantly playing the negative recording about yourself. You believe what you say about yourself more than you believe what anybody else says. Others can tell you repeatedly that God has a great plan for your life. He has a bright future in store for you. But until you get it down on the inside and start replaying it throughout the day, it's not going to do you any good.

Pay attention to how you talk to yourself. Please don't misunderstand, but in my mind all day long I replay the message, "Joel, you have what it takes. You can do what God's called you to do. You're talented. You're creative. You're strong in the Lord. You're well able to fulfill your destiny."

If you too will talk to yourself in the right way, you'll not only enjoy your life more, but you'll rise higher to a new level of confidence, a new level of boldness. I read a study where researchers gave a test group of college students some special eyeglasses that turned everything upside down, totally opposite of what it should be. For the first few days of the experiment, confusion reigned. The students stumbled over the furniture, they couldn't read or write, they had to be led to class, and they could barely function. But slowly, they started adjusting. By the end of the first week, they were able to go to class on their own. They didn't need any help to get around. The researchers were intrigued so they decided to continue the experiment. After one month, the students had totally adapted. Their minds had compensated for their upside-down world, and they could read without any problem. They could write, do their homework, type on the computer—all upside down.

Something similar can happen to us. If we go around with wrong mind-sets long enough, telling ourselves, "Well, I'm not a good parent. I've made too many mistakes. Nothing good ever happens to me," just like those college students, even though it's totally backwards, and not the way God created us, our minds will eventually adapt and adjust, and we will end up living at that level.

Your world may be upside-down already. Maybe you are living far below your potential, feeling bad about yourself, lacking confidence, and wallowing in low self-esteem. Have you considered that it could be a result of what you are constantly speaking to yourself? Your internal dialogue is negative. You have to change that before anything else will change.

I saw a lady on television who had lost 175 pounds. She had surgery to remove the excess skin and everything went great. They showed the before and after pictures, and she looked fantastic. But several months later they went back to interview her and she was so depressed. She would hardly eat anything. They said, "Hey, what's wrong? You look great. You look fantastic."

She said, "Yes, that's what everybody is telling me. But I guess in my mind, I'll always be a fat, unattractive lady."

As I watched, I thought, *You hit the nail on the head. It's in your mind.* She had changed on the outside, but she had not changed on the inside. She was still playing that old negative recording. "I'm fat. I'm unattractive. I'll never be happy." She could have gotten down to ninety pounds, and she still wouldn't have been happy.

Don't listen to voices that are pulling you down. You may not look like you stepped out of a fashion magazine, but I can tell you this: You were made in the image of Almighty God. You will be amazed at how much more you enjoy your life and how much better you feel about you, if you'll learn to talk to yourself in a positive manner. And even when you make mistakes, even when you do wrong, don't go around saying, "Well, I can't do anything right. I'm so clumsy. I'm so slow."

I played sports with people who make the mistake of beating themselves up, calling themselves derogatory names. "You idiot!" "Bill, you sorry thing. You can't make a shot." "What kind of jerk are you?"

I know other people who have gone through setbacks in life—disappointments, failures, bankruptcy, or divorce. They go around so defeated, focused on what went wrong. They allow that negative record to play continually. "You blew it. You had your chance. You messed up your life."

Learn to put on that new recording, tell yourself "I am forgiven. I am restored. God has a new plan. Good things are in store."

I'm not saying simply to take the easy way out. I am saying that it does you no good to go around feeling condemned, disgraced, or disqualified over something that is in the past. I know people who live with a black cloud following them around. It's a vague feeling; they can't even put their finger on it, but something is always telling them, "You're never going to be happy. You might as well forget it."

You cannot sit back and accept those kinds of statements to yourself. You must rise up and start talking to yourself in a new way. All through the day, you should be telling yourself things like, "Something good is going to happen to me. God is pleased with me. I have a bright future. The best is yet to come." You have to change on the inside before it's ever going to happen on the outside.

It would do us all good to lie in bed in the morning and before we get up, think good thoughts about ourselves. *I'm a good parent. I'm a good leader. I'm a good husband. I have a bright future. God is pleased with me.* Learn to think these thoughts on purpose.

I was blessed to be raised by parents who instilled in me this kind of confidence and self-esteem. As I was growing up, my parents always told me that I could accomplish great things; they constantly reminded me that they were proud of me. Having people in our lives who will nurture and encourage us, especially at a young age, when we're forming so many of our thought patterns, is extremely important.

Parents, I would encourage you to instill these qualities in your children. They need your love, your encouragement, your approval, and your affirmation. Don't ever put your children down. Don't say things like "Why can't you make good grades like your brother?" Or "You are just not smart enough to attend college." "If you keep that up, you're not going to amount to anything."

Words are like seeds. They can take root and grow in a person's mind for years. Certainly, when our children are small, we have to correct them, but don't make the mistake of saying things such as, "You are such a bad boy," "You're a bad girl." No, he or she is not a bad person. They may have done something wrong, but they are good children. They're made in the image of Almighty God. God didn't make any junk. Parents, we have a responsibility to instill confidence, self-esteem, and security into our children.

I wonder how many adults struggle today because they didn't get the positive encouragement they needed from their parents or from the people who raised them. Or maybe the parents only corrected the child without showing her the approval side. If you are a parent, please avoid that sad mistake.

My brother Paul and his wife, Jennifer, have the cutest little boy named Jackson. He's always happy and so much fun to be around. Every night when Jennifer takes Jackson to bed, she tells him a story and prays with him. Just before she says good night, she says, "Now, Jackson, let me remind you who you are," then she'll go through this long list of superheroes. "Jackson, you're my Superman. You're my Power Ranger. You're my Buzz Lightyear. You're my Rescue Hero. You're my Lightning McQueen. You're my cowboy. You're my baseball player." Little Jackson just lies there with a big smile on his face, taking it all in.

What is Jennifer doing? She's giving Jackson fuel for his internal dialogue. Even though he's only three years old, Jennifer is saying to him, "Jackson, you are special; you are valuable; you're going to do great things in life." Then she goes through this same routine when she puts my brother Paul to bed! But instead of using Buzz Lightyear, she uses Elvis.

Something funny happened the other day. Paul and Jennifer got home late, so Jennifer put Jackson to bed in a hurry. She didn't take time to go through the long list of superheroes. A few minutes later, she heard this little voice calling out from upstairs. "Mamma, mamma." Jennifer ran to the staircase and called, "Yes, Jackson, what's wrong?" He said, "Mamma, you forgot to tell me who I am."

There's a deeper truth to that simple statement. I have found that if we don't tell our children who they are, somebody else will. I want to tell my children: "You've got what it takes. There's nothing you can't do. Mother and Daddy are behind you. We're proud of you. We believe in you. You are destined to do great things."

Speak words of blessing over your children. Speak victory over their lives. They need your encouragement. They need your approval. Help them to have a big vision for their lives.

When Moses was born, the Egyptian Pharaoh decreed that all the children two years of age and under would be killed. Instead of acquiescing to the absurd, diabolical command, Moses's mother hid him away. Eventually, she put him in a basket and sent him down the Nile River. One of Pharaoh's daughters found him and raised him. Because Moses didn't grow up around a godly father, he didn't have that person speaking blessings into his life.

Many years later, God came to Moses and said, "Moses, I'm choosing you to deliver the people of Israel." Not surprisingly, the first words out of Moses's mouth were, "God, who am I?"

When we don't tell our children who they are and instill confidence and build self-esteem in them, it causes them to struggle with their identity, with who they are, with what they can do. God said, "Moses, don't say, 'Who am I?' You're the one that I've chosen."

Then Moses asked another question. He said, "But, God, who will listen to me? You know I'm not a good speaker. You know I stutter." Notice his lack of confidence. He too was playing the wrong recording in his mind. Possibly his confidence had been undermined by having an absentee father, missing a parent who spoke good things into his life on a regular basis. With God's help, however, Moses overcame that deficit in his upbringing.

Maybe you didn't have a great deal of positive encouragement as a child either. That does not have to hold you back in life. Your earthly father may not have told you who you are, but allow me to help you out. You are a child of the Most High God. You have been crowned with God's glory and honor. You can do all things through Christ. You are full of potential. You are overflowing with creativity. There's nothing in your heart that you cannot accomplish. You have courage, strength, and ability. The favor of God surrounds you wherever you go. Whatever you touch is going to prosper and succeed. You are blessed and you cannot be cursed. That's who you really are. So throw back your shoulders, hold your head up high, and start telling yourself: "I am victorious. I am well able. I am endowed with greatness by God Himself."

You must get your thoughts about yourself moving in the right direction if you truly want to become a better you. All through the day, you should be thinking good things about you. And when the old, negative recordings come to mind, let them remind you that it is time to put on the new recording. Immediately begin quoting some positive affirmations about yourself and about your God. "I am anointed. I am well able. God has good things in store for me!" Keep the right thoughts playing in your mind.

The other day I talked to a young woman in the lobby of Lakewood Church. She was beautiful, and by all outward appearances, she seemed to be happy and on top of the world. On the inside, however, she had a war going on. She didn't like herself. She thought she was unattractive. She thought she was overweight. She had a long list of things she felt were wrong with her.

As I talked with her, I discovered that her father had always put her down. He constantly told her what was wrong with her, what she couldn't do, what she was never going to be. The sad thing is, this young lady in her late twenties had gone through one marriage, gone through a second marriage, and now she was about to end her third marriage.

I told her, "You've got the wrong recording playing on your internal CD player. You're constantly telling yourself, 'I'm fat. I'm unattractive. I have nothing to offer. I'm unlovable.' As long as you're dwelling on those lies, there's going to be a war on the inside. You were not created to live that way. God created you to feel good about yourself. He created you to feel complete, to feel whole, to be confident and secure—not to constantly be against yourself. If you cannot get along with yourself, you'll never be able to get along with other people. It'll spread over into every other relationship."

Maybe there's no peace in your home and the problem is not the other person. You need to get at peace with who you are. Quit allowing the negative voice to play in your mind. Perhaps, like the young woman I mentioned, the root cause was something that happened way back in your life.

Maybe, like many people, you don't know how to turn it off. You think it is normal to go around feeling bad about yourself. You may not have gotten everything that you should have from your parents or the people who raised you, but always remember this: It's not how we start that counts; it's how we finish. Tell yourself every day, "I am the apple of God's eye. I'm His most prized possession. I am crowned with glory and honor. I'm valuable. I'm attractive. I have a bright future in front of me."

Understand that the negative voices always seem to cry out the loudest. You can have twenty people encouraging you and one person will come up and say something negative, and that's what you'll tend to remember. That's what your mind will want to replay again and again. You can do a hundred things right and if you make one mistake, you'll have to fight being guilty and condemned. The negative voices will come at you the strongest, but you must learn to let those go. As long as you stay focused on the negative, you will have a war on the inside. You're not going to feel good about yourself. The only way to change this is to get your internal dialogue going in the right direction. Replace the negative recordings with new, positive, uplifting messages. Start thinking the right thoughts about yourself.

God told the children of Israel in Joshua 5, verse 9, "This day have I rolled away the reproach of Egypt from you." In other words, they didn't feel good about themselves. They had been hurt and mistreated; they were discouraged, even after being delivered from slavery. God came to them and said, "Stop doing that. I am rolling away the reproach from you." I believe the reproach had to be rolled away before they could go into the Promised Land.

It's the same with us. You may be trying to live in victory, trying to be successful, trying to have a good marriage. But you are negative toward yourself. You don't feel good about who you are. You're constantly dwelling on your past hurts and pains. Until you are willing to let go of those offenses and start focusing on your new possibilities, they will tie you down right where you are. You cannot have a bad attitude toward yourself and expect to have God's best. Quit focusing on what you've done wrong. God has already rolled away your reproach—your shame, embarrassment, failures, and setbacks. God has done His part. Now you must do your part. Let it go so you can go into your Promised Land. Start thinking, feeling, and speaking positively about yourself.

The Scripture says, "Our faith is made effectual when we acknowledge everything good in us." [28] Think about this: Our faith is not effective when we acknowledge all our hurts and pains. It's not effective when we stay focused on our shortcomings or our weaknesses. Our faith is most effective when we acknowledge the good things that are in us. Declare affirmations such as "I have a bright future. I am gifted. I am talented. People like me. I have the favor of God."

When we believe in God's Son, Jesus Christ, and believe in ourselves, that's when our faith comes alive. When we believe we have what it takes, we focus on our possibilities.

Unfortunately, most people do just the opposite. They acknowledge everything wrong with them. Even subconsciously, they are constantly playing that negative recording, causing them to have a low opinion of themselves. If you are in that group, you must change that recording.

I may be naïve, but I *expect* people to like me. I expect people to be friendly to me. I expect people to want to help me. I have a positive opinion about who I am because I know whose I am—I belong to Almighty God.

Don't walk into a room timid and insecure, thinking, *Nobody's going to like me in here. Look at them; they're probably talking about me already. I knew I shouldn't have worn this suit. I knew I should have stayed at home.*

No, get your inner dialogue going in a different direction. Develop a habit of being positive toward yourself; have a good opinion about who you are. "Well, Joel, I'm just a housewife. I'm just a businessperson. I'm just a schoolteacher."

No, you are not "just" anything. You are a child of the Most High God. You are fulfilling your purpose. The Lord orders your steps. Goodness and mercy are following you. You are a person of destiny. Knowing and acknowledging these things can boost your confidence sky high.

Get up every morning and say to yourself, "I am blessed. I am equipped. I have the favor of God. This is going to be a great day." All through the day, play that over and over in your mind. Keep the right recording on. Dwell only on positive, empowering thoughts toward yourself. That's when your faith will be energized. Do not make the mistake of merely acknowledging what's wrong with you. Acknowledge what's right with you. Have a good opinion of who you are. If you'll get in this habit of talking to yourself the right way with these positive empowering affirming thoughts, you'll not only have more confidence, you will rise higher and see God's blessings and favor in a greater way.

PART 2: BE POSITIVE TOWARD YOURSELF

1. I refuse to live guilty or condemned because of past mistakes. Instead, I will step into new situations confidently, knowing that I am forgiven by God. I will make this day a fresh beginning.

2. Today, I am choosing to refresh my self-image by speaking positive affirmations and faith-filled words over my life such as:

   "I am blessed; I am prosperous; I am healthy; I am continually growing wiser."

   "I am excelling in my career; God is helping me to succeed."

   "I have a positive opinion about myself because I not only know who I am, but I know *whose* I am—I belong to Almighty God."

3. I am determined to keep my inner dialogue positive about myself. I will reject any negative thoughts toward myself and others, and I will meditate on thoughts such as, "I am valuable. I am well able to do what God has called me to do."

PART THREE

DEVELOP BETTER RELATIONSHIPS

CHAPTER 11

Bringing the Best out of People

When I was in middle school, I was one of the smaller players on the basketball team. In our first game of the season, we were scheduled to face a real good team, boasting a bunch of big guys. Naturally, at my size, it would have been easy to be intimidated by our opponents.

On game day, I was walking through the school hallways in between classes, when my basketball coach called me over to where he was standing in front of several of my friends. He was a big, strong, tough coach, and in his usual gruff manner, he said, "Joel, you're not that tall, but let me tell you, size doesn't matter. What counts is right down in here." He pointed his finger at his chest as he continued. "Joel, you've got a big heart, and you're going to do great this year."

When I heard the coach's words—spoken right in front of my friends—I stood up taller, threw my shoulders back, and smiled even more than usual! You would have thought I was Michael Jordan. I thought to myself, *The coach believes in me!* My confidence shot up to a completely new level, and I played better that year than I'd ever done before. It's amazing what we can accomplish when we know somebody really believes in us.

That coach took a little time to make a big difference. He took time to instill confidence in me. If we're going to bring out the best in people, we too need to sow seeds of encouragement.

"Well, Joel, nobody's encouraging me," someone might say. "Why should I encourage anyone else?"

If you want your life to increase, if you want your life to get better, then you need to help improve somebody else's life. If you will help somebody else become successful, God will make sure that you are successful.

God puts people in our lives on purpose so we can help them succeed and help them become all He created them to be. Most people will not reach their full potential without somebody else believing in them. That means you and I have an assignment. Everywhere we go we should be encouraging people, building them up, challenging them to reach for new heights. When people are around us, they should leave better off than they were previously. Rather than feeling discouraged or defeated, people should feel challenged and inspired after spending any time with you and me.

The Bible says that love is kind.[29] One translation says, "Love looks for a way of being constructive." In other words, love looks for ways to help improve somebody else's life.

You have something to offer that nobody else can give.

Take time to make a difference. Don't just obsess about how you can make your own life better. Think about how you can make somebody else's life better as well. Our attitude should be: Who can I encourage today? Who can I build up? How can I improve somebody else's life?

You have something to offer that nobody else can give. Somebody needs your encouragement. Somebody needs to know that you believe in him, that you're for him, that you think he has what it takes to succeed. If you look back over your own life, most likely you'll find someone who played a pivotal role in helping you get to where you are today. Maybe your parents or a teacher had confidence in you and helped you believe in yourself. Perhaps it was a boss who placed you in a higher position even though you didn't feel qualified at the time. Or a school counselor who said, "You've got what it takes. You can go to this college. You can be successful in that career."

Maybe they saw something in you that you may not have seen in yourself, and they helped you get to that next level. Now, it's your turn to do something similar for somebody else. Who are you believing in? Who are you cheering on? Who are you helping to become successful? Friend, there's no greater investment in life than in being a people builder. Relationships are more important than our accomplishments.

I believe that God is going to hold us responsible for the people He's put in our lives. He's counting on us to bring out the best in our spouse, in our children, and in our friends and our coworkers. Ask yourself, "Am I improving somebody's life, giving that person confidence, or am I just coasting along, consumed with doing my own thing?"

That's something I've loved about Victoria. She has always believed in me; she's my biggest supporter and my biggest fan. Victoria thinks that I'm the greatest person on the face of this earth. Now, I know that's not true, but I like the fact that she thinks I'm great. Victoria thinks that I can do anything. She's always bringing out the best in me.

One time, a number of years ago, we were preparing to build a house. We had sold our other home and had bought property on which we planned to build. I picked up the phone to call our builder friend, to get everything lined up to begin construction, but Victoria stopped me. She said, "Joel, what are you doing? We don't need a builder. You can build the house."

I said, "Victoria, I don't know how to build a house. I don't know anything about construction."

"Sure you do, Joel," Victoria replied, her eyes sparkling with excitement. "You were at our other house practically every day when they were building it. You saw how they did it. You can get those subcontractors lined up as well as anybody else."

Sure enough, she talked me into it, and I built our house. It turned out pretty well, considering that I forgot the plumbing!

One thing I know for sure is that Victoria has confidence in me. I don't believe that I would be standing up, speaking to people every week, if Victoria had not told me years ago that one day I was going to be the pastor of Lakewood Church. Keep in mind that when Victoria first began expressing those convictions, I had never preached a sermon in public, much less on television. Furthermore, I had no desire to do so at the time. Yet as Victoria and I sat listening to my father preach, she'd often say, "Joel, one day, that's going to be you up there. You have so much to offer. One day, you're going to be helping a lot of people."

I didn't think I could do it; I didn't like getting up in front of people. I'd never been to seminary. I had no formal training that qualified me to be a pastor. I replied under my breath, "Victoria, I wish you'd quit saying that. That's just not me. I'm not a preacher."

"No, Joel," she answered, "I can see it in you. You have what it takes." Victoria saw things in me that I didn't see in myself, so she kept watering those seeds of encouragement.

When my father went to be with the Lord, and I first started preaching at Lakewood Church, I was extremely nervous, but two factors helped reduce my fears. One, all the seeds of encouragement that Victoria had sown; the other was the congregation's support. Every time I got up to speak, many of the people of Lakewood cheered me on. They applauded even before I began my message. I could have been a terrible speaker, but they kept cheering me on, giving me the confidence that I needed.

After a few months, I realized that they truly believed in me. I thought, *These people think that I can do it.* It did something on the inside of me as Victoria, my family members, and our congregation at Lakewood Church helped bring out the best in me.

Now, I'm committed to bringing out the best in them and in you. You have things on the inside of you—gifts and talents—that you've not yet dreamed of using. You can go further and accomplish more. Don't settle for the status quo. You can overcome any challenge that's before you. You can break any addiction. You have the power of the Most High God on the inside of you. Start believing in yourself and acting like it's true.

The Bible says in First Corinthians 8, verse 1, that love encourages people to grow to their full stature. When you believe the best in people, you help to bring the best out of them.

Susan Lowell had carved out a successful career, and everything was going great in her life, but she just wasn't satisfied. She had a desire deep down inside to help troubled teenagers. One day, she quit her high-paying job and went to work as a schoolteacher in one of the roughest schools in California, a high school known for drugs, gangs, and other serious problems. Not surprisingly, the school had one of the highest dropout rates in the state. The school board could hardly keep teachers, because the students were so unruly and rebellious. Nobody thought the new lady would last.

But Ms. Lowell took a different approach. On the first day of school, she asked her students to write down their names and addresses and something interesting about themselves. While they were writing, she walked up and down the rows and secretly memorized each student's name. When they finished, she announced to the class they were about to have their first test. The students moaned and groaned. She said, "No, the test isn't for you; this test is for me." She explained, "If I can call each one of you by your correct name, then I pass the test. But if I miss even one of your names, then every one of you will get an automatic 'A' on our first real test."

The students were excited as Ms. Lowell slowly walked up and down the rows, and, one by one, she correctly called out each student's name. The class was duly impressed, and she had their attention. Ms. Lowell spoke softly as she said, "Class, the reason I did this is to show you that you are important to me. When I look at you, I not only like you, but I care about you. That's the reason I'm here."

The students realized that this teacher was different. She was not there simply to get a paycheck; she wasn't trying to get the most compensation for the least amount of work. *This lady believes in us. This lady thinks that we can become something.*

One day Ms. Lowell got word that Armando, one of the roughest students in her class, owed one of the street gangs a hundred dollars. It was an extremely dangerous situation, especially since Armando didn't have the money to pay. Ms. Lowell asked her student to stay after class. When they sat down to talk, she said, "Armando, I've heard about your dilemma and I want to loan you the money to pay your debt, but I'll do it only under one condition."

"What's that?" Armando asked.

She said, "I'll give you this money if you promise to pay me back on the day that you graduate." At the time, Armando was a sopho-more, and of all Ms. Lowell's students, he was one of the least likely to graduate. His older brothers and sisters who had attended the same school before him had not graduated. His parents had only a second-grade education.

Ms. Lowell's act of kindness touched his heart. Nobody had ever shown him that kind of love. Nobody had ever believed in him enough to think that he could actually graduate.

Ms. Lowell had the students keep a journal. The week before, she'd asked them to write down the nicest thing anyone had ever done for them. Armando said, "Ms. Lowell, last week I had to make up something, because I can't ever remember anybody doing anything nice for me. But what you did for me today, I will never forget." He went on to say, "Ms. Lowell, I will not let you down. I will graduate, because if you think I can do it, then I know I can do it."

This teacher believed in her students so much, they began to believe in themselves. Indeed, Armando became the first person in his family ever to earn a high school diploma.

Many people simply need somebody to spark a bit of hope, somebody to say, "Yes, you can do it. You've got what it takes."

Are you believing the best in your own children? Are you instilling the confidence in them that they need, telling them that they're going to do great things in life? Are you believing the best in your loved ones? Maybe some of them have gotten off course. Don't give up on them; don't write them off. Make sure they know that you're concerned. Make sure they know that you really believe in them.

**When you believe the best in people,
you help to bring the best out of them.**

Here's the key: Don't focus on what they are right now. Focus on what they can become. See the potential on the inside. They may have some bad habits, or they may be doing some things that you don't like, but don't judge them for it. Don't look down on them critically. Find some way to challenge them to rise higher. Tell them, "I'm praying for you. I believe you're going to break that addiction. I'm believing for great things in your life."

You'll be pleasantly surprised at how people respond when they know you really care. Everywhere Jesus went, He saw potential in people that they didn't see in themselves. He didn't focus on their weaknesses or their faults. He saw them the way they could become.

For example, the disciple Peter had many rough edges. He was hot tempered, loud, bombastic, and impetuous, but that didn't deter Jesus. Jesus didn't say, "Forget it, Peter. I'm going to find somebody a little more refined than you." Instead, Jesus worked with Peter to bring the best out of him. It was in there. He just had to get it out.

Interestingly, Peter's name literally meant "pebble" or "small stone." However, Jesus saw so much more in Peter. He said, "I'm going to give you a new name. Your new name is going to be Cephas, which means 'a rock.' " In other words, God said, "You are a pebble right now, but when I get finished with you, you're going to be a rock. You're going to be strong, solid, and secure."

As a rule, you never bring out the best in someone by condemning and criticizing, or verbally beating a person down. You bring out the best by love. You bring it out by showing people that you care. Your friends, family members, or coworkers may do some things you don't like or that you find offensive; they may have some bad habits, but don't focus on their weaknesses. Find something they're doing right and encourage them for that.

I'm not saying that you just sweep things under the rug, but wait for the right time and opportunity to deal with those negative actions or attitudes. First, you must build your relationship, gain the person's respect and trust, and you can do that by encouraging and challenging him or her to rise higher.

I've found that if I treat people the way I want them to be, they are much more likely to become that sort of person. They're much more likely to change.

For instance, if your husband is not treating you with as much respect as you know he should, don't sink down to his level and act disrespectful as well. No, sow a seed. Treat him respectfully anyway and watch that man begin to change. If he's lazy, treat him as if he were a hard worker. He may do a thousand things you don't like, but find the one thing on which you can compliment him and encourage him for that.

It is easy to nitpick and find fault, but our goal is to bring out the best in people. Our job is to encourage, build up, to challenge people to rise higher.

I heard about a man who went out to get his newspaper one morning, and when he opened up the front door, a little dog owned by the folks living across the street was bringing his paper to him. The man chuckled, hurried back inside, and got the dog a treat. That little dog left there just as happy as can be.

The next morning, when the man went to pick up his newspaper, he opened the door and found that same little dog sitting there. Next to the dog were eight of the neighbors' newspapers!

Human beings respond similarly to treats—especially when we are treated to praise, admiration, and appreciation. Husbands and wives should be each other's greatest cheerleaders. Take time to praise your wife. Take time to compliment your husband. Don't get lazy in this area. Learn not to take each other for granted.

The other day, Victoria walked by me and I noticed that she looked especially beautiful. She was dressed up, and had her hair all fixed. I thought to myself, *Wow, she looks great today.*

But I was busy working at my desk and didn't want to be interrupted, so I didn't say anything. *Besides,* I thought, *she knows I think she's beautiful. I've told her thousands of times.*

I missed the opportunity to sow a compliment. Later, I realized that I was just being lazy. Sure, Victoria may know that I love and appreciate her; she may know that she is physically attractive to me. But as her husband, I have the responsibility to build her up every chance I get.

I heard somebody say, "Complimenting each other is the glue that holds relationships together." With so many things working against good relationships nowadays it's amazing what a kind word here and there will do.

"Honey, you look beautiful today. Thanks for preparing such a delicious dinner," or, "You did great on your project last week." Short, sincere, natural compliments can help keep our relationships strong.

Complimenting each other is the glue that holds relationships together.

Nearly every time I finish speaking and walk off the platform, Victoria tells me, "Joel, that was great today."

In truth, it may have been the worst message I have ever presented, but that doesn't matter to Victoria. She still encourages me.

We walked off the platform the other day and Victoria said, "Joel, that was spectacular today."

I felt so good. The next Sunday, however, she went back to saying "Joel, that was great today."

"What do you mean, great?" I asked, feigning incredulity. "How about spectacular?"

Victoria just laughed and rolled her eyes. She knows that she's spoiled me!

Be free with your compliments and be quick to vocalize them. Remember, your *thoughts* don't bless anybody but you. You can think good thoughts about somebody all day long, but it's not going to do them one bit of good. You must verbalize those thoughts; speak them out. Every day, try to find somebody you can compliment, someone you can build up. If a waiter at the restaurant gives you good service, don't just think about it. Tell him. "Thanks for being such a fine waiter and taking good care of us today." Those positive words might make his day.

Brent, a man who attends Lakewood Church, was standing in line at the grocery store checkout counter waiting to pay for his selections. The young woman running the register was having a tough time. People in line started getting aggravated and being a bit short with her.

When it was Brent's turn to check out, he decided he wasn't going to add to the problem by responding the way others had done. He smiled and said, "Ma'am, I just want to tell you that I think you're doing a great job. I appreciate you working so hard."

That young woman's countenance brightened instantly. It was as though Brent had lifted a load of heavy bricks off her shoulders. "Sir, I've been working here for three months," the checkout girl said, "and you are the first person to tell me anything like that. Thank you so much."

Our society overflows with critics, cynics, and faultfinders. Many people quickly point out what you are doing wrong, but relatively few take the time to point out anything you are doing right. I don't want to live my life like that. I'm going to be a giver and not a taker. I want to build people up and not tear them down. I'm going to do my best to leave places better off than they were before I passed by.

Be a giver and not a taker.

Recently, I was thinking about the many things in life for which people become known. As I pondered the legacy I would leave, I decided that a hundred years from now, I want to be known as somebody who brought out the best in people, somebody who left the world a better place. Material accomplishments will soon be forgotten. The only thing that lasts is the investment we make in other people's lives.

I want to bring the best out of my wife and children. I want to inspire the best in my friends. I want people to say, "I like being around that Joel Osteen. He encourages me to go higher, to expect more, and to expand my horizons. His actions, attitudes, and the way he treats other people inspire me to be a better individual."

Moreover, I want to spend most of my "discretionary" time with people who will strive to bring the best out of me. The Scripture says, "iron sharpens iron." The way we live our lives with one another should encourage one another to do better.

Ask yourself, Are the people in my life better off or worse off because I passed their way? Am I building them up in our conversations, and bringing out their best, or am I dragging them down? Do I believe in somebody? Do I give them confidence to improve their lives? Or am I focused on myself?

Over the past few years, I've received a number of complimentary letters from famous people—movie stars, government leaders, pro athletes, and the like. I'm flattered and honored by the comments in those letters. But the greatest compliment I ever received came when Victoria stood up in front of our home congregation and said, "After living with Joel all these years, I can tell you that I'm a better person. I've got more confidence. I'm kinder. I have a better attitude. I've grown. And I've been challenged."

Of course, I can say the same thing about the impact she has had on me. She's a "people builder," and we are committed to leaving people better off than they were before they encountered us.

You can be a people builder everywhere you go. That man at the gas station—don't simply pump your gasoline; pump something good into his life. The woman at the office who always seems grumpy—rather than complaining about her, take time to give her a compliment. Build up your friends and coworkers and your boss. Everywhere you go, make positive deposits, instead of negative withdrawals.

When you get up in the morning, instead of applying your energies to how you can be blessed, find some way to be a blessing to someone else. If you will make somebody else's day, God will make yours.

In my life, I've been blessed to have people who believed in me— my parents, my wife, my family. Now, it's my turn. Who am I believing in? Who am I cheering on? Who am I helping to succeed?

If you will make somebody else's day, God will make yours.

Friend, choose to bring out the best in the people that God has put in your life. You're never more like God than when you give, and the closest thing to His heart is helping others. If you will be a people builder, focused on bringing out the best in others, I can promise you this: God will bring out the best in you.

CHAPTER 12

Keep the Strife out of Your Life

Relationships are what really matter in life—our relationship to God, with our spouse, children, extended family members, friends, and others within our communities—yet all too often, we allow these relationships to occupy much lower positions than they deserve on our priority lists. If we are not careful, we can allow something or somebody to drive a wedge between ourselves and the people who are most precious to us.

To maintain healthy relationships, we need to learn how to keep the strife out of our lives. God made each of us as unique individuals. We have different personalities and temperaments; we approach issues in different ways, so we really shouldn't be surprised when we grate against one another occasionally. Too often, though, if someone doesn't agree with our opinion, or see eye to eye with us on some matter, we get bent out of shape and allow strife to foment. I've discovered that just because somebody is not exactly like me, or doesn't do things the way I do them, that doesn't necessarily mean that I am right and they are wrong. We're just different, and our differences can cause friction.

It takes maturity to get along with somebody who is different than you are. It takes patience not to start a dispute over minor issues or become easily offended. If we're going to keep the strife out of our lives, then we must learn how to give people the benefit of the doubt.

We will also need to overlook some things. Every person has faults; we all have weaknesses. We should not expect the people with whom we are in a relationship to be perfect. No matter how great a person he or she may be, no matter how much you love him or her, if you are around that person long enough, you will have an opportunity to be offended. There is no such thing as a perfect spouse, a perfect boss, or even a perfect pastor (although I'm very close!).

If we're putting unrealistic expectations on people, expecting them to be perfect, that is not fair to them, and it will be a source of frustration for us. We're always going to be disappointed.

Some people live with the attitude of, "I'll love you as long as you never hurt me or as long as you never make a mistake." "I'll be your friend as long as you treat me just right." "As long as you do things my way, then I'll accept you, and I'll be happy."

But that is extremely unfair and places too much pressure on that other person. The Scripture teaches that love makes allowances for people's weaknesses. Love covers a person's faults. In other words, you have to overlook some things. Quit demanding perfection out of your spouse, your children, or other people with whom you are in a relationship, and learn to show a little mercy.

I couldn't find a better wife than Victoria. She is an extremely loving, caring, generous person, and yet there are some things I have to overlook, some things for which I have to make allowances. That doesn't mean something is wrong with her; she's just human. If I were a critical faultfinder, keeping an account of everything she did wrong, then our relationship would suffer. Before long, we'd be at odds with each other, arguing, and fighting.

Instead, we make allowances for each other's weaknesses. We've learned not to wear our feelings on our sleeves and not to be easily offended.

Few things are worse than living with a touchy, overly sensitive person. If somebody offends you or does you wrong, learn to shake it off and move on. The Scripture teaches that love believes the best in people.

"Well, my husband hardly spoke to me this morning. He didn't even thank me for cooking dinner the other night," a wife might say.

Remember, love covers a fault. Instead of going through the day offended and upset, consider the fact that he may not have been feeling up to par. Maybe he's under a lot of pressure at work or stressed out over some other matter. Rather than criticizing and condemning, give him the benefit of the doubt and believe the best in him.

My father used to say, "Everybody has the right to have a bad day every once in a while." If somebody does something you don't like, if they insult or offend you unwittingly, simply swallow your pride and say, "I choose to overlook that offense," and move on.

Instead of immediately drifting to the negative and seeing the worst, it could change your life greatly if you would get in a habit of viewing events from a positive perspective and believing the best in people.

The Scripture says that love keeps no record of wrongs done to it.[30] You might see your relationship with someone go to a whole new level if you'd just get rid of the record book. I know people who have a mental list of everything anybody has done wrong to them for the last twenty years. They have a detailed scorecard, listing every time their spouse hurt them, every time their boss was thoughtless or rude, every time their parents missed the grandkids' ball game. Instead of keeping a list of slights or offenses, throw out your negative record book and look for the good.

Steve told me, "Joel, any time my wife and I have a little disagreement, she brings up every mistake I've made for the last ten years. 'Well, you did this last year. Don't you remember that you did that in 2005? Last month you hurt me.' She keeps stirring up dirt from the past."

As long as you are bringing up pain from the past, you are going to have strife in your present.

"But I'm the one that's right!" I hear you lamenting.

Maybe so, but do you want to be right, or do you want to have peace in your home? Do you want to have your way, or do you want to have healthy relationships? Many times, we can't have both. In all of our relationships, especially in marriage, it is vital that we not keep score of offenses.

Christine was driving through an intersection when she accidentally turned too sharply and sideswiped another car. Worse yet, she was driving her brand-new car, a wedding gift from her husband Eric. Christine pulled over to the side of the road and the driver of the other car, an older gentleman, got out of his car and began to examine his severely damaged front bumper. He then stepped over to where Christine was sitting in her car, crying.

"Are you okay, young lady?" he asked kindly.

"I'm fine," Christine sobbed, "but I just got married and my husband gave me this car as a wedding gift; he is going to be so upset. I don't know what I'm going to do."

"Oh, I'm sure it will be okay." The older gentleman tried to console her. "Your husband will understand." They talked for a few minutes before he said, "If I could just get your insurance information, we'll exchange that, and be on our way."

"I don't even know if I have an insurance card," Christine said through her tears.

"Well, it is usually in the glove compartment," the man suggested. "Why don't you check there?"

Christine opened the glove compartment and found the owner's registration and the insurance information. Attached to the envelope containing the insurance card was a note that read, "Honey, just in case you ever have an accident, please remember I love you and not the car."

That's the kind of person I want to be—a person who shows mercy, even in advance of a mistake or a wrong action. Rather than flaunting somebody's failure, learn to cover some of those weaknesses in the people who are close to you.

Choose to Be a Peacemaker

"But Joel, my spouse and I are simply not that compatible. We just can't get along. We are so different."

No, God may have put you with somebody different from you on purpose. That's not a mistake. Your strengths and weaknesses and that other person's strengths and weaknesses may be quite different, but ideally, your strengths can make up for your partner's weaknesses, and his or her strengths make up for your weaknesses. You complement each other. You should *complete* each other, rather than *compete* with each other. The two of you are much more powerful together than you are apart.

But you must study that other person, find out what he likes and dislikes; find out what her pressure points are, and then don't allow the weaknesses to bring conflict into your relationship.

Maybe you're a neat and tidy person. You like everything put perfectly into place, but your husband is sloppy; he tends to leave things lying around the house. You've told him a thousand times not to leave his shoes in front of the TV. Yet you walk in there one evening, and sure enough, his shoes are there. You go find him and say, "When are you ever going to put your shoes away? I'm so tired of cleaning up after you. That's all I ever do!"

No, why don't you be the peacemaker in your family? Quietly put away his shoes and go on your way so you can enjoy the rest of the evening. In other words, quit making a big deal out of something that is relatively minor. That issue is not worth allowing strife in your home.

"I've asked my wife over and over to turn the lights off when she leaves the room," David huffed. "But she always forgets and I have to go back in there and do it."

"No, instead of harping on your wife, why don't you make allowances for her weaknesses just as she does yours?" I said. "After all, it's not going to hurt you to go back in there and turn the lights off. Maybe you could even get a bit of exercise."

"But when is she ever going to change?" David protested.

You could probably answer David's question for him. When he quits nagging her, stops complaining, and develops a better attitude. That's when she's going to change.

Obviously, these are relatively minor issues, but the same principle applies to matters of more significance. When you cover a person's weaknesses and go the extra mile to keep strife out of your home, you are sowing a seed for God to do a work in that other person. Remember: You cannot change people, only God can. You can harp on that person all day long, but your comments will only serve to make matters worse. The result will bring more strife and more division. Nothing will drive the peace out of your home any quicker than constant criticism. Similarly, you can disrupt the atmosphere in your workplace by incessant griping, snipping, and having a critical attitude.

The Bible teaches, "We need to adapt and adjust in order to keep the peace." [31] It doesn't say that other people should adapt and adjust to us. No, if we are going to have peace, *we* have to be willing to change.

You can't have the attitude, "Well, if my wife would start doing what I ask her, then we'd have peace." "If my husband will start picking up his stuff, then we'll get along fine." "If my boss would start treating me right, then I'd quit being so rude to him."

No, we have to make adjustments in order to keep the peace. In other words, you have to swallow your pride sometimes. Maybe you simply put his shoes away. And then don't go announce to him that you did. "Well, I just want you to know I picked up your shoes . . . again . . . today . . . like I do every day."

No, just put them away and keep your mouth closed. You may not realize it, but when you do your part to keep strife out of your relationships, you are honoring God. When you honor God, He will always honor you. When you sow seeds of mercy and kindness, you'll begin to see your relationships improve.

The key is learning to adapt. We have to be willing to make adjustments. Stop waiting for somebody else to do it; instead, you be the peacemaker in your family or in your workplace.

Sometimes we allow strife to smolder because of the smallest, most insignificant things. We argue over things that don't even matter. One time Victoria and I were driving out of our neighborhood, and we stopped to look at a new house that was being built. I simply made the comment, "I wonder why the builder put the garage over there, on that side of the house. That's not the way I would have done it."

Victoria looked at the house and said, "Well, I think he did that so it would give him more room on his lot."

I studied the landscape and considered how the house was situated, and then replied, "No, that wouldn't give him any more room."

"Sure it would, Joel," Victoria answered. "It would give him a lot more space."

Fifteen minutes later, we were still debating why the builder had put the garage where he did. Our voice tones were getting louder, and our words were getting sharper. Finally, it dawned on me, *Why are we arguing over where this guy put his garage? We don't even know the man!* It wasn't worth losing our joy and peace, so Victoria and I simply agreed to disagree.

Pick your battles wisely. Don't quibble over things that don't really matter. We have enough big issues in life with which to deal.

One day Victoria and I were leaving a Houston Astros baseball game at Minute Maid Park downtown. At that time, the ballpark was relatively new and I didn't really know the best way to exit. When I pulled out of the stadium I asked, "Victoria, should I turn right or should I turn left?"

"I think we need to turn right," Victoria answered.

I looked up and down the street, and didn't recognize anything to the right. "No," I said, "I think we need to go left."

She looked around in every direction, and said, "No, Joel. I know we need to go right."

"Victoria, our house is that way," I said, pointing to the left. "I know we need to go in that direction." I pulled out and turned to the left.

She said, "Well, that's fine, but you're going the wrong way."

We had just enjoyed a relaxing time at the ball game and had such a great time together. Now the whole atmosphere in our car changed. We were uptight, tense, and on edge. We were hardly even talking to each other over something so insignificant. If I would have just swallowed my pride and gone her way, it wouldn't have hurt anything. Even if it had been the wrong way, what's ten minutes going to matter? But no, I had to show her that I was right. I had to prove my point.

I started driving . . . and driving . . . and driving all over downtown Houston. I was trying my best to act as if I knew where I was going, but I might as well have been in Japan! I had no idea where we were. I could see the freeway, but I couldn't figure out how to get on it. (Anyone who has ever driven in downtown Houston can probably relate!)

Every time I looked at Victoria, she'd just smile and say, "Well, you should have listened to me. Maybe we'll get home by this time tomorrow." The more she rubbed it in, the more aggravated I became.

Finally, after wandering around downtown for thirty minutes, I said, "All right, fine. We're going back to the ballpark and we're going to see if you can get us home."

She said, "It's about time."

We drove back to the baseball park and she said, "All right, you need to go right, then you go left." As we drove through a part of Houston that I had never seen before, I was hoping so bad that we were lost. I didn't care if we ever got home. I just did not want Victoria to show me up. We went through several side streets, and she finally said, "Okay, take a right."

Sure enough, that put us on the main freeway headed home. I was so shocked. I refused to believe she could do that. I said, "Victoria, how did you know those directions?"

"Oh, there's a little fabric store down here," she said, "that I used to come to all the time."

Don't make the same mistake that I did. Don't be so proud that you always have to prove your point. Swallow your pride and consider somebody else's opinion. You may think you're right, but there's a chance you could be wrong.

I know people who have gotten a divorce all because they stayed stirred up over something equally as silly or ultimately insignificant. They allowed the sore to fester, and before long they were living at each other's throats. Deep down inside, they may really love each other, but through the years, they've allowed strife to drive a wedge into their relationship.

Jesus said, "A house divided is continually being brought to destruction and it will not stand." Notice, if you allow strife into your relationship, it will be brought to destruction. It may not happen overnight; it might not happen in a couple of months or even a few years. If you allow strife to grow by holding grudges, making sarcastic remarks, or otherwise, you may not realize it, but that relationship is in the process of being destroyed. Strife is chipping away at your foundation, and unless you decide to do something about it soon, your life could crumble into a mess. You could very well look up one day and think, *What have I done? I've destroyed this relationship. How could I have been so foolish?*

Don't be hardheaded and stubborn. Maybe you have been at odds with somebody for months, not speaking to them, giving them the cold shoulder. Life is too short to live it that way. If possible, go to that person and make things right—while you still have the opportunity.

I recently spoke with a man who was broken and defeated. When I asked him what was troubling him, he explained how he and his father got at odds with each other over a business decision. They hadn't spoken in over two years. He said, "Joel, I knew deep down inside that I needed to make it right, but I kept putting it off. Then earlier this week, I received a call informing me that my father had suffered a heart attack and died." Imagine what emotional pain that man is living with.

Don't wait until you cannot make amends with someone from whom you are estranged. Do it today; swallow your pride and apologize even if it wasn't your fault. Keep the peace. Understand, it's not always about being right. It's about keeping strife out of your life. You can win every argument, but if it opens the door to turmoil, brings division, and tears you apart, in the end you didn't win at all—and you may have lost a lot.

I believe that God always gives us a warning, a wake-up call of sorts. He may say simply, "Stop being so argumentative. Quit being a faultfinder. Quit keeping your record books. Start being a peacemaker." When we recognize His voice, we need to respond.

"Well, I'll start being a peacemaker as soon as my husband changes," I hear somebody saying. "I'll do it as soon as my boss starts treating me better."

No, if you wait for somebody else to be the peacemaker in your life, you may wait around your whole lifetime, living your life on hold. Peace starts with you; you make the first move.

"But I apologized first last time. That's not fair. It's his turn to apologize."

It may not be fair, but it can keep you together. Swallow your pride. Be the bigger person. When you do that, you are sowing a seed, and God will always make it up to you.

Abraham, the Old Testament patriarch, moved to a new land with his nephew Lot. The land wasn't big enough to support both of them, so the Bible says in Genesis 13, verse 7, that Lot's herdsmen began to get into strife with Abraham's herdsmen.

Abraham dealt with the situation immediately. He knew if he allowed that friction to continue, it would not only affect the herdsmen, it would affect his relationship with Lot, as well. That strife would eventually bring turmoil to the whole family. So Abraham took the high road and let Lot choose the best piece of land. Interesting, isn't it? To avoid strife, Abraham willingly allowed Lot to take advantage of him. He allowed Lot to have it his way even though Abraham was the elder gentleman and should have been able to choose the best piece of land. Sometimes, no matter how much it hurts, you may have to let the other person do it his or her way just so you can avoid unnecessary conflict. It may not be fair. You may know beyond a doubt that you are right and they're wrong, but that doesn't matter. Let it go and trust God to make it up to you.

The Bible reveals that because Abraham kept the peace and refused to get into strife, God honored him by giving him the whole country. If you will choose to keep the peace, even though somebody is doing you wrong, God will bless you with abundance. He will bring you out better off than you were previously.

The Bible doesn't say it is permissible to live in strife as long as it is not your fault. No, when we're in strife, no matter whose fault it is, destruction and turmoil are sure to follow. Moreover, God may ask *you* to make adjustments to keep the peace.

Bill and Mary had major problems in their marriage. They didn't really have a relationship; they merely existed together. Bill was extremely selfish and argumentative. He was just a hard-to-get-along-with, critical, negative person.

Mary, however, genuinely loved God. She went to church every week and did her best to live with integrity. Bill prided himself on being just the opposite. He wouldn't have anything to do with the things of God and often spoke sarcastically about spiritual matters. Mary prayed nearly every day for God to change her husband. Years dragged by, with little improvement.

One day as Mary was praying, she asked God, "Why do I have to live in such a terrible environment? When are You ever going to change my husband?"

God spoke to her deep in her heart and mind, and said, "Mary, I will change your husband as soon as you change."

"God, what do You mean?" Mary cried. "*He's* the problem. Bill is the one who is mean and argumentative. I go to church every Sunday."

God said, "No, you're not doing all that you can to keep the peace. You've become indifferent to this situation." Then God said, "I'm going to hold you responsible because you know the truth. You know the right thing to do, and when you start doing it, I will change Bill."

Mary took God at His word and started making special efforts to keep the peace in her home. In less than a year, Bill began to change, slowly at first, then more dramatically. Today, they are both serving God and loving each other like newlyweds.

The Bible says, "To him that knows what's right and doesn't do it, then it's sin." [23] So often, we wait for the other person to change. We know he is wrong; she is at fault. We have to realize that God holds us responsible to do what we know to do. When we allow strife in our relationships, we open up the door to all sorts of trouble.

A few years ago, Victoria, I, and our two children went for a bike ride together at a park. The day had not gone real well for me, and I was aggravated over something that Victoria had done. I didn't think it was right, and it irritated me. Instead of letting it go, I chose to hold on to it. I could have overlooked it; it wasn't any big deal. I could have shaken it off and enjoyed the day with my family, but I chose to stay sour.

I placed our daughter Alexandra on my bike seat behind me and pulled away from Victoria and Jonathan. The bike trail was rather narrow, approximately four feet wide, and Jonathan had just learned how to ride his bike a few months earlier. He wasn't yet sure of himself, so he had to go slowly.

I was about a hundred yards ahead of Jonathan and Victoria when another biker approached in the opposite direction, racing past me at a high speed. My first thought was, *I hope Jonathan is careful. That guy is flying!*

Sure enough, as the racer approached Jonathan on the narrow path, Jonathan got rattled and turned his bike right into the path of the oncoming cyclist. They collided head-on, with an awful sound of crunching metal. I thought for sure Jonathan had broken an arm or a leg.

I slammed on the brakes, set my bike down, and ran back to Jonathan as fast as I could. I picked him up and was amazed that he wasn't hurt badly. He was skinned up on his legs and his arms, but he didn't have any broken bones. His bike, however, was such a tangled mess he could no longer ride it.

Fortunately, the other rider was okay as well. When everything calmed down, something on the inside of me said, "Joel, you brought all this on yourself. You had the choice to make things right. You had the choice to diffuse strife, but you chose not to."

I knew better, yet I continued to hold on to the offense. I wasn't treating Victoria right, and the accident happened, at least partly as a result. The Scripture says don't give any foothold to the enemy, a foothold of strife, a foothold of arguing, a foothold of unforgiveness. Of course, not every accident is because of strife, but I knew I had brought this one on us, so I apologized to my family members.

When we hardheadedly choose to hold on to strife, we are choosing to step out of God's protection. We step out of God's blessings and favor. Certainly, there are times when we must confront issues head-on, but there are also times that we can choose to avoid strife in a relationship by giving up our right to be right. Take the initiative to keep strife out of your life. Get rid of pettiness that produces division and discord. Make a decision that you're going to make the necessary adjustments so you can live a more peaceful life.

Friend, if you will swallow your pride and do whatever it takes to keep strife out of your life, you will sow seeds for God's blessings and promotion. When you do that, you'll see your relationships begin to flourish. God said, "Blessed are the peacemakers." If you'll have that kind of attitude, your relationships will continually get better and better.

CHAPTER 13

Taking a Stand for Your Family

One of the greatest threats we face in the twenty-first century is not a terrorist attack or an ecological catastrophe, but an attack on our homes. The enemy would love nothing more than to ruin your relationship with your husband or your wife, your parents, or your children. Too many homes are being destroyed through strife, lack of commitment, wrong priorities, and bad attitudes. If we're going to have strong, healthy relationships, we must dig our heels in and fight for our families.

The Old Testament records a time when Nehemiah was rebuilding the walls of Jerusalem. The walls had been torn down years previously, and the enemy was coming against God's people, against their homes, their wives and children, while the men worked on the construction crews. The situation got so bad that Nehemiah instructed his men to work with a hammer in one hand and a sword in the other. He encouraged them, "Men, fight for your sons, fight for your daughters, fight for your wives, fight for your families" (Nehemiah 4:14). He went on to say, "If you will fight, then God will fight."

I believe God is saying something similar to us today. If we will do our part and take a strong stand for our families, God will do His part. He'll help us to have great marriages and great relationships with our parents and children.

Certainly, not everyone will get married, but if a man and a woman choose to marry, two issues must be settled first. Number one: As a couple, we are committed to God. We're going to live a life that honors Him. We will be people of excellence and integrity in all that we do.

161

The second settled issue must be that as a couple, we are committed to each other. Occasionally, we may disagree, say things we shouldn't, we might even pout or get downright angry. But when it's all said and done, we're going to get over it, and we will forgive and move on. Leaving is not an option. We're committed to each other through the good times and the tough times.

If bailing out of the relationship is an option or an alternative, then you will always find some reason to justify it. "Joel, we just can't get along. We're not compatible. We tried, but we just don't love each other anymore."

Truth is, no two people are completely compatible. We have to learn to become one. That means we may have to make sacrifices; we may have to overlook some things. We must be willing to compromise for the good of the relationship.

The perfect spouse does not exist. Victoria sometimes tells people, "Oh, my husband, Joel, is the perfect husband."

Don't believe that for a minute. She is saying that by faith!

Stick with your spouse and make that relationship work. As one lady quipped, "My husband and I got married for better or for worse. He couldn't do any better and I couldn't do any worse."

When you do have disagreements, learn to disagree from the neck up. Don't let it get down in your heart. Victoria and I don't always see eye to eye, but we've learned how to agree to disagree. When you present your case, don't try to make that other person change his or her mind. Give others the right to have their own opinion. If you're not going to be happy unless they agree with you, then really you're simply trying to manipulate your partner. You're trying to force your opinion on that person. The better approach is to present your case, share your heart, and then step back and allow God to work in that person or situation.

As long as we are argumentative and we're trying to force our opinions, then there's going to be strife in our homes. Wherever there's strife, there's confusion. And there's nothing worse than living in a home that's tense. Everybody's on edge. You feel that at any moment something could explode.

You don't have to live that way. Do your best to create an atmosphere of peace and unity in your home. When you're tempted to pop off and say hurtful, critical, counterproductive things that you know you shouldn't, next time you have that opportunity, do yourself a favor. Take a deep breath, pause about ten seconds, and think about what you're going to say before you speak. Words can cut like a knife. You may say them in a matter of seconds, but three months later the person to whom you spoke them may still be feeling the sting.

Have you ever touched the stove and then pulled your hand off immediately? But weeks later, it still stings. That is what hurtful, critical words can do.

Never threaten your spouse with divorce. I've heard people say, "Well, if you ever do that again, I'm out of here." "If you don't do this, I'm leaving."

No, don't even let those words out into the atmosphere. Your words have creative power, and when you speak like that, you're just giving the enemy a right to bring it to pass. Besides, the Bible tells us "to be angry and sin not." Certainly, at times we're going to get angry. Anger is an emotion God built into us. But we don't have to blow up and say hurtful things that are going to damage our relationships. Learn to take a step back, collect your thoughts, and think about what you want to say.

One time, my mother and father got into a disagreement. My dad was extremely upset, so he decided he was going to give my mother the silent treatment. When Mother spoke to him, Daddy would answer back in the shortest, most unfriendly way he could. This went on for an hour or two, and he was doing his best to ignore my mother.

My mother is rather feisty, so she decided to do something about the situation. She went and hid behind a door, and she stayed there as still and quiet as she could be. Before long, my father realized that she wasn't around and he began searching for her. He looked all over the house, and he couldn't find her anywhere. The more he looked, the more frustrated he became. He said, "It's terrible to try to ignore somebody and you can't even find them." This went on for about fifteen minutes.

Finally, Daddy started getting worried. About that time, he walked past the door where my mother was hiding. Quick as a cat, my mother leaped onto my father's back, wrapped her arms and legs around him, and said, "John, I'm not getting off until you cheer up." They laughed so much that my father forgot what he was mad about.

Try to create a fun-filled atmosphere in your home. Everyone experiences stressful times; we all get uptight. We all have disagreements, but we should not allow that to linger. Too often we get complacent. "Well, I know I shouldn't say this, but I'm mad. I'm going to say it anyway." Or "I know I need to forgive, but I don't feel like it." Little by little, the relationship gets worse. Don't play those petty games. Do whatever it takes to keep the peace.

Victoria and I have been married for more than twenty years, and we don't agree on every single thing, but we are committed to each other. We're committed to our children, and to our extended family. We have committed in advance that we will work through any differences with each other that we may have.

Some people are committed while they're dating, or for the first few years of marriage. They're committed while everything is rosy, but how about when the sizzle subsides? Now, instead of scintillating romance, you are picking up his dirty socks or washing his sweaty workout clothes. That takes commitment. Or when you were dating, she always looked perfect, dressed to the nines. You never saw her without her hair in place and her makeup perfectly done. Now, you wake up in the morning and say, "Who is that woman over there?"

But marriage is a commitment, not a feeling.

I heard a true story about the president of a prestigious university. He was an older gentleman and a well-respected leader. Later in his life, his wife developed Alzheimer's. Month after month, her condition grew progressively worse. Several years down the road, the disease had so impaired her mind that she could not even recognize her husband anymore. They were a relatively affluent couple, so the gentleman hired nurses to help care for his ailing wife.

Then one day, he went in and announced to the university board of directors that he was going to resign so he could spend his full time taking care of his wife. The board members tried to talk him out of it, reminding him how needed he was. One board member spoke up and said, "In all respect, sir, why would you want to do this? Your wife doesn't even know who you are."

The university president looked the board member in the eye and said, "I made a commitment to this woman over fifty years ago. She may not know who I am, but I know who she is."

That's the kind of commitment that we need to have in our relationships as well.

Interestingly, God holds the husband and father responsible to keep the family together. The word *husband* comes from a Latin word that means "house band." Think of a rubber band that wraps around something, holding it together. That's a picture of what a good husband is supposed to do for his wife and family.

Solomon was the wisest man who ever lived. His book of wisdom encourages a husband to look his wife in the eyes and tell her, "There are many beautiful women in the world, but you excel them all." Solomon started his day off by praising and encouraging his wife. Men, you can imagine how our relationships would improve if we'd start complimenting our wives like that. Some women haven't had a compliment in years, not because they are undeserving, but because they are not appreciated. All they hear is what they're doing wrong. How the dinner wasn't any good. The kids are too loud.

Listen carefully to the words and tone of voice you use with your spouse. Are you complaining all the time and telling her what she's not doing right? Or are you doing like Solomon—blessing, encouraging, and uplifting that woman?

A Word from the Wise

The Song of Solomon is a biblical love story. In eight short chapters, Solomon praised his wife forty times. He wrote of her strength, beauty, and intelligence.

"Well, Joel, you don't know my wife," Chuck said. "She's the problem. She's argumentative. She's hard to get along with."

"Maybe so, Chuck," I replied, "but if you start praising your wife, if you start telling her how beautiful she is, and how glad you are to have her in your life, when you talk about the good, you will draw out the good. If you talk about the negative, you'll draw out the negative. It's up to you."

Men, learn to speak blessings over your wife and you will see that woman rise to a new level. She will respond to your praise and encouragement. Your words don't have to be poetic, fancy, or profound. Tell her simply but sincerely, "You're a great mother to our children. And you are a great wife to me. I'm so glad I can always count on you."

When you talk about the good, you will draw out the good.

If you'll treat your wife like a queen, she will be much more willing to treat you like a king. As a husband, you must understand that your wife needs your blessing. She needs your approval.

"Well, Joel, I'm just not a real romantic kind of guy," you may be saying. "I don't say all those mushy, gooey things."

Understand, this is not an option; it's a necessity, if you're going to have a healthy marriage. Like Solomon, get in the habit of looking at your wife and saying, "You are beautiful. I'm glad you're in my life. There are a lot of pretty women, but you excel them all."

The Bible says, "The wife is reflection of the man's glory."

If Victoria appeared in public with her countenance downcast, her hair disheveled, and her clothes dirty and wrinkled, her appearance and demeanor would be a be a sad reflection on me. I would need to examine my life and ask myself, "Am I treating her well? Am I making her secure? Does she know I'm proud of her?"

Husband, you need to look at your wife and see if she is reflecting your glory. Your wife should be strong, confident, secure, beautiful, radiant, and healthy. You should see it in her smile. You should see it in the way she carries herself.

I used to play basketball with a guy who disrespected his wife. After the game, he'd say things such as, "Well, I'm going home to see my old lady."

I often wondered, *If you talk about your wife like that, you must not think too much of yourself, either, because she's reflecting your glory.* I'd smile and say, "Well, I'm going home to see Queen Victoria."

It's true! Victoria is the queen of our house. Since I've made her the queen, that makes me the king, and I rather enjoy that.

Because the writer of Proverbs 31 praised his wife, his children rose up and blessed her as well.[33] Unquestionably, when a husband praises and blesses his wife, their children will follow his example. How a man treats his wife will have a profound impact on how his children will respect and honor their mother. Your children subconsciously take in voice tones, body language, and personal demeanor.

And Dad, your daughter will most likely marry somebody much like you. If you are hard-nosed and disrespectful, speaking rude, hurtful things to your spouse, don't be surprised if your daughter gravitates toward somebody with those same characteristics. I realize I need to treat my wife the way I want somebody to treat my daughter.

And Mom, you need to treat your husband the way you want somebody to treat your sons.

Men, open the car door for your wife. Take her coffee in the morning. Go out of your way to show her love, honor, and respect. I heard somebody say, "If a man ever opens the car door for his wife, he's either got a new car or a new wife." Perhaps we need to return to a society that encourages men to respect and honor women.

"If I do that sort of thing, my friends may think I'm a weakling," a guy might say. "They may give me a hard time."

If that's the case, you probably ought to find some new friends. A real man's masculinity is not diminished because he opens the car door for his wife. Being male doesn't necessarily make you a man. Treating people with dignity and respect makes you a man. Taking care of your wife and family makes you a man. Watching over your children makes you a man. Speaking blessings over your wife and kids—that's being a real man.

Granted, you may not have grown up in that kind of loving environment, but you can set a new standard. You can raise the bar.

In the reproduction process, the father provides the child's identity. The female contributes two X chromosomes; the male contributes an X and a Y chromosome. If the father gives the female an X, the child will be a baby girl. If he gives a Y, the baby will be a boy. The mother does not determine the sex of the baby. The child's identity comes through the father.

Father, you need to make especially sure that you affirm your children. You have incredible influence over them. Every day, just as you bless your wife, bless your children as well. Look at each child and say, "I'm so proud of you. I think you're great. There's nothing that you can't do." Your children need your approval. You're helping them to form their identity. If we're too busy as fathers, we're never there, or maybe we're just always correcting our children without providing them with affirmation, our children are not going to be as confident and secure as they should be.

Certainly, there are times when the father can't be there for his children because of other responsibilities. Nonetheless, do your best to keep your priorities in order. No amount of success in your career can make up for failure at home. I've seen some men accomplish great things in the corporate world as business leaders but at the expense of their children. Their children grew up without a father figure.

Fathers, take your children to church; don't send them. Be at their ball games as often as possible. Know who their friends are. Listen to their music. Children are looking for direction and guidance. When that young man comes over to take your daughter out on a date, be the first one at the door. Let him know there's a man in the house watching over that young lady. Parents, we have to fight for our children. If we will fight for them, God will fight with us.

A lifelong friend told me that as a teenager he had a drug problem. I thought that was strange, since I knew him well and remembered him as a good kid. He didn't look or act like someone on drugs. He said, "Yeah, Joel, every Sunday my parents drug me to church. They drug me to Sunday school. They drug me to Bible Study!" He laughed as he said, "And those 'drugs' are still in my veins. They affect everything that I say and do."

Years ago, at the largest game reserve in South Africa, they developed an overpopulation of elephants. The curators decided to take three hundred of the youngest male elephants and separate them from their parents and other adult elephants. The "orphans" were transported to another national park, where the white rhinoceros reigned as the dominant "king of the park." The rhinoceros has no natural enemies. Nothing stalks it, not even a lion, a tiger, or a bear. The rhino is simply too powerful. As such, the curators felt there would be no problem mixing the orphan elephants in with the rhinos. Over time, however, they began to find dead rhinos out in the brush. They couldn't understand what was happening, so they set up surveillance cameras to observe the park. Much to their surprise, they found that those young male elephants, the ones that no longer had a father or mother figure, had formed gangs and they had viciously attacked the rhino population. It's not even in the elephant's God-given natural instincts to act that way, but the lack of parental influence spawned the strange, deadly phenomenon.

I believe a similar plight threatens our children. The reason that children get in trouble can often be traced to the fact that they do not have positive role models in their lives. They don't have anybody speaking blessings over them and praying for them; they don't have father figures, and many don't have healthy, positive mother figures. It doesn't mean these children are incorrigible; it is simply a fact that without parental guidance, children sometimes do things they might not otherwise do if Mom or Dad were around.

We have a responsibility to reach out to children who don't have a father figure or a mother figure. Maybe you can mentor a young man or a young woman. If you really want to be blessed, don't just fight for your family, fight for somebody else's family. Stand in the gap for that single mom or single dad. When you take your son out to hit baseballs, swing by and pick up that young man who doesn't have a father figure. Reach out to some other children. Help them discover their identity.

Mandy grew up in a dysfunctional home. Her father was never around and her mother had plenty of problems of her own. As a teenager, Mandy raised her younger brother. To all observers, it appeared that Mandy was handling the situation reasonably well, but on the inside, she was crying out for help.

One day a friend of hers at school mentioned that her father owned a fast-food restaurant. "Come on down, Mandy. Maybe my dad will give you a job," her friend suggested. Mandy visited the restaurant, and that gentleman not only gave her a job, but he also took her under his wing. He began to watch after her, making sure she changed the oil in her car, checking to see that she was doing okay in school, and on and on. He didn't even realize it, but he became the father figure for which Mandy longed. Years later, when Mandy was about to get married, her real father was nowhere to be found. Can you guess who gave Mandy away at her wedding?

That's right; it was the man from the fast-food restaurant. He made time to care. He fought not only for his own family; he fought for somebody else's child, too. Today, Mandy is healthy, whole, and happily married, much to the credit of a man who became a father figure to her. Stand up for your family and then be "family" to someone else who needs a father, mother, sister, or brother. As you take time for others, God will provide for you.

CHAPTER 14

Invest in Your Relationships

"Just a minute, boys," Terry said as he wheeled his car toward First National Bank's outdoor automated teller machine. "I have to stop and get some money, and then we'll be on our way. I'm glad you guys accepted my invitation to go to the ball game." Terry pulled alongside the money machine and punched in his password. He pressed the keys and entered $200 as the amount of money he wanted to withdraw. The machine buzzed, whirred, and in a few seconds spit out a slip of paper . . . but no money. Terry pulled the paper off the machine, read it, and quickly stuffed it into his pocket. "Silly machine!" he said. "These things never work right. Does anyone have any cash?"

"Yeah, sure. No problem," one of the guys said from the backseat. "I have plenty of cash. You can borrow some from me till Monday." Terry's friends looked at each other knowingly. Whether Terry was willing to admit it or not, they all knew that the reason Terry was unable to make a withdrawal from his account was simple: He hadn't made a deposit into his account. Terry was pretending to be a generous giver, when in fact he was a selfish "taker."

If you want your relationships to thrive, you must invest in them by being a giver rather than a taker. Everywhere you go, strive to make relational deposits into people's lives, encouraging them, building them up, and helping them to feel better about themselves.

Granted, it's not always easy. Some people are difficult to be around, because they tend to draw the life and energy out of you. They're not bad people; they just drain you. They always have a problem, or some major crisis that they are convinced requires your help to solve. They talk all the time, so much so that you can't get a word in edgewise. By the time the conversation is done, you feel as though your emotional energy is gone. Difficult people don't make positive deposits; they are too busy making withdrawals.

Please don't misunderstand. It's okay to be down and discouraged occasionally. Everybody has a right to have a bad day. But if you do that all the time, that's a problem. You're not going to have good friendships if you're always draining the emotional reserves of the people around you.

Let me tell you something that your friends may not tell you: Your family members, friends, and coworkers don't want to hear about your problems all the time. They have enough problems of their own. They're already carrying a heavy load without you dumping your heavy burdens on them, too.

If you're always talking about what's wrong in your life, or how badly people or circumstances are treating you, that's an extremely selfish way to live. Try to get your mind off yourself and quit living with that "What can you do for me?" attitude. Replace it with questions such as, "What can I do to help someone else? How can I make your life better? How can I encourage you?" Make sure you are investing in people, rather than constantly making withdrawals from their emotional reserves.

I like to think of my relationships as "emotional bank accounts." I have an account with every person with whom I have a relationship—whether a family member, a business associate, friends, even some of the people I meet in passing; I have an emotional account with the security guard at work, the man at the gas station, and the waiter at the restaurant. Every time I interact with them, I'm either making a deposit or making a withdrawal from that account.

How do you make a deposit? It can be something as simple as taking the time to walk over and shake that man's hand. "How are you doing today? Good morning. Good to see you."

Just the simple fact that you went out of your way to make him feel important made a deposit into that account. Your act of kindness built trust and respect. You can make a deposit simply by smiling at somebody, acknowledging them, being friendly, being pleasant to them in ordinary circumstances.

When you compliment people, you're making a deposit. Tell that coworker, "That was an outstanding presentation. You did a great job." Tell your husband, "I appreciate what you do for this family." Tell your wife, "You make it so much fun to live around here." When you do such things, you are not merely giving a compliment, you are making a deposit into the account you share with that person.

At home, you can make deposits in your emotional bank accounts by giving your wife a hug and a kiss, telling her that you love her. You make deposits into your accounts with your children by spending time with them, by listening to your daughter when she's playing the piano, by going down to the park and watching your son skateboard.

A subtle yet amazingly effective means of making a deposit is by overlooking a fault. Maybe a coworker is rude to you and he jumps down your throat about some meaningless matter. Instead of retaliating, you let it go. The next day when he apologizes, you say, "Don't even worry. I've already forgiven you. I didn't think twice about it. I knew that wasn't your normal self."

When you do such things, you make huge deposits into your account with that person. Your stock goes up significantly on his scale. Perhaps one day when you're a bit stressed and on edge, and maybe you don't treat him as well as you normally would, you'll have plenty in your account to cover it.

How do we make withdrawals from our relationship accounts? The most common way of making withdrawals is through selfish behavior. When we're thinking only about what we want and what we need, we will inevitably withdraw resources from our relationship accounts. We make withdrawals when we don't take time for people. You go into the office and you just blow past the receptionist. You don't smile or even notice her. Whether your mind was somewhere else or you were simply being rude is irrelevant. You just made a withdrawal from your account with that person; you lowered her opinion of you.

Other ways of making withdrawals include those incidents in which we don't forgive, when we don't keep our commitments, when we don't express appreciation to someone to whom it is due. Maybe somebody does something nice for you by going out of her way, but you take it for granted. You don't say thank you; you're too busy or, worse yet, maybe you feel that you're too important to say something such as, "I appreciate your effort." Failure to appreciate the kindnesses of others will always result in a withdrawal from your account with those people.

The problem in many of our relationships is that our accounts are overdrawn. When we make a mistake and we need a little mercy, understanding, or the benefit of the doubt, that person goes to our relationship account and discovers it is already empty. Now we must live constantly on edge. Minor issues become magnified. We have to guard every little word that we say, because there's no reservoir of grace from which to draw in that relationship. We've exhausted the resources. And that's when little things suddenly turn into big things.

For instance, you correct your teenage son, and seemingly out of the blue, he blows up on you. "Who are you to tell me that?" he rails. "I don't have to listen to you."

Through such statements he is revealing that your relationship account with him is depleted. "You haven't built in trust recently. You haven't taken an interest in me; you haven't let me know that I am important to you."

He's saying, "You're trying to make a withdrawal, but there's nothing in the account, because you haven't made any recent deposits."

That situation doesn't come about overnight. The teenager doesn't wake up one morning and decide he doesn't have any respect for his parents. Rather, through the years he's not been getting what he needs. The deposits in the account between the teenager and his parents have been drained.

If you're going to correct someone, or maybe you're going to offer some constructive criticism, you need to make sure that you've made plenty of deposits into your account with that person. Make sure you've earned that person's respect.

In disciplining your children, ask yourself, "Have I encouraged him? Have I complimented her? Have I been interested in what he's interested in, or have I simply been making withdrawals?" If all your child has heard for the last couple of months is "Clean your room, do your homework, take out the trash, tuck your shirt in, be home by ten . . ." you are merely making withdrawals. And let's face it: Parents must make many withdrawals during their children's teenage years, but you cannot expect to speak effectively into your child's life unless you have first made plenty of deposits. You must invest in that relationship, nurture it, and build trust.

A dad was having a terrible time with his teenage son. They just couldn't seem to get along. They couldn't connect with each other and had little in common. The son was a star athlete, but the dad was more interested in his own career. He was working all the time, and hardly saw any of his son's ball games. Over time, their relationship deteriorated.

One day, the dad recognized that he had to make some changes. He realized if he was ever going to earn his son's respect, and be able to speak into his life, he needed to start making some deposits. He knew that his son was a huge baseball fan, so even though the dad didn't care for baseball, he decided to take a whole month off work and take his son to see every Major League Baseball team play. It was expensive and time-consuming as they traveled to numerous cities all across America. But it was a priceless time of healing, a time when their emotional accounts were replenished. That month-long trip was the catalyst that began a turnaround in that father-son relationship.

When the dad got back home, one of his business partners found out what he had done. He was shocked that this father had put forth such an enormous effort and expense to attend the baseball games with his son. He asked his partner, "Do you really love baseball that much?"

The dad said, "Not at all, but I really love my son that much."

Start investing in your children. You may not be able to do what this man did, but you can take time for your son, let your daughter know that you care. Keep those emotional accounts maxed out.

Deposit Before Withdrawing

It's amazing how people will respond when they know that you're rooting for them, that you are in their corner, wanting them to do well. Oftentimes, they will be willing to change when they know you're not trying to condemn them, that you are not trying to put them down or make them feel bad about themselves. True correction always inspires people to want to do better.

Often after one of our services at Lakewood Church, or at one of our special events around the country, Victoria and I will talk candidly about how things went and what we could have done better. When I have what I think is a good suggestion or some constructive criticism, I don't just get in the car and blurt it out. "Well, Victoria, if you'd have said this or that, things would have been better; if you'd have just done it my way." No, when I have a suggestion that I feel would help her, I always start off with something positive. I'll tell her, "Victoria, you did great up there. You spoke into the people's lives. This point was so good. That was clear and helpful, but maybe next time you could add this, and it would be more effective. You would do even better." When I begin with something positive, the defenses come down, and she's willing to consider my suggestion. She does something similar with me when she notices some area in which I can improve. Rather than condemning each other, we've chosen to encourage each other.

The first thirty seconds of a conversation will determine the next hour.

If you'll make it a priority to keep your emotional accounts full in your relationships, you will have far fewer problems with people receiving suggestions and receiving correction from you. In fact, one expert says the first thirty seconds of a conversation will determine the next hour. So when you have something sensitive to talk about, when you have something that has potential to cause conflict or problems, always start positively. Make sure it is the right time to broach that matter. Make sure that you've thought about how you're going to start the conversation and be aware of your voice tones. Watch your body language. Keep a pleasant expression, and choose to discuss the matter in love.

When you are trying to improve a relationship, if your words or actions cause the other person to become defensive, you've defeated your purpose. They are not going to receive what you have to say. They may get their feelings hurt, or they'll start pointing out your faults. "Well, who are you to tell me that?" he or she may retort. "You're no better than I am! Do you think you're perfect?" If you approach matters in a better way, all that turmoil can be avoided.

Studies show that it takes five positive charges to override one negative charge. In other words, before you correct someone, make sure that you have already given that person five compliments. Sadly, the correction-to-compliment ratio is nearly opposite that in our society today. We hear five things we're doing wrong to every one thing that we're doing right. No wonder our relationships are not what they should be! Our accounts are overdrawn.

It takes five positive charges to override one negative charge.

When we correct people, we should never belittle them or make them feel insignificant. At the office, don't have the attitude, "How could you come up with that? Whose lousy idea was this?" Instead, do your best to find the good in every suggestion, even if you can't use it.

Sometimes, in our organization, somebody may start a new project and it simply doesn't work; it doesn't catch on. We know that we are going to have to discontinue it. However, when that happens, I always go overboard to let the people involved know that I have initiated plenty of projects that haven't worked. For one reason or another, some program that I really thought would fly never made it off the ground. I want my coworkers to know that I'm right there with them. We should never make people feel small for having attempted something great and failing. We should never talk down to someone, whether it is a spouse, a coworker, or a child. Treat people with respect.

Remember, genuine love overlooks a fault. Love makes allowances for mistakes. True love sees the best in every person. If you want to make a huge deposit into somebody's life, when he makes a mistake and he knows he is wrong, don't make a big deal about it. Don't embarrass a child in front of other family members or friends. Don't embarrass an employee in front of his or her coworkers. If you must confront them about a matter, deal with them in private if at all possible, and always do your best to protect their dignity. It does not do anything positive to show somebody up or to humiliate someone in front of others.

Occasionally, you may be tempted to pay back a person for something painful that he or she did to you, but if you succumb to that temptation, in the long run, you will lose out in that relationship. When you embarrass somebody that you could have easily covered for, it will drain your account with that person and destroy any sense of trust and loyalty that existed between the two of you.

Years ago when Colin Powell worked for President Ronald Reagan, he and several other cabinet members came up with a new policy. They were excited about it and went to a meeting with President Reagan to explain the details.

General Powell felt strongly about it because it was his idea, so he was selling the program to the best of his ability. He told President Reagan how helpful the new system could be, but President Reagan wasn't convinced. He saw what he thought were some major flaws in the policy, and he debated Colin Powell back and forth for some time. Finally, even though President Reagan disagreed, he decided to trust General Powell and he accepted the new policy.

Unfortunately, it was a big mistake. The policy totally failed and created a huge mess. At a press conference, President Reagan was questioned about what went wrong. After intense grilling of the president, a reporter finally asked the question that General Powell was hoping wouldn't be asked: "President Reagan, tell us, was this new policy your idea?"

Without hesitation President Reagan said, "I take full responsibility for it." General Powell stood on the side of the room, and when President Reagan looked over at him, the general had tears in his eyes.

President Reagan had just made a huge deposit into his account with Colin Powell. The president had protected Powell's reputation and covered a mistake. As General Powell was leaving the room, he told one of the other cabinet members, "I'll do anything for that man."

If you want to build lifelong, loyal friendships, if you want to build trust, learn to protect your family members and friends even when they make mistakes. Learn to show mercy. Take the heat even though it wasn't your fault. Do your best to protect a reputation. Don't embarrass somebody when you have the opportunity or wherewithal to build up that person.

Certainly, we are not to condone evil or to cover intentional wrongdoing. But whenever it is simply a mistake or a failure on the part of somebody with whom we share an account, do your best to guard that relationship carefully and with integrity.

Everywhere we go we should be making deposits—whether at the grocery store, ballpark, school, or office. Develop a habit of sowing good things into people's lives. Make it your business to help somebody else feel better about himself or herself. Be interested in people. Take time to let someone know that you care. Go out of your way to show somebody that he or she is special. When you leave the office, instead of rushing out of the parking garage, take a few moments to ask the attendant, "How are you doing today? How are you feeling? I'm so glad you are part of this company." Encourage him in some way; make him feel important; help him to know that somebody cares.

Learn to appreciate people. Learn to say thank you. Just because somebody works for you doesn't mean you are exempt from expressing appreciation to that person. "Well, Joel, I pay him good money. I pay her good money. I shouldn't have to coddle him or her." Or "I pay high enough taxes. I shouldn't have to thank that policeman. I shouldn't have to thank that schoolteacher. They should do their jobs." No, learn to sow positive deposits into people's lives.

A while back, I was working at my house out in the yard. It was a hot, humid morning, so I decided to go inside and get some water. On my way, I noticed the garbagemen working their way down the street collecting trash. I thought, *I'll get a couple of extra bottles of water and give some to them.* When they came by our home, I ran out and gave them that water. The response was surprising. You would have thought I had given each of them a hundred-dollar bill. They were so thankful. I didn't think much about it at the time; it was no big deal. But I had just made a deposit into that account.

A few months passed, and one day, Victoria and I were late in getting our trash out. The sanitation truck came by early in the morning and we missed it. I didn't want the trash in the garbage cans to stay out on the street for three or four days, but there was not much I could do about it.

Later that day, those garbage men made a special trip back by our house to see if we'd put our trash out before they went to the dump. That sort of unanticipated, reciprocal help happens frequently when you make deposits into people's lives.

Don't make the mistake of living your life self-centered, rushing through your day concerned only about yourself. Take time for people; make them feel special; learn to appreciate them. When you see your mailman dropping off the mail, call out to him, "Hey, thank you. I appreciate that." When you go to the grocery store, encourage the cashier. Be friendly. Sow a seed with the bank teller, the woman who cuts your hair, the man at the gas station; make a positive deposit in each of their lives as you pass their way.

"Why bother?" you may ask. "I'm never going to have a long-term relationship with them."

Maybe not, but as part of your relationship with God, you can still extend kindness and appreciation to every person you meet. The Scripture says, "We should encourage one another daily."[34] That means every day you should find somebody you can help build up. Each day look for somebody for whom you can make a deposit of encouragement. A simple compliment may turn somebody's whole day around. "You look great today. That color really looks good on you." Or you can tell somebody, "I appreciate you being my friend. That means a lot to me."

I remember when I was at my father's house and he would see the mailman coming, Daddy would get a big smile on his face, and he'd say, "Well, look-ee here, here comes the finest mailman in all the world." That mailman's countenance would light up. My father's simple compliment brightened the man's day. It didn't take a lot of effort; it didn't require much of Daddy's time. He had developed a habit of investing in people, in helping other people to feel better about themselves.

Your words have the power to put a spring in somebody's step, to lift somebody out of defeat and discouragement, and to help propel them to victory. A potentially uplifting deposit such as Daddy made in the life of that postman doesn't take much more than ten or fifteen seconds to make. Yet somebody in your realm of influence may need just such a fifteen-second investment in the account they share with you.

Understand that every person needs encouragement, no matter who he or she is or how successful they appear. Frequently, someone will tell me, "Joel, you've really helped me." Or "You've made such a difference in my life." Every time I hear a statement such as that, it encourages me to be better; it does something deep down on the inside of me that lets me know that my life has significance and that I've been able to make a difference in this world. Everyone you know needs that sort of encouragement.

Husband, your wife can never hear you say too many times, "You're beautiful. I think you're great. I'm so glad that you're my wife." Keep those emotional accounts growing.

Learn to give compliments freely. Learn to be friendly and avoid anything that exudes the attitude that you are so important that you can't take time for somebody who's not up to your level. Instead, make everyone you meet feel important; strive to make every person with whom you have contact feel special. After all, every person you meet is made in the image of God.

Victoria and I share a favorite restaurant, a place with great food, wonderful atmosphere, and valet parking. I noticed, however, that many customers drive up and toss their car keys to the parking attendants, treating them as though they were servants. I refuse to do that. Instead, I always make an effort to be friendly to the valet parking attendants. I'll take fifteen seconds or so and say, "How are you doing? How's everything been going?" It is amazing how that little bit of time and interest makes a deposit in the lives of those young men.

I've also noticed that when Victoria and I leave that restaurant, there may be five or ten people waiting for their cars, but somehow our car always seems to get to the doorway ahead of the others. It almost embarrasses me. I never ask the parking guys to do anything special for us, nor do we expect it. Yet they do it.

I'm convinced that people want to be good to you when you have sown good things into their lives. I probably haven't spoken to those young men more than five minutes in my whole lifetime, but they know I've made some deposits into my emotional account with them.

Rather than trying to figure out what everybody can do for you, start looking for things that you can do for somebody else. Make relational deposits wherever you go. Be a giver rather than a taker. As you do so, your relationships will not only get better, but you also will see God's favor in a greater way, and you will experience more of His blessings.

CHAPTER 15

Being Good to People

Do you want to get more out of life? Who doesn't, right? Okay, try this: Get up every day and rather than trying to be blessed, do everything in your power to be a blessing to someone else. If you will do that for six weeks—trying to be a blessing to someone every day—your life will be filled with so many blessings you won't be able to contain them all.

I've discovered that if I meet other people's needs, God will meet mine. If I make somebody else happy, God will make sure that I'm happy. Every day, we should look for opportunities to be good to people. Maybe you can buy somebody's lunch, or give someone a ride, babysit somebody's children, tip a little more than is expected. Get in a habit of doing some good for somebody every day. Don't make the mistake of living selfishly. That's one of the worst prisons you could ever live in. You were not created to be focused only on yourself. Almighty God made you to be a giver. The best way for you to be fulfilled is to get your mind off yourself and reach out to others.

If I meet other people's needs, God will meet mine.

Get up in the morning with the attitude, "Who can I be a blessing to today? Who can I encourage? Where is there a need that I can meet?"

I don't believe that we see enough good works today. We hear a lot about success and about the good things that God wants to do for us, but let's not forget we are blessed, so we can be a blessing. We are blessed so we can share God's goodness wherever we go. If you want to make an impact on somebody's life, you don't necessarily have to preach a sermon to that person; just be good to them. Your actions will speak much louder than your words. You can say, "I love you and I care about you," but we demonstrate true love by what we do.

If I love you, I'll go out of my way to help you. If I love you, I'll give you a ride to work or school, even though I have to get up earlier than usual to do it. If I love you, I'll babysit your children when I know that you're not feeling well. True love turns words and feelings into action.

Learn to be good to people in your everyday life. When you go to the lunchroom, bring your coworker back a cup of coffee. You may be thinking, *I'm not going to do that. He never does anything for me.*

Be bigger than that; do it unto God. Don't miss an opportunity to do something good for someone. On the freeway, when traffic backs up, let that car squeeze in front of you. At the grocery store, when you have a large basket full of groceries and the person behind you is carrying just a few, let him or her go ahead of you. In the parking lot, when you pull up to that last spot at the same time as another car, back up and let the other person have that space. Prefer them over you. Be good to them.

"Well, I thought that was God's favor, helping me beat them to the parking spot," you might say.

No, that's our old selfish nature wanting to be first. If you will be good to people, you will have more of God's favor than you will ever need.

When you are eating at a restaurant, be a good tipper. Please don't leave that young waitress a dollar bill when you just spent thirty dollars to eat. "But Joel, I shared my testimony. I invited her to come to church."

No, you canceled out your testimony with your lousy tip.

Victoria and I went to a restaurant where we had eaten a number of times before. We practically knew the menu by heart, and we knew exactly what we wanted. When we sat down, we ordered right away. I was hungry, but it seemed to take forever for the cooks to prepare our food. We waited and waited. It didn't make sense. The restaurant wasn't even busy. When the waitress finally brought the food, our order was incorrect. She returned my dinner to the kitchen, and it was another long delay. Finally, I got tired of waiting and began eating off Victoria's plate. It was the worst service that we'd ever had in that restaurant.

When it came time to pay the bill and leave a tip, I thought, *God, now You just saw what happened. And I know that You're a just God. Surely, You don't expect me to leave a good tip.*

Almost immediately, I knew I was wrong. I said, "Okay, God; how about five percent?"

Let me tell you a secret. Don't ever negotiate with God, because you will never win. I said, "Okay, God, how about ten percent, fifteen percent? That's the normal amount. God, You know that's the going rate. I should be able to do that." But I still didn't have any peace. I knew God was saying, "Don't miss this opportunity to do good. Don't miss this opportunity to show My mercy." We can be good to people when they're good to us. That's easy. But God wants us to be good to people even when they're not so good to us.

I eventually changed my attitude and thought, *I'm not just going to give this girl a tip, I'm going to sow a seed in her life. I'm going to go the extra mile and be good to her.* We left a twenty-dollar tip for a thirty-dollar meal. But we did it as sowing a seed.

A few weeks later, I received a letter from that young lady. I had no idea that she had recognized Victoria and me; she hadn't given us any indication that she knew us.

Her letter began by asking, "Do you remember me? I'm the girl who waited on you at what was probably your worst restaurant experience ever?"

I smiled as I read and thought, *I know exactly who you are.*

She went on to tell how she had been raised in a good Christian family. They went to church every Sunday, but in her late teens, her family was hurt by a leader in their congregation. Somebody did them wrong. Consequently, the entire family had given up on God and dropped out of church. Over the last year or two, however, they had been watching me on television. The waitress related in her letter, "I told my parents I know those people are real. Something on the inside tells me they're sincere and we need to get back in church."

She continued, "Joel, when you and your wife came in the restaurant, and we got your order all mixed up, most people would have really gotten aggravated and upset, but you two were so nice and kind. And on top of that, you left us that big tip." She said, "That confirmed what I already knew in my heart. I went home and told my parents what happened, and now we've gotten our lives back on track, and we're worshiping the Lord at Lakewood every Sunday morning."

When you show love, you are showing God to the world.

Learn to be good to people. That's one of the best witnesses we can possibly have. Now, when I tip people, I tell Victoria, "We're going to sow a seed into their life. Here's an opportunity to do good." When I leave that place, I want them to be able to say, "That couple sure is generous; they are good to people."

The world does not need to hear another sermon nearly as much as it needs to see one. Learn to give your time, your money, and an encouraging word; meet a need. When you show love, you are showing God to the world.

Don't worry about it if you don't get any credit. If that young lady hadn't written to Victoria and me, it wouldn't have mattered one bit. I would still feel that we did the right thing. When you let somebody in traffic in front of you, you may never see that person again. When you give somebody twenty dollars simply because you felt compassion in your heart, you may never hear back from them. That's okay; God is keeping the records. He sees every act of kindness you show. He sees every time you are good to somebody. He hears every encouraging word you speak. God has seen all the times you went out of your way to help somebody who never said thank you. Your good deeds do not go unnoticed by Almighty God.

In fact, the Scripture teaches that when you do things in secret, without getting any credit, you will receive a greater reward. It's one thing to make a big splash and let everybody know how generous you are, but if you really want to be blessed, do something good for somebody and don't tell anybody about it. Leave some cash in an unmarked envelope on the desk of that coworker who's struggling. At the restaurant, buy somebody's dinner and remain anonymous. Clean up the kitchen at the office and don't tell anybody that you did it. When you do things in secret, when nobody thanks you and you don't get any credit, you are sowing a seed for God to do great things in your life.

I want to be the kind of person that does good for people whether I get paid back or not, whether they say thank you or they don't. I don't want to do something kind so I can be seen. I don't want to do it so people can say, "Look how great he is." No, I want to do it unto God. I believe when we have that kind of attitude, we will see God's favor in ways we've never seen before.

At a tollbooth on a busy section of the freeway, instead of paying the normal one-dollar toll, a man often gave the clerk five dollars and paid for the next four cars behind him. When that next car pulled up, the clerk told the driver, "Your toll has already been paid by somebody in front of you." It happened so frequently that eventually, a reporter heard about the generosity and wrote about it in the news.

It's amazing how just one little act of kindness can brighten somebody's whole day. Who knows, maybe that person whose toll was paid was down and discouraged, or otherwise stressed out, but then the clerk said, "Your toll has been paid." Maybe the passengers in the four cars following the phantom toll payer were about to go home uptight and irritated, but suddenly, they were going home to be a better father or a better wife all because somebody sowed a seed, somebody didn't miss an opportunity to do good.

I wonder what our world would be like if every person would find some way to do good every single day. What would our cities be like? What would our offices be like? What would our schools be like if we made it a priority to brighten somebody else's day, to do something good for somebody else?

The Bible says, "Every opportunity we have we should do good to people."[35] That means we need to be proactive, on the lookout for opportunities. Who can I bless today? For whom can I do a favor? You can't sit back and wait for the need to come to you; go after it.

Be sensitive; pay attention to the people around you. If you see one of your friends wearing the same clothes over and over again, step up and say, "Let me give you a new suit or two." Or "Take this gift certificate and go get yourself some new clothes."

Maybe you overheard one of your coworkers saying, "Next week, I have to take my car in to the shop. I don't know how I'm going to get to work."

Tell your coworker, "Let me swing by in the mornings and pick you up."

"No, that's too far. My home is out of your way."

"It's okay; no big deal. I'll be glad to do it."

Listen to what people are saying around you.

Of course, we can't spend all our time and money like that. Most of us could probably do more than we are currently in this regard, though. The Scripture says people will know us by our fruit.[36] They're not going to know us by how many verses of Scripture we quote. They won't know us by how many bumper stickers we have on our car. People are going to know that we're believers when we meet real needs by doing good works.

You may have plenty of money. If so, when you see that single mom who's really struggling, why don't you pay her rent for a month or two? Tell her, "Let me pick up the car payment for the next several months. Let me lighten the load just a little." Jesus said, "When you do it to the least of one of these, it's like you're doing it unto Me." [37]

Moreover, it says in Proverbs, when you give to the poor, you are lending to God. You may not be able to do that, but you can babysit some children. Why don't you give a young couple or a single mom a break one night? Say, "You go do something special for yourself. Here's a gift certificate. You go up to the mall. You go get your nails done. You go get a massage, or whatever you want, but our family is going to keep your children tonight."

Perhaps you can be a mentor to a young man or young woman who doesn't have a positive role model in his or her life. That doesn't take a lot of money. It just takes time and somebody who cares, somebody who is willing to make a difference.

A young man who sings in our Lakewood children's choir comes from an extremely dysfunctional family. His father is in prison, his mother has a serious drug addiction, and he was not receiving the care and attention that he really needed. Somehow, one of our families at Lakewood came across the boy's path, and they took an interest in him. They had a son the same age as this young man, so they started taking the young man to church and showing him love. He began to see what a family was all about, as he received the love and attention that he needed. He'd never been to church before, but he loved coming to Lakewood. That was the highlight of his week. He couldn't wait till Sundays.

He eventually got involved in our children's choir and discovered that he loved to sing. Now the family that had taken an interest in the boy not only had to bring him to church on Sunday, but they also had to bring him back during the week for choir practice. It was more time, effort, and energy, but they never complained. They gladly did it. They were sowing into his life.

Unfortunately, that young man lost his mother in a tragic accident at home. She died right before his eyes. Of course, he was devastated and heartbroken. A couple of days after the funeral, the family members and relatives gathered in that home to try to figure out what they were going to do. But this young man was nowhere to be found. They finally went to his room and found his door closed. When they opened it, they discovered the young man listening to his choir tapes, practicing for his next song, getting ready for that next special.

When I heard about that incident, I wondered what that young man would have done had somebody not taken an interest in him. How would he have coped in that situation, if that surrogate family had not taken time to care? What if they had been too busy? What if they had the attitude, We'll take you to church, but we're not going to take you to choir practice; that's just asking too much.

No, they were willing to be inconvenienced. They sacrificed their own time and resources to help meet that boy's need. They took time to care, and that's what true living is all about. The closest thing to the heart of God is helping people who are hurting. If we're too busy for our friends and neighbors, and for the less fortunate, then we're too busy. Our priorities are out of line.

The Scripture says that in the last days the love of the great body of people will grow cold.[38] That simply means that people will be so busy, they'll be so focused on their own needs, they'll be so caught up in their drive for success they won't take time to make a difference.

Friend, don't let that description apply to you. All around you people are hurting. They need your love and your encouragement. Don't miss the miracle of the moment. You may have someone in your life right now who needs your time and energy. Are you paying attention?

Maybe one of your coworkers is just about on the brink of giving up. He desperately needs your encouragement. She needs you to take her to lunch and let her know that you care. Don't be too busy. Don't be insensitive to the needs around you. Be willing to be inconvenienced.

When you study the life of Jesus, you'll notice that He always took time for people. He was busy. He had places He wanted to go, but He was always willing to change His plans to do good for somebody else. As He walked through the villages, people called out to Him, "Jesus, please come over here and pray for us." He would stop and go out of His way to bring healing to those people. One time they came up to Him and said, "Jesus, please come to our city, our relative is so sick. You've got to pray for him." Jesus changed His plans and went that way.

When they tried to bring the little children to Jesus, the disciples said, "No, don't bother Him. He's busy. He's too important."

Jesus said, "No, no; let the children come to Me."

It's so easy for us to get caught up in our own little worlds and focus only on ourselves. "I've got my plans. Don't get me off my schedule." Instead, take time for people. Don't miss any opportunities to do good. Make a difference in somebody's life. It doesn't have to be something big. Often, small gestures of love and kindness can make a big difference. A women's group at our church makes blankets, and then the women embroider Scripture verses on them and take them to cancer patients at M. D. Anderson Cancer Center, in Houston. Those handmade blankets remind the men and women struggling with cancer that somebody cares; the expression of love gives them an extra ray of hope. Those ladies are using their talents to do something good for somebody else.

You may not have a lot of extra money, but maybe you can make a blanket or bake a cake. You can mentor a young man. You can visit the nursing home. You can get involved in a prison outreach and encourage the inmates to trust God. Do something good for somebody.

O. A. "Bum" Phillips, the legendary NFL football coach, retired from the game a number of years ago, but Phillips isn't really retired. He's at the prisons every chance he gets, encouraging the prisoners and giving them hope. That's what life's all about—doing something good for somebody else. John Bunyan, the author of the classic *Pilgrim's Progress,* said, "You have not lived today until you have done something for someone who can never repay you."

"But, Joel, I bought this book to find out how I could get blessed," you may be saying. "I wanted how to find out how I could get my needs met."

Friend, this is exactly how it happens. If you will meet somebody else's needs, God will meet yours. What you make happen for others, God will make happen for you. When I start to feel discouraged or down, or feeling as though I have the weight of the world on my shoulders, I go up to the hospital and pray for people. I find when I start giving encouragement, giving people hope, my joy quickly returns. It changes my focus.

A while back, I was at one of the hospitals praying for a family. As I left their room, four or five people came up to me and asked me to go into their loved ones' room and pray for them. I gladly did it. One family member asked, "Would you go in there and pray for our father?"

"Sure I will," I said, "but why don't you come with me?"

They said, "No, we'll wait out here, if you don't mind." I went in and talked with the man and treated him as if he were my best friend. I prayed a strong prayer over him. When I came out of the room, his family was so surprised. One of them said, "Joel, we can't believe that he let you pray for him. He makes fun of us for watching you on television."

I thought, *If I had known that earlier, I might have prayed differently!* Regardless of what he thought of me, I was refreshed by praying for him.

There are two kinds of people in this world: givers and takers. Be a giver and not a taker. Make a difference in somebody's life.

You are never more like God than when you give.

I heard a story about a young boy who lived in the inner city. He was about eight years old, and his family was extremely poor. One cold fall day, he was up at the local store looking in the window admiring a pair of tennis shoes. As he stood there, cold and barefoot, a lady came along and said, "Young man, what are you doing staring so intently in this window?"

Under his breath, and almost shyly, he said, "Well, I was just sort of praying and asking God if He'd give me a new pair of tennis shoes."

Without hesitation, the woman took him into the store and very gently and lovingly washed his cold dirty feet. Then she put a brand-new pair of socks on him and told him to pick out three new pairs of tennis shoes. He couldn't believe it. He was so excited. He had never owned a new pair of shoes. He'd always worn hand-me-downs.

After the woman paid for the purchases, she returned to the little boy. He looked at her in disbelief. Nobody had ever taken that kind of interest in him. With tears running down his cheeks, he said, "Lady, can I ask you a question? Are you God's wife?"

Friend, you are never more like God than when you give, when you take time for people, when you do something good for somebody who can never repay you. Don't get sucked into society's narcissistic way of thinking—it's all about me, me, me! You will never be happy catering to yourself. Real joy comes as you give your life away.

Do you really want to be a better you? Make a decision with me that you're going to start being good to people. Pay attention to those around you—your friends, coworkers, relatives, even strangers. Listen to what they're saying. Be sensitive and don't miss any opportunity to do good. Remember, true love is always backed up with actions.

ACTION POINTS

PART 3: DEVELOP BETTER RELATIONSHIPS

1. I will help somebody else become successful and trust God to make me successful. This week I will build up, encourage, or otherwise improve the lives of at least three people.

2. I will (on purpose) find somebody that I can be good to today. I will attempt to make somebody's day. I will look for ways to be a blessing, especially to someone who cannot repay me.

3. I will be determined to keep strife out of my home. I will remind myself regularly:

   "I am a peacemaker, not a troublemaker."

   "I will overlook minor matters and I will forgive quickly."

   "I choose to see the best in other people."

   "I appreciate my spouse, my family members, my friends, and my coworkers."

4. Today I will make relational deposits in the lives of people around me. I will give compliments freely and seek to make every person I meet feel important.

PART FOUR

FORM BETTER HABITS

CHAPTER 16

Feed Your Good Habits

An old Cherokee tale tells of a grandfather teaching life principles to his grandson. The wise old Cherokee said, "Son, on the inside of every person a battle is raging between two wolves. One wolf is evil. It's angry, jealous, unforgiving, proud, and lazy. The other wolf is good. It's filled with love, kindness, humility, and self-control.

"These two wolves are constantly fighting," the grandfather said.

The little boy thought about it, and said, "Grandfather, which wolf is going to win?"

The grandfather smiled and said, "Whichever one you feed."

Feeding unforgiveness, impatience, low self-esteem, or other negative traits will only make them stronger. For instance, maybe you complain frequently about your job. You're always talking negatively about your boss, how that company doesn't treat you right, and how you can't stand the drive to work. Ironically, when we complain, we feel a sense of release. It feels good to feed those negative thoughts. But the wolf we feed will always want more.

The next time you are tempted to complain, ask yourself, "Do I really want to keep feeding this negative habit?" "Do I really want to stay where I am?" Or, "Do I want to starve this complaining spirit and step up higher?"

If you will start feeding peace, patience, kindness, gentleness, humility, and self-control, you will see those character traits developing in your life. Make the better choice and instead of complaining about going to work, learn to say, "Father, I thank you that at least I have a job. And these people may not be treating me right, but I'm not working for man; I'm working unto You." When you do that, you're feeding the right thing and the new habit develops.

A habit is an acquired, learned behavior that we do without even thinking about it. It's almost involuntary. We've done it so much it becomes practically second nature. If we have good habits, that may be fine. But sometimes our habits are keeping us from God's best, and we may not even realize it.

Many of the habits that we've developed stem from the culture in which we were raised. If you grew up in a home where people were disorganized, sloppy, or perpetually late, you may have formed some of those same negative habits. Or if you were raised around people who tended to be harsh, sarcastic, or rude, you may have picked up some of that same behavior. You may not even realize that such attitudes and behaviors are offensive, since that is all you've ever known.

On the other end of the spectrum, some people grow up around people with positive habits such as neatness, godliness, cleanliness, and order. Many people have established positive habits concerning diet and exercise. Other individuals have a habit of getting up at a particular time and going to bed at a time that will allow his or her body to rest and be refreshed. These are positive learned behavior patterns.

Your habits—whether good or bad—will greatly determine your future. One study says that 90 percent of our everyday behavior is based on our habits. Let that sink in for a moment: From the time we get up in the morning to the time we go to bed at night, 90 percent of what we do is habitual behavior. That means how we treat people, how we spend our money, what we watch, what we listen to—90 percent of the time, we're on autopilot. We do what we've always done. It is no wonder that if you want to change your life, you must start by consciously changing your everyday habits. You can't keep doing the same things you have been doing and expect to get different results.

To become a better you, take inventory of your habits. Do you have a tendency to be negative in your thoughts and conversations? Are you always late to work? Do you worry all the time? Do you overeat? Do you regularly succumb to addictions?

Understand, your habit may not be legally, ethically, or morally wrong. It can be a seemingly innocuous action or attitude, a little thing, but if you don't do something about it, you can go for years wasting time and energy, being unproductive and unprofitable. That is not God's best.

The good news is you can change. You can develop better habits. Most studies of habitual behavior indicate that a habit can be broken in six weeks; some studies tell us that you can break a habit in as little as twenty-one days. Think about that. If you will discipline yourself for a month or so, and be willing to suffer through the pain of change, you can rid yourself of a negative behavior, form a new healthy habit, and rise to a new level of personal freedom.

The Apostle Paul said, "All things are permissible to me, but not all things are profitable. All things are lawful, but I will not be mastered by anything." Notice, Paul is saying in effect, "I'm going to rid myself of anything that is not profitable or productive in my life." He was saying, "I'm not going to stay under the control of any bad habits."

It's a fact: Successful people develop better habits. That's why even professional golfers practice hitting golf balls nearly every day. Some pros hit as many as five hundred to a thousand balls a day when they are not competing in tournaments. They work for hours to repeat their golf swing so they can do it without even thinking about it. Then, when they get in a tournament under intense pressure, their bodies perform the correct swing almost automatically. No wonder those golfers are successful! They have formed successful habits.

If you have a bad habit of not getting to work on time, change that behavior. People who get ahead in life are usually punctual. Get up fifteen minutes earlier on days you must go to work, attend school, or go to a meeting. Plan your travel so you can arrive with time to spare. Establish a new routine of being on time. Don't allow yourself to be late when punctuality is such an easy habit to develop.

People who get ahead in life usually get there on time.

Or if you have a habit of eating a bunch of junk food and drinking several sodas every day, commit yourself to forming better eating habits. Don't go on a crash diet; just change one small thing at a time. Before long, you will notice a marked difference in your energy level as well as your personal appearance.

Our habits become part of our character. If you allow yourself to be disorganized or you are always running late, that becomes a part of who you are. If you've trained yourself to get upset and have a fit whenever you don't get your way, unfortunately those bad habits become a part of you, too. The first step toward changing is to identify what's holding you back. Identify any bad habits and then make a decision to do something about them.

How do we change a habit? Simple: Quit feeding the bad habit. You have to starve your bad habits into submission and start nourishing your good habits.

I heard somebody say, "Bad habits are easy to develop but difficult to live with." In other words, it's easy to pop off and be rude, saying whatever you feel and making snide, cutting, sarcastic remarks. That's easy. But it's difficult to live in a home filled with strife and tension.

It's easy to spend money that we don't have and charge everything on our credit cards. It's hard to live with the pressure of not being able to pay our bills. It's easy to give in to temptation and do whatever we feel. It's difficult to live in bondage, feeling guilty and condemned.

Consider a person with a chemical addiction. It is easy to get hooked. It may seem fun and exciting at first. Before long, however, that addiction controls the person. He becomes a slave to it. Bad habits are easy to acquire but hard to live with.

On the other hand, good habits are difficult to develop. A good habit results from a desire to work and sacrifice, and sometimes a willingness to endure pain and suffering. But good habits are easy to live with. For instance, at first it's hard to hold your tongue and overlook an offense when someone criticizes or insults you. It's hard at first to forgive. But it sure is easy to live in a home filled with peace and harmony.

If you are willing to be uncomfortable for a little while, so you can press past the initial pain of change, in the long run, your life will be much better. Pain doesn't last forever; in fact, once you develop the new habit, the pain often disappears.

Victoria knows that I won't argue with her. We don't allow strife and conflict in our home. In our marriage, it's not hard for me to overlook things or to forgive an offense, because I've simply trained myself to be a peacemaker. I've trained myself to apologize even when it's not my fault, which of course is every time we have a disagreement!

However, in the early years of our marriage, I didn't respond that way. Instead, I'd put up a good argument, and I'd tell her what I thought and the way I felt it should be. One day I realized, *That's not the way God wants me to live.* That's not His best. I could hear the still, small voice down inside, saying, "Joel, let it go. You're better than this. Don't live on this low level."

I recognized that I had to make a decision: Did I want to prove I was right, or did I want to have peace in our home? I began to change, and relinquishing my right to fight gradually got easier. Today, it's not difficult at all for me to be easygoing; it has become part of my character. It's natural to me. Truth is, I could still be floundering where I was twenty years ago, when Victoria and I first married: arguing, pouting when I didn't get my way, and always wanting to have the last word.

Thankfully, I developed better habits. I pressed past the pain of change and today I can say it has been worth it. Sure, I have other areas in which I need to improve—maybe one or two!

If you, too, will press past the initial pain—whether it takes a week, a month, or a year—eventually the pain will go away, and you will not only enjoy your life a lot more, but you'll be living at a much higher level.

Delayed Reactions

The subtle danger associated with many bad habits is that we may not suffer their consequences until later on in life. If you abuse your body with tobacco or alcohol, it may be years before you develop cancer, emphysema, or cirrhosis of the liver. If you mistreat your body by eating poorly and working long hours all the time, getting insufficient nutrition and rest, you may get away with it for a while, but one day those bad habits will catch up with you. If you're rude and harsh to your family, friends, and coworkers, they may put up with it now, but one day you could be a very lonely person. People may tolerate your insolence for a season, but eventually your relationships will suffer.

Usually, when we consider habits, we tend to think of destructive patterns such as drug addictions, alcoholism, or some other kind of abuse. Yet the habits that are likely to make or break most people are much more mundane. Look at your everyday habits. If you waste four or five minutes each day trying to find things that you have misplaced—your keys, cell phone, glasses, notebook, or something else—at the end of a year, you will have wasted almost a week of your life. The Bible tells us to make the most of our time. Living sloppy and disorganized is not being a good steward of the time that God has given to you.

I heard somebody say, "Habits are like gravity; they will always pull you toward them." If you develop good habits, they'll make your life easier, more successful, and more productive. You won't be struggling constantly to do the right thing. When you practice good habits, your life will produce good fruit. You'll be happy, naturally, and you will experience God's abundant life. But if you establish bad habits, they will inevitably drag you down. You'll gravitate toward them.

Certainly, if you've been set in your ways for twenty or thirty years, you may not overcome that habit you want to change in a mere twenty-one days. But if you will make up your mind, and ask God for His help in breaking that habit, it won't take you years to do it either. Make a decision to change, stick with it, and you will be amazed how soon you begin to form that new habit. It will get easier every day, to the point when, eventually, you'll do the right thing automatically. You won't even have to think about it.

When Victoria and I first got married, we often misplaced our car keys. I'd come home and put them on the table, or maybe take them up to the bedroom with me. Victoria might leave them in her purse or put them in the kitchen. It seemed like every time we got ready to leave, we'd have to search to find the car keys. One day, I realized how much time we were wasting. I found a hammer and two little nails and

I pounded those nails right inside a cabinet by our back door so we could hang our keys on them. The next few times I came home, I did the same thing as I'd always done. Without even thinking about it, I took the keys up to our bedroom or left them in my gym bag. I had to remind myself, *Go back downstairs, and put the keys where they now belong, on the tiny nails in the closet.* I did this day after day after day.

Changing a habit is not easy at first, but eventually, once you retrain yourself, the new habit comes naturally. Now, Victoria and I don't even think about where we are supposed to keep our car keys. When we go home, we go right to the cabinet and hang up the keys. A habit works that way whether positively or negatively. Repeated behavior tends to become almost automatic.

Friend, don't stay stuck in a bad habit. Make a decision that you are going to develop better habits. To change, you must be consistent. You have to do it day in and day out. You need to have a "no exceptions" policy. That means no matter how you feel, no matter how much you want to go back to your old ways, you're going to stick with your new plan. No exceptions.

A second key to change is that you must be willing to press past the pain and discomfort at the beginning of your new regimen. After all, if you've trained your body in a certain way year after year, you've developed behavior patterns to which you have grown accustomed. Don't be surprised if your own body revolts against you when you try to establish new patterns. But if you will discipline yourself and stand your ground, in a few months, you can form new habits and your life will be much more rewarding.

For a runner preparing to race in competition, the first few days of conditioning are awful. His stomach wrenches, his legs ache, and at every turn the temptation to quit looms. As he conditions his body day after day, he is able to run farther, faster, with less fatigue and fewer interruptions in his progress.

Understand, once you get past that initial pain, establishing the new and better pattern will be much easier. Think of a rocket being launched into space. Liftoff takes an enormous amount of thrust. The majority of the energy expended in that launch is spent as the spacecraft breaks free of earth's gravitational pull. Once it pushes into outer space, it is much easier to keep moving forward. In the same way, when it comes to breaking habits, if you can just get past the first few weeks, it will get easier, and one day you will be home free.

Think about all the people you know who are trying to lose weight. The diet business is a multibillion-dollar industry nowadays. Although diets can be helpful at times, the long-term solution to keeping your weight under control is not to run from one new "wonder" diet to another. Most of the success achieved by those kinds of diets is temporary. Unfortunately, most dieters end up regaining that weight—and more!

The better way to get your weight under control and maintain it is to establish new habits. Start exercising, start watching what you eat, when you eat, and how much you eat. Granted, it's not always easy; especially at first, you will have to be extremely disciplined. Every time you resist a temptation, every time you make a better choice, it will get easier. One day, you'll notice that you are living a healthier and more productive life.

Remember, in forming a new habit, it is always the most difficult at the beginning. You'll be tempted to turn around or to return to your old routine, but you don't have to give in.

You may say, "But Joel, I just couldn't live without that bowl of ice cream before I go to bed each night."

Yes, you *can* live without it, and you will probably live longer and better without it! If you are going to break that habit, the first step is to quit going into the kitchen late at night. The Bible says to run from temptation, so whether it is sexual temptation or sugar temptation, the key to success is the same: You have to stay far away from it!

When you go to the grocery store, don't even go down the aisle where all that delicious, *fattening* ice cream is hiding, waiting to seduce you. Don't make excuses such as, "Well, I'm just going to pick up this one half gallon of Cookies and Cream in case we have some guests come over."

No, you know you will be the only guest who eats that ice cream. Stay far away from it. Run from that temptation. Don't make eating right harder on yourself than it has to be. I'm teasing (a little), but seriously, you cannot mistreat your body and expect it to function the way God intended.

Time for a Change

Just as some people don't manage their diets well, others don't manage their time well. They're not living a balanced life; consequently they are stressed out, always run-down. They've gotten into a habit of overworking. They rarely relax; they hardly ever exercise. They never take any free time for themselves. Unless they make changes and bring some balance into their lives, one day, that's going to catch up to them. You can live stressed out for a while, especially when you're young. But don't be surprised when your body suffers the consequences.

It's much better to develop good habits right now. Look at the way you live, and ask, "Why am I doing what I'm doing? Is this something that's been passed down to me by my family? Is this a good habit? Is it helping me become a better person?" If, in your analysis, you discover some habits that are not productive or profitable, dare to make the changes that will help you to replace them. Make sure that you're not allowing anything but God to master you.

I'm familiar with a woman who was trying to quit smoking, after having been addicted to cigarettes for many years. She was determined that "this time" she was going to stop. And she did well for several weeks. But one day, she had an argument with her husband. She became aggravated and upset, so she went down to the store and bought a package of cigarettes. She thought, *I'll show him, I'm going to smoke this whole pack!*

But when she started to light up the first cigarette, something down inside her said, "You are about to waste all you've been through. If you smoke that cigarette, you will have to start all over and retrain yourself from the beginning, just because you can't control your emotions."

When she thought about the toil and discipline it had taken to kick the habit, and about all she had been through, and how much she had already endured to get to that point, she made a decision.

She put down those cigarettes and determined never to pick them up again.

You will always have plenty of excuses and rationalizations why you should not change. You can usually find a reason to give up, turn around, go back, and keep living the same way you've always lived. Don't be surprised when you are tested. Simply remember that the Scripture says, "There is no temptation that will come to you that you can't overcome. God will always make a way of escape." [39] No matter how intense the pressure, or how difficult it seems, you need to know that you can withstand it. God will help you. He will make a way of escape, but you must take it.

It's not so much that we *break* bad habits; we must *replace* them.

If you see an area where you're not responding in a positive manner, don't make excuses. Take responsibility and say, "I recognize what's happening and I choose to change. I'm going to develop better habits."

In reality, it's not so much that we *break* bad habits; we must *replace* them. In other words, if you have a problem with worry, and your mind is always racing ninety miles per hour—worried about your children, worried about your finances, worried about your health—you need to recognize that worry is a bad habit you've developed. It is hard to worry and trust God at the same time. God wants your mind to be at peace. You can rest assured, knowing that God has you in the palm of His hand. When you've been worrying for a long time, however, it's almost second nature to you; you don't even think about it. You just get up in the morning and start worrying about what the day will bring.

In most cases, you can't simply decide to stop worrying. You have to replace the negative thoughts with positive faith-filled thoughts. Then every time you're tempted to worry, use that temptation as a reminder to dwell on good things. The Scripture tells us to "Dwell on things that are pure, things that are wholesome, things that are of a good report." [40] If you will replace those thoughts of worry with thoughts of hope, faith, and victory, then you will retrain your mind.

Do that day in and day out, and before long, you will have formed a habit of dwelling on good things, and you'll have broken that old habit of worry.

The key to success is to find something with which you can replace the negative habit. If you habitually run to the kitchen and eat every time you are stressed out, find someplace else to go, something else to do. When you feel tense, go outside and take a walk. It doesn't have to be a two-mile jog. Simply walk around the block or down the street. When you come back, stay busy and stay out of the kitchen!

"Practice makes perfect," the saying goes. That may be so, but sometimes we practice the wrong things. I've had people tell me, "Joel, I'm just a real negative person. My parents were negative. My grandparents were negative. This is just who I am."

With all due respect, that's *not* who you really are. That's who you are *allowing* yourself to be. That is not the person God made you to be. God made you to be free. He didn't make you to be bound by addictions. He didn't make you to be disorganized, hot-tempered, frustrated, or negative. God made you as a person of excellence. He made you to be happy, healthy, and whole. But too often, we've developed wrong mind-sets. We tell ourselves, "I can't change. I can't break this habit." No, the problem is we're practicing the wrong things.

Interestingly, the Apostle Paul said in Romans, chapter 7, "The things I want to do I don't. And the things I don't want to do, I end up doing." Paul was struggling to do the right thing. In verse 19, he gives us insight into why he was having that struggle. He said, "For I failed to practice the things I desire to do." He was basically saying, I haven't developed good habits in these areas. I'm not practicing what I know I should be doing. Truth is, we are all practicing something, and the way to develop good habits is by practicing the right things. You may be good at losing your temper because you practice it a couple of times a week. Some people are good at being impatient because they practice it every morning on the drive to work. I know people who are good at being negative because they constantly practice negative thinking. Remember, repetition is what forms a habit. That's what puts us on autopilot. So we have to make sure we are practicing the right things.

For instance, every one of us should be practicing forgiveness. The next time somebody offends or hurts you, don't return evil for evil. Immediately forgive the person who hurt you; let it go and start practicing forgiveness.

Let's practice being disciplined in our spending and making good financial choices. Many people are way out of balance in their finances because they've developed bad habits, such as spending money that they don't have and charging purchases on their credit cards. It doesn't take a lot of wisdom to realize that paying twenty-some percent interest on a credit card is not a good thing.

I've heard people say, "Joel, I just can't make it without my credit cards. I can't live without them." You can make it, but you may be a little uncomfortable. You may have to suffer through that period of change. As my father often said, "Learn to sit on an apple box until you can afford a chair." What he was really saying was if you'll use what you have wisely, then God will give you more. Many people today are praying for a miracle; they're praying for a financial break-through. I say this respectfully, but often we don't really need a miracle, we just need to develop better spending and saving habits. I know some people—if God blessed them with a million dollars tomorrow, a year from now, they'd be in the same financial difficulty. They'd have the same problems. Why? They have not developed good spending and saving habits.

We need to think long and hard before we buy something that puts us deeply into debt. Do you really need that fancy car? Do you really need that extra toy? Financial counselors say that if we paid with cold, hard cash for everything we purchase, in a year we would save an average of $900. Why? When you dole out that money, one bill at a time, it makes you think, *Do I really want to give up my cash for this item?* Paying cash is a lot more thought provoking than simply swiping a credit card through a scanner.

Keep in mind, financial pressure is usually listed as one of the top three reasons why modern marriages fall apart. If you want your marriage to last, develop good spending and saving habits. It is never too late to start doing the right thing. If you'll do your part, God will do His. He will promote you; He'll give you increase, but first you must be a good caretaker of what you have.

A young couple at Lakewood had about $40,000 in credit card debt. They were embarrassed and distraught over it. They didn't see any way out. In the natural, it looked impossible.

Then one day, they took a step of faith; they swallowed their pride and met with one of our financial counselors at the ministry. That counselor studied their finances and gave them instructions in how they could overcome their financial problems, step by step.

The couple committed themselves to getting out of debt, and for three years they didn't go out to eat, they didn't take vacations, they didn't buy extra clothes. They lived on a bare-bones budget. It was uncomfortable. It was a sacrifice.

But they were overturning years of wrong choices, forming better habits, and establishing a foundation for years of right choices. They quit using their credit cards. They learned the difference between their wants and their needs. They started practicing discipline and self-control. Three years later, that young couple is totally debt-free and God is blessing them. They're seeing increase and promotion. And it all started when they decided to form better habits. They drew a line in the sand and said, "That's it. We're not living like this anymore."

The first step to overcoming any habit or addiction is to identify what's holding you back. But don't stop there. Make a decision to do something about it. Take action. Don't be too embarrassed to seek help. People struggle with chemical addictions, sexual addictions, and all sorts of other maladies. It may be an anger addiction. You just can't control your temper. Understand that you can change. Freedom is available. Don't believe the lie that you're stuck and you'll never get any better. God already has a path of success laid out for you.

But you must do your part and be willing to walk it out. The next time that temptation comes, the first thing you should do is pray. Get God involved in your situation. We cannot defeat bad habits in our own strength. Ask God to help you. When you feel your emotions getting out of hand, and you are tempted to rudely tell somebody off, pray right then and there, under your breath, "God, I'm asking You to help me. Give me the grace to keep my mouth closed and the courage to walk away."

The Scripture tells us, "Pray that you don't come into temptation." [41] It doesn't say, "Pray that you'll never be tempted." We're all going to face temptation. God says, "When that temptation comes, ask Me for my help." In any area that you're trying to change—even small things—seek His help. "God, I'm about to walk through this kitchen and I can smell the chocolate chip cookies, so I'm asking You to help me resist the temptation to break my diet." "Father, all my friends are going out partying tonight and I know down inside, it's not right. God, I'm asking You to help me make the best choice. Help me stay on Your best plan."

"Joel, that's difficult. It's hard not to go out with my friends, hard not to use my credit cards, hard not to speak my mind."

Yes, that's difficult. But living in bondage is even more difficult. Feeling bad about yourself because you know you're living below your potential is even harder. There's nothing worse than going through the day with little things holding you back that you know good and well you can beat.

Maybe you are struggling with addictions, or you battle with your temper or impatience. Possibly, you are living in mediocrity, simply because you are allowing something small to control you. Let me tell you what you already know: You are better than that. You are a child of the Most High God. You have His royal blood flowing through your veins. Don't just sit back and settle where you are. No obstacle in your life—large or small—is insurmountable. It doesn't matter whether it's a critical spirit or an addiction to cocaine, God's power in you is greater than the power that's trying to hold you back. Fight the good fight of faith. Don't let anything or anyone on earth master you. Your attitude should be, "That's it. I'm not staying where I am. I'm moving up higher. I know I'm better than this."

Tap into God's power within you and stop saying, "I can't break that habit." Instead, start declaring every day: "I am free. I can do all things through Christ. No weapon formed against me is ever going to prosper." Remember what Jesus said: "Whom the Son sets free is free indeed." Start declaring that over your own life.

It says in Philippians, chapter 2, we have to work out our salvation. That means we have all these good things on the inside, but we must do our part to see those things brought to fruition in our lives. You have the seed of Almighty God. He's already put in you self-control, discipline, kindness, forgiveness, patience, and more. Because of your faith in Him, these qualities are already in you, but it's up to each one of us to work it out. The good does not come into being automatically. It comes about only when we make good choices. Not once in a while, but consistently, over and over again.

My personality type is such that I am intensely goal oriented. I'm structured and organized. If I tell you I'm going to be somewhere at noon, I'm not going to be ten minutes late; I'm going to be ten minutes early. I'm disciplined when it comes to getting things done.

Even with the good in our personalities, there are always other areas that we have to work on. While I am naturally disciplined and focused, I'm not naturally patient. I don't like to wait. I like to get somewhere, get it done, and move on. It's easy for me to be impatient, so I realize that's an area I have to improve. I can't just sit back and say, "Well, I'm not a patient person; that's not the way God made me." No, I know patience is on the inside of me, but I have to do my part to work it out. Sometimes it's funny how God will use people and circumstances to try to help us come up higher.

For instance, the freeway system in Houston has taught me a whole lot about patience. I used to practice being stressed out and uptight every time traffic backed up. Now I've learned to relax, go with the flow, and stay in peace. I've worked some of that patience from the inside to the outside, to my thoughts, to my behavior, to my attitude.

Also God has used my beautiful wife, Victoria, to help me work out my salvation. When we first got married, and we were about to leave the house to go somewhere, I'd say, "Victoria, are you ready?"

She'd say, "Yes, I'm ready. I'll be right there."

With my personality type, I would get in the car and wait. After all, to me, "I'm ready" means we're leaving right now. But Victoria's personality is laid-back and easygoing; nothing's a big deal. She's the most patient person in the world. So when she says, "I'm ready," she means that as a relative term. She means, "I'm generally ready, so in the next ten or fifteen minutes, I'll begin to mosey my way toward the back door."

When this happened in the early days of our marriage, I used to sit in our car and get frustrated and aggravated. "I thought she said she was ready," I'd fume to myself. "When is she coming?"

Now, after more than twenty years of marriage, I've learned that when Victoria says, "I'm ready," it is similar to the two-minute warning in football. The clock says two minutes to go, but if you know anything about football, you understand that it is going to be at least another ten or fifteen minutes. Now, when Victoria says she's ready, I just go sit down, look over some sermon notes, watch television, or relax for a few minutes. I stay in peace, rather than getting uptight. God has used Victoria to bring patience out of me!

How did I develop patience? By practicing it. Over time, I developed better habits.

Maybe patience is not a problem for you; you may be the most patient person in the world. But you spend half your life discouraged and depressed. You too must work the joy from the inside to the outside. You need to get up in the morning and say with David, "This is the day that the Lord has made. I will rejoice and be glad. I'm going to be happy today." Focus on what's right; not on what's wrong. Work out your salvation. Don't believe those lies that you've given birth to before: "I just can't control my temper. I'm just hotheaded." No, self-control is in you; God put it in there. The problem is you just haven't worked it out yet.

The way you work it out is by exercising your muscles in that area. If you want to work out kindness, start by encouraging people. Start giving compliments. You can't sit back and wait for God to change you into a kind, loving person. You must work it out by developing a habit of being kind to people.

Moreover, we should always keep new goals in front of us. Our attitude should be, I'm going to practice treating my family better. I'm going to come up higher in how I honor and respect my spouse. I'm going to be more loving and generous to my children. Don't just work on overcoming bad habits; work on strengthening and improving good habits.

You may have some areas in your life that you need to get under control. God is saying, "Don't put it off any longer. Today is the day to start. Today can be a new beginning." If you'll take this to heart and be willing to press past the pain of change, a year from now, you won't be the same person. You'll be free from addictions, free from bad attitudes, free from the bondage that's been holding you back.

Make sure you are practicing the right things. Starve any bad habits and feed your good habits. If you do this, you will rise higher and God will pour out His blessings and favor in your life. Friend, don't let anything master you. Develop better habits. Get rid of anything that is not producing good fruit in your life.

Remember, your habits today will determine your future. Examine your life, take inventory of your habits, and when you find something that's not right, be quick to change. In the process, you will establish the habit of becoming a better you.

CHAPTER 17

Develop a Habit of Happiness

Many people don't realize that much of the manner in which we approach life—our attitudes, and our demeanor—is learned behavior. These habits have formed by repetition throughout the years. If we've spent years focusing on what's wrong rather than what's right, then these negative patterns are going to keep us from enjoying our lives.

We acquired many of our habits from our parents or from the people who were around us as we grew up. Studies tell us that negative parents raise negative children. If your parents focused more on what was wrong, living stressed out, uptight, or discouraged, there's a good possibility that you have developed some of those same negative mind-sets.

I often have people tell me, "Well, Joel, I'm just a worrier. I'm just uptight. I'm not a friendly sort of person."

No, please understand, those are habits that you have developed. And the good news is you can "reprogram" your own "computer." You can get rid of a negative mentality and develop a habit of happiness.

The Bible says, "Rejoice in the Lord always." [42] One translation simply says, "Be happy all the time." That means no matter what comes our way, we can have smiles on our faces. We should get up each morning excited about that day. Even if we are facing difficult or negative circumstances, we need to learn to keep a positive outlook. Many people are waiting for their circumstances to be worked out before they decide to be happy. "Joel, as soon as I get a better job; as soon as my child straightens up; as soon as my health improves."

No, the bottom line is if you're going to be happy, you need to make a decision to be happy right now.

Happiness does not depend on your circumstances; it depends on your will. It's a choice that you make. I've seen people go through some of the most awful, unfortunate situations, yet at the time you would never know they were having a problem. They had a smile on their face and a good report on their lips. In spite of their dire dilemmas, they remained positive, upbeat, and energetic.

**Happiness does not depend on your circumstances . . .
It's a choice that you make.**

Other people in similar circumstances—and some in far less severe situations—insist on wallowing in despair; they're down, depressed, discouraged, and worried. What makes the difference?

It's all in how they've trained their mind. One person has developed a habit of happiness. She is hopeful, trusting, believing for the best. The other person has trained his mind to see the negative. He's worried, frustrated, and constantly complaining.

If you are going to develop a habit of happiness, you must learn to relax and go with the flow, instead of getting frustrated. You have to believe that God is in control, and that means you have no need to be stressed out and worried. Moreover, you have to be grateful for what you have, rather than complaining about what you don't have. A habit of happiness boils down to staying on the positive side of life.

Each day is full of surprises and inconveniences, so you must accept the fact that not everything is going to always go your way. Your plans are not always going to work out just as you scheduled them. When that happens, make a willful decision that you are not going to let the circumstances upset you. Don't allow stress to steal your joy. Instead, be adaptable and adjustable and seek to make the best of a bad situation.

One of the best things I've ever learned is that I don't have to have my way to be happy. I've made up my mind that I'm going to enjoy each day whether my plans work out, or whether they don't.

Our attitude should be, *I'm going to enjoy today even if I have a flat tire on the way home. I'm going to enjoy each day even if it rains out my ball game. I'm going to be happy in life even if I don't get that promotion that I was hoping for.*

When you have that kind of attitude, minor irritations or inconveniences that may have stressed you out will cease to be a source of frustration. You don't have to live all uptight. Understand, you can't control people, nor can you change them. Only God can do that. If somebody is doing something that's getting on your nerves, you might as well leave that up to God. Quit allowing somebody else's quirk or idiosyncrasy to get the best of you.

If your husband is fifteen minutes late coming from work and dinner gets a little cold, that ruins your entire evening. No, don't be so rigid and set in your ways. Life is too short to live it stressed out. Besides, prolonged stress can damage your health and significantly shorten your life. I don't want to die early because I got upset every time I was stuck in traffic. I don't want to live with knots in my stomach because some person is not doing what I want him to do or because my big weekend was rained out.

It's not worth it. You can choose to be more flexible and have a more easygoing attitude. Think about this. Ten years from now, many of the things that you are allowing to create stress in your life won't even matter. You won't remember the fact that your golf game was rained out last Tuesday. You won't care that you were stuck in traffic.

One time, Victoria and I had the perfect vacation planned. We had been looking forward to it for several months. It was an opportunity for just the two of us to get away together and take a break for a few days. The closer I got to the vacation dates, the more excited I became. I had my tickets and I was ready to go.

My mother had been dealing with a hip problem due to a bout with polio she had suffered when she was a child. When the doctors had done their best to treat my mother with medicine, they decided that they were going to have to replace her hip, so they scheduled her for surgery. Something came up right at the last minute, and they had to reschedule that surgery. The postponed surgery date fell on the exact same day we planned to leave for our big trip. I had a tough decision whether I was going to go on vacation or stay home and take care of my mother. We decided to stay home. At first, we were disappointed; it was a bit of a letdown, but we decided that we weren't going to let that steal our joy.

Mother had the surgery, and that week while I was at the hospital visiting her, I must have prayed for twenty or thirty other people, too. At one point, I was going from hospital room to hospital room, as one family after another asked me to pray for their loved one. At the end of that week, I felt more refreshed and more relaxed than I would have had I gone on vacation.

We could have let that stress us. We could have said, "God, it's not fair. We had this planned for a long time. Why is this happening to us?"

Instead, we simply remained adaptable and adjustable. The Bible says in Romans 8:28, "That all things work together for good when you love the Lord." I don't know why Mother's surgery fell on the exact same day as our vacation. I don't know what all the factors were, but I do know this: God worked it out for our good. I know, too, even when my plans don't work out, even when things don't go my way, because I am honoring God and striving to keep the right attitude, God will make it up to me.

He'll do the same for you. When your plans don't work out, don't get negative and sour. Don't start complaining, "I can't believe this is happening to me. God, I just can't afford this delay." God may be protecting you from an accident. How do you know God has not allowed that delay so you can meet somebody He really wants you to know? Learn to go with the flow. Don't get upset and let minor interruptions steal your joy.

Sometimes our plans may be interrupted because God has somebody He wants us to touch or something special He wants us to do. Many times we don't even realize such "behind the scenes" events are happening, but God is using us.

Recently, my son Jonathan and I went to one of our favorite

restaurants to eat. A large party had arrived ahead of us, and the hostess informed us that we would have a forty-five-minute wait. We couldn't wait that long and were disappointed, since we had really been looking forward to eating there. But we decided to take it all in stride. I told Jonathan, "Let's go down to that little hamburger place and eat." I hadn't been to that hamburger place more than twice in my life. But when we went in, I noticed a well-dressed man sitting at one of the front tables; he was all by himself. As Jonathan and I passed by him, I glanced at him, nodded my head, and smiled. No big deal. We proceeded to the counter and ordered our food.

A few days later, I received a note from that man. He said that he was at one of the lowest points in his life and that he had rarely ever prayed before, but that morning he prayed, and said, "God, if You are real, show me some kind of sign." In his letter, he wrote, "When my eyes met your eyes, something on the inside of me happened. I've never felt love like that before."

Now, what is amazing to me is I didn't feel anything at all—apart from hunger pangs. I just wanted to eat. Looking back, though, I realize God changed my plans on purpose. God interrupted my plans so that I could see that man, and in some small way, so Jonathan and I could be part of the answer to that man's prayer. Sometimes God may lead you an entirely different way, just so you can give somebody a smile, just so you can say hello. Your very countenance can give people hope. God can cause people to look at you and see His love and compassion.

I don't believe any of that would have happened if I had been stressed out. I doubt that I would have carried that same anointing if I had been all upset and frustrated because one of our favorite restaurants didn't have room for us.

When you are inconvenienced, and things don't go your way, don't give in to the temptation to get bent out of shape. Not only is it going to cause you problems, but it also may prevent God from using you in the way He really wants to.

Sometimes, everything that can go wrong will. When you have one of those days, dig your heels in, make a decision you're going to keep a smile on your face, and just go with the flow, knowing that God is still in control. Victoria and I were aboard a flight recently, returning home to the United States, when, for no reason at all, they upgraded us to first class. It was simply the favor of God that allowed us to sit in the front row of that plane.

We travel a great deal, so when I get back to town, I like to hit the ground running. We were scheduled to land in Houston around noon, and I had already scheduled the rest of my day. I wanted to go eat lunch at a favorite restaurant, play with our kids, go work out, and do a few other things. I had it all planned out, and I figured that since Victoria and I were going to be the first ones off the plane, we could get through customs and immigration rather quickly.

The plane landed and just as I had planned, Victoria and I made a hasty exit. Evidently four or five other international flights had landed just prior to our arrival, because the customs area was as crowded as I had ever seen it. The line was backed up all the way to the jetways. At least a thousand people stood in that line. One look and I knew that it could take an hour or two to clear customs and immigration, and that was going to throw my plans completely off schedule.

I decided I wasn't going to get uptight, but that I was going to believe for the favor of God. I sort of joked with Victoria, saying, "Watch this, Victoria. Somebody's going to come get us, and take us right up front." I prayed, "God, please give me Your favor. God, cause us to stand out in the crowd," and on and on.

The line seemed to surge with even more people, but I remained undaunted. I was expecting God's favor, so I had stood off to the side and momentarily got out of the line so I could look up toward the front. That's when I noticed a woman coming toward me. She was dressed in a uniform, wore a badge, and was carrying a walkie-talkie. She was some sort of official, I knew. I told Victoria, "Here she comes. She probably attends Lakewood." I was so excited. I knew she was going to take me up to the front of that line.

Sure enough, the woman came right up to me. She said, "Sir."

I smiled real big. I said, "Yes, ma'am," already reaching for my carry-on bag so I could step to the front of the line.

She said, "Would you please get back in the line?"

"God? That is not what I was praying for."

My whole day went like that. Not one of my plans turned out. But thank God, I have learned to be adaptable and adjustable. I've made up my mind I'm going to enjoy every day whether I get my way or not.

Make a decision that you're going to be happy even if you get stuck in traffic, even if the waitress spills something on your new coat, even if you have to wait in that long line.

Understand, God did not create you to be a negative-thinking person. He didn't make any of us to live depressed, stressed out, worried, or frustrated. God intends for you to be happy, peaceful, contented, and to enjoy your life. God wants us to be examples of what it means to live a life of faith. When people see us, they should see so much joy, peace, and happiness that they will want what we have.

Take an honest look at your life. Are you as happy as you know you should be deep down inside? Do you get up each day excited about your future? Are you enjoying your family? Enjoying your friends? If not, what is stealing your joy and causing you to get upset? Why are you worried? Identify what it is. Take inventory and then take it one step further. Begin retraining your mind in those particular areas.

Many times, you can make a small change—a minor adjustment in your attitude, or a minor adjustment in how you treat people; a minor adjustment in how you respond to problems—and it will make a huge difference in your life and in your level of joy.

Years ago, the Russian scientist Ivan Pavlov did an experiment with some dogs. He studied their habits and how they responded to certain situations. Every time he fed them, he rang a bell. When the dogs saw the food, they became excited and started salivating. They couldn't wait to eat.

Over the next couple of weeks, every time Pavlov fed the dogs, he made sure he first rang that bell. After a while, the dogs associated the ringing of the bell with the presence of food.

A few weeks later, Pavlov decided to try something different. He started ringing the bell at odd times when he wasn't feeding the dogs, just to see what they would do. Interestingly, every time he rang the bell, even though there was no food within sight or smell, the dogs began salivating. In their minds, they were about to eat. Pavlov called this a "conditioned response."

Something similar can happen in us. We can allow ourselves to develop all sorts of negative conditioned responses. For instance, we get stuck in traffic and almost instantly our blood pressure shoots sky high. We get all upset. Or maybe at the office somebody doesn't speak to us, somebody intentionally ignores us. Instead of letting it go and giving that person the benefit of the doubt, we get offended. We've conditioned ourselves to respond in a certain way. We've allowed these negative mind-sets to steal our joy.

To develop a habit of happiness, you must retrain those negative responses. When you get up in the morning, you may feel discouraged or depressed. You may not feel like going to work. But instead of dragging through the day, thinking, *Nothing good ever happens to me; this is going to be a lousy day,* break out of that rut. No matter what those circumstances look like, say, "This is the day the Lord has made. I'm going to enjoy it. I'm going to be happy today." Speak that out by faith. Every time you do, you are retraining your mind. You're forming a new habit of happiness. Just as we can form negative habits of defeat, discouragement, bitterness, or self-pity, we can get in the habit of enjoying every single day.

Train your mind to see the good. Be grateful for what you have and get rid of any negative conditioned responses.

Friend, there's too much sadness in our world today. Many people are even sick physically because they are living so stressed out, uptight, and worried. Granted, depression may be caused by a chemical imbalance, but I see too many people dragging around defeated and depressed because they habitually focus on the negative. They focus on their problems, on what's wrong, rather than what's right; or what they lost or can't do, rather than what they can do with what they have left.

Change your focus. You can have a tiny problem, but if you stay focused on it, it will seem to get bigger and bigger. Don't magnify your problem; magnify your God. Step out of doubt and step into faith. Get out of that discouragement and come over into joy. Make a decision that you are going to live your life happily.

Don't magnify your problem; magnify your God.

I don't mean that you feel on top of the world all the time. That's not realistic. I'm talking about being content. In fact, one definition of joy is "calm delight." That means you are at peace, you have a smile on your face. You are excited about your future. Sure, you may have some problems. We all have obstacles to overcome. But we know God is in control. We know He has us in the palm of His hand.

The key is to retrain our mind to move away from negative conditioned responses. I know some people who actually get depressed every Monday morning. They don't like their jobs, they dread going to work, and every week, they develop a bad case of the Monday Morning Blues.

Oddly enough, researchers purport that we are 70 percent more likely to have a heart attack Monday morning than any other time of the week because people are more uptight and stressed out on Monday than on any other day.

In contrast, the Apostle Paul said, "I have learned how to be content no matter what state I'm in." Think about that. He said, "*I have learned* to be content." In other words, "This didn't happen automatically. I had to train my mind to stay at peace. I had to train my mind to look on the bright side. I had to train my mind to focus on the good."

We must do the same thing. Happiness is not going to fall on us. It's a choice we have to make. Being positive doesn't necessarily come naturally. We have to make that decision daily. Our mind, left alone, will often drift toward the negative. If we don't stay on the offensive, little by little we will grow more sullen; we won't smile as much. Soon, we're not as much fun to be around. We start to find fault. We start to get critical.

Instead, refuse to allow these negative habits to take hold. When you get out of bed in the morning, put a smile on your face. Set the tone right at the start of the day. If you don't set the tone, somebody else will set it for you.

"Joel, if I smile or act as though I'm in a good mood, I'm just faking it, because really I'm depressed. I've got so many problems."

You need to realize that when you smile, it's an act of faith. When you smile, you're sending a message to your whole body, announcing that everything is going to be all right. If you will develop this positive attitude of faith, you will sow a seed for God to work in your life.

I read about a young couple in college, studying to get their degrees. They lived in an apartment complex next door to another young college couple, so the two couples soon became good friends. They had a lot in common.

The second couple, however, seemed to get all the breaks. They lived in the corner apartment, and it was much bigger and nicer than the other units in that complex were. They furnished their apartment with brand-new furniture. The other couple barely had any furniture, and the pieces they did have were old hand-me-downs. The one couple wore nice clothes, the latest fashions, while the other couple wore the same clothes again and again. At one point, both of the men were trying to get an assistant teaching job at the university. Once again, the second man got it.

The first young man was extremely frustrated that he couldn't seem to get any breaks. To top things off, at Christmastime, the second couple received a brand-new fancy sports car from their parents. The first couple drove an old beat-up pickup truck. It didn't have any air-conditioning, and they lived in a hot and humid part of the country. Many times they'd be driving to class in the morning, sweating and miserable, and they'd look over to see their friends in that brand-new sports car.

As this sort of thing continued, the young man got more negative and more depressed. He started complaining about their circumstances, and before long he was at odds with his wife. They started arguing and fighting. Ironically, they had never before had problems in their relationship, but negative attitudes will quickly spread to every area of our lives and drag us down.

One day, this young man was in his statistics class on campus. He'd spent several hours entering an enormous amount of data into his computer. He was working on this long, complicated equation. He had to get the numbers all lined up. He got them in the right order in the right column, and then he hit the "enter" key on his computer, asking it to give him the answer. As he did, he sat back and folded his arms. He thought it would take ten to fifteen minutes for the computer to analyze and calculate all that information. But much to his surprise he looked up to find that the computer was already finished. He couldn't believe it. He thought, *That is amazing! It took me hours to put this in, and the computer gave me the answer in less than one-tenth of a second.* About that time, the professor came by and noticed that the student looked perplexed and befuddled.

"What's wrong?" the professor asked.

"Well, sir, nothing's wrong. I just spent all this time putting data in the computer, and I don't really see how it could calculate it that rapidly."

The professor smiled and said, "Let me explain." He told the student how the computer takes every bit of data, and it gives it either a positive electrical impulse or a negative electrical impulse, and then stores it away. Then the computer simply recalls the information and combines it in the right order. It does it so quickly because the information has already been categorized.

Then the professor said something that really got the young man's attention. He said, "The computer works much like the human brain. Before anything ever goes into our mental computer, before any sight, sound, taste, feel, or intuition gets stored in the brain, it's first stamped either positive or negative. That sensation is permanently stored in our memory. That's why sometimes you can't remember a person's name, but you can remember how you felt about that person." The professor went on to say, "But unlike a computer, every person develops a habit of mainly programming their mind positive or negative."

The professor's words turned on a light in that young man's mind. He realized he had gotten in the habit of making himself miserable. Without even knowing it, he had been stamping everything in his life as a "negative." When he saw his friends next door, all he could see

was what they had and he didn't. "They've got a bigger apartment . . . negative. They've got a better car . . . negative. They get all
the breaks . . . negative." He realized that the reason he wasn't enjoying his life was that he was categorizing everything he was putting
into his mental computer as negative.

Unquestionably, what you put into your heart and mind is what
you're going to get out. Sure, you may have negative circumstances.
Maybe you didn't get good breaks. Maybe you didn't get the position
you were longing for. Now instead of automatically stamping it "negative" and storing it away, turn your attitude around. Remind yourself,
"I know God has something better in store for me. I know when one
door closes, God can open another door." When you do that, you will
take that negative situation, turn it around, and stamp it "positive."

You can do this even in your most difficult times. Maybe you lost
a loved one. I know that can be painful, but our attitude should be,
"I know where they are. They're in a better place, a place of joy, a
place of peace." When we do that, we're stamping that experience as
a "positive."

Pay attention to what you're feeding yourself. Are you storing
away more positive or more negative? You cannot mentally brand
everything as negative and expect to live a positive, happy life.

"I got caught in traffic last week, and I missed an important
meeting."

No, turn it around and declare, "Father, I thank you that you have
me at the right place at the right time. I am not going to get
depressed. I believe you're directing my steps and you're going to
turn that missed meeting around and use it for my good."

When you do that, you're turning around the negative and stamping it positive. In the process, as you grow more accustomed to this
sort of mind-set, you will discover that you are developing a habit of
happiness.

Our brain possesses a fascinating function known as the "reticular
activating system." It's a function through which our minds eliminate
the thoughts and the impulses deemed unnecessary. For instance,
years ago, my sister Lisa lived in a townhome right beside the railroad tracks. Two or three times a night, a train rumbled by, loudly

sounding its whistle as it passed her window. That train literally shook that place. When Lisa first moved in, the train awakened her no matter how deeply she was sleeping. But after living there for several weeks, an amazing thing happened. Those trains could pass by in the middle of the night, and Lisa would hardly even notice. Several months later, Lisa was able to sleep all through the night.

One time, I stayed at her house, and that train came by in the middle of the night. I think I jumped three feet off the bed. It sounded like the world was coming to an end.

The next morning, I asked Lisa, "How do you sleep here with that train going by in the night?"

"What train?" she asked.

The reticular activating system in her mind processed the sound of the train going by and allowed her to sleep right through it.

In a similar manner, we can train our minds in such a positive fashion that when negative, discouraging thoughts come, they won't affect us anymore. When that thought of fear comes, learn to tune it out as Lisa did. Or that depressing thought of "It's going to be a lousy day"—tune it out. If you'll keep it up, before long, your mind's reticular activating system says, "He doesn't need this information. She's not paying attention. Don't even send the thought of fear or worry." Certainly, that is an oversimplification of the mental process, but just as Lisa was able to tune out the sounds of that train, I believe we can tune out negative messages. We can tune in to thoughts of joy, peace, faith, hope, and victory, as we learn to turn around negatives and stamp everything positive.

"Well, Joel, my children are not doing well. They've gotten off course. I'm so worried about them." No, just turn that around: "Father, thank you that my children are blessed, they're making good decisions. I declare what Your Word says, 'As for me and my house, we will serve the Lord.'"

"Well, Joel, it's my finances. Gas prices are so high. Business is slow. I don't see how I'm going to make it."

No, tune that out and start tuning in, "God is supplying all of my needs. Everything I touch prospers and succeeds. I am blessed. I cannot be cursed."

Following the devastation of Hurricane Katrina, I was watching a special news program one day as reporters were interviewing people in New Orleans who had gone through the hurricane. Person after person told his or her story, and most of them were extremely negative and bitter, blaming other people, blaming the government, blaming God.

One young woman stepped up to the microphone, and I could tell immediately that she had a different attitude. She had a big smile, and her face almost seemed to glow.

The reporter asked her somewhat sarcastically, "Okay, tell us your story. What's wrong?"

"Nothing's wrong," the woman said. "I'm not here to complain. I'm simply here to thank God that I'm still alive and I have my health. I thank God that my children are okay."

The reporter was taken back. Everyone else had been complaining about not having any electricity or water. It was more than a hundred degrees and they had no air-conditioning. The reporter probed further, "Well, what about your power? Do you have any air-conditioning?"

The woman said, "No, I not only don't have any power, I don't even have my home. It was swept away in the flood." Then she smiled as she said, "I'll tell you what I do have." She reached down and picked up her Bible. "I have my hope, I have my joy, I have my peace," she said. With a radiant countenance, she continued, "I know God is on my side."

That woman chose to take a heartrending, negative, unfortunate situation, and she chose to turn it around; she stamped "positive" on it. She refused to tune in thoughts of self-pity. She refused to allow her negative circumstances to steal her joy. She was saying in effect, "I know God is still in control of my life. He said a little sparrow would not fall to the ground without Him seeing it. So I know He's watching over me. I know He's going to take care of my children and me."

Train your mind to see the good. Get rid of any negative, conditioned responses. Everybody around you may be complaining, but you can find the good in every situation. If you'll do what the Scripture says, you can indeed be happy at all times.

CHAPTER 18

Handling Criticism

"I can't believe she said that about me!" Tera said through her anger and tears. "I don't want to work with someone that I can't trust, someone who is going to say one thing to my face and then do the exact opposite behind my back."

"She didn't really mean it," Tera's friend Bonnie tried to console her. "She's always that way. She criticizes everybody; it's her way of trying to feel good about herself."

"Well, maybe so, but she didn't win any points with me."

Every one of us will have times when we are criticized, sometimes fairly, but more often unfairly, creating stress in our hearts and minds and tension in our relationships. Somebody at work or in your social circle speaks negatively about you or blames you for something, trying to make you look bad, or blowing some minor incident out of proportion. Usually, your critics have no interest in helping you; they are simply trying to drag you down.

Certainly, constructive criticism can be helpful. An insightful point of light presented by someone who truly has your best interests at heart can illuminate an area where you need to improve. Sad to say, most criticism is not intended to build up another person; quite the opposite. It is not given in the spirit of blessing, but is more often presented with an intentional sting. The criticism that hurts the worst is frequently undeserved and unfair. Such criticism is a reflection more of the critic than of the person being criticized.

I've found that unwarranted criticism is most often based on jealousy. It stems from a competitive spirit. You have something that somebody else wants. Instead of being happy for you, instead of keeping a good attitude, knowing that God can do something similar for anyone who trusts Him, jealousy rises up in the critical person. They try to cover their own insecurity by being critical, cynical, caustic, or snippy toward others.

The more successful you are, the more criticism you will encounter. If you get that promotion at the office, don't be surprised when your critics come out of the woodwork.

"Well, he's not that talented," someone might say. "She's just a manipulator, always playing up to the boss."

Or your friends may be fine as long as you are single. Once you are married, however, they start saying things such as, "I can't believe he married her. She has no personality whatsoever."

Unfortunately, not everybody will celebrate your victories with you. Not all your single friends may jump up and down when you marry the man of your dreams. Your coworkers may not sing your praises when you get that promotion. Sadly, for some people, your success evokes that jealous, critical spirit rather than appreciation and compliments.

Here's the key to handling criticism: Never take it personally. Many times, it's not even about you, even though it may be directed at you. If the critic weren't tearing you apart, he'd be complaining about somebody else. It's something on the inside of the critical person that lashes out at others. Unless they deal with it, it's going to keep them from rising higher.

One of the most important things I've ever learned is to celebrate other people's victories. If your coworker gets the promotion you wanted, yes, there is a tendency to be jealous. Sure, there's a tendency to think, *Why didn't that happen for me? I work hard. That's not fair.*

Celebrate other people's victories.

However, if we'll keep the right attitude and be happy for other people's success, at the right time God will open up something even better for us. I've found that if I can't rejoice with others, I'm not going to get to where I want to be. Many times, God has a promotion in store, but first He sends along a test. He wants to see if we're ready. When our best friends get married, while we're still single, can we be happy for them? Or when our relatives move into their dream house, and we've been praying for years to own a home but are still renting a crowded apartment. That's a test. If you get jealous and critical, your attitude will trap you right where you are. Learn to celebrate other people's victories. Let their success inspire you. Know that if God did something so marvelous for them, He can certainly do it for you.

If you are going to become better, you will need to know how to deal with critics—people who are talking about you, judging you, or maybe even making false accusations. In Old Testament times, these people were called "slingers." When an enemy attacked a city, their first priority was to pry the stones off the wall that was protecting that city. They would then sling those stones into the city's wells. The attackers knew if they could clog the wells with stones and interrupt the flow of water, eventually the people within the walls would have to come out.

Do you see the parallel? You have a well of good things on the inside, a well of joy, peace, and victory. Too often, we let the slingers clog up our wells. Perhaps somebody speaks derogatorily about you, but instead of letting it go, you dwell on it, growing more and more upset. Before long, you think, *I'm going to get even; I'm going to pay them back. They are speaking untruths about me; let me tell you what I know about them.*

Instead, make it a priority to keep your well pure. If somebody is critical of you, trying to show you in a bad light, recognize that is a stone coming your way. If you dwell on it, or get upset and revengeful, the person who threw that stone has accomplished his or her goal. Another stone landed in your well. Now your joy, peace, and victory become more restricted. They don't flow like they should.

Truth is, we all have some slingers in our lives, people who try to bring us down with their words or actions. They may be a friend to your face, but you know behind your back, they would shred you if given an opportunity.

The way you overcome unwarranted criticism is by not allowing yourself to take revenge or even harboring an attitude that wants revenge. Don't sink down to their level and start talking badly about them. Most of all, don't get defensive or try to prove that you're right and your critic is wrong. No, the way you defeat a slinger is to shake it off and keep moving forward. Keep your eyes on the prize; stay focused on your goals and do what you believe God wants you to do.

This is what Jesus told His disciples to do when He sent them out to various towns to teach the people, to heal the sick, and to care for their needs. Jesus knew His followers would sometimes suffer rejection. Not everybody would like them or gladly receive their message. Some people would get jealous and start talking negatively about them, trying to make them look bad. Jesus knew the slingers would be out there, so He instructed His disciples, "When you go into a town, whoever will not receive and welcome your message, when you leave that place, shake the dust off of your feet." [43]

Notice, He didn't say *if* they treat you poorly, if they start talking about you and spreading rumors; He said *when* they do these things. Jesus did not advise His disciples to become defensive or worried. Nor did He instruct them to defend their reputations and set the record straight. He simply said, "Shake the dust off of your feet." That was a symbolic way of saying, "You're not going to steal my joy. You may reject me or speak badly about me, but I'm not going to sink down to your level. I'm not going to fight with you. I'm going to let God be my vindicator."

Sometimes when you leave the workplace, you simply have to shake it off. People backbiting, playing politics, trying to bring you down—leave it; don't lug that heavy, worthless load home. Shake it off. Sometimes even leaving a relative's house, you may have to say, "I'm shaking this off. I'm not going to drink of their poison."

"I heard one of my competitors at work is talking about me," Rick said. "I'm not going to take that. I'm going to fight fire with fire. I'm going to let him have it."

"You could do that," I told him, "but that's not the way to win. Instead, let God be your vindicator. If you'll stay on the high road, God will fight your battles for you. You never really win by sinking down to your critics' level and attacking them personally. Rise above that."

When somebody is critical or negative toward you, your attitude should be, "I'm better than that. I'm not going to let their stone clog up my well. I'm not going to let their jealous spirit poison my life. I'm going to stay full of joy."

Perhaps you have not been shaking things off, and recently you have let the slingers get the best of you; you've been dwelling on their criticism, fretting about who's talking negatively about you or who has rejected you. You feel sluggish because your well is nearly clogged up. It's time to clear out the rocks and keep your inner well fresh and clean.

Once the Apostle Paul was shipwrecked on a small island. He went to pick up some firewood and a poisonous snake bit him. The people thought he would die immediately. That's what it feels like when somebody criticizes us, when somebody is talking behind your back, trying to put you in a bad light; we can feel the sting of his or her words. I love what Paul did. One translation says, "He simply shook it off." It was as though he was saying, "No big deal. I'm not going to let this thing bother me. It may be poisonous, it may look bad, but I know God is in control. I know God can take care of me."

Miraculously, that snakebite didn't even harm Paul. Although it was dangerous and poisonous, Paul knew the secret of simply shaking it off.

Many people let negative words or other people's opinions totally ruin their lives. They live to please other people and honestly think that they can be happy by trying to keep everyone else happy. They don't want anybody to say a negative word about them.

That's simply impossible. You have to accept the fact that not everybody is going to like you, not everybody is going to accept you, and you certainly cannot keep everybody happy. Some people will find fault, no matter what you do. You can be there for them a thousand times in a row, but they will remind you repeatedly of that one time when you couldn't show up. Life is too short to try to keep people like that happy.

Yes, we should be kind and loving, but don't spend too much time trying to please somebody who is impossible to please. Until they deal with their own issues on the inside, they're not going to be happy. Say, "I'm not going to play up to them. I'm not going to try to keep them happy, because I know no matter what I do or don't do, a month later, they're going to be running me down." Tremendous freedom results when you accept the fact that not everybody is going to like you.

The Scripture says in Proverbs, "A gossiping, fault-finding tongue is like a venomous snake." A person's words can poison your life, if you allow them to do so. The longer you think about it, the more venom goes into you.

If somebody relates something uncomplimentary that another person may have said about my family or me, I try to stop them as quickly as possible. I'll say, "I don't really want to hear that. I don't want that poison to get inside me." I've found it's a lot easier to shake things off if you don't know all the details. If somebody is talking about you, don't go home and call seven of your friends and say, "What did you hear about this?" Just shake it off. Remember, most of the time, it's not really about you. It's about the fact that they haven't dealt with that jealous, critical spirit on the inside.

We can't live with an idealistic view of life thinking, *I'm a good person. I'm kind and loving. Nobody is going to talk badly about me.*

Unfortunately, sometimes, the nicer you are, the more people will talk about you. The good in you seems to stir up the bad in them. They feel convicted by the purity of your heart. You can feed the poor; you can mow your neighbor's lawn; you can take in a person who needs a place to live temporarily. You'd think your critics would be happy. But no, here comes that jealous spirit: "Well, who does he think he is? Mr. Goody Two-shoes? Why does she get to work early every day? He's just playing up to the boss. Why is she so friendly to everybody all the time? She's just trying to get something."

The best thing you can do is ignore the slingers. They won't put forth the effort to be their best, so they feel like they need to tear you down to help ease their consciences. When you hear those negative comments or false accusations, just remind yourself, "No big deal, it's just another slinger. I've already made up my mind: No more stones are going into my well. I'm going to live my life in freedom."

Slingers' comments are nothing more than distractions, trying to get you to lose focus on what you should be doing. You shouldn't waste five seconds of your emotional energy trying to figure out why somebody said something or what they really meant. You only have so much energy each day. So shake off a distraction immediately so you can use your strength positively. Otherwise, if you allow yourself to focus on the distraction, you'll go to work and not be able to give it your best. You'll come home and not really want to interact with your family, because you will be emotionally drained. You got distracted and poured all your energy into something that really didn't even matter.

Run Your Own Race

Recognize that you cannot stop people from talking negatively. If you are trying to be the "gossip police," hoping to make sure that nobody ever says a negative thing about you, you're going to live a frustrated life. No, accept the fact that certain people are going to make cutting remarks. But you are better than that; you don't have to drink of their poison. You can rise above it. You can stay on the high road and enjoy your life anyway.

Don't spend all your time trying to win over your critics; just run your own race.

I don't have time to sit around thinking about all the people who don't like me. I realize that every day is a gift from God, and my time is too valuable to waste it trying to please everybody. No, I've accepted the fact that not everybody is going to like me and not everybody is going to understand me. You don't have to try to explain yourself. Don't spend time trying to win over your critics; just run your own race.

I start every morning searching my own heart. I make sure, to the best of my ability, that I'm doing what I believe God wants me to do. As I follow the Scripture and I feel in my own heart that my life is on course, that's all that matters. I can't afford to let critics and negative voices distract me—and neither can you!

Some people spend more time focused on what other people are saying about them than they do thinking about their own dreams and goals. But understand that if you're going to do anything great in life—whether you want to be a great teacher, a successful businessperson, or a champion athlete—not everybody is going to be your cheerleader. Not everybody is going to be excited about your dream. In fact, some people are going to be downright jealous. They will find fault and criticize. It is crucial that you learn to shake off unwarranted criticism. Because the moment you start changing so you can please people, you will be taking a step backwards. Sure, you could say, "I'm not going to show up early at work anymore because my coworkers are starting to talk about me." Or "I'm not going to buy that car that I really want, because I know people are going to judge, people are going to condemn me." No, I've found that no matter what you do or don't do, somebody won't like it, so don't waste your time worrying about it. Do what God has put in your heart and trust Him to take care of the critics.

One thing that I'm good at is staying focused. I don't allow what people are saying to distract me. I realize that not everybody is going to understand me. I also recognize that it is not my job to spend all my time trying to convince them to change their minds. I'm called to plant a seed of hope in people's hearts. I'm not called to explain every minute facet of Scripture or to expound on deep theological doctrines or disputes that don't touch where real people live. My gifting is to encourage, to challenge, and to inspire.

I've heard people say, "Well, that Joel Osteen; he's not enough of this," or, "He's too much of that." If I changed with every critic, I would be living in a revolving door! I believe that one reason God has promoted me is that I have stayed true to who I am. I refuse to let people talk me out of doing what I know in my heart God wants me to do.

Maybe you need to get free from trying to please everybody as well. Stop worrying that somebody might criticize you. Remember that if you are criticized when you are trying to make a positive difference in the world, you're in good company. Jesus was perpetually criticized for doing good. He was even criticized for healing a man on the Sabbath. He was criticized for going to dinner with a tax collector. The critics called Him a friend of sinners. He was criticized for helping a woman in need, somebody that they were about to stone. Jesus didn't change in a futile attempt to fit into everybody's mold. He didn't try to explain Himself and make everybody understand Him; He stayed focused and fulfilled His destiny.

This truth really helped to set me free. There was a time in my life when I wanted everybody to like me. If I heard one negative comment, I thought, *Oh, no. I've failed. What have I done wrong? What do I need to change?*

One day I realized it's impossible for everybody to like me, and if someone chooses to misinterpret my message or my motives, there's nothing I can do about it anyhow. Now I don't let my critics upset me or steal my joy. I know most of the time it's not about me. The success God has given me stirs up the jealousy in them.

If you're making a difference in your family, or at the office, or in your workplace, you will always have your share of critics. Don't allow them to stress you out. Simply recognize that the higher you go, the more visible a target you will be and the more critics will want to take shots at you.

The Apostle Paul had great crowds following him. But time and time again, people became jealous; they got all stirred up, and on several occasions ran him out of town. What did Paul do? Did he get depressed and say, "God, I'm trying to do my best, but nobody understands me"? No, he shook the dust off his feet. He was saying in effect, "It's your loss, not mine, because I'm going to do great things for God. I'm not going to allow your rejection or your negative words to keep me from my destiny." His attitude was, "Sling all you want to. I have a cover on my well. I'm not going to let you poison my life." I heard somebody say, "If people run you out of town, just get to the front of the line and act like you're leading the parade." In other words, shake it off and keep moving forward.

I love the Scripture "No weapon formed against us will prosper, but every tongue raised against us in judgment, You will show to be in the wrong."[44] You may have to endure some people speaking against you, but if you can just stay on the high road and keep doing your best, you will prove their criticism invalid. Moreover, God will pour out His favor on you, in spite of your critics.

Understand that your destiny is not tied to what people are saying about you. Some critical people in Houston predicted that Lakewood Church would never be able to meet in the arena known as the Compaq Center. They told us we didn't have a chance. In fact, at a business luncheon attended by numerous high-level city leaders, one man told the people at his table, "It will be a cold day in hell before Lakewood Church ever gets the Compaq Center."

When I heard about that remark, I just shook it off. I knew our destiny was not tied to one dissenter. I knew that remark was nothing more than a distraction. I also realized that not everybody was going to understand our decision to move the church. I heard people saying, "Why do they need to move? Why do they want a bigger church? Why are they leaving their roots?" Many times, I was tempted to get in there and try to explain it, hoping to convince them that our moving was a good idea. I knew not everybody wanted to understand. And I guess today is a cold day in hell because Lakewood Church has now been worshiping God in the location formerly known as the Compaq Center since July 2005.

Friend, your destiny is not determined by your critics. God has the final say. Quit listening to what the naysayers are telling you and stop living to please people. Shake that off and keep pressing forward in life.

Your destiny is not determined by your critics.

Another important key is not to allow the criticism to change you. We need to be tough on the outside, but you have to stay tender on the inside. Often we become hard and calloused by criticism. If we're not careful, when critical people talk behind our backs, it's easy to let their poison get on the inside of us and start to change us. But you must keep your heart pure and stay true to who God has made you to be.

Sometimes when people see little quirks in our personality, or even something about our appearance, they make fun of it. If we learn of it, we tend to overcompensate, and it starts affecting our personality and the way we carry ourselves. But we cannot let cutting remarks and insensitive words cause us to become self-conscious.

A high school friend of mine was popular, fun, and outgoing, but he had an unusual high-pitched laugh. One day, a couple of our friends started making fun of him, going around the school imitating his laugh. They didn't mean any harm. They were just teasing, trying to have fun. I noticed how that young man started to change, though. He quit laughing as much. He became much more quiet and reserved. Where he once was gregarious and the life of the party, little by little he tucked his true personality inside a shell. He lost his confidence, became insecure, and started overcompensating. That's what happens when we don't shake things off.

You may have some distinct features or personality traits. But know this: God made you like you are on purpose. If people are making fun of you or causing you to feel overly self-conscious, just shake it off. Don't let their comments or actions stick to you.

For example, I smile a lot. In fact, I smile all the time. I can't help it. I've been doing it since I was a little baby. When I was seven years old, I was in a car accident and I suffered a severe gash on my head. Some friends came up to the emergency room to see me, and they were worried that I'd be upset and crying. When they came in, I was lying on the emergency room table. They later told me, "Joel, when we walked in there, you were smiling from ear to ear."

That's just the way God made me. Sometimes people make fun of me for smiling so much. You'd think they'd be happy that somebody is smiling instead of frowning. I've heard people say, "Why does he smile so much?" Almost as if to say, "There's something wrong with him."

A few months after my father went to be with the Lord and I began ministering, somebody started calling me the Smiling Preacher. The nickname really caught on. Shortly after that, a well-known reporter interviewed me and asked rather sarcastically, in a demeaning tone, "What do you think about being known as the Smiling Preacher?"

My answer surprised him. I said, "I kind of like it. I'm happy. I believe God wants us to be happy, so that's just fine with me." His jaw dropped open, as though he didn't know what to think.

I don't want to allow what other people say or what other people think to change me from being who God made me to be. You too should be confident in who you are.

The other day I saw a parody that somebody produced about me. It was a television clip of me speaking and every time I smiled, my front teeth would *ping*, and a star rose off my teeth, sort of like a toothpaste commercial. When I saw the parody, I laughed—probably more than the people who watched it with me. I thought to myself, *That doesn't bother me one bit. I smile a lot. If somebody doesn't like it, I'll just smile some more.* Who knows? Maybe Crest or Colgate will want to sponsor our television program!

You ought to be able to laugh at yourself. Don't let unwarranted criticism create stress in your life. Stay focused on what God has in store for you.

CHAPTER 19

Keep Yourself Happy

One of the most important keys to a better life is to keep yourself happy, rather than living to please everybody else. It's easy to take on a false sense of responsibility, thinking that it is our job to keep everybody happy, to "fix" this person, to rescue that person, or to solve another person's problem.

Certainly, it is noble and admirable to want to help as many people as possible, and it is always good to reach out to others in need. Too often, though, we get out of balance. We're doing everything for everybody else, but we're not taking any time to keep ourselves healthy. I've discovered that when I try to keep everybody around me happy by trying to meet all their needs, I'm the one who ends up suffering.

God does not want you to sacrifice your happiness to keep somebody else happy. At first brush, that may sound a little selfish, but there's a tenuous balance here. Your first priority is to take care of yourself. To do so, you must recognize that some people are still not going to be happy no matter what you do for them, no matter how nice you are, no matter how much time and energy you give them. They have their own issues with which to deal or things inside that they need to resolve.

You should not take responsibility for someone else's poor choices. If you do, before long, that person will be controlling you and manipulating you.

Maybe you are stressed because you are allowing someone else to dull your happiness—it may be a spouse, a child, a friend, or a neighbor. They won't do right. They're always dumping their problems on you. They expect you to bail them out of every problem and keep them cheered up. Now you are frustrated because you are spending so much time and energy on them. It seems like every time you get that person fixed up, he or she is back a week later with that same problem. If you continue to help them, you're not only hurting yourself, but you are doing them a disservice as well. You've become a crutch to them. Because as long as they know they can come running to you, making you feel guilty and talking you into solving all their problems, then they will never deal with the real issues. They won't change.

Truth is, some people don't really want to be helped; they don't want to change. They like the attention their perpetual dilemmas bring them. Sometimes, the best thing you can do for somebody like that is *not* to help them.

Consider a small child. If every time that child throws a fit, you come running over and give him exactly what he wants, he will continue that pattern. The child knows what he has to do to get his way, and he will try to use that to control you. But if the child yells and screams, and you don't give in, you just ignore it or reprimand him for his behavior, it won't be long before he realizes that throwing a fit isn't working.

The same principle is true for adults. As long as you allow somebody to pressure you into doing what he or she wants, he or she will continue to do it.

But, friend, life is too short to go through it being controlled and manipulated by people who refuse to make good choices on their own. Please understand: You are not responsible for everybody else's happiness. You are responsible for your own happiness. If people are controlling you, it's not their fault; it's your fault. You must learn to set some boundaries. Quit allowing them to call you at all hours of the day and night to dump their problems on you. Quit catering to them and giving in every time they throw a fit. Quit lending them money every time they make poor choices. Let them take responsibility for their actions.

You needn't be harsh or uncaring, but sometimes we can be so good-hearted and generous that we allow people to control us. At some point we have to realize that we are not helping that person anymore. Beyond that, now they are hurting us.

Many people go around all upset, frustrated, and discouraged because they've made the mistake of taking on a false sense of responsibility for somebody close to them who won't do what is right. They carry a heavy load, trying to fix the person, or trying to keep someone else happy.

You can be free from all that if you will just give those people to God. Quit trying to be the keeper of the universe. That's not your job. You can't make everybody do what's right. You can't make your children serve God. You can't force your relative to make good decisions. Take the pressure off yourself and let God deal with them.

"But, Joel, if I don't loan them money they may lose their house," I hear someone saying. "If I don't call him every morning, he will get angry at me." Or "If I don't give in when she throws a fit, she may not talk to me for two weeks."

All that *may* be true. But do you want to live the next twenty years like that? Or do you want to help that person get free? Because you are not doing anyone a favor by allowing him or her to control you. In fact, in a sense, you are hurting that person because you are allowing him or her to take the easy way out.

I realize that at first, it may be difficult to say no to the stress-inducing controller, but if you'll put your foot down and make these necessary changes, in the long run your life and that other person's life are both going to be much better.

Linda and Troy's marriage was miserable. Linda came from an extremely negative family environment where she had endured many unfair hardships growing up. Unfortunately, she dragged her unhappiness and negativism right into her marriage with Troy. If she didn't get her way, she would pout or throw a tantrum. Sometimes, she would pout for two or three days. She was always having some kind of crisis where she needed attention. She was miserable and she did her best to make everyone around her equally as miserable.

Troy was a good man and a good husband, so he did almost anything he could to keep Linda happy. He was always encouraging her, trying to fix her problems, and letting her know she was going to be okay. For three years, he catered to her every need, giving up his own happiness in a futile attempt to keep Linda happy. Then one day it dawned on him that she was never going to change. He finally was fed up. He realized that although he had good intentions, he was not helping her anymore; he was hurting her. He had become her crutch.

Troy boldly went to Linda and said, "Honey, I love you, but I realize there's nothing I can do to keep you happy. I've done everything I can. So I'm just letting you know that I'm finished trying."

Troy's honest and heartfelt statement stunned Linda, forcing her to look inside herself and deal with the real issues. Beyond that, as Troy followed through and no longer coddled her, Linda had to take responsibility for her own actions. That wake-up call took place more than twenty years ago, and today their marriage is stronger than ever.

If you are in a relationship with somebody similar to Linda, don't allow that person to steal your joy. Do not go through life unhappy because somebody close to you is unhappy. If they insist on making poor choices, choosing to live depressed and in the pits, be kind and courteous, but don't get in the pits with them. At the right time, and in a controlled voice, tell that person, "If you don't want to be happy, that's fine, but you're not going to keep me from being happy."

Certainly, there's a very fine line here, but you are not responsible for your spouse's happiness. Nor are you responsible for your children's happiness. All of us are responsible to keep ourselves happy.

If you are on the flip side of this issue, and you are the person who is doing the controlling, pardon me for being so blunt, but it is time for you to grow up and take responsibility for your own life. Quit relying on that other person to carry you. Quit demanding that your spouse cheer you up every day and work constantly to keep you encouraged. That's not fair to the other person. Stop manipulating that person when he or she does not comply with your wishes or do what you want. No, take responsibility and learn to keep yourself happy.

I'm not talking today about being selfish or self-centered. We should be givers. But there's a big difference between giving and allowing somebody to control you and make you feel guilty until you do what they want. God has not called you to be unhappy simply to keep somebody else happy. Again, if you are allowing that, the other person is not the only one at fault. You may have taken on a false sense of responsibility and now you are allowing them to control you.

God has not called you to be unhappy simply to keep somebody else happy.

If you are in a relationship where you do the majority of the giving and always encourage or rescue the other person, that is a clear sign that something is out of balance. You've become a crutch. And unless you make some changes, the relationship will continue to flounder. You must take a stand. You can do it in love, but you need to go to that person and say, "I love you, but I'm not going to allow you to keep dumping your problems on me and making my life miserable. I'm not going to let you keep draining all my time and energy. You have to take responsibility and learn to keep yourself happy."

"Well, Joel, if I do that, they may get their feelings hurt," I hear you saying. "They may get angry."

Yes, they might. But that is between them and God. When you stand before God, He's not going to ask you, "Did you keep everybody around you happy?" He's going to ask you, "Did you fulfill the call that I placed on your life?"

Ben was thirty-one years of age and still living at home. He was lazy and undisciplined, and wouldn't go out and get a job. He just liked to sit around the house and watch television. Ironically, he didn't think that he had a problem. He didn't see anything wrong with that lifestyle; in fact, as far as he was concerned, life was great.

Ben's parents catered to him constantly because they loved their son and didn't want to be too hard on him. Occasionally, they tried to get him to go out and apply for a job, but he ignored their requests and refused to take any initiative. Why should he? He had no motivation.

The situation continued year after year. One day, Ben's parents were so distraught by their son's sluggardly behavior, they went to a professional counselor for help. The parents explained the situation to the doctor and told him how their son was extremely lazy. "Doctor, on top of all of this, our son doesn't even think that he has a problem," one of the parents lamented.

The doctor's reply shocked the parents. He said, "Well, I agree with your son. He doesn't have a problem. *You* have the problem because you have delivered him out of all his problems." He went on to say, "You have buffered him from any pain, and you have helped him avoid responsibility for his own life. If you want your son to get better, you need to give him back his problem."

The parents were too stunned to speak, so the doctor continued, "You must stop making it so easy on him. Quit delivering him out of all his trouble."

It is difficult to understand, but it is not always the best thing to rescue somebody and make his life easy. It's not always best to solve his problems for him. Sometimes you have to say, "I love you, but if you're going to live in my household, you're going to have to get up and go get a job. You're going to have to start taking some responsibility."

The Bible says, "If you don't work, you won't eat." You may need to say, "If you don't go get a job, you're about to find out what it means to go on a long, long fast!"

I heard somebody say that there are two important qualities all of our children need to have. They need to be grateful and they need to be eager. If they're not grateful, they will take everything for granted. They will expect everybody to give them what they need on a silver platter.

They also need to be eager—eager to learn, eager to serve, eager to achieve, eager to be better than they are currently. Sometimes as parents, we like to make life too easy for our children. Victoria and I have some help around the house and the easy thing is to let the housekeeper make sure our children's rooms are clean. But I know that is not the best thing. As I write these words, our children are twelve and eight, and every morning they make their own beds, get their own clothes together, and get dressed by themselves. When they come downstairs, they have their chores to do. Sure, Victoria or I could do it ourselves, or we could pay somebody to do those same chores. But

I know that if we make it too easy for our children, they will develop the wrong habits and mind-sets, and our excessive kindness will actually hurt our children later on in life.

Adults, too, need to be grateful and eager. I have a tendency to want to help everybody. I want to solve all their problems. "Let me do it for you." But I have to realize that's not always the best. Several years ago, I ran into a homeless man who was about my age. He asked me for some money, and I was about to hand him a twenty-dollar bill, but I felt a check in my heart and mind, so instead of handing him some money and going on my way, I engaged the homeless man in conversation.

As we talked, he told me his story, how he had gone from city to city and had lived a rough life. He tried to hold down a job, but it just didn't work out.

I felt compassion for the man, and I really wanted to help him, so I invited him to church. I said, "Hey, I'm a pastor of a church here in town. Where are you on Sunday mornings? I'll have somebody come by and pick you up."

"Oh, no; I can't come to church," he said. "I don't have time to come to church."

I thought, *Man, what are you going to be doing? You don't have to mow your lawn. You don't have to clean your house!*

The more I talked to him, the more I realized he didn't want to be helped. He didn't want to change. He preferred to take the easy way out. He just wanted my money. Please understand, I'm not saying he didn't have a hard life, but when people don't want to change, when they don't want to be helped, we do them a disservice by delivering them out of all their problems. I could have easily given him that money and been on my way, but I didn't want to do anything to prolong his misery. Yes, we should help the needy, but there comes a point where if you continue to help somebody who refuses to try to help himself or herself, you are actually hurting that person more than you're helping.

Too often, we are controlled by others more than we realize. "I've got to work sixty hours a week or my boss will look down on me. He won't invite me to important meetings. He'll leave me out."

No, recognize what's happening. You are being manipulated and you need to set some boundaries. Go to your boss and say, "Here's what I'm able to do. I cannot work late every night. I have a family. I have other commitments. When I am here at work, I'll give you one hundred ten percent, but when the workday is over, I will leave the work here and go home."

You need to confront it. Don't allow yourself to be manipulated or coerced into doing something out of guilt. Start paying attention to why you respond certain ways and why you do certain things.

Maybe you are operating more out of guilt than out of desire or destiny. You are working late night after night because you feel guilty about leaving when others in the office are staying. Or maybe you are helping somebody because you feel guilty, you're overcommitted, worn out, and run down because you're afraid you're going to hurt somebody's feelings. This is all rooted in that taking on a false sense of responsibility, trying to keep everybody happy.

You should not feel guilty because you can't meet the demands that others arbitrarily put on you. You must change how you respond. If every time you disagree with your spouse, you get the cold shoulder and life is miserable for the next four hours, that's a form of manipulation. The next time something similar happens, you need to address it. Don't respond the same way. "Well, she's ignoring me. I'll show her. I'll go to the ball game!" Or "I'll go play golf." Or "I'm going shopping!"

No, if you'll change how you respond and not give in and not play those games, it will force the other person to change how he or she responds.

Say a person invites you to an event, so you check your schedule and realize you are too busy to attend, but you feel the pressure to acquiesce. You know the person will get upset if you decline. You may even fall out of their good graces.

You must recognize that is a controlling spirit, and you need to be able to say, "I would love to go, I'm sorry. I'm just not going to be able to accept your invitation." If they can't understand, then that's their problem.

To reduce your stress, be aware of high-maintenance people in your life. These people are almost impossible to keep happy. You have to call them so many times a week. You must respond at their beck and call. If not, they're going to get upset; they'll be disappointed in you. And they'll attempt to make sure you feel guilty about it!

I've found that high-maintenance people are usually controllers. They're not interested in you; they're interested in what you can do for them. They're interested in how you can make their life better. If you fall into the trap of trying to keep them happy, you're going to be weary and worn out, and you're going to be frustrated in your own life.

Many years ago, I attempted to help a married couple. They were fine people and I really liked them. In fact, when they moved to another state, I gave them some money and I tried to stay in touch. If they ever needed anything, I was always available. But it seemed like I was never doing enough. They were never happy.

I was being kind and generous, but they never saw any of that. They continually found some reason to complain, to find fault, or to make me feel guilty, as though I was not doing enough to help them.

One day I realized that they are just high-maintenance people and I am not responsible to keep them happy. I can't make them like me. I can't make them be grateful. I need to just run my race and not allow them to steal my joy.

I continued to be their friend, but I had to step back and let them work on making themselves happy. That made me very happy! That's a very freeing way to live.

Examine how you spend your time and check your motives as to why you do what you do. Is it out of guilt? Is it because somebody is manipulating or controlling you? If so, make some changes. If you don't take control of your life, others will, and they may take you places you don't want to go. You must be secure enough in yourself to tell people no. If you refuse a friend's invitation to dinner and he or she gets upset, understand something: He is not responding out of love or friendship; that person is attempting to manipulate you. She is using you for what she wants.

A true friend understands. A true friend doesn't get upset when you can't meet every one of his or her requests.

These days, I get numerous invitations to speak in all sorts of venues, and I'm always honored to be asked. But between my obligations to Lakewood Church and to my family, I'm not able to accept most invitations, even those from close friends or people that I've loved and respected for many years. At first, it was extremely difficult for me to say no to requests, because I don't like to disappoint people. But I've learned that I must take care of myself. That's my first priority. After that comes my family.

The first few times I declined those invitations, I was nervous, wondering what people would think. *They may think that I've gotten a big head,* I fretted, *that I think I'm too important.* But every time those people wrote back, they said, "Joel, it's no big deal. It's no problem. Whenever you can come, the invitation is always open." That is a true friend, somebody who is not merely concerned for his own interests. A true friend will not try to pressure you and make you feel guilty when you don't do exactly as she wants.

It is liberating to understand that you don't have to keep everybody happy. More important, I really believe that if you live your life just trying to please people, you will not be able to fulfill your God-given destiny.

When I went away to college, after my first year, I knew deep down on the inside that I was supposed to come back to Lakewood and start a television outreach. I felt it so strongly. But I was concerned about what my parents were going to think. After all, my brothers and sisters had all graduated from college. My brother Paul had spent twelve years or more in study and preparation to be a surgeon, so when I left school and went back home, I didn't know how my parents would respond.

I talked to my father about it one day, and he was open to the possibilities. He said, "Joel, that'd be great. Just do what you feel good about doing." Daddy was fine with my leaving school and developing the television ministry at Lakewood. My mother, however, was a different story. Mother needed prayer! She couldn't stand the thought of one of her children not graduating from college.

That was tough for me. As I said, I don't like to disappoint people, especially my parents. But I finally had to make the decision to do what I felt good about. I had to follow my own heart. Of course, my mother eventually came around. I told her the other day, "Mother, I didn't graduate from college, but I'm doing pretty well today!"

Sometimes, you're not going to be able to keep everybody happy, even your closest loved ones. Of course, we should honor our parents, respect them, and listen to their advice. In the end, you have to follow your own heart. An intriguing Scripture verse says, "They have made me a keeper of the vineyards, but my own vineyard I have not kept."[45] Solomon was saying, "I was real good at keeping everybody else happy. I kept my parents happy, I kept my family happy. I took care of all my relatives and my friends. But in doing so, I neglected to take care of myself."

Too often, we live to please everybody else, but we neglect to take time to please ourselves. We end up allowing somebody else to run and control our lives.

If you allow them, some people will draw all the time and energy right out of you. You would see your life go to a new level if you dared to confront those people and start making the necessary changes.

I'm not saying it's going to be easy. If people have controlled you for a long time, they're not going to like your putting your foot down. Always do what you must in love, be kind and respectful, but stand firm and make a decision that you will live in freedom.

If you are the controller rather than the person being controlled, you too need to change. You're not going to be blessed by manipulating people to get your way. Quit pressuring people into doing what you want. Take the high road, walk in love, and you'll see your relationships and life become so much better.

Let this be a turning point. If you have been living to please everybody else, or constantly trying to fix everything, rid yourself of that false sense of responsibility. Yes, reach out to others. Yes, be kind and be compassionate. But make sure that you're keeping yourself happy. After God, you are your first priority.

Friend, if you will run your race and not let people control you and manipulate you, you'll not only have less stress and more time and energy, but I also believe you'll be happier, and you will be free to fulfill the best plan that God has for you.

PART 4: FORM BETTER HABITS

1. I will examine my daily routine and identify any habits that are affecting my life negatively. I determine today that I will begin to break at least one of those negative habits and replace it with a positive habit instead.

2. I will beware of negative conditioned responses; I will train my mind to see the good. I will relax and learn to go with the flow.

3. I will not be distracted by my critics. I realize that not everyone will agree with me, or cheer me on, but I will stay focused on what I am called to do. Today, I will seek fresh ways to use the gifts, talents, and resources God has given me.

4. I recognize that I am not responsible for the happiness of everybody around me. Today I will be aware that I am responsible for keeping myself happy. I will be kind to everyone around me, but I refuse to be manipulated. I will not take on a false sense of responsibility for the actions or attitudes of others.

PART FIVE

EMBRACE THE PLACE WHERE YOU ARE

CHAPTER 20

Embrace the Place Where You Are

Do you know someone who is not happy with where he or she is in life? She is frustrated because she is not married, and her internal body clock is sounding an alarm. Or he is upset because somebody is not treating him fairly on his career path. They are constantly worried, trying to reason things out, trying to change things that only God can change.

I believe that we create much of our own unhappiness and frustration by constantly resisting and fighting against situations and circumstances occurring in our lives. We don't understand why our prayers aren't being answered, why things aren't changing sooner. "Why has this happened to me?" Consequently, we live with unrest and uneasiness on the inside.

Learn to relax and accept the place where you are. Admittedly, it may not be a great place right now. We all have things we want to see changed, things we want to happen sooner. If we really believe that God is in control and is directing our steps, then we must believe that we are exactly where we are supposed to be. We needn't be wrestling with life and resisting our circumstances all the time.

Yes, we should resist the enemy; we should resist sickness and other robbers of joy. Now, that doesn't mean that every minute we must be fighting and struggling. Some people seem to wear themselves out, constantly praying, resisting, and rebuking. They beg, "Please, God, you've got to change this situation. Change my husband. I don't like my job. My child won't do right."

No, turn all of that over to God. Your attitude should be: "God, I'm trusting You. I know that You are in control of my life. I may not understand everything that is happening, but I believe You have my best interests at heart. I'm not going to go around resisting and struggling. I'm going to relax and enjoy my life." Friend, if you can sincerely pray such a prayer, it can take an enormous amount of pressure off you.

The Bible says to "Be still, and know that I am God." [46] Notice, you need to get still. You need to be at peace with where you are right now. Things may not be perfect. You may have some areas in which you need to improve. But as long as you are living with worry and stress, you are tying the hands of Almighty God. If you could get to a place of peace, God could fight your battles for you. He can turn your negative situations around and use them for good.

Scripture records, "Those who have believed enter in to the rest of God." [47] Being in God's rest means that although you may have a problem, you trust Him to take care of it. It means that you may have a situation that you don't understand, but you are not constantly trying to figure it out. It means you have a dream in your heart, but you are not in a hurry, you're not frustrated because it hasn't come to fruition yet. In other words, when you are really in God's rest, you know that God has you in the palm of His hand. No matter where you are, you accept it as the place God wants you to be.

I'm not saying that God wants you to stay there, but if you are truly trusting Him, if you believe He is in control, then wherever you are—in either good circumstances or bad—that is where you are supposed to be. Maybe something unfair has happened; maybe somebody is not treating you right, or you are struggling financially. Still, that doesn't give you the right to live upset and frustrated.

We have to understand that God has promised He will use whatever comes into our lives for our good. He will use that difficulty to do a work in you. What you are facing currently may not be good, but if you'll keep the right attitude, He'll use it for your good.

You may be saying, "Joel, you don't understand my circumstances. I'm doing the right thing, but the wrong things are happening to me." Or "I'm in a lousy marriage." Or "People aren't treating me right."

Please don't use that as an excuse to live your life in the doldrums or in the pits. Consider the Old Testament character Joseph. He spent thirteen years in prison charged with a crime that he didn't commit. He could have constantly fought that. He could have spent all his time trying to figure out why the horrific events happened to him. He could have easily lived his life upset, negative, and bitter, but he didn't. He simply embraced the place where he was and made the best of a bad situation. His attitude was "God, this is where You have me right now. I may not like it. I may not understand it. I don't think it's fair, but I'm not dwelling on any of that. I'm going to keep doing my best, knowing that in the end, You are going to use this to my advantage."

That's exactly what God did for him. God will do the same thing for you if you will keep your attitude positively focused on Him.

You may be frustrated because you are not yet married. You're not going to be happy until you find a mate. Instead, relax and enjoy the place where God has you right now. Being frustrated will not make it happen any sooner, and perpetually fretting about your marital status may slow down the process. You pray every five minutes, telling God what to do and how to do it. You have your ideal man all picked out— what he should look like, what kind of car he should drive, how tall he should be, how much money he should make. "God, I've got to get married. I can't take it another month."

No, you have already expressed your desire to God. Why don't you just relax and say, "God, not my will but Yours be done. I'm turning this over to You. I believe You have my best interests at heart."

It is okay to be honest and pray, "God, you know I'd like to see it happen today. But I'm going to trust You and believe that at the right time, You are going to bring the right person into my life." That's what it means to trust God. You can quit trying to figure it all out on your own.

One of my favorite Scripture verses is Romans 8:28: "All things work together for good to those who love God." [48] If you can stay in an attitude of faith, God will cause every situation to work for your good.

"Well, Joel, these people at work aren't treating me right. I'm uncomfortable. I don't like it. I want to get out of this situation."

No, we can't pray away everything uncomfortable in our lives. God is not going to remove every difficulty from you instantly. He uses those things to refine us, to do a fresh work in us. In the tough times, God develops our character. The fact is, we don't grow nearly as much when everything is easy; we grow when life is difficult, when we are exercising our spiritual muscles, in the pressure spots.

Of course, none of us enjoys being uncomfortable, but it will help you to press through difficult times if you can remember that God is going to get some good out of your discomfort. You will come out of that situation stronger than before, and God is getting you prepared for greater things.

But you have to pass the test. If you are dragging around worried, trying to figure everything out, and fighting against everything that's not going your way, you will simply prolong the process. You must recognize you are where you are for a reason. It may be because of your choices, or maybe it is merely an attack of the enemy. Whatever it is, God will not allow anything to come into your life unless He has a purpose for it. You may not like it; you may be uncomfortable. But if you'll keep the right attitude, in the end, you will come out stronger and better off than you were before.

Understand that your faith will not instantly deliver you out of every problem. Instead, your faith will carry you through the problem. If God removed some of the things that you are praying for Him to remove right now, you wouldn't be prepared for the promotion that He has in store for you. He's using what you are currently going through to get you ready for the good things to come. If you are not getting your way, it doesn't mean that God doesn't love you. If your prayers aren't being answered in the way you want, or on your timetable, it doesn't mean that God is angry with you or that He is trying to punish you.

**Faith doesn't always instantly deliver you,
but it always carries you through.**

Get a bigger vision than that. Maybe it means God has something better in store. Maybe it means He's protecting you from danger up ahead. Or maybe God is just trying to do a work in you so He can take you to a whole new level. Why don't you quit resisting everything that's going on in your life? Quit fighting against everything that doesn't go your way.

"It seems like God never answers my prayers," someone may say. "He never does what I want."

Maybe God *is* answering your prayers; He's simply saying no. Or maybe He's saying it's not the right time. Or maybe He's saying, "I'm not going to remove that obstacle until you change your attitude and quit complaining about it." Make some simple adjustments, and you will see things begin to improve.

I thank God that He didn't answer some of my prayers, because sometimes what I thought was the best for me wasn't the best at all. Nevertheless, if you push and manipulate, trying to make things happen, God will sometimes let you have your way—and you will have to learn His lessons the hard way.

I've seen people jump into a relationship or a business deal that they didn't feel good about, but they wanted it so badly. God is a gentleman. If you insist, He will back off and let you do things your way. Most of the time when we do that, though, we end up settling for second best.

If events are not happening as quickly as you would like, or if you are not seeing circumstances change in your favor, open your grip on the situation; relax and learn to trust God. Know this: God is on your side. He is not trying to hold you back. Nobody wants you to fulfill your destiny more than Almighty God. Nobody wants you to see your dreams come to pass any more than He does. He put the dream in your heart in the first place. Let Him lead you and guide you.

I believe one of the best prayers that we could ever pray is "God, not my will, but Your will be done." I pray it in some form every day: "God, open up the right doors and close the wrong doors." If you will stay open to His direction, and follow your heart, God will protect you. It says in Proverbs, "If you acknowledge God in all your ways, He will direct your paths." [49] One translation says, "He'll crown your efforts with success."

Not long ago, some of our staff members and I were flying to another city aboard a small airplane. The aircraft had only one seat on each side of the aisle. After we took off, I wanted to get my tray table out so I could make some notes. The tray table on this particular plane came right out of the side, beneath my window. There was a little sign that said "pull," so I pulled, but I couldn't get it open. It was stuck. My friend Johnny was sitting across the aisle, so I looked over at his tray table, which he had pulled out with ease, and his window looked exactly like mine. I went back to work, trying to extricate my table, yanking on it even harder. I thought, *I'm going to get this tray table out if it's the last thing I ever do!*

I tugged and pulled, and it still wouldn't come out. About that time, Johnny came over and started pulling on the table release, and he couldn't get it out either. One of our other staff members tried as well. Nothing happened. Finally, I sat down across the aisle in a different seat. That's when I looked up and noticed right above that window where we had been pulling was a little sign in big bold letters. It read, "No tray table this seat. Emergency exit only."

I said, "Dear God, thank you for not letting me have my way. Thank you for not opening up that door." Thank goodness the people who designed that plane knew there'd be people like me on board. They put a latch up top, where you had to use both hands to open the emergency door. Otherwise, pulling that latch may indeed have been one of the last things that I ever did!

Thank God, He knows what's best for us. Thank God that He's merciful and He doesn't always give us our way.

I've learned that when my prayers aren't being answered, or when things aren't happening as fast as I would like, that either means that God is protecting me from danger up ahead, it's not the right time, or God has something better in store.

The first year I went away to college, I applied for a job at the university television studio. The school owned a large, well-known production facility, and I'd always wanted to be a part of it. Television production was my passion. The first week of school, I met with the production manager in charge of all the cameramen and hiring all the assistants. At that point, I had several years of camera experience under my belt.

The production manager went out of his way to be kind to me. He took a couple of hours to show me around, and we seemed to really hit if off. When it came time for me to leave, he said, "Joel, I'll call you later this week and I'll let you know about the job."

That week went by, and I didn't hear from him. The next week, nothing. The following week, still no word. Finally, I called him, and he was always either busy or out of town. It was the strangest thing: I didn't think I would have any problem getting that job, but the door simply wasn't opening. Worse yet, I wanted it so badly, but I could see it just wasn't meant to be. Finally, I accepted it and embraced the thought, "No big deal. I'm just going to let it go."

In retrospect, I now realize that if I had taken that position, I probably would not have returned to Lakewood Church to start a television outreach. I know my personality. I would have been so caught up in the excitement and I would have loved it so much, I'm sure I just would have stayed right there at the university TV station.

But God knows what's best for us. Although that job looked great to me at the time, I didn't know where God was taking me. I didn't know what He had in store. Had I remained there, I would have missed what God wanted me to do at Lakewood, and you would probably not be reading this book.

Too often, we're shortsighted. We can see only a little ways down the road, and even that we see through a glass dimly. God, though, can see the big picture. He knows when something is going to be a dead end. He knows when someone is going to be a distraction that will hinder us from our destiny.

Some of the things you may be frustrated about right now, ten years from now you will look back at and thank God for not answering that prayer the way you wanted or for not opening up that door. You may not be able to see it right now, but that's what faith is all about. Why don't you trust God? Believe that He has you in the palm of His hand and know that when it comes time for God to open a door, no man can keep it shut. No obstacle is too high.

Your enemies may be powerful, but our God is all-powerful. When God says it's time to promote you, you are going to be promoted. The good news is that your promotion will not be one second late. *Suddenly,* God can turn any situation around. *Suddenly,* God can cause a door to open. All it takes is one touch of God's favor.

Our attitude should be "I'm not going to live upset and frustrated. I know that everything is going to be all right. I know that in the end, it is all going to work out to my advantage."

You may be going through some tough times. But remember, God has promised He will never let you go through more than you can handle.

"Joel, I don't understand why this has happened to me. Why haven't my prayers been answered? Why did I get sick? Why did my marriage not last?"

Some things you may never understand this side of heaven. If you are always trying to figure it out, it will only bring frustration and confusion. Learn to trust God, and know that as long as you're doing your best, as long as you're keeping your heart pure before God, you are exactly where you're supposed to be. It may not be easy, but in the end, God is going to use it to your advantage.

One of the most important aspects of faith is trusting God even when we don't understand. A good friend of mine contracted cancer. I called him to encourage him, and I thought he'd be all down and depressed, but I was pleasantly surprised. He said, "Joel, I'm at peace. I don't like this, but I know God is still in control. And I believe in my heart that He's going to bring me through this thing."

Even in your times of greatest difficulty, even if the bottom falls out, you don't have to be distraught and let yourself get all worked up. Sometimes we think we always must be praying, resisting, quoting the Scriptures every minute. Certainly, there's nothing wrong with that. But remaining at rest, remaining in peace, keeping your joy, keeping a smile on your face, that's all part of fighting the good fight of faith as well.

If you're in a hard place, be encouraged in knowing that God is still in control of your life. He made your body. He knows your circumstances. Don't sit around depressed and discouraged. Your attitude should be "God, I'm trusting You. I know You can do what men can't do, and I'm committing my life into Your hands." That attitude of faith pleases God. People who have a made-up mind. People who say, "God, I'm going to trust You if I get my way or if I don't get my way. I will trust You in the good times or the tough times."

God, I'm going to trust You if I get my way or if I don't.

Recall those three Hebrew teenagers in the Old Testament who wouldn't bow down to King Nebuchadnezzar's golden idol. The king got so upset that he ordered them thrown into a fiery furnace.

The Hebrew boys said, "King, we're not worried about it. We know that our God will deliver us. *But even if He doesn't,* we're still not going to bow down." Notice, they embraced the place where they were, even though it was difficult, even though they didn't like it.

You can do something similar. Quit living frustrated because your prayers weren't answered the way you wanted. Quit being depressed because you're not as far in your career as you had hoped, or because you have a problem in your marriage, or in your finances. No, just keep pressing forward. Keep your joy and enthusiasm. You may not be exactly where you hoped to be, but know this: God is still in control of your life. Moreover, as long as you keep passing the tests, no forces of darkness can keep you from fulfilling your God-given destiny.

You can have that heavy burden lifted off you. You don't have to fight and struggle all the time, trying to change everybody and everything. No, just embrace the place where you are and believe that God is in control. He's doing a work in you. He's guiding and directing you.

If you are currently in a storm, or if you are facing some severe difficulties, hear God speaking to your heart these words: "Rise above it. Quit fighting. Quit trying to change things that only I can change."

Believe that God has a great plan for your life. Friend, if you'll learn to embrace the place where you are, you can rise higher. You'll overcome every obstacle, and you can live that life of victory that God has in store for you!

CHAPTER 21

It Is Well with My Soul

Have you ever noticed that it is in the difficult times that we grow stronger? That's when we are being stretched. That's when God is developing our character and preparing us for promotion.

We may not like it; stretching can sometimes be uncomfortable. But if we can keep the right attitude, we will come out better than we were before.

The key to passing the test is to remain in peace, at rest. When you're in peace, you have power. When you're at rest, God can fight your battles for you. Many people wear themselves out, frustrated because they don't have the job they want, upset because a child won't do right, worried over a health problem. No, turn all that over to God and be willing to go through tough times with a good attitude.

In Colossians, chapter 3, Paul prayed that the people would have the strength to endure whatever came their way. Think about that. The great Apostle Paul didn't pray that God would remove every difficulty. He didn't pray that God would deliver them instantly. He prayed that they'd have the strength to go through it.

Sometimes we pray, "God, you've got to get me out of this situation today. I can't stand it any longer. If it goes on another week, I'm not going to make it." But a better way to pray is, "Father, please give me the strength to go through this with a good attitude. Help me to keep my joy. Help me to keep my peace." Our circumstances are not going to change until we change.

But you may say, "It is so difficult. I have a serious health problem. And I have this situation at work . . ." No, you have the power of the

Most High God on the inside of you. You can withstand anything that comes your way. You are more than a conqueror, a victor and not a victim. Sure, we'd all love God to deliver us instantly. Most of the time, though, that's not the way He works. Make a decision to turn the situation over to God and then stop worrying about it. Don't allow it to dominate your thoughts and words; instead, move to that place of peace and rest. Even though the situation may be hard, and you may not like it, you are growing.

God has a plan and a purpose for everything. We may not be able to see it right now. But God has promised He will not allow anything to come into our lives unless He can ultimately get some good out of it. This should take all the pressure off us. That means if our prayers aren't being answered in the way we want, God must have something better in store. He knows what's best, so you can believe that all things are going to work together for your good. Don't live stressed out when the pressure times come.

Determine in your heart and mind "I'm not going to be depressed because my business hasn't grown as I wanted it to." Or "I refuse to lose heart merely because my child is not doing right. No, I'm going to stay in peace, trusting God, knowing that at the right time, God is going to turn it around and use it to my advantage." That's an incredibly liberating way to live.

You may suffer from stomach problems, headaches, ulcers, and all sorts of other ailments; possibly, you can't sleep well at night, because your mind is perpetually rerunning images of you fighting against everything that isn't going your way. You're trying to change things that only God can change. When God is not moving in the situation, either it is not the right time, or He is doing a work in you. Center your mind in that place of peace where you can truly say, "All right, Father; not my will but Yours."

When you understand this principle, it makes life so much easier. You won't live frustrated because your plans didn't work out. You don't have to be disappointed for a month because you didn't get the promotion you wanted. You don't have to get upset because somebody is being unfair to you. You know that God is in control and He has you exactly where He wants you. As long as you keep trusting Him,

God is going to fight your battles for you. That's what it says in the book of Exodus, chapter 14. "If you will remain at rest and hold your peace, then the battle is not yours, but the battle is the Lord's."

Consider this: God wants you to remain at rest, to keep your peace of mind. As long as we're upset, frustrated, and all bent out of shape, God will back away and wait. To show God that we are trusting Him, we must stay in peace; keep a smile on your face; have a good attitude day in and day out. When you are consistent, when you're stable, and when you're not moved by your circumstances, you are proclaiming, "I believe that God is in complete control of my life."

I used to play basketball with my friends several times a week. One night after the game, it was still rather early, so I asked one of the guys if he wanted to stop and get something to eat. He casually answered, "No, Joel, I've got to go up to the hospital. I'm taking chemotherapy."

"You've got to be kidding!" I said. "You're doing what?"

"This is my second bout with cancer," he replied, "so I take chemo three times a week."

I was amazed. I didn't even know anything was wrong with him. He always had a smile on his face, always was upbeat, and had an attitude of faith. He looked as if he were on top of the world.

Other people in similar situations drag around, wallowing in self-pity, defeated and blaming God. But not him. He knew that God was still in control. Even though he didn't like his circumstances, even though he was uncomfortable, he didn't allow it to get him down. His attitude was "I'm not going to sit around feeling sorry for myself. I'm not going to let this disease take over my life. I'm going to deal with it and move on." And he did exactly that. Several years later, he's cancer-free. God has totally healed him. I saw him not long ago. He's as healthy as he can be.

You may be fighting some serious battles, but the good news is, God is bigger than anything that you're facing. He can make a way even when it looks like there is no way. Don't quit living your life. Don't let that obstacle be the central focus of your existence. Keep pressing forward, trusting God, and knowing that as you believe, all things are possible. It may look dark and bleak right now, but the

Scripture says, "Weeping may endure for a night, but joy comes in the morning." [50] It doesn't matter what the situation looks like in the natural, because our God is a *supernatural* God. When you are trusting in Him, you can rest. You needn't be stressed out or worried. You know that everything is going to be all right. You know that God has you in the palm of His hand. As you continue in peace, God will make sure that you fulfill every single day that He has ordained for you. The Bible says: "No man can snatch you out of God's hands." That means no sickness is too great, no enemy too powerful. If God be for you, who dare even be against you? Even when you are uncomfortable, remind yourself that you will come out better than you entered that situation. Even in the worst-case scenario—if we die—we go to heaven to be with the Lord!

Some people's faith is tied to their circumstances: When their circumstances are good, their faith is up; when the circumstances are adverse, their faith is down. You don't have to live that way. When you know that God is directing your steps, you can be consistent. No matter what comes into your life, God will use that for your good.

Sometimes God may ask us to go through things to help somebody else. He might put you in an uncomfortable place so you can be the answer to someone's prayer.

"Joel, I can't stand my job. These people get on my nerves. They irritate me. I shouldn't have to put up with them."

Have you ever considered that God may have you there on purpose, so He can do a work in them? Maybe God wants you to speak a word of hope into somebody's life; perhaps He is counting on you to let your light shine. Maybe God wants you to plant a seed of faith, so He can change their hearts.

Mary Anne endured some difficult and unfair experiences growing up. Not surprisingly, her first marriage didn't last long, so she soon married a second man and set about making his life miserable. She wasn't trying to be difficult; she was simply so wounded and hurt, she couldn't trust anybody. She was a negative and bitter person.

Curtis, Mary Anne's husband, considered leaving her numerous times. He had every reason, and nobody who knew the couple would have blamed him. But he knew deep inside that he was supposed to stay with Mary Anne. He later told me, "Joel, it was the most difficult thing that I ever did. I was uncomfortable. I didn't like it. I didn't understand it." But Curtis stuck with her and was willing to pay the price to get her some help. Today Mary Anne is healthy and whole, and their relationship is strong.

Mary Anne realized what a gift she had been given. She said, "Joel, what if Curtis had been like my former husband and had taken the easy way out? What if he had not cared enough to stick with me? I'd be in an asylum or a cemetery today."

As much as you desire to become a better you, it is important to understand that not everything God does is about you. Sometimes God asks you to suffer for somebody else. Sometimes God takes you through challenging experiences so you can help others in need. Precisely at that point, we need to say, "God, I'm trusting You. I believe that You are in control. Even though I don't understand this and it's not necessarily something I may have chosen, I'm going to stick with it, and with Your help, I will maintain a good attitude."

You may not always feel like doing it, but do it as a sacrifice to God because you love and trust Him. God rewards such an attitude. Don't give up on that husband or wife; don't give up on those children. Don't write off your self-serving coworkers. Keep loving them, keep praying for them and encouraging them. God is keeping the records. As you sow seeds to help someone else, God sees, and He will reward you.

Sometimes we can get so focused on what we want that we let it consume us. I've known people who are not going to be happy until they get married. They're not going to be happy until their business grows or until they get out of a certain situation. No, it's imperative that we turn those situations over to God and learn to be content right where we are. When we turn loose of our will, and our way, God works wonders.

My sister Lisa and her husband Kevin desired to have a baby, but Lisa just couldn't conceive. She went through all sorts of fertility treatments, and they spent a lot of money. After several years, the doctor said, "Lisa, I'm sorry. There's nothing more we can do for you. You are not going to be able to have any children."

Lisa was so disappointed and discouraged. She had spent a great deal of time, energy, and money. She was always praying, believing, and doing everything she could. She was nearly consumed by her desire to have a baby. And now she was just emotionally and physically drained. One day she got tired of struggling and fighting. She said, "God, I'm not going to ask You another time about having this baby. You already know what I want. I'm just turning it all over to You." She later said, from that day forward, she did her best not to worry about it. She no longer begged God for a baby. Instead, anytime she thought about it, she thanked God that He was still in control. Really, she was saying, "God, not my will, but Yours be done."

A few months after that, Lisa and Kevin received a call from a friend of ours about adopting twin baby girls. Long story short, they ended up doing exactly that. A few years later, they adopted another child, a baby boy. Today they have three beautiful children. But nothing changed until Lisa turned loose of her consuming desire to have a child.

Sometimes we can get so consumed with our dreams or overcoming an obstacle, that's all we think about, talk about, and pray about, and we're not going to be happy unless it comes to pass exactly the way we want it. That leads to frustration, and if we're not careful, possibly to resentment. When you sense that happening, you must get back to that place of rest and peace where you can honestly say, "God, I trust You. I believe that You know what's best for me. And God, even if this doesn't work out the way I want, I'm not going to be unhappy. I'm not going to let this ruin the rest of my life. I'm making a decision that I'm going to be content right where You have me today."

One of my favorite stories in church history is that of Horatio G. Spafford, a wealthy lawyer and businessman who lived back in the 1800s. Spafford's story is not the success story, however, that we seek nowadays. In fact, he encountered horrendous tragedy in his life. His wife and four daughters were on a ship crossing the Atlantic Ocean when the vessel collided with another ship, and all four Spafford daughters lost their lives along with more than two hundred other people. Spafford's wife sent a telegram informing her husband of the terrible news.

Horatio Spafford booked passage across the Atlantic Ocean to be reunited with his grieving wife. At one point, the captain notified him that they were passing the spot where he believed Spafford's daughters had died. Horatio Spafford stared solemnly at the rolling waves, and that night he wrote the words to what would become a beloved hymn of the Christian faith: "When peace like a river attendeth my way, when sorrows like sea billows roll, whatever my lot, You have taught me to say, It is well, it is well with my soul."

No matter what comes our way in life, we need to be able to say, "It is well with my soul. Life may have thrown me some curves, but it is well with my soul. All my dreams may not have come to pass just yet, that's okay. I'm not in a hurry. I know in God's timing they will.

"My plans didn't work out. But nonetheless, it is well with my soul. I received a bad report from the doctor, things don't look good. But I know God has another report. I know He can do what men can't do. And whatever happens to me, it is well, it is well with my soul." That's the kind of attitude we need to have.

You may need to get a new perspective. Perhaps you have been too focused on what you don't have, what you can't do, and what's wrong in your life. Maybe you've been telling God every five minutes what to do and how to do it, and letting Him know that you are not going to be happy unless it turns out exactly like you want it.

Make a decision to turn it over to God. Psalm 55:22 says: "Cast your burdens on the Lord. Release the weight of them and God will sustain you." No matter how dark and gloomy it looks in your life right now, if you can release the weight of those burdens, you will rise higher and you will see the sun break forth in your life.

This starts by believing that God is in control. In the following chapters, we'll look more closely at how that works out in our lives, but in the meantime, you can decide right now that you will trust Him wherever you are. When you do that, the battle is not yours; the battle is the Lord's. Ask God to give you the strength to endure. And rest assured, He will take care of you, even in the midst of life's most vicious storms.

CHAPTER 22

Stay in Peace

Did you know that you can have peace even in the midst of diffi-cult circumstances? Many people are trying to get rid of their problems, hoping they will then be happy; then they can start enjoy-ing their lives. But God wants us to learn to have peace in the midst of the storms. He wants us to have peace even when things aren't going our way—when your boss isn't treating you right, you didn't get the promotion you wanted, your child isn't doing what he should. If we make the mistake of basing our peace on our circumstances, we'll never experience God's best, because something will always upset us. You're never going to get rid of life's little aggravations. You will never get to a point where you don't have challenges or opportunities to get discouraged. We have to change our approach to life.

The Apostle Paul experienced all kinds of heartache. People had done unfair things to him, others had lied about him. Nevertheless, he said, "In spite of all these things, we are more than conquerors." That's the kind of attitude we need to have. Don't use your faith to try to get rid of all your problems. Use your faith to remain calm in the midst of your problems.

Jesus was asleep on a small boat when suddenly a huge storm arose. The winds were fierce and strong, batting the boat back and forth. The disciples got all upset and were afraid. They finally said, "Jesus, please get up. We're about to perish!"

Jesus got up and simply spoke to the storm. He said, "Peace, be still." Instantly, the wind subsided, and the Sea of Galilee turned to a glassy calm. The reason Jesus was able to bring peace to that situation was because He had peace inside Himself. He was in the storm, but He didn't let the storm get in Him.

You can be in the storm, but don't let the storm get in you.

Peace is not necessarily the absence of trouble, nor is it always the absence of enemies. You can have trouble and conflict all around you on the outside, yet have real peace on the inside.

You may be upset and worried about some aspect of life. Perhaps you are concerned about your finances, or there's a situation at work that is unjust or unfair, and you are letting that situation rile you on the inside. Day after day, it weighs on you, draining your joy, your energy, and your enthusiasm. You have let the storm get on the inside, and you need to make some changes.

"As soon as I get through this, then I'm going to get back to being my normal self," you may be saying.

No, you know that when this challenge is over, there will be something else that can steal your peace. You've got to change your approach and stop allowing those things to upset you. Instead, turn that situation over to God.

Understand that until you get to this place of peace, God can't really work in your life the way He wants to, because God works where there is an attitude of faith and expectancy, not attitudes of unbelief, worry, despair, and discouragement. Every day you will have opportunities to lose your peace. Somebody may be rude to you on the phone. You want to jump right down their throat. Instead, say to yourself, "No, I'm going to stay at peace. I'm not going to allow him to upset me."

Or perhaps your boss doesn't give you the credit you deserve. You didn't get the big promotion for which you were hoping. Say something such as "That's okay. I know God is in control. I know God has something better in store for me."

"Well, I'm upset because this man walked out of our relationship," Suzanne says. "It was wrong. It was just so unfair. I want to call him up and let him have a piece of my mind."

"No, hold your peace," I advised. "If you'll stay calm and at rest,

God will bring somebody better into your life. He'll take what the enemy meant for evil and turn it all around and use it for your advantage. But you've got to do your part and hold your peace. Don't live life upset, worried, and frustrated."

Sometimes we lose our peace over things we can't change. You can't change the traffic in the morning. You might as well just stay calm. You can't make your spouse or your boss or your neighbor do what's right. Only God can. You might as well enjoy your life while God is in the process of changing things in the lives of people around you.

One time Victoria and I and our kids were going on vacation to Branson, Missouri. It was Christmas season and the airports were crowded. We had to change planes in Memphis, so we had a brief layover. We got off the plane and our kids were hungry, so we stopped to get them something to eat, and then we took off toward the gate. It seemed to take forever to get there. We had to catch a shuttle bus, and then we ran the rest of the way. When we got to the gate, the plane was still there, but the main door at the jetway was closed. I begged the woman behind the counter to get our family on that plane. I prayed for God's favor. I smiled real big. I was as friendly as I could be . . .

But none of that worked.

I don't want to sit in this airport for three or four hours waiting for the next flight, I thought. I could feel myself starting to get stressed. I had to make a choice right then and there: Was I going to keep my peace or was I going to give it away? I kept about half of it!

When we finally got to Branson, I got off the plane and an older couple approached me. The woman said, "I hate to bother you, but I've got to tell you, I really love you. I listen to you all the time; I just enjoy you so much." On and on she went, just heaping compliments on me. I started to feel better, and the sting of the missed flight didn't smart quite so badly. I noticed that her husband was looking at me as if to say, "Who in the world is this guy?" as his wife continued to gush. As we were finally leaving, I overheard her say, "Oh, honey, you know who he is. That's the guy that sings 'Achy Breaky Heart.' "

I thought, *It's going to be one of those days!*

We have to learn to keep our peace, even when people don't have a clue who we are, even when we get caught in traffic, even when we miss the flight, even when our plans don't work out.

How do you know that's not where God wants you to be? How do you know God is not protecting you from an accident? I love the Scripture in Proverbs that says, "Since the Lord is directing our steps, why do we try to figure out everything that happens along the way?" Just go with the flow. Quit worrying about things you can't change. Turn the situation completely over to God, knowing that He is in control of your life.

One of the best ways that we can show God we are trusting Him is by simply remaining calm. When you get to that point where the storm is raging, people are treating you unfairly, or maybe you've received a bad report from the doctor, or you just lost your job, in the natural you should be discouraged; you should be upset, but instead, you have a smile on your face. You still have a spring in your step. You are at peace. What you're really saying is, "God, I trust You. I know You are bigger than this sickness. I know You're bigger than this marriage struggle. I know You are bigger than my enemies."

Be the type of person who remains calm in the midst of the storm. When somebody is saying critical things about you, remind yourself (and others, if necessary), "That's okay, I know God is in control. I know God will fight my battles for me."

"Well, aren't you going to at least respond? Aren't you going to set the record straight?"

"No, I know God will be my vindicator. If I have been wronged, He will make things right."

Somebody may say, "I heard you got a bad report from the doctor. I'm sure you're all upset."

"No, I'm not upset," you can reply. "I'm at peace. I know my life is in the palm of God's hand."

"Well, I heard you're up against some big enemies," somebody else warns.

"Yes, that's true, but I'm not worried. I know God is bigger. Nobody can stand against my God. With men it may be impossible, but with God all things are possible."

Recently, I was waiting patiently in my car for a particular parking spot. The man was about to pull out, and I was sitting there with my turn signal blinking. I'd been there long enough that it was quite obvious I was going to pull into the spot as soon as it was vacated. When the driver backed out his car, however, he blocked me for a couple of seconds, and another car pulled in the spot right in front of me. I couldn't believe it! There was no doubt in my mind that the person who pulled into the parking spot must have seen me waiting. I had to make a decision. Was I going to lose my peace, or was I going to stay calm and overlook it? Was I going to get upset, or was I going to sow it as a seed and trust God to make it up to me?

In the natural, I wanted to blow my horn and let him know what I thought. The thought crossed my mind, *Well, I'll wait till he goes inside, and then I'll go let a little air out of each tire!*

But I decided, *This is not worth losing my peace over. I'm just going to bless him and move on.* I whispered a quick prayer for the rude driver and then pulled out to look for another parking spot.

Don't allow anyone to steal your peace. Understand that there will always be people around you who are able to aggravate you if you allow them. And usually you cannot just pray them away. Even if they did leave, God would probably send two more people to replace them! Maybe people at your office are gossiping about you, talking behind your back, or acting in some condescending manner toward you. They get on your nerves, and if you were operating under your own power, you would want to get in there and argue with them. But if you'll just hold your peace, if you'll be the bigger person and take the high road, if you will overlook those things, God will fight your battles.

Throughout Scripture, the person who truly trusts in God is compared to an eagle. The eagle has some pests, one of which is a crow. He's always squawking, always causing the eagle trouble. The truth is we all have a few crows in our life. You may have an entire flock of them, along with a few chickens and turkeys, as well!

Certain people can rub us the wrong way; they can irritate us if we allow them. We need to take a lesson from the eagle instead. When the eagle is out flying, often a crow will come up right behind him and start to pester him, aggravating and annoying him. Although the eagle is much larger, it cannot maneuver quickly. To get rid of his pest, the eagle simply stretches out his eight-foot wingspan and catches some of the thermal currents, and he rises up higher and higher. Eventually, he gets to an altitude where no other bird can live. The crow can't even breathe up there. On rare occasions, eagles have been spotted at altitudes as high as 20,000 feet, nearly as high as a jet flies.

In the same manner, if you want to get rid of your pest, you need to rise higher. Don't ever sink down to the opposition's level. Don't argue; don't try to pay somebody back; don't give them the cold shoulder. Be the bigger person. Overlook their faults. Walk in love and dare to bless even your enemies. In the long run, crows can't compete with eagles.

Friend, you are an eagle. You've been made in the image of Almighty God. Learn to live above your circumstances. Rise above the petty politics at the office. Don't let people pull you into strife and division and get you all upset or gossiping.

Always remember, the turkeys, chickens, and crows cannot live at the altitude for which you were designed to soar. God is in complete control of your life. He's promised if you will remain at rest, He'll make your wrongs right. He'll bring justice into your life. You don't have to worry, nor must you be controlled by your circumstances. You can do as the eagle and rise up above.

You won't see an eagle pecking around in the chicken coop with a bunch of chickens. An eagle lives in the high places, where he's close to God.

Moreover, when the storms come, an eagle doesn't simply go through the storm. No, he puts his wings out and catches a little more wind and he rises above it. He'll rise higher until he's completely above all that turmoil. That eagle is not concerned about the storm he's facing. He doesn't get upset. He knows he has a way out.

No doubt, he probably could fight his way through the storm, struggle and strain, and come out weary, worn, and all beat up. What a shame for him to live that way when God has given him the ability to rise above it.

Yet that is what many of us do. God has given us His peace. He's told us to cast our cares on Him. He said if we'll just remain at rest,

He will fight our battles for us. Too often, though, we allow ourselves to become worried and upset. We let people steal our joy. We get bent out of shape if our plans don't work out exactly as we had hoped. Or maybe we're frustrated because our boss or our husband or wife is not doing what we want them to do.

You may not be able to change certain aspects of your life, but you can rise above them. Turn those situations over to God. Make a decision today that you are not going to allow those things to upset you and bother you anymore.

Interestingly, the crow has to flap his wings tenaciously simply to fly. He has to work constantly. The chicken can barely get off the ground; no matter how much he flaps his wings, he's not going far. Yet an eagle merely catches the right wind currents and he'll soar. He doesn't have to be like the crow, working and straining all the time. He just puts his wings out and rests in what God has given him, letting the winds carry him.

If you are always frustrated, trying to fix everything in your life, trying to straighten this person out for what he or she said about you, worried about your health, worried about your finances, you're acting like that crow. You're working and working, flapping and flapping. Friend, life doesn't have to be that way. Why don't you relax? God is in complete control of your life. He said He'd never leave you nor forsake you. He said He'd be the friend that sticks closer than a brother.

You may say, "I don't see how my business can make it." Or "I don't see how I can possibly resolve these problems."

The Scripture says that the things we see with our natural eyes are only temporary. That means they are subject to change. All it takes is one touch of God's favor, and God can turn around any situation. Suddenly, God can prosper your business. God can give you one idea or one new account that will cause your business to take off. God can bring somebody into your life who will really love you. He can cause you to be at the right place at the right time. In any situation, God can turn it around in a split second of time.

Make a decision today that you are going to enter into God's rest. You're not going to live worried anymore. You're not going to let people steal your joy. You're not going to give up on the dreams that God has placed in your heart. Perhaps you need to get a new perspective, a fresh outlook. Maybe you've been in a difficult situation for a long time. It just doesn't look like it's going to get any better. The storm is raging and you are discouraged. Life looks gloomy and you have found yourself living lower than you believe God intends. You need to do like that eagle and rise higher, above the circumstances.

At times, I have been on an airplane about to take off and the skies outside are gray and overcast, almost depressing. Then the plane races down the runway and takes off, climbing through the clouds. Finally, we break through the dismal skies, and behold, up above the clouds the sun is shining and the sky is bright blue. You can tell the air is crystal clear.

Now, here's what intrigues me: The sun was shining the whole time. I just had to get a higher perspective to see it. Similarly, the clouds in your life are only temporary. It may look dark and dismal right now, but the sun is up there, shining brightly. One of the best things you can say to yourself when you are tempted to get discouraged is, "This too shall pass. It is not going to last forever. The clouds will dissipate one day, and I will see the goodness of God again in my life."

Friend, get a higher perspective. God is on your side. There's nothing too difficult for Him. Lay aside anything that is weighing you down, so you can live free from worry, frustration, or discouragement, knowing that God is in complete control. When life gets tough and things don't go your way, don't be a crow or a chicken. Be the eagle God made you to be. Stretch your wings and rise to the level where God wants you to live. You were made to soar; you were made for more.

CHAPTER 23

Remember the Good

The Psalmist said, "I recall the many miracles God has done for me. They are constantly in my thoughts. I cannot stop thinking about them." [51] Notice, he said thoughts of God's goodness were constantly in his mind. That's a great way to live!

Too often, though, we remember what we should forget—our disappointments, hurts, and failures—and we forget what we should remember—our victories, successes, and the good times.

In the Old Testament, God commanded His people to celebrate certain feasts so they would not forget what He had done for them, and so they could pass on those inspiring stories to the next generation. Several times a year, the Israelites stopped whatever they were doing and everybody celebrated how God brought them out of slavery, or how God defeated this enemy, or how He protected them against that calamity. These celebrations were not optional; they were commanded, and the people were required to attend and remember God's goodness to them.

In other places, the Bible records how God's people put down "memorial stones." These large markers were to remind the people of specific victories God had given them. Every time they or future generations passed by a memorial, they would remember the mighty things God had done.

We need to do something similar. Take time to remember your victories, and celebrate what God has done in your life. Put out some memorial stones.

This is one of the best ways to build your faith and keep yourself encouraged. Remember the time that God made a way for you when it looked as if there was no way. Remember when you were so lonely, and God brought somebody special into your life. Recall how God has healed you or someone you know; think of how He protected you in the storm, guided you, blessed you. If you will get this awareness of God's goodness down on the inside, you won't go around thinking, *Well, I wonder if I'll ever get out of this mess? I wonder if God's ever going to work in my life.*

No, you'll be saying, "I know if God did it for me once, He'll do it for me again!"

It would do you good to review God's goodness to you on a regular basis—simply thinking about the major victories in your life, the unexpected successes, or the times when you knew that God intervened in your circumstances. Remember the day your children were born. Remember how God gave you that job. Remember when God brought that special person into your life. Remind yourself how you fell in love and got married; thank God for your spouse and your family. Remember what God has done for you.

I do this often and on purpose. I think about the time I walked into a jewelry store in Houston, Texas, as a young man in my early twenties. I was minding my own business, hoping to purchase a watch battery, and out walked the most beautiful woman that I'd ever seen. The moment I saw Victoria, I thought to myself, *God, you just answered my prayers!* We dated for a year and a half and she couldn't keep her hands off me, so we got married! At least that's the way I remember it. But I don't take meeting and marrying Victoria for granted. That wasn't a coincidence or a lucky break. That was God directing my steps and causing me to be at the right place at the right time. When I remember that, it reminds me that God is in control of my life. It gives me confidence to know that if God was directing my steps back then, God can direct my steps today.

When we learn to recall the good things God has done, it helps us to stay in an attitude of faith and to remain grateful. It's hard to go around complaining when you are constantly thinking about how good God has been to you. It's hard to get negative and to veer off into unbelief when you are always talking about God's blessings and favor in your life.

"Well, Joel, if God would do something like that for me—if He'd bring me a beautiful wife, or if He'd bring me somebody great—I'd have something good to recall as well."

No, God has done something for every one of us. We merely need to go back and remember where we came from. Maybe you used to think or speak negatively. You were depressed and defeated. Today, though, you are rising higher; you know you are a victor and not a victim. Perhaps at one point you suffered with all kinds of addictions and bad habits. But God supernaturally delivered you, and today you are healthy and whole. Thank God for what He has done. Remember how He set you free. Remembering where you came from is one of the best ways to keep yourself encouraged.

Sometimes we take these things for granted. Some people don't even realize that it was God at work in their life.

One man I heard about was driving around in a crowded parking lot, trying to find a space. He finally got so frustrated, he said, "God, if You will give me a parking space, I'll attend church every Sunday."

Just then, a car backed out of the front row, and the frustrated driver pulled into the open spot. He looked up and said, "Never mind, God. I just found one."

Too often, we forget God is the Giver of all good things. God is the one who caused us get that "lucky break." He's the one who caused us to be at the right place at the right time. How many times have you been driving on a busy highway and you said to yourself, "Whew! That car almost hit me. Another split second and I would have had an accident." That was God's hand of protection. Understand that there's no such thing as a coincidence when your life is directed by God. When something good happens to you, be sensitive, recognize the work of God, and learn to recall it often.

Shortly after Victoria and I were married, I was driving on a Houston freeway by myself. It was a Monday afternoon, and it had been pouring down rain for nearly twenty minutes. I was driving in the second lane from the left, and when I changed lanes I sloshed through a large puddle of water. My tires lost traction and the car hydroplaned. I lost control of the car and headed straight toward the concrete barrier in the center of the highway. I smashed into that median strip traveling at a speed of about fifty miles per hour. When I hit the barrier, it catapulted me back across the freeway and spun my car violently out of control.

I didn't have time to pray; I didn't have time to quote the Ninety-first Psalm. I didn't have time to call the 24-Hour Prayer Hotline. I only had time to say "Jesus!" As I spun back across that freeway, I found myself looking straight into the headlights of an oncoming eighteen-wheeler, a heavy tractor trailer truck. It looked like I could reach out and touch his front grill. I couldn't have been five or six feet away. I closed my eyes, expecting to hear the crunch of metal at any moment, assuming my life was over.

Somehow, someway, however, I suddenly found myself in the ditch on the other side of the freeway. I had crossed six lanes of traffic during rush hour in Houston, Texas, and no other vehicle had crashed into me!

After I checked to make sure I still had all my body parts, I climbed out of my car. As I did, I noticed that the eighteen-wheeler—the truck that had almost hit me—had pulled over to the side of the freeway and was backing up. It took about ten minutes for the truck to ease back to where I was.

The driver bounded out of the truck's cab and ran to where I was leaning against my car. The first thing he said to me was, "Boy, you must be living right."

I sort of laughed and said, "What do you mean?"

"I don't know how I missed you," the trucker said, shaking his head. "You were right in front of me, and I tried to swerve, but my rig is fully loaded. I couldn't do it. So, I just braced myself and got ready for the collision."

A quizzical look spread across the man's face as he said, "I know this sounds odd, but right at the last moment, I felt this pocket of wind push me into the other lane."

I thought to myself, *He may call it a pocket of wind, but I know that was the angel of the Lord. That was God's hand of protection.*

For me, that is another memorial stone that I can put out in my life. I know if it were not for the goodness of God, I might not be here today. But God showed up and made a way when it looked like there was no way. I don't take that for granted; I remember the great things God has done in my life, and I thank Him for them.

I encourage you to keep a notebook, something like a diary or a journal. When something happens in your life that you know is God, write it down. You know God opened up a door. Add that to your list. You know God spared your life or you know God spoke to you a specific word of direction; make a note of that, too. You were down and discouraged, ready to give up, when God quickened a Scripture to your heart and it lifted your spirits. Write that down. Keep a running record of the good things that God has done for you.

It need not always be something big; to others it may seem quite insignificant. But you know it is God guiding your life. You may unexpectedly meet somebody. They introduce you to another person, and that leads to you getting a new client. Write that down. Maybe you are driving down the highway, and you see a new billboard that sparks an idea that you take to the office. The bosses like it and your idea leads to a promotion. Recognize that is God at work in your life. Write that down.

Then on a regular basis, get that notebook out and read about all the great things God has done in your life. You will be encouraged! When you recall how God opened up this door for you, protected you over here, restored you there, healed you there, your faith will increase. Especially in times of difficulty, when you are tempted to get discouraged, get that notebook out and read it again. If you do that, you will not go through the day discouraged and defeated. You will know that God is in control of your life. He is holding you in the palm of His hand, and He will take care of you.

CHAPTER 24

God Is in Control

To truly become a better you, it is imperative to believe that God is in control of your life. Too many people go around worried and upset. They're always trying to figure everything out. How am I going to get out of this problem? How can I change my child? When am I ever going to get married? Why won't my dreams come to pass?

But that's not the way God wants us to live. When we truly trust Him and believe that He's in control, we can rest. There's a peace in our hearts and minds. Deep down on the inside, we know that everything is going to be all right.

Many times, the reason we lose our peace and begin to worry is because we don't see anything happening in the areas we are praying about or believing for. Everything looks the same month after month, year after year. But we have to understand that God is working behind the scenes in our lives. He has already prearranged a bright future for you. And if the curtain were pulled back so you could peer into the unseen realm, you would see God fighting your battles for you. You'd find your heavenly Father getting everything arranged in your favor. You'd see how God is getting ready to open a door and bring an opportunity across your path. I'm convinced that if we could really see how God is orchestrating everything behind the scenes, we wouldn't worry. We wouldn't live stressed out anymore.

God is working behind the scenes in our lives.

The fact is we all have difficulties; we all have things in life that can steal our joy, steal our peace. We have to learn to turn them over to God and say, "Father, I'm trusting You. I believe that You are in control. And even though I may not see anything tangible happening, I believe You are working in my life, going before me, making my crooked places straight, and causing me to be at the right place at the right time."

You may be trying to figure everything out, trying to solve every problem. But it would take so much pressure off you, and you would enjoy your life so much more, if you could just learn to relinquish control and start believing that God really is directing your steps.

The Bible reminds us, "For it is God who is all the while at work in you." Notice, God doesn't work for a while, then go off on a two- or three-year vacation, and then come back and work a little more. God is constantly at work in your life. That means that although you may not be able to see it, God is arranging things in your favor. He is getting the right people lined up to come across your path. He is looking years down the road and getting everything perfectly in order, lining up solutions to problems you haven't even considered yet. He has the right spouse for you and the right spouse for your child. He has the best opportunities, the best doors He plans to open for you. God is constantly working behind the scenes in our lives.

"Well," you say, "Joel, I've been praying for my child for two years, but I don't see anything happening." "I've been believing for my finances to improve, but they continue to dwindle." Or "I've been praying for the right person to come into my life, but it's been four years."

No, you don't know what God is doing behind the scenes. Don't get discouraged just because you don't see anything happening. That doesn't mean God is not working. In fact, many times God works most when we see it the least.

When we're in one of those dry seasons and we don't see anything happening, that is simply a test of our faith. We have to dig in our heels and show God what we're made of. A lot of people get negative and discouraged. "Well, I never get any good breaks. I knew nothing good would ever happen to me." "I knew I'd never get out of this problem."

No, you've got to zip that up. If you want to pass the test, you need to put a smile on your face and say, "I may not see anything happening, but I know God is working in my life."

"My child may not be doing right, but I know it's only a matter of time. As for me and my house, we will serve the Lord."

"My finances may look the same, but I'm not worried about it, I know I am blessed. I cannot be cursed. I know in my due season at the exact right time, things are going to change in my favor." When we have this attitude of faith, we will see God do great things in our lives.

Many times God is working and we may not recognize it. We need to be more aware of God's goodness. When you get a good break, when things change in your favor, when you find yourself at the right place at the right time, recognize that this is not mere coincidence; that is God directing your steps; that is God at work in your life. If you'll be aware, it will encourage you and build your faith.

Every one of us can look back in our lives and see critical moments that had to be the hand of God. It's almost as though we can connect the dots. I can see how I met this person over here and I got this break and it caused me to get this job and that's where I met my spouse. And if I had not been at this exact place, I'd never have gotten this other promotion and on and on.

That's not a lucky break; that's God's hand of favor. All the while, God is working behind the scenes.

I remember as a young couple, Victoria and I found a home that we really liked. It was a run-down house but on a nice piece of property. And we knew it was for us. In the natural, it didn't make a lot of sense. We were leaving a beautiful townhome. Yet we knew that's what God wanted us to do. So we took a step of faith and we bought the run-down house. The day we closed on it, we were standing out in the front yard and a Realtor stopped by and offered us much more than we had paid. We thought, "What's going on?" We didn't understand it. Come to find out, they were in the process of changing the deed restrictions in that neighborhood. And several years later, we sold that property for twice as much as we paid for it. That was God causing us to be at the right place at the right time.

Understand that the Creator of the Universe is working in your life.

You may be doing the same thing you've done month after month, year after year, but then all of a sudden, you bump into a person who offers you a new position; you get one idea that takes you to a new level. You are at the right place at the right time, and you meet the man or woman of your dreams. God could have been working on that ten years earlier, getting everything lined up, and then suddenly it all comes together. Suddenly your due season shows up.

Here, years and years before, you could have thought, *Nothing's happening in my life. I'll probably never get out of this problem.* Yet, the whole time, God was at work. Things were happening behind the scenes.

I'm asking you to not fall into that trap of dragging through life with no joy, no enthusiasm, and thinking nothing good is happening. You've got to shake that off and start believing that right now—not two weeks from now, but right now—God is working in your life. Right now, God is arranging things in your favor. Right now, God is fighting your battles for you. Right now, God is making your crooked places straight. And you may not see it come to pass today, but here's the key: Every day you live with faith and expectancy brings you one day closer to seeing it come to pass. If it doesn't happen today, your attitude should be "No big deal. I know it may happen tomorrow. If it doesn't happen tomorrow, it may happen the next day. But whenever it does or doesn't happen, it's not going to steal my joy; I'm not going to live frustrated. I know God is in control and at the exact right time, it's going to come to pass. And in the meantime, I'm going to relax and just enjoy my life." You've got to believe God is in control. Believe God is working behind the scenes in your life.

The Scripture says, "God is effectually at work in those who believe." [52] Notice, His power is activated only when we believe. God can work in your behalf your whole lifetime and you never really get the full benefit of it because you didn't believe. Sure, you may get a break here or there, but when you really believe, when you really get up every day expecting good things, you're going to see more of God's favor. You're going to see what He's been doing behind the scenes.

And even when we have problems, even when things come against us, we have to believe that God already has the answer. In other words, that problem is no surprise to God. That child who won't do right. That financial difficulty. Being lonely. That doesn't have God baffled. God already has the answer. He knows the end from the beginning. God knows every trial we're ever going to face in the future. He knows every difficulty we're ever going to go through. The good news is God already has the solution. He has already made a way of escape. That tells me we don't have to live life worried. We don't have to go around all stressed out. God has it all under control.

When we're tempted to get negative and start complaining, we need to just turn it around. Our attitude should be "I know God is working on this problem. I know He's in the process of changing things, getting the right people lined up, softening the right hearts. And I believe God will not only bring me out, but He will bring me out better off than I was before." When we have this kind of attitude, it takes all the pressure off us. We can relax and enjoy our lives. We know God is in control. We know as long as we believe, God is all the while working for our good.

It's encouraging to look back over your life and see the things that had to be God. I know a young woman who met her husband on the side of the road. She had a flat tire on the freeway during rush hour, and he stopped to help change it. They started dating, and today they're happily married.

Now, think about the chances of those circumstances coming together. That had to be the hand of God. God was saying to that woman, "It's your due season. You've been faithful. You have passed the test. Now, let me show you what I've been doing behind the scenes all these years." He had that young man move from another city. He gave him the right job and worked the details of his life so he was coming down the freeway at the exact right time. Only God can orchestrate that.

Take the pressure off yourself and start believing that God is in control of your life.

When we were negotiating to get the Compaq Center, we needed ten votes from the city council members. We had worked for two years and had gone through several other votes. When it came down to the final vote, we had exactly ten votes—the minimum that we needed. But unfortunately, just a few days before the vote, we received word that one of the council members had changed his mind. He wasn't even going to show up at the last vote, equating to a vote against us—a vote we sorely needed.

We were terribly discouraged. The situation looked hopeless. It seemed that all our hard work and prayers had been in vain. But we decided to go back and meet with another council member to see if he might change his mind. He's a young Jewish man, a fine gentleman, but he had staunchly opposed Lakewood's acquiring of the Compaq Center for more than two years. Nevertheless, we thought, *What can it hurt to ask him to reconsider?*

At the last moment, the man with whom we met changed his mind. It was his vote that gave us the number we needed to secure the Compaq Center as the new Lakewood Church facility.

I talked to the man later and I asked him, "What was it that really changed your mind?"

He said, "Joel, I received a call from an old friend of mine. She's an elderly Jewish lady. I hadn't talked to her in years, and I really respect her. But she told me in no uncertain terms that I was to vote for your church." He went on to say, "Even though thousands of your church members called my office encouraging me to vote yes, and even though you and your team were very persuasive, it was that lady that changed my mind."

Now consider this: As far as I know, I have never met that woman. I didn't ask her to call. To this day, I don't know who she is. All I know is that while we were doing all that we could do, God was working behind the scenes in a way we could never have done on our own. What we couldn't do in our own ability and strength, God caused somebody else to do for us.

God knows who can influence your life. He knows who should put in a good word for you. You may not ever even know how or why it happened. Why was somebody good to you? Why did you get that break? That was God ordering your steps. For years, He was working behind the scenes, but in a moment of time, it all came together.

Don't go through the day thinking, *My situation is probably never going to change. I'll never get out of debt. I'm going to have to live with this disease for the rest of my life. I don't think I'll ever get married.* No, when you do that, you are tying the hands of Almighty God. And when you are tempted to lapse into negative thoughts and attitudes, turn it around and say, "I know God is working in my life. I know my due season is on its way and one day, I'm going to see all that God has been doing behind the scenes on my behalf." Then go out each day, expecting good things, knowing that the Creator of the Universe is directing your steps.

A while back, I talked to a gentleman who designed the freeway entry and exit ramps for parts of downtown Houston near the Compaq Center more than thirty-five years ago. He told how he had drawn the exit ramps so people could pull into the parking lots with ease. Recognizing that large crowds would be drawn to the downtown arena, he worked with the city to time all the traffic lights in the area to make it easier, more convenient, and the most beneficial for people wanting to attend events at the Compaq Center.

I thought, *That's another sign of God's goodness. Over thirty-five years ago, God was working behind the scenes, prompting people to make it easier to get to our church, so people could find hope and help.* As the engineer and I talked, I laughed and told him, "I would have thanked you back then, but I was only three years old!"   .

Certainly, over the years, the arena has been used for basketball games, concerts, and other events. But I believe those were all secondary. I believe God had it planned out a long time ago that Lakewood Church would be sending out hope to the world from that location.

In the same way, I believe God is working behind the scenes in your life. He is doing things that are going to thrust you to a whole new level. You may not see the culmination of it for years, so you must learn to trust Him. Stop worrying, don't allow yourself to become frustrated because your dream is not happening as quickly as you would like. In God's perfect timing, His plan for your life will come to fruition.

Look for God's Hand in Everyday Life

Trust God even in the small things in your life. About six months ago, I received some disappointing news about a certain situation. It was going to be a pain to deal with, and I didn't know how it was going to turn out. At first, I was tempted to worry and try to figure it all out. In stressful situations such as that, if we're not careful, we can allow our minds to conjure up all the worst possible scenarios. Negative voices will tell you, "You're going under. You're not going to be able to pay your bills. You may lose your house."

You may have a pain in your side, and your mind frets, "Oh, no! That's serious; you'd better get to the doctor."

No, we must choose to control our thought life. We have to believe God is still working in the situation.

When I received the disappointing news, I was at the office, about to get on the elevator, but just then, off stepped a woman I've known since I was a little boy. She has always loved me and prayed for me. Yet because of our schedules, I probably hadn't bumped into her for four or five years. We greeted each other with a hug and before she opened her mouth, I knew what she was going to say. She said, "Joel, I still pray for you every single day."

I thought, *This is not a coincidence.* That was God ordering my steps to be at the right place, just so He could encourage me. That was God's way of saying, "Joel, everything is under control. Everything is going to be all right. Just stay at peace. Stay at rest."

If we will pay attention, we will often detect God's activity; we'll know that He is speaking to us, guiding us, directing our steps.

The den of the townhouse in which my parents once lived had large windows that looked out onto the courtyard. Birds flitted back and forth between the trees in the yard. One bird in particular became a favorite of my mother's. Every day a beautiful little cardinal would perch on one of the branches right by the window. My mother enjoyed having it there. She got to the point where she looked forward to seeing it each day. Like clockwork, the little bird showed up and spent the afternoon in the courtyard. This went on for five or six months, but eventually the friendly little bird quit coming by. I tried to give my mother my pet hamster to console her, but she didn't want that!

About a year later, my father went to be with the Lord. Now Mother was at home by herself. She had to make some adjustments. I'm sure at times she was tempted to be lonely, tempted to get down and discouraged.

Then one day, the little cardinal came back. To some people, that may have been coincidence, or merely an explainable function of nature. But to my mother and our family, that was God saying, "I still have a plan. I'm still in control."

Throughout life, if we will be sensitive, if we'll be aware, we will see the hand of God even in little things. That's God letting us know He's still working behind the scenes.

A friend of mine has what the doctors say is terminal cancer. They're not giving him any hope. But the other day, his four-year-old son came in with his Bible. He opened it up and said, "Daddy, I want you to read this Scripture right here." The little boy can't read yet, so he didn't know what passage he was pointing to, but when the father read the Scripture, it spoke right to his heart. It was John 11:4, a passage where Jesus said, "This sickness shall not end in death. But it is for the glory of God."

My friend took that to heart. He felt that was God saying, "I know what you're going through. I've seen every tear you've shed. It may not look possible to you, but remember, I'm the God of the impossible. Keep believing. Keep trusting. I'm still in control."

These little signs are simply glimpses that God gives us to build our faith. They are reminders He is working behind the scenes. Our responsibility is to be sensitive to His leading, to be on the lookout for His hand moving in our everyday circumstances. If you are tuned in to God, you will soon recognize that most of the time, you don't simply bump into somebody. You didn't just get a lucky break. You don't just happen to be at the right place at the right time. God has been directing your steps.

The last weekend that Lakewood Church met at our Northeast Houston location proved to be an emotional experience for me. I had attended services on that campus with my family my whole life. I had grown up there. Although I was excited about moving downtown, in a way it was sad leaving that place. Memories of so many marvelous things that had happened there flooded my mind as I drove to the final Saturday evening service. I was reflecting on all that God had done, when I looked up in the sky and saw a beautiful rainbow. It looked as though one end of it was literally touching the church on the northeast side, and the other was reaching out across the city of Houston toward downtown. It was almost as if God was putting His stamp of approval on our move, saying, "I'm pleased. Your work here is done. It is time for a new beginning."

You may say, "Well, Joel, I've seen rainbows before, and they never meant anything to me."

That's because this promise is for believers! You must believe God is at work in your life, and then be on the lookout to see His hand shaping the events. It may be that a Scripture jumps out at you one day while you're reading. Perhaps it will be a small bird in your backyard. Or maybe you will see a rainbow in the sky and know that it is your time to step into a fresh start. God gives us these little glimpses to build our faith, to let us know that He is still in control and working behind the scenes.

Even in our dark times, God is still working in our lives. Some young parents told me about their daughter who is now in heaven. When she was three years old, she contracted a serious illness that confined her to bed as death ominously approached. The parents were distraught and in so much pain. They rarely left their daughter's side at the hospital.

Toward the end, the little girl drifted in and out of a coma. The parents knew they were about to lose her. But just before she died, she smiled with the most peaceful look on her face, and said, "Look, Mommy. Look, Daddy. Jesus is saying it's okay to come." She closed her eyes and breathed her final breath.

Even when we don't think that we'll ever smile again, God is there. He is the friend who sticks closer than a brother. He has a new beginning for you. The Bible says, "Weeping may endure for a night, but joy comes in the morning." [53]

Dare to trust Him today. Dare to believe that even in your disappointments, heartaches, and pains, God is right there with you. He said He would never leave you nor forsake you.

You don't have to figure everything out. You may not know what your future holds. But as long as you know who holds your future, you're going to be okay. God has been working behind the scenes in your life over the years.

I don't know what He has in store for my future, but I know I'm excited about it. It puts a spring in my step to think that the God who created heaven and earth and flung the stars into space cares so much about you and me that He is constantly working for our good. To know that God is bigger than anything you will ever face, and to know that He is already lining up answers for problems that you may not even encounter for ten or twenty years should give you incredible confidence as you enjoy your life today.

Whatever your circumstances are—whether good or bad—you need to know that God already knows about them, and He is working behind the scenes to arrange future events in your favor. Learn to trust Him. Quit worrying about it. Reject anything that hints at frustration or impatience. Remember, when you believe, you activate His power. And keep in mind that just because you don't see anything happening, that doesn't mean God is not working. Why don't you relinquish control and say, "God, I'm going to trust You. I know You have a great plan for my life."

When you do that, you will feel an enormous weight lift off you. And you'll not only enjoy your life more, but you will see more of God's blessings and favor. You will become a better you!

ACTION POINTS

PART 5: EMBRACE THE PLACE WHERE YOU ARE

1. I know that God works where there is an attitude of faith and expectancy. I will turn my situation over to God. I will not allow myself to worry or become frustrated. I will recognize that God is working behind the scenes, even when I cannot see external evidence of positive change.

2. I will look for glimpses of God's goodness in the little things of my life. I will recognize His blessings in nature, and I will be more aware of His work in the ordinary areas of life—a kind word from a stranger, a rainbow in the sky, a bird perched on my windowsill, a flower blooming in a field.

3. Today I will declare God's favor in my life. I will speak aloud statements such as:
   "Thank you, Father, for working in my life. Although I cannot see it yet, I know you are arranging things in my favor."
   "I know the clouds will dissipate, and I will see the favor of God in my life again."
   "I am looking for one touch of God's favor that can turn my circumstance around to my advantage and for His honor."

4. I acknowledge that God has me right where I am for a reason. He is directing my steps; I'm where I am supposed to be, and even if it is not a good place, God is giving me the strength to be here, and I know there will be good days ahead. God has me in the palm of His hand, and He will protect me and guide me to His best. Today I choose to be a positive influence on someone else by the way I handle my situation.

PART SIX

DEVELOP YOUR INNER LIFE

CHAPTER 25

Rising Higher

G od's plan for each of our lives is that we continually rise to new levels. But how high we go in life, and how much of God's favor and blessings we experience, will be directly related to how well we follow His directions.

Throughout life, God will deal with us and bring areas to light where we need to improve. He often speaks to us through our conscience, or through a still, small voice. He knows the things that are holding us back. He knows our weaknesses, faults, and the inner secrets that we keep hidden. When He brings these matters to our attention, if we want continued success and blessings, we have to be willing to face the truth about ourselves and take the corrective measures God commands.

Many people don't realize the importance of dealing with such issues. Consequently, they remain stuck in a rut—a rut in their marriage, or in their finances, or in their careers. They casually sweep the dirt under the rug as if it doesn't matter, hoping that nobody will notice. All the while, they ignore the still, small voice.

Sometimes we think, *It's too hard to obey. I know I should forgive that person, but he hurt me so badly.* Or, *I know I need to get in shape, but I don't really have the time. I know I need to quit working so much, but I need the extra money.*

It is important to understand that everything God tells us is for our good. God never holds us back from His best. Nor does He purposely make our lives more difficult. Quite the contrary, your heavenly Father is waiting for your obedience so He can release more of His favor and blessing in your life.

Are there things in your life that God has been dealing with you about that you have been putting off? Maybe you keep procrastinating or ignoring His leading about getting your finances in order, being less judgmental, keeping strife out of your home, or making peace with somebody at work. Pay attention to what God is saying to you.

Perhaps God has been dealing with you about your close friends, the people you most frequently choose to be around. Maybe you know some of your friends are not a good influence and they are pulling you down, but you keep making excuses. "I don't want to hurt their feelings. Besides, if I didn't hang around them, I may not have any other friends." But the fact is, if you will do what you know is right, God will give you new friends. Not only that, He'll give you *better* friends—people who will lift you up rather than drag you down. Yes, you may go through a season of loneliness as you make the transition, but I would rather be lonely for a little while, knowing that I'm rising higher, knowing that I'm going to fulfill my destiny, than let people pollute me and keep me from being all God created me to be.

Anytime you obey, a blessing will follow. Why? Because you are sowing a seed to grow and rise higher. It may not happen overnight, but at some point, in some way, you will see God's goodness in your life to a greater measure.

Any time you obey, a blessing will follow.

My question to you is: How high do you want to rise? Do you want to continue to increase? Do you want to see more of God's blessings and favor? If so, the higher we go, the more disciplined we must be; the quicker we must obey. If we're hanging around people who compromise and cheat on their spouses and have no integrity, we're just asking for trouble.

"Well, Joel, they are good people, and their conduct doesn't affect me. It doesn't seem to hurt me one bit."

No, you don't know how much your association with them is

holding you back. You don't know what God wants to release, but He cannot and will not until you get away from those negative influences. If you will do as He says, you would see God's favor in a new way, and your entire life would rise to a higher level.

Understand, the longer we delay dealing with a character issue, the more difficult it is to do later on. You'd be far better off if you'd learn to obey God's promptings quickly. The moment you feel the uneasiness, the moment an inner alarm sounds and something says, "This isn't right," take the proper steps to move away from that action, comment, or attitude. That may well be God talking to you—trying to keep you on His best path for your life.

God has given us our own free will. He will not force us to do what is right. He won't force us to make good decisions. It's up to each one of us individually to pay attention to the still, small voice; at the same time, we mustn't get so busy or self-directed that we miss what God is trying to tell us. Learn to act on His leading.

God's directions often affect the most practical aspects of our lives. Recently, a young woman told me that she felt a strong urge to go to the doctor to get a medical checkup. She looked as healthy as could be, and she was active, energetic, and exercised regularly. Nevertheless, the feeling persisted: "Go see the doctor. Go get a checkup." That still, small voice was speaking to her. For several weeks, she ignored it and put it off. "Oh, I'm fine. That's not a message for me."

But she couldn't get away from it. She finally decided to schedule an appointment with her doctor. During a routine checkup, the doctor discovered a small cyst in her body, and found that it was malignant. Thankfully, he was able to remove it completely, because it hadn't spread. The young woman required no further treatment. But after the operation, the doctor told her, "It's a good thing you came in when you did, because a couple of years later, this could have been a major problem, possibly even life-threatening."

The young woman was so grateful. She later told me, "Joel, I know that was God. I would not have gone to the doctor for that checkup had it not been for God's promptings."

We need to listen to the still, small voice. God knows what's best for us.

I've had people come to me with tears in their eyes, saying, "Joel, I knew I should have kept the strife out of my family; I knew I should have spent more time with them. I knew I shouldn't have been so hard to get along with."

Isn't it amazing that we can know the right thing to do, yet still ignore it? Don't let that be you. Be obedient now, so you won't have regrets later on.

Victoria and I were married in 1987 and for the first few years, like any young couple, we were trying to learn how to live together as one. The problem was that she wasn't learning the way I wanted her to. We didn't have major difficulties, just minor irritations. I'd argue over things that didn't matter, always wanting to have my way, not willing to compromise. I'll never forget—God spoke to me back then, not aloud, but deep inside. He said, "Joel, if you don't make changes and do your part to keep the peace in the family, you're not only going to change the beautiful girl you married, but it's going to cause you major problems in the future." That was all the warning I needed. Thank God, I was smart enough to heed that warning, and we stopped arguing over little things and were willing to make compromises and adjustments in our marriage. Today, we're as happy as could be and have a great relationship.

God may be dealing with you about your words, cautioning you against saying so many hurtful, sarcastic, critical things. You've developed a bad habit, and you know down inside, it is destroying your relationship. Don't be hardheaded. Don't wait till the sirens go off before you do something. In most instances, God will not hit somebody over the head with a baseball bat and say, "Hey, you're ruining your marriage. You're going to end up hurt and lonely."

No, He whispers it in a still, small voice. We have to be sensitive and pay attention to His leading and then do whatever it is that He tells us to do to make life better.

Too often we make excuses. "Well, I know I should treat my spouse better. I know I can be disrespectful, but she's disrespectful to me. I know I have a chip on my shoulder. I know I'm hard to get along with, but I've been through a lot in life. It's just not fair."

Those excuses will cause us to remain stuck right where we are. The way to rise higher is by staying open and dealing with issues as God brings them to light. It may be something as simple as how you speak to your spouse, your tone of voice, body language, or facial expressions. If you come across as harsh or short or too direct, you can hurt someone with your words—especially someone who loves you.

On the other hand, if you will listen to that inner voice of conviction when it says, "That's not right. You can do better. You can be kinder," and make some simple adjustments, you will see that relationship go to a new level.

I know some people who are extremely jealous. They see somebody who is blessed and prospering, and rather than being happy for that person and rejoicing, the jealous person seeks to find fault. Interestingly, that person could have enjoyed the same success and fulfillment, but he or she was unwilling to pay the price. That person wasn't willing to obey his or her conscience, to discipline himself or herself, or to make the sort of sacrifices the successful person made to get ahead.

Any one of us can rise higher. There is no limit to what God will do in your life, if you will learn to obey quickly and deal with the issues He brings to light, even the small things.

Some time ago, I was watching a minister on television. He's a fine man and he has a great ministry. As I was watching, though, I began to critique the production of the program. My background involves television production, so I naturally thought, *Why did they put the camera there? That background doesn't look good. He shouldn't be wearing that. And that light is not adjusted right.*

Within minutes, I'd found a dozen things that I would have done differently. About that time, I felt that still, small voice saying, "Joel, don't be critical. Look for the good. Look what they're doing right. Look at all the people they are helping."

I felt that conviction, and I could have easily blown it off and ignored it. Nobody would have known. But I've learned to quickly say, "Father, forgive me. Help me to never be critical. Help me to do better. Help me to always see the good."

That was an opportunity for me to come up higher. God showed me something, although small, that held the potential to keep me from being my best. I'm not perfect, but I've learned to deal with things like that. I've learned to stay open and look for ways that I can improve. I know God always has more in store, so I don't want to compromise or live in complacency.

You can do a lot in life and get away with it. You can run with the wrong crowd and still get to heaven. You can treat people disrespectfully or be sloppy in your business affairs and still live in relative comfort. But I'm talking about rising higher. I'm talking about being the very best that you can be.

For instance, perhaps God is dealing with you about your finances. Maybe you are living above your means, spending more than you can afford.

Too often, we made a purchase that we didn't feel good about. We bought a house, a car, or a boat that we couldn't afford or didn't really need. The alarm was going off even as we signed the papers, but we ignored it, and now we're in a financial bind.

It is much better to obey all along the way, and then you won't have to deal with many of these issues. This is one of the most important principles you can ever learn. Follow peace; listen to your conscience; deal with the issues God brings to light. Don't put it off. The longer you put it off, the more difficult it will be.

Many people wonder why they're not happy, why they are not blessed and increasing in influence, why they can't sleep well at night. Often it is because their conscience is not clear. We cannot bury things in our subconscious minds and expect to rise higher and enjoy God's best.

When King David committed adultery with Bathsheba, he tried to cover it up. Making matters worse, he sent Bathsheba's husband to the front lines of the battle and then ordered his general to pull back, resulting in certain death. For one full year, David pretended that everything was okay; he went on with life and business. No doubt, he thought, *If I don't deal with it, if I ignore it, it won't bother me; it won't affect me.*

That year was one of the worst of David's life. He was miserable. The Scripture says he was also weak; he grew sick physically and had all kinds of problems. That is what happens when we refuse to deal with things. We step out of God's protection and favor. When we live with a guilty conscience, we don't feel good about ourselves, so we take it out on other people. Many times, just like David, we're weak, defeated, living in mediocrity. It's because of the poison on the inside.

But, friend, none of us needs to live that way. Our God is a forgiving, merciful God. When you make a mistake, you don't have to hide it. When you do wrong, don't run away from God. Run to God.

After a year of living in denial, King David finally admitted his sin and his mistakes after a prophet confronted the king about his misdeeds. David said, "God, I'm sorry. Please forgive me. Create in me a clean heart. Restore the joy of my salvation." When David sincerely did that, God restored him. That's how David got his joy, peace, and victory back, and although he had failed miserably, he went on to do great things.

Now think about it: David could have been stuck right there in defeat, in mediocrity for the rest of his life had he refused to deal with that issue. But he chose to change, and God helped him to do it.

Are there things in your life that you are refusing to deal with? When you ask for forgiveness, God can restore you. That's when He'll put you back on your best path. That's when He'll give you a new beginning.

Keep in mind, God deals with each of us individually. We are all at different levels, so we should never compare ourselves to others. Too often, when we compare ourselves with others, we tend to make excuses for ourselves. For instance, maybe all your friends are going to see a movie, but you read the review and don't feel good about it. You know it would not be God's best for you. Your inner alarm goes off and your conscience cautions you, "You are better than that; don't willingly take dirt into your mind."

Right there is an opportunity for you to rise higher. Sure, you could attempt to quiet your conscience and say, "Oh, it's not going to hurt me. I'm strong and besides, all my friends love God. They attend church. They're good people. They are going to see that movie."

No, maybe your friends are at a different stage in their spiritual walk than you. Or perhaps they are ignoring God's voice speaking to them; maybe they would be much more blessed if they would quit giving in and living at such a low level. You must do what you feel good about in your own heart. It may cost you a few friendships. It may mean that you spend a few lonely nights. Or maybe you can't play on a team that parties after every game.

Remember that anything God asks you to do is for your benefit. It's so He can ultimately release more of His favor in your life.

Moreover, anything God asks of us, He always gives the grace to do it. If God asks you to forgive somebody, you may not think you can, but if you will take that step of faith, God's grace will be there to help you. You don't get the grace unless you step out. You have to make the first move. God will see that step of faith and He'll give you supernatural strength to help you overcome any obstacles standing in the way of doing the right thing.

Friend, God has great things in store for you. Don't get stuck in a rut and settle for mediocrity, bad habits, or bad attitudes. Pay attention to the still, small voice on the inside. Deal with the issues God brings to light and learn to obey quickly. Remember: How high you go in life will be directly related to how obedient you are.

The Scripture says, "To whom much is given, much is required." [54] God is preparing you for greater things. He's going to take you further than you thought possible, so don't be surprised when He asks you to think better of yourself and to act accordingly.

CHAPTER 26

Develop a Tender Conscience

Your conscience is often called the compass of the soul. It works like an inward monitor, similar to an alarm. When you're about to do something that is not beneficial or something that will get you into trouble, your conscience causes you to feel uneasy. Don't ignore that warning. That's your conscience helping you to know what is right and what is wrong. One of the best friends you can ever have is your own conscience.

We could avoid a great deal of trouble and heartache if we would maintain a more tender conscience. I hear people say all the time, "I know I shouldn't do this, but . . ." Or "I know I shouldn't say this, but . . ." Or "I know I shouldn't buy this, but . . ."

They know what they should do. The alarm is going off. They can feel that sense of disapproval, but they choose to disobey their own conscience. Someday they will look back and recognize how God tried to warn them again and again.

Don't make the mistake of overriding your conscience. Respect it. Just as you respect your boss or someone else with authority over you, learn to treat your conscience in the same way. God will use your conscience to help lead you and keep you out of trouble. Perhaps you are in a conversation with your spouse and things are heating up. You can feel yourself getting aggravated, wanting to continue the argument more forcefully, when suddenly, that inner alarm goes off. Something down inside says, "Let it go. Drop it. Bite your tongue. Walk away. Keep the peace."

That's your conscience trying to keep you out of trouble. That's

God trying to warn you. Too many times we ignore it and choose to do our own thing. We end up having a big argument and getting all upset, ruining the rest of the evening. It could have been avoided if we would have paid attention to what our conscience was trying to say to us.

Learn to be sensitive. Stop when your conscience says stop. Quit having to have the last word. Pay attention to what you're feeling inside, and don't override your own conscience.

One time, my father was driving down the road, about to get on the freeway. He was in a big hurry, running late to a meeting. Traveling well over the speed limit, he came up to a big curve in the road. Just then, that alarm went off inside. Something said, "You'd better slow down. A policeman is around the corner."

My father later told how that word came to him so distinctly. He felt it strongly, but he was in a hurry so he ignored it and didn't pay any attention. Sure enough, when he got around the corner, a police officer stood there holding out his radar gun. The police officer flagged my dad over. When the officer approached my father's car window, Daddy had a big smile on his face. He said, "Officer, you are never going to believe this, but God told me you were up here."

The officer looked at my father as if he were from another planet. He took my father's license and returned to his patrol car. He came back a few minutes later, shaking his head. He said, "Listen here, preacher, I'm going to let you go, but the next time God speaks to you, you'd better listen."

Don't override your own conscience. When you feel uncomfortable down inside, pull back and pay attention to what God is trying to say to you. You may be in the middle of a conversation. All of a sudden, the alarm goes off, and you know you need to button your lip or walk away. Don't ignore that warning from your conscience. You may be ready to buy something or about to eat something or about to make some less than noble plans when that inner siren goes off. If you will learn to be sensitive and listen to your conscience, God will keep you out of trouble. He will help you make good decisions. He can protect you from danger.

I recently encountered Peter, a young man who did some contract labor for us, and when I saw him, I almost didn't recognize him. He looked as though he had been in some type of accident. His face was bruised, and the skin around both his eyes was black and purple. He had some stitches on his arm. I said, "Peter, what in the world happened to you? Were you in a wreck or something?"

"No, Joel," he said. "A couple of nights ago, I was carjacked."

"What?"

"Yeah, I was on my way home from work, and I stopped at the traffic light, and these guys came up to me and pulled me out of my car. I didn't have a wallet, so they just beat me up and left me there."

"That's awful, Peter."

"Yes, but, Joel, the funny thing was, on my way home that night, something told me to not go that way. Right down in here as distinct as it could be"—Peter pointed to his chest—"something said, 'You'd better go another way.' It was so strong that I even debated it in my mind. I said to myself, 'I always go this way. This is the quickest way. Why should I go another way?'"

This young man was not a religious person, but he said, "I know that was God trying to warn me. I know that was God trying to protect me." He paused and looked at me, and said, "Joel, if I had only listened, I could have avoided this pain."

Before you step into trouble or make a poor decision, God will always provide a warning for you. An alarm will sound inside. The caution may not be as dramatic as Peter's, but if you'll be sensitive and pay attention, God will lead you and will help you to avoid unnecessary turmoil.

Most of the time, deep down inside, we know what we should do, but too often, we simply choose not to do it. Understand, every time you ignore your conscience, the next time that voice will speak more softly. Unfortunately, you can get to the place where you have totally drowned out the voice of your conscience.

For instance, maybe you're about to say something rude to someone and all of a sudden that check goes off inside. You feel that sense of uneasiness as something tells you to bite your tongue. But if you ignore that prompt and choose to override it, you will feel guilty as a result. If you don't go back and make things right and apologize, then the next time you're in that situation, the alarm won't be quite as loud. The voice won't be quite so strong. You can get to the place where you have overridden your conscience so often that it becomes desensitized. That's why we need to pray every day, "God, help me to develop a tender conscience. Keep me sensitive to Your voice."

Recently, I met a man whose family lives in another country while he has been in the United States for several years working with his company. He told me how he came to be intimately involved with another woman. They have been in a relationship for a couple of years, but he feels guilty about it. He said, "Joel, I just feel terrible. I know that this relationship is not right. I really want to change, but I just can't seem to do it."

"You are in an interesting situation," I told him. "You are the exception to the rule, because most people who have been overriding their consciences that long no longer care. They don't feel anything. They're not concerned."

"Really?" he asked. "What do you think I should do?"

"First of all, you should thank God that you still have a tender conscience and be grateful that you still have that concern." I then challenged him to make the necessary changes before that uneasiness wore off.

Any insensitivity to God's voice should concern us—especially when we have been willfully doing wrong for so long that it no longer bothers us, or we no longer regard it as wrong. We've grown numb in that area. Again, that is why we should pray every day, "God, help me to stay sensitive to Your voice. Don't let me get calloused, cold, or numb in any area of my life, in my attitude, or in how I treat people, or in what I say or what I do. God, help me to have a tender conscience."

Friend, God rewards obedience. Get into God's best path. Don't keep overriding your conscience. If you will be honest with yourself and have the desire to change, God will help you to do it. It is better to go through a little pain of change than it is to go twenty or thirty years stuck in mediocrity.

I have found that the more obedient we are, the easier it becomes. Obedience breeds obedience. Unfortunately, the opposite is also true.

Disobedience breeds more disobedience. Consequently, you can increase the sensitivity of your conscience or you can decrease it. Every time you obey, your conscience becomes more tender. When you obey, you're letting in a little more light. Your heart will be a little softer and you'll respond more quickly. You can get to the point where you are so sensitive that when you first feel that uneasiness, it will get your attention and cause you to make changes. Really, that's the kind of people God wants us to be. When we hear the still, small voice, when we first feel that little nudge, we are quick to take action.

Understand this: When you live an obedient life, God's blessings will chase you down and overtake you. When you obey, you cannot outrun the good things of God.

God does not expect you to change overnight. He is not going to be disappointed with you or write you off if you don't turn your life around in one week's time. No, all He asks is that you keep making progress. He doesn't want you to be at this same place next year. He will lead you in His own special way, and if you will be sensitive and do your best to keep your own conscience clear, God will be pleased, and He'll release more of His blessings in your life.

God meets us at our own level. I don't have to keep up with you, and you don't have to keep up with me. I just have to be true to my own heart. I know the areas in which God deals with me most frequently, and I do my best not to go against my own conscience. That's what I'm challenging you to do as well.

A young man with whom I attended college had a habit of being short with people. Sometimes, he was downright rude. One day we were at a restaurant together with a group of guys from the school, and the waiter mixed up my friend's order. My friend jumped down the waiter's throat. I mean he let him have it and embarrassed him in front of all of us.

After we got back to the dorm, my friend came into my room about an hour later and asked if he could borrow my car. I said, "Sure you can, but where are you going at this late hour?"

"Joel, I feel terrible," he said. "I treated that waiter so badly, I can't even sleep. I'm going to go back there and apologize to him."

That young man changed over the course of that year. He went from being hard, cold, and rude to being one of the kindest, most considerate people you could ever meet. God will help you to change, if you will simply work with Him.

None of us is perfect. We all make mistakes, but we can learn to obey our own consciences if we can be big enough to say, "I'm sorry, I didn't treat you right, I'll do better next time." If you will be sensitive and maintain a clear conscience, there's no limit to what God will do in your life. In contrast, when you have a guilty conscience, you don't feel good about yourself. You're not happy; you can't pray with boldness; you feel condemned. You don't expect good things, and you usually don't receive them.

At that point, the best thing you can do is go back and make things right. Like that young man, swallow your pride and be quick to obey. Apologize to the people you have offended. Don't live with a guilty conscience.

Or maybe you need to say, "God, I'm sorry; please forgive me for having such a critical attitude toward that person."

When you do that, your conscience will relax. That heavy burden will be lifted off you; you'll be able to sleep well. Not only that, but God will help you do better next time.

Years ago, one time after a service, my father came back into the television production area. Four or five crew members and I were gathered there, and when my dad walked in, we were all laughing and having a good time. Something really funny had just happened. For some reason, my father thought that we were making fun of someone in the service, but it didn't have anything to do with that.

Now, ordinarily, my father was a very kind and compassionate person, but this incident seemed to set him off. He began to chew us out, letting us know that we should not be making fun of people, and on and on. I said, "Daddy, it had nothing to do with that; it was totally unrelated," but he didn't accept that.

He left, and, of course, the guys on the crew and I felt bad about the misunderstanding. When I got home that night a couple of hours later, my father came into my room. "Joel, I've got to talk to you," he said. "I blew it tonight. I know I was wrong. I know I made a mistake, and I'm asking you to forgive me please. I want to apologize." Before I'd gotten home, my dad had called each of those other young men as well and apologized to them. It must have been close to midnight, but he would not go to bed with that heaviness on his heart.

What an impression that made upon me! What an impression it made upon those other young men. My father was the boss, but he was not too proud to admit that he had made a mistake and needed to apologize. See, my father had a tender conscience. No wonder God blessed him. No wonder God used him in a great way.

If we can learn to have that kind of sensitive, pure heart and be quick to obey, quick to forgive, quick to apologize, quick to change our attitudes, we will be pleasing to God.

Live your life with a clear conscience. Get into God's best plan. The Scripture says in Matthew 6:22 that the lamp of the body is the eye. Your "spiritual eye" is your conscience. Jesus goes on to say that if the eye is clear, the whole body will be filled with light. In other words, if your conscience is clear, life is good. You're going to be happy. You will have a positive vision and will enjoy God's blessings.

If your conscience is clear, life is good.

Then the next verse describes many people today. It says in the *Amplified Version,* "If our conscience is full of darkness, then how dense will that darkness be." Many people are living with a heaviness hanging over their lives. They have some nagging feeling, something's always bothering them. They're not happy. The problem is they don't have a clear conscience. They've ignored the warnings for too long. They've gotten hard and cold in certain areas.

That insensitivity won't change until you make the proper adjustments. If there are things that you are doing that you know you should not be doing, then make some adjustments. Or if there are things that you *should* be doing and you're not, then make those changes. As I've said, it may not be something big. You may not be living in some sordid sin, but maybe God is dealing with you about having a better attitude, about spending more time with your children, about eating healthier. Whatever it is, make a decision that you're going to pay more attention to your conscience and that you are going to be quick to obey. That's when the heaviness will leave. I like what the Apostle Paul said in Acts 23. He said, "I have always lived before God with a clear conscience."

That should be our goal as well. When our conscience is clear, condemnation flees. When we have a clear conscience, we can be happy. Other people may try to judge us or condemn us, but that negative input will bounce right off us.

Sometimes people say, "Joel, why don't you do more of this or more of that?"

I know I'm not perfect, but I also know this: My conscience is clear before God. I know that I'm doing my best to please Him. That's why I can sleep well at night. That's why I can lie down in peace. That's why I have a smile on my face. Friend, keep your conscience tender, and you will discover that life keeps getting better and better.

CHAPTER 27

Dealing with the Root Issues

I heard about a man who owned a bunch of horses, and one day one of the horses kicked a wood fence and scraped his leg badly. The owner took the horse to his barn, cleaned the wound, and bandaged the animal's leg. A few weeks later, the man noticed that the horse was still bothered by that bruise. The owner called a veterinarian to come examine the horse. After checking the animal, the vet prescribed some antibiotics.

Almost immediately, the horse responded positively to the medication and began to do much better. A month or two went by, however, and the owner noticed that the injury still had not healed; it actually appeared to be worse than ever. So the vet put the horse back on antibiotics.

Once again the animal responded and was fine for a few weeks, but then the process repeated itself. The wound simply would not heal. Finally, the owner loaded up the horse and took him down to the veterinarian's clinic. He knew he had to find out why this wound wouldn't heal. In the clinic, the veterinarian put the horse under anesthesia and began to probe the injured leg. Once he got deep enough, the vet discovered a large sliver of wood that had gone far below the skin when the horse had hit the fence many months previously. The vet realized that every time the horse went off the antibiotic, the infection caused by that foreign object returned. They had been treating the symptoms rather than treating the true source of the horse's pain.

We do something similar many times. We fix the surface things.

"Let me clean up my behavior. Let me just turn over a new leaf. I'm going to try being more friendly, more loving and kind. I'm not going to spend so much money, or use credit cards to get into debt. I'm not going to manipulate people anymore. I won't get so angry and upset." It's good that we're trying to improve, but so often we are not dealing with the real source of the problem. No matter how much we want to be better, that issue just keeps coming back, and we can't seem to get free.

It is usually easier to make excuses for our behavior, to pass the blame and try to justify our behavior. But if we want to experience God's best, we must learn to take responsibility for our thoughts, words, attitudes, and actions.

Too many people never really look inside and get honest with themselves. They don't get down to the root of the problem. Instead, they simply deal with the fruit, the surface issues. They may be negative, or they can't get along in relationships. Perhaps they have low self-esteem, severe financial problems, or some other chronic problem. They try to improve their behavior, and that is admirable, but many times their efforts produce only temporary results because they refuse to deal with the bad root. Consequently, they continue to produce bad fruit.

The Bible teaches that we should not let a root of bitterness spring forth and contaminate our whole lives. It's like having a weed out in your front yard. You can pull that weed, but if you merely clip it off at the surface, you are not really getting down to the roots. A couple of days later, you look out in your yard, and you have that same weed to deal with again.

For lasting, positive change, you must go deeper and not merely look at what you do, but ask yourself, "What is the root of this problem?" "Why do I act this way?" "Why am I out of control in this area?" "Why am I always so defensive?" "Why do I feel that I must repeatedly prove myself to everybody?"

Only as you get to the root and start dealing with the source of the problem can you realistically expect positive changes.

We need to examine carefully the areas in which we constantly struggle. Is our spouse really at fault? Is it really our circumstances, upbringing, or environment? Or could it be that we have something buried deep within that is causing us to "be infected"?

This is especially important in the area of your relationships. Many people have a root of rejection—they have been through hurts in the past. Somebody did them wrong, and rather than letting it go, they hold on to it. That bitterness poisons every part of the person's life.

I know people who have a root of insecurity that causes them to feel defensive. They're always trying to prove to somebody else who they are. As long as they have that bad root, they're going to continue to produce the wrong kind of fruit.

So often we can't seem to get along with a particular person, and we're sure it must be his or her fault. We're sure it's our spouse. We're sure it's our boss or coworkers. But wait. Could the problem be you? Could it be that you have a root of pride that is causing you to withhold forgiveness or is blinding you to somebody else's opinion? We can try to correct all these things on the surface, but that's similar to merely putting a fresh bandage on that horse's leg. The problem will keep coming back until we get to the real source.

Shawna and Andy were always having problems in their marriage, especially in the area of communication. When they engaged in conversation, if Andy didn't agree with Shawna, she would get extremely defensive. She'd get all upset, lose her cool, and they'd end up having an argument. "Why can't you just let me have my opinion?" Andy said. "Why do you have to get so upset when I don't agree with you? Haven't you ever heard that if two people agree on everything in a marriage, one of them is unnecessary?"

Shawna didn't have a good answer, but she obstinately opposed Andy's opinions when he disagreed with her. This went on year after year, and the tension created by this situation tore at the fabric of their marriage.

One day Shawna decided to get honest with herself. She looked deep down on the inside, and as she did, she realized that the reason she became defensive so easily was that she was intensely insecure. She had been through a lot of hurt and pain in her lifetime. She had experienced a devastating dose of rejection from a previous relationship. Now every time Andy didn't agree with her, Shawna felt that he was rejecting her. Rather than agreeing to disagree on some matters, Shawna took it personally. She tried to control and manipulate Andy to keep that tension from sprouting in their relationship.

Shawna realized that the true source of the problem wasn't that they couldn't communicate; it was her own insecurity. It didn't happen overnight, but as Shawna began to deal with these feelings, asking God to help her, little by little things began to change. Slowly, Shawna and Andy's relationship improved, but the key was she got to the root. Once she took care of the bad root, eventually the fruit took care of itself.

We have to understand that most of our problems have deeper roots. We might be amazed at how many things affect us negatively, and we are trying to solve the problem simply by dealing with the fruit—often treating surface issues for years on an endless treadmill.

The children of Israel were doing something similar. They wandered around in the wilderness between Egypt and the Promised Land of Canaan for forty years—a trip that should have been a mere eleven-day journey. The root cause of their problem was that they had developed a victim mentality. Granted, they had been treated horribly during the last portion of their time in Egypt; they had been through many painful, unfair experiences while in slavery. The inner pain followed them, even after God had miraculously delivered them from bondage. Out in the desert, they blamed Moses for their lack of food and water; they blamed the past, complained about the food, and fretted over their enemies. It never dawned on them that they were a part of the problem. Because of their lack of faith, they kept going around the same mountain year after year, never making any real progress.

Perhaps you have been stuck at the same place in your life for far too long. Maybe you are stuck in a sour marriage or a dead-end career. Or maybe you are stuck in a quagmire of debt or negative attitudes; you are often hard to get along with, defensive, or critical.

It's time to get up and get going. Our prayer should be, "God, please show me the truth about myself. I don't want to be at this same place next year, so if I have things holding me back, show me what they are. Help me, Father, to change. Help me to get to the root of my problems."

God is knocking on the door of new rooms in our hearts, maybe rooms that we haven't let Him enter previously. The only way He'll come in is if we invite Him. The doorknob is on the inside. I have discovered that I can allow God in some rooms of my heart, yet keep Him out of other rooms. Some of those rooms can be painful or embarrassing. Hidden in some of those rooms are hurts and wounds from the past. It's where our weaknesses and shortcomings are tucked away. Rather than dealing with the issues and cleaning the crud out of those dark corners, we keep those rooms locked. We make excuses for our behavior; we blame other people. Sometimes, we even blame God.

"That's just the way I am," someone might say.

God continues to knock. If we want to get to the source, then we must look inside; we must allow God to shine the floodlight of His Word in every room of our heart. When we have feelings that we know are wrong, rather than hiding them and trying to bury them away in one of these rooms, the best thing we can do is to be honest and ask, "God, why do I feel this way?" "Why can't I get along with my spouse?" "Why do I try to manipulate everybody?" "God, why do I always have to have my way?" "Why do I get upset so easily?" If you will be honest and willing to face the truth rather than hiding behind excuses, God will show you some answers to those questions. As you begin to act on that truth, you can come up higher.

If you're impatient, be honest enough to say, "God, show me why I'm so impatient. And then please help me to deal with it."

When you feel resentment toward another person, tending to be critical or finding fault, the first thing you should do is to pray, "Please, God, show me why I don't like this person. What's wrong on the inside of me? God, am I jealous of her position, jealous of his money, jealous of their talents? God, please show me the truth about myself. I don't want to go around that same mountain another year. I want to come up higher; I want to enter my Promised Land."

Make sure that you're not carrying around excess baggage. If you have areas in your life in which you constantly struggle and you can't seem to get free, then you need to ask God to show you what's holding you back. Ask God to show you if you have any bitter roots that you need to get rid of. If God brings something to light, then be bold enough to deal with it.

You *can* be happier, you can have better relationships, you can break free from anything that's holding you back, but you have to do your part. Be honest and face the truth about yourself. Let's not do as the children of Israel did in the years following the Exodus, thinking our lack of progress is somebody else's fault.

I know digging out those roots can be painful. The easy thing is to concentrate on surface issues, to maintain the status quo. The easy thing is to avoid change. There is a pain associated with coming up higher. It's uncomfortable to be honest and really deal with these issues. It can be uncomfortable to have to forgive an offense when it was somebody else's fault. It's hard to admit sometimes, "I'm holding on to the bitterness." Or, "I'm defensive because I'm so insecure." Or "I'm hard to get along with because I'm dragging all my baggage from the past." Moreover, don't be surprised if, as you shed the superficial layers and really get honest, you feel a little pressure. Please understand that this discomfort is only temporary. It's a growing pain, and once you get past that point, you're going to move up to a new level of victory. The pain of change is much less than the pain of staying in mediocrity.

Perhaps you have been spinning your wheels, going around in circles year after year, and are not really happy. You need to be honest enough to say, "God, show me what it is. Am I relying on other people to make me happy? Do I have unrealistic expectations? Am I going to be happy only if I get married? Am I allowing my circumstances to keep me down? God, show me the truth about myself."

Not too long ago a man told me that whenever he took time to enjoy his life, he felt guilty about it. He felt condemned, as though he were doing something wrong. Over the years, he engrossed himself in his work. He became a workaholic, not taking any time for himself, not taking any time for his family. Ironically, his overworking was all because of these feelings of guilt. His life was out of balance. This went on year after year until one day he decided to get honest and let God in that room of his heart. He said, "God, why do I feel this way? Why do I feel guilty when I just want to go out and have fun, to enjoy being with my family?"

He realized that as he was growing up his father was extremely strict. He came from a military family, and his dad didn't allow any fun in the house. Everything was serious. He didn't really know what it was like to have a normal childhood. He was taught to work, to be serious, with little to no playtime. Now an adult himself, he realized that he had become just like his father. Those thoughts, those attitudes, those habits were what he had learned early on—not that they were right, but that's all that he had known. Once he recognized what the source was, he was able to break that heaviness and really start enjoying his life.

You may have come out of an abusive situation. Maybe somebody else caused you a lot of heartache and pain; perhaps the people who raised you were unkind, or somebody with whom you shared a relationship used or abused you. They made poor decisions, and now you are dealing with the ramifications of those decisions. But please don't let that be an excuse. You can come up higher. You can set a new standard.

Understand that if you want to get to the source of the problem, you cannot just sit by idly and remain passive. You've got to come to the point where you say, "I am sick and tired of being sick and tired. We may have been this way a long time, but I'm not going to dance around this issue. I'm going to get to the source, and I'm going to start making better decisions for my family and for me."

One of the first things we must do is to stop making excuses. We have to quit blaming the past. You may have been through a lot of heartache. That may be the reason you struggle with bad habits or why you have trouble in relationships. Perhaps you suffer from low self-esteem. That may be the reason, but don't use that as an excuse to stay the way you are. Take responsibility. Many people have had unfair things happen, and they go their whole lifetime allowing that experience to poison them. They're angry. They've got a chip on their shoulder, they are hard to get along with. "Well, Joel, if you'd been through what I've been through, you'd act this same way."

No, that may be the reason you act that way, but thank God, you don't have to stay that way. You can come up higher, but you must take responsibility. You have to be willing to face the truth and say, "This is not right. I refuse to live upset and angry. I don't want to be hard to get along with. God, I'm asking You to help me to change." If you have that attitude, God will always help you.

A woman came up to me in the church lobby one time. She said, "Joel, I wish you would pray for me. I'm about to get married again for my fifth time." She continued in a pious tone, "I want you to agree with me in prayer that this man will be the one who finally starts treating me right."

I wanted to ask her, "Have you ever thought about what the common denominator is in all these marriages? It's you! Something's wrong on the inside."

After we prayed, I asked her, "Does anybody else in your family struggle with these same kinds of difficulties?"

"Oh, yes," she said. "My mother has been married four times and she's just about to get another divorce."

I thought, *The enemy loves us to perpetuate those negative cycles, passing them down from one generation to the next. If we don't take responsibility and do something about it, it will keep repeating itself. Our children, grandchildren, and great-grandchildren will all have to deal with it.*

If I have bad habits, if I have insecurities, if I have wrong thinking, I want to be honest and open enough to deal with it and not make excuses, not blame my past, my parents, my circumstances, or my spouse. I can't change any of that, but I can change me.

"But if you knew my family, you'd realize that we are so dysfunctional. We have so many bad habits. We're so messed up."

I say this respectfully: Almost every family has some dysfunction. Don't use that as an excuse. We all have things to deal with and overcome.

Some people say, "I'm depressed because my parents were so depressed," or "I'm hot-tempered just like my father." "I'm a worrywart, because my mother always worried."

No, you can change. You are a child of God, so you have the greatest power in the universe inside you. You can break any addiction and overcome any stronghold. You can defeat any bondage. The Scripture says, "Greater is He that's in you than he that's in the world." [55] That means there is no obstacle on this planet that you cannot overcome. You can fulfill your God-given destiny. You can accomplish your dreams. You may have had a negative history, but please understand, you don't have to have a negative future. What's important is not where you've come from. What matters is where you are going.

One of the main ways we can honor God is by taking responsibility for our actions, not blaming our past, not blaming our circumstances. We must get down to the root, so we don't go through life trying to pick off the bad fruit. Take responsibility. Rise up and do something about it. You can experience the good things of God. I know if you will face the truth about yourself, get to the source of your issues, and make the adjustments God asks, I can promise that your inner life will improve, you will have better relationships, and you will be happier and more fulfilled.

ACTION POINTS

PART 6: DEVELOP YOUR INNER LIFE

1. Today I will be aware of the issues God brings to light in my life, and I will be quick to obey and make the necessary changes so I can move up higher.

2. I will pay more attention to my conscience, listening to the still, small voice within. I will do my best to keep my conscience tender by being quick to respond to His leading.

3. I refuse to make excuses for myself; I will look inside and deal with the root, not simply the fruit. I will probe beyond the surface symptoms and get down to the source of my problems. I choose to overcome any unfair experiences by looking for the good God is bringing out of them.

PART SEVEN

STAY PASSIONATE
ABOUT LIFE

CHAPTER 28

Plan for Blessing

If you want to become a better you, it is important to put the right actions along with your faith. It's not enough to believe, as important as that may be. We have to take it one step further and start expecting. While we are expecting good things from God, we should be making plans. We need to talk as if what we are praying about is going to happen. We should dare to step out in faith and act like it's going to happen.

When a couple is expecting a baby, they make all sorts of preparations. Why? Because they know a child is on its way. The fact is, in the early stages of the pregnancy, they haven't seen the baby or touched it. Yet they have faith in the doctor's report, so they start making preparations.

God has put dreams in every one of our hearts. We all have things for which we are believing—perhaps you are believing to overcome an illness, believing to get out of debt, or believing to accomplish your dreams. Here's the key: We have to go beyond believing. True faith puts action behind it. If you're sick, you need to start making plans to get well. If you're struggling in your finances, start making plans to prosper. If your marriage is on the rocks, start making plans to see that relationship restored. Lay your faith on the line.

Too often, we say that we are believing God for good things, yet with our actions, we're doing just the opposite. Understand that your faith will work in either direction, positively or negatively. I know some people who plan to get the flu. At the grocery store, I hear them predicting their future: "Well, it's flu season. I had better pick up some

329

of this flu medicine just in case. After all, it was bad last year. I got lucky and didn't get it. But I'll probably get it this year." They talk as though it is sure to happen. They take it even further and put actions behind their negative faith, by purchasing the flu medicine. Not surprisingly, a few weeks later they come down with the flu. Their faith worked, albeit negatively. They expected the flu, made plans for it, and they got it. Remember, your faith will work in either direction.

Please don't misinterpret what I am saying. It is prudent to take precautions; we have medicine at our house. However, I don't think we should run to the pharmacy every time a television commercial announces that flu season is here.

Funny, sometimes we put more faith in those commercials than we do in what God says. I love what it says in Psalms: "A thousand may fall at my side, ten thousand at my right hand; but it will not come near my dwelling." [56] Everybody at work may be getting the flu, everybody at school may have it, but I believe God has put a hedge of protection around me, and I'm going to stay in faith and not make plans to get it.

If we read the news long enough, and watch all the studies, they'll nearly talk us into having heart disease, high cholesterol, diabetes, and all sorts of ailments. "Well, you know what they say, one in four people gets cancer," a pessimistic friend points out.

Maybe that's true, but let's believe we will be among the three who don't get it instead of one of those who do. It is just as easy to believe for the positive as it is the negative. Start making plans to live a long healthy life. When you face sickness—and we all have things come against us from time to time—don't just give up and start making plans to live with it. I've had people tell me, "Well, Joel, I'm learning to live with my arthritis. I'm learning to live with my high blood pressure."

No, that's not *your* high blood pressure; that's not *your* sickness. Quit taking ownership of it and start making plans to get well. Our attitude should be, this sickness didn't come to stay, it came to pass. Say things such as, "I know with long life, God is going to satisfy me. So I declare it by faith, I'm getting better and better every day in every way."

Don't quit dreaming. Keep the vision in front of you. A friend of mine was in an accident where both of his knees were crushed. The doctor told him he would be fortunate to walk, but he would certainly never run or play sports again. My friend was so disappointed. After being in the hospital for over three months, the first thing he did when he was discharged was to join a health club. He took a step of faith. The fact is, he couldn't go to the club for over a year. He was too weak, but he made up his mind he was not going to sit back and plan on staying in that wheelchair; he was making plans to be up walking again. That was more than five years ago, and today that young man can outrun me. He defied the odds. What happened? He started making plans to rise up out of that injury. He could have easily let the doctor's negative words sink in, convincing him to give up, and settle for mediocrity. Instead, he believed God and began making plans to be well.

Maybe you've had some negative things happen to you or some negative comments spoken over you. Don't allow those negatives to take root. Keep believing for good things. And remember, faith is always in the now. Get up every morning saying, "Father, I thank You that right now You are working in my life. I thank You that right now I'm getting better. Right now things are changing in my favor."

Stay in the now; faith is always in the present.

Avoid Planning for Defeat

We frequently prepare for the wrong things. A man told me that when his father got up in years, he had a terrible time with his eyesight. He got to the point where he couldn't read anymore. This was a common malady for the older members of their family. This man was already making plans to have poor eyesight. He said, "Joel, I love to read. So I've started buying all of my books on CD now. That way I can listen to them just in case something ever happens to my eyesight."

That's planning for the wrong things. That's putting your faith in the negative, allowing—even welcoming—it to come to pass. I told him, "You need to keep buying regular books that you always read. And even when you get older, don't start buying these large-print books just because some of your friends are, or it makes it a little easier for you. No, if you don't need it, don't take the easy way out. And even if you do need it, put that off until you cannot read the smaller print anymore. Don't give up any ground."

Victoria has always had good eyesight, twenty-twenty vision. But over the last couple of years she's developed some difficulty in reading print up close. I've tried to get her to go see the eye doctor, but she wouldn't do it. She could not stand to think about the fact that her vision might be impaired a bit.

Finally, I talked her into it. She went to the optometrist, and he said her eyes were strong. She needed the lowest-power reading glasses, the kind you can buy over the counter at the grocery store. Still, it has been like pulling teeth for her to give in to wearing those things. I love the fact that she's not going to just sit back and accept it; she stands against it. She has put it off and put if off and put it off. We'll go to a restaurant and she'll have to hold the menu eighteen inches away just to see it! It's like my dad used to say: "God, You're either going to have to heal my eyes or lengthen my arms." Victoria refuses to sit back and say, "Well, I guess I'm getting older." Or "I guess my vision is going downhill." No, she will not make plans for defeat.

I read a study the other day. It included a chart that showed how at different ages, certain parts of our bodies start to decline. According to the research, when we get to be thirty years old, our hearing diminishes so much every year. We lose so much muscle mass every year. Our brain cells decrease by a certain percentage each year. If you start believing all those reports and acting on them, no wonder your body is falling apart! The other day someone told me, "Joel, I just turned sixty and I can't hear as well as I used to. I knew this day was coming. Everybody told me my hearing would go down."

I told the person, "You are agreeing with the wrong voices. Quit putting your faith in the wrong places, and start agreeing with what God says about you. It says in Deuteronomy 34, verse 7, that when Moses was a hundred and twenty years old, his eye was not dim and his natural strength was not abated. That means he could still see clearly, he could hear clearly, he was strong and healthy. I don't know about you, but I'm going to believe to live out my days like Moses. Instead of listening to all these negative reports, let me give you a different report. Let me give you a study found in God's Word. It says in effect, 'At sixty, you're still supposed to hear well. At seventy, your mind is supposed to be as sharp as it was when you were twenty-five. At eighty, you're supposed to be full of joy, full of life, full of energy.' Why don't you start making plans to live a long, healthy, satisfied life?"

Back in the early 1990s, we were remodeling the old sanctuary at Lakewood Church, especially the platform area. At that time, my father was more than seventy years old. One of the architects I was working with said, "Joel, your dad's getting a little older. Don't you think we should put a wheelchair ramp up to the side of the platform, just in case he ever needs a wheelchair?" The architect was a nice man, and he meant well. But I thought to myself, *You don't know my father. If he heard you say that, he would chase you out of this county.* My dad was never planning on being in a wheelchair.

Don't make plans to get old and bent over and not be able to do anything. Keep your faith out there. Speak words of health over yourself. Talk about the long life God is giving you, then put some actions behind it.

I know a man in his nineties who still lives in his own home alone, and his bedroom is on the second floor. That means several times every day he goes up and down those stairs. His children and grandchildren have tried to talk him into moving into one of the empty bedrooms downstairs, but he won't do it. His mind is made up. He said, "Joel, I know if I give in, I'll never be able to go back up those stairs."

He's probably right. Certainly, we should use common sense; we have to be realistic. What I'm saying is don't make plans for defeat. Everybody around you may be getting old and cranky, complaining that this part of his body doesn't work or that part of her body is failing, but you can be the exception. Believe to live a long, healthy life.

My father wanted to preach for as long as he lived. He didn't want to retire. He used to tell me, "Joel, I will never have a stroke." He was saying that by faith because he struggled with high blood pressure his entire life. He would say, "I'll never be incapacitated. I'll never come to the place where I cannot preach."

And true to his faith, my father preached just eleven days before he went to be with the Lord. God gave him the desires of his heart, because he was bold enough to put his faith out there. He believed he was going to be productive right up until the day that he died, and he was.

It's easy to think, "Well, the law of entropy is setting in: Everything is moving toward disintegration. So of course my body is debilitating. That's just a part of getting older. This doesn't work. That doesn't work. Can't see. Can't hear. Cranky."

No, don't fall into that trap—especially not the cranky part. There are enough cranky people in the world already! Make plans to be healthy, to be full of joy, to be productive right up to the day God calls you home.

In the Old Testament, when Caleb was eighty years old, he said, "God, give me another mountain." He was saying, "Give me something else to do. Give me another assignment." Notice, he was planning on living out his life in victory. He could have said, "God, just let me retire. My back is hurting. I can hardly see anymore. Medicare wouldn't pay for that latest prescription. I'm so aggravated."

No, he was strong, energetic, and ready for the next challenge—even at eighty years of age. You are never too old to do something great for God. You can be sure that regardless of your age God has important plans for you to fulfill. You are not just taking up space, waiting to go to heaven. Get your joy back; get your enthusiasm back. Don't wither up like a prune; instead, make plans to live every day joyfully, vibrantly alive, healthy, and productive.

An older couple came to one of Lakewood's leadership conferences, and during a question-and-answer session, they stood up and the man said, "Joel, we're not real sure what we're supposed to be doing at our age."

He said that they were in their nineties. This man was dressed to the nines; his skin looked great. His eyes sparkled with life. His wife was the epitome of grace and beauty. They were a sharp, striking older couple.

I told them, "One thing you need to do for sure is to go around and let other people see you. Be an example. Your joy, your health, your peace, your victory is an inspiration to others." I said, "You need to let the younger generation—which, in your case, is anyone under eighty—see how you can be up there in years and still be healthy, joyful, and peaceful."

That elderly couple inspired me! I tell Victoria every week I'm believing for at least forty more good years of strong, productive ministry. Forty years of sharing God's Word, encouraging people, building the kingdom. Not thirty good years, and then the last ten, my back's hurting, this doesn't work, that doesn't work, no joy, no peace. No, I've got my faith out there. I'm believing that at eighty years old, I'm going to be just as vibrant as I am right now. I will still have my hair, still be telling my jokes, still be teasing my brother Paul. I'm making plans to live a long, healthy, prosperous, joy-filled, abundant life. Why don't you do the same thing?

I know a lady who went through an extensive medical checkup when she was about seventy years old. After the doctors compiled all of her information, they gave her an average life expectancy. Based on their findings, her health, her genetics, and her family history, they estimated that she'd probably live to be around seventy-five years old.

The doctors might as well have told her that she was going to die the next day. She got so depressed that she wouldn't come out of her house. She lost her joy and her peace. Basically, she just gave up living her life. This went on for a while, until one day, her family brought her to see me. I told her, "Don't make plans for the worst. Don't let the negative take root. God can do what man's human intelligence and medical science can't do. And I found sometimes these experts, even though they're fine people, they can be wrong." We talked further, and I tried to encourage her. I could tell by the expression on her face that she was filling up with faith. Today, that woman is eighty-one years old and as healthy and vibrant as can be.

When I saw her recently, she said, "Joel, I've already beaten it by six years."

I laughed and said, "Yeah, and when you make it to ninety, we're going to have a real party around here!" And we will.

While it is important that you don't let negative thoughts and declarations take root, it is equally important to set high goals for your life. My father always believed that he would live to preach into his nineties. He didn't quite make it, but he used to say, "I'd rather shoot high and miss it than shoot low and make it." Keep a high goal. I used to play basketball with a gentleman who was in his seventies. He was in great shape and could run up and down the court with the twenty-year-olds. One day he said, "Joel, it's funny. When I was forty, my doctor told me that my knees wouldn't hold up playing this much, but I just kept playing. At fifty, he told me my back would start hurting if I kept running and jumping like this. But I just kept on. At sixty, he told me I could never keep up physically, but I can still run with the young guys." He said, "I went back at seventy, and finally the doctor told me to just keep playing as much as I want."

I laughed and asked him, "How long are you going to play?"

He smiled and said, "I'm going to play until I get old."

I like that. Old is a state of mind. Your body may age, but if you'll stay young in your spirit, your body will age even better. This man had the heart of a twenty-five-year-old. He was always grateful and happy, always in a good mood. You could tell that he wasn't making plans to get old and worn out. He was planning on living out his life joyfully, vibrantly, and in good health.

Maybe you have a history of serious illnesses in your family. You must stand against those diseases and believe God for good health. You can be the exception. You can be the one to start a new standard for your family. Here's what you have to do: You must think differently, and you need to take a different tack, take different actions. You cannot prepare for defeat and expect to live in victory. Keep your faith working for you, rather than against you.

Grandmother Osteen, my grandmother on my father's side, was a feisty woman. She stood only about five feet tall, but she had a big faith. One time, when she was older in life, she went to see her doctor. He said, "I'm sorry, Mrs. Osteen, but you're in the beginning stages of Parkinson's disease."

Well, Grandmother Osteen didn't know what that was, but she was sure she didn't want to have any part of it. She bristled back and she got real stern. She said, "Listen here, doctor, I'll not have that. I refuse to have it. I'm too old to have it."

She went home and never did come down with Parkinson's disease. She just kept doing what she'd always been doing, planning on living a long, healthy life. She didn't let the negative words take root.

I realize that we can't just wish things away; sometimes we can't even pray them away, but we *can* decide what we're going to plan for. We can plan to get old and lose our health, or we can plan to live a long, healthy, blessed, prosperous life.

What are you planning for today? Sickness or divine health? To barely get by or to be blessed? To stay where you are or to rise higher and accomplish your dreams? According to our actions or lack of action, we are making plans for something.

There's an interesting story in the Bible about a widow. Her husband died and she didn't have enough money to pay her bills. The creditors were coming to take her two sons as payment. The only thing she had of any value was a small pot of oil. Elisha the prophet showed up at her home and he instructed her to do something rather unusual. He said, "Go out to all your neighbors and gather up as many large empty containers that you can find, big jars that can be used to hold oil." Elisha told her specifically, "Don't get just a few; get as many as you can possibly find."

No doubt, in the natural, it seemed like the woman was simply wasting her time. Elisha knew he had to get her faith going in the right direction. She had been sitting around long enough preparing for defeat. Now he was trying to get her to start preparing for victory. So she gathered up all sorts of empty containers, brought them home, and Elisha told her to pour the oil that she had into one of the other containers. At first, it looked as though she was merely going to transfer it from one container to another, but the Scripture says her oil never ran out. She kept pouring and pouring and pouring. God supernaturally multiplied it until every single container was completely full. If she would have gotten a dozen more containers, they would have been full as well. Friend, we are the ones who limit God; His resources are unlimited. If you will believe Him for more, regardless of your circumstances, He can provide—even if it takes a miracle to do so!

Let me challenge you. Have a big dream for your life. Make provision for abundance.

"I'd love to pay my house off," I hear you say. "I'd love to get out of debt, but I don't see how it could happen for me. I've gone as far in my career as I can go. I'd love to send my children to college, but it's so expensive these days."

No. Are you making provisions? Do you have a savings account opened up? Do you have any containers? "Well, Joel, that'd be kind of foolish to have an account and not have anything to put in it."

The woman in Elisha's day did precisely that. She took a step of faith. It's not enough just to believe. Put actions behind your faith. Do what you can. Are you being your best on the job, showing up early, going the extra mile, doing more than expected? Are you dressing for success? You may have only one suit. Clean it up, press it, and wear it like you own the place. Are you talking successful talk? "Well, everybody gets promoted except me. They're talking about laying off people at my job, and last week my washing machine broke. If it's not one thing, it's another."

No, dwelling on that sort of talk will only prepare you for defeat. Change your attitude and change what you're saying. Start saying, "This is going to be a blessed day; I'm having a good month. This is the best year of my life. I know great things are in store. Goodness and mercy are following me. God's favor is surrounding me. I am expecting increase, promotion, and abundance." Don't stop there; start making plans to prosper. Prepare to succeed, not to fail.

When my father went to be with the Lord back in 1999 and I stepped up to pastor the church, one of the first things I did was to cancel our weekly television time. I thought, *I've never preached before and I'm sure not going to get on television and preach.* So I called our representative from the main national network on which we were broadcasting at the time. He was a good friend, and I told him what had happened and how we were going to have to cancel our broadcast. What was I doing? I was making plans for defeat. I was making plans to do poorly. I didn't think I could preach; I couldn't imagine that anybody would want to listen to me, so I put actions behind my faith. But I was stretching my faith in the wrong direction.

When I got home that night, I casually mentioned to Victoria what I'd done. She said, "Joel, you need to get that time back. People all over the country are waiting to see what's going to happen to Lakewood."

When she said that, something resonated within me, and I knew that it was right. We immediately took steps to get the broadcast time back, and today the broadcast goes out all over the world. Many times, with our own actions, we are limiting God. Had I not taken a step of faith in the right direction, I don't know if we'd be on television today. We cannot prepare for defeat and expect to have victory.

Maybe you are preparing to fail, preparing to barely get by or to lose your health. Start preparing for good things; prepare for success, prepare for abundance. Prepare for victory. Prepare for a long life. Prepare for good health. Get your faith going in the right direction. Start making plans to live a blessed, prosperous, healthy, joy-filled, abundant, long life. If you do this, God will do more than you can even ask or think. He will pour out his blessings and favor and you will become a much better you!

CHAPTER 29

Keep Singing Your Song

One of the secrets to becoming a better you is to keep singing the song that God has put in your heart—even if you can't carry a tune in a bucket! Let me explain. Too many people go around negative and discouraged, allowing their problems and circumstances to weigh them down. They live stressed out, dragging through each day, not really excited about life. I've had people tell me, "Joel, I've got too many problems to enjoy life." Or "The reason I'm discouraged and not happy is because I have all these things coming against me."

The fact is, God has put a well of joy on the inside of each one of us. Our circumstances may be negative; things may not be going our way. But if we can learn to tap into this joy, we can still be happy. We can live with enthusiasm in spite of what comes against us.

One of the keys is found in Ephesians 5:18. It says, "Ever be filled with the Spirit." Notice, you don't just get filled one time and then you live happily ever after. The Scripture says to be ever filled. That means we can be filled on a continual basis. How can we do this?

The next verse reveals the secret: "By speaking to yourselves in psalms and hymns, by making melody in your heart, and by being grateful." In other words, the way to keep your life full of joy and the way to overcome the pressures of life is by keeping a song of praise in your heart. All through the day, we should be singing, if not aloud then at least silently allowing a song of praise to dance through our minds. You may not actually vocalize words and music. You may simply express a grateful attitude. In your thoughts, you are thinking about God's goodness. Or maybe you go around humming a tune to a song. Maybe it's something as simple as whistling while you work, but throughout the day, you're making melody in your heart. Under your breath, you're saying, "Lord, thank You for this day. Thank You that I'm alive and healthy."

When you do that, you are filling up on the inside; God is replenishing your strength; He's refilling your supply of joy and peace. The very things that so often become depleted through the stress, disappointments, and rigors of the day, God wants to refresh in your life. When you keep singing that song of praise, you can be continually refilled, filling up faster than the depletion caused by life taking a toll on you. That's how we stay full of the Spirit.

"Well, I went to church on Sunday," Mike said. "I read my Bible before I went to work. Isn't that enough?"

No, this is an ongoing process. To be ever filled means we have to get in a habit of being refilled throughout the day—especially on those tough days.

Think back to when somebody gave your child some helium-filled balloons on her birthday. For the first few days following the party, the balloons remain bright and beautiful. They fly high at the end of their strings, bobbing in the wind. If you let go, the balloons would take off into the air. In a couple of days, though, the balloons begin to shrivel and shrink, sinking down, lower, smaller, weaker. Day by day, the balloons drop lower and lower. Finally, they land on the floor, totally deflated. The balloons have lost their life and attractiveness, not to mention their potential to rise higher.

Ironically, all you'd have to do to replenish those balloons and give them a fresh new start and appeal is to fill them back full of helium. If you did so on a regular basis, those balloons would last for months, bringing happiness and joy to all who saw them.

The same principle is true regarding our lives. Throughout the day, no matter how filled we are at the start, we "leak"; we get pressured or stressed; life happens. You get stuck in traffic, and a little helium goes out. You find out you didn't get the contract you were hoping for, and a little more escapes your balloon. You get home at the end of a hard day only to discover that your child is not feeling well and you must deal with that. The dog got into the trash, you have to clean up that mess, and your balloon loses a little more of its shape. The only way to stay full and to keep your joy and peace is to have this song of praise in your heart.

Understand, I'm not saying that you have to burst out in song, but I am suggesting that in your thoughts, you continually express a grateful attitude. Under your breath, throughout the day, you are thanking God for all He has done for you and your family. When you are working around the house, instead of complaining, you're whistling a tune. While you are cleaning up the dishes, you have some good praise music on in the background. You're humming along with it.

What's happening? You are making melody in your heart, and when you do that, you are continually filled up with God's love, joy, and peace.

Everywhere my father went, he was either singing or praying or whistling. Sometimes, when he would whistle incessantly, it would get on my mother's nerves. She'd say, "John, would you quit whistling? Can we have some peace around here?"

He'd say, "Oh, Dodie, I'm just happy. I'm just giving God praise."

She'd say, "John, you are whistling the tune to *The Andy Griffith Show.* You are not giving God praise."

The song didn't matter to my dad; what mattered was his attitude. My father was joyful when he was whistling. In his mind, he was saying, "God, I'm happy. God, I love You. I'm grateful to be alive." He always had a song of praise in his heart.

When you are doing the dishes, you can stand at the sink and complain, "Nobody appreciates me; all I do is work around here." Or you can choose to hum a song of praise and thanks. It's up to you.

"Well, I'm not musically inclined," you might say. "I can't sing very well."

Neither can I. But this isn't merely about music; this is an attitude. In our thoughts, we are grateful. We are excited about the future. We are expecting good things from God, so we allow a song to play continually in our minds. Any of us can do that. And yes, if you choose, you can sing in the shower or while driving to work. When you do this, you're making melody in your heart.

Not long ago, I woke up in the middle of the night and I could hear myself singing a song that I've known since I was a little boy. The words were right out of the Scripture: "You, oh Lord, are a shield unto me. The glory and the lifter of my head." Over and over, not out loud, but deep inside me, a song of praise was gushing out. As it did, God was filling me up anew.

When you're driving to work, play an inspiring praise CD. Make use of that time. At your house, put on some good uplifting music. Pay attention to what's going into you. Be aware of what you're feeding yourself.

A while back, I was driving and scanning the radio dial at the same time. I came across a station that plays oldies. When I turned it on, the first thing I heard was, "You're no good, you're no good, you're no good. Baby, you're no good."

I thought, *I don't need to hear that! I have enough things to deal with each day without putting that junk into me.*

Talk about leaking! If you listen to negative material like that, don't be surprised when you find yourself feeling totally deflated.

That's what many people do today. In their thoughts, they have no song. They dwell on negative issues, the people who hurt them, how much work they have to do, how unfair life is. Then they wonder why they don't have any energy, why they don't enjoy raising their children, why they dread going to work. It's because they've lost their song. They're not replenishing what's being taken out of them. You must stay on the offensive and make sure you have more positive input than negative.

It's interesting how little children—even toddlers—become invigorated if you put on some good music. They start swaying, dancing, and clapping. The music energizes them. Interestingly, you don't have to teach them to do that. You don't have to say, "I'm about to turn on the music; get ready to move."

It comes naturally to them because God has put a song in their heart. In the same way, God has put rhythm in every one of us. Too often, we allow the pressures of life to weigh us down. We had this song when we were children. We were happy, carefree, excited about life. But over time, we've developed new habits: being sour, dragging through the day, not really being excited about life. We need to rediscover childlike faith, and when we do, we will also discover the song within us.

One day, our seven-year-old daughter Alexandra came in early in the morning. She was dressed and ready to go to school, so happy, so enthusiastic. She smiled real big and said, "Daddy, guess what? I've already sung two songs, and I've already done two cartwheels."

I looked her in the eyes and I said, "Sweetheart, I love your enthusiasm. No matter what comes your way, keep singing those songs and keep turning those cartwheels."

Interesting to me, Victoria and I never asked Alexandra to sing. She just sings. I can hear her all through the day. It's because God has put a song in her heart. Start the day by making melody in your heart unto God, singing a song of praise. That's what I do. In the shower, I sound great! I don't know what happens when I step out! I like to start my day with a song of praise. Even if you don't do it out loud, at least do it on the inside. You may even want to try a few cartwheels, as well!

Whatever you do, get your song back. If you need to change some of your habits and quit dwelling on the negative, do it! Things may not be perfect in your life, but it could be a whole lot worse. Stop dwelling on what's wrong and start being grateful for what's right. Throughout the day, thank God for His goodness. Meditate on His promises. If you'll get your song back, you'll not only enjoy life more, but you will see things change in your favor.

My grandmother learned how to do this. Growing up, my siblings and I used to go over to my grandparents' home a lot. Every time I saw Grandmother, she was humming a tune. You couldn't hear her unless you were right next to her, but while ironing the clothes, she was at peace; she had a smile on her face, just humming along. In everything she did—doing the dishes, cooking dinner, traveling with my grandfather—she was constantly making melody in her heart. I cannot remember one time that I ever saw my grandmother upset, frustrated, stressed out, or worried. She was one of the most peaceful, joyful people that I've ever known. Even when things didn't go her way, her attitude was, "I'm not going to worry about it. I know that everything is going to be all right."

One time, my grandparents came over to our house for Thanksgiving dinner, and my grandmother forgot the turkey—the main dish. But it did not ruin her day. It did mine, but not hers. She stayed in peace. She just laughed and said, "Can you believe I did that?" Nothing took away her song. No wonder she lived a long, healthy life. She was always making melody in her heart unto God.

It Starts in Your Heart

I wonder how much more you and I would enjoy our lives if we'd be a little bit more like her. How would our attitude change if we did not take everything so seriously, and refused to allow every setback or disappointment to depress us for two weeks. How much better our lives could be if we'd simply keep the song of praise in our hearts!

Maybe lately you have noticed that you don't smile as much as usual; you don't laugh much anymore. You have allowed the burdens of life to weigh you down. Perhaps you have settled into enduring your life and not really enjoying it. You don't have the fire and enthusiasm you once had.

This can all change, but it requires a decision on your part. You must develop some new habits. Number one: Develop a habit of smiling on purpose. "But I don't feel like smiling. I have a lot of problems, a lot of things coming against me," you might say.

No, sometimes you have to smile by faith. If you'll smile by faith, soon the joy will follow. Smiling sends a message to your whole body that everything is going to be okay. When you smile, chemicals are released throughout your physical system that make you feel better. Beyond that, when you smile you'll have more of God's favor. It will help you in your career. Smiling will help you in dealing with people. Numerous studies show that people who smile and are friendly, people who have a pleasant demeanor, get more breaks than other people who are solemn and unfriendly.

I read where a major corporation planned to hire five hundred new employees. They interviewed five thousand people and they automatically disqualified any candidate who smiled fewer than four times during the interview.

Develop a habit of smiling on purpose.

Somebody has said your smile is a million-dollar asset. If you're not using it, you're doing yourself a disservice. "Well, Joel, I don't think it matters whether I smile or not."

God is concerned about your countenance. Fifty-three times in the Scripture, He mentions it. When you smile, it's not only good for yourself, but it's a good witness to others. They will want the sort of happiness that you have. It's one thing to talk about our faith, but it's a far better thing to live it out. One of the best witnesses we could ever have is simply to be happy, to have a smile, to be friendly and pleasant to be around.

Some people always seem to look as though they've lost their last friend. Even when they go to church, they look as though they were attending God's funeral!

Somebody asks, "How're you doing?"

"Oh, I'm just trying to hold on till Jesus comes," the starched-faced person replies.

No, we're not supposed to be merely holding on or dragging through life. Get your song back. Quit allowing the burdens of life to weigh you down.

Sure, sometimes you think, *I have a lot coming against me. I'm dealing with some difficult issues.* But the truth is, we all have tough times, hard things to handle, or heavy loads to carry. Don't allow your problems and circumstances to steal your joy.

And don't allow someone else to rob you of God's best. Too many people are being dragged down because somebody in their life is negative. Somebody else won't do right. Maybe you work around people who always complain. Or you live with somebody who seems perpetually discouraged and wants to wallow in self-pity. Don't get into the pit with them. Keep your song.

Several years ago, I was walking through a large field covered with brown weeds. Everywhere I looked, I saw nothing but dried-up, dead, unattractive weeds. As I came to a certain point on the path, however,

I noticed one beautiful flower, colorful and radiant. It had bloomed right there in the midst of all those weeds. I immediately thought, *That's the way we're supposed to be.* We may have a lot of problems; you may have a lot of negative people around you. But don't sink down to their level; just bloom right where you are. You may be married to an old weed, but you can still bloom. You may work around a bunch of weeds—people who complain, gossip, bad-mouth the company, the boss, or one another.

You may not be able to change them, but you can bloom right there amidst all the weeds. Put a smile on your face and have a grateful attitude. Don't let anyone else drag you down. Instead, by your example, pull them up; make them want what you have.

Declare today, "I'm not allowing another problem, another circumstance, or another person to keep me from giving God praise. I'm going to bless the Lord at all times. I'm going to get my song back."

I recognize that our problems are real, and at times, life is extremely difficult. But after you get through this problem, after you overcome this challenge, there will always be another challenge to overcome. There'll be something else to deal with. If you are waiting for all of your problems to go away before you decide to get your song back, you will miss the joy of living.

The Apostle Paul had all sorts of difficulties, all kinds of challenges. But he said, "In all these things we are more than conquerors." Notice, he didn't say, "When these difficulties are done, I'm going to be happy." No, he said, "In the middle of this adversity, I'm going to enjoy my life anyway."

Number one: Get in a habit of smiling on purpose. Number two: Check your posture. Make sure you stand up tall, put your shoulders back and hold your head up high. You are a child of the Most High God. You are not supposed to go around slumped over, feeling sloppy, weak, inferior, and thinking that you're unattractive.

The Scripture says, "We are ambassadors of Christ." [57] That means you represent Almighty God. Represent Him well. Even many good, godly people have gotten into a bad habit of slumping and looking down. When you do that, subconsciously you are communicating a lack of confidence, a lack of self-esteem. You need to put your shoulders back, hold your head up high, and communicate strength, determination, and confidence. Subconsciously, you're saying, "I'm proud of who I am. I know I'm made in the image of Almighty God. I know I am the apple of God's eye."

Much of communication is nonverbal. When I first started ministering publicly, and I really wanted to make a point, I'd stick my neck out and lean over. I was trying to be real emphatic and demonstrative. But a friend of mine who deals in communication suggested, "Joel, you're doing just the opposite. When you stick your head out and you're all bent over, that's a sign of weakness. You would communicate much more effectively if you'd put your shoulders back and hold your head up high. That's a position of strength and confidence, and people will receive more of what you have to say."

Our body language is communicating constantly, so make sure yours is saying what you want to say. Your countenance, smile, posture, and how you carry yourself may make a world of difference in becoming a better you.

As a young man, I noticed this quality about a friend of ours, an older gentleman. He looked like a statesman; his posture was perfect, his manner of dress impeccable. He was always kind, compassionate, and considerate. He is now in his eighties and he carries himself exactly the same way. When I see him, I think of a prince or a king. He looks like royalty. That's the way you and I should be. Not in arrogance. I'm not saying to be proud and puffed up. I'm talking about living with a calm, quiet confidence. We know we are representing Almighty God. Let's learn to walk tall.

Certainly, your personality plays a part in this. Some people are naturally more confident. Some people naturally smile more often. I probably smile in my sleep. You may be just the opposite. But don't use that as an excuse to go through life sour and unfriendly. I've had to make changes, too. While I smile a lot naturally, I am by nature rather quiet and reserved. I have had to train myself to be more confident and to speak up.

You may have a lot of confidence, but you're too serious, you don't smile nearly enough. You can train yourself to smile more often. The best smile, of course, starts on the inside. In fact, the Scripture implies that our joy can overflow. That means we should have so much joy that when other people get around us, it rubs off on them. When they leave, they should be happier, encouraged, inspired, better off than they were before.

Notice when you get around people, are you always taking and never giving? Are you counting on them to cheer you up? It should be the opposite. You need to start making melody in your own heart. Maybe you received a bad report from the doctor, and it takes the wind out of your sail. That's when you have to dig your heels in and say, "God, I know you're still in control. I'm going to keep a smile on my face and I'm going to give You praise anyway."

The Scripture tells us to offer unto God the sacrifice of praise,[58] but that doesn't mean it is always easy to do so. Nevertheless, our attitude should be, "God, I know when I keep my song and stay grateful it not only activates your power, but it also replenishes me. It fills me up. So despite my circumstances, I choose to give you praise anyway."

Friend, you can choose what kind of song you're going to have. Don't be lazy in your thought life; speak to yourself in psalms and hymns. You talk to yourself throughout the day. Perhaps you have been talking to yourself in the wrong way. You need to start declaring, "This is going to be a good day. Thank you, Lord, for your strength. Thank you, Lord, for my health."

Get your song back. Say things such as, "Father, thank You for this day. Thank You that I'm alive." Every time you do that, God will fill you afresh with His joy, His peace, His strength, His victory, and His favor. And when you're full of God's love and power, a natural by-product is that you start looking for the good things of God in your life. Let's look at that more closely in our next chapter.

CHAPTER 30

From Believing to Expecting

I hope that by now you are making preparations for the good things God has in store for you. God has put dreams and desires in every one of our hearts. We all have promises that we're standing on, things that we believe will come to pass. But almost always there's a time of waiting involved. Maybe you're waiting for a relationship to improve, waiting to get married, waiting for a promotion, or perhaps you are waiting to overcome an illness.

Much of life is spent waiting. There's a right way to wait and a wrong way. Too often when things don't happen on our timetable we get down and discouraged. Even though we have the promise in our heart, we give up and settle for the status quo. I believe it's because we're not waiting the right way.

The Bible says, "Be patient as you wait." [59] Notice, it doesn't say *if* you wait, it says *as* you wait. The passage goes on to say, "See how the farmer waits expectantly." That's the key: We have to wait with expectancy. We're not supposed to sit around thinking, *My situation is never going to change. I prayed, I believed. But I don't see how I can ever get out of this mess.*

No, to wait with expectancy means that we are hopeful and positive. We get up every morning expecting good things. We may have problems, but we know this could be the day God turns it around. This could be the day I get the break that I need.

Waiting should not be a passive thing. Waiting the correct way means you are on the lookout. You talk as if what you believe is going to happen. You act as though it's going to happen. You are making preparations.

If you are expecting someone for dinner, you don't wait until the guest shows up at your door before you prepare for the meal. Most likely you start early in the day. You make sure the house is clean. You may go to the grocery store the day before; perhaps you will buy some flowers for the table and swing by the bakery to get your favorite dessert—low-fat, of course. You make all these preparations. Why? Because you're expecting someone.

We need a similar attitude while we're waiting for God's promises to come to pass. It's not enough merely to pray. We must put actions behind our prayers. The Scripture says: "Faith without corresponding actions is dead." [60] In other words, we can believe one way, we can talk one way, but if we're not putting the right actions behind our faith, it's not going to do any good.

I talked to Scott, a young man who has a dream to go to college. But nobody in his family has gone beyond high school. He immediately began listing all of his obstacles. "Joel, I don't know if I can afford it. I don't know if I'll make good enough grades. I don't know if they'll accept me. I don't know what my other family members will think." He was about to talk himself out of his dream.

Finally, I stopped him and said, "Scott, why don't you take a step of faith? Put some actions behind your prayers and at least fill out an application. Go tour the campus. Talk to the counselors. Make preparations to succeed. If you'll do what you can, then God will do what you can't."

Too often, we're believing one way, but actions are demonstrating the opposite—we're actually preparing for defeat. Maybe you come from a long line of divorce in your family. Instead of being afraid of ever getting married or worrying that your marriage will end in divorce, you need to start planning what you're going to do on your first wedding anniversary, and on your fifth anniversary, and on your twenty-fifth anniversary. Speak words of vitality and life regarding your marriage. Don't say, "I'm not sure our marriage is going to survive this strain." Not any of this, "If we make it, maybe we'll go on a cruise next year." Get rid of the "if" and start saying, "*When* we make it!"

I tease Victoria that I have already planned our fiftieth wedding anniversary. The way I figure, after sticking with me for all those years, I'm going to take that girl to Dairy Queen!

Seriously, though, stay hopeful and positive, and make preparations to succeed. We must understand there's a difference between believing and expecting. You can believe to have a child and not even be pregnant. But once you go from believing to expecting, you kick into a different gear. When you are expecting, you'll go furnish the nursery. You'll buy clothes for a baby that's not here. You'll call your friends and relatives and let them know the good news. "Mom! Dad! A baby is on its way." Even in the early stages of pregnancy, you start making all sorts of preparations. It affects your attitude, what you eat and drink, how you exercise, talk, and think.

Interestingly, you may go several months and say, "I look the same. I don't feel all that different."

It doesn't matter what you see or feel. You received a report from the doctor that says a baby is on its way. That's all you need to know to start making preparations.

There's a difference between believing and expecting.

You need to do something similar when God puts a dream in your heart. Maybe one of His promises comes alive in your heart and mind, and for the first time, you dare to believe that your family can be restored. You know you can be healthy again. You know you can accomplish your dreams. The first thing is you have to let the seed really take root. But you can't stop there. You must move on from believing to expecting.

"I'm doing that," you might say, "but I don't see anything happening. My finances aren't improving. I don't see any doors opening. My health is slipping rather than improving."

Scripture teaches, "We walk by faith, not by sight."[61] If you can see everything happening, you don't really need any faith. But when you have nothing to stand on in the natural—and you start acting as though God's Word is true, being positive and hopeful—you are putting actions behind your faith. That gets God's attention. That's what causes Him to work supernaturally in your life. What happened? You went from believing to expecting.

That's what the leadership of Lakewood Church did when we were negotiating to move our congregation to the Compaq Center, former home of the National Basketball Association's Houston Rockets. I announced to the congregation that we were going to raise funds to renovate the center before we really knew for sure that it was going to be ours. After we won the main city council vote, a company filed a lawsuit to try to keep us from moving in. Our attorneys told us there was no guarantee that we would win, and even if we did, the case could be tied up in the courts for up to ten years through various appeals.

From a logical business standpoint, I should have waited to see how everything was going to turn out. But down inside, I knew God wanted us to go forward. So I went from believing to expecting, and we started making preparations. Just like a young couple preparing the nursery, we started drawing the new plans, doing the studies, putting the vision out there.

It wasn't always comfortable or easy. Many times, I'd wake up in the middle of the night in a cold sweat. Those negative voices would pummel my mind, saying, "Joel, what are you going to do if you don't get that building? You're going to look like a fool! You've already encouraged people to donate their money to the cause. You're going to have to give their money back." And on and on.

I'd say, "God, I know You're in control, and I'm not going to be moved by what I don't see. I know You are bigger than our obstacles. And God, I believe at the right time, You will change things in our favor."

A year and a half later, that's exactly what happened.

How does the farmer wait? Expectantly. How does he take care of his seed? By watering it, by pulling the weeds, by keeping the soil soft.

How do we water our seeds? By staying full of praise. By getting up every morning and thanking God that the answer is on the way. When negative thoughts threaten that it's never going to happen, you're never going to get well; you're never going to get out of debt, pull those weeds by simply saying, "God, I know You are faithful. My trust and confidence is in You. I know You have great things in store for my life." You protect your seed by having a grateful attitude of expectation.

Are you believing or are you expecting?

"Well, Joel, I'd like to get out of debt," you might say. Or "I'd like to have a nice house one day. But my business is so slow. And the cost of living is so high. I don't see how it could ever happen for me."

That kind of thinking will keep you right where you are. Decide to wait with expectancy. Declare, "God, I know You can do what men can't do. You are my provider; my job is not my source, the economy is not my source. But God, I know You are my source."

Get a bigger vision; get rid of that limited mentality and start making preparations for God's blessings, even if it's in some small area.

Years ago, I went to the apartment of Peter and Becky, some friends of mine. It was a small place, and even though they were happy and content, they knew God had put bigger things in their hearts. As an act of faith, when the young couple bought furniture for their den, they bought pieces that were much too large for the size of the small room. The couches were crammed against each other, with tables on each end. I could barely step by them.

Naturally, I didn't say anything about it, but it looked odd to me. A few minutes later, Becky said, "Joel, you'll have to excuse our den. We bought this furniture for our *new* house."

I didn't know they were moving, so I said, "Really, where are you going?"

They laughed and Peter replied, "We don't know yet. We just know we're not staying here. This is only temporary."

They were saying, "This is not our destiny. We're not going to sit back and accept this. God has put bigger things in our hearts and we're making preparations to rise higher."

They stayed in that apartment for several years, and when I'd see them in passing, I often asked, "Have you moved yet?"

"Not yet."

"When are you moving?"

Their answer was always, "Soon!" I never heard them speak out discouraging words. I never saw them down and defeated. They stayed hopeful and expectant.

One day, Becky got a huge break at work, resulting in a promotion and a sizable increase in her salary. Suddenly, things started falling into place.

Can you guess where that oversized furniture is now?

No, it's not in their new home. They gave it to another young couple who are believing for their dream home, and Becky and Peter purchased brand-new furniture for their new home.

You get God's attention when you put actions behind your faith. Why not take a step of faith, plant a seed, do something that indicates to you and others that you are planning to succeed?

You may be facing sickness and disease. Maybe you got some bad news concerning your health. Well, don't start planning your funeral. Don't sit around depressed thinking about all the other people who have died from that same disease. Start making plans to get well.

When my father was preparing for open-heart surgery, it was an extremely serious situation. The doctors gave us no guarantees that it would turn out okay.

Instead of moping around in defeat, my father had us bring his tennis shoes and his running suit up to the hospital and put them right beside his bed. The facts said that he would not be up running anytime soon. But every day as he recovered, he'd look at those tennis shoes. In his mind, he was saying, *One day soon, I'm going to be running again. One day I'm going to be healthy. One day I'm going to be strong.* He was watering his seed, living expectantly, and that is what gave him the strength to carry on.

The Scripture says, "Those who wait upon the Lord"[62] will have their strength renewed. The Amplified Bible expands what it means to "wait on the Lord." It says, "Those who expect, who look for, and hope in Him." What might happen if we were to live with expectancy, stay hopeful, and make preparations for the goodness of God?

This Scripture goes on to say, "We will mount up with wings like the eagle. You will run and not get tired. You will walk and not faint." In other words, you will not stay down; you will overcome life's challenges.

If you can just get up every morning expecting God to turn your problems around for good, if you can stay positive and hopeful, then God promises He will give you a supernatural strength that will cause you to soar like the eagles.

Put Some Action Behind Your Prayers

Remember, though, you need to put some actions behind your prayers. You may already be praying and believing; that's good. But don't stop there; keep pressing in closer to God. Move deeper to not only believing God can do something in your life, but expecting that God will do great things in, for, and through you.

A minister I know had a dream to go all over the world and share God's Word. But at the time, he didn't have a single open door, not one invitation.

Instead of getting down and discouraged, thinking, *I must have missed it. This must not be for me,* he took a step of faith. He went out and bought a brand-new set of luggage. He had hardly traveled more than a few miles beyond his hometown, and in the natural he had much better things on which he could have spent his money. But deep down, he knew that one day, God was going to open doors of opportunity for him. The minister kept his faith fresh and strong.

About six months later, he received his first invitation to speak outside his church. He was so excited that he brought it up and showed it to my father. Today that man travels all over the world. He has more invitations than he could ever possibly accept. He went from believing to expecting to receiving. Notice how he put action behind his faith. We cannot be passive and have God's best. When we're really expecting, we're on the lookout for opportunities. We're doing everything we can to make our dreams come to pass.

When my sister Tamara was about seven years old, she decided she wanted some rabbits. We lived out in the country and we already had a couple of dogs, and even some chickens. But Tamara wanted some rabbits, too. She went to my father and said, "Daddy, would you please get me some rabbits?"

My father was generous and good to his children, but he had

endured enough problems with our chickens. They frequently escaped their pen or the yard, and we had to go round them up from our neighbors.

Daddy said, "Tamara, I love you, but we are not going to get any rabbits." Well, he might as well have told that to a tree for all Tamara heard him; she paid no attention. Instead, she kept acting like she was going to get those rabbits.

It reminded me of a time when Jesus was walking down the road on His way to pray for a little girl who was sick. Along the way, though, he encountered several delays and interruptions. Finally, the people came up and said to his disciples, "Tell Jesus not to bother coming. It's too late. The little girl has died."

The Scripture says, "[Jesus,] overhearing but ignoring."[63] Now, there's a principle: Sometimes, to stay in faith, you must ignore a negative report. Sometimes people will try to talk you out of your dreams. Sometimes medical science will tell you there's nothing more they can do for you. Sometimes our own thoughts can even try to convince us of all the reasons why our dream, goal, or prayer request is not going to happen.

Jesus heard the bad news, but He chose to ignore it. He chose to not allow it to influence Him. That's what my sister Tamara did. Every two or three days, she went back to my father and asked him again, "Daddy, have you thought any more about those rabbits? I really would like to have one."

"Tamara, I don't have to think about it," Daddy said. "We are not getting any rabbits."

A couple of days later, Tamara asked again. "Daddy, I'd still like to have a rabbit." This went on for two or three months. Tamara was determined that one day she was going to have those rabbits.

At one point, I could tell she was wearing my father down. He said, "Tamara, even if I wanted to get you rabbits, I have no idea where to get one."

"I do!" Tamara responded. "I know exactly where they are. I've already seen the place."

He said, "Show me." They got in the car and drove about fifteen minutes down the highway. About two hundred yards off the main road, way back in the woods, was a small sign. On it in handwritten letters were the words: "Rabbits for Sale."

Tamara was on the lookout. And when you have a dream in your heart, you'll see things that other people don't see. My family and I had traveled up and down that road hundreds of times, yet none of us had ever seen that sign. Finally, my father said, "Tamara, I'd love to get you rabbits, but we don't have any place to keep them."

She said, "Yes, we do. I've already had Paul make me a cage."

Needless to say, Tamara got her rabbits.

A lot of times, we are waiting for God to do something. "God, just give it to me on a silver platter."

But we must do our part by making preparations. Do some research, sow some seeds, and then stay expectant.

"Well, Joel, what if I do that and it doesn't happen?"

What if you do this and it *does* happen? Even if it doesn't turn out the way you had hoped, you'll still be better off to live your life positively and hopeful.

Many people are waiting for their situation to change, and while they're waiting to get the break they need, they get all sour. "Nothing good ever happens to me." "When am I going to get married?" "When am I going to get out of this problem?"

No, you need to turn that situation over to God.

In the Old Testament, David said, "God, my times are in your hands." He was saying, "God, I don't know when it's going to happen, but I know You know what's best for me, so I'm going to expect good things. And even if it doesn't happen today, I'm not going to go to bed disappointed. I'll keep trusting that I am one day closer to seeing it come to pass."

Start making preparations to live a blessed life. Keep your vision in front of you and don't believe the "never" lies: I'll never get well. I'll never see my dreams come to pass. No, shake that off, and stay positive and expectant.

Don't believe the "never" lies.

You may say, "I did this. I prayed, I believed, I expected. But my loved one died. I just don't understand it."

No, God still has a great plan for your life. You cannot let one setback or even a series of disappointments keep you from pressing forward and believing for God's best.

John and Karen had become estranged from their son. Some things had happened, causing them to be at odds with each other. The young man wouldn't talk to his mother or father, wouldn't come visit them, and wouldn't have anything to do with them. This went on month after month, until it looked as if they would never be reconciled.

But John and Karen refused to give up on their son. They took a step of faith and bought their son a Bible. They even had his name engraved on the front of it. The young man had never had anything to do with the things of God, so by all outward appearances, it seemed that his parents were wasting their money. They put the Bible on their coffee table anyway, and every time they walked by it, they thanked God that one day their son would be back home. One day, he would get back on the right course.

A few years later, they got a phone call from their son. "Mom and Dad," he said, "I want to come home." God supernaturally restored that relationship and today, I see that young man in church all the time, and he's carrying a Bible—but not just any Bible. He's clutching that Bible with his name engraved on it, the same one that sat on that coffee table all those years.

John and Karen waited expectantly. They made preparations for their son to come back home, and today their entire family is reaping the benefits.

Stacey was so tired of being overweight. She had tried every diet that came along, yet nothing seemed to work. Finally, she gave up and resigned herself to being overweight, even though she knew that wasn't God's best for her.

In any area of life, it is easy to settle for mediocrity. But one day, Stacy got fed up. She put her foot down and started applying actions to her prayers. She went to the mall and purposely bought a new outfit that was two sizes too small for her. She knew she couldn't wear it.

What was she doing? She was preparing to lose the weight. She went from believing to expecting. She later told me that she put that outfit in her closet right by her mirror so she could see it every day. It inspired her. Every time she saw it, she'd say, "Father, thank You that I'm going to lose this weight. Thank You that every gland, every organ, every cell in my body functions normally. Thank You that I have discipline and self-control."

When I next saw her, she was wearing her new outfit. She said, "Joel, I not only lost thirty pounds, but I feel better today than I've ever felt before."

God rewards people like that—people who keep the vision in front of them. Stay determined. Tamara would have never gotten those rabbits if she had not already had the cages built. Lakewood Church would never have been able to secure our new building had we not pressed through those obstacles.

Stretch your faith. Put some actions behind what you are believing God to do for you. Maybe you've just about given up on what God has put in your heart. You think your life is never going to get any better.

It can, but you must rekindle that fire.

"Well, Joel, it's been a long, long time . . ."

The Scripture says, "Though the vision tarries, wait earnestly for it." Notice, we can't wait passively; we must wait earnestly and expectantly. What will happen when you do that? The Scripture passage goes on to say, "The vision will not be one second late." That means when we stay in faith, positive, expectant, and hopeful, then all the forces of darkness cannot keep God from bringing those promises to pass.

You may remember Gavin MacLeod, the actor probably best known for playing the captain on *The Love Boat*, a popular television show years ago. He and his wife Patti had been married for seven years. They hit some bumps along the road and Gavin left.

He later told how he got caught up in his career and wasn't making good choices. He and Patti divorced and Patti was devastated. She never wanted the breakup of their marriage.

Instead of just giving up and accepting their divorce, every day she started thanking God that one day Gavin would be back home and their relationship would be restored. She took it one step further and started putting actions behind her faith.

Patti later told how every night at the dinner table, instead of setting one place setting, she would set two place settings. She was making preparations for Gavin to come back home.

Three years later, Patti heard a knock on the front door. She opened it and there stood Gavin. She smiled and said, "Come on in. Your dinner is getting cold." They remarried shortly thereafter.

How are you waiting for the good things of God? Learn to wait with expectancy. Get up every morning and water your seeds by thanking God that the answer is on the way. Then take it one step further and start making preparations for the dreams God has planted in your heart. Talk like it's going to happen, act like it's going to happen. Keep the right attitude. If you will go from believing to expecting, God promises that in due season, at the right time, He will bring you the desires of your heart.

CHAPTER 31

Stay Passionate About Life

If you want to become a better you, it is imperative that you appreciate the good things that God has done for you. Too many people have lost their passion for life. They've lost their enthusiasm. At one time, they were excited about their dreams. They got up every day with purpose and with passion. But now because of the time that's passed, the disappointments they have experienced, and the pressures of life, they're not excited about them anymore. They've lost their fire.

At one time maybe you were excited about that person to whom you are married. You were so in love and so passionate, but now that relationship has become stale. You are going through the motions of life, getting up, going to work, coming home. But God does not want us to live that way. We should get up every day with enthusiasm, excited about that day. We should be grateful that we're alive, grateful for the opportunities in front of us, grateful for the people in our lives.

Understanding that most of life is rather routine, anything can become stagnant if we allow it to do so. You can have an exciting job, but it can become boring. Or you can be married to a fine, loving, caring person, but if you don't nourish that relationship and put something into it, over time, it is likely to get stagnant. We have to work at it if we're going to stay fresh. It doesn't automatically happen.

We need to stir ourselves up every day. The Apostle Paul told Timothy, "Fan your flame." He was saying, "Timothy, don't let your fire go out. Stay passionate about your life. Stay enthusiastic about your dreams."

Maybe right now, you are having difficulty being excited about your life, but keep your hope alive. You may have just a tiny flicker, and that fire is barely burning. You're about to give up on one of your dreams. Or maybe in that relationship, you're not excited about it anymore. But the good news is the fire is still in there, and if you will do your part to fan the flame, it can burst forth into passion once again. That means instead of dragging around finding every reason you can to be unhappy, you must change your focus. Quit looking at what's wrong in your life and start being grateful for what's right in your life. Your attitude should be: "I am not going to live my life defeated and depressed. My dreams may not have come to pass yet; I may have some obstacles in my path, but I know God is still in control, I know He's got great things in store for me, so I'm going to get up each day excited about my life."

**Quit looking at what's wrong in your life
and start being grateful for what's right.**

Everything may not be perfect in your life, but if you don't learn to be happy where you are, you will never get to where you want to be. You may not have the perfect job, but you should thank God that at least you are employed. Some people would love to have your job. Fan your flame and go to work with a new enthusiasm. Don't drag into the workplace with a long face and then waste half the day playing on the Internet. Instead, give your employer 100 percent. Do your work with all your heart, to the best of your ability. Stay passionate about it. Everybody else may be slacking off; everybody else may have a sour attitude. But you are not everybody else; you are a child of the Most High God. Don't be part of the problem; be part of the solution.

Enthusiasm is contagious. If you go into your workplace with a smile on your face, full of life, full of joy, full of victory, before long, you'll rub off on others. That whole place will come up to a higher level, thanks to you.

The Bible says to "never lag in zeal, but be aglow and on fire serving the Lord." [64] Do you get up each morning passionate about your dreams? Are you grateful for the home in which you live?

"Oh, I'm living in a tiny apartment," you may say. "I can't stand it. I want a bigger house."

No, you must learn to be happy right where you are. Understand that it dishonors God for us to go around complaining and thinking about everything that's wrong in our lives. You may not be living in your dream house, but you should thank God you have a roof over your head. Thank God you're not homeless, living out there in the elements.

"My husband and I don't have anything in common. We don't get along anymore."

Well, he may not be the perfect husband. But you can thank God that at least you have somebody to love. Do you know how many people are lonely today? Believe it or not, some woman would be glad to have your husband. Be grateful for that man. Be grateful for that woman.

Every day is a gift from God.

We need to recognize that every day is a gift from God. What a shame to live any day in a negative and defeated mind-set.

Certainly, we all have obstacles in our path and challenges to overcome, but our attitude should be, "Thank God, I'm alive. I live in a great country. I have family. I have opportunity. So I'm going to make the most of this day and give it my best."

"Well, Joel, I would do that, but I just found out I have to work late next week. I have to go on a business trip. I've got to take care of these kids all day."

No, you don't *have* to do anything; you get to do it. God is the One who has given you breath. You wouldn't be able to work late next week if God hadn't opened up that door of opportunity. You need to change your perspective. Don't do things out of obligation or because you have to—do them with an attitude of gratitude. In other words, "I don't have to go to work today; I get to go to work." "I don't have to take care of these children, they're a blessing; I get to take care of them." "I don't have to give; I get to give."

The Scripture says, "When we are willing and obedient, we will eat the good of the land."[65] It's one thing to be obedient. That's good. That's better than not doing it. But if you really want to experience God's best, you need to be more than obedient; you have to be willing. You have to do it with the right attitude.

For instance, it's one thing to give because you have to. It's another thing to give because you want to. It's one thing to go to work to pick up a paycheck. It's another thing to go to work to be a blessing to somebody else. It's one thing to stay married to that person because it's the right thing to do. People may look down on you if you don't. But it's another thing to stay married to that person and to treat him or her with respect and honor and help your partner reach a higher level. That's being willing and obedient. When you do the right thing with the right motives, there's no limit to what God will do in your life. It is important that we get beyond mere obedience. That's easy, anybody can do that. To become a better you, take the next step and be willing to do the right thing with a good attitude.

**When you do the right thing with the right motives,
there's no limit to what God will do in your life.**

Roger was down and discouraged so he went to see his minister for some advice. "Nothing's going right in my life," Roger said. "I don't have any reason to be excited."

The minister thought for a moment and then said, "All right, let's do a simple exercise." He took out a legal pad and drew a line right down the center. "On the left side, we're going to list all of the good things in your life, everything that's going right. And on this other side, we'll list all your problems and all these things that are bothering you."

Roger laughed skeptically and said, "Okay, but I'm not going to have anything to put on the asset side."

The minister said, "Fine, let's just go through the exercise."

Roger put his head down.

The minister said, "I'm so sorry to hear that your wife passed away."

At that, Roger snapped to attention. "What are you talking

about?" he asked. "My wife didn't pass away. She's alive and healthy."

"Oh, really?" The minister wrote on the asset side: "Has a wife, alive and healthy." Then he said, "I'm so sorry to hear that your house burned down."

"What?" Roger cried. "My house didn't burn down. I have a beautiful house."

"Oh, really?" the minister said, as he wrote on the asset side of the ledger: "Has a beautiful house." Then he said, "I'm really sad to hear that you lost your job. You got laid off."

"Where are you getting all this nonsense?" Roger asked incredulously. "I've got a great job."

"Oh, really?" the minister said, as he raised his eyebrows and wrote down, "Has a great job."

About that time, Roger caught on. He said, "Give me that list." The minister passed the yellow legal pad to Roger, who proceeded to list several dozen more good things in his life. By the time he was finished, he left the minister's office with a different attitude. His circumstances hadn't changed, but his perspective was completely different.

It's so easy to get focused on what's wrong and to take for granted what's right, what is going well. When you focus on the good, that's when you bolster your enthusiasm and passion. If you struggle with staying excited and passionate about your life, you too need to make a list of all the things for which you can be grateful. Write down all the things God's blessed you with. If you have your health, write it down. "I'm healthy." If you can see, write it down. "I can see." If you're good-looking (like me!), write it down. "I'm good-looking." If you have a job, write "I've got a job. I've got family. I have several close friends. I have great children." Make that list and every day before you leave the house, read over it two or three times. It is important to get your mind going in the right direction, because your life will follow your thoughts.

At the first of the day, set the tone. If you can go out with a grateful attitude and a positive frame of mind, you'll not only feel better, but you also will draw in the good things of God. We attract what we continually think about. If you get up thinking, *My life is dragging;*

nothing good ever happens to me. I know my marriage isn't going to last, you attract defeat, failure, and mediocrity. However, if you can learn to turn it around and go out with a grateful attitude, thinking about how blessed you are and how good God's been to you, then you will draw in the goodness of God.

We attract what we continually think about.

Sometimes we lie in bed in the morning thinking, *I don't want to go to work today. I've got so many problems. I'm sick and tired of cleaning this house.*

Unfortunately, you just paved the way to have a lousy day. You made preparations for defeat.

When those negative, discouraging thoughts come, you must turn them around. Get your list out and read over it again. Remind yourself, "I'm alive. I'm healthy. I've got a great spouse. I have beautiful children. I have so many good things." Put that list on your bathroom mirror, on your desk, or some place where you can see it throughout the day. Read over it occasionally as you go about your normal routine, and it will help you to stay excited about your life.

Another important key to fanning your passion is to keep fresh goals before you. Some people have lost their passion for life simply because they're not pursuing anything. But understand that God created us to be always reaching for something beyond where we are presently. If you live with low motivation, few dreams, and no realistic goals, you are bound to become stagnant. On the other hand, if you will continue to pursue a new goal, it will keep you fresh and excited about life. Your goal needn't be lofty or grandiose. It may be a goal to finish school, or to be a better parent, or to increase your income. Still, have something out in front of you. Always be growing and never allow yourself to become complacent. After you accomplish one goal, immediately set another. Keep moving; keep looking for new challenges.

If you're not healthy, have a dream to get healthy. If you're in debt, let your dream be, "I'm going to get out of debt and be a blessing to others as well." Then get up each day knowing that you're pressing toward that goal.

"Well, Joel, I'm retired," you might be saying. "I'm just kicked back, taking it easy." No, even though you are retired from your job, you never retire from the life of service God has for you. It is unhealthy to not have something to pursue every day.

Years ago, my father and I met Jacques Cousteau, the famous underwater explorer. Daddy and I were on a flight down to the Amazon jungle and Mr. Cousteau was on the same flight, so we engaged in conversation. He was probably in his early eighties, yet he was incredibly passionate about his life. He began telling us about a new project he was working on, excitedly explaining it in great detail. As we were about to leave, he told us about his ten-year plan and all that he hoped to accomplish. I thought, *Most people his age are not thinking ahead much more than a week or a month. But Jacques Cousteau is still thinking ten years down the road.* No wonder he was so vibrantly alive.

If your assignment right now is to raise your children, do it with passion; do it with enthusiasm. Maybe you have a dream to start a business, a dream to own your own home, a dream to be in the ministry. Keep it in front of you and keep pressing toward it.

The Scripture says in Proverbs, "Where there is no vision, the people perish." My dad kept a globe everywhere he worked—at his chair at home where he studied and on his desk at the office. Daddy's passion was to share God's love all over the world, and that globe reminded him of that. Even later in my father's life when he had to go on dialysis, he asked us to check to see if they could do dialysis in India. Although Daddy never made it back to India once he started dialysis, that didn't keep him from dreaming. In fact, that was one of the things that helped him to get up every day with enthusiasm in spite of his adversity.

Maybe you have some obstacles or challenges in your path as well. That's fine, but don't give up on your dreams. God still has something important for you to do. However, if you make the mistake of dwelling on the wrong things, before long you'll be planning your own funeral. No matter what the situation looks like in the natural, keep your dreams alive. You may be a mother raising small children and you're facing a serious illness. Keep a picture of your children in front of you. Get up every day and say, "I'm going to be here to raise my children. I'm going to live and not die."

Or perhaps you are struggling financially, but you have a dream of owning your own home. Keep that dream alive. Put up a picture of the home you would like to have. Keep it in front of you. You need something to be striving toward, then work and save and make wise financial choices, and you will be surprised how your dream can become a reality.

Remember the Miracle

Sometimes we lose our enthusiasm because we let what once was a miracle become too common to us. We get used to it and it becomes routine. For instance, maybe at one time you were excited about your job. You prayed and believed and you know God opened up that door for you. God supernaturally gave you that position, and you couldn't wait to get to work every morning. You got there and gave it 100 percent. Now, a few years later, the newness has worn off. It's become routine, and you don't really enjoy going to work anymore, and you have become discouraged. Do you know what has happened?

You let your miracle become common. You need to go back and remember how God brought you to where you are. You need to fan your flame.

I'm not saying that we never want to move on, but too many times we are taking things for granted that we should still be excited about.

A friend of mine complained incessantly about his job. He told me how the company wasn't treating him right. He wasn't being paid enough money. He couldn't stand his boss. On and on it went. One day, the company announced that they were going to downsize and lay off about half of the employees and it looked as though he was going to get laid off. Amazingly, my friend really started liking his job.

At the last minute, his company decided to keep him on, and you would have thought he'd just won the lottery! It's interesting how things like that can change our perspective. You may be a lot more excited about your job if you realize that you may not always have it.

Or maybe you would be much more excited about your marriage partner if you thought you were about to lose that person. At one time, you were so excited that you couldn't keep your eyes off him or her. But over the years you've allowed yourselves to grow stale, stagnant, and apart. You don't enjoy each other like you should. You don't have time for hugs and kisses and compliments. You're too busy to talk at night. You might miss your favorite TV program.

No, don't take that other person for granted. Do whatever you have to do to get that spark back and rekindle the relationship that brought you together in the first place. Bring some freshness to your marriage. Get out of your normal routine and do something different.

I am a person of habit, and I have to make myself get out of my normal routine. For instance, Victoria and I have a date night every Friday night. Usually we simply go out to eat, take some time to talk, and enjoy being together. But we've also done more adventurous activities for our date nights as well. Not long ago, we went and rode go-karts. Another time, we took our bikes down to the park and rode them around.

It takes a little creativity, but with effort you can do something to bring some freshness to your relationship. Don't lose that enthusiasm for the other person. Don't let that miracle, that relationship with the person God has brought into your life become so commonplace that you take it for granted.

Maybe at one time, you were excited about that house God's given you. You prayed, you believed, and you know God opened up the door. But now you think, I have to clean this place, my gutters are messed up, my dishwasher quit working. Taxes are so high.

You are focused on the wrong things. God blessed you with that house. No doubt, at one time it was a dream come true. Don't allow it to become commonplace.

We should never lose the amazement of what God has done. Every time I drive by Lakewood Church, I am amazed. And I've made up my mind that twenty years from now, I'm still going to be amazed. As I drive into Lakewood's parking lot, I say, "God, You've done more than we could ever ask or think."

God told some people in the book of Revelation, "I'm not happy with you because you've left your first love." In other words, you're not excited about what I've done for you. Too often, we do the same thing. We let something that was so great at one time become routine and we don't appreciate it as we should.

I heard a reporter ask a famous heart surgeon how he kept his excitement. This man had developed a certain procedure and he had performed it more than a thousand times. By now, the operation was considered routine and ordinary.

The reporter asked the surgeon, "Do you ever get tired of doing it?"

"No," he said, "because I act like every operation is my first one."

He was saying, "I don't take for granted what God has allowed me to do. I don't want to let it become so common that it doesn't excite me anymore."

Maybe God has done great things in your life. He's taken you further than you could dream. He's brought great people into your life. He's opened up great doors. Don't get so accustomed to those things that they don't excite you anymore. Choose to remain passionate, living every day with enthusiasm.

Sometimes I hear people complain about their children. "Well, I'd be more enthusiastic if I didn't have to stay here and take care of my children all day."

No, you're missing the point. Your children are a miracle, and if you want evidence of that, simply think back to the day they were born. No doubt you had tears running down your cheeks. You were so overjoyed. You knew each child was a gift from God. Don't allow that sense of awe to disappear with time.

Recently, I was in a hurry to leave the house and trying to get the family rounded up and out the door. Somebody had given us a label maker—a little machine that prints out labels—and our children loved to play with it. Jonathan had the label maker out and was typing a message.

I said, "Jonathan, put that thing away. We've got to go."

He said, "Daddy, just give me a few more seconds. I want to finish this up."

"No, Jonathan," I said. "Put it up. We have got to go right now." He and I bantered back and forth and I was getting all uptight. Finally, he got finished and printed out the label. It read: "BEST DADDY IN THE WORLD."

I thought, *Well, maybe we can stay here a little longer and print a few more of these labels!*

Sometimes we get in such a hurry that we miss the miracles all along the way. Take time for your children. Look in their eyes every day and tell them how much you love them, how proud you are of them. Think of the joy and the fulfillment they bring you. That alone should be enough to cause us to get up each day with enthusiasm. And when you're tired of cleaning up after them or tempted to have a bad attitude, learn to turn it around. Say, "Father, thank You for these children. Thank You for each of these gifts that You've given me."

Miracles are all around us. The people in your life, the doors God has opened, the things that have happened along the way are not by accident. It was God's favor that caused you to be at the right place at the right time. You met someone and fell in love. Or you qualified for that home and you know that by all usual means you would not have done so. Or you got that promotion unexpectedly. These are not coincidences. God was directing your steps, so don't take it for granted.

Miracles are all around us.

What are you focused on today? Are you becoming a better you? Is there peace in your home and in your heart and mind? Are you happy, at rest, and enjoying life? We need to realize that this day is unique and irreplaceable. We need to make the most of it, and live like it could be our last.

An elderly couple I knew were tremendous role models, always smiling and encouraging other people, and everyone loved them—especially the young people. Moreover, after decades of marriage, they still treated each other with honor and respect.

In her mid-eighties, the woman went home to be with the Lord. At the funeral, her husband, also an octogenarian, told an interesting story. He said, "About fifteen years ago, I had a heart attack. When my wife came to the hospital, she said, 'Honey, this just shows us how fragile life really is. You could have died.' She said, 'From now on, every night before we go to bed, I want us to kiss seven times just to show how much we love each other, just to show that we're not taking each other for granted.' And so, for these last fifteen or twenty years, we never went to sleep without kissing seven times."

Don't you love that? That woman lived every day like it could be her last. She went to be with the Lord on a Tuesday, but Monday night, she kissed her husband seven times. Monday night, she told him how much she loved him. And when her life was over, she had no regrets. She made every day special. The last day of her life, she lived it loving, caring, at peace, and enjoying every moment. That's the way I want to live.

Friend, this day is a gift, so make the most of it. Shake off anything that hints of self-pity or discouragement and find some reason to be grateful.

Becoming a better you is all in how you choose to view life. I heard a story about two men who were patients in the same hospital room. Every day, the man closest to the window shared with his friend what he saw outside, describing it in great detail, so his roommate could enjoy the view, even though he was confined to his bed.

"Today, I see a beautiful sunrise," he'd say. "The kids are out there playing. The trees are blooming," and on and on. Each day, the bedridden patient looked forward to hearing his roommate's report on the outside world. It was the highlight of his day.

One day, the patient next to the window became so excited. "Oh, you should see it! There's a parade coming by, with a marching band, kids and adults celebrating something and having such a good time."

After several weeks, the patient next to the window passed away, so his friend asked the nurse if he could have the bed by the window, so he could see all the great scenes of activity outside.

"Why, certainly," the nurse replied, as she and an orderly moved the patient to the bed next to the window. But when the man looked out the window, much to his surprise, all he could see was a brick wall. About fifteen feet away stood another wing of the hospital. The patient called the nurse back in, and said, "Hey, wait a minute! What's going on? My friend who passed away described all those beautiful scenes for several weeks, and I can't see anything but a wall!"

The nurse smiled and said, "Sir, didn't you realize that your friend was blind? He chose to see a beautiful life from the inside out."

No matter what twists and turns life takes, you can find the good if you look for it. If we have the right attitude, we can see the sun shining even when it's cloudy. We can stay full of joy and keep getting better, even when things don't go our way.

My prayer is that God would give us a spirit of gratitude, that we'd always focus on the good and never take life for granted. If you will trust God each day and live according to His plan for your life, you will be happier, healthier, and you'll rise higher than you ever imagined possible.

Make a decision that you're going to live every day with enthusiasm. Get up each morning and think about all the things for which you can be grateful. If you need to, make a list. Keep it in front of you and then go out each day pursuing your God-given dreams.

The Bible says, "To set your mind and keep it set on the higher things." [66] I believe the higher things are the positive things, so first thing every day, set your mind in the right direction. Set your mind for success and victory. Set in your mind that you are going to enjoy this day. Then rise higher and get into the jet stream of God!

Remember, friend, you have seeds of greatness in you. You weren't made to be stagnant; rise out of complacency; keep growing, keep reaching for new heights. Your best days are still out in front of you.

You have not seen, heard, or imagined the great things God has in store for you. As you keep stretching to the next level, improving your life, and reaching for your highest potential, you will not only give birth to your dreams, but you will become a better *you*, better than you ever dreamed possible!

ACTION POINTS

PART 7: STAY PASSIONATE ABOUT LIFE

1. Today, I will look for tangible ways that I can stay passionate about life. I will develop a habit of smiling on purpose. I will keep singing a song of joy in my heart, despite the circumstances. I will have a grateful attitude, recognizing this day is a gift.

2. I will exercise my faith in a positive direction, preparing for success, and expecting God's best in my life. This week, I will tell someone close to me that I am planning to live a long, healthy, prosperous life. I will take action to fill my life with healthy activities, while eliminating any unhealthy actions, attitudes, or lifestyle issues.

3. I choose to move from believing to expecting. Today I will reach for something beyond where I am presently. I will actively pursue new goals, keeping them out in front of me, and expecting to meet them.

4. I will be continually aware that becoming a better me is all in how I choose to view life. I will constantly look for ways to improve my life; I will choose to be kind to people; I will seek more vibrant relationships with the people closest to me, and I will actively pursue a deeper relationship with God.

5. I choose to live this day passionately as a positive reflection of God in our world. I will put actions behind my faith and leave a lasting legacy for my family and the world.

WE CARE ABOUT YOU!

I believe there is a void in every person that only a relationship with God can fill. I'm not talking about finding religion or joining a particular church. I'm talking about developing a relationship with your heavenly Father through His Son, Jesus Christ. I believe that knowing Him is the source of true peace and fulfillment in life.

I encourage you to pray, "Jesus, I believe You died for me and rose from the dead, so now I want to live for You. I am turning away from my sins and placing my trust in You. I acknowledge You as my Savior and Lord, and I'm asking You to guide my life from now on."

With that simple prayer, you can get a fresh, clean start, and establish a close relationship with God. Read the Bible every day; talk to God through prayer, and attend a good Bible-based church where you can find friends who will lift you up rather than pull you down. Keep God in first place in your life and follow His principles; He will take you places you've not yet imagined!

For free information on how you can grow stronger in your spiritual life, we encourage you to contact us. Victoria and I love you, and we will be praying for you. We'd love to hear from you!

To contact us, write to:

Joel and Victoria Osteen
P.O. Box 4600
Houston, TX 77210–4600

Or you can reach us online at www.joelosteen.com.

NOTES

1. See Romans 11:29.
2. Psalm 30:5.
3. See Isaiah 28:16 and Romans 10:11.
4. See Psalm 139:16.
5. See Revelation 12:11.
6. See 2 Corinthians 5:17.
7. See Genesis 2:7.
8. Galatians 3:29.
9. See Isaiah 61:7.
10. Galatians 3:13.
11. John 8:36.
12. Proverbs 26:2.
13. James 5:16.
14. See Ephesians 6:12.
15. 1 Chronicles 4:40.
16. See Romans 7:19.
17. See Ephesians 6:14.
18. See Philippians.
19. Hebrews 4:16.
20. Luke 15:20.
21. Matthew 22:39.
22. See Hebrews 12:1–2.
23. Matthew 3:17.
24. See Ephesians 1:4–14.
25. James 3:10.
26. See Romans 4:17.
27. See Jeremiah 1:4–9.
28. Philemon 1:6.
29. 1 Corinthians 13:4.
30. 1 Corinthians 13:5.
31. See Romans 12:16.
32. See James 4:17.
33. See Proverbs 31:28.
34. See Hebrews 3:13.
35. Galatians 6:10.
36. See Luke 6:43–45.
37. See Matthew 25:40.
38. See 2 Timothy 3:1–5.
39. See 1 Corinthians 10:13.
40. Philippians 4:8.
41. See Matthew 26:41.
42. 1 Thessalonians 5:16.
43. Matthew 10:14.
44. Isaiah 54:17.
45. Song of Solomon 1:6.
46. Psalm 46:10.
47. Hebrews 4:3.
48. Romans 8:28 NKJV.
49. Proverbs 3:5–6.
50. Psalm 30:5.
51. Psalm 77:11.
52. 1 Thessalonians 2:13.
53. Psalm 30:5.
54. Luke 12:48.
55. 1 John 4:4.
56. Psalm 91:7.
57. See 2 Corinthians 5:20.
58. See Hebrews 13:15.
59. See James 5:7.
60. See James 2:17.
61. 2 Corinthians 5:7.
62. Isaiah 40:31.
63. Mark 5:36.
64. Romans 12:11.
65. Isaiah 1:19.
66. See Colossians 3:2.

ABOUT THE AUTHOR

Joel Osteen is the pastor of a new generation. Called by many "America's voice of hope," Joel has been recognized as one of the 10 Most Fascinating People by Barbara Walters.

Joel Osteen reaches a huge audience in the United States and across the globe. Tens of millions of people in more than a hundred nations worldwide are inspired through his weekly television broadcasts, his *New York Times* bestselling books, his sold-out international speaking tours, and his weekly top-ten podcasts.

Joel and his wife, Victoria, are the pastors of America's largest church—Lakewood Church in Houston, Texas.